INSTRUCTOR'S ANNOTATED EDITION

THIRD EDITION

IMMAGINA

L'ITALIANO SENZA CONFINI

Anne Cummings
El Camino College

Gloria Pastorino
Fairleigh Dickinson University

VISTA®
HIGHER LEARNING

Boston, Massachusetts

D0905688

On the cover: **Teseo Screpolato** (*Cracked Theseus*) by artist Igor Mitoraj, from a 2016-2017 exhibition at the archaeological site of Pompeii

Creative Director: José A. Blanco

Publisher: Sharla Zwirek

Editorial Development: Judith Bach, Armando Brito, Deborah Coffey, Joanna Duffy, Catalina Pire-Schmidt

Project Management: Rosemary Jaffe, Faith Ryan

Rights Management: Ashley Poreda, Jorgensen Fernandez

Technology Production: Kamila Caicedo, Jamie Kostecki, Paola Ríos Schaaf

Design: Daniela Hoyos, Radoslav Mateev, Gabriel Noreña, Andrés Vanegas

Production: Oscar Díez, Sebastián Díez, Daniel Lopera

Student Edition (Perfectbound) ISBN: 978-1-54330-335-3
Student Edition (Casebound-SIMRA) ISBN: 978-1-54330-337-7
Instructor's Annotated Edition ISBN: 978-1-54330-338-4

Library of Congress Control Number: 2018939735

1 2 3 4 5 6 7 8 9 TC 23 22 21 20 19 18

Printed in Canada.

INSTRUCTOR'S ANNOTATED EDITION

Table of Contents

The Vista Higher Learning Story

Your Specialized Foreign Language Publisher

Independent, specialized, and privately owned, Vista Higher Learning was founded in 2000 with one mission: to raise the teaching and learning of world languages to a higher level. This mission is based on the following beliefs:

- It is essential to prepare students for a world in which learning another language is a necessity, not a luxury.
- Language learning should be fun and rewarding, and all students should have the tools they need to achieve success.
- Students who experience success learning a language will be more likely to continue their language studies both inside and outside the classroom.

With this in mind, we decided to take a fresh look at all aspects of language instructional materials. Because we are specialized, we dedicate 100 percent of our resources to this goal and base every decision on how well it supports language learning.

That is where you come in. Since our founding, we have relied on the invaluable feedback of language instructors and students nationwide. This partnership has proved to be the cornerstone of our success by allowing us to constantly improve our programs to meet your instructional needs.

The result? Programs that make language learning exciting, relevant, and effective through:

- unprecedented access to resources
- a wide variety of contemporary, authentic materials
- the integration of text, technology, and media, and
- a bold and engaging textbook design.

By focusing on our singular passion, we let you focus on yours.

The Vista Higher Learning Team

VISTA®
HIGHER LEARNING

500 Boylston Street, Suite 620, Boston, MA 02116-3736 TOLL-FREE: 800-618-7375
TELEPHONE: 617-426-4910 FAX: 617-426-5209 www.vistahigherlearning.com

Getting to Know *Immagina*, Third Edition

Immagina, Third Edition, is a market-leading intermediate Italian program designed to provide students with an active and rewarding learning experience as they strengthen their language skills and develop their cultural competency. **Immagina** takes an interactive, communicative approach. It focuses on real communication in meaningful contexts to develop and consolidate students' speaking, listening, reading, and writing skills. **Immagina** features a fresh, magazine-like design that engages students while integrating thematic, cultural, and grammatical concepts within every section of the text.

NEW! to the Third Edition

- One new **Galleria di persone illustri** per lesson, featuring four prominent Italian creators

- Three new authentic short films: **Due piedi sinistri** (Lesson 2), **Stanza 8** (Lesson 7), and **Il sarto dei tedeschi** (Lesson 8)

- Two new **Letteratura** readings: **Va' dove ti porta il cuore** by Susanna Tamaro (Lesson 1) and **L'estate fredda** by Gianrico Carofiglio (Lesson 8)

- Three new **Immagina** section paragraphs about Italian cuisine

- Task-Based Activities—for more language practice

- Oral Testing Suggestions rewritten as Partner Chat activities offered as online assessments

- Online interactive Student Edition (vText) now included with Supersite access

- All instructor resources now available online

Plus, the original hallmark features of *Immagina*

- Authentic dramatic short films by well-known Italian-speaking filmmakers tie together the lesson themes and grammar structures.

- Short and comprehensible literary and cultural readings recognize and celebrate the Italian-speaking world.

- Contemporary cultural presentation of the everyday life of Italian speakers and their diverse cultures

- Emphasis on authentic language and practical vocabulary for communicating in real-life situations

- Clear and well-organized grammar explanations highlight the most important concepts of Intermediate Italian.

- Groundbreaking, text-specific technology (Supersite) specially designed to expand students' learning and instructors' teaching options

*Students must use a computer for audio recording.

	PER COMINCIARE	CORTOMETRAGGIO	IMMAGINA
Lezione 1 **Sentire e vivere** 	**I rapporti personali** .... 4 la personalità lo stato civile i rapporti i sentimenti	*La scarpa* (5 min.) .... 6 Regista: Andrea Rovetta	GLI ITALIANI NEL MONDO *Italiani: un popolo in movimento* .... 12 L'Italia celebrata negli Stati Uniti; Italiani famosi nel mondo....... 13 **GALLERIA DI PERSONE ILLUSTRI:** Ennio Morricone, Miuccia Prada, Lorenzo Da Ponte, Cristoforo Colombo........... 14
Lezione 2 **Vivere insieme** 	**Città e comunità** .... 44 luoghi e indicazioni la gente le attività il trasporto per descrivere	*Due piedi sinistri* (6 min.) .... 46 Regista: Isabella Salvetti	ROMA E L'ITALIA CENTRALE *Roma: un museo all'aperto!* .... 52 Le regioni del Centro Italia; San Francesco d'Assisi .... 53 **GALLERIA DI PERSONE ILLUSTRI:** Sofia Loren, Giulio Andreotti, Maria Montessori, Claudio Baglioni 54
Lezione 3 **Distrarsi e divertirsi** 	**I passatempi** .... 84 lo sport il tempo libero lo shopping e l'abbigliamento	*Bulli si nasce* (16 min.) ..... 86 Regista: Massimo Cappelli	TOSCANA E FIRENZE *In giro per Firenze* .... 92 La Vespa; L'Arcipelago Toscano .. 93 **GALLERIA DI PERSONE ILLUSTRI:** Leonardo da Vinci, Michelangelo Buonarroti, Margherita Hack, Dante Alighieri. 94
Lezione 4 **Il valore delle idee** 	**La giustizia e la politica** ... 124 le leggi e i diritti la politica la gente la sicurezza e i pericoli	*Mare nostro* (18 min.) ..... 126 Regista: Andrea D'Asaro	MILANO E LA LOMBARDIA *Milano: capitale del nord* ..... 132 Il gorgonzola; Terra dei laghi ... 133 **GALLERIA DI PERSONE ILLUSTRI:** Antonio Stradivari, Valentino Garavani, Caravaggio, Mina 134

STRUTTURE	CULTURA	LETTERATURA	

STRUTTURE	CULTURA	LETTERATURA	

	PER COMINCIARE	CORTOMETRAGGIO	IMMAGINA

STRUTTURE	CULTURA	LETTERATURA	

Icons

Familiarize yourself with these icons that appear throughout **Immagina**.

 Presentational content for this section available online

 Textbook activity available online

 Partner Chat or Virtual Chat activity available online

 Pair activity

 Group activity

Additional practice on the Supersite, not included in the textbook, is indicated with this icon feature:

 Practice more at **vhlcentral.com**.

The *Immagina*, Third Edition, Supersite

The **Immagina**, Third Edition, Supersite is your online source for integrating text and technology resources. The Supersite enhances language learning and facilitates simple course management. With powerful functionality, a focus on language learning, and a simplified user experience, the Supersite offers features based directly on feedback from thousands of users.

Student Friendly

Make it a cinch for students to track due dates, save work, and access all resources.

Set-Up Ease

Customize your course and section settings, create your own grading categories, plus copy previous settings to save time.

All-in-One Gradebook

Add your own activities or use the grade adjustment tool for a true, cumulative grade.

Grading Options

Choose to grade student-by-student, question-by-question, or spot check. Plus, give targeted feedback via in-line editing and voice comments.

Accessible Student Data

Conveniently share information one-on-one, or issue class reports in the formats that best fit you and your department.

Instructor resources include:

- A gradebook to manage classes and grades, view rosters, and set assignments
- A communication center for announcements and notifications
- Downloadable and editable task-based activities, sample syllabus, sample lesson plan, and Testing Program
- Instructor Resources (answer keys, audioscripts, videoscripts, translations, grammar slides, and teaching suggestions)
- **NEW!** Online Instructor's Edition with teaching suggestions, annotations, and the ability to add notes.
- Online administration of quizzes and exams with time limits and password protection
- Customize assessments by adding, removing, or editing questions and providing section references.
- Tools to add your own content to the Supersite:
    - Create and assign Partner Chat and open-ended activities
    - Upload and assign videos and outside resources
- Single sign-on feature for integration with your LMS
- Lab and Testing Audio Program MP3 files
- Live Chat for video chat, audio chat, and instant messaging
- Forums for oral assignments, group discussions, and projects
- vText—the online, interactive student edition with access to Supersite activities, audio, and video

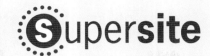

Each section of the textbook comes with resources and activities on the **Immagina**
Supersite, many of which are auto-graded with immediate feedback. Visit **vhlcentral.com**
to explore this wealth of exciting resources.

PER COMINCIARE	• Audio of the **Vocabulary** • Textbook and extra practice activities • Partner Chat and Virtual Chat activities for increased oral practice
CORTOMETRAGGIO	• Streaming video of the short film with instructor-controlled options for subtitles • Audio of the **Vocabulary** • Pre- and post-viewing activities • Textbook and extra practice activities
IMMAGINA	• Main **Immagina** cultural reading • **Progetto** research activity • **Galleria di persone illustri** readings • Textbook and extra practice activities
STRUTTURE	• Textbook grammar presentations • Textbook and extra practice activities • Partner Chat and Virtual Chat activities for increased oral practice • **Sintesi** composition engine writing activity
CULTURA	• Audio of the **Vocabulary** • **Cultura** reading • Textbook and extra practice activities
LETTERATURA	• Audio of the **Vocabulary** • Audio-synced, dramatic reading of the literary text • Textbook and extra practice activities • **Tema** composition activity
LABORATORIO DI SCRITTURA	• **Saggio** composition engine writing activity
VOCABOLARIO	• Audio of the **Vocabulary** • Vocabulary Tools: customizable word lists, flashcards with audio

Plus! Also found on the Supersite:

• Lab audio MP3 files
• Forums for oral assignments, group presentations, and projects
• Live Chat tool for video chat, audio chat, and instant messaging
• Communication center for instructor notifications and feedback
• A single gradebook for all Supersite activities
• WebSAM—the online Student Activities Manual (Workbook, Lab Manual)
• vText—the online, interactive student edition with access to Supersite activities, audio, and video

Students must use a computer for audio recordings.

Immagina Film Collection

Fully integrated with your textbook, the **Immagina** Film Collection features dramatic short films by Italian filmmakers. These films are the basis for the pre- and post-viewing activities in the **Cortometraggio** section of each lesson. The films are a central feature of the lesson, providing opportunities to review and recycle vocabulary from **Per cominciare**, and previewing and contextualizing the grammar from **Strutture**.

These films offer entertaining and thought-provoking opportunities to build listening comprehension skills and your cultural knowledge of Italian speakers.

Besides providing entertainment, the films serve as a useful learning tool. As you watch the films, you will observe characters interacting in various situations, using real-world language that reflects the lesson themes as well as the vocabulary and grammar you are studying.

LEZIONE 1
La scarpa
(5 minuti)

A woman wakes up to some unexpected bad news. Thinking quickly, she races across town to meet her boyfriend at the train station one last time, but will she arrive in time to speak her mind?

LEZIONE 2
NEW! Due piedi sinistri
(6 minuti)

A teenage boy is keen on befriending a fellow soccer fan until something about her gives him pause. Can a friendship blossom between two young people no matter their differences?

LEZIONE 3
Bulli si nasce
(16 minuti)

Thanks to "good" genes and persistent parents, Ale became a schoolyard king. What else is he genetically destined for?

LEZIONE 4
Mare nostro
(18 minuti)

When Marcello's ordinary fishing trip suddenly goes terribly wrong, he learns a lesson in what it means to rely on one's fellow man. How will he react when someone needs to rely on him?

LEZIONE 5
Dove dormono gli aerei
(18 minuti)

In a crowded airport, an independent, extroverted little boy and a shy girl become friends. While they run off to play, they unknowingly leave worried parents, paranoid airport staff, and a forgotten backpack in their wake.

LEZIONE 6
Lacreme napulitane
(19 minuti)

Northerners and Southerners historically don't get along. What will happen when a reserved **Milanese** and an outspoken **Napoletano** are stuck together on the long journey to Milan?

LEZIONE 7
NEW! Stanza 8
(9 minuti)

Two couples at opposite ends of a hospital waiting room anxiously await the results of their child's surgery. The surgeon finally delivers the news, setting the four parents' lives on a common course.

LEZIONE 8
NEW! Il sarto dei tedeschi
(15 minuti)

A tailor in 1940s Italy is approached by a high-ranking client with a new request. The money and prestige of this assignment may change his image in the community. Could this be his finest suit yet?

LEZIONE 9
Il numero di Sharon
(5 minuti)

Andrea chats online with Lisa and falls in love. A blackout leaves him with an incomplete phone number, but he is determined to find her. After all; there are only about a thousand possible numbers.

LEZIONE 10
Rischio d'impresa
(14 minuti)

Balancing a career and a family is difficult. For Marina, breaking the news of a big promotion to her husband might be even harder.

Immagina and the *World-Readiness Standards for Learning Languages*

Since 1982, when the *ACTFL Proficiency Guidelines* were first published, that seminal document and its subsequent revisions have influenced the teaching of modern languages in the United States. **Immagina** was written with the concerns and philosophy of the *ACTFL Proficiency Guidelines* in mind. It emphasizes an interactive, proficiency-oriented approach to the teaching of language and culture.

The pedagogy behind **Immagina** was also informed from its inception by the *Standards for Foreign Language Learning in the 21st Century*. First published under the auspices of the *National Standards in Foreign Language Education Project*, the Standards are organized into five goal areas, often called the Five C's: Communication, Cultures, Connections, Comparisons, and Communities. National Standards icons appear on the pages of your IAE to call out sections that have a particularly strong relationship with the Standards.

Since **Immagina** takes a communicative approach to the teaching of Italian, the Communications goal is an integral part of the student text. Diverse formats (discussion topics, role-plays, interviews, oral presentations, and so forth) promote authentic communicative exchanges in which students provide, obtain, and interpret information, as well as express emotions or opinions. Interactive **Comunicazione, Sintesi,** and **Analisi** activities allow students to synthesize grammatical, cultural, and thematic material to expand their communicative abilities. In addition to oral skills, written communicative skills are strengthened through a wide array of practical and creative tasks.

Immagina also stresses cultural competency and the ability to make connections as invaluable components of language learning. The **Cortometraggio, Immagina, Cultura,** and **Letteratura** sections all provide students with the opportunity to acquire information, to expand cultural knowledge, and to recognize distinctive viewpoints. Through connections with multiple disciplines such as film, literature, and art, students are exposed to various cultural practices and perspectives of Italian speakers. **Nota culturale** sidebars provide additional opportunities for students to connect to language through culture.

Students develop further insight into the nature of language and culture through comparisons with their own. Compelling discussion topics throughout the text encourage students to compare new information with familiar concepts and ideas. In addition, the clear, comprehensive grammar explanations in **Strutture** allow students to compare and contrast the grammatical structures of their own language with those presented in **Immagina**.

Finally, **Immagina** encourages students to expand their use of language beyond the classroom setting and participate in broader, richer Italian-speaking communities. In the **Immagina** section of each lesson, outside projects provide access to a wealth of opportunities for students to expand their use of Italian outside the classroom.

As you become familiar with the **Immagina** program, you will find many more connections to the *World-Readiness Standards for Learning Languages*. We encourage you to keep its goals in mind and to make new connections as you work with the text and ancillaries.

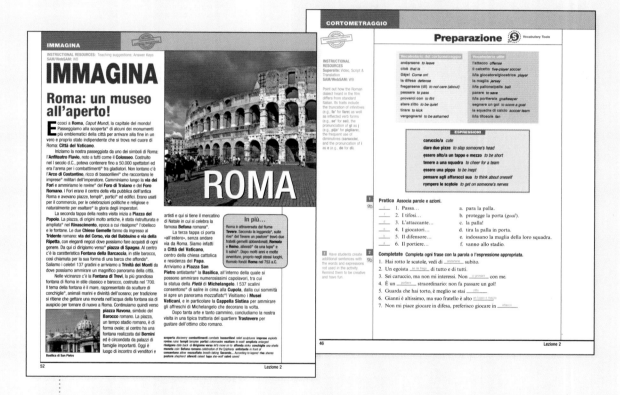

Communication Understand and be understood: read and listen to understand the Italian-speaking world, converse with others, and share your thoughts clearly through speaking and writing.

Cultures Experience Italian-speaking cultures through their own viewpoints, in the places, objects, behaviors, and beliefs important to the people who live them.

Connections Apply what you learn in your Italian course to your other studies; apply what you know from other courses to your Italian studies.

Comparisons Discover in which ways the Italian language and Italian-speaking cultures are like your own—and how they differ.

Communities Engage with Italian-speaking communities locally, nationally, and internationally both in your courses and beyond—for life.

SOMMARIO

outlines the content and themes of each lesson.

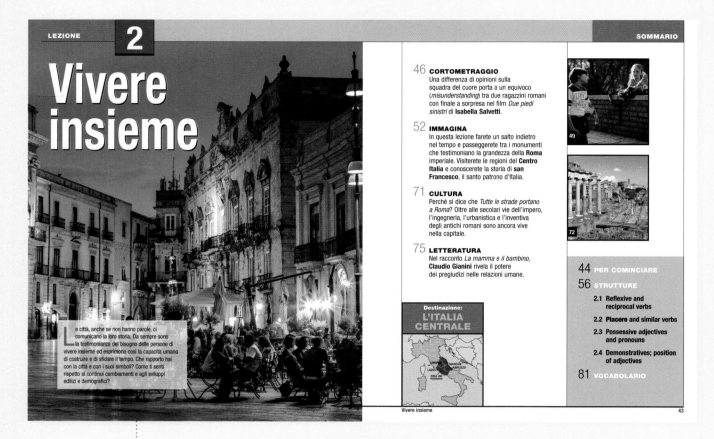

Lesson opener The first two pages introduce students to the lesson theme. Dynamic photos and brief descriptions of the theme's film, culture topics, and readings serve as a springboard for class discussion.

Destinazione A locator map highlights each lesson's region of focus.

Lesson overview A lesson outline prepares students for the linguistic and cultural topics they will study in the lesson.

ⓢupersite

Supersite resources are available for every section of the lesson at **vhlcentral.com.** Icons show you which textbook activities are also available online, and where additional practice activities are available. The description next to the ⓢ icon indicates what additional resources are available for each section: videos, audio recordings, readings and presentations, and more!

PER COMINCIARE

practices the lesson vocabulary with thematic activities.

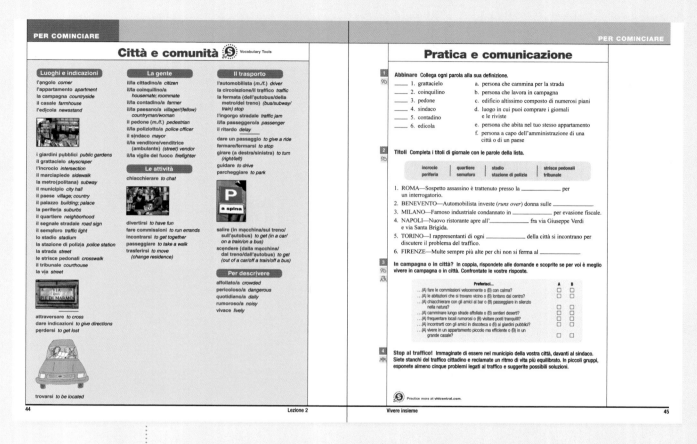

Vocabulary Easy-to-study thematic lists present useful vocabulary.

Photos and illustrations Dynamic, full-color photos and art illustrate selected vocabulary terms.

Pratica This set of activities practices vocabulary in diverse formats and engaging contexts.

ⓢuper**site**

- Audio recordings of all vocabulary items
- Textbook activities
- Partner Chat and Virtual Chat activities for increased oral practice
- Additional activities for extra practice

CORTOMETRAGGIO

features award-winning short films by contemporary Italian filmmakers.

Films Compelling short films let students see and hear Italian in its authentic contexts. Films are thematically linked to the lessons.

Scene Video stills with captions from the film prepare students for the film and introduce some of the expressions they will encounter.

Nota culturale These sidebars with cultural information related to the **Cortometraggio** help students understand the cultural context and background surrounding the film.

Supersite

- Streaming video of short films with instructor-controlled subtitle options
- Audio recordings of vocabulary terms

PREPARAZIONE & ANALISI

provide pre- and post-viewing support for each film.

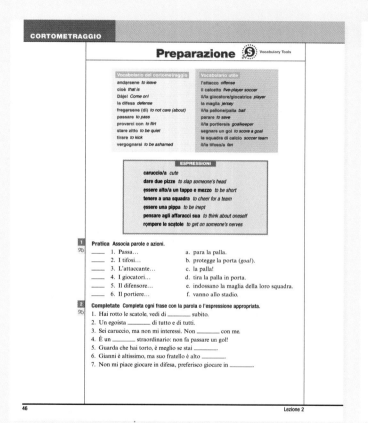

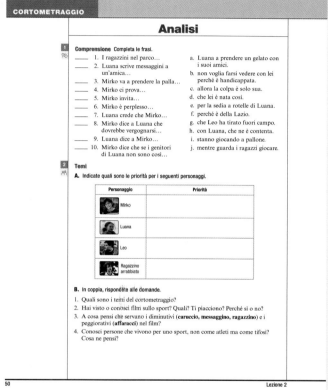

Preparazione Pre-viewing activities set the stage for the film by providing vocabulary support, background information, and opportunities to anticipate the film content.

Analisi Post-viewing activities check student comprehension and allow them to explore broader themes from the film in relation to their own life.

Supersite

- Textbook activities
- Additional activities for extra practice

IMMAGINA

simulates a voyage to the featured country or region.

Magazine-like design Each reading is presented in the attention-grabbing visual style you would expect from a magazine.

Region-specific readings Dynamic readings draw students' attention to culturally significant locations, traditions, and monuments of the country or region.

Galleria di persone illustri **profiles** Brief descriptions provide a synopsis of the featured person's life and cultural importance. Colorful photos show their artistic creations.

Activities The activities check students' comprehension of the **Immagina** and **Galleria di persone illustri** readings and lead you to further exploration.

Supersite

- Cultural readings
- Textbook activities and online-only comprehension activities
- **Progetto** research activity

STRUTTURE

presents grammar points key to intermediate Italian in a graphic-intensive format.

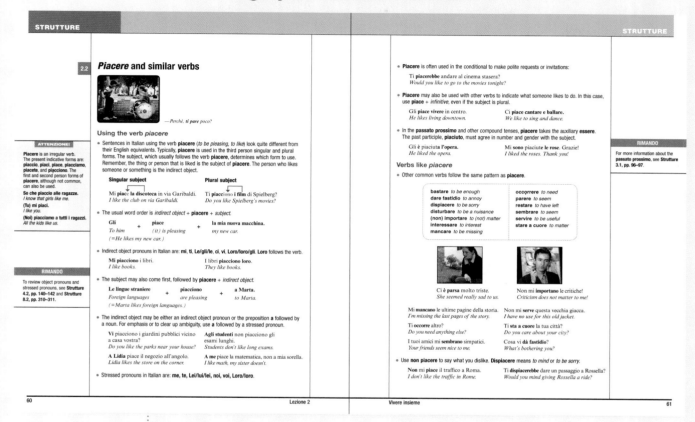

STRUTTURE

2.2 *Piacere* and similar verbs

—*Perché, ti pare poco?*

Using the verb *piacere*

- Sentences in Italian using the verb **piacere** (*to be pleasing, to like*) look quite different from their English equivalents. Typically, **piacere** is used in the third person singular and plural forms. The subject, which usually follows the verb **piacere**, determines which form to use. Remember, the thing or person that is liked is the subject of **piacere**. The person who likes someone or something is the indirect object.

Singular subject	Plural subject
Mi piace **la discoteca** in via Garibaldi.	Ti piacciono **i film** di Spielberg?
I like the club on via Garibaldi.	*Do you like Spielberg's movies?*

- The usual word order is *indirect object* + **piacere** + *subject*.

Gli	+	piace	+	la mia nuova macchina.
To him		*(it) is pleasing*		*my new car.*
(=He likes my new car.)				

- Indirect object pronouns in Italian are: **mi, ti, Le/gli/le, ci, vi, Loro/loro/gli. Loro** follows the verb.

Mi **piacciono** i libri.	I libri **piacciono loro.**
I like books.	*They like books.*

- The subject may also come first, followed by **piacere** + *indirect object*.

Le lingue straniere	+	piacciono	+	a Marta.
Foreign languages		*are pleasing*		*to Marta.*
(=Marta likes foreign languages.)				

- The indirect object may be either an indirect object pronoun or the preposition **a** followed by a noun. For emphasis or to clear up ambiguity, use **a** followed by a stressed pronoun.

Vi piacciono i giardini pubblici vicino a casa vostra?	Agli **studenti** non piacciono gli esami lunghi.
Do you like the parks near your house?	*Students don't like long exams.*
A **Lidia** piace il negozio all'angolo.	A **me** piace la matematica, non a mia sorella.
Lidia likes the store on the corner.	*I like math, my sister doesn't.*

- Stressed pronouns in Italian are: **me, te, Lei/lui/lei, noi, voi, Loro/loro.**

60   Lezione 2

STRUTTURE

- **Piacere** is often used in the conditional to make polite requests or invitations:

  Ti **piacerebbe** andare al cinema stasera?
  Would you like to go to the movies tonight?

- **Piacere** may also be used with other verbs to indicate what someone likes to do. In this case, use **piace** + *infinitive,* even if the subject is plural.

Gli **piace vivere** in centro.	Ci **piace cantare e ballare.**
He likes living downtown.	*We like to sing and dance.*

- In the **passato prossimo** and other compound tenses, **piacere** takes the auxiliary **essere.** The past participle, **piaciuto,** must agree in number and gender with the subject.

Gli è piaciuta **l'opera.**	Mi sono piaciute **le rose.** Grazie!
He liked the opera.	*I liked the roses. Thank you!*

Verbs like *piacere*

- Other common verbs follow the same pattern as **piacere.**

bastare *to be enough*	**occorrere** *to need*
dare fastidio *to annoy*	**parere** *to seem*
dispiacere *to be sorry*	**restare** *to have left*
disturbare *to be a nuisance*	**sembrare** *to seem*
(non) importare *to (not) matter*	**servire** *to be useful*
interessare *to interest*	**stare a cuore** *to matter*
mancare *to be missing*	

Ci è **parsa** molto triste.	Non mi **importano** le critiche!
She seemed really sad to us.	*Criticism does not matter to me!*

Mi **mancano** le ultime pagine della storia.	Non mi **serve** questa vecchia giacca.
I'm missing the last pages of the story.	*I have no use for this old jacket.*
Ti **occorre** altro?	Ti **sta a cuore** la tua città?
Do you need anything else?	*Do you care about your city?*
I tuoi amici mi **sembrano** simpatici.	Cosa vi **dà fastidio?**
Your friends seem nice to me.	*What's bothering you?*

- Use **non piacere** to say what you dislike. **Dispiacere** means *to mind* or *to be sorry.*

Non mi **piace** il traffico a Roma.	Ti **dispiacerebbe** dare un passaggio a Rossella?
I don't like the traffic in Rome.	*Would you mind giving Rossella a ride?*

Vivere insieme   61

Integration of *Cortometraggio* Photos with quotes or captions from the lesson's short film show the new grammar structures in meaningful contexts.

Charts and diagrams Colorful, easy-to-understand charts and diagrams highlight key grammar structures and related vocabulary.

Grammar explanations Explanations are written in clear, comprehensible language for reference both in and outside of class.

Attenzione These sidebars expand on the current grammar point and call attention to possible sources of confusion.

Rimando These sidebars reference relevant grammar points actively presented in **Strutture.**

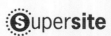

- Grammar presentations

STRUTTURE

progresses from directed to communicative practice.

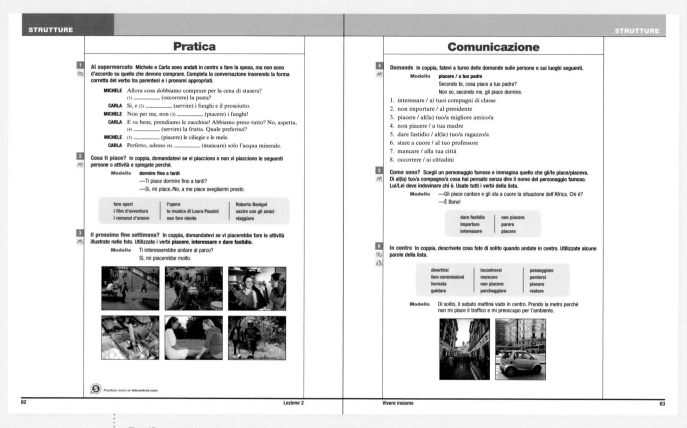

Pratica Directed exercises support students as they begin working with the grammar structures, helping them master the forms they need for personalized communication.

Comunicazione Open-ended, communicative activities help students internalize the grammar point in a range of contexts involving pair and group work.

Nota culturale Where appropriate, sidebars explain cultural references embedded in activities and expand the culture content of each lesson.

Supersite

- Textbook activities
- Partner Chat and Virtual Chat activities for increased oral practice
- Additional activities for extra practice

SINTESI

brings together the lesson grammar and vocabulary themes.

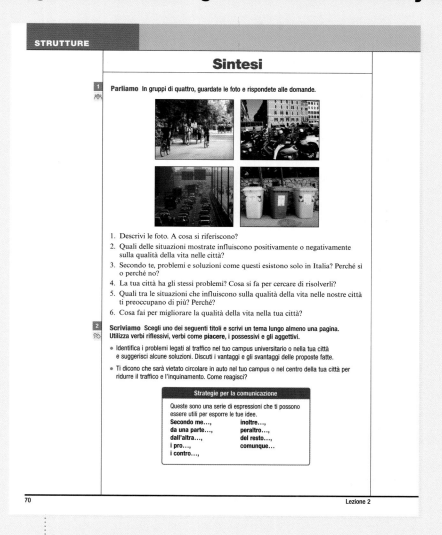

Parliamo Realia and photography serve as springboards for pair, group, or class discussions.

Scriviamo Gives students the opportunity to use the grammar and vocabulary of the lesson in engaging, real-life writing tasks.

Strategie Tips, techniques, key words, and expressions help students improve their oral and written communication skills.

Supersite

• Composition engine for writing activity

CULTURA

features a dynamic cultural reading.

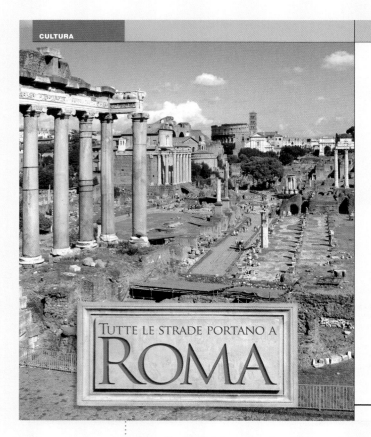

CULTURA

Readings Brief, comprehensible readings present students with additional cultural information related to the lesson theme.

Design Readings are carefully laid out with line numbers, marginal glosses, and box features to help make each piece easy to navigate.

Photos Vibrant, dynamic photos visually illustrate the reading.

Ⓢupersite

• Cultural reading

• Additional activities for extra practice

LETTERATURA

showcases literary readings by well-known Italian writers.

Letteratura Comprehensible and compelling, these readings present new avenues for using the lesson's grammar and vocabulary.

Design Each reading is presented in the attention-grabbing visual style you would expect from a magazine, along with glosses of unfamiliar words.

ⓢupersite

- Dramatic recordings of each literary selection bring the plot to life
- Audio-sync technology for the literary reading highlights text as it is being read out loud

PREPARAZIONE & ANALISI

activities provide in-depth pre- and post-reading support for each selection in Letteratura and Cultura.

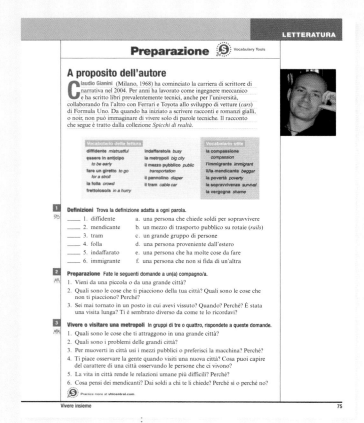

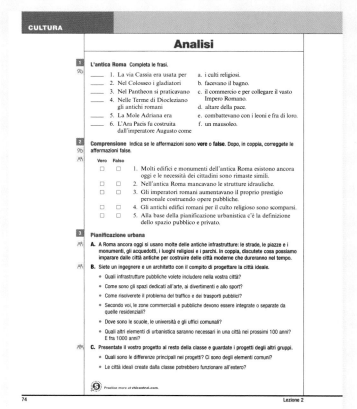

Preparazione Vocabulary presentation and practice, author biographies, and pre-reading discussion activities prepare students for the reading.

Analisi Post-reading activities check student understanding and guide them to discuss the topic of the reading, express their opinions, and explore how it relates to their own experiences.

Supersite

- Audio recordings of vocabulary terms

- Textbook activities

- Additional activities for extra practice

- **A proposito dell'autore/dell'autrice** reading with online-only activity

LABORATORIO DI SCRITTURA

synthesizes the lesson with a writing assignment.

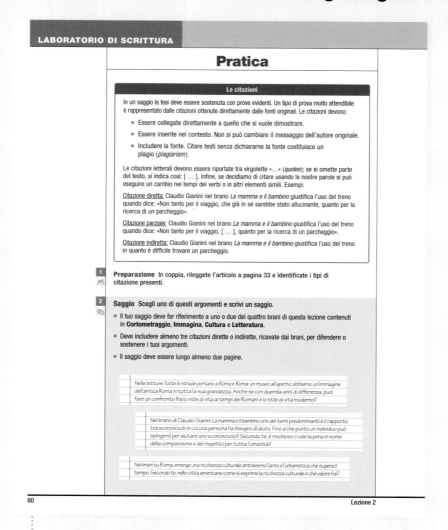

LABORATORIO DI SCRITTURA

Pratica

Le citazioni

In un saggio la tesi deve essere sostenuta con prove evidenti. Un tipo di prova molto attendibile è rappresentato dalle citazioni ottenute direttamente dalle fonti originali. Le citazioni devono:

- Essere collegate direttamente a quello che si vuole dimostrare.
- Essere inserite nel contesto. Non si può cambiare il messaggio dell'autore originale.
- Includere la fonte. Citare testi senza dichiararne la fonte costituisce un plagio (*plagiarism*).

Le citazioni letterali devono essere riportate tra virgolette «...» (*quotes*); se si omette parte del testo, si indica così: [...]. Infine, se decidiamo di citare usando le nostre parole si può eseguire un cambio nei tempi dei verbi o in altri elementi simili. Esempi:

Citazione diretta: Claudio Gianini nel brano *La mamma e il bambino* giustifica l'uso del treno quando dice: «Non tanto per il viaggio, che già in sé sarebbe stato allucinante, quanto per la ricerca di un parcheggio».

Citazione parziale: Claudio Gianini nel brano *La mamma e il bambino* giustifica l'uso del treno quando dice: «Non tanto per il viaggio, [...], quanto per la ricerca di un parcheggio».

Citazione indiretta: Claudio Gianini nel brano *La mamma e il bambino* giustifica l'uso del treno in quanto è difficile trovare un parcheggio.

1 **Preparazione** In coppia, rileggete l'articolo a pagina 33 e identificate i tipi di citazione presenti.

2 **Saggio** Scegli uno di questi argomenti e scrivi un saggio.

- Il tuo saggio deve far riferimento a uno o due dei quattro brani di questa lezione contenuti in **Cortometraggio**, **Immagina**, **Cultura** e **Letteratura**.
- Deve includere almeno tre citazioni dirette o indirette, ricavate dai brani, per difendere o sostenere i tuoi argomenti.
- Il saggio deve essere lungo almeno due pagine.

Nelle letture *Tutte le strade portano a Roma* e *Roma: un museo all'aperto*, abbiamo un'immagine dell'antica Roma in tutta la sua grandezza. Anche se con duemila anni di differenza, puoi fare un confronto fra lo stile di vita ai tempi dei Romani e lo stile di vita moderno?

Nel brano di Claudio Gianini *La mamma e il bambino* uno dei temi predominanti è il rapporto tra sconosciuti in cui una persona ha bisogno di aiuto. Fino a che punto un individuo può spingersi per aiutare uno sconosciuto? Secondo te, è rischioso o vale la pena in nome della compassione e del rispetto per tutta l'umanità?

Nei brani su Roma, emerge una ricchezza culturale attraverso l'arte e l'urbanistica che supera il tempo. Secondo te, nelle città americane come si esprime la ricchezza culturale e che valore ha?

80   Lezione 2

Preparazione & Pratica Writing strategies with practice help students develop their ability to draft clear, logical essays.

Saggio Writing topics bring the lesson together by asking students to construct and defend a thesis in the context of the lesson theme, film, and readings they have studied.

Supersite

- Composition engine for writing activity

VOCABOLARIO

summarizes the active vocabulary in each lesson.

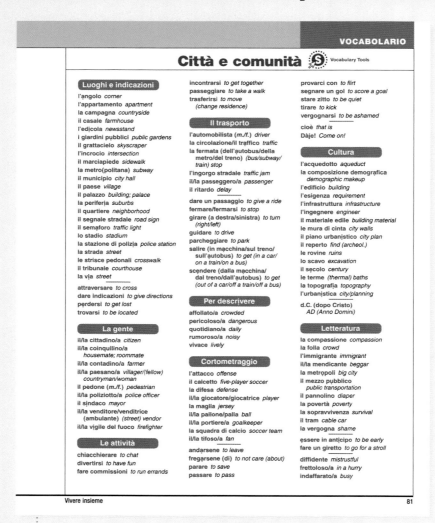

VOCABOLARIO

Città e comunità — Vocabulary Tools

Luoghi e indicazioni

l'angolo *corner*
l'appartamento *apartment*
la campagna *countryside*
il casale *farmhouse*
l'edicola *newsstand*
i giardini pubblici *public gardens*
il grattacielo *skyscraper*
l'incrocio *intersection*
il marciapiede *sidewalk*
la metro(politana) *subway*
il municipio *city hall*
il paese *village*
il palazzo *building; palace*
la periferia *suburbs*
il quartiere *neighborhood*
il segnale stradale *road sign*
il semaforo *traffic light*
lo stadio *stadium*
la stazione di polizia *police station*
la strada *street*
le strisce pedonali *crosswalk*
il tribunale *courthouse*
la via *street*

attraversare *to cross*
dare indicazioni *to give directions*
perdersi *to get lost*
trovarsi *to be located*

La gente

il/la cittadino/a *citizen*
il/la coinquilino/a *housemate; roommate*
il/la contadino/a *farmer*
il/la paesano/a *villager/(fellow) countryman/woman*
il pedone (m./f.) *pedestrian*
il/la poliziotto/a *police officer*
il sindaco *mayor*
il/la venditore/venditrice (ambulante) *(street) vendor*
il/la vigile del fuoco *firefighter*

Le attività

chiacchierare *to chat*
divertirsi *to have fun*
fare commissioni *to run errands*

incontrarsi *to get together*
passeggiare *to take a walk*
trasferirsi *to move (change residence)*

Il trasporto

l'automobilista (m./f.) *driver*
la circolazione/il traffico *traffic*
la fermata (dell'autobus/della metro/del treno) *(bus/subway/train) stop*
l'ingorgo stradale *traffic jam*
il/la passeggero/a *passenger*
il ritardo *delay*

dare un passaggio *to give a ride*
fermare/fermarsi *to stop*
girare (a destra/sinistra) *to turn (right/left)*
guidare *to drive*
parcheggiare *to park*
salire (in macchina/sul treno/sull'autobus) *to get (in a car/on a train/on a bus)*
scendere (dalla macchina/dal treno/dall'autobus) *to get (out of a car/off a train/off a bus)*

Per descrivere

affollato/a *crowded*
pericoloso/a *dangerous*
quotidiano/a *daily*
rumoroso/a *noisy*
vivace *lively*

Cortometraggio

l'attacco *offense*
il calcetto *five-player soccer*
la difesa *defense*
il/la giocatore/giocatrice *player*
la maglia *jersey*
il/la pallone/palla *ball*
il/la portiere/a *goalkeeper*
la squadra di calcio *soccer team*
il/la tifoso/a *fan*

andarsene *to leave*
fregarsene (di) *to not care (about)*
parare *to save*
passare *to pass*

provarci con *to flirt*
segnare un gol *to score a goal*
stare zitto *to be quiet*
tirare *to kick*
vergognarsi *to be ashamed*

cioè *that is*
Dàje! *Come on!*

Cultura

l'acquedotto *aqueduct*
la composizione demografica *demographic makeup*
l'edificio *building*
l'esigenza *requirement*
l'infrastruttura *infrastructure*
l'ingegnere *engineer*
il materiale edile *building material*
le mura di cinta *city walls*
il piano urbanistico *city plan*
il reperto *find (archeol.)*
le rovine *ruins*
lo scavo *excavation*
il secolo *century*
le terme *(thermal) baths*
la topografia *topography*
l'urbanistica *city/planning*

d.C. (dopo Cristo) *AD (Anno Domini)*

Letteratura

la compassione *compassion*
la folla *crowd*
l'immigrante *immigrant*
il/la mendicante *beggar*
la metropoli *big city*
il mezzo pubblico *public transportation*
il pannolino *diaper*
la povertà *poverty*
la sopravvivenza *survival*
il tram *cable car*
la vergogna *shame*

essere in anticipo *to be early*
fare un giretto *to go for a stroll*

diffidente *mistrustful*
frettoloso/a *in a hurry*
indaffarato/a *busy*

Vivere insieme   81

Vocabolario All the lesson's active vocabulary is grouped in easy-to-study thematic lists and tied to the lesson section in which it was presented.

Supersite

• Audio for all vocabulary items
• Vocabulary Tools

Instructor Resources

Immagina, Third Edition, offers a wide array of resources to support instructors and students. Below is a list of the key instructor support materials.

Instructor's Annotated Edition

This edition of **Immagina** contains activity answers, tips, suggestions, ideas for expansion, and more—all conveniently overprinted on the Student Edition page.

Online Instructor's Edition

Available on the Supersite for anytime access, with teaching suggestions, annotations, and the ability to add notes.

Supersite

The password-protected Instructor Supersite allows instructors to assign and track student progress through its course management system. Instructors have full access to the Student Supersite, and seamless integration with the **Immagina**, Third Edition, **WebSAM** and **vText**. Instructor Resources for easy access and download include:

- sample syllabus and lesson plan
- scripts and translations for the **Cortometraggio** films
- teaching suggestions for **Immagina** sections
- Student Activities Manual (SAM) Answer Key
- Grammar presentation slides

For more details about the Supersite, see pages IAE-12 and IAE-13.

Testing Program

The Testing Program is delivered in ready-to-print PDF and also in editable DOCX. Tests and exams can be downloaded from the Supersite or assigned online. The testing materials include lesson tests, a midterm exam, a final exam, and answer keys. An optional listening comprehension activity with the corresponding scripts and MP3 files is provided for each test and exam, and Oral Testing Suggestions are offered as Partner Chat activities.

Program Components

Student Edition vText
This virtual, interactive Student Edition provides a digital text, plus links to all Supersite activities and media.

Student Activities Manual (SAM)
The **Student Activities Manual** consists of two parts: the **Workbook** and the **Lab Manual**.

- #### Workbook
  The **Workbook** activities focus on developing students' reading and writing skills. Each workbook lesson reflects the organization of the corresponding textbook lesson; it begins with **Per cominciare**, followed by **Cortometraggio**, **Immagina**, and **Strutture**. Each lesson ends with **Sintesi**, which develops students' writing skills through a longer, more focused assignment.

- #### Lab Manual
  The **Lab Manual** activities focus on building students' listening comprehension and speaking skills as they reinforce the vocabulary and grammar of the corresponding textbook lesson. Each Lab Manual lesson contains a **Per cominciare** section followed by **Strutture**, and ending with **Vocabolario**, a complete list of the active lesson vocabulary.

WebSAM
Completely integrated with the **Immagina** Supersite, the **WebSAM** provides access to online **Workbook** and **Lab Manual** activities with instant feedback and grading for select activities. The complete audio program is accessible online in the **Lab Manual** and features record-submit functionality for select activities. The MP3 files can be downloaded from the **Immagina** Supersite and can be played on a computer, portable MP3 player or mobile device.

Immagina, Third Edition, Supersite
Included with the purchase of every new Student Edition, the Supersite (**vhlcentral.com**) gives students access to a wide variety of interactive activities for each section of every lesson of the student text, including auto-graded activities for extra practice with vocabulary, grammar, video, and cultural content; reference tools; the short films, the Lab Program MP3 files, and more.

Teaching with *Immagina*

Orienting Students to the Textbook

Have students flip through **Lezione 1**, and explain that all lessons are organized in the same manner. Emphasize that all sections occupy either a full page or spreads of two facing pages. Call students' attention to the use of charts, diagrams, word lists, and activities. Provide a brief overview of the main sections of each lesson: **Per cominciare, Cortometraggio, Immagina, Strutture, Cultura, Letteratura, Laboratorio di scrittura,** and **Vocabolario**. Then point out the **Attenzione!, Rimando,** and **Nota culturale** sidebars and explain that these boxes provide useful lexical, grammatical, and cultural information.

Flexible Lesson Organization

To meet the needs of diverse teaching styles, institutions, and instructional objectives, **Immagina** has a very flexible lesson organization. You can begin with the lesson opener spread and progress sequentially through the lesson, or you may rearrange the order of the material in each lesson to suit your teaching preferences and students' needs. If you do not want to devote class time to teaching grammar, you can assign the **Strutture** explanations for outside study, freeing up class time for working with the activities.

Identifying Active Vocabulary

The thematic vocabulary lists in **Per cominciare** are active vocabulary, as are all words and expressions in the **Vocabolario** boxes of the **Cortometraggio, Cultura,** and **Letteratura** sections. Words in the charts, lists, and sample sentences of **Strutture** are also part of the active vocabulary load. At the end of each lesson, the **Vocabolario** section provides a convenient one-page summary of the items students should know and that may appear on quizzes and exams.

Note that the marginal glosses from the readings and film captions are presented for recognition only. They are not included in testing materials, although you may wish to make them active vocabulary for your course, if you so choose. The additional terms and lexical variations provided in the annotations of the Instructor's Annotated Edition are also considered optional.

Suggestions for Using
Sommario and *Per cominciare*

Lesson Theme and Vocabulary

- Use the title, photo, and text on the lesson opening page as a springboard to introduce the themes and vocabulary of the lesson. Use the discussion questions in the introductory paragraph and **Preview** annotation for partner, group, or class activities.

- Allow time for students to scan the table of contents and flip through the pages of each lesson, much as they would a magazine. Have students point out sections that appeal to them and briefly describe the cultural and thematic content of each lesson.

- To prepare students for new material, have them review what they already know about each theme by brainstorming related vocabulary words they have already learned.

- Introduce the new vocabulary by describing words and categories, then asking students yes/no or multiple-choice questions.

- Introduce the new vocabulary using Total Physical Response (TPR) or interactive class games such as Charades or Pictionary.

- Tell students that they will see some of the vocabulary in the context of a short film and ask them to look at the vocabulary and predict what they think the film might be about.

- Use the lab materials in class to introduce vocabulary and develop listening skills, or assign lab and workbook activities for extra practice outside of class.

Pratica

- The **Pratica** exercises can be done orally as class, pair, or group activities. One pair activities may also be completed online as Partner Chat or Virtual Chat activity. They may also be assigned as written homework.

- Insist on the use of Italian during partner, chat, and group activities. Encourage students to use the language creatively.

- Have students form pairs or groups quickly. Assign or rotate partners and group members as necessary to ensure a greater variety of communicative exchanges.

- Allow sufficient time for pair and group activities (between five and ten minutes depending on the activity), but do not give students so much time that they lapse into English and socialize. Always give students a time limit for an activity before they begin.

- Circulate around the room and monitor students to make sure they are on task. Provide guidance as needed and note common errors for future review.

- Remind students to jot down information during pair and group discussion activities so they can report the results to the class.

- Encourage students to practice more online on the **Immagina** Supersite.

Suggestions for Using *Cortometraggio*

The **Cortometraggio** section of the student text and the **Immagina** Film Collection were created as interlocking pieces. All photos in the **Cortometraggio** section are video stills from the short films. These dramatic films highlight the themes and language of each lesson and provide comprehensible input at the discourse level. The films and corresponding activities offer rich and unique opportunities to build students' listening skills and cultural awareness.

Depending on your teaching preferences and school facilities, you might show the films in class, or you might assign them for viewing outside the classroom at **vhlcentral.com**. You could begin by showing the first film in class to teach students how to approach viewing a film and listening to natural speech. After that, you could work with the **Cortometraggio** section and have students view the remaining films outside of class. No matter which approach you choose, students have the support they need to view the films independently and process them in a meaningful way. Here are some strategies for coordinating the film with the subsections of **Cortometraggio**.

Preparazione

- Preview the vocabulary in **Preparazione** using the activities provided and the suggestions for teaching vocabulary on page IAE-34.
- Initiate group discussion of important themes and issues. Ask students to discuss recent films of the same genre or that touch on similar themes.

Scene

- The poster, photos, and text in **Scene** may be used in a variety of ways. Before they view the film, you might ask students to read or act out the dialogues, invent endings, or make predictions based on the photos and captions. You may also use the scenes while viewing, pausing for discussion at each of the scenes pictured. You may even choose to play the film first as an introduction to the lesson, returning to the scenes and text later for reinforcement.
- Use the **Nota culturale** sidebar to provide background information and cultural context before viewing the film, as a starting point for enrichment activities or projects, and to make connections to cultural information in other sections of the text.
- Use the film to introduce or reinforce the themes, vocabulary, and grammar points in each lesson, pausing and replaying examples of important words, structures, or concepts. If students need additional support before or while viewing, print the scripts (available on the **Immagina** Supersite) and provide them to students. Students may read them ahead of time and look up unknown words, or follow along as they watch.
- Before you show the film, ask students to read the **Sullo schermo** activity. Have them complete it while they watch the film.

Analisi

- Have students scan the comprehension questions before viewing the film. Pause the film after key scenes to ask related questions. Replay scenes as needed.
- Ask students to compare the plot, characters, and endings to their earlier predictions.
- Assign expansion and follow-up activities based on the film, such as film reviews, ideas for sequels, alternate endings, and comparisons with other **corti** or recent movies.

Suggestions for Using *Immagina*

The **Immagina** section is designed to be visually stimulating. It gives students the opportunity to get acquainted with Italian geography, history, architecture, traditions, and celebrities through engaging readings about the region of focus. In addition to the general suggestions listed here, the Instructor's Resources, available on the **Immagina** Supersite, contain specific teaching ideas and activities for every **Immagina** section.

- Use the locator map in the lesson opener to help students become familiar with the region(s) of focus.

- Use the main feature and photo of **Immagina** to introduce the region of focus. The feature articles can be assigned for outside reading or you may use them in class to develop reading skills.

- Use the shorter readings as you would a travel brochure to highlight must-see locations or iconic people in each region. Encourage students to bring in photographs from their own travels or assign group projects to research important cities, parks, architecture, or museums, according to the theme of each lesson.

- Check comprehension using the **Vero o falso?** and **Quanto hai imparato?** activities.

- Depending on your teaching preferences and time constraints, you may wish to use all of the **Progetto** features or you might select some for large oral projects. You may choose to have all students complete each **Progetto** or you may assign one or two small groups for each lesson.

- Use the **Comprensione** activity to quickly check that students understood the content of the **Galleria di persone illustri** paragraphs, then allow them to select one of the **Scrittura** topics for writing practice. Print out additional examples of the celebrities' work for use in class discussion. You may wish to incorporate additional readings from **Galleria di persone illustri** authors into the **Letteratura** section, focusing on genre, theme, or specific literary techniques. The films of famous directors and actors can be assigned for outside viewing and integrated with the **Cortometraggio** section. You may also have students select figures in the **Galleria di persone illustri** section for oral and written projects, such as mock interviews and biographies.

Suggestions for Using *Strutture*

Grammar Explanations

- Have students read the explanations at home and come to class with any questions. If necessary, explain the grammar in Italian and keep explanations to a minimum, about five to ten minutes for each point. Class time should be devoted to the **Pratica** and **Comunicazione** activities.

- Introduce new grammar in context, using short narrations, guided discussions, brief readings, or realia. Call on students to share what they already know about each grammar point.

- Use other sections of the text to introduce or reinforce grammatical concepts. Pause the **Cortometraggio** film to discuss uses of each structure, or have students jot down examples as they watch. Have students take notes of key structures as they read the **Cultura** and **Letteratura** selections.

Pratica, Comunicazione, and *Sintesi*

- The **Pratica** exercises can be done orally as class, pair, or group activities. They may also be assigned as written homework.

- Activities marked with a ⌕ mouse icon are also available on the Supersite with auto-grading or they can be submitted online for instructor grading. These activities may be assigned as homework; depending on students' success rate, devote additional time to the explanation or to extra **Pratica** activities before moving on to **Comunicazione**.

- Insist on the use of Italian for all pair and group activities.

- Have students form pairs or groups quickly or assign them yourself for variety. Allow sufficient time for **Comunicazione** activities (between five and ten minutes), but do not give students too much time or they may lapse into English and socialize. Always give students a time limit for an activity before they begin.

- Circulate around the room to answer questions and keep students on task.

- Encourage students to practice more online on the **Immagina** Supersite.

- Use **Sintesi** activities to review all four grammar points and to make connections with the theme, vocabulary, and culture of the lesson. Encourage debate and open discussion.

Suggestions for Using *Cultura*

Preparazione

- Preview the vocabulary in **Preparazione** using the activities provided and the suggestions for teaching vocabulary on page IAE-34.
- Refer students to the **Immagina** section for background information and cultural context.

Cultural Readings

- Talk to students about how to become effective readers in Italian. Point out the importance of using reading strategies. Encourage them to read every selection more than once. Explain that they should read the entire text through first to gain a general understanding of the main ideas without stopping to look up words. Then, they should read the text again for a more in-depth understanding of the material.
- Discourage students from translating the readings into English and relying too heavily on a bilingual dictionary. Tell them that reading directly in the language and using context to infer the meaning of unfamiliar words will help them grasp the ideas better and improve their ability to discuss the reading in Italian.
- Use the reading to reinforce the themes and linguistic structures of each lesson.

Analisi

- Have students scan the comprehension questions before reading, then pause after each paragraph to ask related questions. Ask students to summarize the reading orally or in writing.

Suggestions for Using *Letteratura*

Preparazione

- Preview the vocabulary in **Preparazione** using the activities provided and the suggestions for teaching vocabulary on page IAE-34.
- Have students read the background information about each author.
- Introduce important themes and literary techniques used in the reading and call attention to genre and style. Encourage students to think about other works they have read in Italian or English of the same genre or that make use of similar themes and techniques.

Literary Readings

- Talk to students about how to become effective readers in Italian. Point out the importance of using reading strategies. Encourage them to read every selection more than once. Explain that they should read the entire text through first to gain a general understanding of the plot or main ideas without stopping to look up words. Then, they should read the text again for a more in-depth understanding of the material.
- Discourage students from translating the readings into English and relying too heavily on a bilingual dictionary. Tell them that reading directly in the language and using context to infer the meaning of unfamiliar words will help them grasp the ideas better and improve their ability to discuss the reading in Italian.
- Use the reading to reinforce the themes and linguistic structures of each lesson.

Analisi

- Have students scan the comprehension questions before reading, then pause after each paragraph to ask related questions. Ask students to summarize the reading orally or in writing.
- For the **Tema** activities (and other writing assignments), have students maintain a writing portfolio so they can periodically review their progress. The Composition Engine on the Supersite allows you to edit a student's draft. Have students create a running list for their reference of the most common grammatical or spelling errors they make for use when writing, when revising their work, or for peer editing. Explain your grading system for writing assignments. This rubric could be used or adapted to suit your needs.

Evaluation			
Criteria	**Scale**		**Scoring**
Appropriate details	1 2 3 4	Excellent	18–20 points
Organization	1 2 3 4	Good	14–17 points
Use of vocabulary	1 2 3 4	Satisfactory	10–13 points
Grammatical accuracy	1 2 3 4	Unsatisfactory	<10 points
Mechanics	1 2 3 4		

Suggestions for Using *Laboratorio di scrittura*

- The **Laboratorio di scrittura** essays are best suited as written homework. The preparation activities may be done orally in pairs or groups.

- Encourage students to be creative in their writings, but remind them to follow the essay requirements carefully and use vocabulary they know, rather than relying on a dictionary.

- Encourage students to use the check lists provided in the **Punti per la revisione dei saggi** appendix of the student edition to review their work before handing in a draft or the final essay.

- Allow class time for peer review of drafts; remind students to be tactful in their comments and to give positive feedback while reading with a critical eye.

- Make a list of frequent errors and review the material with the class.

- Explain to students how you will grade their writing. For example, you could use the rubric on the previous page and adapt it to suit your needs.

Course Planning

The **Immagina** program was developed with the need for flexibility and manageability in a wide variety of academic situations in mind. The following sample course plans illustrate how **Immagina** can be used in courses on either semester or quarter systems. You should, of course, feel free to organize your courses in the way that best suits your students' needs and your instructional goals.

Two-Semester System

This chart shows how **Immagina** can be completed in a two-semester course. Please see the **Sommario** (IAE-6–10) for a breakdown of the material covered in each lesson.

Semester 1	**Semester 2**
Lessons 1–5	Lessons 6–10

Quarter System

This chart illustrates how **Immagina** can be used in the quarter system. If you wish to have more time for review at the end of the course, you may choose to teach four lessons in the first quarter instead of three. Keep in mind, however, that you will need to adjust testing materials accordingly in the **Testing Program** (available on the Supersite).

Quarter 1	**Quarter 2**	**Quarter 3**
Lessons 1–3	Lessons 4–6	Lessons 7–10

Reviewers

We extend a special thank you to the contributing writers and editors whose hard work was essential to bringing **Immagina**, Third Edition, to fruition.

Vista Higher Learning would also like to offer sincere thanks to the many instructors nationwide who reviewed **Immagina**. Their insights, ideas, and detailed comments were invaluable to the final product.

Dr. Anna Gray
Miami University, OH

Pia L. Bertucci, PhD
The University of South Carolina, SC

Sarah Annunziato
University of Virginia, VA

Costantina Tolu
Cunningham, NV

Susan Amatangelo
College of the Holy Cross, MA

Mary Sisler, PhD
Hamilton College, NY

Jonathan Druker
Illinois State University, IL

Jonathan R. Hiller
Adelphi University, NY

Magda Pearson
Florida International University, FL

Maria Mann
Nassau Community College, NY

Mariagabriella Gangi
University of Massachusetts-Lowell, MA

Andrew Korn
University of Rochester, NY

Alessia Blad
University of Notre Dame, IN

Stella Mattioli
University of Virginia, VA

Adrienne D'Agostino
Malden High School, MA

Antonina Campisciano Ungaro
Maine East High School, IL

Gina Gallo Reinhard
Bristol Central, CT

Dr. Linda De Caterina
San Diego City College, CA

Manuela Biancotti
St. Thomas Aquinas High School, FL

Antonella Dell'Anna
Arizona State University, AZ

Annelise M. Brody
Washington University, MO

Gina R. Pietrantoni
Arizona State Unviersity, AZ

Carmen De Lorenzo
Michigan State University, MI

Julia Ombres
Duquesne University, PA

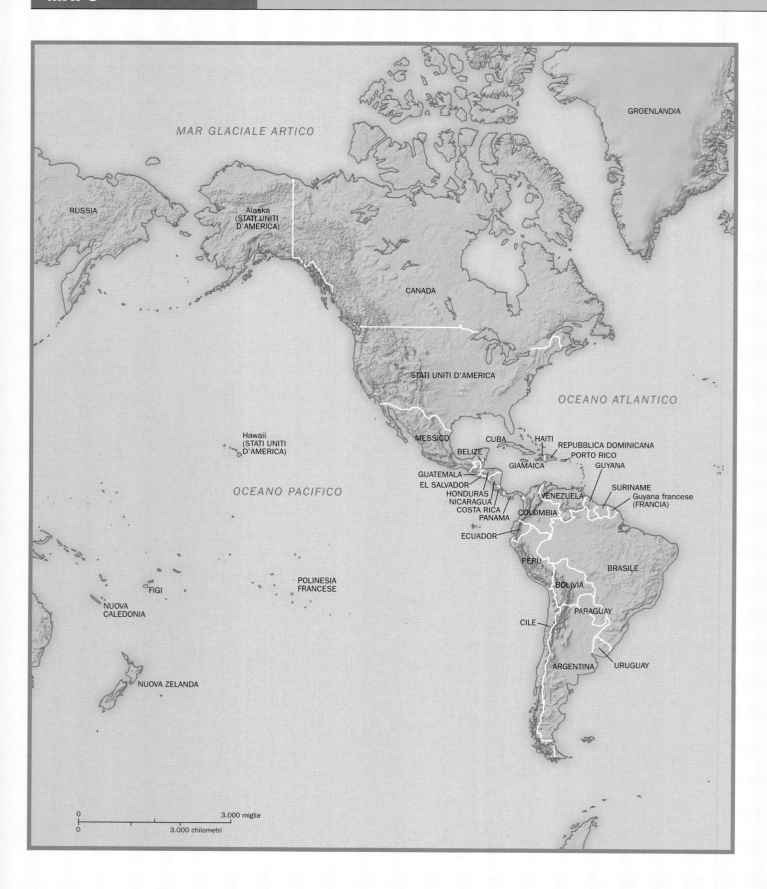

MAR GLACIALE ARTICO

GROENLANDIA

RUSSIA

Alaska
(STATI UNITI
D'AMERICA)

CANADA

STATI UNITI D'AMERICA

OCEANO ATLANTICO

Hawaii
(STATI UNITI
D'AMERICA)

MESSICO

CUBA

HAITI

REPUBBLICA DOMINICANA
PORTO RICO

BELIZE

GIAMAICA

GUYANA

OCEANO PACIFICO

GUATEMALA
EL SALVADOR
HONDURAS
NICARAGUA
COSTA RICA
PANAMA

VENEZUELA

SURINAME
Guyana francese
(FRANCIA)

COLOMBIA

ECUADOR

PERÙ

BRASILE

BOLIVIA

POLINESIA
FRANCESE

FIGI

NUOVA
CALEDONIA

PARAGUAY

CILE

ARGENTINA

URUGUAY

NUOVA ZELANDA

0   3.000 miglia
0   3.000 chilometri

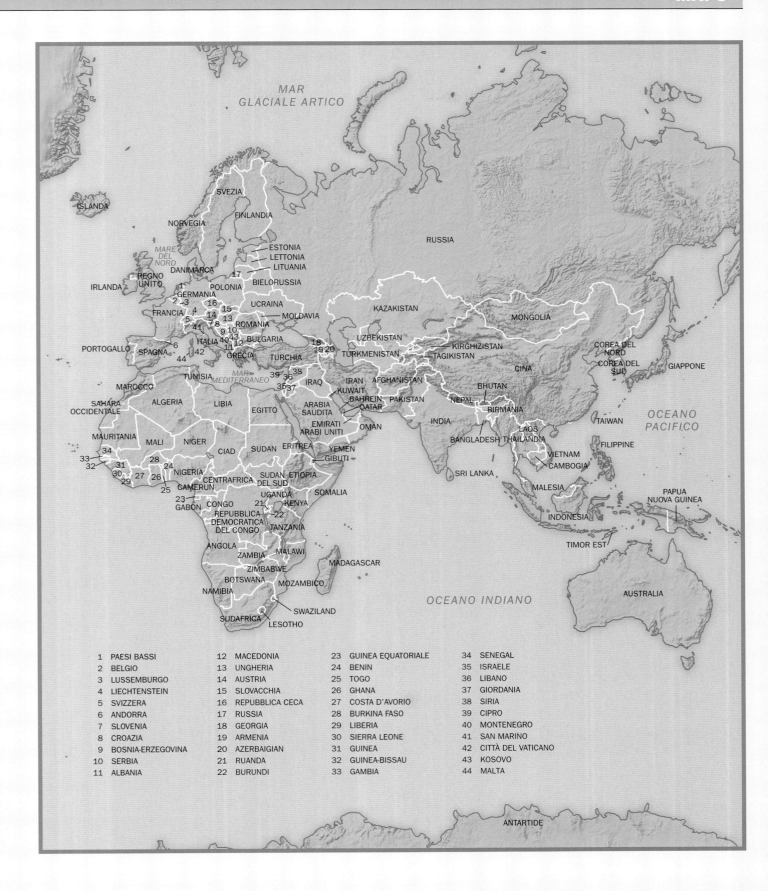

MAR GLACIALE ARTICO

ISLANDA

SVEZIA

NORVEGIA

FINLANDIA

MARE DEL NORD

ESTONIA
LETTONIA
LITUANIA

DANIMARCA

REGNO UNITO

IRLANDA

17

BIELORUSSIA

RUSSIA

1 POLONIA
GERMANIA
2 3
FRANCIA   4   14 15
5   13
7   8
41 9 10
ITALIA 40 43
11   42
44

UCRAINA

MOLDAVIA

ROMANIA

BULGARIA

KAZAKISTAN

MONGOLIA

PORTOGALLO   SPAGNA   6

GRECIA

18
19 20

UZBEKISTAN

TURKMENISTAN

KIRGHIZISTAN

TAGIKISTAN

CINA

COREA DEL NORD
COREA DEL SUD

GIAPPONE

TURCHIA

MAR MEDITERRANEO

TUNISIA

39 36 38
35 37

IRAQ

IRAN   AFGHANISTAN

KUWAIT
BAHREIN   PAKISTAN
QATAR

NEPAL

BHUTAN

BIRMANIA

TAIWAN

OCEANO PACIFICO

MAROCCO

ALGERIA

LIBIA

EGITTO

ARABIA SAUDITA

EMIRATI ARABI UNITI

OMAN

INDIA

LAOS
THAILANDIA

VIETNAM
CAMBOGIA

FILIPPINE

SAHARA OCCIDENTALE

MAURITANIA

MALI

NIGER

CIAD

SUDAN

ERITREA

YEMEN
GIBUTI

BANGLADESH

SRI LANKA

MALESIA

PAPUA NUOVA GUINEA

34
33
32
31
30 27 26
29   25

28

24

NIGERIA

CAMERUN

23
GABON

CONGO

CENTRAFRICA
SUDAN DEL SUD

ETIOPIA

UGANDA   KENYA
21
22

SOMALIA

REPUBBLICA DEMOCRATICA DEL CONGO

TANZANIA

INDONESIA

TIMOR EST

ANGOLA

ZAMBIA

MALAWI

ZIMBABWE

MADAGASCAR

AUSTRALIA

NAMIBIA

BOTSWANA

MOZAMBICO

OCEANO INDIANO

SUDAFRICA   LESOTHO

SWAZILAND

1	PAESI BASSI	12	MACEDONIA	23	GUINEA EQUATORIALE	34	SENEGAL
2	BELGIO	13	UNGHERIA	24	BENIN	35	ISRAELE
3	LUSSEMBURGO	14	AUSTRIA	25	TOGO	36	LIBANO
4	LIECHTENSTEIN	15	SLOVACCHIA	26	GHANA	37	GIORDANIA
5	SVIZZERA	16	REPUBBLICA CECA	27	COSTA D'AVORIO	38	SIRIA
6	ANDORRA	17	RUSSIA	28	BURKINA FASO	39	CIPRO
7	SLOVENIA	18	GEORGIA	29	LIBERIA	40	MONTENEGRO
8	CROAZIA	19	ARMENIA	30	SIERRA LEONE	41	SAN MARINO
9	BOSNIA-ERZEGOVINA	20	AZERBAIGIAN	31	GUINEA	42	CITTÀ DEL VATICANO
10	SERBIA	21	RUANDA	32	GUINEA-BISSAU	43	KOSOVO
11	ALBANIA	22	BURUNDI	33	GAMBIA	44	MALTA

ANTARTIDE

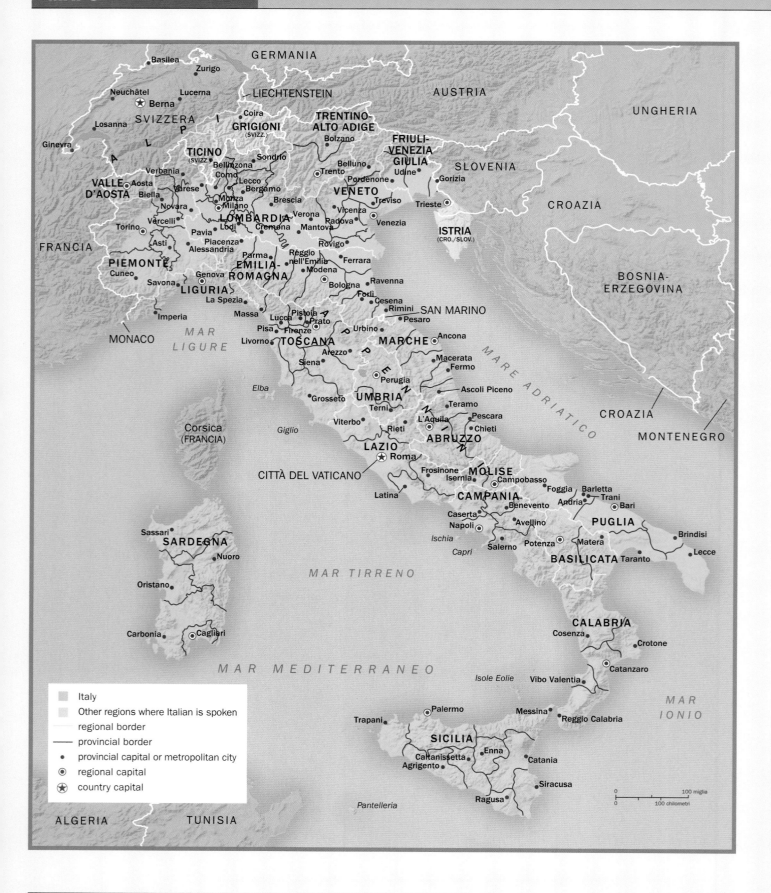

Italy

Other regions where Italian is spoken

regional border

provincial border

• provincial capital or metropolitan city

◉ regional capital

✪ country capital

500 miglia

0   500 chilometri

Paesi dove l'italiano
è una lingua ufficiale

MARE DI
BARENTS

MARE DI
NORVEGIA

ISLANDA

Reykjavik

SVEZIA

FINLANDIA

NORVEGIA

Helsinki

RUSSIA

Oslo

Stoccolma

Tallinn

ESTONIA

Mosca

MARE
DEL NORD

DANIMARCA

MAR BALTICO

Riga

LETTONIA

LITUANIA

Copenaghen

RUSSIA

Vilnius

Minsk

Dublino

IRLANDA

BIELORUSSIA

REGNO
UNITO

PAESI
BASSI

Berlino

Varsavia

Kiev

Londra

Amsterdam

POLONIA

UCRAINA

OCEANO
ATLANTICO

Bruxelles

GERMANIA

LUSSEMBURGO

BELGIO

Praga

Lussemburgo

REPUBBLICA
CECA

SLOVACCHIA

Parigi

LIECHTENSTEIN

Bratislava

Vienna

MOLDAVIA

Budapest

Chisinau

AUSTRIA

Berna

Vaduz

SLOVENIA

UNGHERIA

FRANCIA

SVIZZERA

Lubiana

Zagabria

ROMANIA

Bucarest

MAR NERO

ITALIA

CROAZIA

Monaco

BOSNIA
ERZEGOVINA

Belgrado

PORTOGALLO

Andorra la Vella

SAN
MARINO

Città di
San Marino

Sarajevo

SERBIA

COSSOVO

BULGARIA

MONACO

Pristina

MONTENEGRO

Sofia

Ankara

ANDORRA

Roma

Podgorica

Skopje

Lisbona

Madrid

Corsica

CITTÀ DEL
VATICANO

Tirana

MACEDONIA

TURCHIA

SPAGNA

ALBANIA

Sardegna

GRECIA

Atene

Nicosia

Sicilia

CIPRO

Algeri

Tunisi

La Valetta

MALTA

Rabat

ALGERIA

TUNISIA

MAR MEDITERRANEO

MAROCCO

Tripoli

Il Cairo

LIBIA

EGITTO

THIRD EDITION

IMMAGINA

L'ITALIANO SENZA CONFINI

Sentire e vivere

L'essere umano è un animale sociale. Abbiamo bisogno degli altri per sentirci vivi. Amici, famiglia, compagni di vita, colleghi di lavoro, ma anche incontri con nuove persone, ci permettono di confrontarci, di esprimere i nostri sentimenti e quindi (*therefore*) di imparare a capire noi stessi. In una società che cambia e che diventa sempre più multietnica, che rapporto hai con gli altri? Ti senti meglio da solo o in mezzo ad altre persone? Prova a riflettere e a capire perché.

8

32

GLI ITALIANI NEL MONDO

PREVIEW Point to the photo on the previous page and to the photo of three young people on this page. Engage students in a discussion about friendship and relationships. **Dove avete conosciuto i vostri amici? A scuola? Nel vostro quartiere? Sulla rete? Quali sono le caratteristiche di un(a) buon(a) amico/a?**

I rapporti personali  Vocabulary Tools

La personalità

affascinante *charming*

affettuoso/a *affectionate*
attraente *attractive*
geniale *great*
idealista *idealistic*
insicuro/a *insecure*
(im)maturo/a *(im)mature*
(dis)onesto/a *(dis)honest*
orgoglioso/a *proud*
ottimista *optimistic*
pessimista *pessimistic*
prudente *careful*
sensibile *sensitive*
timido *shy*
tranquillo/a *calm*
umile *humble*

Lo stato civile

divorziare (da) *to divorce*
fidanzarsi (con) *to get engaged (to)*
sposarsi (con) *to get married (to)*

celibe *single (m.)*
divorziato/a *divorced*
fidanzato/a *engaged; fiancé(e)*
nubile *single (f.)*
sposato/a *married*
vedovo/a *widowed; widower/widow*

Explain that **sposarsi (con)** is a reflexive verb, while **sposare** is followed by a direct object.

I rapporti

l'amicizia *friendship*

l'anima gemella *soul mate*
l'appuntamento *date*
il colpo di fulmine *love at first sight*
il/la compagno/a *partner*
la coppia *couple*

il matrimonio *wedding*
i pettegolezzi *gossip*

avere fiducia (in) *to trust*
condividere *to share*
contare su *to rely on*
lasciare *to leave*
mentire *to lie*
meritare *to deserve*
rompere con *to break up with*
uscire con *to go out with*

comprensivo/a *understanding*
(in)dimenticabile *(un)forgettable*
(in)fedele *(un)faithful*

ATTENZIONE!

Generally, Italian words are stressed on the second-to-last syllable. To aid with pronunciation, when words do not follow this rule and are presented in a vocabulary or grammar feature, this text uses a dot under the stressed vowel: (1) when a word is stressed on the third or fourth syllable from the last (**parole sdrucciole e bisdrucciole**), and (2) when a diphthong is broken because the **i** or **u** is stressed (ex.: **farmacia**, **paura**). In addition, it is sometimes used for clarification when presenting difficult words or when contrasting words.

I sentimenti

adorare *to adore*
amare *to love*
arrabbiarsi *to get angry*

avere vergogna (di) *to be ashamed (of)*
dare fastidio (a) *to annoy*
disturbare *to bother*
innamorarsi *to fall in love*
odiare *to hate*
provare *to feel*
sentirsi *to feel*
sognare *to dream*
volere bene a *to feel affection for*

ansioso/a *anxious*
contrariato/a *annoyed*
deluso/a *disappointed*
depresso/a *depressed*

emozionato/a *excited*
entusiasta *enthusiastic*
geloso/a *jealous*
preoccupato/a *worried*
stufo/a *fed up*

SINONIMI
avere vergogna (di) ←→ vergognarsi (di)
avere fiducia (in) ←→ fidarsi (di)
la personalità ←→ il carattere

Give students examples with **provare** and **sentirsi**. Ex.: **provare odio/rancore**; **sentirsi felice**.

INSTRUCTIONAL RESOURCES
Audioscripts, Answer Keys, Lab MP3s
SAM/WebSAM: WB, LM

Pratica e comunicazione

1

L'intruso Trova la parola che non c'entra.

1. affascinante   ottimista   timido   (nubile)
2. avere fiducia   (odiare)   adorare   volere bene
3. (prudente)   ansioso   preoccupato   stufo
4. sposato   divorziato   fidanzato   (contrariato)
5. arrabbiarsi   odiare   (innamorarsi)   dare fastidio
6. orgoglioso   (vedovo)   ottimista   immaturo
7. (pettegolezzi)   coppia   anima gemella   matrimonio
8. depresso   emozionato   (geniale)   preoccupato

2

Sinonimi Inserisci la parola o l'espressione più adeguata per ogni situazione.

anima gemella	colpo di fulmine	entusiasta	idealista
ansioso	deluso	geloso	indimenticabile

1. Ieri sera sono uscito con Giulia; è stata una serata bellissima che non dimenticherò mai. _indimenticabile_
2. La settimana scorsa mio fratello ha conosciuto Elena e si è innamorato subito di lei. _colpo di fulmine_
3. L'estate scorsa ho mangiato in un famoso ristorante, ma il cibo non era buono come mi avevano detto. _deluso_
4. Domani inizio un nuovo progetto e sono molto contento. _entusiasta_
5. Mio cugino non è felice quando la sua fidanzata esce con le amiche; ha paura che lei incontri un altro uomo. _geloso_
6. Mia sorella ha finalmente trovato l'uomo perfetto per lei. _anima gemella_

3

Introverso o estroverso? Rispondi alle domande e poi calcola il tuo punteggio. Confronta il risultato del tuo test con quello di un(a) compagno/a.

Sì	Qualche volta	No		Punteggio
☐	☐	☐	1. Diventi ansioso/a quando c'è tanta gente?	**Sì** = 0 punti
☐	☐	☐	2. Ti imbarazza mostrare le tue emozioni?	**Q.v.** = 1 punto
☐	☐	☐	3. Hai paura di essere il primo/la prima a parlare?	**No** = 2 punti
☐	☐	☐	4. L'idea di avere un appuntamento con qualcuno che non conosci ti fa paura?	**Risultati**
☐	☐	☐	5. Ti disturbano le persone che ti fanno tante domande?	**Da 0 a 7 punti** Hai la tendenza a essere introverso/a. Esci più spesso.
☐	☐	☐	6. Hai paura di parlare in pubblico?	
☐	☐	☐	7. Durante un viaggio in treno o in aereo cominci a parlare con chi ti è seduto vicino?	**Da 8 a 11 punti** Non sei né introverso/a né estroverso/a. Hai un buon equilibrio.
☐	☐	☐	8. Ti senti più felice quando sei in compagnia di altre persone?	**Da 12 a 20 punti** Hai la tendenza ad essere estroverso/a. Ascolti sempre gli altri?
☐	☐	☐	9. Dici mai di essere d'accordo con qualcuno solo per evitare una discussione?	
☐	☐	☐	10. Ti senti molto in imbarazzo in alcune situazioni?	

1 Explain that **volere bene a** (*to feel affection for*) is generally used for friends and family members. **Amare** is used in romantic relationships. Example: **Ti voglio bene, mamma./Ti amo, Sara.**

1 To check comprehension, ask students to describe what the three similar words in each group have in common.

1 Have pairs of students add two more groups of new vocabulary words. Then call on volunteers to indicate the word that does not belong.

2 Have pairs of students create situations for two additional vocabulary words. Then call on each pair to read their situations while the rest of the class guesses what is being described.

3 Before assigning the activity, ask if anyone has ever taken a personality test. Have students predict their results.

3 After students complete the test, ask: **Ti sorprende il risultato del test? Perché?**

TEACHING OPTION Have students describe their **anima gemella** using the new vocabulary.

Practice more at **vhlcentral.com**.

INSTRUCTIONAL RESOURCES
Supersite: Video, Script & Translation
SAM/WebSAM: WB

Preparazione  Vocabulary Tools

Vocabolario del cortometraggio

il binario *train track*
buttare via *to throw away*
la colpa *fault*
la piattaforma *platform*
resistente *sturdy*

Vocabolario utile

la commessa *saleswoman*
indossare *to wear*
mettersi *to put on (clothing, shoes)*
l'orario *schedule*

la scatola *box*
i tacchi alti/bassi *high/low heels*
truccarsi *to put on make up*
la vetrina *shop window*
vendicativo/a *vengeful*

ESPRESSIONI

basta *enough*
come può essere finita? *how can it be over?*
dai! *come on!*
perché fai così? *why are you doing this?*

---

1 Ask students to compare their answers and then to report them to the class.

1 **Un'avventura in treno** Elisa va in treno a Milano. Usate le parole dalla lista del vocabolario per completare la storia.

Pronto, parla la polizia? Ho bisogno d'aiuto. Oggi è il compleanno di mia sorella Giulia che vive a Milano; io abito a Venezia e volevo andare a trovarla in treno. Stamattina prima di andare alla stazione ho controllato l'(1) ___orario___: c'era un treno per Milano che partiva alle 11 dal (2) ___binario___ numero 8. Poi sono andata a comprare il regalo per Giulia. Nella (3) ___vetrina___ di un negozio ho visto dei bellissimi guanti neri, eleganti e (4) ___resistenti___ allo stesso tempo. Con il freddo che fa a Milano in inverno bisogna (5) ___indossare___ spesso i guanti. Sono entrata per comprarli e ho chiesto alla (6) ___commessa___ di metterli in una (7) ___scatola___. C'era molto traffico. Il treno stava quasi per partire quando sono finalmente arrivata alla stazione. Ho dovuto correre per non perderlo! Per fortuna avevo i (8) ___tacchi bassi___; con quelli alti non sarei mai arrivata in tempo.

Una volta sul treno, mi sono seduta per qualche minuto e poi sono andata a prendere un caffè nel vagone ristorante. Quando sono ritornata al mio posto la scatola non c'era più! Pronto?

Pronto? Oh, no! Il mio telefonino si sta scaricando! Pronto? Polizia?

2 Encourage students to use words that describe feelings from the previous section.

2 **Continuate la storia** Secondo voi, cosa è successo alla scatola? Scegliete una conclusione e commentate la vostra scelta.

- Elisa ritrova il regalo e festeggia con la sorella.
- Elisa non ritrova il regalo e nella confusione perde anche il telefonino.
- La polizia arriva e pensa che Elisa sia la ladra.

3

Cosa fareste? In coppia, rispondete a queste domande.

1. Quali situazioni vi causano stress? Parlate delle vostre esperienze.
2. Vi siete mai trovati in una situazione particolarmente stressante? Descrivete la situazione.
3. Quali sentimenti avete provato? Come avete reagito?
4. Secondo voi, quale effetto ha lo stress sulle persone?

4

Come reagiresti?

A. Scegli la reazione che corrisponde meglio alla tua personalità.

4 As a warm-up, ask students: **Come reagite a un evento triste? E a un evento felice? Siete molto emotivi o più controllati? Estroversi o introversi?**

Test della **Personalità**

1. **Aspetti una mail da una persona con cui vorresti avere una relazione.**
   - **a.** Controlli l'e-mail ogni cinque minuti.
   - **b.** Hai da fare (*You have things to do*) ma controlli l'e-mail ogni volta che puoi.
   - **c.** Non ti preoccupi troppo e controlli l'e-mail normalmente.

2. **La mail che ricevi da un tuo professore o dal tuo capo è scritta tutta in lettere maiuscole (*uppercase*).**
   - **a.** Pensi che la persona che ti scrive sia molto arrabbiata con te.
   - **b.** Pensi che sia un errore.
   - **c.** Non lo noti.

3. **Una persona che conosci è molto triste.**
   - **a.** Anche tu ti senti triste come quella persona.
   - **b.** Provi compassione per la persona.
   - **c.** Pensi che i sentimenti degli altri non ti riguardino.

4. **Hai una brutta notizia da riferire a qualcuno.**
   - **a.** La riferisci subito, faccia a faccia. È il modo migliore.
   - **b.** Eviti (*avoid*) la persona per qualche giorno prima di riferire la notizia.
   - **c.** Preferisci mandare una mail che parlare faccia a faccia.

5. **Il tuo telefonino squilla (*rings*) alle tre di notte. Qual è la tua prima reazione?**
   - **a.** Ti preoccupi: deve essere successo qualcosa di grave.
   - **b.** Ti arrabbi per essere stato/a svegliato/a così all'improvviso.
   - **c.** Non lo senti e continui a dormire.

6. **Compri qualcosa on-line. Quale metodo di spedizione preferisci?**
   - **a.** Posta celere (*express*): sei impaziente.
   - **b.** Posta normale: sai aspettare.
   - **c.** Posta assicurata: non si sa mai.

B. In coppia, confrontate le vostre reazioni. Avete personalità simili o diverse?

5

Immaginate In coppia, guardate le immagini e immaginate una storia.

- Cosa fa la donna? Quali sono i suoi sentimenti?
- Perché guarda le scarpe in vetrina?
- Chi è l'uomo? Qual è il rapporto tra i due personaggi?
- Come sono le loro rispettive personalità?

5 After students have come up with their own narration, ask them to share it with the rest of the class.

 Practice more at **vhlcentral.com**.

Video

Trama *Una donna riceve una brutta notizia per telefono e ha pochi minuti per reagire. Cosa farà per risolvere la situazione?*

DONNA Ciao amore! Perché non sei qui?

UOMO Sono in stazione. Devo dirti una cosa. È finita. Devo dirti che è finita, basta. Dai, ciao.

DONNA Ti prego di non buttar via tutto! Siamo stati benissimo insieme.

COMMESSA Signorina, la carta!
DONNA Dopo, dopo! Taxi!

DONNA In stazione!

DONNA Ehi...

🔗 Sullo **SCHERMO**

Mentre guardi il corto completa queste frasi.

1. Il telefono ___d___.
2. L'uomo è ___c___.
3. Nella vetrina c'è ___a___.
4. La donna lascia ___e___.
5. La donna prende ___b___.

a. un paio di scarpe
b. un taxi
c. alla stazione
d. sveglia la donna
e. la carta di credito

Analisi

1

Comprensione Indica se l'affermazione è **vera** o **falsa**. Dopo, in coppia, correggete le affermazioni false.

Vero	Falso		
☑	☐	1.	La donna è felice quando risponde al telefono.
☐	☑	2.	L'uomo è innamorato della donna.
☐	☑	3.	L'uomo è all'aeroporto.
☐	☑	4.	La donna si veste con calma.
☑	☐	5.	La donna corre per strada.
☑	☐	6.	La donna compra un paio di scarpe.
☐	☑	7.	La donna prende la metropolitana.
☑	☐	8.	Alla stazione la donna si cambia le scarpe.
☑	☐	9.	L'uomo sta salendo sul treno quando arriva la donna.
☐	☑	10.	L'uomo sorride alla fine del film.

2

I protagonisti Descrivi le personalità e i sentimenti della donna e dell'uomo nel corto, mettendo le parole della lista vicino al personaggio appropriato. Dopo, in coppia, confrontate le vostre descrizioni. Some answers will vary.

a. ansioso/a	**d. intelligente**	**g. stufo/a**
b. contrariato/a	**e. onesto/a**	**h. tranquillo/a**
c. sensibile	**f. sicuro/a**	**i. vendicativo/a**

 **Donna: personalità e sentimenti**
a, b, c, d, i

 Uomo: personalità e sentimenti
b, c, e, f, g, h

Opinioni

A. Sei d'accordo con queste affermazioni?

Affermazioni	sono d'accordo	non sono d'accordo
1. L'uomo e la donna stavano insieme da molti anni.	☐	☐
2. La donna è vanitosa.	☐	☐
3. L'uomo è egoista.	☐	☐
4. La vendetta è una soluzione a molti problemi.	☐	☐
5. Le separazioni sono sempre dolorose.	☐	☐
6. L'amore è un sentimento pericoloso.	☐	☐
7. Lo shopping è un'attività terapeutica.	☐	☐
8. Una persona si può giudicare dalle scarpe che indossa.	☐	☐
9. Le emozioni possono influenzare il nostro modo di vestire.	☐	☐
10. È importante seguire la moda per avere successo.	☐	☐

B. In coppia, spiegate le ragioni delle vostre risposte. Ci sono delle ragioni personali o delle esperienze passate che hanno motivato le vostre risposte? Quali?

2 Before completing the activity, review the **Per cominciare** vocabulary by asking each student to express an emotion with a facial expression; the rest of the class should guess the emotion being expressed. After completing the activity, ask students to expand their descriptions to include physical attributes, style of clothing (and shoes!), and to try to guess what the characters' professions, hobbies, and friends might be like.

3 Encourage students to share their opinions with the rest of the class. If there is controversy about a particular topic, divide the class into two teams and ask them to debate the issue. Ask everyone to give at least one opinion.

4 **Commenti** In coppia, rispondete a queste domande.

1. La donna aveva già un piano (*plan*) preciso quando ha deciso di uscire o le è venuta un'idea quando ha visto le scarpe in vetrina?

2. Che conclusione vi aspettavate quando l'uomo e la donna si sono incontrati alla stazione?

3. Quale potrebbe essere un titolo alternativo per questo film?

4. Il film è una riflessione sulle relazioni fra donne e uomini o è, più semplicemente, una storia superficiale con un finale a sorpresa?

5. Vi ricordate un altro film o un'altra storia con un finale inaspettato? Quale?

5 **Modi di comunicare**

A. Qual è il modo migliore di comunicare emozioni e sentimenti? In coppia, indicate i vantaggi e gli svantaggi per ogni mezzo di comunicazione.

mezzo di comunicazione	vantaggi	svantaggi
una lettera		
una mail		
una telefonata		
una conversazione faccia a faccia		
un SMS (*text message*)		
Altro?		

B. Ora descrivete qual è il mezzo di comunicazione migliore nelle seguenti situazioni.

- Devi lamentarti con la compagnia della tua carta di credito perché ha aumentato il tasso d'interesse.

- Devi comunicare al(la) tuo/a coinquilino/a che stai per lasciare l'appartamento che condividete.

- Devi fare dei piani per il fine settimana con il/la tuo/a migliore amico/a.

- Devi dire ai tuoi genitori che non hai superato (*passed*) un esame importante.

6 **Una conversazione** In coppia, inventate una conversazione basata su una di queste situazioni e poi recitatelo davanti alla classe.

A

L'uomo e la donna si incontrano alcuni mesi dopo. Immaginate la prima conversazione fra i due. Si riconciliano?

B

Hai un appuntamento con un(a) ragazzo/a. Sei molto nervoso/a e non sai cosa indossare. Chiedi l'opinione del(la) tuo/a coinquilino/a.

7 **Scriviamo** Racconta la storia del corto dal punto di vista di un altro personaggio: per esempio, l'uomo, la commessa del negozio di scarpe, l'autista del taxi, o viaggiatore alla stazione che osserva la scena finale.

4 Ask an additional question: **C'è qualcosa di «italiano» in questo film? Che cosa?**

6 Give students an additional, more open ended option: **Pensate ad una situazione difficile e immaginate il dialogo fra le due persone coinvolte: qual è il problema? Perché è una situazione stressante? Nel dialogo esprimete i vostri sentimenti e suggerite una o più soluzioni al problema.**

7 While students are preparing to write, ask **Come interpreta i sentimenti dei personaggi il nuovo narratore? Come cambia la storia?**

Practice more at **vhlcentral.com**.

INSTRUCTIONAL RESOURCES: Teaching suggestions; Answer Keys
SAM/WebSAM: WB

IMMAGINA GLI ITALIANI

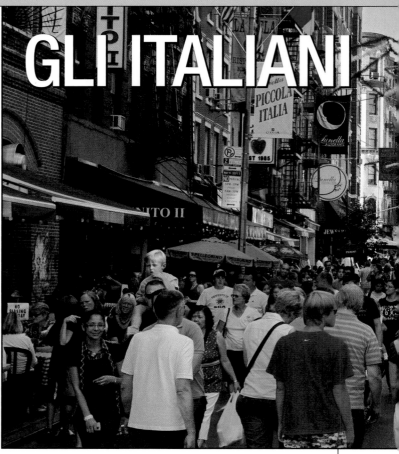

Italiani: un popolo in movimento

«Tutto il mondo è paese» dice un proverbio che sembra definire la condizione degli **emigrati**° italiani nel mondo. Anche se l'Italia è un paese relativamente piccolo, gli italiani che vivono in altre parti del mondo sono moltissimi. Oggi si contano quasi cinque milioni di italiani all'estero e circa 80 milioni sono gli **oriundi**, cioè persone nate fuori dall'Italia da genitori di origine italiana. Il paese che ospita° il maggior numero di oriundi italiani è il Brasile, seguito da Argentina, Stati Uniti, Francia e Canada.

Perché ci sono così tante comunità di origine italiana nel mondo? Chi sono e cosa fanno gli emigrati italiani? La ricerca di un lavoro è sempre stata la prima ragione che ha spinto° e ancora spinge gli italiani a lasciare il loro paese. È necessario, però, distinguere gli **emigranti**° del secolo° scorso da quelli attuali. Gli emigranti del XX secolo sono partiti soprattutto dopo la prima e la seconda guerra mondiale. Negli Stati Uniti erano impiegati nella costruzione di ferrovie e strade e spesso erano minatori°. In Germania, Canada e Australia lavoravano nel settore edile°. In Argentina hanno collaborato alla realizzazione di grandi infrastrutture e molti hanno lavorato nell'agricoltura.

Grazie ai sacrifici dei primi emigrati e alla veloce integrazione delle **seconde generazioni**, oggi gli oriundi italiani sono presenti in ogni settore dell'economia dei nuovi paesi, dall'agricoltura, all'industria e ai servizi. In molti casi sono piccoli imprenditori°, hanno aperto bar, ristoranti e pasticcerie. Negli Stati Uniti si registrano discendenti di italiani anche nei settori della politica e del cinema, e fra la classe dirigente° dell'industria e della finanza.

In molte città statunitensi ci sono dei quartieri con comunità italiane, spesso conosciute come *Little Italy*. La ***Little Italy*** originale, e forse più grande e famosa, è a New York. Ci sono quartieri italiani anche a Boston (il **North End**), Chicago, San Francisco, San Diego, Toronto e Montreal (**Petite Italie**).

Negli ultimi vent'anni la tipologia dell'italiano che si trasferisce all'estero è cambiata. Gli emigranti del dopoguerra avevano poca o nessuna conoscenza della lingua parlata nel nuovo paese ed erano costretti° a cercare lavoro e fortuna lontano dall'Italia. I nuovi emigranti sono spesso giovani specializzati, con un alto livello di istruzione, in genere una laurea, che scelgono di emigrare per poter mettere alla prova° le loro potenzialità, soprattutto nella ricerca accademica. Anche il rapporto con la **madrepatria**° è cambiato: per i primi emigranti il sogno era quello di tornare in Italia e molti lo hanno fatto. I giovani di oggi, in genere, mantengono un rapporto stretto° con la loro nazione d'origine soprattutto grazie alle tecnologie e a Internet, ci tornano per le vacanze, ma di solito si stabiliscono° definitivamente nel nuovo paese.

In più...

L'emigrazione dall'Italia verso l'estero inizia alla fine del 1800. Il periodo con il più alto numero di emigranti è quello tra il 1950 e la fine degli anni '60. Le regioni di provenienza sono soprattutto quelle del Sud, in particolare la Sicilia. Nel XX secolo sono emigrati **30 milioni** di italiani di cui 10 milioni sono tornati in Italia.

emigrati *people who left their country and live abroad* **ospita** *hosts* **spinto** *pushed*
emigranti *people who leave their country to move abroad* **secolo** *century* **minatori** *miners*
settore edile *building sector* **imprenditori** *entrepreneurs* **classe dirigente** *executives*
costretti *forced* **mettere alla prova** *to test* **madrepatria** *homeland* **rapporto stretto** *close connection* **si stabiliscono** *they settle*

NEL MONDO

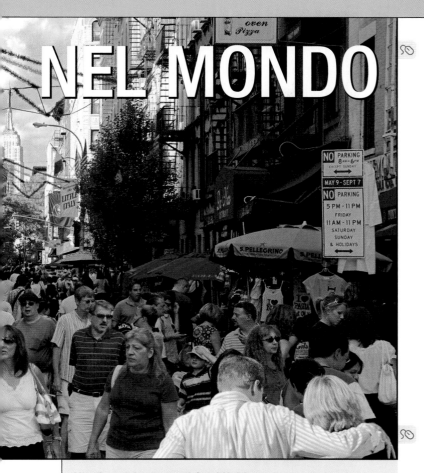

🔊 **Vero o falso?** Indica se ogni frase è **vera** o **falsa**. Correggi le frasi false. *Some answers will vary.*

1. Il maggior numero di emigranti italiani vive negli Stati Uniti. *Falso. Il paese con il maggior numero di emigranti dall'Italia è il Brasile.*

2. Gli emigranti del XX secolo venivano soprattutto dalle regioni del Sud Italia. *Vero.*

3. Gli italiani di seconda generazione si sono integrati bene nel mondo del lavoro. *Vero.*

4. I nuovi emigranti italiani hanno buone possibilità di successo all'estero. *Vero.*

5. Gli italiani che emigrano oggi hanno una buona istruzione. *Vero.*

6. La maggior parte degli emigranti dei nostri giorni vuole tornare a vivere in Italia. *Falso. La maggior parte degli emigranti di oggi si stabilisce nel nuovo paese.*

7. Alcuni dei festival italiani in America sono celebrazioni in onore dei santi. *Vero.*

8. Esempi di italiani famosi all'estero si trovano solo negli Stati Uniti. *Falso. Si trovano anche in altri paesi come l'Australia.*

🔊 **Quanto hai imparato?** Rispondi alle domande.
Some answers will vary.

1. Qual è la ragione da sempre alla base dell'emigrazione dall'Italia? *la ricerca del lavoro*

2. Quali erano le condizioni degli emigranti del XX secolo? *Avevano poca o nessuna conoscenza della nuova lingua; erano costretti a emigrare.*

3. In quali settori operavano gli emigranti del secolo scorso? *settore edile, agricoltura, realizzazione di infrastrutture, miniere*

4. Quali sono le caratteristiche del nuovo emigrante italiano? *più istruito, sceglie di andare all'estero, si stabilisce nel nuovo paese*

5. Che cosa vogliono celebrare gli italiani all'estero con i loro festival? *i santi, l'eredità, la cultura e i valori italiani*

6. Quali sono alcune delle invenzioni realizzate da italiani emigrati all'estero? *il prototipo del telefono e la radio*

L'Italia celebrata negli Stati Uniti I festival italiani negli Stati Uniti sono numerosi. Alcuni hanno un tema, come il **Festival di Sant'Antonio e Santa Lucia** a Boston, in cui si celebrano i santi con messe° e processioni. A San Francisco c'è la **Parata° dell'eredità culturale italiana**, che ricorda l'arrivo di Colombo sulle coste americane. In ogni caso, i festival sono un'occasione per la celebrazione dell'eredità° culturale e dei valori° italiani e la gente festeggia con giochi tradizionali, cibo, vino, musica e artigianato tutto rigorosamente «Made in Italy».

Italiani famosi nel mondo Molti italiani e discendenti di italiani hanno raggiunto la fama e il successo in ogni parte del mondo e in ogni settore: dal cinema alla musica alla scienza. **Antonio Meucci** realizza un primo prototipo di telefono a New York; **Guglielmo Marconi** sceglie la Gran Bretagna e l'America per i suoi esperimenti di radio-trasmissione°. Anche oggi in molti nomi famosi si nasconde° un'origine italiana: **Martin Marcantonio Luciano Scorsese, Robert Mario De Niro, Leon Panetta, Janet Napolitano** e molti altri!

Antonio Meucci

messe *masses* **parata** *parade* **eredità** *heritage* **valori** *values* **esperimenti di radio-trasmissione** *radio-transmitter experiments* **si nasconde** *it is hidden*

🔊 **Progetto**

Dove sono gli italiani negli Stati Uniti e in Canada?

- Cerca le maggiori comunità italiane negli Stati Uniti e in Canada.

- Scegli una comunità italiana e raccogli informazioni sulla sua storia.

- Confronta i tuoi risultati con il resto della classe.

GALLERIA DI PERSONE ILLUSTRI

STILISTA
Miuccia Prada (1948–)

Miuccia Prada è una famosa stilista e imprenditrice (*entrepreneur*) italiana a capo dell'omonima (*of the same name*) casa di moda. Nata a Milano nel 1948, Miuccia inizia a lavorare nell'azienda di famiglia negli anni Settanta. Grazie alla sua visione e alla conduzione manageriale del marito Patrizio Bertelli, Miuccia riuscirà a trasformare Prada in una delle più influenti case di moda al mondo. Gli anni Ottanta rappresentano una svolta (*turning point*) per l'azienda che crea il famoso logo, lancia le iconiche borse nere in nylon high-tech e presenta la prima linea di scarpe e di *prêt-à-porter*, definendo il carattere minimalista del marchio (*brand*). Il decennio successivo vede il debutto della linea Miu Miu, di una linea maschile e di una sportiva. Secondo *Forbes*, Miuccia è la terza donna più ricca d'Italia, con un patrimonio di 4,1 miliardi di dollari, e il settimanale *Time* l'ha inserita insieme al marito tra le 100 coppie più influenti al mondo.

COMPOSITORE
Ennio Morricone (1928–)

Ennio Morricone è universalmente riconosciuto come uno dei più importanti autori della musica cinematografica. Durante i suoi quarant'anni di brillante carriera ha lavorato con registi di ogni nazionalità, scrivendo musiche per più di 500 film e serie TV. Morricone ha saputo creare colonne sonore memorabili per ogni tipo di situazione e genere cinematografico, dal western all'italiana, a cui deve la fama, al cinema hollywoodiano. Dagli anni Settanta lavora a Hollywood dove collabora con registi come John Carpenter, Oliver Stone e Quentin Tarantino, scrivendo le musiche per numerose pellicole premiate all'Academy Award. Il compositore romano ha ricevuto moltissimi premi, tra cui l'Oscar onorario alla carriera e una statuetta per le partiture del film di Quentin Tarantino, *The Hateful Eight*.

LIBRETTISTA

Lorenzo Da Ponte
(1749–1838)

Lorenzo Da Ponte occupa un posto d'onore tra i librettisti italiani del Settecento. Originario della comunità ebraica di Ceneda (oggi Vittorio Veneto), Da Ponte trascorre (*spends*) la sua gioventù in giro per (*all over*) l'Europa, finché non giunge a (*until he reaches*) Vienna dove diventa poeta di corte dell'imperatore Giuseppe II. Qui ha la possibilità di collaborare con numerosi musicisti per i quali produrrà una quarantina di libretti di successo. Memorabile è la sua collaborazione con Mozart per la creazione di *Le nozze di Figaro*, *Don Giovanni* e *Così fan tutte*.

Dopo un periodo a Londra, Da Ponte si trasferisce negli Stati Uniti. Passa il resto della sua vita a New York dove insegna lingua e letteratura italiana finché nel 1825 diventa il primo professore di letteratura italiana nella storia della Columbia University.

ESPLORATORE

Cristoforo Colombo
(1451–1506)

Cristoforo Colombo è un importante navigatore ed esploratore che contribuisce a memorabili imprese (*feats*) e scoperte geografiche nel XV e nel XVI secolo. Nato a Genova, Colombo intraprende la professione di mercante e all'età di soli quindici anni aveva già navigato verso la Grecia, il Portogallo e l'Inghilterra. Si trasferisce in Portogallo quando aveva trent'anni e lì si convince dell'esistenza di un'altra terra oltreoceano (*overseas*), secondo lui l'Asia. Nessun navigatore era mai tornato dopo aver salpato (*set sail*) nell'Oceano Atlantico verso occidente, ma, sicuro delle proprie convinzioni, ottiene i finanziamenti dai re di Castiglia e Aragona. Il 3 agosto 1492 salpa dalla Spagna e giunge (*reaches*) all'odierna (*today's*) San Salvador, Bahamas, il 12 ottobre. Seguono altri tre viaggi per le Americhe che sono però meno fortunati e lo portano alla rovina.

Comprensione

Rispondere Rispondi alle domande.

1. Che cosa fa a Hollywood Ennio Morricone?
   Collabora con registi scrivendo le musiche per numerose pellicole.

2. Quanti Oscar ha ricevuto Morricone?
   Ne ha ricevuto due.

3. Come si chiama il marito di Miuccia Prada?
   Si chiama Patrizio Bertelli.

4. Che cosa lancia Prada negli anni Novanta?
   Lancia la linea Miu Miu, una linea maschile e una sportiva.

5. A quanto ammonta il patrimonio di Miuccia Prada secondo *Forbes*?
   Ammonta a 4,1 miliardi di dollari.

6. Quanti libretti di successo produce Lorenzo Da Ponte quando si trova alla corte di Vienna?
   Produce una quarantina di libretti di successo.

7. Che cosa nasce dalla collaborazione tra Mozart e Lorenzo Da Ponte?
   Nascono le opere *Le nozze di Figaro*, *Don Giovanni* e *Così fan tutte*.

8. Dove muore Lorenzo Da Ponte?
   Muore a New York.

9. Dov'è nato Cristoforo Colombo?
   È nato a Genova.

10. Chi ha finanziato il primo viaggio di Cristoforo Colombo verso le Americhe?
    L'hanno finanziato i re di Castiglia e Aragona.

Scrittura

Scrivi sull'argomento Scegli uno dei seguenti argomenti e scrivi un paragrafo seguendo le indicazioni.

- **La colonna sonora** L'importanza della colonna sonora per un film è indubbia (*undeniable*). La musica e i suoni completano le pellicole accompagnando ed emozionando lo spettatore. Qual è la tua colonna sonora preferita? A quale film appartiene e perché ti è piaciuta.

- **Coppie influenti** Il settimanale *Time* ha inserito Miuccia Prada e il marito tra le coppie più influenti al mondo. Conosci altre coppie famose che gestiscono (*manage*) un'azienda insieme con successo? Secondo te, che qualità deve avere una coppia per poter lavorare insieme?

- **Italiani famosi in America** Lorenzo Da Ponte e Cristoforo Colombo sono due esempi di italiani che hanno legami (*bonds*) importanti con l'America. Conosci altri italiani legati storicamente e culturalmente agli Stati Uniti?

 Practice more at **vhlcentral.com**.

INSTRUCTIONAL RESOURCES `1.1`
Audioscripts, Answer Keys, Lab MP3s, Grammar Presentation Slides
SAM/WebSAM: WB, LM

The present tense: regular verbs

*Il treno **parte** dal binario 9.*

Subject pronouns

- In Italian, the subject pronouns are:

	1st person	**2nd person**	**3rd person**	
Singular	io *I*	tu/Lei *you/you (formal)*	lui *he*	lei *she*
Plural	noi *we*	voi/Loro *you/you (formal)*	loro *they (m./f.)*	

- Italian subject pronouns are used much less frequently than their English counterparts because the verb form usually identifies the subject.

> **Mangiamo** spesso al ristorante.
> *We often eat at the restaurant.*

> **Abiti** ancora a Roma?
> *Do you still live in Rome?*

- Subject pronouns add emphasis with words such as **neanche**, **soltanto**, and **anche**; they also add emphasis when placed after the verb. Before the verb, subject pronouns prevent ambiguity or contrast subjects.

> **È lei** che odia la pizza.
> *She's the one who hates pizza.*

> **Neanche noi** siamo sposati.
> *We aren't married either.*

> **Lui** ha un fratello e **lei** ha una sorella.
> *He has a brother and she has a sister.*

> **Anche tu** puoi venire alla festa.
> *You can come to the party, too.*

- Use **Lei** and **Loro** to address people formally. **Voi**, rather than **Loro**, is typically used for both the formal and informal second person plural, especially in speaking. That style will be followed in this book.

> Buonasera, signori, **Loro** desiderano?
> *Good evening, ladies and gentlemen, what would you like?*

> Ehi, ragazzi, partite anche **voi** domani?
> *Hey, guys, are you leaving tomorrow too?*

The present tense

- The present indicative tense expresses actions and circumstances in the present. It has three equivalents in English.

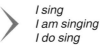

canto ➤ *I sing*
I am singing
I do sing

- To form the present indicative of the three regular verb conjugations, drop the ending of the infinitive (**–are**, **–ere**, or **–ire**) and add the appropriate endings to the stem.

	parlare	**prẹndere**	**dormire**	**capire**
io	parlo	prendo	dormo	capisco
tu	parli	prendi	dormi	capisci
lui/lei/Lei	parla	prende	dorme	capisce
noi	parliamo	prendiamo	dormiamo	capiamo
voi	parlate	prendete	dormite	capite
loro/Loro	parlano	prẹndono	dọrmono	capịscono

- There are two types of **–ire** verbs. Verbs conjugated like **capire** insert **–isc–** between the stem and the ending of all forms except the first and second person plural. Verbs conjugated like **dormire** do not require insertion of **–isc–**.

- Most **–ire** verbs that do not require insertion of **–isc–** have a consonant five letters from the end of the infinitive: **aprire**, **coprire**, **dormire**, **offrire**, **partire**, **scoprire**, **seguire**, **sentire**, **servire**, **soffrire**, etc.

- Spelling changes are required in the present indicative of some **–are** verbs. To avoid a double **i**, drop the **i** of the **tu** and **noi** stems of most verbs ending in **–iare**.

cominciare	cominci̶ + i/iamo	cominci (tu) / cominciamo (noi)
cambiare	cambi̶ + i/iamo	cambi (tu) / cambiamo (noi)
lasciare	lasci̶ + i/iamo	lasci (tu) / lasciamo (noi)
sbagliare	sbagli̶ + i/iamo	sbagli (tu) / sbagliamo (noi)
studiare	studi̶ + i/iamo	studi (tu) / studiamo (noi)

- When the **i** of the stem is stressed in the first person of the present indicative, in verbs ending in **–iare** like **inviare** and **sciare**, do not drop the **i** of the stem in the **tu** form.

sciare	scịo (io)	scịi (tu)
inviare	invịo (io)	invịi (tu)

- Add an **h** to the **tu** and **noi** forms of verbs ending in **–care** and **–gare** to maintain the hard sound of the **c** and **g**.

cercare	cerch + i/iamo	cerchi (tu) / cerchiamo (noi)
spiegare	spiegh + i/iamo	spieghi (tu) / spieghiamo (noi)

- Use the simple present tense for ongoing actions that began in the past. Use **da** (*for; since*) to indicate when the action first began. Use **da quando** or **da quanto tempo** when asking *How long?* or *Since when?*

Da quanto tempo sei fidanzata?
How long have you been engaged?

Sono fidanzata **da** sei mesi.
I've been engaged for six months.

Da quando escono insieme Mario e Carla?
Since when have Mario and Carla been going out?

Escono insieme **dal** mese scorso.
They've been dating since last month.

Remind students that –isc– verbs are denoted in vocabulary lists by (–isc–) after the infinitive.

You may want to point out to students that some –ire verbs such as **mentire**, **nutrire**, and **tossire** can be conjugated either with or without –isc–, but that one form generally prevails (**mento**, **nutro**, and **tossisco**).

Provide the infinitive of verbs ending in –iare, then ask students to say the **tu** form aloud. Here are a few to get you started: **inviare, studiare, sbucciare, sciare, cambiare, cominciare, arrabbiare, lasciare, sbagliare, iniziare, spogliare**, etc.

Give students a list of spelling change verbs (**pagare, spiegare, mancare, cominciare, lasciare, sbagliare**, etc.), then randomly pick subject pronouns to go with a given verb. Call on students to give the appropriate form, indicating any spelling changes. For example, you say "**tu, spiegare**" and the student should reply "**Spieghi, con l'acca.**"

ATTENZIONE!

Verbs with a root ending in **–gn** —such as **guadagnare** (*to earn*), **insegnare** (*to teach*), and **sognare** (*to dream*)—can be spelled with or without the **i** in the first person plural.

guadagniamo or **guadagnamo**
sogniamo or **sognamo**

Pratica

Nota CULTURALE

«Le bomboniere» sono oggetti ricordo che si regalano ad amici e parenti in occasioni importanti come un matrimonio. Le accompagnano i **«confetti»**, piccole caramelle fatte di mandorle° ricoperte di zucchero. Sempre in numero dispari°, generalmente cinque, augurano° successo e prosperità. Solitamente i confetti sono rosa o azzurri per il battesimo di una bambina o di un bambino, rossi per la laurea, bianchi per il matrimonio e argentati° o dorati rispettivamente per le nozze d'argento e le nozze d'oro (venticinque e cinquant'anni di matrimonio).

mandorle *almonds* **dispari** *odd* **augurano** *wish* **argentati** *silver coated*

1 Ci sposiamo o ci lasciamo? Attilio e Luciana sono una coppia in crisi. Completa il paragrafo coniugando al presente il verbo fra parentesi.

Attilio e Luciana sono fidanzati da molti anni, ma da qualche tempo lei gli (1) ___mente___ (mentire), o almeno così lui sospetta, su un'amicizia con un compagno di scuola, Mario. Attilio è preoccupato perché (2) ___circolano___ (circolare) già molti pettegolezzi!

Luciana non (3) ___capisce___ (capire) il comportamento di Attilio, che lei considera troppo geloso. Lei è una ragazza molto fedele e Mario è il suo migliore amico. Così, un giorno, Luciana decide: «(4) ___Chiedo___ (Chiedere) a Mario di fare da testimone (*witness*) al mio matrimonio con Attilio!»

Attilio, intanto, (5) ___preferisce___ (preferire) non parlare dell'argomento con Luciana: non le (6) ___telefona___ (telefonare) e non (7) ___apre___ (aprire) la sua casella di posta elettronica da ormai quindici giorni. Poi, un giorno, finalmente (8) ___decide___ (decidere) anche lui: «(9) ___Lascio___ (lasciare) Luciana e (10) ___cerco___ (cercare) la mia vera anima gemella!» Cosa succede? Attilio lascia Luciana?

2 Che disastro! Ecco qual è la situazione una settimana prima delle nozze (*wedding*) di Attilio e Luciana. Scrivete le frasi con i soggetti e i verbi nella lista.

> **Modello**   **Attilio / perdere / carta di credito**
> Attilio perde la carta di credito.

1. pasticcere / chiudere / per ferie   Il pasticcere chiude per ferie.
2. testimoni / partire / per un viaggio di lavoro   I testimoni partono per un viaggio di lavoro.
3. fratello di Attilio / perdere / anelli   Il fratello di Attilio perde gli anelli.
4. prete (*priest*) / cadere / dalle scale   Il prete cade dalle scale.
5. ristorante / cambiare / indirizzo   Il ristorante cambia indirizzo.
6. negozio di bomboniere / finire / confetti   Il negozio di bomboniere finisce i confetti.
7. genitori di Luciana / invitare / anche i cugini americani   I genitori di Luciana invitano anche i cugini americani.
8. cugini americani / arrivare / una settimana prima   I cugini americani arrivano una settimana prima.

3 Chi trova un amico... Unite gli elementi delle tre colonne per creare delle frasi complete.

> **Modello**   I miei genitori condividono le gioie (*joys*) e i dolori del matrimonio.

A	B	C
i miei genitori	odiare	il suo compagno di stanza
io	contare su	il traffico
la mia migliore amica	condividere	la sorella di Luisa
le mie compagne di classe	ammirare	la sua amica del cuore
mia madre	cercare	la sua anima gemella
mia sorella	mentire a	le gioie e i dolori del matrimonio
noi	disturbare	le persone oneste
?	?	?

 Practice more at **vhlcentral.com**.

Comunicazione

4

Conversazione Con un(a) compagno/a, descrivete a turno ogni persona usando il verbo corrispondente.

> **Modello**   **mio fratello / preferire**
>
> —Mio fratello preferisce lavorare la sera tardi.
>
> —Anche mia sorella. Lei preferisce fare i compiti dopo le sei di sera.

1. la mia migliore amica / disturbare
2. io e mia madre / condividere
3. i miei compagni di classe / studiare
4. io / contare su
5. io e mia madre / condividere
6. tu e i tuoi amici / adorare

4 Encourage students to expand on their statements by adding information about other people. Example: **Mia sorella non mi disturba mai. I miei genitori, invece, mi disturbano sempre mentre guardo la TV**.

5

Da quanto tempo...? Fatevi delle domande usando i verbi della lista.

> **Modello**   **studiare**
>
> —Da quanto tempo studi italiano?
>
> —Studio italiano da due anni.

- amare
- ascoltare
- condividere
- conoscere
- abitare
- scrivere
- seguire
- ?

5 As an expansion, ask volunteers to repeat the interview asking **da quando** rather than **da quanto tempo**. Example: **Da quando conosci il tuo fidanzato?** → **Conosco il mio fidanzato dal 2007.**

6

Una chiacchierata In coppia, fatevi domande usando questi verbi. Potete parlare dei temi suggeriti o di altri.

> **Modello**   **provare un senso di insicurezza**
>
> —C'è qualche situazione in cui provi sempre un senso di insicurezza?
>
> —Sì. Provo sempre un senso di insicurezza quando devo parlare in pubblico perché sono timido.

1. provare un senso di: (in)sicurezza / solitudine / benessere / felicità / depressione
2. raccomandare: un film di un regista italiano / un gruppo musicale italiano / un libro di uno scrittore o un artista italiano
3. ricordarsi: quando hai imparato a nuotare / di una persona che ti ha influenzato / del tuo primo bacio
4. sognare di: visitare un luogo particolare in Italia / rivedere una persona speciale, forse lontana

6 Explain that **sognare** (item 4) uses the preposition **di** only when followed by a verb. Otherwise, no preposition is used. Example: **Sogno di fare un viaggio intorno al mondo./ La notte scorsa ho sognato Giacomo**.

7

Tra moglie e marito... Ecco Attilio e Luciana, finalmente sposi! Ma la vita matrimoniale è solo l'inizio di un'avventura... In coppia, usate i verbi della lista per parlare della vita di Attilio e Luciana dopo il matrimonio e dei loro progetti nell'immediato futuro.

cambiare	decidere	partire
capire	guadagnare	perdere
cercare	mentire	preferire
cominciare	offrire	trovare

> **Modello**   —Attilio trova lavoro in banca.
>
> —Luciana domani parte per cercare lavoro in Inghilterra.

7 Explain that the title refers to an Italian expression (**Tra moglie e marito non mettere il dito!**), meaning that friends should not interfere with the private matters of a husband and a wife.

7 Encourage students to give unexpected twists to the story. Then ask volunteers to share their story with the class, who will vote on the funniest story.

INSTRUCTIONAL RESOURCES 1.2
Audioscripts, Answer Keys, Lab MP3s, Grammar Presentation Slides
SAM/WebSAM: WB, LM

ATTENZIONE!

Omit the indefinite article in these two cases:

- before unmodified nouns designating profession or religion

È professoressa.
She's a professor.

but

È una professoressa molto divertente.
She's a very funny professor.

- after **che** in the expression *What a…!*

Che bel pupazzo di neve!
What a nice snowman!

ATTENZIONE!

The definite article is also used when talking about certain illnesses or ailments (**Luca ha la febbre**). It may also be used before names of languages (**L'italiano è la mia lingua preferita**).

ATTENZIONE!

Remember to use the definite article **le** when telling time for all numbered hours, except one o'clock, which takes a singular article (**l'una**). Don't forget to use the indefinite article **un** for quarter past an hour or quarter to the next hour.

Explain to students that **con** may also be contracted, though less frequently than the prepositions in the table. The contracted forms are **col**, **collo**, **coll'**, **colla**, **coi**, **cogli**, and **colle**.

Articles

- Definite and indefinite articles must agree in number and gender with the nouns they modify. They vary in form for pronunciation purposes, and in spelling depending on the word they precede.

Definite articles (*the*)

Before...	masc. sing.	fem. sing.	masc. pl.	fem. pl.
most consonants	**il** padre	**la** madre	**i** genitori	**le** sorelle
s + cons., **z**, **y**, **x**, **ps**, **gn**	**lo** psicologo	**la** zia	**gli** studenti	**le** scuole
a vowel	**l'**uomo	**l'**amica	**gli** uomini	**le** amiche

Indefinite articles (*a; an*)

Before...	masculine	feminine
most consonants	**un** fratello	**una** cugina
s + cons., **z**, **y**, **x**, **ps**, **gn**	**uno** stadio	**una** zia
a vowel	**un** amore	**un'**amica

- Use the definite article in these circumstances.

when referring to specific people or things	**Il** cane che abbaia si chiama Nobile. *The dog that is barking is named Nobile.*
with last names and titles of people	Ho visto **il** signor Bianchi stamattina. *I saw Mister Bianchi this morning.*
with geographical names such as countries, continents, large islands, regions, and mountains	**La** Sardegna è un'isola molto bella. *Sardinia is a very beautiful island.*
with days of the week or time expressions, to mean *every* or *each*	Abbiamo lezione **il** martedì e **il** giovedì. *We have class on Tuesdays and Thursdays.*
with the hour (when telling time)	Sono **le** undici. *It's eleven o'clock.*
when describing body parts, such as hair or eye color	La mia fidanzata ha **gli** occhi blu e **i** capelli biondi. *My fiancée has blue eyes and blonde hair.*
when referring to general categories and abstract ideas	Grazie a Meetic ho conosciuto **l'**amore… *Thanks to Meetic I found love…*

- When the definite article follows the prepositions **a**, **di**, **da**, **in**, and **su**, the article and the preposition form a contraction.

	+il	+lo	+l'	+la	+i	+gli	+le
a (*in; at*)	al	allo	all'	alla	ai	agli	alle
di (*of*)	del	dello	dell'	della	dei	degli	delle
da (*from; for*)	dal	dallo	dall'	dalla	dai	dagli	dalle
in (*in*)	nel	nello	nell'	nella	nei	negli	nelle
su (*on; about*)	sul	sullo	sull'	sulla	sui	sugli	sulle

Pratica e comunicazione

1

A ciascuno il suo Carla ha un sogno: lavorare in un'agenzia matrimoniale (*matchmaking service*). Leggi cosa pensa dei suoi amici e completa le frasi usando la forma corretta degli articoli determinativi o indeterminativi.

1. Maria è _una_ ragazza matura, ma troppo orgogliosa. Ha bisogno di _un_ uomo con _un_ carattere dolce e forte.

2. _La_ fidanzata di Giorgio è sensibile, ma molto timida. Quando vede Giorgio diventa rossa come _un_ peperone!

3. Giorgio è _una_ persona molto superficiale. Gli piacciono tutte _le_ studentesse della scuola!

4. Lucia è _una_ donna affascinante ma rompe con tutti _i_ fidanzati dopo qualche settimana. Può andare bene per _un_ seduttore come Giorgio.

5. Carlo, invece, è _un_ ragazzo molto simpatico e carino. Ha _gli_ occhi neri, _i_ capelli scuri, _il_ naso dritto e _una_ voce profonda e affascinante! Forse va bene per me!

2

Ugo e Flavia Leggi la storia di Ugo e Flavia e inserisci gli articoli determinativi, combinandoli con le preposizioni quando è necessario.

1. Ugo e Flavia si incontrano _il_ lunedì prima di andare a scuola, (da) _dalle_ 7.00 (a) _alle_ 8.00.

2. Quando Flavia scende (da) _dall'_ autobus, Ugo è già (su) _sul_ marciapiede che l'aspetta.

3. Poi, insieme, vanno (in) _nel_ bar (di) _del_ centro e prendono un cappuccino e una brioche per colazione.

4. Si raccontano _le_ cose che hanno fatto durante _il_ fine settimana e parlano (di) _dei_ loro progetti per _i_ giorni successivi.

5. Poi si rimettono _gli_ zaini (su) _sulle_ spalle e vanno verso _la_ scuola, mano (in) _nella_ mano.

3

Chi cerca trova! In coppia, fatevi delle domande per capire quanto siete simili o diversi.

A che ora	comprare	a	casa
Chi	invitare	da	discoteca
Come	mangiare	in	famiglia
Cosa	ritornare		luce
Quando	spegnere (*turn off*)		ristorante
Quante volte	telefonare		supermercato

4

L'anima gemella Scrivi una lettera a «La Posta del cuore di Carla» per trovare la tua anima gemella. Descrivi la tua donna/il tuo uomo ideale in otto frasi, usando le preposizioni articolate, le parole della lista e altre parole imparate in questa lezione.

appuntamento	condividere	coppia	fiducia	matrimonio
cercare	contare su	credere	lasciare	mentire

Practice more at vhlcentral.com.

INSTRUCTIONAL RESOURCES **1.3**
Audioscripts, Answer Keys, Lab MP3s, Grammar Presentation Slides
SAM/WebSAM: WB, LM

Explain to students that, while some words may look like masculine and feminine forms of the same noun, they may actually be completely different words with unrelated meanings. A few examples are: **il pasto** (*meal*), **la pasta** (*noodles*); **il caso** (*case*), **la casa** (*house*); **il banco** (*counter*), **la banca** (*bank*); **il mostro** (*monster*), **la mostra** (*exhibition*).

RIMANDO

For more information about feminine profession words, see **Nota culturale, p. 125.**

ATTENZIONE!

Ogni (*each, every*) and **qualche** (*some*) may only be used with singular nouns.

ogni giorno
every day

qualche volta
sometimes

RIMANDO

To learn about placement of adjectives and demonstrative adjectives, see **Strutture 2.4, p. 68.**

To learn about comparatives and superlatives, see **Strutture 7.1, pp. 262–264.**

Gender and number

- All nouns in Italian are characterized by their gender (masculine or feminine) and number (singular or plural). Adjectives agree in number and gender with the nouns they modify.

Gender

- Most Italian nouns end in a vowel. Nouns ending in **–o** are usually masculine and nouns ending in **–a** are usually feminine. Nouns ending in **–e** can be either masculine or feminine. While there is no sure way to determine the gender of a noun just by looking at the ending, there are a few general tendencies.

- To make the feminine form of some nouns, replace the masculine ending with the feminine ending.

change in ending	masculine → feminine
o → a	ragazz**o** → ragazz**a**
e → essa	student**e** → student**essa**
e → a	signor**e** → signor**a**
ore → rice	att**ore** → att**rice**
a → essa	poet**a** → poet**essa**

- Some nouns denoting traditionally male professions or activities are used in the masculine form to refer to women, for example, **l'ingegnere** (*engineer*) and **l'architetto** (*architect*). The accompanying articles and adjectives should also be used in the masculine form. On the other hand, **la guida** (*guide*) and **la spia** (*spy*) are always feminine in gender, even when referring to a man.

> Mia zia Rita è **un noto architetto**.
> *My aunt Rita is a well-known architect.*

> James Bond è **una spia famosa**.
> *James Bond is a famous spy.*

- Some nouns have the same ending for masculine and feminine forms; the gender can be determined by the context or the article. For example, **il/la pianista** (*pianist*) and **lo/la psichiatra** (*psychiatrist*) end in **–a**, but can be either masculine or feminine.

> **L'artista** (*m.*) si chiama **Leonardo**.
> *The artist's name is Leonardo.*

> **L'artista** (*f.*) si chiama **Artemisia Gentileschi**.
> *The artist's name is Artemisia Gentileschi.*

- Adjectives, like nouns, have masculine and feminine forms and tend to follow the same rules as nouns. Most masculine adjectives end in **–o**, and most feminine adjectives end in **–a**. Adjectives ending in **–e** can modify either masculine or feminine nouns.

> Marcell**o** è molto sensibil**e**.
> *Marcello is very sensitive.*

> **La** mia gatt**a** non è affettuos**a**.
> *My cat isn't affectionate.*

- Not all adjectives follow the rules of **–o**, **–a**, or **–e** endings. Some common adjectives end in **–ista** (**ottimista**, **pessimista**, and **idealista**, for example) and describe both masculine and feminine nouns. Other adjectives such as **viola**, **rosa**, **blu**, **ogni**, and **qualche** are invariable and have only one form.

> **un bambino ottimista**
> *an optimistic boy*

> **la camicia blu**
> *the blue shirt*

Plurals

All nouns are either singular or plural; adjectives that modify them must agree with them in gender and number.

- Singular nouns and adjectives ending in –**o** or –**e** typically become –**i** in the plural. Singular nouns and adjectives ending in –**a** typically become –**e** in the plural.

fratell**o** > fratell**i**
scarp**a** > scarp**e**

ristorant**e** > ristorant**i**
intelligent**e** > intelligent**i**

- As you know, some singular nouns and adjectives ending in –**a** can be masculine or feminine. Form their plural by replacing the –**a** with –**i** for the masculine form and with –**e** for the feminine form.

il pianist**a** ottimist**a** > i pianist**i** ottimist**i**
la pianist**a** ottimist**a** > le pianist**e** ottimist**e**

- Some nouns and adjectives form plurals according to other patterns for purposes of pronunciation or gender distinctions.

	singular → plural	example	common exceptions
retain hard sound of consonant by adding an –**h** in the plural	stress on syllable before –**co**: –**co** → –**chi**	parco → parchi	amico/greco/nemico/porco → amici/greci/nemici/porci
	–**ca** → –**che**	banca → banche	
	–**go** → –**ghi**	albergo → alberghi	
	–**ga** → –**ghe**	lunga → lunghe	
change sound of consonant	stress on second syllable before –**co**: –**co** → –**ci**	dinamico → dinamici	carico → carichi
	–**ologo** → –**ologi**	biologo → biologi	monologo → monologhi
	–**fago** → –**fagi**	sarcofago → sarcofagi	
unstressed –**i**	–**io** → –**i**	negozio → negozi	orecchio → orecchie
	–**cia** → –**ce**	faccia → facce	camicia → camicie
	–**gia** → –**ge**	spiaggia → spiagge	grigia → grigie
stressed –**i**	–**io** → –**ii**	zio → zii	
	–**cia** → –**cie**	farmacia → farmacie	
	–**gia** → –**gie**	bugia → bugie	

- You must memorize the irregular plural forms of certain nouns. Some examples are **la moglie → le mogli, l'uomo → gli uomini, il dio → gli dei, il tempio → i templi, l'ala → le ali, la mano → le mani.**

- Some nouns are invariable: they do not change from the singular to the plural. Articles and adjectives can help you determine whether these nouns are singular or plural. Invariable words include some words of foreign origin that end in a consonant (such as **bar**, **film**, and **sport**), words that end in an accented vowel or have only one syllable (such as **re**, **sci**, **virtù**, or **città**), and words that are shortened forms of longer words (such as **cinema**, **foto**, and **radio**).

Remind students to use the masculine plural form of the adjective when referring to two or more nouns of different genders. Example: **Maria e Robertino sono simpatici**.

As you go through the chart, explain any unknown examples and have students use them in sentences.

Tell students they must learn to recognize the plural patterns, adding new words as they learn them.

ATTENZIONE!

Masculine words ending in –**ma** or –**ta** that are Greek in origin form their plurals by changing –**a** to –**i**. Some examples are **il programma/i programmi** and **il poeta/i poeti**. Feminine words ending in –**i** that are Greek in origin do not change in the plural. Some examples are **la crisi/le crisi** and **la tesi/le tesi**.

ATTENZIONE!

A number of masculine nouns that end in –**o** have a feminine plural form ending in –**a**. Many, but not all of them, refer to parts of the body.

il labbro (*lip*) → **le labbra**

il braccio (*arm*) → **le braccia**

il ginocchio (*knee*) → **le ginocchia**

il ciglio (*eyelash*) → **le ciglia**

l'uovo (*egg*) → **le uova**

Pratica

1 For expansion, have students work in pairs to provide the plural form for each item. Remind them that the plural of indefinite articles is made with the preposition **di** combined with the definite article. Example: **un'auto nuova; delle auto nuove**.

1

Maschile o femminile? Colloca l'articolo indefinito davanti a ogni nome e concorda l'aggettivo.

Modello auto / nuovo   un'auto nuova

1. braccio / forte — un braccio forte
2. camera / oscuro — una camera oscura
3. cinema / aperto — un cinema aperto
4. crisi / lungo — una crisi lunga
5. foto / bello — una foto bella
6. ingegnere / abile — un ingegnere abile
7. labbro / carnoso — un labbro carnoso
8. mano / leggero — una mano leggera
9. moglie / affettuoso — una moglie affettuosa
10. poeta / romantico — un poeta romantico
11. problema / politico — un problema politico
12. professore / severo — un professore severo
13. radio / alternativo — una radio alternativa
14. studente / serio — uno studente serio
15. tesi / difficile — una tesi difficile
16. uovo / fresco — un uovo fresco
17. viaggio / avventuroso — un viaggio avventuroso
18. virtù / raro — una virtù rara

2 Ask pairs of students to write out a detailed description of an imagined person in the consulate waiting room and read it to the class. The rest of the students will determine why each person described is likely to be going to Italy.

2

Al consolato italiano Al consolato italiano di New York ci sono molte persone. Leggi le descrizioni e cambia il genere delle parole sottolineate (*underlined*).

1. La stanza è piena di gente. C'è la professoressa Simonetti che parla con due studenti americani che hanno bisogno di un visto (*visa*) per andare in Italia. *il professor / studentesse americane*
2. Nell'angolo (*corner*), un uomo anziano e un bambino irrequieto aspettano che la mamma finisca di parlare con il console. *una donna anziana / una bambina irrequieta / il papà*
3. La donna è un'importante scrittrice, che deve andare in Italia per una conferenza. *L'uomo / un importante scrittore*
4. In seconda fila ci sono due ragazze italiane allegre e spiritose che devono rinnovare il passaporto. *ragazzi italiani allegri e spiritosi*
5. Dietro, una ragazza alta dall'aria intellettuale disegna su un quaderno bianco. Ha un vestito colorato molto stravagante. Forse è un'artista principiante che vuole andare in Italia in cerca di ispirazione. *un ragazzo alto / un artista principiante*

3 Invite pairs of students to describe other common assumptions about Italy and Italians and to read them to the class. Write the sentences on the blackboard and ask the class to give the plural forms.

3

Gli stereotipi Paolo vive a New York con una famiglia americana per imparare l'inglese. La famiglia ha molti stereotipi sull'Italia e gli italiani, e Paolo non è d'accordo. Riscrivi le frasi cambiando al plurale le parole sottolineate, come nell'esempio.

Modello L'automobilista italiano è sempre poco prudente.
Non tutti gli automobilisti italiani sono sempre poco prudenti.

1. Un figlio vive in famiglia fino a trent'anni perché è immaturo. *Non tutti i figli vivono in famiglia fino a trent'anni perché sono immaturi.*
2. La moglie prepara un pranzo squisito per il marito. *Non tutte le mogli preparano pranzi squisiti per i mariti.*
3. La coppia che si incontra sulla spiaggia divorzia presto. *Non tutte le coppie che si incontrano sulle spiagge divorziano presto.*
4. L'italiano è ottimista anche di fronte alla avversità. *Non tutti gli italiani sono ottimisti anche di fronte alle avversità.*
5. Il negozio di alimentari è sempre chiuso tra le 13.00 e le 16.00. *Non tutti i negozi di alimentari sono sempre chiusi tra le 13.00 e le 16.00.*
6. Il bar ha sempre un televisore per vedere la partita di calcio. *Non tutti i bar hanno sempre dei televisori per vedere le partite di calcio.*
7. Il ragazzo italiano arriva sempre tardi all'appuntamento. *Non tutti i ragazzi italiani arrivano sempre tardi agli appuntamenti.*
8. Un artista deve vivere a Firenze per produrre un'opera geniale. *Non tutti gli artisti devono vivere a Firenze per produrre delle opere geniali.*

 Practice more at **vhlcentral.com**.

Comunicazione

4

Il mondo come lo vorrei! In coppia, completate le frasi usando almeno tre aggettivi. Se volete, potete usare alcune parole della lista.

comprensivo	fedele	leale	silenzioso
educato	geloso	rumoroso	socievole
esperto	istruito	severo	tranquillo

1. L'amico/a ideale è...
2. Il marito/La moglie ideale è...
3. Il professore ideale è...
4. Il fratello/La sorella ideale è...
5. Il vicino di casa ideale è...
6. Il gatto ideale è...

5

Dio li fa e poi li accoppia! In coppia, fatevi queste domande e decidete se l'altra persona può essere un(a) compagno/a di stanza ideale in un viaggio di studio. Aggiungete quattro domande libere alla lista.

1. Sei ordinato/a?
2. Hai un carattere allegro?
3. Sei una persona matura?
4. Cosa fai nel tempo libero?
5. Come sono i tuoi amici?
6. Come ti descrivono i tuoi genitori?

6

In centro Con un(a) compagno/a, trovate almeno tre modi per descrivere ciascuna foto. Confrontate le vostre descrizioni con un altro gruppo e discutete le differenze con la classe.

4 Remind the students that **educato** means *well-mannered*, while **istruito** means *educated*.

5 Have the students rank all the questions from most to least important and have them explain their choices.

6 Tell students to use as many descriptive adjectives as possible, and remind them to make all necessary agreements.

INSTRUCTIONAL RESOURCES **1.4**
Audioscripts, Answer Keys, Lab MP3s, Grammar Presentation Slides
SAM/WebSAM: WB, LM

ATTENZIONE!

To say *there is/are*, use **c'è/ci sono**.

C'è uno stadio qui vicino.
There is a stadium nearby.

Ci sono sempre problemi.
There are always problems.

Remind students that the third person singular forms of **essere** and **dare** require a grave accent. Ask them what the words would mean without the accent. **È** = *is*, **e** = *and*; **dà** = *gives*, **da** = *from*.

ATTENZIONE!

The verb **avere** is used in many idiomatic expressions whose English equivalents use the verb *to be*. These include **avere fame/sete** (*to be hungry/thirsty*), **avere sonno/paura** (*to be sleepy/afraid*), **avere…anni** (*to be…years old*), and so on.

ATTENZIONE!

Dare, **fare**, and **stare** are also used in a number of idiomatic expressions: **dare un esame** (*to take a test*), **fare spese** (*to go shopping*), **fare i compiti** (*to do one's homework*), **fare bel/brutto tempo** (*to be nice/nasty weather*), **fare colazione** (*to have breakfast*), **stare bene/male** (*to be well/ill*), **stare per** (*to be about to*).

On the board, list the verbs **fare**, **dare**, and **stare** in three columns. Ask students to provide as many expressions as they can under each verb. You may also want to provide expressions they may not be familiar with, such as **fare due passi**, **fare quattro chiacchiere**, **stare tranquillo**, **stare da solo**, etc.

The present tense: irregular verbs

—Non **può** *finire così!*

- Many Italian verbs are irregular in the present tense. Two of the most important irregular verbs are **essere**, *to be*, and **avere**, *to have*.

ẹssere		avere	
sono	siamo	ho	abbiamo
sei	siete	hai	avete
è	sono	ha	hanno

I miei figli **sono** gemelli. **Hanno** sedici anni.

- Only four **–are** verbs are irregular.

andare (*to go*)	**dare** (*to give*)	**fare** (*to do/make*)	**stare** (*to stay*)
vado	do	faccio	sto
vai	dai	fai	stai
va	dà	fa	sta
andiamo	diamo	facciamo	stiamo
andate	date	fate	state
vanno	danno	fanno	stanno

- Although the conjugations of irregular verbs must be memorized, some follow similar patterns, making them easier to learn. The verbs below, for example, insert **–g–** in the first person singular and third person plural forms.

porre (*to put*)	**rimanere** (*to remain*)	**salire** (*to go up*)	**tenere** (*to hold*)	**venire** (*to come*)
pongo	rimango	salgo	tengo	vengo
poni	rimani	sali	tieni	vieni
pone	rimane	sale	tiene	viene
poniamo	rimaniamo	saliamo	teniamo	veniamo
ponete	rimanete	salite	tenete	venite
pọngono	rimạngono	sạlgono	tẹngono	vẹngono

Oggi rimango a casa.
I'm staying home today.

Neanch'io vengo alla festa.
I'm not going to the party either.

- Four very common **–ere** verbs are also irregular.

dovere *(to have to, must)*	potere *(to be able, can)*	sapere *(to know)*	volere *(to want)*
devo	posso	so	voglio
devi	puoi	sai	vuoi
deve	può	sa	vuole
dobbiamo	possiamo	sappiamo	vogliamo
dovete	potete	sapete	volete
dęvono	pọssono	sanno	vọgliono

RIMANDO

For more information about **dovere**, **potere**, and **volere**, see **Strutture 4.4, p. 150.** For the distinction between **sapere** and **conoscere**, see **Strutture 7.4, p. 276.**

Point out that **dovere** has two possible conjugations in the first person singular and the third person plural: **devo** or **debbo**, **devono** or **debbono**.

As you go over the irregular verbs in the section, have pairs of students ask each other questions and give answers using the verbs in the charts.

- Some irregular verbs add regular present tense endings to irregular stems. The conjugations of **bere**, **dire**, and **tradurre** use stems derived from Latin roots: **bev–**, **dic–**, and **traduc–**.

bere *(to drink)*	dire *(to say)*	tradurre *(to translate)*
bevo	dico	traduco
bevi	dici	traduci
beve	dice	traduce
beviamo	diciamo	traduciamo
bevete	dite	traducete
bęvono	dịcono	tradụcono

- The conjugations of **accogliere**, **cogliere**, **scegliere**, and **togliere** follow a similar pattern. The first person singular and third person plural have **–lg–** before the endings, but all the other forms are like the infinitive, **–gl–**.

accọgliere *(to greet)*	cọgliere *(to pick)*	scẹgliere *(to choose)*	tọgliere *(to remove)*
accolgo	colgo	scelgo	tolgo
accogli	cogli	scegli	togli
accoglie	coglie	sceglie	toglie
accogliamo	cogliamo	scegliamo	togliamo
accogliete	cogliete	scegliete	togliete
accọlgono	cọlgono	scẹlgono	tọlgono

- **Uscire** (*to go out/exit*) and **riuscire** (*to succeed*) are irregular and must be memorized.

	uscire		riuscire
esco	usciamo	riesco	riusciamo
esci	uscite	riesci	riuscite
esce	ẹscono	riesce	riẹscono

Play a game. Have students draw a square with nine boxes on a sheet of paper, like a tic-tac-toe game. Have them write in each box one of the infinitives from the charts in this section, plus a subject pronoun. Randomly announce different infinitives until a student gets three in a row, vertically, horizontally, or diagonally. To claim a "win" (or prize, if you are giving them), the student must give the three infinitives, say the subject pronoun, and indicate the corresponding verb form. This activity can also be done in teams.

Pratica

1 As an expansion, ask pairs of students to write a description of a character mentioned in the activity and to share it.

1 Completare Completa le frasi con la forma corretta dei verbi.

1. Serena e Bruno __stanno__ (stare) insieme da tre anni e adesso __fanno__ (fare) progetti di matrimonio.

2. Lucia __fa__ (fare) colazione ogni giorno al bar e poi __va__ (andare) in ufficio a piedi.

3. I miei amici __hanno__ (avere) un esame domani, quindi __rimangono__ (rimanere) a casa a studiare stasera.

4. Vittoria __dà__ (dare) lezioni private di italiano e __traduce__ (tradurre) dall'inglese.

5. «Perché quando __vengo__ (venire) a trovarti tu mi __accogli__ (accogliere) sempre così freddamente?»

6. Ogni volta che io __tolgo__ (togliere) la giacca di papà dalla poltrona, lui __viene__ (venire) da me e mi __pone__ (porre) la solita domanda: «Sono io disordinato, o sei tu maniaca dell'ordine?»

2 Ask pairs of students to continue the dialogue mentioning things that they know about the Italian-American community.

2 As an expansion, ask students to search the Web for at least two Italian-American associations and to get information to share with the class (in Italian) about their mission and activities. They could be asked to indicate which of the two associations they prefer and why.

2 Incontro Antonio, napoletano, e Marco, romano, sono due vecchi amici. Dopo alcuni anni si incontrano per caso a New York. Completa il dialogo usando i verbi della lista nella forma corretta. Alcuni verbi si usano più di una volta!

andare	fare	sapere
essere	potere	uscire

MARCO Antonio, ciao! Non ci (1) __posso__ credere! Anche tu (2) __sei__ qui a New York!

ANTONIO Ciao, Marco! Che bello rivederti! Sì, studio qui già da tre mesi. Ma... non capisco... oggi la città (3) __è__ più vivace del solito e poi dalle finestre (4) __esce__ un buon profumo di dolci familiari. Che succede?

MARCO Ma come, non lo (5) __sai__? Oggi è il 19 settembre: la festa di san Gennaro! (6) __È__ un giorno importante per la comunità italo-americana.

ANTONIO Davvero? E cosa (7) __fanno__?

MARCO Tutto quello che (8) __fate__ voi a Napoli! Cucinano gli struffoli, (9) __vanno__ a messa e portano la statua di san Gennaro in processione per le strade di Little Italy. Perché non (10) __andiamo__ anche noi alla festa?

3 The phrase **tagliare e cucire** (cut and sew), is related to **pettegolezzi** because it implies that you look at people for so long and with such attention that you could measure their sizes and make a piece of clothing for them!

3 Pettegolezzi Parlate di voi stessi e degli altri usando le parole delle due liste.

A	B
Il professore/La professoressa di italiano	andare
Il/La mio/a vicino/a (*neighbor*)	dire
I genitori di...	fare
Io	stare
Tu	venire
La mia amica	rimanere
?	?

 Practice more at **vhlcentral.com**.

Comunicazione

4

Confronti Con un(a) compagno/a, descrivete le persone della lista usando le espressioni date. Motivate le vostre scelte e poi confrontate le vostre descrizioni con quelle di un altro gruppo.

4 Before beginning, brainstorm other celebrities for students to use in the activity.

Modello   È evidente che Madonna fa ginnastica perché è in ottima forma.

avere voglia di	fare ginnastica	stare bene
avere paura	fare shopping	stare male
avere ragione	fare un viaggio	stare da solo/a
avere torto	fare finta di (*to pretend*)	stare per
?	?	?

- Mariah Carey
- Brad Pitt
- Taylor Swift

- Beyoncé
- Will Smith
- Robert De Niro

- Miley Cyrus
- Johnny Depp
- Ben Stiller

5

Interpretiamo Guardate le immagini e rispondete alle domande.

1. Chi sono queste persone?
2. Con chi sono?
3. Dove sono?

4. Cosa fanno?
5. Come stanno?
6. Di che cosa parlano?

6

Gli affari degli altri

A. Usando i verbi e le espressioni della lista, formulate almeno sei domande da fare al(la) vostro/a compagno/a e poi intervistatelo/a.

6 Encourage students to use expressions indicating surprise or scandal while listening to their classmates' reports. Example: **Non ci posso credere! Che strano! Roba da pazzi! Figurati! Ma va!**

avere fame	bere	fare colazione
avere fretta	dare un esame	rimanere a casa da solo/a
avere paura	fare i compiti	scegliere
avere sete	fare il bagno	stare bene/male
avere sonno	fare spese	tenere

B. A gruppi di quattro o cinque, riassumete le cose che avete saputo del(la) vostro/a compagno/a e condividetele con gli altri.

Sintesi

1

Parliamo Sandra è negli Stati Uniti per lavoro e condivide l'ufficio con Bruno. Leggete l'e-mail di Sandra a Maria e rispondete alle domande.

Da:	Sandra <smancini@libero.it>
A:	Maria Farnetti <mfarnetti@libero.it>
Oggetto:	uno strano collega d'ufficio

Cara Maria, finalmente sono a New York! Qui è tutto così diverso dall'Italia! Le vie sono larghe e spaziose e i grattacieli (*skyscrapers*) sono immensi. C'è sempre traffico, notte e giorno, e gente che cammina lungo i marciapiedi (*sidewalks*). Qui fa già freddo, ma l'ufficio del mio collega Bruno è molto caldo. Troppo! Penso spesso a mia nonna, che ripete sempre di fare economia, di spegnere le luci e il riscaldamento (*heating*)... E poi, è tutto molto silenzioso... tutti lavorano nel loro ufficio e quando si incontrano parlano a voce bassa.
Il nostro dipartimento di italiano è il più rumoroso!

C'è un gatto in ufficio. È carino ed affettuoso, ma sale continuamente sulla mia scrivania e riempie la mia sedia di peli (*hairs*). Come faccio a dire a Bruno che odio i gatti? Non voglio offenderlo, ma non voglio condividere l'ufficio con un collega a quattro zampe (*paws*)! Forse posso chiedere un altro ufficio al capo del dipartimento...
Dammi un consiglio, tu che sai sempre tutto!

A presto, Sandra.

1. Cosa fa Sandra negli Stati Uniti?
2. Cosa colpisce (*strikes*) l'attenzione di Sandra a New York?
3. Perché Sandra pensa spesso alla nonna?
4. Quali sono gli aspetti degli Stati Uniti che forse non piacciono a Sandra? Siete d'accordo con lei? Perché?
5. Cosa può fare Sandra per liberarsi del gatto senza offendere Bruno?
6. Hai un collega, un compagno di scuola, un vicino o un compagno di stanza che ti rende difficile la vita? Cosa fai per risolvere il problema?

2

Scriviamo Scrivi un'e-mail di tre paragrafi, scegliendo uno dei seguenti titoli:

- Descrivi a un amico/un'amica una situazione nuova che ti preoccupa o in cui per qualche motivo ti senti a disagio (*uncomfortable*).
- Scrivi a Sandra dei suggerimenti per risolvere il problema del gatto in ufficio. Prova a suggerire soluzioni e a lasciare aperta la possibilità di altre proposte.

Strategie per la comunicazione
Suggerimenti per scrivere un'e-mail informale Ecco alcuni consigli per scrivere un'e-mail informale ma corretta: • Saluto iniziale: Cara Sandra/Ciao Sandra • Ringraziamenti: grazie/grazie mille/ti ringrazio per (l'aiuto, il consiglio, la disponibilità, ecc.) • Saluto finale: A presto/Ciao

Teach students additional vocabulary that they can use to answer the questions: **spreco** (*waste*), **al massimo** (*at the highest setting*), **allergico/a** (*allergic*).

Point out that in Italian it would be rude to start a letter just with the name of the addressee and that a salutation is always required at the end.

Preparazione

 Vocabulary Tools

Vocabolario della lettura

approfondire *to study in-depth*
il/la bisnonno/a *great-grandfather/mother*
la cassata *Sicilian dessert*
il/la curatore/curatrice *curator*
il ricordo *memory*
il retaggio *heritage*

il quartiere *neighborhood*
vergognarsi (si vergogna) *to get embarrassed*
la sfogliatella *Neapolitan pastry*
lo spumone *a type of gelato*
il tiramisù *"pick-me-up" coffee dessert*
utile *useful*

Vocabolario utile

il bar *café*
il biscotto *cookie*
i cantucci *Tuscan almond biscotti*
il vassoio *tray*

1

Pratica Inserisci le parole nuove negli spazi.

1. La materia che vorrei ___approfondire___ di più è l'informatica.
2. Il ___tiramisù___ è un dolce a base di caffè, mascarpone e biscotti.
3. Soho è uno dei ___quartieri___ più famosi di New York.
4. Mia cugina è molto timida: si ___vergogna___ di parlare in pubblico.
5. I figli e nipoti degli immigrati sono spesso interessati al loro ___retaggio___ culturale.
6. Anche dopo tanti anni ho ancora dei bellissimi ___ricordi___ del nostro viaggio a Genova.

2

Intervista In coppia, intervistate degli altri studenti.

1. Cosa ti ha spinto (*drove you*) a studiare l'italiano?
2. Quali lingue sono simili all'italiano? Perché?
3. Hai imparato altre lingue in passato? Quali?
4. Secondo te, quali sono i vantaggi di parlare più di una lingua?
5. Quale altra lingua vorresti studiare? Perché?
6. Pensi che studiare l'italiano ti aiuterà a imparare anche altre lingue? Perché?

3

Quartieri e specialità In coppia, rispondete alle domande.

1. C'è un quartiere italiano nella tua città? E altri quartieri etnici? Come sono?
2. Ci sono ristoranti tipici? Negozi con prodotti importati?
3. Quali sono le specialità italiane che hai assaggiato (*tasted*)?
4. Quali sono le specialità italo-americane? Perché sono diverse, secondo voi?

---

2 Ask pairs to report their findings to the rest of the class.

3 Ask students to share the descriptions of ethnic neighborhoods that they know of or where they grew up and/or where they live now with the rest of the class. Make a list on the board and ask students to provide lists of the features of each neighborhood. Are there restaurants they would recommend? Important landmarks to visit?

Nota CULTURALE

Secondo il più recente censimento ufficiale, gli **italo-americani sono** circa 18 milioni, cioè il 6% della popolazione degli U.S.A. e ne costituiscono il quarto gruppo etnico. Fra questi, **solo 724.632 parlano italiano** a casa. **L'Associazione delle lingue moderne** (*MLA*) ha annunciato che, dal 2006 al 2009, il numero di studenti universitari iscritti a corsi d'italiano negli Stati Uniti ha continuato ad aumentare.

PERCHÉ STUDI L'ITALIANO?

Reading

widespread

link

Quali sono le ragioni più diffuse° per imparare l'italiano? Per chi è di origine italiana c'è un legame° personale nel rapporto con i nonni o altri parenti
5 che ancora parlano la lingua o un dialetto. Molti hanno il desiderio di recuperare il proprio retaggio culturale: il ricordo di un piatto speciale, di una tradizione, di immagini e racconti che vengono da
10 un'altra epoca. Anche la lettura di un libro o una scena di un film possono far nascere la curiosità di conoscere meglio la propria storia. Ci sono poi studenti con interessi che li portano a contatto diretto con
15 l'Italia di ieri e di oggi: musica, cinema, ingegneria, architettura e storia dell'arte, teologia, moda, studi classici, medicina,

law

giurisprudenza°, design, sport, economia e commercio e altro ancora. C'è anche
20 chi vuole imparare la lingua perchè si è innamorato di una persona o di una città. E tu, perché studi l'italiano? Con questa domanda siamo andati al Caffè Vittoria nel *North End*, il quartiere italo-americano
25 di Boston.

Il primo a rispondere è Tom, un italo-americano: «Mia nonna parla un misto di

dialect from Palermo, Sicily

would speak 30

fit in

italiano e dialetto palermitano°, ma non li ha insegnati alla mia mamma. Voleva che i suoi figli parlassero° bene l'inglese per potersi inserire° meglio nella società statunitense e non essere considerati stranieri. Ma adesso le cose sono cambiate e i sentimenti anti-italiani che si ricorda mia
35 nonna non esistono più. Da quando ho cominciato a studiare l'italiano due anni fa, parliamo per telefono molto più spesso. Però si vergogna quando parla perché non vuole che io impari il palermitano».

40 Manuel, un argentino di origine italiana che studia al MIT, ci ha detto: «Sto studiando ingegneria e voglio lavorare in Italia. Nessuno nella mia famiglia parla l'italiano, anche se riusciamo a
45 capirlo perché è così simile allo spagnolo e specialmente allo spagnolo argentino in cui si usano tante parole italiane. Non so

I don't even know

neanche° esattamente la storia di come il

mio bisnonno sia arrivato a Buenos Aires; so solo che si chiamava come me: Emanuele
50 Ricasoli. Ho potuto seguire solo 3 semestri di italiano all'università, ma l'estate scorsa ho partecipato a uno stage° a Venezia e

internship

ho fatto una vera immersione nella lingua italiana di 3 mesi. Forse non bisogna dire
55 'immersione' parlando di una laguna... »

Erin, un'americana di origine irlandese che è curatrice di un museo, ci ha raccontato che viaggia spesso in Italia, specialmente a Firenze, sia per lavoro che°
60

sia... che *both... and*

per le vacanze. «All'università ho studiato la storia dell'arte italiana, ma non ho avuto l'opportunità di approfondire la lingua. La prima volta che sono andata in Italia ho imparato qualche parola.
65 Poi ho incominciato a studiare l'italiano seguendo dei corsi di lingua e letteratura. Certamente l'italiano mi è stato utile anche professionalmente, ma la cosa più bella è stata l'amicizia con gli altri studenti
70 dei corsi. Siamo ancora in contatto».

Tom, Manuel ed Erin sono solo tre esempi di persone che hanno scelto di imparare l'italiano, ma le loro storie sono simili a molte altre. E tu, perché
75 stai studiando l'italiano? Perché non ci racconti anche tu la tua storia? ■

Il Caffè Vittoria

È il primo bar italiano del North End di Boston, aperto nel 1929. Per i residenti è un locale° per rilassarsi, incontrarsi, chiacchierare e guardarsi intorno; per i turisti è un viaggio nel tempo. Oltre al caffè espresso offre sfogliatelle, tiramisù, gelati e spumoni. Nelle vetrine e all'interno c'è una collezione di antiche macchine per fare l'espresso. Con tanti clienti abituali e turisti di passaggio curiosi di assaggiare le specialità, i camerieri passano di corsa° tenendo magicamente in equilibrio cappuccini e caffè sul vassoio. Accanto e di fronte al Caffè Vittoria ci sono altri bar e pasticcerie italiane come Mike's Pastry.

locale *spot* **corsa** *rush by*

Analisi

1 **Comprensione** Scegli la risposta giusta.

1. Tom vuole parlare al telefono in italiano con _____.
   a. gli amici a Firenze   b. la sua mamma   (c.) sua nonna

2. La nonna di Tom è _____.
   a. napoletana   (b.) siciliana   c. abruzzese

3. Una delle ragioni per cui Manuel studia l'italiano è per _____.
   a. andare a Venezia   (b.) lavorare in Italia   c. parlare con i suoi nonni

4. Il bisnonno di Manuel è emigrato in _____.
   (a.) Argentina   b. Australia   c. Brasile

5. Erin ha imparato l'italiano _____.
   (a.) seguendo dei corsi di lingua   b. studiando la storia dell'arte
   c. frequentando il *North End*

2 As a warm-up for this activity, point out factors that draw attention to a certain language or culture. For example, *The Lord of the Rings* films increased tourism to New Zealand. Encourage students to come up with more examples.

2 As a follow-up question, ask students: **Secondo voi, ci sono delle mode per quanto riguarda le lingue?**

2 **Lingue e culture** In coppia, rispondete alle domande a turno. Dopo confrontate le vostre risposte con quelle di un'altra coppia.

1. Con quale delle persone intervistate ti identifichi di più? Perché?

2. Quali lingue potevi studiare al liceo? Quale hai scelto?

3. Quali corsi di lingua puoi frequentare all'università?

4. Ci sono dei film o dei libri che ti hanno fatto venir voglia di viaggiare o/e di imparare una lingua? Quali?

3 **Tre generazioni** In gruppi di quattro, parlate della famiglia nelle foto.

- Che legame (*link*) c'è tra le persone nelle foto?
- Da dove sono emigrati? In che paese sono andati?
- Perché sono emigrati?

- Cosa speravano di trovare?
- Cosa hanno portato con loro?
- Cosa hanno trovato?

The family featured in these photos is a typical example of Italian immigration all over the world and back to Italy.

Donato e Rosa Corbo;
figli: Nicola, Mario e Maria
Italia → Argentina, 1954

Mario e Amelia Corbo;
figli: Mario, Luis, Sandra
Argentina → Australia, 1974

Gaby Corbo (figlia di Nicola)
Argentina → Italia, 2008

4 **Scrittura** Scegli uno di questi argomenti e scrivi una composizione.

- Come è arrivata in questo Paese la tua famiglia? Avete dei rapporti con il vostro Paese di origine? Racconta la storia della tua famiglia in tre paragrafi.

- Scrivi una lettera a un amico/un'amica per convincerlo/a a studiare una lingua straniera.

Practice more at
vhlcentral.com.

Preparazione

 Vocabulary Tools

A proposito dell'autrice

Susanna Tamaro (Trieste, 1957) è autrice di oltre 20 libri tra cui libri per bambini, regista televisiva e di un film, autrice di testi di canzoni e articoli su importanti riviste cattoliche. Nel 1994 con *Va' dove ti porta il cuore* raggiunge un successo di pubblico straordinario (15 milioni di copie vendute, tradotto in 43 paesi), non ripetuto neanche nel seguito *Ascolta la mia voce*, pubblicato nel 2006. Il romanzo nel 2011 è stato inserito nella lista dei 150 «grandi libri» che hanno segnato la storia d'Italia al Salone del Libro di Torino e nel 1996 ha ispirato il film omonimo (*of the same title*). Susanna Tamaro ha continuato a scrivere libri che parlano di temi universali con un linguaggio semplice.

Vocabolario della lettura		Vocabolario utile
abbaiare *to bark*	**il lupo** *wolf*	**il desiderio** *wish*
il bassotto *basset hound*	**il muso** *muzzle*	**l'entusiasmo** *enthusiasm*
il botolo *mutt*	**la razza** *race*	**inaspettato/a** *unexpected*
il cane da caccia *hunting dog*	**la taglia** *size*	**la nostalgia** *nostalgia*
il canile *dog shelter*	**la volpe** *fox*	**la scelta** *choice*
la gabbia *cage*	**il volpino** *Pomeranian*	
il lassie *collie*	**la zampa** *paw*	

1

Definizioni Trova la definizione adatta a ogni parola.

<u>e</u> 1. il botolo   a. la grandezza di cose, animali e persone

<u>g</u> 2. il lupo   b. braccio e mano, o gamba e piede, degli animali

<u>a</u> 3. la taglia   c. la ricerca di animali per ucciderli e mangiarli

<u>f</u> 4. la volpe   d. la faccia degli animali

<u>b</u> 5. la zampa   e. un cane piccolo e antipatico

<u>d</u> 6. il muso   f. un animale noto per la sua furbizia (*cunning*)

<u>c</u> 7. la caccia   g. un animale simile al cane, presente in molte fiabe

2

Preparazione Fate le seguenti domande a un(a) compagno/a.

1. Hai o hai avuto un animale domestico? Quale? Come si chiama?

2. Ti ricordi di una tua scelta di bambino/a che ha sorpreso i grandi (*adults*)?

3. Ti ricordi di qualcosa che per te era logica da bambino ma che i grandi non capivano? Secondo te, i bambini vedono le cose con più chiarezza (*clarity*)?

3

Gli animali domestici In gruppi di tre o quattro, rispondete a queste domande.

1. Che valore ha la presenza di un animale in una casa? È un membro della famiglia? Che tipo di sostegno (*support*) morale dà un animale?

2. È giusto educare gli animali domestici a non sporcare, a non fare rumore in casa, a non distruggere le cose o questo significa snaturarli (*denature*)?

Nota
CULTURALE

In *Va' dove ti porta il cuore* l'autrice fa riferimento al libro dell'autore francese Antoine de Saint-Exupéry, *Il Piccolo Principe*. Pubblicato nel 1943, è uno dei libri più letti al mondo ed è stato tradotto in 300 lingue. Il piccolo principe spiega a un pilota in panne° nel deserto che è venuto sulla Terra° per cercare una pecora° che mangi i baobab che soffocano° il suo pianeta. L'incontro con il pilota è solo l'ultimo di una serie con animali, fiori e persone. Una volpe, in particolare, gli insegna il significato dell'amicizia. Susanna Tamaro inizia il suo libro con il racconto di un'amicizia improbabile, ispirandosi al romanzo di Saint-Exupéry.

in panne *broken down* **Terra** *Earth* **pecora** *sheep* **soffocano** *suffocat*

 Practice more at **vhlcentral.com**.

VA' DOVE TI PORTA IL CUORE

(FRAMMENTO)

Susanna Tamaro

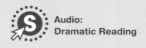

Audio: Dramatic Reading

Sei partita da due mesi e da due mesi, a parte una cartolina nella quale mi comunicavi di essere ancora viva, non ho tue notizie°. Questa
5 mattina, in giardino, mi sono fermata a lungo davanti alla tua rosa. Nonostante° sia autunno inoltrato°, spicca° con il suo color porpora°, solitaria e arrogante, sul resto della vegetazione ormai spenta°.
10 Ti ricordi quando l'abbiamo piantata? Avevi dieci anni e da poco avevi letto *Il Piccolo Principe*. Te l'avevo regalato io come premio° per la tua promozione. Eri rimasta incantata° dalla storia. Tra
15 tutti i personaggi, i tuoi preferiti erano la rosa e la volpe; non ti piacevano invece i baobab, il serpente, l'aviatore, né tutti gli uomini vuoti e presuntuosi° che vagavano° seduti sui loro minuscoli pianeti. Così una
20 mattina, mentre facevamo colazione, hai detto: «Voglio una rosa.» Davanti alla mia obiezione che ne avevamo già tante hai risposto: «Ne voglio una che sia mia soltanto, voglio curarla, farla diventare
25 grande.» Naturalmente, oltre° alla rosa, volevi anche una volpe. Con la furbizia° dei bambini avevi messo il desiderio semplice davanti a quello quasi° impossibile. Come potevo negarti° la volpe dopo che ti
30 avevo concesso° la rosa? Su questo punto abbiamo discusso a lungo, alla fine ci siamo messe d'accordo per un cane.

La notte prima di andare a prenderlo non hai chiuso occhio. Ogni mezz'ora
35 bussavi° alla mia porta e dicevi: «Non riesco a dormire.» La mattina alle sette avevi già fatto colazione, ti eri vestita e lavata; con il cappotto addosso° mi aspettavi seduta in poltrona. Alle otto e
40 mezza eravamo davanti all'ingresso° del canile, era ancora chiuso. Tu guardando tra le grate dicevi: «Come saprò qual è proprio° il mio?» C'era una grande ansia° nella tua voce. Io ti rassicuravo°,
45 non preoccuparti, dicevo, ricorda come il piccolo principe ha addomesticato la volpe.

Siamo tornate al canile per tre giorni di seguito°. C'erano più di duecento cani là dentro e tu volevi vederli tutti.
50 Ti fermavi davanti a ogni gabbia, stavi lì immobile e assorta° in un'apparente indifferenza. I cani intanto° si buttavano tutti contro la rete°, abbaiavano, facevano salti, con le zampe cercavano di divellere°
55 le maglie°. Assieme a° noi c'era l'addetta° del canile. Credendoti una ragazzina come tutte le altre, per invogliarti° ti mostrava gli esemplari più belli: «Guarda quel cocker», ti diceva. Oppure: «Che te ne
60 pare di quel lassie?» Per tutta risposta emettevi una specie di grugnito° e procedevi senza ascoltarla.

Buck l'abbiamo incontrato il terzo giorno di quella via crucis°. Stava in uno
65 dei box° sul retro°, quelli dove venivano alloggiati° i cani convalescenti. Quando siamo arrivate alla grata, invece di correrci incontro assieme a tutti gli altri, è rimasto seduto al suo posto senza neanche alzare
70 la testa. «Quello», hai esclamato tu indicandolo con un dito. «Voglio quel cane lì.» Ti ricordi la faccia esterrefatta° della donna? Non riusciva a capire come tu volessi entrare in possesso di quel botolo
75 orrendo. Già perché Buck era piccolo di taglia ma nella sua piccolezza raccoglieva° quasi tutte le razze del mondo. La testa da lupo, le orecchie morbide° e basse da cane da caccia, le zampe slanciate° quanto quelle
80 di un bassotto, la coda spumeggiante° di un volpino e il manto nero focato° di un dobermann. Quando siamo andate negli uffici per firmare le carte, l'impiegata ci ha raccontato la sua storia. Era stato
85 lanciato° fuori da un'auto in corsa° all'inizio dell'estate. Nel volo si era ferito° gravemente e per questo motivo una delle zampe posteriori pendeva° come morta.

Buck adesso è qui al mio fianco°.
90 Mentre scrivo ogni tanto sospira° e avvicina la punta° del naso alla mia gamba. Il muso e le orecchie sono diventati ormai quasi bianchi e sugli occhi, da qualche tempo, gli si è posato° quel velo che sempre
95 si posa sugli occhi dei cani vecchi. Mi commuovo° a guardarlo. È come se qui accanto ci fosse una parte di te, la parte che più amo, quella che, tanti anni fa, tra i duecento ospiti del ricovero°, ha saputo
100 scegliere il più infelice e brutto. ∎

Glosses (right/left margins):
news; Even though; late / stands out; crimson; faded; prize; enchanted; presumptuous / wandered; in addition to; cleverness; almost; deny you; granted; knocked; on; entrance; exactly; anxiety / reassured; in a row; immersed; meanwhile; wire netting; rip off; mesh / Together with / employee; encourage you; grunt; difficult journey; cages / back; housed; appalled; gathered; soft; slender; effervescent; seal-like; thrown / running; injured; hung; side; sighs; tip; set; it moves me; shelter

1 Ask students if they have aging pets and if they display affection differently. How do relationships between humans and animals evolve over time?

Comprensione Scegli quale frase è vera in ogni coppia di opzioni.

1. (a.) Una ragazza è partita e dà poche notizie di sé.
   b. Una ragazza è partita e scrive molte cartoline.

2. a. La ragazza a dieci anni amava tutti i personaggi de *Il Piccolo Principe*.
   (b.) La ragazza a dieci anni amava solo due personaggi de *Il Piccolo Principe*.

3. a. A dieci anni la bambina aveva ottenuto una rosa e una volpe.
   (b.) A dieci anni la bambina aveva ottenuto una rosa e un cane.

4. (a.) La bambina prima di andare al canile non ha chiuso occhio.
   b. La bambina prima di andare al canile ha dormito benissimo.

5. (a.) La bambina aveva paura di non riconoscere il suo cane.
   b. La bambina sarebbe stata contenta di avere un cane qualunque (*whichever*).

6. (a.) L'addetta del canile propone solo cani di razza.
   b. L'addetta del canile chiede di considerare i cani che si buttano contro la rete.

7. a. Buck è un cane vivace e bello.
   (b.) Buck è un cane malato e bruttissimo.

8. a. Buck adesso è ancora attivo e ci vede bene.
   (b.) Buck adesso è vecchio e quasi cieco (*blind*).

2 Explain that **meticcio** is a term that derives from the Spanish *mestizo* and Portuguese *mestiço* and designates someone born from the union of a white European and an indigenous person of the Americas.

Opzioni Scegli una risposta e poi con un(a) compagno/a discuti perché ti sembra giusta.

1. Buck è un cane _____.
   a. di razza mista, felice e esuberante
   b. che non voleva essere adottato perché era quasi morto
   (c.) ferito e convalescente, meticcio (*mixed breed*), brutto ma tenero
   d. un cane senza una zampa

2. La rosa è _____.
   a. bianca e rosa e della ragazza che è partita
   b. della persona che parla, che la cura e le dà da bere
   c. di un giardiniere che l'ha piantata dieci anni fa con la ragazza
   (d.) della ragazza che era bambina quando han piantato la rosa rossa

3. La bambina aveva chiesto _____.
   (a.) una rosa e una volpe
   b. una rosa e un baobab
   c. una rosa e un cane
   d. una rosa e un serpente

4. La bambina è stravagante perché _____.
   a. vuole un cane malato e scostante (*off-putting*)
   (b.) non vuole un cane di razza ma uno che ha bisogno di lei
   c. vuole un cane di razza ma non trova la sua preferita
   d. vuole duecento cani che saltano e abbaiano

5. Buck è _____.
   (a.) la parte più bella e vera della ragazza che se n'è andata
   b. un cane ormai cieco e inutile
   c. un cane che pensa sempre alla ragazza che se n'è andata
   d. un cane poco affettuoso

3

Personaggi Scegli gli aggettivi che descrivono meglio i tre personaggi.

abbandonato/a	brutto/a	furbo/a	tenero/a
accomodante	commosso/a	nostalgico/a	vecchio/a
analitico/a	curioso/a	paziente	
ansioso/a	egoista	sofferente	

1. Chi scrive _accomodante, commossa, nostalgica, paziente_

2. La ragazza che è partita _analitica, ansiosa, curiosa, egoista, furba_

3. Buck _abbandonato, brutto, sofferente, tenero, vecchio_

4

Opinioni In coppia, rispondete alle seguenti domande.

1. Secondo te, chi scrive è una madre, un padre, una nonna, un nonno, uno zio o una zia, o semplicemente un amico o un'amica? Perché? Come cambia il racconto se è una persona più grande a parlare o una coetanea (*peer*) della ragazza che è partita?

2. È meglio prendere un animale da tenere in casa da un allevatore (*breeder*) o da una struttura per animali randagi (*stray*) o abbandonati? Perché?

3. Siamo noi che scegliamo gli animali o loro che scelgono noi?

4. Cosa faresti a chi abbandona gli animali domestici? Perché credi che la gente li abbandoni? Ci sono circostanze che giustificano questo atto?

5. Hai mai desiderato una cosa (un animale, un viaggio, un'esperienza) perché lo avevi letto in un libro o visto in un film? Quale?

5

Inventa una storia In gruppi di tre o quattro, scrivete un dialogo su come vi comportereste se doveste scegliere un animale tra molti nelle gabbie di un canile. Secondo quali criteri scegliereste un animale, e quale animale?

6

Come continua? In gruppi di tre, scegliete una possibile continuazione delle pagine che avete letto tra le tre proposte. Scrivete una storia da leggere poi al resto della classe.

1. Buck è molto malato e muore. Chi scrive lo dice alla ragazza che torna.

2. Chi scrive sta morendo e non si può più prendere cura di Buck.

3. La ragazza non riceve la lettera e, quando torna, la rosa è appassita (*wilted*). Chi scrive e Buck sono spariti (*disappeared*) e nessuno sa dove sono.

7

Tema Scrivi due paragrafi su un tuo animale domestico e su come è diventato parte della famiglia. Descrivi cos'è, come si chiama, di che colore è, etc. Parla di come ha cambiato la tua vita e quella della tua famiglia. Se non hai un animale, descrivi l'animale che vorresti avere.

4 As a follow-up activity, have students do an online search for **campagna contro l'abbandono dei cani** to see which ads they find. Ask which one is their favorite, why they think it is particularly effective or ineffective, and if they can come up with one of their own.

6 Collect the written stories for a group grade, taking into account creativity, grammatical accuracy, and use of vocabulary. Students should put effort into imagining how the story continues. While groups are working, circulate and provide additional vocabulary if necessary. Have groups read their stories to the class.

7 Remind students to use the vocabulary they have learned in this lesson in their **tema**. Have them exchange papers with a classmate for peer-editing. Each student should write his or her own **tema** and provide comments to a partner.

Practice more at **vhlcentral.com**.

Pratica

La tesi e gli argomenti

Un saggio accademico si divide, in genere, in tre parti: un'introduzione in cui si presenta la tesi; una discussione in cui si presentano gli argomenti per difendere la tesi; e una conclusione. Una tesi è un'idea che si deve sostenere o difendere con degli argomenti. La tesi deve essere:

- **chiara e concisa:** non presentare argomenti troppo diversi altrimenti risulta imprecisa e diventa molto complicato difenderla e giungere a una conclusione coerente.

- **obiettiva:** anche se sono richieste opinioni personali, la tesi deve essere esposta in un linguaggio obiettivo e basarsi su prove evidenti.

- **originale:** la tesi non deve prospettare argomenti ovvi; deve condurre a una conclusione creativa e originale.

   Gli argomenti che si usano per presentare o difendere la tesi possono esprimere:

- **autorità,** quando si riporta l'opinione di un personaggio di prestigio o di un esperto.

- **esemplificazione,** quando si usano citazioni ed esempi.

- **confutazione,** quando si respingono argomenti contrari alla posizione di chi scrive la tesi.

- **analogia,** quando si mettono a confronto due fatti o situazioni.

- **opinione comune,** quando si fa riferimento a opinioni generali, a favore o contrarie alla tesi sostenuta.

1

Preparazione A quali categorie appartiene ognuno di questi argomenti?

1. Oggi tutti i giovani si trovano d'accordo…: **Confutazione/opinione comune**
2. Mentre le persone nel XIX secolo conducevano vite semplici, senza mezzi di comunicazione moderni, ai nostri giorni invece…: **Analogia/confutazione**
3. Già nel 1960, un famoso professore di… aveva difeso la teoria…: **Analogia/autorità**

2

Saggio Scegli uno di questi argomenti e scrivi un saggio, lungo almeno due pagine.

- Il tuo saggio deve far riferimento ad almeno uno dei quattro brani studiati in questa lezione e contenuti in Cortometraggio, Immagina, Cultura e Letteratura.

- Deve includere almeno due tipi diversi di argomenti ed esempi tratti dai brani proposti nella lezione.

- Deve far risaltare la tua tesi personale.

   1. Al giorno d'oggi, il bilinguismo e il multilinguismo rappresentano un vantaggio o possono essere motivo di discriminazione? Perché?

   2. La fine di una relazione segna solo un fallimento o può essere l'inizio di una riflessione su cui costruire i nostri futuri rapporti con gli altri?

   3. In relazione agli esempi studiati nei brani di questa lezione, come definiresti le tue idee di amore e rispetto per un'altra persona?

I rapporti personali

 Vocabulary Tools

La personalità

affascinante *charming*
affettuoso/a *affectionate*
attraente *attractive*
geniale *great*
idealista *idealistic*
insicuro/a *insecure*
(im)maturo/a *(im)mature*
(dis)onesto/a *(dis)honest*
orgoglioso/a *proud*
ottimista *optimistic*
pessimista *pessimistic*
prudente *careful*
sensibile *sensitive*
timido *shy*
tranquillo/a *calm*
umile *humble*

Lo stato civile

divorziare (da) *to divorce*
fidanzarsi (con) *to get engaged (to)*
sposarsi (con) *to get married (to)*

celibe *single (m.)*
divorziato/a *divorced*
fidanzato/a *engaged; fiancé(e)*
nubile *single (f.)*
sposato/a *married*
vedovo/a *widowed; widower/widow*

I rapporti

l'amicizia *friendship*
l'anima gemella *soul mate*
l'appuntamento *date*
il colpo di fulmine *love at first sight*
il/la compagno/a *partner*
la coppia *couple*
il matrimonio *wedding*
i pettegolezzi *gossip*

avere fiducia (in) *to trust*
condividere *to share*
contare su *to rely on*
lasciare *to leave*
mentire *to lie*
meritare *to deserve*
rompere con *to break up with*

uscire con *to go out with*

comprensivo/a *understanding*
(in)dimenticabile *(un)forgettable*
(in)fedele *(un)faithful*

I sentimenti

adorare *to adore*
amare *to love*
arrabbiarsi *to get angry*
avere vergogna (di) *to be ashamed (of)*
dare fastidio (a) *to annoy*
disturbare *to bother*
innamorarsi *to fall in love*
odiare *to hate*
provare *to feel*
sentirsi *to feel*
sognare *to dream*
volere bene a *to feel affection for*

ansioso/a *anxious*
contrariato/a *annoyed*
deluso/a *disappointed*
depresso/a *depressed*
emozionato/a *excited*
entusiasta *enthusiastic*
geloso/a *jealous*
preoccupato/a *worried*
stufo/a *fed up*

Cortometraggio

il binario *train track*
la colpa *fault*
la commessa *saleswoman*
l'orario *schedule*
la piattaforma *platform*
la scatola *box*
i tacchi alti/bassi *high/low heels*
la vetrina *shop window*

buttare via *to throw away*
indossare *to wear*
mettersi *to put on (clothing, shoes)*
truccarsi *to put on make up*

resistente *sturdy*
vendicativo/a *vengeful*

Cultura

il bar *café*
il biscotto *cookie*
il/la bisnonno/a *great-grandfather/ mother*
i cantucci *Tuscan almond biscotti*
la cassata *Sicilian dessert*
il/la curatore/curatrice *curator*
il quartiere *neighborhood*
il retaggio *heritage*
il ricordo *memory*
la sfogliatella *Neapolitan pastry*
lo spumone *a type of gelato*
il tiramisù *"pick-me-up" coffee dessert*
il vassoio *tray*

approfondire *to study in-depth*
vergognarsi (si vergogna) *to get embarrassed*

utile *useful*

Letteratura

il bassotto *basset hound*
il botolo *mutt*
il cane da caccia *hunting dog*
il canile *dog shelter*
il desiderio *wish*
l'entusiasmo *enthusiasm*
la gabbia *cage*
il lassie *collie*
il lupo *wolf*
il muso *muzzle*
la nostalgia *nostalgia*
la razza *race*
la scelta *choice*
la taglia *size*
la volpe *fox*
il volpino *Pomeranian*
la zampa *paw*

abbaiare *to bark*

inaspettato/a *unexpected*

Vivere insieme

Le città, anche se non hanno parole, ci comunicano la loro storia. Da sempre sono la testimonianza del bisogno delle persone di vivere insieme ed esprimono così la capacità umana di costruire e di sfidare il tempo. Che rapporto hai con la città e con i suoi simboli? Come ti senti rispetto ai continui cambiamenti e agli sviluppi edilizi e demografici?

Destinazione:

L'ITALIA CENTRALE

UMBRIA
MARCHE
LAZIO
ABRUZZO
Città del Vaticano

PREVIEW Invite students to share their views on city life, having them cite some of their favorite cities. Have them comment on the statement: **[Le città] sono da sempre la testimonianza del bisogno delle persone di vivere insieme.** Elicit reactions and opinions on whether it is essential for people to live in close proximity to others, or if one can live a satisfying life alone.

Città e comunità Vocabulary Tools

Luoghi e indicazioni

l'angolo *corner*
l'appartamento *apartment*
la campagna *countryside*
il casale *farmhouse*
l'edicola *newsstand*

i giardini pubblici *public gardens*
il grattacielo *skyscraper*
l'incrocio *intersection*
il marciapiede *sidewalk*
la metro(politana) *subway*
il municipio *city hall*
il paese *village; country*
il palazzo *building; palace*
la periferia *suburbs*
il quartiere *neighborhood*
il segnale stradale *road sign*
il semaforo *traffic light*
lo stadio *stadium*
la stazione di polizia *police station*
la strada *street*
le strisce pedonali *crosswalk*
il tribunale *courthouse*
la via *street*

attraversare *to cross*
dare indicazioni *to give directions*
perdersi *to get lost*

trovarsi *to be located*

La gente

il/la cittadino/a *citizen*
il/la coinquilino/a *housemate; roommate*
il/la contadino/a *farmer*
il/la paesano/a *villager/(fellow) countryman/woman*
il pedone (*m./f.*) *pedestrian*
il/la poliziotto/a *police officer*
il sindaco *mayor*
il/la venditore/venditrice (ambulante) *(street) vendor*
il/la vigile del fuoco *firefighter*

Le attività

chiacchierare *to chat*

divertirsi *to have fun*
fare commissioni *to run errands*
incontrarsi *to get together*
passeggiare *to take a walk*
trasferirsi *to move (change residence)*

SINONIMI
automobilista ←→ autista
passeggiare ←→ fare una passeggiata
trasferirsi ←→ traslocare
ingorgo stradale ←→ coda
giardini pubblici ←→ villa (Southern Italy)
affollato/a ≠ deserto/a

Point out that **ritardo** is also used in the expression **essere in ritardo**.

Point out that the **poliziotti** and **carabinieri** enforce different laws. The **poliziotti** are a civil corps dependent on the **Ministero degli Interni**. They usually operate in urban areas. The **carabinieri** are a military corps dependent on the **Ministero della Difesa**. They operate in urban and rural areas. A **vigile urbano** is a local official who enforces traffic laws.

Point out that **traffico** and **circolazione** are sometimes interchangeable. Ex.: Il **traffico/ La circolazione oggi è intenso/a**. However, the expression **c'è traffico** means **cattiva circolazione** and the expression **non c'è traffico** means **buona circolazione**.

Il trasporto

l'automobilista (*m./f.*) *driver*
la circolazione/il traffico *traffic*
la fermata (dell'autobus/della metro/del treno) *(bus/subway/train) stop*
l'ingorgo stradale *traffic jam*
il/la passeggero/a *passenger*
il ritardo *delay*

dare un passaggio *to give a ride*
fermare/fermarsi *to stop*
girare (a destra/sinistra) *to turn (right/left)*
guidare *to drive*
parcheggiare *to park*

salire (in macchina/sul treno/ sull'autobus) *to get (in a car/ on a train/on a bus)*
scendere (dalla macchina/ dal treno/dall'autobus) *to get (out of a car/off a train/off a bus)*

Per descrivere

affollato/a *crowded*
pericoloso/a *dangerous*
quotidiano/a *daily*
rumoroso/a *noisy*
vivace *lively*

Point out that **strada** is a general term for any road connecting two places, while **via** usually refers to a street in a city or village. **Via** is used in addresses: **via Garibaldi, n. 10**.

Point out that an **edicola** sells newspapers, magazines, and bus tickets. **Tabacchi** sell bus tickets, postcards, stamps, cigarettes, and lottery tickets. **Tabacchi**, which originally sold salt and tobacco, have distinctive blue or black signs with a white **T** in the middle.

INSTRUCTIONAL RESOURCES
Audioscripts, Answer Keys, Lab MP3s
SAM/WebSAM: WB, LM

Pratica e comunicazione

1

Abbinare Collega ogni parola alla sua definizione.

_c_ 1. grattacielo

_e_ 2. coinquilino

_a_ 3. pedone

_f_ 4. sindaco

_b_ 5. contadino

_d_ 6. edicola

a. persona che cammina per la strada

b. persona che lavora in campagna

c. edificio altissimo composto di numerosi piani

d. luogo in cui puoi comprare i giornali e le riviste

e. persona che abita nel tuo stesso appartamento

f. persona a capo dell'amministrazione di una città o di un paese

2

Titoli Completa i titoli di giornale con le parole della lista.

| incrocio | quartiere | stadio | strisce pedonali |
| periferia | semaforo | stazione di polizia | tribunale |

1. ROMA—Sospetto assassino è trattenuto presso la ___stazione di polizia___ per un interrogatorio.

2. BENEVENTO—Automobilista investe (*runs over*) donna sulle ___strisce pedonali___.

3. MILANO—Famoso industriale condannato in ___tribunale___ per evasione fiscale.

4. NAPOLI—Nuovo ristorante apre all'___incrocio___ fra via Giuseppe Verdi e via Santa Brigida.

5. TORINO—I rappresentanti di ogni ___quartiere___ della città si incontrano per discutere il problema del traffico.

6. FIRENZE—Multe sempre più alte per chi non si ferma al ___semaforo___.

3

In campagna o in città? In coppia, rispondete alle domande e scoprite se per voi è meglio vivere in campagna o in città. Confrontate le vostre risposte.

Preferisci...	A	B
...(A) fare le commissioni velocemente o (B) con calma?	☐	☐
...(A) le abitazioni che si trovano vicino o (B) lontano dal centro?	☐	☐
...(A) chiacchierare con gli amici al bar o (B) passeggiare in silenzio nella natura?		
...(A) camminare lungo strade affollate o (B) sentieri deserti?	☐	☐
...(A) frequentare locali rumorosi o (B) visitare posti tranquilli?	☐	☐
...(A) incontrarti con gli amici in discoteca o (B) ai giardini pubblici?	☐	☐
...(A) vivere in un appartamento piccolo ma efficiente o (B) in un grande casale?	☐	☐

4

Stop al traffico! Immaginate di essere nel municipio della vostra città, davanti al sindaco. Siete stanchi del traffico cittadino e reclamate un ritmo di vita più equilibrato. In piccoli gruppi, esponete almeno cinque problemi legati al traffico e suggerite possibili soluzioni.

S Practice more at **vhlcentral.com**.

1 Divide the class into teams and read these words out loud: **cittadino**, **paesano**, **pedone**, **poliziotto**, and **sindaco**. After each word, allow the students time to write as many related words as possible. The team with the most responses at the end wins.

2 Have groups of students invent headlines with unused vocabulary. The class can vote on the headline that is funniest, scariest, most/least believable, etc.

3 Divide the class into two groups to debate the pros and cons of city life and country life.

3 Point out that the preposition **in** is used in phrases with **campagna** and **centro**: **andare/stare/vivere in campagna/centro**.

4 Give groups of students a specific role (parents taking their children to school, people going to work, doctors, firemen, etc.). Have each group invent a story in which they did not reach an important destination because of the traffic. Have them present their stories to the class. The group that uses the most vocabulary words wins.

Preparazione  Vocabulary Tools

Vocabolario del cortometraggio

andạrsene *to leave*
cioè *that is*
Dạje! *Come on!*
la difesa *defense*
fregạrsene (di) *to not care (about)*
passare *to pass*
provarci con *to flirt*
stare zitto *to be quiet*
tirare *to kick*
vergognarsi *to be ashamed*

Vocabolario utile

l'attacco *offense*
il calcetto *five-player soccer*
il/la giocatore/giocatrice *player*
la maglia *jersey*
il/la pallone/palla *ball*
parare *to save*
il/la portiere/a *goalkeeper*
segnare un gol *to score a goal*
la squadra di calcio *soccer team*
il/la tifoso/a *fan*

ESPRESSIONI

caruccio/a *cute*
dare due pizze *to slap someone's head*
ẹssere alto/a un tappo e mezzo *to be short*
tenere a una squadra *to cheer for a team*
ẹssere una pippa *to be inept*
pensare agli affaracci sua *to think about oneself*
rọmpere le scạtole *to get on someone's nerves*

1

Pratica Associa parole e azioni.

_c_ 1. Passa…	a. para la palla.
_f_ 2. I tifosi…	b. protegge la porta (*goal*).
_d_ 3. L'attaccante…	c. la palla!
_e_ 4. I giocatori…	d. tira la palla in porta.
_b_ 5. Il difensore…	e. indossano la maglia della loro squadra.
_a_ 6. Il portiere…	f. vanno allo stadio.

2

Completate Completa ogni frase con la parola o l'espressione appropriata.

1. Hai rotto le scatole, vedi di _andartene_ subito.
2. Un egoista _se ne frega_ di tutto e di tutti.
3. Sei caruccio, ma non mi interessi. Non _ci provare_ con me.
4. È un _portiere_ straordinario: non fa passare un gol!
5. Guarda che hai torto, è meglio se stai _zitto_.
6. Gianni è altissimo, ma suo fratello è alto _un tappo e mezzo_.
7. Non mi piace giocare in difesa, preferisco giocare in _attacco_.

3

Sondaggio In piccoli gruppi, chiedete ai vostri compagni se sono d'accordo o no con le seguenti affermazioni e perché. Poi condividetele con la classe.

Affermazione	D'accordo		Perché?
	Sì	No	
1. È importante avere solo amici che hanno le nostre stesse opinioni.			
2. I bambini non si fissano (*fixate*) su difetti fisici.			
3. Ci sono difetti fisici che impediscono di avere una vita normale.			
4. Ci sono cose più importanti dello sport.			
5. È giusto discriminare chi pensa diversamente.			

3 Ask these follow-up questions: **Fino a che punto ti spingeresti per difendere un'opinione? Pensi che manifestare aggressività nel tifo sportivo sia un modo di non essere aggressivi in altri aspetti della vita?**

4

Espansione In gruppi di tre o quattro, discutete i seguenti temi.

1. Usciresti con qualcuno che tifa (*roots*) per una squadra diversa dalla tua?

2. Usciresti con qualcuno che vota per un partito diverso dal tuo?

3. Quali sono gli argomenti che possono distruggere una coppia, secondo te?

4. C'è una cosa su cui sei irremovibile (*adamant*)? Su cosa non scenderesti mai a compromessi?

5. Ti è mai capitato di non notare un difetto fisico di qualcuno che ti piace?

6. Cambieresti mai opinione su una cosa importante per amore?

5

Descriviamo Come sono i personaggi di questo film?

A. In coppia, guardate le immagini del film e descrivete l'aspetto fisico e la personalità dei personaggi. Poi immaginate che ruolo hanno nel film.

5 After students have watched the film and completed the **Preparazione** activities, have them compare their predictions with what actually happens in the film.

B. Descrivete questi cinque personaggi (fisico, stato d'animo [*mood*], carattere) e immaginate la storia associata a queste quattro immagini.

Practice more at **vhlcentral.com**.

Video

ANDREA D'ADDARIO
PRESENTA

DUE
PIEDI
SINISTRI

DIRETTO DA
ISABELLA SALVETTI

SCRITTO DA NICOLA GUAGLIANONE

CON
MARIA ELENA SCHIORLIN E GABRIELE SGRIGNUOLI

FOTOGRAFIA MICHELE D'ATTANASIO | MONTAGGIO DARIO INCERTI | MUSICHE MAMMOOTH, ALTON D. TERRY
COSTUMI ILARIA CAPANNA | SCENOGRAFIA VALERIA BEVILACQUA | FONICO MARCO DE CAROLIS

 Lea Film* | I FILM GOOD

TEACHING OPTION Point out that the expression **due piedi sinistri**, like its English
equivalent *two left feet*, does not apply to sports in Italian. Mirko is innovating, a sign
of his keen intellect.

Trama *Alcuni ragazzini° giocano a calcio in un parco. Uno di loro si ferma a parlare con una ragazzina che sta guardando seduta dietro a un muretto° mentre manda messaggi a un'amica. L'approccio° finisce male per differenze filosofiche.*

Nota CULTURALE

Calcio e calcetto, rivalità tra squadre

Il calcio è lo sport più popolare in Italia e anche il più democratico: per giocarlo non c'è bisogno di attrezzature° speciali ma solo di una palla e di una superficie piana°, oltre° a abilità e capacità di correre per 90 minuti muovendo una palla con i piedi. Se non si hanno undici giocatori per squadra, ogni° combinazione di giocatori dispari funziona lo stesso. Il calcetto si gioca in squadre di cinque giocatori. Ci sono città o regioni in Italia che hanno due squadre di calcio in serie A° e la rivalità tra le tifoserie° è molto intensa. Nel cortometraggio la rivalità è tra tifosi della Roma (maglia rossa) e della Lazio (maglia bianco-celeste), che geograficamente è la regione in cui si trova° la città di Roma. Altre rivalità storiche sono tra Milan e Inter (a Milano) e Juventus e Torino (a Torino).

attrezzature *equipment* **superficie piana** *flat surface* **oltre** *on top of* **ogni** *any* **serie A** *first division* **tifoserie** *supporters* **si trova** *is found*

RAGAZZINO Dai, passa!

TEACHING OPTION Have students read the **Nota culturale**, then ask who plays a sport. Explain that in Italy anyone can usually find somewhere to play after school without belonging to a formal team. Explain that the name of a team is preceded by a definite article, often feminine because it is short for **la squadra: la Roma** is the team from the city of Rome; **la Lazio** is the team from the Lazio region. However, the article is sometimes masculine: **il Milan, il Torino, il Napoli.**

RAGAZZINO Ma che ci posso fare se questo è encefalitico°?
LEO Aho', encefalitico ci sarai°!

MIRKO Scusa.
LUANA Di che?
MIRKO È colpa dell'amico mio. Ci ha° due piedi sinistri.

BIONDINO Ma a lui non gliene frega niente del pallone. L'importante è mangiare, vero Leo?
LEO Appunto. Andiamoci a pigliare° un gelato.

MIRKO Lo vedo che è una sedia a rotelle°, ma che è, tua?
LUANA Sì…
MIRKO Tutta tua?!
LUANA Sì…
MIRKO Cioè, non te l'ha prestata nessuno?

MIRKO Ti devi vergognare° perché sei della Lazio. Tiè°! Ci hai pure l'aquilotto°, ci hai!

ragazzini *kids* **muretto** *low wall* **approccio** *pick-up* **Ci ha** *He has* **encefalitico** *dim-witted* **ci sarai** *is what you are* **pigliare** *to get* **rotelle** *wheels* **vergognare** *to be ashamed* **Tiè!** *There!* **aquilotto** *eagle*

EXPANSION Ask students to give examples of variants of popular sports that, like **calcetto**, require fewer players or less gear than their professional counterparts.

🔊 Sullo SCHERMO

Indica se le affermazioni sono **vere** o **false**.

F	1.	Mirko passa la palla a tutti.
V	2.	Luana scrive messaggi a un'amica.
V	3.	A Leo piace soprattutto mangiare.
F	4.	I ragazzini che giocano sono della Lazio.
F	5.	Luana sta studiando.
V	6.	Mirko offre un gelato a Luana.

Analisi

2 Explain that diminutives and augmentatives are widely used in Italian. They express more than just nuances in physical size; for instance, **un muretto** is a smaller **muro**. However, **un fiorellino** is not just a small flower; the word also implies prettiness and fragility.

2 Play Antonello Venditti's song *Grazie Roma* to show the extent of fans' love for a team. Although Venditti wrote it in 1983 to celebrate the second **scudetto** (*shield*) symbolizing the national championship victory of team **Roma**, it is still a popular song.

1

Comprensione Completa le frasi.

___i___ 1. I ragazzini nel parco…

___j___ 2. Luana scrive messaggini a un'amica…

___g___ 3. Mirko va a prendere la palla…

___h___ 4. Mirko ci prova…

___a___ 5. Mirko invita…

___e___ 6. Mirko è perplesso…

___b___ 7. Luana crede che Mirko…

___f___ 8. Mirko dice a Luana che dovrebbe vergognarsi…

___d___ 9. Luana dice a Mirko…

___c___ 10. Mirko dice che se i genitori di Luana non sono così…

a. Luana a prendere un gelato con i suoi amici.

b. non voglia farsi vedere con lei perché è handicappata.

c. allora la colpa è solo sua.

d. che lei è nata così.

e. per la sedia a rotelle di Luana.

f. perché è della Lazio.

g. che Leo ha tirato fuori campo.

h. con Luana, che ne è contenta.

i. stanno giocando a pallone.

j. mentre guarda i ragazzi giocare.

2

Temi

A. Indicate quali sono le priorità per i seguenti personaggi.

Personaggio	Priorità
Mirko	
Luana	
Leo	
Ragazzino arrabbiato	

B. In coppia, rispondete alle domande.

1. Quali sono i temi del cortometraggio?
2. Hai visto o conosci film sullo sport? Quali? Ti piacciono? Perché sì o no?
3. A cosa pensi che servano i diminutivi (**caruccio, messaggino, ragazzino**) e i peggiorativi (**affaracci**) nel film?
4. Conosci persone che vivono per uno sport, non come atleti ma come tifosi? Cosa ne pensi?

3

Dialogo In coppia, immaginate come potrebbe continuare la conversazione tra Mirko e Luana dopo che lei ha capito che la discriminazione è per la Lazio e non per l'handicap. Poi condividete il dialogo con il resto della classe.

4

Discussione In gruppi di tre o quattro, discutete le seguenti affermazioni.

1. Quando si gioca a uno sport tra amici, se uno non è bravo non deve giocare.
2. Le rivalità sportive sono stupide.
3. L'opinione degli amici sul/sulla (potenziale) compagno/a è molto importante.
4. Le persone vanno accettate per quello che sono, non per le scelte sportive, religiose, politiche, ecc.

5

Intervista In coppia, fatevi a turno le seguenti domande.

1. Hai mai parlato a qualcuno che non conoscevi solo perché era carino/a?
2. Cosa diresti per provarci con qualcuno?
3. Qual è un approccio (*pick-up line*) che ha funzionato con te?
4. Come ti liberi di (*get rid of*) qualcuno che non ti piace?

6

Situazioni In piccoli gruppi, improvvisate dei dialoghi basati su queste situazioni e poi recitateli per tutta la classe.

A. Immaginate che Mirko e Luana giochino una partita a calcio balilla (*table football*), lui con i colori della Roma e lei con quelli della Lazio. Come si svolge la partita?

B. Immaginate che Mirko porti Luana a prendere il gelato con i colori della Lazio sulla sedia a rotelle: cosa dicono gli amici?

7

Scriviamo In uno o due paragrafi, descrivi una situazione in cui hai dovuto scegliere tra una cosa e una persona.

 Practice more at **vhlcentral.com**.

3 Have students write out their scene. Then, ask them to perform it for the rest of the class. Have the class vote for the most creative, funniest, etc., scene or the one that incorporates the most new vocabulary or recycles the most grammar.

4 Ask if there are famous rivalries between teams in sports that students might be more familiar with, and have them name the rivals. Ask how differences of team affiliation manifest themselves among their fans.

INSTRUCTIONAL RESOURCES: Teaching suggestions; Answer Keys
SAM/WebSAM: WB

IMMAGINA

Roma: un museo all'aperto!

E ccoci a **Roma**, *Caput Mundi*, la capitale del mondo! Passeggiamo alla scoperta° di alcuni dei monumenti più emblematici della città per arrivare alla fine in un vero e proprio stato indipendente che si trova nel cuore di Roma: **Città del Vaticano**.

Iniziamo la nostra passeggiata da uno dei simboli di Roma: l'**Anfiteatro Flavio**, noto a tutti come il **Colosseo**. Costruito nel I secolo d.C., poteva contenere fino a 50.000 spettatori ed era l'arena per i combattimenti° tra gladiatori. Non lontano c'è l'**Arco di Costantino**, ricco di bassorilievi° che raccontano le imprese° militari dell'imperatore. Camminiamo lungo la **via dei Fori** e ammiriamo le rovine° del **Foro di Traiano** e del **Foro Romano**. I Fori erano il centro della vita pubblica dell'antica Roma e avevano piazze, templi°, portici° ed edifici. Erano usati per il commercio, per le celebrazioni politiche e religiose e naturalmente per esaltare° la gloria degli imperatori.

La seconda tappa della nostra visita inizia a **Piazza del Popolo**. La piazza, di origini molto antiche, è stata ristrutturata e ampliata° nel **Rinascimento**, epoca a cui risalgono° l'obelisco e le fontane. Le due **Chiese Gemelle** fanno da ingresso al **Tridente** romano: **via del Corso, via del Babbuino e via della Ripetta**, con eleganti negozi dove possiamo fare acquisti di ogni genere. Da qui ci dirigiamo verso° **piazza di Spagna**. Al centro c'è la caratteristica **Fontana della Barcaccia**, in stile barocco, così chiamata per la sua forma di una barca che affonda°. Saliamo i celebri 137 gradini e arriviamo a **Trinità dei Monti** da dove possiamo ammirare un magnifico panorama della città.

Nelle vicinanze c'è la **Fontana di Trevi**, la più grandiosa fontana di Roma in stile classico e barocco, costruita nel '700. Il tema della fontana è il mare, rappresentato da sculture di conchiglie°, animali marini e divinità dell'oceano; per tradizione si ritiene che gettare una moneta nell'acqua della fontana sia di auspicio per tornare di nuovo a Roma. Continuiamo quindi verso **piazza Navona**, simbolo del **Barocco** romano. La piazza, un tempo stadio romano, è di forma ovale; al centro ha una fontana realizzata dal **Bernini** ed è circondata da palazzi di famiglie importanti. Oggi è luogo di incontro di venditori e artisti e qui si tiene il mercatino di Natale in cui si celebra la famosa **Befana** romana°.

Basilica di San Pietro

ROMA

La terza tappa ci porta «all'estero», senza andare via da Roma. Siamo infatti a **Città del Vaticano**, centro della chiesa cattolica e residenza del **Papa**. Arriviamo a **Piazza San Pietro** antistante° la **Basilica**, all'interno della quale si possono ammirare numerosissimi capolavori, tra cui la statua della *Pietà* di **Michelangelo**. I 537 scalini consentono° di salire in cima alla **Cupola**, dalla cui sommità si apre un panorama mozzafiato°! Visitiamo i **Musei Vaticani**, e in particolare la **Cappella Sistina** per ammirare gli affreschi di Michelangelo che decorano la volta.

Dopo tanta arte e tanto cammino, concludiamo la nostra visita in una tipica trattoria del quartiere **Trastevere** per gustare dell'ottimo cibo romano.

In più...

Roma è attraversata dal fiume **Tevere**. Secondo la leggenda°, sulle rive° del Tevere un pastore° trovò due fratelli gemelli abbandonati, **Romolo** e **Remo**, allevati° da una lupa° e li salvò°. Dopo molti anni e molte avventure, proprio negli stessi luoghi, Romolo fondò **Roma** nel 753 a.C.

scoperta *discovery* **combattimenti** *combats* **bassorilievi** *relief sculptures* **imprese** *exploits* **rovine** *ruins* **templi** *temples* **portici** *colonnades* **esaltare** *to exalt* **ampliata** *enlarged* **risalgono** *date back* **ci dirigiamo verso** *let's move on to* **affonda** *sinks* **conchiglie** *sea-shells* **moneta** *coin* **Befana romana** *celebration of the Epiphany* **antistante** *in front of* **consentono** *allow* **mozzafiato** *breath-taking* **Secondo...** *According to legend* **rive** *shores* **pastore** *shepherd* **allevati** *raised* **lupa** *she-wolf* **salvò** *saved*

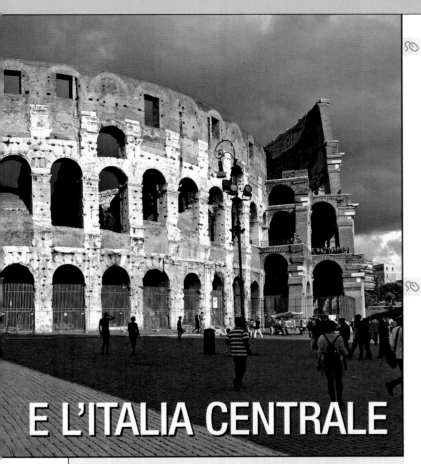

E L'ITALIA CENTRALE

Le regioni del Centro Italia Tra le regioni del Centro Italia ci sono **Lazio**, **Umbria**, **Marche** e **Abruzzo**. Le coste sono bagnate dal **mar Tirreno** a ovest e dal **mare Adriatico** ad est. L'interno è attraversato dagli **Appennini** con la montagna più alta, il **Gran Sasso** (2.912 metri), in Abruzzo. Il **Centro** è caratterizzato da paesaggi collinari° con foreste e laghi, soprattutto in Umbria e Lazio, e splendidi litorali° come il **Conero** nelle Marche.

San Francesco d'Assisi **San Francesco**, nato ad **Assisi** in Umbria nel 1181 o nel 1182, è uno dei santi più cari agli italiani. Francesco, figlio di un ricco mercante, dopo una guerra tra Assisi e Perugia, si converte° e si dedica completamente alla vita spirituale. Abbandona ogni suo bene° e vive tra i poveri e i lebbrosi° per aiutarli e per diffondere la Parola di Dio. San Francesco fonda l'ordine dei frati° francescani ed è l'autore del **Cantico delle Creature**. Dal 1939 è il **santo patrono°** d'Italia e la sua festa si celebra il 4 ottobre.

collinari *hilly* litorali *coasts* si **converte** *is converted* bene *property* lebbrosi *lepers* frati *friars* patrono *patron saint*

Vero o falso? Indica se ogni frase è **vera** o **falsa**. Correggi le frasi false. Some answers will vary.

1. I gladiatori combattevano al Colosseo. Vero.

2. I Fori erano luoghi utilizzati solo per le celebrazioni religiose. Falso. Erano utilizzati anche per il commercio e le celebrazioni politiche.

3. Trinità dei Monti e piazza di Spagna sono due luoghi vicini. Vero.

4. Piazza Navona era un Foro romano. Falso. Era uno stadio.

5. La montagna più alta degli Appennini si trova in Abruzzo. Vero.

6. San Francesco è il santo protettore d'Italia. Vero.

Quanto hai imparato? Rispondi alle domande. Some answers will vary.

1. In che epoca è stato costruito il Colosseo? I secolo d.C.

2. Chi ha realizzato i Fori? vari imperatori

3. Che cos'è il Tridente? tre strade di Roma: via del Corso, via del Babbuino e via della Ripetta.

4. Perché la Fontana della Barcaccia ha questo nome? Perché ha la forma di una barca che affonda.

5. Qual è il tema che ha ispirato la costruzione della Fontana di Trevi? il mare

6. Che cos'è la Cappella Sistina? una cappella con gli affreschi di Michelangelo

7. Dove si trova la Città del Vaticano? a Roma

8. Quali sono le caratteristiche naturali delle regioni del Centro? colline, foreste, laghi e montagne

9. Chi era san Francesco? Era figlio di un mercante che diventò frate per aiutare i poveri e i lebbrosi. Ha fondato l'ordine dei frati francescani. È il santo patrono d'Italia.

10. In che stagione si celebra la festa di san Francesco? autunno

Progetto

L'Impero Romano

Quanto era grande l'Impero Romano? Che lingua si parlava nell'Impero?

Vai in rete e cerca informazioni sull'estensione dell'Impero al massimo del suo splendore.

- Crea una mappa dell'Impero Romano.
- Scopri quali sono le lingue di oggi che hanno sostituito il latino parlato all'epoca dell'Impero.
- Cerca almeno tre luoghi con resti di edifici e strutture romane.
- Confronta i tuoi risultati con il resto della classe.

GALLERIA DI PERSONE ILLUSTRI

PAROLE COLTE

il cantautore *singer-songwriter*
laurearsi *to graduate*
la pellicola *movie*
il protagonista *main character*
recitare *to act*

POLITICO
Giulio Andreotti (1919–2013)

Giulio Andreotti è stato un politico, scrittore e giornalista. Protagonista indiscusso della vita politica italiana, ha ricoperto (*held*) ruoli governativi al massimo livello per oltre quarant'anni. Principale esponente della Democrazia Cristiana, il partito in carica dal secondo dopoguerra al 1994, Andreotti è stato a capo di sette governi, ministro della Repubblica per ventisette volte, e senatore a vita dal 1991. A oggi, Andreotti è il politico con il maggior numero di incarichi governativi nella storia della Repubblica Italiana. Viene anche ricordato per i suoi scritti di memorialistica, tra i più celebri: *De Gasperi visto da vicino* (1966) e *A ogni morte di papa. I papi che ho conosciuto* (1980). Nel 2008 il regista Paolo Sorrentino ha dedicato ad Andreotti il film *Il divo*, vincitore di numerosi premi.

ATTRICE
Sofia Loren (1934–)

Sofia Villani Scicolone, in arte Sofia Loren, è nata a Roma il 20 settembre 1934. Arriva tra le finaliste nel concorso di bellezza Miss Italia a sedici anni. Nel 1954 la sua carriera prende una svolta (*turn*) con il ruolo in *L'oro di Napoli*. Nel 1957 si sposa con il produttore Carlo Ponti, compagno con cui trascorrerà (*will spend*) tutta la vita. Nel 1958 firma un contratto con la Paramount Pictures e inizia così a collezionare una moltitudine di successi con pellicole di stampo hollywoodiano. Recita in inglese con stelle del cinema americano, affermandosi (*establishing herself*) come icona del cinema italiano. I film più famosi che l'hanno vista protagonista sono: *La ciociara* (1960); *Matrimonio all'italiana* (1964); *That's Amore* (1995). Vincitrice di due Oscar, nel 1999 l'American Film Institute ha inserito Sofia al ventunesimo posto tra le più grandi star della storia del cinema.

PEDAGOGISTA

Maria Montessori
(1870–1952)

Maria Montessori è stata una pedagogista e medico italiana, nota principalmente per l'omonimo metodo educativo da lei sviluppato. Una tra le prime donne in Italia a laurearsi in medicina nel 1896, inizia a lavorare come assistente in una clinica psichiatrica dell'Università di Roma e si dedica ai bambini con problemi psichici. Nei primi anni del Novecento apre la sua prima «Casa dei Bambini», in cui utilizza un nuovo e innovativo sistema educativo, e intorno al 1920 nasce il movimento montessoriano. La teoria sulla quale si basa il metodo pedagogico della Montessori è «aiutiamoli a fare da soli». Secondo la pedagogista è necessario fornire al bambino gli strumenti per fare da solo, affinché sviluppi la capacità di eseguire i gesti quotidiani senza dover ricorrere all'aiuto di un adulto. Nel corso della sua vita riceve numerosi riconoscimenti, tra cui la candidatura al premio Nobel per la pace. Il metodo educativo di Maria Montessori gode tutt'ora (*still enjoys*) di grande popolarità in tutto il mondo, e le scuole montessoriane di ogni ordine e grado sono attualmente circa 22.000.

CANTANTE

Claudio Baglioni
(1951–)

CLAUDIO BAGLI

Claudio Baglioni è un cantautore nato a Roma. I primi passi nel mondo della musica li compie (*achieves*) a soli tredici anni quando partecipa ad un concorso canoro (*singing*) arrivando finalista. Nel 1965 riceve in regalo la sua prima chitarra che imparerà a suonare da autodidatta (*self-taught*) esercitandosi su canzoni di Fabrizio De André. Nel 1972 esce *Questo piccolo grande amore*, album che lancia e afferma Baglioni come cantautore romantico per eccellenza degli anni Settanta. Nel 1981 esce *Strada facendo*. L'album lo fa vincere il premio come miglior cantante dell'anno al concorso *Vota la Voce* e il premio miglior cantautore assegnato (*awarded*) dall'Associazione Critici Discografici. Nel 1990 Baglioni è vittima di un tremendo incidente che mette a rischio la sua carriera per via di un profondo taglio (*cut*) alla lingua. Il cantautore riesce a rimettersi e otto anni dopo realizza il sogno di una vita, esibendosi allo Stadio Olimpico di Roma. Oggi si presta anche al piccolo schermo: nel febbraio del 2018 ha infatti presentato il festival musicale di Sanremo.

Comprensione

Vero o falso? Indica se ogni affermazione è vera o falsa. Correggi le frasi false.

1. Sofia Loren vince il concorso di bellezza Miss Italia.
   Falso. Arriva tra le finaliste.

2. Carlo Ponti è stato l'unico marito di Sofia Loren.
   Vero.

3. Giulio Andreotti entra a far parte della vita politica italiana a quarant'anni.
   Falso. Andreotti lavora in politica per oltre quarant'anni.

4. La Democrazia Cristiana è stata il partito politico egemonico in Italia dal dopoguerra al 1994.
   Vero.

5. Andreotti diventa senatore a vita nel 1972.
   Falso. Diventa senatore a vita nel 1991.

6. Maria Montessori è la prima donna a laurearsi in medicina in Italia.
   Falso. È tra le prime donne a laurearsi in medicina in Italia.

7. La carriera di Maria Montessori inizia in una clinica psichiatrica di Roma.
   Vero.

8. Maria Montessori riceve il premio Nobel per la pace.
   Falso. Viene nominata al Nobel.

9. Nel 1965 Baglioni riceve in regalo una chitarra da Fabrizio De André.
   Falso. Riceve la chitarra in regalo e impara a suonarla usando canzoni di De André.

10. Baglioni partecipa a Sanremo come concorrente.
    Falso. Partecipa come presentatore.

Scrittura

Scrivi sull'argomento Scegli uno dei seguenti argomenti e scrivi un paragrafo seguendo le indicazioni.

- **Metodo Montessori** Una coppia di tuoi amici sta pensando di iscrivere il loro figlio ad una scuola materna Montessori e chiede la tua opinione. Documentati sul metodo Montessori e riassumi in un paragrafo i punti principali del sistema educativo montessoriano. Indica se sei favorevole o contrario al metodo e spiega le tue ragioni.

- **Democrazia Cristiana** Un amico sa che studi italiano. Ha sentito nominare la Democrazia Cristiana nel film *Il divo* e ti chiede informazioni su questo partito politico. Fai una ricerca e spiegagli in un paragrafo la storia della Democrazia Cristiana.

- **Divismo cinematografico** Perché un attore diventa un divo? Fai una ricerca sul concetto di divismo cinematografico, spiega di che cosa si tratta e quali sono i divi più popolari del XX secolo.

 Practice more at vhlcentral.com.

INSTRUCTIONAL RESOURCES **2.1**
Audioscripts, Answer Keys, Lab MP3s, Grammar Presentation Slides
SAM/WebSAM: WB, LM

Remind students that infinitives of reflexive verbs end in **–arsi**, **–ersi**, or **–irsi** and that **–si** is attached to the infinitive after dropping the last **–e**.

Pantomime a few of the reflexive verbs for students, having them guess the infinitive. Then ask for volunteers from the class to play charades. You may provide them with the verbs if you wish.

ATTENZIONE!

When a reflexive verb is used with **potere**, **volere**, and **dovere**, the reflexive pronoun may attach to the infinitive or precede the conjugated verb.
Adriana vuole riposarsi.
Adriana si vuole riposare.
Adriana wants to rest.

RIMANDO

For more information about the use of **potere**, **dovere**, and **volere**, see **Strutture 4.4, p. 150**.

Have students sort the verbs related to daily routines chronologically.

RIMANDO

In compound tenses, reflexive and reciprocal verbs are conjugated with **essere** and require agreement between the subject and the past participle. See **Strutture 3.1, pp. 96–97**.

Reflexive and reciprocal verbs

- Reflexive verbs describe an action that the subject of the verb does to or for himself, herself, or itself (the action is "reflected" back on the subject of the verb). Reflexive verbs are always used with a reflexive pronoun: **mi**, **ti**, **si**, **ci**, **vi**, or **si**.

*—E certo che **mi vergogno**!*

Reflexive verbs		
lavarsi	**vedersi**	**vestirsi**
mi **lavo**	mi **vedo**	mi **vesto**
ti **lavi**	ti **vedi**	ti **vesti**
si **lava**	si **vede**	si **veste**
ci **laviamo**	ci **vediamo**	ci **vestiamo**
vi **lavate**	vi **vedete**	vi **vestite**
si **lạvano**	si **vẹdono**	si **vẹstono**

- Reflexive pronouns precede conjugated verbs, but are attached to infinitives after dropping the final **–e**. The reflexive pronoun always matches the subject of the sentence, even when it is attached to the infinitive.

  Mi alzo presto ogni giorno.   Preferisco **alzarmi** presto.
  I get up early every day.   *I prefer to get up early.*

- Many common reflexive verbs are used to describe routines.

addormentarsi *to fall asleep*	**fermarsi** *to stop (oneself)*	**riposarsi** *to rest*
alzarsi *to get up*	**incontrarsi** *to meet*	**sbrigarsi** *to hurry*
annoiarsi *to get bored*	**lavarsi** *to wash oneself*	**sdraiarsi** *to lie down*
asciugarsi *to dry up*	**mẹttersi** *to put on (clothes)*	**svegliarsi** *to wake up*
divertirsi *to have fun*	**pẹrdersi** *to get lost*	**truccarsi** *to put on make-up*
farsi la barba *to shave*	**pettinarsi** *to comb one's hair*	**vestirsi** *to get dressed*

- When parts of the body or clothing are mentioned with Italian reflexive verbs, use the definite article, not the possessive adjective as in English.

  Ci laviamo le mani.   In inverno **mi metto** i guanti.
  We wash our hands.   *In winter I put on my gloves.*

- Some verbs that express feeling, state of mind, or attitude are used in the reflexive form even though they do not literally express a reflexive action.

accorgersi *to realize* **annoiarsi** *to get/be bored* **arrabbiarsi** *to get mad/angry* **dimenticarsi** *to forget*	**lamentarsi** *to complain* **pentirsi** *to regret* **preoccuparsi** *to worry* **ricordarsi** *to remember*	**sentirsi** *to feel* **stufarsi** *to be fed up* **vantarsi** *to brag* **vergognarsi** *to be ashamed*

Perché **si arrabbia**? Non ho fatto niente!
Why is he getting mad? I didn't do anything!

Mi annoio sempre quando sono con Massimo.
I am always bored when I am with Massimo.

- Some verbs change meaning when they are used with a reflexive pronoun.

non-reflexive	reflexive
alzare *to raise*	**alzarsi** *to get up*
chiamare *to call*	**chiamarsi** *to be named*
fermare *to stop (someone/something)*	**fermarsi** *to stop (oneself); to stay*
mettere *to put*	**mettersi** *to put on (clothes)*
muovere *to move (someone/something)*	**muoversi** *to move (oneself)*
svegliare *to wake someone*	**svegliarsi** *to wake up*

Hai chiamato Lola?
Did you call Lola?

Si chiama Lola.
Her name is Lola.

- Reflexive pronouns are also attached to the familiar forms (**tu**, **noi**, and **voi**) of the imperative when the command is affirmative, but can precede or follow negative forms. The reflexive pronoun always precedes a formal command.

Non **ci fermiamo**.
Non **fermiamoci**.
Let's keep going.

Prego, **si accomodi**.
Please sit down.

- The plural forms of certain verbs can be used with the plural reflexive pronouns **ci**, **vi**, or **si** to express reciprocal actions—actions that people do to or for each other.

abbracciarsi *to hug each other* **aiutarsi** *to help each other* **amarsi** *to love each other*	**baciarsi** *to kiss each other* **conoscersi** *to know each other* **parlarsi** *to speak to each other*	**scriversi** *to write to each other* **telefonarsi** *to phone each other* **vedersi** *to see each other*

I miei fratelli **si telefonano** ogni sabato.
My brothers call each other every Saturday.

Non **ci parliamo** più perché lavori troppo.
We don't talk anymore because you work too much.

ATTENZIONE!

Certain verbs are used in the reflexive form for emphasis, especially when spoken. Some verbs in this category are **bersi**, **mangiarsi**, **comprarsi**, and **prendersi**.

Mi sono mangiata una bella pizza.
I had myself a nice pizza.

ATTENZIONE!

Some verbs can be used either reflexively or non-reflexively.

Ho perso le chiavi stamattina.
I lost my keys this morning.

Mi sono persa stamattina.
I got lost this morning.

Give students an example of a verb that is non-reflexive and ask them to come up with an example of its reflexive counterpart. You may also do the opposite. You say: **Guardo la TV**. They say: **Mi guardo allo specchio**.

RIMANDO

For more information about the **imperative**, see **Strutture 4.3, pp. 146–147.**

ATTENZIONE!

To differentiate reciprocal from reflexive actions, you may add phrases such as **l'un l'altro/a** (*one another*), or **reciprocamente** (*mutually*).

Victor e Paolo si aiutano l'un l'altro.
Victor and Paolo help one another.

To reinforce the idea of reciprocity, hold up pictures of one person doing an action, then of two people doing the same action with each other. Alternatively, have one student model an action (**Mariela parla**), then have another join the first so the action is reciprocal (**Mariela e Josh si parlano**). Ask students to say what they see.

Pratica

1

Il lunedì mattina Completa il brano e descrivi quello che fanno Guido ed Elena il lunedì mattina. Utilizza la forma corretta dei verbi riflessivi.

accorgersi	farsi la barba	pettinarsi
addormentarsi	incontrarsi	prepararsi
alzarsi	lamentarsi	svegliarsi
asciugarsi	mettersi	truccarsi

Guido ed Elena (1) _si svegliano_ presto la mattina, (2) _si alzano_ subito e (3) _si preparano_. Elena fa la doccia, (4) _si asciuga_ i capelli, (5) _si trucca_ e prepara la colazione. Anche Guido fa la doccia, (6) _si fa la barba/ si pettina_, (7) _si pettina/ si fa la barba_ e va a fare colazione. Dopo colazione Guido ed Elena (8) _si mettono_ il cappotto ed escono di corsa. Alcune volte Guido (9) _si accorge_ di aver dimenticato le chiavi della macchina sul tavolo e così deve rientrare a prenderle. Di solito Guido ed Elena (10) _si incontrano_ per pranzo in una tavola calda vicino al lavoro. La sera tornano a casa tutti e due stanchi. Elena (11) _si lamenta_ del lavoro che non le piace e Guido prepara la cena. Dopo cena guardano la TV e spesso (12) _si addormentano_ sul divano.

2

Cosa fanno? In coppia, descrivete cosa fanno le persone nelle foto. Utilizzate i verbi riflessivi. Suggested answers.

1. Marco _si addormenta_ invece di pulire la casa.

2. Quando Sara vede Paolo con un'altra ragazza, _si arrabbia_.

3. Antonio e Paola _si divertono_ in piscina.

4. Noi _ci incontriamo_ al caffè.

5. Andrea _si sveglia_ tardi la domenica.

6. A volte _mi perdo_ quando viaggio.

 Practice more at **vhlcentral.com**.

Comunicazione

3

E tu? In coppia, fatevi a turno le seguenti domande. Rispondete con frasi complete e spiegate le vostre risposte.

1. A che ora ti svegli di solito il sabato mattina?
2. Ti alzi sempre appena ti svegli?
3. Ti prepari subito?
4. Di solito, a che ora ti addormenti durante il fine settimana?
5. Cosa fai per rilassarti dopo una lunga giornata?

6. Come ti vesti per uscire con i tuoi amici?
7. Tu e i tuoi amici vi vestite mai in modo elegante? In quali occasioni?
8. Ti diverti quando vai a una festa? E quando vai a una riunione di famiglia? Spiega perché.
9. Impieghi molto tempo a prepararti prima di uscire? Che cosa devi fare?
10. Ti preoccupi del tuo aspetto? Spiega perché sì o perché no.

11. Tu e i tuoi amici vi telefonate o vi scrivete sms?
12. Ti arrabbi spesso? Con chi e perché?
13. Conosci qualcuno che si arrabbia spesso? Con chi e perché?
14. Ti scusi mai per delle cose che hai fatto?
15. Ti sbagli mai quando giudichi qualcuno?

4

Al caffè Immagina di essere in un caffè e un tuo amico non trova più il portafoglio. Cosa fate? Lavorate in gruppi di tre e ricreate la scena utilizzando almeno cinque dei verbi della lista.

accorgersi	fermarsi	perdersi
alzarsi	incontrarsi	preoccuparsi
arrabbiarsi	lamentarsi	ricordarsi
dimenticarsi	pentirsi	sbrigarsi

INSTRUCTIONAL RESOURCES
Audioscripts, Answer Keys, Lab MP3s, Grammar Presentation Slides
SAM/WebSAM: WB, LM

2.2

Piacere and similar verbs

—*Perché, **ti pare** poco?*

Using the verb *piacere*

- Sentences in Italian using the verb **piacere** (*to be pleasing, to like*) look quite different from their English equivalents. Typically, **piacere** is used in the third person singular and plural forms. The subject, which usually follows the verb **piacere**, determines which form to use. Remember, the thing or person that is liked is the subject of **piacere**. The person who likes someone or something is the indirect object.

Singular subject

Mi **piace la discoteca** in via Garibaldi.
I like the club on via Garibaldi.

Plural subject

Ti **piacciono i film** di Spielberg?
Do you like Spielberg's movies?

- The usual word order is *indirect object* + **piacere** + *subject*.

Gli + **piace** + **la mia nuova macchina.**
To him + *(it) is pleasing* + *my new car.*
(=He likes my new car.)

RIMANDO

To review object pronouns and stressed pronouns, see **Strutture 4.2, pp. 140–142** and **Strutture 8.2, pp. 310–311.**

- Indirect object pronouns in Italian are: **mi**, **ti**, **Le/gli/le**, **ci**, **vi**, **Loro/loro/gli**. **Loro** follows the verb.

Mi piacciono i libri.
I like books.

I libri **piacciono loro**.
They like books.

- The subject may also come first, followed by **piacere** + *indirect object*.

Le lingue straniere + **piacciono** + **a Marta.**
Foreign languages + *are pleasing* + *to Marta.*
(=Marta likes foreign languages.)

- The indirect object may be either an indirect object pronoun or the preposition **a** followed by a noun. For emphasis or to clear up ambiguity, use **a** followed by a stressed pronoun.

Vi piacciono i giardini pubblici vicino a casa vostra?
Do you like the parks near your house?

Agli studenti non piacciono gli esami lunghi.
Students don't like long exams.

A Lidia piace il negozio all'angolo.
Lidia likes the store on the corner.

A me piace la matematica, non a mia sorella.
I like math, my sister doesn't.

- Stressed pronouns in Italian are: **me, te, Lei/lui/lei, noi, voi, Loro/loro**.

- **Piacere** is often used in the conditional to make polite requests or invitations:

> Ti **piacerebbe** andare al cinema stasera?
> *Would you like to go to the movies tonight?*

- **Piacere** may also be used with other verbs to indicate what someone likes to do. In this case, use **piace** + *infinitive*, even if the subject is plural.

> Gli **piace vivere** in centro.
> *He likes living downtown.*

> Ci **piace cantare e ballare.**
> *We like to sing and dance.*

- In the **passato prossimo** and other compound tenses, **piacere** takes the auxiliary **essere**. The past participle, **piaciuto**, must agree in number and gender with the subject.

> Gli **è** piaciut**a l'opera.**
> *He liked the opera.*

> Mi **sono** piaciute **le rose**. Grazie!
> *I liked the roses. Thank you!*

Verbs like *piacere*

- Other common verbs follow the same pattern as **piacere**.

bastare *to be enough*	**occorrere** *to need*
dare fastidio *to annoy*	**parere** *to seem*
dispiacere *to be sorry*	**restare** *to have left*
disturbare *to be a nuisance*	**sembrare** *to seem*
(non) importare *to (not) matter*	**servire** *to be useful*
interessare *to interest*	**stare a cuore** *to matter*
mancare *to be missing*	

Ci **è parsa** molto triste.
She seemed really sad to us.

Non mi **importano** le critiche!
Criticism does not matter to me!

Mi **mancano** le ultime pagine della storia.
I'm missing the last pages of the story.

Non mi **serve** questa vecchia giacca.
I have no use for this old jacket.

Ti **occorre** altro?
Do you need anything else?

Ti **sta a cuore** la tua città?
Do you care about your city?

I tuoi amici mi **sembrano** simpatici.
Your friends seem nice to me.

Cosa vi **dà fastidio**?
What's bothering you?

- Use **non piacere** to say what you dislike. **Dispiacere** means *to mind* or *to be sorry*.

> **Non** mi **piace** il traffico a Roma.
> *I don't like the traffic in Rome.*

> Ti **dispiacerebbe** dare un passaggio a Rossella?
> *Would you mind giving Rossella a ride?*

For more practice of the infinitive with **piacere**, ask students about their daily activities. Ex:
—Studi molto, Robert?
—Sì, studio molto.
—Ti piace studiare?
—Sì, (No, non) mi piace studiare.
Give an appropriate reaction depending on the answers.
Ex.: **Bravo, Robert!/ Che peccato!**

RIMANDO

For more information about the **passato prossimo**, see **Strutture 3.1, pp. 96–97**.

Remind students that the past participle of **piacere** takes an **–i** before the normal **–uto** ending for **–ere** verbs in order to maintain the correct pronunciation.
Have students practice the past participle agreement by asking them questions in the present, then adding «E ieri?»
—Ti piacciono i dolci?
—Sì, mi piacciono.
—E ieri?
—Sì, mi sono piaciuti.

Point out that **importare** is most commonly used in negative statements. It can be also used with **di**. In these cases, the verb is always used in the third person singular. Ex.: **Non mi importa delle critiche./ Non ci importa del calcio!/ Non mi importa nulla di quello che dicono!**

Have students create an example sentence with each verb in Italian. Then ask which verbs are used like their English equivalents, such as **dare fastidio**.

Pratica

2 After the activity, do a survey of the students' answers and write the results on the board.

3 Compare students' weekday activities with what they would like to do. Ex.: **Il lunedì hai lezione. Cosa ti piacerebbe fare invece di venire a lezione?**

1 **Al supermercato** Michele e Carla sono andati in centro a fare la spesa, ma non sono d'accordo su quello che devono comprare. Completa la conversazione inserendo la forma corretta del verbo tra parentesi e i pronomi appropriati.

MICHELE Allora cosa dobbiamo comprare per la cena di stasera? (1) __Ci occorre__ (occorrere) la pasta?

CARLA Sì, e (2) __ci servono__ (servire) i funghi e il prosciutto.

MICHELE Non per me, non (3) __mi piacciono__ (piacere) i funghi!

CARLA E va bene, prendiamo le zucchine! Abbiamo preso tutto? No, aspetta, (4) __ci serve__ (servire) la frutta. Quale preferisci?

MICHELE (5) __Mi piacciono__ (piacere) le ciliegie e le mele.

CARLA Perfetto, adesso (6) __ci manca__ (mancare) solo l'acqua minerale.

2 **Cosa ti piace?** In coppia, domandatevi se vi piacciono o non vi piacciono le seguenti persone o attività e spiegate perché.

Modello **dormire fino a tardi**

—Ti piace dormire fino a tardi?

—Sì, mi piace./No, a me piace svegliarmi presto.

fare sport	l'opera	Roberto Benigni
i film d'avventura	la musica di Laura Pausini	uscire con gli amici
i romanzi d'amore	non fare niente	viaggiare

3 **Il prossimo fine settimana?** In coppia, domandatevi se vi piacerebbe fare le attività illustrate nelle foto. Utilizzate i verbi **piacere**, **interessare** e **dare fastidio**.

Modello Ti interesserebbe andare al parco?

Sì, mi piacerebbe molto.

 Practice more at **vhlcentral.com**.

Comunicazione

4

Domande In coppia, fatevi a turno delle domande sulle persone e sui luoghi seguenti.

> **Modello** **piacere / a tuo padre**
> Secondo te, cosa piace a tuo padre?
> Non so, secondo me, gli piace dormire.

1. interessare / ai tuoi compagni di classe
2. non importare / al presidente
3. piacere / al(la) tuo/a migliore amico/a
4. non piacere / a tua madre
5. dare fastidio / al(la) tuo/a ragazzo/a
6. stare a cuore / al tuo professore
7. mancare / alla tua città
8. occorrere / ai cittadini

5

Come sono? Scegli un personaggio famoso e immagina quello che gli/le piace/piaceva. Dì al(la) tuo/a compagno/a cosa hai pensato senza dire il nome del personaggio famoso. Lui/Lei deve indovinare chi è. Usate tutti i verbi della lista.

> **Modello** —Gli piace cantare e gli sta a cuore la situazione dell'Africa. Chi è?
> —È Bono!

dare fastidio	non piacere
importare	parere
interessare	piacere

5 For a related game, divide the class into small groups. Give group members a photograph of a famous person from current events, recent movies, or popular music. Have students take turns describing the person's likes and dislikes and guessing his/her identity.

6

In centro In coppia, descrivete cosa fate di solito quando andate in centro. Utilizzate alcune parole della lista.

divertirsi	incontrarsi	passeggiare
fare commissioni	mancare	perdersi
fermata	non piacere	piacere
guidare	parcheggiare	restare

6 Have students share their experience with the rest of the class.

> **Modello** Di solito, il sabato mattina vado in centro. Prendo la metro perché non mi piace il traffico e mi preoccupo per l'ambiente.

INSTRUCTIONAL RESOURCES
Audioscripts, Answer Keys, Lab MP3s, Grammar Presentation Slides
SAM/WebSAM: WB, LM

2.3

Possessive adjectives and pronouns

—*Vedi d'andartene sennò chiamo **mio fratello.***

RIMANDO

To review articles, see **Strutture 1.2, p. 20.**

- Possessive adjectives and pronouns indicate ownership, possession, or relationships. In Italian, possessive adjectives and possessive pronouns have the same forms, which include the definite article in most cases.

English meaning	singular		plural	
	masculine	feminine	masculine	feminine
my/mine	il mio	la mia	i miei	le mie
your/yours	il tuo	la tua	i tuoi	le tue
your/yours (*formal*)	il Suo	la Sua	i Suoi	le Sue
his/her(s)/its	il suo	la sua	i suoi	le sue
our/ours	il nostro	la nostra	i nostri	le nostre
your/yours	il vostro	la vostra	i vostri	le vostre
their/theirs	il loro	la loro	i loro	le loro

RIMANDO

To review gender and number, see **Strutture 1.3, pp. 22–23.**

Possessive adjectives

- Possessive adjectives (**gli aggettivi possessivi**) usually precede the noun that they modify. They must agree in number and gender with the noun they modify, not the owner of the object.

Ecco **il mio** palazzo.
Here's my apartment building.

Dove sono **i tuoi** genitori?
Where are your parents?

ATTENZIONE!

To clarify, you may use **di lui** or **di lei** to indicate *his* or *her(s)*.
Ada è amica di lui, non di lei.
Ada is his friend, not hers.

- In Italian, there is no difference between *his* and *her*. Use the context to determine the meaning.

Roberto non ha voglia di vendere **il suo** motorino.
*Roberto doesn't want to sell **his** scooter.*

Fiammetta non ha voglia di vendere **il suo** motorino.
*Fiammetta doesn't want to sell **her** scooter.*

ATTENZIONE!

When a preposition precedes the article used with a possessive adjective, combine the preposition and article as you normally would.
Il mio telefonino è nella mia camera.
My cell phone is in my room.

Diamo questi fiori alle tue amiche.
Let's give these flowers to your friends.

- The possessive adjective may be omitted in Italian when the relationship or ownership is obvious, such as when referring to body parts or clothing.

Ho telefonato **alla mamma**.
*I called **my** mom.*

Mi metto **le** scarpe.
*I put on **my** shoes.*

- To express the idea *of mine, of yours,* and so on, use an indefinite article, a number, or a demonstrative adjective with the appropriate form of the possessive adjective.

Due tuoi coinquilini sono venuti da me.
Two of your roommates came by my place.

Questa mia compagna di classe si chiama Paola.
This classmate of mine is called Paola.

- With the exception of **loro**, which always requires the definite article, possessive adjectives are generally used *without* the definite article when referring to singular, unmodified family members. Use the definite article when the noun referring to a family member is plural and when it is a modified or affectionate form, such as **mamma** or **papà**. Compare:

Nostro fratello studia a Napoli. *Our brother studies in Naples.*	*but*	**I nostri fratelli** studiano a Roma. *Our brothers study in Rome.*
Mia sorella ha ventotto anni. *My sister is twenty-eight years old.*	*but*	**La mia sorellina** ha otto anni. *My little sister is eight years old.*
Tuo cugino abita a Roma. *Your cousin lives in Rome.*	*but*	**Il tuo cugino preferito** abita a Perugia. *Your favorite cousin lives in Perugia.*

- Possessive adjectives are used without the definite article in some common expressions. Note that the possessive adjective follows the noun in these expressions.

Festeggiamo **a casa nostra**. *Let's celebrate at our house.*	È **colpa mia**. *It's my fault.*
Preferisce fare **a modo suo**. *He prefers doing things his way.*	Vorrei farlo **per conto mio**. *I want to do it on my own.*

Possessive pronouns

- Possessive pronouns replace nouns, and must agree in number and gender with the nouns to which they refer.

Il tuo gatto ha sempre fame, ma **il mio** mangia poco. *Your cat is always hungry, but mine doesn't eat much.*	La nostra è una buona squadra, ma **la vostra** è fantastica! *Our team is good, but yours is fantastic!*
Ecco **la tua borsetta**, ma dov'è **la mia**? *There's your purse, but where is mine?*	Se non trovi **il tuo iPad**, prendi **il mio**. *If you can't find your iPad, take mine.*

- The definite article is almost always used with possessive pronouns, even when referring to a single family member.

Hai visto mio fratello? No, ma ho visto **il suo**. *Have you seen my brother? No, but I saw hers.*	Il quartiere di Michele è tranquillo, ma **il tuo** è molto rumoroso. *Michele's neighborhood is quiet, but yours is very noisy.*

- When the possessive pronoun follows the verb **essere**, the definite article is generally omitted. However, the article may be used after **essere** for clarification or emphasis.

Questi CD sono **nostri**? *Are these our CDs?*	*but*	Questi CD sono **i nostri o i tuoi**? *Are these CDs ours or yours?*
È **tuo** questo telefonino? Sì, è **mio**. *Is this your cell phone? Yes, it's mine.*	*but*	È **il tuo** telefonino o **il mio**? *Is that your cell phone or mine?*

You may want to point out that this rule is not always followed. **Mamma** and **papà** can be used without the definite article. **Nonno/a** can be used with the definite article even when it is not modified.

Remind students that **loro** is invariable, but that the definite article must agree in number and gender with the noun it modifies.

Some other idiomatic expressions you may want to share with students are: **da parte sua** (*on his/her behalf*), **a vostra disposizione** (*at your disposal*), **affari miei** (*my business*).

ATTENZIONE!

Possessive pronouns may be used to refer to family.

I suoi non abitano in Umbria.
His parents don't/family doesn't live in Umbria.

Un grande abbraccio **ai tuoi**.
A big hug to your parents/family.

To get students to practice possessive pronouns, ask them questions using possessive adjectives and have them answer using a pronoun in the negative, following up with someone else's item(s).

–Sono i tuoi libri?
–No, non sono i miei, sono i suoi.
–Mi dai la tua matita?
–No, non ti do la mia, ti do la loro.

Pratica

1

Trasforma Inserisci l'aggettivo possessivo e il pronome possessivo corrispondente.

Modello **Il palazzo di Luisa** il suo palazzo / il suo

1. L'appartamento di Marco ___il suo appartamento___ / ___il suo___
2. L'automobile tua e di Paolo ___la vostra automobile___ / ___la vostra___
3. Le biciclette dei bambini ___le loro biciclette___ / ___le loro___
4. Il paese mio ___il mio paese___ / ___il mio___
5. La via tua ___la tua via___ / ___la tua___
6. Il casale mio e di mio fratello ___il nostro casale___ / ___il nostro___

2 Have students retell the story from the perspective of different people. Give them the beginning and ask them to continue the story. Ex.: **La settimana scorsa nostra nonna ha organizzato…**

2

La riunione di famiglia Giulia racconta della riunione di famiglia a cui ha partecipato la settimana scorsa. Completa il brano con gli aggettivi possessivi giusti.

La settimana scorsa (1) ___mia___ (mia / la mia) nonna ha organizzato una festa per il suo 80° compleanno e ha voluto attorno a sé tutti i suoi cari. C'erano proprio tutti e finalmente dopo tanto tempo ho potuto rivedere (2) ___mio___ (mio / il mio) cugino Giovanni, che studia a Firenze. È stata una bellissima festa. (3) ___I miei___ (Miei / I miei) zii hanno regalato alla nonna una bella spilla (brooch) d'oro. (4) ___Le mie___ (Mie / Le mie) cugine hanno cantato la canzone preferita della nonna. (5) ___Mio___ (Mio / Il mio) fratello ha organizzato le foto dei momenti più belli della vita di (6) ___nostra___ (nostra / la nostra) nonna. Ovviamente (7) ___la mia___ (mia / la mia) mamma si è commossa (was moved) e (8) ___il mio___ (mio / il mio) papà l'ha presa in giro (made fun of her).

3 Have students come up with similar questions to ask a partner about things in the classroom. Ex.: **Questa è la tua penna? Questo è lo zaino di Cristiano?**

3

Di chi è? Il tuo coinquilino sta controllando quali oggetti gli appartengono. In coppia, rispondete a turno alle domande con i pronomi possessivi.

Modello **Questa è la tua calcolatrice?** Sì, è la mia./No, non è la mia.

1. Questo è il tuo cellulare? il mio
2. Questa è la calcolatrice dei tuoi genitori? la loro
3. Questo è il mio asciugamano? il tuo
4. Queste sono le foto di tuo cugino? le sue
5. Questi sono gli appunti di Sabrina? i suoi
6. Questi sono i CD miei e di mio fratello? i vostri

4 Have pairs of students extend the conversation, providing an imaginative finale.

4 Have pairs of students re-create the conversation, modifying it to talk about their own neighborhoods.

4

Un incontro inaspettato Due amiche si incontrano alla fermata dell'autobus e parlano di dove abitano. Completa il dialogo con gli aggettivi e i pronomi possessivi.

ROBERTA Quanto tempo! Non ci vediamo da una vita. Abiti sempre in centro?

ALESSIA No, mi sono trasferita in un'altra zona.

ROBERTA Raccontami, com'è (1) ___il tuo___ quartiere? (2) ___Il mio___ è così caotico!

ALESSIA (3) ___Il mio___ è molto tranquillo. Anche se (4) ___mio___ marito dice che è troppo tranquillo. Però ci sono molti giardini pieni di fiori e piante.

ROBERTA Che bello! (5) ___I nostri___ invece sono quasi abbandonati. (6) ___Le mie___ figlie non vogliono mai andare a giocare fuori. E (7) ___le tue___ come stanno?

ALESSIA Stanno bene, crescono in fretta! Ah, ecco (8) ___il mio___ autobus, devo andare, a presto!

ROBERTA (9) ___Il mio___ è in ritardo… A presto!

Practice more at **vhlcentral.com**.

Comunicazione

5

Intervista In coppia, a turno, fatevi le seguenti domande e aggiungetene altre. Rispondete utilizzando gli aggettivi possessivi.

1. Hai fratelli o sorelle? Come si chiamano?
2. Quanti anni ha tuo padre?
3. Dove lavora tua madre?
4. Dove vivono i tuoi cugini?
5. Quando vedi i tuoi nonni?
6. Quali lingue parla la tua famiglia?

6

I vicini di casa Descrivi le persone della foto con cinque o sei frasi; utilizza gli aggettivi e i pronomi possessivi.

7

Cosa porteresti con te?

A. L'estate prossima ti trasferisci in una nuova città. Fai una lista degli oggetti personali che porti con te.

> **Modello** L'estate prossima vado a vivere per due mesi a Rimini. Di sicuro porto con me i miei CD musicali preferiti, le mie scarpe da ginnastica per le passeggiate in collina, la mia macchina fotografica per fare foto bellissime...

B. In piccoli gruppi, condividete e discutete le vostre liste. Scrivete negli spazi giusti gli oggetti simili e quelli diversi. Dopo domandate e spiegate perché volete portare le cose nella lista di oggetti diversi.

> **Modello** Io voglio portare la mia Wii ma tu non vuoi portare la tua. Perché?

oggetti simili	oggetti diversi

INSTRUCTIONAL RESOURCES
Audioscripts, Answer Keys, Lab MP3s, Grammar Presentation Slides
SAM/WebSAM: WB, LM

2.4

Demonstratives; position of adjectives

Demonstratives

- The demonstrative adjectives **questo** and **quello** correspond to *this* and *that*, respectively. They agree in number and gender with the nouns they modify. **Questo** has four forms, but may be abbreviated to **quest'** before a singular noun or adjective that begins with a vowel. **Quello**, like the definite article, has seven forms.

masc./sing.	fem./sing.	masc./pl.	fem./pl.
questo poliziotto	**questa** farmacia	**questi** quartieri	**queste** macchine
quest'anno	**quest'**amica		

masc./sing.	fem./sing.	masc./pl.	fem./pl.
quel segnale	**quella** città	**quei** tribunali	**quelle** cose
quell'amico	**quell'**edicola	**quegli** angoli	**quelle** amiche
quello stadio	**quella** strada	**quegli** zii	**quelle** banche

- **Questo** and **quello** may also be used as demonstrative pronouns. Used as a pronoun, each has only four forms ending in **–o**, **–a**, **–i**, or **–e**.

    Non mi piace **quell'appartamento** in via Roma; preferisco **questo**.
    I don't like that apartment on via Roma; I prefer this one.

Position of adjectives

- Most adjectives follow the nouns they modify. There are, however, a dozen or so common adjectives that usually precede the noun. They are typically adjectives of beauty, age, quality, or size, but you must memorize them to avoid making mistakes. Some of them are **bello, bravo, brutto, buono, cattivo, nuovo, vecchio, piccolo**, and **grande**.

    Roma è una **grande città**.
    Rome is a big city.

- Some adjectives change meaning depending on whether they are placed before or after the noun they modify.

caro	un **caro** amico	a *dear* friend
	un quaderno **caro**	an *expensive* notebook
povero	un **povero** ragazzo	a *poor (unfortunate)* boy
	un ragazzo **povero**	a *poor (penniless)* boy
vecchio	una **vecchia** amica	an *old (longtime)* friend
	un'amica **vecchia**	an *old (elderly)* friend

- The singular form of **buono** follows the pattern of the indefinite article when it precedes a noun. **Bello**, like **quello**, follows the pattern of the definite article when used before a noun.

- **Grande** may be shortened to **gran** in front of masculine or feminine nouns beginning with a consonant (except **s** + *consonant*, **z** or **ps**). Before words beginning with a vowel, it may be shortened to **grand'**.

Pratica e comunicazione

1 🎧

Perugia Una guida sta parlando ai turisti di Perugia. Completa il brano con la forma giusta degli elementi tra parentesi.

GUIDA Buongiorno a tutti e benvenuti a Perugia. Perugia è una città antica e ricca di storia. Ci sono (1) ___molti___ (molto) monumenti e (2) ___molte___ (molto) fontane. Ci sono (3) ___bei___ (bello) palazzi, ristrutturati di recente. (4) ___Questa___ (questo) è una delle più antiche università d'Italia e (5) ___quella___ (quello) è una famosa università per stranieri. Se mi seguite, ora vi mostro uno dei monumenti più importanti di Perugia: (6) ___quelle___ (quello) sono le antiche mura della città.

TURISTA Scusi, ma cosa sono (7) ___quegli___ (quello) edifici in fondo alla piazza?

GUIDA (8) ___Quelli___ (Quello) sono il Palazzo dei Priori e la cattedrale di San Lorenzo. E non dimenticate di ammirare l'(9) ___antica___ (antico) Fontana Maggiore. Ora, prima di lasciarvi liberi di girare da soli, voglio consigliarvi un (10) ___buon___ (buono) ristorante per il pranzo. A più tardi.

2 🎧 👥

Dialoghi In coppia, create dei piccoli dialoghi con gli elementi forniti. Fate tutte le modifiche necessarie.

Modello **Lei / visitare / chiesa**
—Vuole visitare questa chiesa o quella chiesa?
—Non voglio visitare né questa né quella.

1. Tu / affittare / appartamenti
2. Voi / visitare / giardini pubblici
3. Lui / comprare / motorino
4. Loro / fotografare / fontane
5. Lei / preferire / quartiere
6. Voi / guidare / automobile

3 🎧

Le città Crea delle frasi con gli elementi forniti. Fai tutte le modifiche necessarie e stai attento alla posizione degli aggettivi!

Modello **Ad Ascoli Piceno c'è una (piazza / grande / bello).**
Ad Ascoli Piceno c'è una gran bella piazza.

1. A Urbino c'è un (museo/grande/molto). museo molto grande
2. A Pisa c'è una (torre/pendente/famoso). famosa torre pendente
3. A Milano c'è un (grattacielo/grande/nuovo). nuovo grande grattacielo
4. A Viterbo ci sono (rovine/romano/antico). antiche rovine romane
5. Ad Assisi c'è un (festival/grande/invernale). grande festival invernale
6. A Orvieto ci sono due (teatri/importante/nuovo). importanti nuovi teatri

4 👥

Chi sono? In coppia, inventate un'identità per ogni personaggio. Scrivete almeno tre frasi per ogni foto. Utilizzate i dimostrativi e gli aggettivi che avete imparato in questa lezione.

Modello Questa è Francesca. È una brava giornalista...

3 You may wish to share the phrase "BAQS in front" with your students to remind them that adjectives of beauty, age, quality, and size tend to precede the nouns they modify.

Practice more at vhlcentral.com.

Sintesi

1

Parliamo In gruppi di quattro, guardate le foto e rispondete alle domande.

1. Descrivi le foto. A cosa si riferiscono?
2. Quali delle situazioni mostrate influiscono positivamente o negativamente sulla qualità della vita nelle città?
3. Secondo te, problemi e soluzioni come questi esistono solo in Italia? Perché sì o perché no?
4. La tua città ha gli stessi problemi? Cosa si fa per cercare di risolverli?
5. Quali tra le situazioni che influiscono sulla qualità della vita nelle nostre città ti preoccupano di più? Perché?
6. Cosa fai per migliorare la qualità della vita nella tua città?

2

Scriviamo Scegli uno dei seguenti titoli e scrivi un tema lungo almeno una pagina. Utilizza verbi riflessivi, verbi come **piacere**, i possessivi e gli aggettivi.

- Identifica i problemi legati al traffico nel tuo campus universitario o nella tua città e suggerisci alcune soluzioni. Discuti i vantaggi e gli svantaggi delle proposte fatte.

- Ti dicono che sarà vietato circolare in auto nel tuo campus o nel centro della tua città per ridurre il traffico e l'inquinamento. Come reagisci?

Strategie per la comunicazione
Queste sono una serie di espressioni che ti possono essere utili per esporre le tue idee.

Secondo me...,	**inoltre...,**
da una parte...,	**peraltro...,**
dall'altra...,	**del resto...,**
i pro...,	**comunque...**
i contro...,	

Preparazione  Vocabulary Tools

Vocabolario della lettura

l'acquedotto *aqueduct*
d.C. (dopo Cristo)
  AD (Anno Domini)
l'edificio *building*
l'esigenza *requirement*
il materiale edile
  building material

le mura di cinta *city walls*
il piano urbanistico *city plan*
il reperto *find (archeol.)*
le rovine *ruins*
lo scavo *excavation*
il secolo *century*
le terme *(thermal) baths*

Vocabolario utile

**la composizione
  demografica**
  demographic makeup
l'infrastruttura
  infrastructure
l'ingegnere *engineer*
la topografia *topography*
l'urbanistica *city planning*

1 Encourage students to continue the association game by asking them to name actual monuments and sites: **Qual è il nome di una chiesa? Di un monumento? Di un museo?** and the reverse: **Che cos'è il Colosseo? Che cos'è San Pietro? Che cosa sono gli Uffizi?** and so on.

1

La città Associa le parole nelle due colonne.

__e__ 1. le rovine
__d__ 2. le terme
__a__ 3. il materiale edile
__c__ 4. l'acquedotto
__b__ 5. l'ingegnere

a. il cemento
b. il piano urbanistico
c. le opere idrauliche
d. i bagni
e. i resti

2

Il centro Completa il paragrafo.

| acquedotto | edificio | mura di cinta | rovine |
| composizione demografica | infrastrutture | piano urbanistico | topografia |

Il patrimonio artistico delle città antiche è spesso concentrato nel centro storico. Nella (1) __topografia__ di Firenze, per esempio, il Duomo è un (2) __edificio__ dominante. Altri monumenti ed elementi come i parchi e le (3) __mura di cinta__ intorno alla città hanno influenzato lo sviluppo del (4) __piano urbanistico__ moderno. Con l'arrivo degli immigranti nelle città italiane è cambiata la (5) __composizione demografica__, creando nuove necessità nella pianificazione urbanistica.

Nota CULTURALE

All'inizio del 200 d.C., l'**imperatore Caracalla** fece costruire delle magnifiche terme dove gli antichi romani potevano fare il bagno freddo, tiepido o caldo, consultare una biblioteca con testi in greco e in latino, scambiarsi notizie e pettegolezzi° e fare esercizi di ginnastica, come in una palestra° di oggi. L'ingresso costava poco per permettere a tutti di usare i bagni. Dal 1937 le rovine delle terme di Caracalla vengono usate come teatro per concerti e opere liriche.

pettegolezzi *gossip* **palestra** *gym*

3

La tua città In coppia, descrivete la città dove siete nati o la città dove abitate.

1. Quali sono i monumenti principali della tua città?
2. Ci sono elementi che dominano la topografia della tua città?
3. Come coesistono gli edifici antichi e quelli recenti? C'è armonia o contrasto?
4. Dove vai quando vuoi rilassarti? E quando esci con gli amici?
5. Pensi che la tua città sia ben organizzata?

Ask students for examples of old or ancient structures they know that have been rehabilitated or **restaurate** for new uses, such as **fabbriche** remodeled into **appartamenti**, **ville** now used as **musei**, and so-on.

3 Ask students to describe their partners' city and favorite places for the rest of the class.

TUTTE LE STRADE PORTANO A
ROMA

Reading

Nel cuore della città, dietro a edifici monumentali, la gente affolla° il grande mercato all'aperto. Il mercato è circondato da ampi° portici dove è piacevole intrattenersi a conversare o a fare uno spuntino°. Vicino alla piazza in cui domina la statua equestre dell'imperatore alcune persone si apprestano° a visitare gli uffici municipali. Tutto intorno ci sono statue di personaggi illustri, botteghe con merci° esotiche, taverne, un tempio, una palestra e due biblioteche. Un gruppo di studenti seduti sotto un albero ascolta il suo maestro. Siamo nel centro politico, economico, religioso e sociale di Roma, ideato per rispondere alle esigenze di tutti i suoi cittadini. Potrebbe essere un'immagine contemporanea: invece è il Foro Romano della capitale imperiale.

Con il passare dei secoli, il piano urbanistico della città, influenzato dalle tradizioni etrusche ed elleniche°, si è trasformato. Oltre a° voler ingrandire° la capitale con opere pubbliche, ad esempio nel settore idraulico, ogni re e imperatore romano desiderava aumentare anche il proprio prestigio personale realizzando dei monumenti. Le risorse° umane e i materiali edili abbondavano° nella zona: marmo° travertino, schiavi° e tanto spazio.

Le grandi opere nel settore idraulico includono la costruzione della Cloaca Massima, una condotta° della rete fognaria°, e la realizzazione di 1.482 chilometri di acquedotti, fontane e terme come quelle di Caracalla e di Diocleziano. L'imperatore Augusto impreziosì la città con opere di alto valore artistico come l'Ara Pacis, un altare alla pace. Tito e Costantino fecero costruire degli archi trionfali per celebrare le loro vittorie militari.

Per il divertimento dei cittadini furono° anche costruiti teatri come il famoso teatro di Marcello e anfiteatri come il Colosseo. Per il culto religioso

crowd

spacious 5

to have a snack

get ready to 10
(do something)

goods

15

20

Etruscan and Greek
Apart from/expand 25

30

resources
were plentiful/marble
slaves

35

pipe
sewer line

40

45

were

furono innalzati templi come il Pantheon (e altri che divennero° poi chiese e basiliche) e gli imponenti mausolei di Augusto e la mole Adriana (in seguito Castel Sant'Angelo). Le mura di cinta

50

became

Roma sotterranea

La metropolitana di Roma, paragonata° a quelle delle altre capitali, non è molto estesa. La Soprintendenza Archeologica spesso interrompe la costruzione di una nuova linea a causa della ricchezza di reperti storici che si trovano stratificati sotto la città. La difficoltà degli scavi è anche dovuta alla conformazione del terreno e al complesso iter burocratico° dei progetti urbani.

paragonata *compared* **iter...** *bureacratic process*

di Roma, erette° a scopo strategico e difensivo, si modificarono seguendo l'espansione della città e dell'impero e furono costruite grandi strade come la Salaria, la Cassia e la Flaminia. Insieme al porto di Ostia sul Mediterraneo e a quelli fluviali° sul Tevere, le vie romane facilitavano i trasporti e i collegamenti in tutto l'impero. La crisi del III secolo d.C. rallentò° la grande attività edilizia dell'impero, a eccezione della costruzione delle mura aureliane e delle prime catacombe cristiane.

55 *built*

60

river (adj.)

slowed down

65

La definizione dello spazio privato e pubblico è alla base della pianificazione urbanistica di Roma. Lo sviluppo di una città antica è diverso dal piano regolatore di una metropoli moderna nella quale si devono prendere in considerazione le esigenze del trasporto pubblico e dello scorrimento del traffico delle automobili. Comunque, a Roma ancora oggi si usano molte delle antiche infrastrutture: le piazze, i monumenti e molti degli acquedotti; anche le rovine del Foro sono rimaste luogo di passeggiate, conversazioni, commercio e riflessione. ∎

70

75

80

Analisi

1

L'antica Roma Completa le frasi.

_c_ 1. La via Cassia era usata per
_e_ 2. Nel Colosseo i gladiatori
_a_ 3. Nel Pantheon si praticavano
_b_ 4. Nelle Terme di Diocleziano gli antichi romani
_f_ 5. La Mole Adriana era
_d_ 6. L'Ara Pacis fu costruita dall'imperatore Augusto come

a. i culti religiosi.
b. facevano il bagno.
c. il commercio e per collegare il vasto Impero Romano.
d. altare della pace.
e. combattevano con i leoni e fra di loro.
f. un mausoleo.

2

Comprensione Indica se le affermazioni sono **vere** o **false**. Dopo, in coppia, correggete le affermazioni false.

Vero	Falso	
☑	☐	1. Molti edifici e monumenti dell'antica Roma esistono ancora oggi e le necessità dei cittadini sono rimaste simili.
☐	☑	2. Nell'antica Roma mancavano le strutture idrauliche.
☑	☐	3. Gli imperatori romani aumentavano il proprio prestigio personale costruendo opere pubbliche.
☐	☑	4. Gli antichi edifici romani per il culto religioso sono scomparsi.
☑	☐	5. Alla base della pianificazione urbanistica c'è la definizione dello spazio pubblico e privato.

3

Pianificazione urbana

A. A Roma ancora oggi si usano molte delle antiche infrastrutture: le strade, le piazze e i monumenti, gli acquedotti, i luoghi religiosi e i parchi. In coppia, discutete cosa possiamo imparare dalle città antiche per costruire delle città moderne che dureranno nel tempo.

B. Siete un ingegnere e un architetto con il compito di progettare la città ideale.

- Quali infrastrutture pubbliche volete includere nella vostra città?
- Come sono gli spazi dedicati all'arte, ai divertimenti e allo sport?
- Come risolverete il problema del traffico e dei trasporti pubblici?
- Secondo voi, le zone commerciali e pubbliche devono essere integrate o separate da quelle residenziali?
- Dove sono le scuole, le università e gli uffici comunali?
- Quali altri elementi di urbanistica saranno necessari in una città nei prossimi 100 anni? E fra 1000 anni?

C. Presentate il vostro progetto al resto della classe e guardate i progetti degli altri gruppi.

- Quali sono le differenze principali nei progetti? Ci sono degli elementi comuni?
- Le città ideali create dalla classe potrebbero funzionare all'estero?

Practice more at **vhlcentral.com**.

Preparazione Vocabulary Tools

A proposito dell'autore

Claudio Gianini (Milano, 1968) ha cominciato la carriera di scrittore di narrativa nel 2004. Per anni ha lavorato come ingegnere meccanico e ha scritto libri prevalentemente tecnici, anche per l'università, collaborando fra l'altro con Ferrari e Toyota allo sviluppo di vetture (*cars*) di Formula Uno. Da quando ha iniziato a scrivere racconti e romanzi gialli, o noir, non può immaginare di vivere solo di parole tecniche. Il racconto che segue è tratto dalla collezione *Spicchi di realtà*.

Vocabolario della lettura		Vocabolario utile
diffidente *mistrustful*	**indaffarato/a** *busy*	**la compassione** *compassion*
essere in anticipo *to be early*	**la metropoli** *big city*	**l'immigrante** *immigrant*
fare un giretto *to go for a stroll*	**il mezzo pubblico** *public transportation*	**il/la mendicante** *beggar*
la folla *crowd*	**il pannolino** *diaper*	**la povertà** *poverty*
frettoloso/a *in a hurry*	**il tram** *cable car*	**la sopravvivenza** *survival*
		la vergogna *shame*

1

Definizioni Trova la definizione adatta a ogni parola.

___f___ 1. diffidente   a. una persona che chiede soldi per sopravvivere

___a___ 2. mendicante   b. un mezzo di trasporto pubblico su rotaie (*rails*)

___b___ 3. tram   c. un grande gruppo di persone

___c___ 4. folla   d. una persona proveniente dall'estero

___e___ 5. indaffarato   e. una persona che ha molte cose da fare

___d___ 6. immigrante   f. una persona che non si fida di un'altra

2

Preparazione Fate le seguenti domande a un(a) compagno/a.

1. Vieni da una piccola o da una grande città?

2. Quali sono le cose che ti piacciono della tua città? Quali sono le cose che non ti piacciono? Perché?

3. Sei mai tornato in un posto in cui avevi vissuto? Quando? Perché? È stata una visita lunga? Ti è sembrato diverso da come te lo ricordavi?

3

Vivere o visitare una metropoli In gruppi di tre o quattro, rispondete a queste domande.

1. Quali sono le cose che ti attraggono in una grande città?

2. Quali sono i problemi delle grandi città?

3. Per muoverti in città usi i mezzi pubblici o preferisci la macchina? Perché?

4. Ti piace osservare la gente quando visiti una nuova città? Cosa puoi capire del carattere di una città osservando le persone che ci vivono?

5. La vita in città rende le relazioni umane più difficili? Perché?

6. Cosa pensi dei mendicanti? Dai soldi a chi te li chiede? Perché sì o perché no?

 Practice more at **vhlcentral.com**.

2 Ask if any students have ever returned to their old home. Have them describe their feelings. Write nouns on the board: happiness, melancholy, nostalgia, disconnect, etc.

3 Point out that public transportation in Italy, both within cities and nationwide, is generally affordable and reliable. Trains and buses are cheap and reach most destinations. It is possible to live and travel without owning a car, however many people use a car to get to work. This creates huge parking problems, especially in big cities, and often takes longer than the train.

LA MAMMA E IL BAMBINO

Claudio Gianini

Era tanto tempo che non tornavo più nella città in cui sono nato e nella quale sono vissuto per oltre trent'anni della mia vita. In realtà non abito poi così lontano, quaranta chilometri appena, da non poterci venire più di frequente. Semplicemente non ho occasioni particolari per farlo. Tranne° oggi.

La mia Milano. Quanti ricordi sono evocati dai clacson° delle vetture°, dal rumore caotico del traffico, dallo sferragliare° dei tram. Un'onda° di emozioni mi assale appena scendo dal treno delle Ferrovie Nord Milano. Un treno da Far West, come dico spesso ridendo. In effetti mancano solo le frecce°, scagliate° dagli archi dei pellerossa durante un qualche attacco ai visi° pallidi e piantate° nel legno° dei vagoni° attorno ai finestrini.

Ho viaggiato con il treno perché il luogo in cui devo recarmi è a pochi metri dalla Stazione di Piazza Cadorna. Sarebbe stato masochismo puro venirci con l'automobile. Non tanto per il viaggio, che già in sé sarebbe stato allucinante°, quanto per la ricerca di un parcheggio. Meglio quindi il mezzo pubblico.

Mentre attraverso la strada guardo già il portone° del palazzo presso il quale ho il mio appuntamento. Un'occhiata all'orologio mi conferma che sono in anticipo. Ho almeno il tempo per fare un giretto, per immergermi° nella folla di gente frettolosa e indaffarata, per tornare a vivere il gusto della vita frenetica della grande metropoli. Una donna, forse filippina, mi viene incontro spingendo una carrozzina° con dentro un marmocchio°. Mi fissa° per un istante negli occhi. Io ricambio° con fermezza il suo sguardo°. Mi ferma, e io so già cosa vuole. Inizia a parlare, mentre la mia mente sta preparando un rifiuto°.

«Posso farti una domanda?», mi chiede. Ha negli occhi una luce di rassegnata° speranza. Gli anni passati a fermare in quel modo gente diffidente le hanno insegnato a leggere sui visi, tra le pieghe di sorrisi compiacenti o di smorfie° sdegnose°.

«Se so rispondere... », dico con tono lievemente ironico.

«Te lo chiedo come a un fratello», prosegue. Dai suoi occhi è sparita° la rassegnazione ed è rimasta solo la speranza. Forse ritiene già un grosso successo il fatto che io l'abbia almeno degnata° di un minimo di considerazione.

«Mi compri dei pannolini per mio figlio?», continua la donna indicandomi la farmacia che si trova alle mie spalle.

Il rifiuto che avevo pensato sale veloce alle mie labbra, prima ancora che le sue parole mi arrivino al cervello e scendano al cuore, prima che tocchino corde diverse da quelle solitamente fatte vibrare dalle pretese° di qualche spicciolo°. Bastano due passi e la folla si richiude attorno a noi, separandoci. Frazioni di secondo, nelle quali infine realizzo che la preghiera appena ricevuta era una sincera richiesta° d'aiuto.

Quella mamma aveva calpestato° il proprio orgoglio°. Non voleva soldi, voleva direttamente qualcosa di necessario per il suo bambino. Mi giro, torno sui miei passi°, voglio correggere quello che adesso riconosco come un errore. In fondo°, quanto mi può costare un pacco di pannolini? Ma non vi° è più traccia° della donna. Sembra che la folla l'abbia ingoiata°.

Chissà° se qualcun altro, meno pronto di me a presentare un rifiuto, porrà rimedio al mio sbaglio°? ∎

> «Posso farti una domanda?», mi chiede.

Glosses (right margin):

- resigned
- grimaces/disdaining
- disappeared
- deigned
- demands/small change
- demand
- had trampled upon
- pride
- steps
- after all
- (=ci) there
- trace
- swallowed
- Who knows
- mistake

Glosses (left margin):

- Except for
- car horn/cars
- clanging/wave
- arrows/shot
- faces
- stuck/wood
- wagons
- devastating
- entrance door
- immerse myself
- pram
- kid/stares
- return
- gaze
- refusal

Analisi

1 Point out that **marmocchio** is a disparaging term, like "brat." Point out also that Filipinos are very well integrated in Italy, and that it is unlikely for a Filipino woman to beg in **piazza Cadorna**. The protagonist's uncertainty about the ethnicity of the woman may indicate that he unthinkingly considers all foreigners as potential beggars, with no distinction of nationality.

1

Comprensione Indica se ogni affermazione è **vera** o **falsa**. Dopo, in coppia, correggete le affermazioni false.

Vero	Falso	
☑	☐	1. Il protagonista ha preso il treno per andare a Milano.
☐	☑	2. Il protagonista è in ritardo.
☑	☐	3. Il protagonista vede una donna con un marmocchio in una carrozzina che lo guarda fisso.
☑	☐	4. Secondo il narratore, la donna è filippina.
☐	☑	5. Il protagonista compra i pannolini.
☑	☐	6. Il protagonista cambia idea.

2

Opzioni Scegli la frase corretta tra le due.

1. a. Il protagonista lavora a Milano.
   b.) Il protagonista vive fuori Milano.
2. a.) Il protagonista si emoziona rivedendo Milano.
   b. Il protagonista resta indifferente rivedendo Milano.
3. a.) Il viaggio in treno è un'avventura da film western.
   b. Il viaggio in treno è comodo e tranquillo.
4. a. Trovare parcheggio non sarebbe stato un problema.
   b.) Trovare parcheggio sarebbe stata una tortura.
5. a. Il narratore dà soldi alla donna.
   b.) Il narratore non fa il favore chiesto.

3

Pensaci su Scegli la risposta più appropriata. Dopo, in coppia, discutete le frasi che avete segnato con **d**.

1. La donna spera di _____.
   a. aver trovato una persona gentile   b. aver trovato il padre di suo figlio
   c. riuscire a prendersi cura di (*take care of*) suo figlio   d.) sia a che c
2. Il protagonista _____.
   a. ha un atteggiamento ironico   b. è subito compassionevole
   c. è pieno di pregiudizi   d.) sia a che c
3. La donna è _____.
   a. una mendicante professionista   b.) una persona orgogliosa ma disperata
   c. una ladra   d. una bugiarda
4. Il narratore _____.
   a. pensa a lungo prima di dare una risposta   b. cerca di nascondersi tra la folla
   c.) impulsivamente dice sempre di no a chi non conosce   d. aiuta la donna
5. La metropoli _____.
   a.) può essere impersonale   b. favorisce la comprensione tra le persone
   c. è il posto ideale per conoscere stranieri   d. aiuta il dialogo
6. Qualcuno tra la folla _____.
   a. aiuta sicuramente la donna   b.) forse aiuterà la donna   c. andrà in farmacia
   d. darà soldi alla donna

4

Cosa pensate? In coppia, rispondete alle seguenti domande.

1. A chi si riferiscono queste frasi? Che aggettivi usereste per descrivere le emozioni di entrambe le persone?
«Ha negli occhi una luce di rassegnata speranza.»
«Ha negli occhi sospetto e sfiducia.»

2. Secondo te, cosa pensa la donna quando dice queste frasi? Descrivi le sue emozioni.
«Posso farti una domanda?»
«Te lo chiedo come a un fratello.»

3. Perché chiede dei pannolini invece dei soldi per comprarli?

4. Secondo te, chiede sempre soldi o oggetti ai passanti?

5. Come immagini che potrebbe proseguire il dialogo se il narratore la ritrovasse?

5

Tu cosa faresti? Dai la tua opinione personale.

1. Perché credi che il narratore sia così antipatico, persino (*even*) ironico?

2. Il viaggio in treno è paragonato a un Far West da fumetti (*cartoonish*). L'idea dei «buoni» (i visi pallidi) contro «i cattivi» (i pellerossa) è un'indicazione del pregiudizio che il narratore avrà verso la donna. È possibile non avere pregiudizi? Ci sono pregiudizi nei confronti di specifici gruppi etnici nel tuo paese? Per esempio?

3. Cosa faresti se fossi la donna del racconto?

4. Ti sei mai trovato/a in una situazione simile?

5. Sei mai stato/a vittima di pregiudizi?

6. Se tu fossi il narratore, cosa faresti? Saresti così pronto a dire di no? Perché sì o perché no?

6

Dialogo In coppia, create un finale diverso. Immaginate il dialogo che il narratore e la donna avrebbero potuto avere. Scrivete almeno otto frasi e poi recitatele.

 NO! Il narratore dice di no. La folla non li separa. Cosa risponde la donna?

 SÌ! Il narratore dice di sì. Cosa succede?

7

Tema Scegli uno dei seguenti argomenti e scrivi una breve composizione.

● Hai mai incontrato una persona per la strada che ti ha chiesto qualcosa? Come hai reagito? Ti sei sorpreso/a della tua reazione? Pensi che avresti potuto comportarti diversamente? Non deve essere per forza un incontro con un mendicante o un'esperienza negativa: può anche essere una bella esperienza.

● Descrivi le tue emozioni quando sei andato per la prima volta in una grande città. Se vivi in una grande città, descrivi cosa provi quando vai fuori città.

6 Have groups of students re-write the whole story as a play, adding characters (depending on how large is the class), and perform it in class memorizing their lines at home or reading off flash cards. Make sure they write on the board words they may use in their skit if the whole class does not know them.

Nota
CULTURALE

Milano è la seconda città più grande d'Italia dopo Roma. Il comune ha una popolazione di un milione e trecentomila abitanti e l'area metropolitana supera gli otto milioni di abitanti. Più del 21% degli abitanti del comune di Milano sono immigranti. È raro sentire di incidenti dovuti alla convivenza° di tante culture diverse.

convivenza coexistence

Comunità d'immigranti con più di 10.000 abitanti a Milano	
Egitto	52.450
Filippine	48.651
Romania	47.564
Repubblica Popolare Cinese	35.746
Perù	32.988
Ecuador	26.165

(Fonte: www.tuttitalia.it)

5 Point out that **pellerossa** e **viso pallido** are not intended to be politically incorrect terms. They bring to mind John Wayne films and Italian graphic novels such as *Tex Willer*. Just as history has recognized that native cultures have been systematically exterminated, the narrator of this story realizes that his own antagonistic attitude has prevented him from seeing that the woman was not a professional beggar.

 Practice more at vhlcentral.com.

Pratica

Le citazioni

In un saggio la tesi deve essere sostenuta con prove evidenti. Un tipo di prova molto attendibile è rappresentato dalle citazioni ottenute direttamente dalle fonti originali. Le citazioni devono:

- Essere collegate direttamente a quello che si vuole dimostrare.
- Essere inserite nel contesto. Non si può cambiare il messaggio dell'autore originale.
- Includere la fonte. Citare testi senza dichiararne la fonte costituisce un plagio (*plagiarism*).

Le citazioni letterali devono essere riportate tra virgolette «...» (*quotes*); se si omette parte del testo, si indica così: [...]. Infine, se decidiamo di citare usando le nostre parole si può eseguire un cambio nei tempi dei verbi o in altri elementi simili. Esempi:

<u>Citazione diretta:</u> Claudio Gianini nel brano *La mamma e il bambino* giustifica l'uso del treno quando dice: «Non tanto per il viaggio, che già in sé sarebbe stato allucinante, quanto per la ricerca di un parcheggio».

<u>Citazione parziale:</u> Claudio Gianini nel brano *La mamma e il bambino* giustifica l'uso del treno quando dice: «Non tanto per il viaggio, [...], quanto per la ricerca di un parcheggio».

<u>Citazione indiretta:</u> Claudio Gianini nel brano *La mamma e il bambino* giustifica l'uso del treno in quanto è difficile trovare un parcheggio.

Point out to students the difference between Italian and English quotation marks. «...» "..."

To help students cite quotations, distribute some examples of quotes from famous Italian authors and have students practice changing them into indirect quotes.
«Quanto piace al mondo è breve sogno». (Petrarca)
«Il compito degli uomini di cultura è più che mai oggi quello di seminare dei dubbi, non già di raccogliere certezze». (Bobbio)
«Nessun maggior dolore che ricordarsi del tempo felice nella miseria». (Dante, *Inferno* V)

---

1 **Preparazione** In coppia, rileggete l'articolo a pagina 33 e identificate i tipi di citazione presenti.

2 **Saggio** Scegli uno di questi argomenti e scrivi un saggio.

- Il tuo saggio deve far riferimento a uno o due dei quattro brani di questa lezione contenuti in **Cortometraggio**, **Immagina**, **Cultura** e **Letteratura**.
- Deve includere almeno tre citazioni dirette o indirette, ricavate dai brani, per difendere o sostenere i tuoi argomenti.
- Il saggio deve essere lungo almeno due pagine.

> Nelle letture *Tutte le strade portano a Roma* e *Roma: un museo all'aperto*, abbiamo un'immagine dell'antica Roma in tutta la sua grandezza. Anche se con duemila anni di differenza, puoi fare un confronto fra lo stile di vita ai tempi dei Romani e lo stile di vita moderno?

> Nel brano di Claudio Gianini *La mamma e il bambino* uno dei temi predominanti è il rapporto tra sconosciuti in cui una persona ha bisogno di aiuto. Fino a che punto un individuo può spingersi per aiutare uno sconosciuto? Secondo te, è rischioso o vale la pena in nome della compassione e del rispetto per tutta l'umanità?

> Nei brani su Roma, emerge una ricchezza culturale attraverso l'arte e l'urbanistica che supera il tempo. Secondo te, nelle città americane come si esprime la ricchezza culturale e che valore ha?

Città e comunità  Vocabulary Tools

Luoghi e indicazioni

l'angolo *corner*
l'appartamento *apartment*
la campagna *countryside*
il casale *farmhouse*
l'edicola *newsstand*
i giardini pubblici *public gardens*
il grattacielo *skyscraper*
l'incrocio *intersection*
il marciapiede *sidewalk*
la metro(politana) *subway*
il municipio *city hall*
il paese *village*
il palazzo *building; palace*
la periferia *suburbs*
il quartiere *neighborhood*
il segnale stradale *road sign*
il semaforo *traffic light*
lo stadio *stadium*
la stazione di polizia *police station*
la strada *street*
le strisce pedonali *crosswalk*
il tribunale *courthouse*
la via *street*

attraversare *to cross*
dare indicazioni *to give directions*
perdersi *to get lost*
trovarsi *to be located*

La gente

il/la cittadino/a *citizen*
il/la coinquilino/a *housemate; roommate*
il/la contadino/a *farmer*
il/la paesano/a *villager/(fellow) countryman/woman*
il pedone (m./f.) *pedestrian*
il/la poliziotto/a *police officer*
il sindaco *mayor*
il/la venditore/venditrice (ambulante) *(street) vendor*
il/la vigile del fuoco *firefighter*

Le attività

chiacchierare *to chat*
divertirsi *to have fun*
fare commissioni *to run errands*

incontrarsi *to get together*
passeggiare *to take a walk*
trasferirsi *to move (change residence)*

Il trasporto

l'automobilista (m./f.) *driver*
la circolazione/il traffico *traffic*
la fermata (dell'autobus/della metro/del treno) *(bus/subway/train) stop*
l'ingorgo stradale *traffic jam*
il/la passeggero/a *passenger*
il ritardo *delay*

dare un passaggio *to give a ride*
fermare/fermarsi *to stop*
girare (a destra/sinistra) *to turn (right/left)*
guidare *to drive*
parcheggiare *to park*
salire (in macchina/sul treno/sull'autobus) *to get (in a car/on a train/on a bus)*
scendere (dalla macchina/dal treno/dall'autobus) *to get (out of a car/off a train/off a bus)*

Per descrivere

affollato/a *crowded*
pericoloso/a *dangerous*
quotidiano/a *daily*
rumoroso/a *noisy*
vivace *lively*

Cortometraggio

l'attacco *offense*
il calcetto *five-player soccer*
la difesa *defense*
il/la giocatore/giocatrice *player*
la maglia *jersey*
il/la pallone/palla *ball*
il/la portiere/a *goalkeeper*
la squadra di calcio *soccer team*
il/la tifoso/a *fan*

andarsene *to leave*
fregarsene (di) *to not care (about)*
parare *to save*
passare *to pass*

provarci con *to flirt*
segnare un gol *to score a goal*
stare zitto *to be quiet*
tirare *to kick*
vergognarsi *to be ashamed*

cioè *that is*
Dàje! *Come on!*

Cultura

l'acquedotto *aqueduct*
la composizione demografica *demographic makeup*
l'edificio *building*
l'esigenza *requirement*
l'infrastruttura *infrastructure*
l'ingegnere *engineer*
il materiale edile *building material*
le mura di cinta *city walls*
il piano urbanistico *city plan*
il reperto *find (archeol.)*
le rovine *ruins*
lo scavo *excavation*
il secolo *century*
le terme *(thermal) baths*
la topografia *topography*
l'urbanistica *city/planning*

d.C. (dopo Cristo) *AD (Anno Domini)*

Letteratura

la compassione *compassion*
la folla *crowd*
l'immigrante *immigrant*
il/la mendicante *beggar*
la metropoli *big city*
il mezzo pubblico *public transportation*
il pannolino *diaper*
la povertà *poverty*
la sopravvivenza *survival*
il tram *cable car*
la vergogna *shame*

essere in anticipo *to be early*
fare un giretto *to go for a stroll*

diffidente *mistrustful*
frettoloso/a *in a hurry*
indaffarato/a *busy*

Distrarsi e divertirsi

La vita di tutti i giorni è frenetica e faticosa. Ognuno dovrebbe trovare del tempo da dedicare al proprio benessere psico-fisico. Abbiamo a disposizione tantissime opportunità: possiamo fare delle passeggiate in città o a contatto con la natura, incontrare gli amici al caffè con i quali fare due chiacchiere, rilassarsi in casa con un bel libro, andare in palestra o dedicarsi a uno sport. Ognuno è diverso e dà sfogo allo stress della routine in modo diverso. Tu che cosa preferisci? Quale attività ti rilassa e ti dà la carica giusta per affrontare una nuova giornata?

89

112

Destinazione:
TOSCANA

PREVIEW Invite students to
comment on the picture on
the previous page. Do they
prefer to occupy their free
time with sports or other
physical activities like the
people in the photo, or do
they prefer other leisurely
activities? After students have
explained their preferences,
expand the conversation by
asking if both relaxation and
exercise are important for a
well-balanced person. Which
is more important? Why?

I passatempi  Vocabulary Tools

Lo sport

l'allenatore/allenatrice *coach*
l'alpinismo *mountain climbing*
l'arbitro *referee*

l'automobilismo *car racing*
il calcio *soccer*
il campo di/da gioco *playing field*
il canottaggio *rowing*
il club sportivo *sports club*
l'equitazione *horseback riding*
la gara *race*
il giocatore/la giocatrice *player*
il pareggio *tie*
il pattinaggio (sul ghiaccio) *(ice-)skating*
il pugilato *boxing*
lo sci (di fondo) *(cross-country) skiing*

la squadra *team*
il/la tifoso/a *fan*
―――――
allenarsi *to train*
andare in palestra *to go to the gym*
farsi male *to injure oneself*
scalare *to climb*
segnare (un gol) *to score (a goal)*
vincere/perdere/pareggiare (una partita) *to win/lose/tie (a game)*

INSTRUCTIONAL RESOURCES
Audioscripts, Answer Keys, Lab MP3s
SAM/WebSAM: WB, LM

Supply the students with more vocabulary related to soccer: **tirare, passare, dribblare, parare, commettere un fallo**.

Il tempo libero

il biglietto *ticket*
il biliardino *foosball*
il biliardo *billiards*

l'escursionismo *hiking*
il gioco di società *board game*
il gruppo (musicale) *band*
il luna park *amusement park*
la mostra *exhibition*
la prima *opening night*
gli scacchi *chess*
lo spettacolo *show*
il videogioco *videogame*
―――――
applaudire *to clap*
fare campeggio *to camp*

fare la fila *to wait in line*
festeggiare *to celebrate*
giocare a nascondino *to play hide-and-seek*
prendere qualcosa da bere/ mangiare *to get something to drink/eat*
valere la pena *to be worth it*
―――――
buffo/a *funny*
da non perdere *must-see*
tutto esaurito *sold out*

SINONIMI E CONTRARI
biliardino ↔ calciobalilla
fare campeggio ↔ campeggiare
farsi male ↔ infortunarsi
firmato ↔ di marca
passato di moda ↔ fuori moda
il pugilato ↔ la boxe
scalare ↔ arrampicarsi
sostituire (–isc) ↔ cambiare
raffinato ≠ rozzo
fare la fila ≠ saltare la fila
applaudire ≠ fischiare

Lo shopping e l'abbigliamento

l'abito da sera *evening dress*
il cappotto *coat*
il centro commerciale *mall*
l'impermeabile *raincoat*
le infradito *flip-flops*
i saldi (di fine stagione) *(end-of-season) sales*
le scarpe da ginnastica/ tennis *sneakers*

i tacchi alti *high heels*
il vestito (da uomo/donna) *suit/dress*
―――――
cambiare *to exchange*
dare un'occhiata *to take a look*
provare *to try on*
―――――
alla moda *fashionable*
firmato/a *designer brand*
passato/a di moda *out-of-style*
raffinato/a *refined*

Point out that a film or a play may be **buffo/a** or **divertente**, but also **triste, a lieto fine, con finale aperto**. A film may be **d'azione, dell'orrore, giallo, di fantascienza, comico,** or **drammatico**.

Explain that **abbigliamento** is a non-count noun indicating clothing in general, while **vestito** or **abito** indicates something concrete. A single piece of clothing is referred to as **un capo d'abbigliamento**.

Clarify that **tifoso** is used only for teams, while **fan** is used for people. Ex. **Sono un tifoso della Roma e un fan di Francesco Totti**.

Point out that most Italian stores will not allow customers to return (**portare indietro**) items for a refund. Some may let customers exchange items.

Pratica e comunicazione

1 **Categorie** Trova nella lista le parole che appartengono a ciascuna categoria.

applaudire	cappotto	infradito	scacchi	tutto esaurito
biliardo	impermeabile	prima	tacchi alti	videogioco

Giochi   (1) ___videogioco___ , (2) ___biliardo___ , (3) ___scacchi___

Teatro   (4) ___applaudire___ , (5) ___prima___ , (6) ___tutto esaurito___

Abbigliamento (7) ___cappotto___ , (8) ___impermeabile___

Scarpe   (9) ___infradito___ , (10) ___tacchi alti___

2 **Ne vale la pena?** Completa la conversazione utilizzando le parole appropriate della lista.

allenarmi	calcio	pareggio	segnare	vincere
arbitro	campo da gioco	partita	tifosi	una partita

MARCO   Ciao, Giorgio! Che ti è successo alla gamba?

GIORGIO Mi sono fatto male giocando a (1) ___calcio___ ieri.

MARCO   Fai come me: segui il calcio dalla poltrona!

GIORGIO No, Marco, questo mai! Io sono un vero sportivo: preferisco stare sul (2) ___campo da gioco___ .

MARCO   Non dire così! I (3) ___tifosi___ sono importanti quanto i calciatori per (4) ___vincere una partita___ !

GIORGIO È vero, ma quelli che vengono allo stadio contano di più di quelli che guardano la (5) ___partita___ in TV! Ora, che per un po' di tempo non potrò più (6) ___allenarmi___ , andrò allo stadio ogni domenica con tutta la famiglia!

MARCO   Ma hai fatto in tempo a (7) ___segnare___ almeno un gol prima di farti male?

GIORGIO A dir la verità, mi sono fatto male tirando in porta (*shooting a goal*). Il pallone è entrato, ma l'(8) ___arbitro___ ha fischiato fallo di mano (*hand-ball*) e la partita è finita in (9) ___pareggio___ .

MARCO   Vedi? Ho ragione io! Non ne vale la pena!

3 **Conversazione** In coppia, fatevi queste domande e confrontate le vostre risposte.

1. Come preferisci impiegare il tempo libero? Qual è il tuo passatempo preferito?
2. Quale sport segui? Quale ti piace di più? Qual è la tua squadra preferita?
3. Cosa indossi quando pratichi il tuo sport o il tuo passatempo preferito?
4. Ti sei mai fatto male praticando uno sport?
5. Qual è lo spettacolo che hai visto più di recente? Ti è piaciuto? Perché?
6. Cosa indossi di solito per una serata galante?

4 **Il tempo libero** Immaginate di avere una settimana libera e fate dei progetti. Cosa volete fare nel tempo a disposizione? Dove volete andare? Perché? Discutete con i vostri compagni e scrivete un programma per la settimana.

Nota CULTURALE

Il **calcio** è sicuramente lo sport italiano più seguito. Ogni città e piccolo paese ha la propria squadra di calcio. Sono molti gli italiani che amano il calcio o, più propriamente, amano seguire il calcio la domenica, dalla poltrona di casa propria.

Ci sono però anche gruppi di ragazzi (o adulti) che si riuniscono nel fine settimana per giocare a una versione ridotta del calcio, il «**calcetto**». Nel calcetto ci sono solo cinque giocatori per squadra, anziché undici, e il campo è molto più piccolo di un campo di calcio classico. Quando si gioca a calcetto, non c'è un arbitro, perché lo scopo del gioco è divertirsi e non vincere la partita. Spesso la serata si conclude in pizzeria.

Preparazione  Vocabulary Tools

Vocabolario del cortometraggio

il bullo bully
competitivo/a competitive
l'ecografia ultrasound
il fenomeno phenomenon
improvvisare to improvise
l'orgoglio pride

l'ottico optician
prenatale prenatal
il/la quattrocchi four eyes
il/la secchione/a student
  who studies too hard
sminuire (–isc) to play down

Vocabolario utile

il burattino puppet
la coincidenza coincidence
la genetica genetics
le lenti a specchio mirrored lenses
la merendina snack
la suora nun

ESPRESSIONI

prendere di mira to target
prendere in giro to make fun of
tutto va per il meglio everything is turning out for the best

1

Pratica Scegli la risposta giusta.

1. Quando due amici si incontrano per caso si tratta di _____.
   a. una secchiona   (b.) una coincidenza   c. un fenomeno

2. L'ottico fa _____.
   (a.) gli occhiali   b. le merendine   c. l'ecografia

3. I burattini sono un tipo di _____.
   (a.) marionette senza fili   b. occhiali a specchio   c. asteroidi

4. L'ecografia prenatale si fa prima che il bambino _____.
   a. vada a scuola   b. compia due anni   (c.) nasca

5. Quando gli altri studenti chiamano un compagno «quattrocchi» _____.
   a. gli prendono gli occhiali   (b.) lo prendono in giro   c. lo ammirano

2

Secondo te

A. Quali attributi contribuiscono al successo?

CARATTERISTICA	SÌ	NO	CARATTERISTICA	SÌ	NO
Orgoglio	☐	☐	Rispetto per l'autorità	☐	☐
Senso di responsabilità	☐	☐	Spirito d'indipendenza	☐	☐
Iniziativa	☐	☐	Aggressività	☐	☐
Rispetto per le regole	☐	☐	Determinazione	☐	☐
Spirito ribelle	☐	☐	Pazienza	☐	☐
Timidezza	☐	☐	Compassione	☐	☐

B. In piccoli gruppi, confrontate le vostre risposte. Poi rispondete insieme a queste domande.

1. La timidezza è davvero il contrario dell'aggressività?
2. È possibile essere responsabili e ribelli allo stesso tempo?
3. Ci sono delle persone che hanno uno spirito indipendente anche quando rispettano l'autorità?
4. Pensate a dei personaggi famosi: quali caratteristiche hanno? Ci sono delle apparenti contraddizioni in queste caratteristiche?

3

Ingegneria genetica In coppia, immaginate e descrivete il/la vostro/a figlio/a ideale. Poi rispondete insieme alle domande.

Sesso (maschio o femmina)	
Carattere	
Intelligenza (quoziente)	
Abilità e talento (accademico, artistico, sportivo, ecc.)	
Preferenze (opinioni, amici, attività, cibi, ecc.)	

1. Avete scelto un(a) figlio/a con caratteristiche simili alle vostre?
2. Quali caratteristiche sono invece diverse dalle vostre? Perché avete scelto così?
3. Siete d'accordo su tutti gli attributi o avete fatto dei compromessi? Se sì, quali?
4. Pensate che vostro/a figlio/a avrà successo nella vita? In cosa? Perché?

3 Ask each pair to report the similarities and differences in their ideal child to the class.

4

Intervista In coppia, fatevi a turno queste domande.

1. Quali dei tuoi gusti e interessi sono simili a quelli dei tuoi genitori?
2. Che interessi avevi da piccolo/a? Sono ancora gli stessi o sono cambiati con il passare degli anni?
3. Qual è l'attività a cui dedichi più tempo in questo momento? Perché?
4. Che cosa ha influenzato di più le tue scelte personali e accademiche fino a oggi? L'opinione dei tuoi genitori o quella dei tuoi amici?
5. Quali elementi saranno più importanti per il tuo futuro? Assegna un punteggio da 1 a 5 ai seguenti.

- il successo professionale
- la salute
- la felicità in famiglia e con gli amici
- l'intelligenza
- la bellezza

4 Ask each pair to report their responses to the rest of the class, encouraging other students to ask further questions and to explore how genetics shape us.

5

La scuola In piccoli gruppi, rispondete e commentate le risposte.

- Ci si può dedicare agli studi e allo sport senza sacrificare i rapporti con gli altri?
- Cosa pensi dei gruppi di amici che si formano a scuola? Ti hanno mai fatto sentire incluso/a o escluso/a? Perché?
- Quale delle tue caratteristiche rende i tuoi genitori orgogliosi di te?

5 Circulate among the groups facilitating discussion and encouraging students to draw upon their own childhood experiences with sports or other competitive activities.

6

Immaginate Guardate le immagini in piccoli gruppi e immaginate insieme chi sono e come sono i personaggi del corto. Che rapporto c'è tra di loro? Come sono le loro rispettive personalità?

Practice more at vhlcentral.com.

 Video

Soggetto e sceneggiatura FEDERICA PONTREMOLI musica GIULIANO TAVIANI fotografia RAOUL TORRESI (A.I.C.) montaggio FABIO NUNZIATA scenografia ANTON SPAČAPAN VONČINA trucco ed effetti speciali DALIA COLLI fonico in presa diretta MASSIMO TONIUTTI costumi LORENZA FRAGIACOMO montaggio del suono CLAUDIO MARANI per DG MEDIA prodotto da ANTONELLA PERRUCCI e AMEDEO BACIGALUPO

TEACHING OPTION Explain the Italian expression **belli si nasce, non si diventa** (*beauty is born, not made*) and ask students to comment on the pun in the title. To highlight the irony in the story, ask them to imagine how they would react if they found out their child would have an unusual characteristic, such as an extreme talent for music or great physical beauty.

Trama *Ale è nato con le caratteristiche genetiche di un bullo eccezionale, ma con il tempo deve anche accettare le altre caratteristiche che fanno parte della sua natura.*

ALE Quel giorno mamma e papà erano molto agitati. Andavano dal dottore per sapere se ero un maschio o una femmina.
MARIA Ho capito, il solito problema: loro volevano una femmina, ma poi sei arrivato tu e allora...

PADRE Nostro figlio è un bullo! Dottore, è una notizia bellissima!
MADRE Oh, Dio, il nostro piccolo bulletto!
PADRE Ha detto «bullo», il dottore; non sminuire. (*Al dottore*) Era «bullo», no?

ALE All'asilo° poi sono diventato un fenomeno e tutti riconoscevano la mia natura.
MARIA È andata avanti così fino alla quarta elementare°?
ALE Sì, un vero successo.

MARIA Hai cambiato scuola?
ALE No, non è per quello.
MARIA Qualche compagno ti ha preso di mira?

ALE Mi mancavano quattro decimi ipometropi°, come a mia madre.
MARIA Un bullo quattrocchi non si è mai visto.

ALE Occhiali da vista con lenti a specchio! Nessuno si sarebbe accorto del mio problema. Anzi, a scuola il mio prestigio aumentò°.

asilo *kindergarten* **quarta elementare** *fourth grade*
ipometropi *nearsighted* **aumentò** *grew*

Sullo SCHERMO

Mentre guardi le scene principali del film scegli la risposta corretta:

1. Quando vanno dal dottore i genitori sono molto _____.
   a. delusi
   b. agitati
2. Il dottore è sorpreso di vedere che il bambino sarà _____.
   a. un bullo perfetto
   b. un maschio
3. Nel film Ale ha _____.
   a. un cappello e uno zaino blu
   b. un cappello e uno zaino nero
4. All'inizio Maria prova _____.
   a. orgoglio per Ale
   b. compassione per Ale
5. I bambini dell'asilo _____.
   a. hanno paura di Ale
   b. vogliono imitare Ale
6. Ale va dall'ottico perché ha bisogno _____.
   a. degli occhiali da vista
   b. degli occhiali da sole

Analisi

1

Comprensione Indica se l'affermazione è **vera** o **falsa**. Dopo, in coppia, correggete le affermazioni false.

Vero	Falso	
☐	☑	1. I genitori di Ale volevano che diventasse un calciatore.
☑	☐	2. La mamma di Ale ha bisogno degli occhiali.
☐	☑	3. I genitori sono disperati che Ale sia un bullo.
☑	☐	4. I genitori non sono contenti che Ale assomigli a loro.
☑	☐	5. Ale resta calmo quando gli rompono gli occhiali.
☑	☐	6. Alla fine del film Maria rivela una caratteristica inaspettata.

2

Chi lo dice?

A. Associa personaggi e affermazioni.

_f_	1. Mio figlio ha gli occhiali. È colpa mia!	a. il dottore
_g_	2. Non essere impertinente!	b. il padre
_h_	3. Voglio seguire la mia natura.	c. i bulli
_c_	4. Adesso ti rompiamo gli occhiali!	d. la suora
_a_	5. I test sono tutti positivi.	e. la secchiona
_e_	6. Ale non vede la lavagna.	f. la mamma
_d_	7. I bambini dell'asilo hanno tanta paura di Ale!	g. la maestra
_b_	8. Mi piace fare il teatro dei burattini.	h. Ale

B. In coppia, scrivete quattro nuove affermazioni e scambiatele con un'altra coppia; poi associate le rispettive affermazioni ai personaggi del film.

3

Chi è responsabile?

A. Indica le persone che hanno creato queste situazioni.

> Ale | i bulli | il dottore | i genitori | Maria

1. Ale ha gli occhi della mamma e le orecchie del papà. _i genitori_
2. I bambini piccoli sono tormentati. _Ale_
3. I genitori di Ale fanno l'ecografia. _il dottore_
4. Ale racconta la sua storia. _Maria_
5. Ale ha sempre gli occhiali rotti. _i bulli_

B. In gruppi di tre, confrontate le vostre risposte. Poi rispondete alle seguenti domande.

- Pensi che Ale cambi durante il film? Come?
- Cosa imparano i genitori di Ale?
- Cosa capisce Ale alla fine?
- Come si sente Ale alla fine del film?

- Chi sono le vittime nel film? Chi sono i bulli?
- Ci sono dei personaggi stereotipati nel film? Chi sono?
- Chi è responsabile del fatto che Ale sia un bullo?

4

Opinioni In coppia, decidete se siete d'accordo o no con queste affermazioni. Spiegate il perché.

Affermazioni	sono d'accordo	non sono d'accordo
1. I nostri gusti dipendono esclusivamente dalla nostra natura.	☐	☐
2. I nostri genitori o le esperienze che facciamo influiscono sulla nostra personalità.	☐	☐
3. Andare all'asilo aiuta i bambini a socializzare.	☐	☐
4. Le scuole pubbliche sono migliori delle scuole private.	☐	☐
5. Gli sport di squadra sono migliori degli sport individuali.	☐	☐
6. Studiare da soli è più efficace che studiare in gruppo.	☐	☐
7. Per i miei genitori il successo accademico è più importante del successo nello sport.	☐	☐

5

I passatempi

A. In gruppi di tre, fate una lista dei vantaggi e degli svantaggi di queste attività. Poi presentate la lista al resto della classe.

> **Modello**   **suonare uno strumento**
>
> Vantaggi: È rilassante; si può far parte di un'orchestra…
>
> Svantaggi: Bisogna fare pratica spesso; ci vogliono molti anni per…

- studiare in biblioteca
- Facebook
- leggere
- guardare la TV
- giocare con i videogiochi
- mandare sms
- Twitter
- il vostro passatempo preferito

B. Commentate i vantaggi e gli svantaggi delle attività che fate nel tempo libero, a scuola o all'università.

6

Una conversazione In coppia, improvvisate una conversazione per una di queste situazioni.

A

Siete una giovane coppia che aspetta un bambino. Il dottore vi rivela che sarà una campionessa di calcio con notevoli abilità linguistiche. Qual è la vostra reazione? Come aiuterete la vostra bambina a sviluppare le sue abilità naturali? Dove abiterete? In quali scuole la manderete a studiare?

B

Maria e Ale si incontrano dieci anni dopo, quando sono all'università. Qual è la loro reazione nel rivedersi dopo tanto tempo? Come sono cambiati? Che cosa studiano? Quali sono i loro passatempi? Cosa si dicono?

7

Scriviamo Scegli uno di questi argomenti e scrivi una breve composizione.

- Quali caratteristiche fisiche o mentali sono necessarie per eccellere nel campo che preferisci? Descrivi quello che ti appassiona: una professione, un passatempo o altro.

- Sei un(a) giornalista e vuoi scrivere un articolo sulle scuole che hai frequentato, specialmente su come le attività del dopo-scuola aiutano gli studenti a fare amicizia e a sviluppare un senso di gruppo o di squadra.

- Se potessi acquisire una caratteristica o un'abilità, quale sarebbe? Come la useresti?

5 Help students share their lists by creating a scoreboard on the blackboard.

6 Help students be creative in their dialogues by circulating among the groups and asking "what if" questions.

7 Help students adapt and personalize the topics to make them more relevant to their own lives.

Practice more at **vhlcentral.com**.

INSTRUCTIONAL RESOURCES: Teaching suggestions; Answer Keys
SAM/WebSAM: WB

IMMAGINA

TOSCANA E FIRENZE

In giro per Firenze

Firenze, capoluogo della regione Toscana e città ricca di opere d'arte uniche al mondo, è considerata la **culla del Rinascimento°**. Proveremo a suggerirvi degli itinerari artistici alla scoperta di alcuni dei tesori di questa storica città.

Vi consigliamo di iniziare con la **Galleria dell'Accademia** dove è conservato uno dei capolavori° di **Michelangelo**, la statua del *David*, scolpita in un unico pezzo di marmo° e considerata da molti il più alto esempio di bellezza maschile rinascimentale. Da qui potrete continuare a piedi verso **piazza del Duomo** dove si trova **Santa Maria del Fiore**, il Duomo di Firenze progettato° nel XIII secolo. La **Cupola** è uno dei simboli di Firenze e un esempio dell'ingegneria innovativa di **Brunelleschi**, uno dei maggiori architetti del Rinascimento. Di fronte al Duomo c'è il **Battistero**, tra i monumenti più antichi della città. L'esterno è in marmo bianco e verde, le porte in bronzo sono divise in pannelli incisi° e all'interno ci sono elaborati mosaici. La porta principale, completamente dorata, è nota come la **Porta del Paradiso** ed è opera di **Lorenzo Ghiberti**. A fianco del Duomo si innalza° il **Campanile**, ai cui lavori collaborò anche **Giotto**.

Dalla cima° del Campanile e della Cupola potrete godere° di una vista panoramica su Firenze. Nelle vicinanze c'è la basilica di **Santa Maria Novella** con la sua spettacolare facciata° in marmo e all'interno preziosi affreschi e vetrate°.

In **piazza della Signoria** potrete inoltre° visitare **Palazzo Vecchio**, che da diversi secoli è il municipio° di Firenze. Nelle vicinanze si trova uno dei musei più ricchi di raccolte d'arte del mondo: la **Galleria degli Uffizi**. Qui sono conservati° i più famosi dipinti di **Botticelli**, tra cui la **Nascita di Venere** e la **Primavera**, oltre alle opere di importanti pittori del tardo **Medioevo** e del Rinascimento come **Cimabue**, **Raffaello**, **Michelangelo** e **Leonardo da Vinci**.

La visita continuerà al **Museo Nazionale del Bargello** con la sua collezione di sculture, tra cui il *David* in bronzo di

Ponte Vecchio

Donatello. Non lontano potrete visitare la chiesa di **Santa Croce** con gli affreschi di Giotto e le tombe dell'astronomo e filosofo **Galileo Galilei**, di Michelangelo e di **Niccolò Machiavelli**, storico e politico rinascimentale.

L'ultimo itinerario vi farà attraversare il fiume **Arno** passando per il **Ponte Vecchio**, noto per le sue botteghe artigiane e orafe°. Vi troverete nella zona denominata **Oltrarno**, dove sorgono altri due musei importanti: il colossale **Palazzo Pitti** e la **Cappella Brancacci**. Palazzo Pitti ospita eccezionali opere di pittura e scultura e comprende la Galleria Palatina che conserva molte delle collezioni della famiglia Medici, grande protagonista della storia politica e artistica di Firenze. La Cappella Brancacci, situata all'interno della chiesa di **Santa Maria del Carmine**, ospita gli affreschi di **Masaccio**, tra cui la *Cacciata di Adamo ed Eva dal paradiso terrestre.* In quest'opera l'artista introduce l'uso della prospettiva°, che sarà un elemento fondamentale dell'arte rinascimentale.

Dopo questa visita avrete avuto un assaggio° delle bellezze artistiche di Firenze e magari° sarete desiderosi di conoscerne altre.

In più...

La storia di Firenze è stata caratterizzata dall'ascesa° e dal declino di famiglie importanti. La famiglia **Antinori** ha avuto un ruolo significativo nella vita economica della città. Gli Antinori iniziarono a commerciare tessuti° alla fine del XIII secolo arrivando fino in Francia e, nel corso dei secoli, hanno ricoperto anche cariche politiche. Ancora oggi la famiglia Antinori contribuisce alla ricchezza cittadina con la produzione del **Chianti**, un vino riconosciuto in tutto il mondo.

culla... *cradle of the Renaissance* **capolavori** *masterpieces* **marmo** *marble* **progettato** *planned* **pannelli...** *engraved panels* **si innalza** *it rises* **cima** *top* **godere** *to enjoy* **facciata** *façade* **affreschi...** *frescoes and stained glass windows* **inoltre** *furthermore* **municipio** *city hall* **conservati** *preserved* **botteghe...** *craftsmen and goldsmiths' shops* **prospettiva** *perspective* **assaggio** *taste* **magari** *perhaps* **ascesa** *rise to power* **tessuti** *fabrics*

Vero o falso? Indica se ogni frase è **vera** o **falsa**. Correggi le frasi false. Some answers will vary.

1. I lavori per il Campanile di Firenze iniziarono nel Rinascimento. Falso. I lavori iniziarono alla fine del Medioevo, nel XIII secolo.

2. Palazzo Vecchio è la sede politico-amministrativa di Firenze. Vero.

3. Molti degli affreschi di Masaccio sono conservati al Museo del Bargello. Falso. Il Bargello è un museo di sculture. Gli affreschi di Masaccio si trovano nella Cappella Brancacci.

4. Palazzo Pitti ha all'interno altri musei. Vero.

5. La famiglia Antinori oggi produce tessuti. Falso. Produce vino.

6. La Vespa è un'automobile prodotta dalla Piaggio. Falso. La Vespa è uno scooter.

7. L'isola di Montecristo è l'isola più grande dell'Arcipelago Toscano. Falso. L'isola d'Elba è l'isola più grande.

8. I più famosi dipinti di Botticelli si trovano nella Galleria degli Uffizi. Vero.

Quanto hai imparato? Rispondi alle domande. Some answers will vary.

1. Quale famosa statua è conservata nella Galleria dell'Accademia di Firenze? i *Prigioni*, il *San Matteo* o il *David* di Michelangelo

2. Quali sono alcune caratteristiche di Santa Croce? affreschi di Giotto; tombe di Galileo, Michelangelo e Machiavelli

3. Che tipo di negozi ci sono su Ponte Vecchio? botteghe artigiane e orafe

4. Che cos'è l'Oltrarno? un'area dopo Ponte Vecchio; l'area dove si trovano Palazzo Pitti e la Cappella Brancacci

5. Perché è famosa la famiglia Antinori? produzione di tessuti nei secoli scorsi; cariche politiche; produzione di vino oggi

6. Quali sono alcuni dei prodotti attuali (*current*) delle industrie Piaggio? motocicli e scooter

La Vespa Lo scooter **Vespa**, una delle icone italiane più conosciute nel mondo, è uno dei prodotti delle industrie toscane **Piaggio**. La sede della Piaggio è a Pontedera, in provincia di Pisa. La Piaggio inizia la sua attività alla fine del 1800 con la produzione di materiale per ferrovie°, ma ben presto si dedica alla costruzione di aerei. Negli anni '20 e '30 produce automobili ed elicotteri finché, nel 1946, brevetta° e commercializza la Vespa, seguita da altri motocicli come il **Ciao** e il **Sì**.

L'Arcipelago Toscano La Regione Toscana ha 397 chilometri di litorale° bagnato dal mar Tirreno. Al largo della costa ci sono sette isole maggiori e alcune minori che fanno parte dell'**Arcipelago Toscano**. La più grande e conosciuta è **l'isola d'Elba**, famosa per aver ospitato Napoleone Bonaparte durante il suo esilio e oggi ricercata° destinazione turistica. Altre isole dell'arcipelago sono **l'isola del Giglio** e **l'isola di Montecristo**.

ferrovie *railways* **brevetta** *patents* **litorale** *coast* **ricercata** *in great demand*

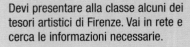

Progetto

Devi presentare alla classe alcuni dei tesori artistici di Firenze. Vai in rete e cerca le informazioni necessarie.

- Ricerca sei opere famose presenti nei musei o nelle chiese di Firenze (possono essere opere di pittura, scultura, mosaici, ecc.).

- Per ogni opera scrivi una didascalia (*caption*) con informazioni sull'autore, l'epoca in cui ha vissuto e le caratteristiche artistiche dell'opera.

- Presenta il tuo lavoro alla classe.

GALLERIA DI PERSONE ILLUSTRI

SCULTORE, PITTORE
Michelangelo Buonarroti (1475–1564)

Michelangelo Buonarroti nasce a Caprese, in provincia d'Arezzo. Considerato uno dei più grandi artisti di sempre, inizia la sua formazione a dodici anni. Spinto (*Driven*) dall'interesse per la  scultura, completa la sua formazione ai Giardini di San Marco, una libera scuola di scultura finanziata da Lorenzo de' Medici. Il signore di Firenze rimane talmente colpito (*struck*) dalla bravura di Michelangelo che lo invita a risiedere nella residenza della famiglia Medici. Michelangelo si trasferisce a Roma e lì gli viene commissionata la sua prima grande opera, la *Pietà*, nella Basilica di San Pietro. Torna poi a Firenze per creare una delle sue più celebri sculture, il *David*, ma appena lo termina ritorna a Roma per lavorare alla Cappella Sistina. Il celeberrimo artista fiorentino muore a Roma all'età (*age*) di ottantanove anni.

PITTORE, SCIENZIATO
Leonardo da Vinci (1452–1519)

Leonardo, nato a Vinci nel 1452, incarna l'ideale di uomo rinascimentale abile in tutte le arti. Intorno ai diciassette anni si trasferisce con la famiglia a Firenze. Durante i dodici anni di formazione e sperimentazione che trascorre (*spends*) a Firenze, Leonardo entra nelle grazie di Lorenzo de' Medici. Viene denunciato per sodomia e nonostante l'accusa venga successivamente ritirata, questo episodio fa sì che sia escluso dal gruppo di artisti che Lorenzo de' Medici invia al Papa Sisto IV per affrescare la Cappella Sistina. Deluso, lascia Firenze e si stabilisce a Milano. Nei sedici anni che trascorre a Milano, Leonardo esegue alcune tra le sue opere più celebri:  *L'ultima cena* (*The Last Supper*), la *Dama con l'ermellino* e la *Vergine delle rocce*. Dopo una serie di viaggi ritorna a Firenze e tra varie nuove opere inizia quella della *Gioconda* (*Mona Lisa*). Nel 1516 accetta l'invito del re di Francia e si stabilisce ad Amboise dove muore tre anni dopo.

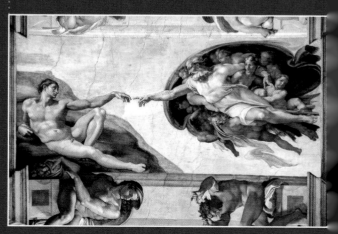

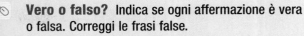

ASTROFISICA

Margherita Hack
(1922–2013)

Margherita Hack è stata un'importante astrofisica e divulgatrice scientifica italiana. Viene ricordata a livello mondiale per gli importanti studi di astrofisica.

Margherita, fiorentina di nascita, si laurea alla facoltà di fisica con una tesi in astrofisica. Dopo aver lavorato all'osservatorio di Merate per una decina di anni, si trasferisce a Trieste dove lavora alla radioastronomia, lo studio delle stelle nella gamma (*range*) delle onde radio. Occupa la cattedra di professore di astronomia all'Università di Trieste dal 1964 al 1992 e inizia a collaborare con molte università straniere. Margherita è la prima donna a dirigere un osservatorio in Italia e grazie a lei l'Osservatorio Astronomico di Trieste diviene (*becomes*) un centro internazionale. Margherita svolge (*carries out*) un'importante attività di divulgazione scientifica e contribuisce alla ricerca per lo studio e la classificazione di molte stelle.

POETA, SCRITTORE

Dante Alighieri
(1265–1321)

Dante Alighieri è considerato lo scrittore italiano più importante tra il Duecento e il Trecento. La vita del poeta fiorentino viene segnata dall'amore platonico per Beatrice, una giovane che vede per la prima volta quando aveva nove anni. La figura di Beatrice è presente in molte opere del poeta, a cominciare dalla prima, le *Rime*, poesie giovanili influenzate dalla poetica stilnovistica. Seguono «romanzo» autobiografico in prosa e versi

Vita nova, il *Convivio*, il *De monarchia* e il rivoluzionario *De vulgari eloquentia*, un trattato linguistico che parla delle varietà e delle qualità della lingua volgare e la mette sullo stesso piano della prestigiosa lingua latina. Ma il capolavoro di Dante è la *Divina Commedia*, riconosciuto a livello mondiale. Nel 1300 Dante viene accusato di corruzione e condannato all'esilio (*exile*). Inizia così la sua peregrinazione (*wanderings*) per tutta l'Italia che termina nel 1321 a Ravenna, dove muore di malaria.

Comprensione

Vero o falso? Indica se ogni affermazione è vera o falsa. Correggi le frasi false.

1. Leonardo dipinge la *Gioconda* a Firenze.
   Vero.

2. Leonardo fa parte del gruppo di artisti che hanno lavorato alla Cappella Sistina.
   Falso. È escluso dal gruppo.

3. Michelangelo inizia la sua formazione ai Giardini di San Marco.
   Falso. Completa la sua formazione ai Giardini di San Marco.

4. Michelangelo torna a Roma per lavorare alla Cappella Sistina.
   Vero.

5. Lorenzo de' Medici conosceva sia Michelangelo che Leonardo.
   Vero.

6. Beatrice è la musa ispiratrice di molte opere di Dante.
   Vero.

7. Il *De vulgari eloquentia* è una poesia autobiografica.
   Falso. È un trattato linguistico.

8. La *Divina Commedia* è l'opera più celebre di Dante.
   Vero.

9. Margherita Hack nasce a Firenze.
   Vero.

10. Margherita Hack è stata la direttrice dell'Osservatorio Astronomico di Trieste.
    Vero.

Scrittura

Scrivi sull'argomento Scegli uno dei seguenti argomenti e scrivi un paragrafo seguendo le indicazioni.

- **Il Rinascimento italiano** Quali sono i fondamenti del Rinascimento italiano? Quali arti comprende? Scrivi dei suoi maggiori esponenti e delle opere rappresentative di questo periodo.

- **La *Divina Commedia*** Di che cosa parla il capolavoro letterario di Dante? Perché il poeta è considerato il padre della letteratura e della lingua italiana? Fai una ricerca e scrivi sull'argomento.

- ***L'ultima cena* di Leonardo** La tua famiglia si sta preparando per un viaggio in Italia. Tu vuoi assolutamente includere *L'ultima cena* nel vostro itinerario. Scrivi un'e-mail alla tua famiglia raccontando la storia di questo capolavoro e i motivi per cui vale la pena vederlo.

 Practice more at **vhlcentral.com**.

INSTRUCTIONAL RESOURCES `3.1`
Audioscripts, Answer Keys, Lab MP3s, Grammar Presentation Slides
SAM/WebSAM: WB, LM

ATTENZIONE!

Note that it is common to use the **passato prossimo** where in English you would often use the simple past. The **passato prossimo** may be translated in several ways:

Lui **ha perso** la partita.
*He **has lost/lost/did lose** the game.*

Ieri Luisa **è rimasta** a casa.
*Yesterday Luisa **stayed** home.*

TEACHING OPTION Divide the class into small groups. Give groups two minutes to think of as many –**are**, –**ere**, and –**ire** verbs as possible. When time is up, invite students to ask each other questions using the **passato prossimo** of the verbs. Encourage them to use expressions such as **ieri**, **l'anno scorso**, and **tre giorni fa**.

To help students master the irregular past participles, encourage grouping similar participles together. Example: **scritto**, **fatto**, **detto** or **chiesto**, **rimasto**, **risposto**.

ATTENZIONE!

Here are some –**are** and –**ire** verbs with irregular past participles.
aprire → ap**erto**
dire → **detto**
fare → **fatto**
morire → **morto**
offrire → off**erto**
venire → ven**uto**

The *passato prossimo* with *avere* and *essere*

—**Ho visto** *cosa è* **successo**. —*Il giorno stesso* **sono andato** *dall'ottico.*

- Use the **passato prossimo** to express an action completed in the past. This compound tense is formed by combining the present tense of an auxiliary verb (**avere** or **essere**) with the past participle of the main verb. When the verb is conjugated with **essere**, the past participle must agree in gender and number with the subject of the verb.

Transitive verbs		Intransitive verbs	
ho		sono	
hai		sei	andat**o**/a
ha		è	
abbiamo	perdut**o**	siamo	
avete		siete	andat**i**/e
hanno		sono	

- The past participle of regular verbs is formed as follows.

–are → –ato	–ere → –uto	–ire → –ito
parlare → parl**ato**	potere → pot**uto**	finire → fin**ito**

- Many past participles from the second conjugation verb group (–**ere**) are irregular. Here is a partial list.

bere → be**vuto**	essere → **stato**	rimanere → rima**sto**
chiedere → chie**sto**	leggere → le**tto**	rispondere → rispo**sto**
chiudere → chiu**so**	mettere → me**sso**	rompere → ro**tto**
correggere → corre**tto**	nascere → **nato**	scegliere → sce**lto**
correre → cor**so**	perdere → per**so**	scendere → sce**so**
cuocere → co**tto**	piangere → pia**nto**	scrivere → scri**tto**
decidere → deci**so**	prendere → pre**so**	smettere → sme**sso**
dipingere → dipi**nto**	raccogliere → racco**lto**	vedere → **visto**/ved**uto**
discutere → discu**sso**	ridere → ri**so**	vincere → vi**nto**

- Transitive verbs employ **avere** as their auxiliary verb; the past participle ends in **–o**. Verbs that are intransitive usually require **essere** as their auxiliary; the past participle must agree in gender and number with the subject of the verb and will end in **–o, –a, –i,** or **–e**.

Transitive verb (takes **avere**, past participle ends in **–o**)

Paola **ha scalato** una montagna.
Paola climbed a mountain.

Marcello **ha segnato** un gol.
Marcello scored a goal.

Intransitive verb (takes **essere**, past participle agrees with subject)

Paola **è caduta.**
Paola fell.

I giocatori **sono andati** in palestra.
The players went to the gym.

- Intransitive verbs often express either physical movement or, in contrast, lack of movement. They also indicate changes in state.

movement	**andare, arrivare, cadere, entrare, fuggire, partire, passare, (ri)tornare, salire, saltare, scendere, uscire, venire**
lack of movement	**essere, restare, rimanere, stare**
change of state	**crescere, divenire, diventare, impazzire, morire, nascere, risultare, sparire**

- Some verbs, like **cambiare, cominciare, finire, iniziare,** and **passare,** can be used both transitively and intransitively. Compare:

Carlo **ha finito** le linguine.
Carlo finished the linguine.

Lo spettacolo **è finito** alle 10.30.
The show ended at 10:30.

- Not all intransitive verbs are conjugated with **essere**. Some intransitive verbs that describe common activities are conjugated with **avere**. These include **camminare, dormire, nuotare, saltare,** and **viaggiare**.

Ieri notte **abbiamo dormito** solo due ore!
We only slept two hours last night!

Laura **ha viaggiato** molto.
Laura has travelled a lot.

- Reflexive and reciprocal verbs, as well as the verb **piacere**, always require **essere** as their auxiliary. The past participle must agree with the subject of the verb.

Paola **si è allenata** in palestra.
Paola worked out at the gym.

Le amiche **si sono telefonate**.
The friends called each other.

A Luigi **sono piaciuti** i tuoi amici.
Luigi liked your friends.

Non mi **sono piaciute** le lasagne.
I did not like the lasagna.

- If a direct object pronoun precedes a verb in the **passato prossimo**, the past participle must agree with it. Remember that the past participle of transitive verbs (those verbs that are conjugated with **avere**) otherwise ends in **–o**.

Dove **hai comprato** le scarpe da ginnastica?
Where did you buy your sneakers?

Le ho comprate al centro commerciale.
I bought them at the mall.

ATTENZIONE!

When the verb acts upon, or has the potential to act upon an object, it is transitive. When the verb cannot be followed by a direct object, it is intransitive. Compare:

Transitive verb:
Ho comprato un gioco di società.
I bought a board game.

Intransitive verb:
Quando siete arrivati?
When did you arrive?

RIMANDO

The verbs **dovere, potere,** and **volere**, when combined with an infinitive in the **passato prossimo**, generally use the auxiliary verb employed with that infinitive. See **Strutture 4.4, p. 150**.

Ho potuto comprare i biglietti.
I was able to buy the tickets.

Siete dovuti partire alle otto.
You had to leave at eight o'clock.

RIMANDO

To review reflexive and reciprocal verbs, see **Strutture 2.1, pp. 56–57**.

RIMANDO

You will learn more about object pronouns in **Strutture 4.2, pp. 140–142**.

Pratica

1 **Francesco Totti** Completa il paragrafo su Francesco Totti, un famoso giocatore italiano, usando il **passato prossimo** dei verbi tra parentesi.

Francesco Totti (1) ___è nato___ (nascere) a Roma il 27 settembre 1976. Dall'età di 16 anni fino a oggi, (2) ___ha giocato___ (giocare) solo nella Roma. Il 4 settembre del 1994, (3) ___ha segnato___ (segnare) il suo primo gol in Serie A e da quel momento non (4) ___ha smesso___ (smettere) di stupirci (*astonish us*). Nel 1998 (5) ___è diventato___ (diventare) il capitano della Roma. Pelé, il famoso giocatore brasiliano, lo (6) ___ha incluso___ (includere) nella lista dei 125 più grandi giocatori viventi. Nel 2003 Totti (7) ___ha scritto___ (scrivere) un libro: *Tutte le barzellette su Totti (raccolte da me)*. Le librerie italiane (8) ___hanno venduto___ (vendere) moltissime copie e Totti (9) ___ha donato___ (donare) i guadagni (*proceeds*) all'Unicef e ad altre associazioni di beneficenza. Nel 2005 il calciatore (10) ___ha sposato___ (sposare) la famosa presentatrice televisiva Ilary Blasi. Dopo un infortunio (*accident*) che lo (11) ___ha tenuto___ (tenere) lontano dal campo da gioco per tre mesi, Totti (12) ___è tornato___ (tornare) a giocare con la Nazionale nei campionati mondiali del 2006, in cui la nazionale di calcio italiana (13) ___ha vinto___ (vincere) il titolo di Campione del Mondo.

2 **Un fine settimana particolare** Completa la conversazione tra Luisa e Mara con la forma corretta dei verbi.

andare	cadere	discutere	fare	passare	studiare
annoiarsi	costruire	essere	farsi male	sentire	venire

LUISA Cosa (1) ___hai fatto___ questo fine settimana?

MARA (2) ___Sono andata___ a Sant'Anna di Stazzema, vicino a Lucca, per un Campo di Educazione alla Pace.

LUISA Interessante. Racconta!

MARA Eravamo in tutto trenta ragazzi e (3) ___abbiamo discusso___ di temi legati alla nonviolenza e alla solidarietà internazionale. (4) ___Sono venuti___ anche ospiti e relatori (*guests and speakers*) stranieri. (5) ___È stata___ un' esperienza indimenticabile.

LUISA Sant'Anna di Stazzema... (6) ___ho sentito___ questo nome...

MARA Probabilmente lo (7) ___hai studiato___ a scuola...

LUISA Ma sì, certo: Sant'Anna è il luogo in cui, durante la seconda guerra mondiale, i nazisti hanno sparato su tantissimi civili!

MARA Esatto. Per ricordare quell'evento gli abitanti (8) ___hanno costruito___ il Museo della Memoria: da non perdere! E tu, come (9) ___hai passato___ questo fine settimana?

LUISA Sono restata qui, a Firenze, ma non (10) ___mi sono annoiata___. Ho partecipato alla Maratona della Pace, con altre 10.000 persone! Peccato però che (11) ___sono caduta___ e (12) ___mi sono fatta male___ alla caviglia (*ankle*)!

MARA Allora, il prossimo anno vieni con me. È meno pericoloso.

Practice more at
vhlcentral.com.

Comunicazione

3
Cos'è successo? In coppia, guardate le immagini e immaginate una storia per ogni situazione.

Modello Marilena ha ricevuto una lettera da suo fratello che è andato in vacanza ai Caraibi. Il fratello ha deciso di rimanere lì. Si è sposato...

| Marilena | Marco e Gloria | Patrizia | Giorgio e Luana |

3 Ask students to read their stories to the class. Have the students vote on the most amusing story.

4
Hai una buona memoria? Ecco una lista di attività. Quando è stata l'ultima volta che avete fatto queste cose? In coppia, fatevi queste domande a turno.

Modello guardare una partita di calcio
—Quando è stata l'ultima volta che hai guardato una partita di calcio?
—Ho visto una partita di calcio domenica scorsa.
—Chi ha giocato?

1. andare in vacanza
2. scrivere un'e-mail
3. guardare un film
4. cenare al ristorante
5. mandare un sms
6. leggere un libro
7. fare una fotografia
8. andare in palestra
9. perdere qualcosa
10. farsi male

4 Ask the students to pick an activity they have done recently from the list. Their partner can then ask questions to guess the activity: **Quando lo hai fatto? Dove lo hai fatto? Cosa hai fatto dopo? I tuoi genitori si sono arrabbiati? È stata una brutta esperienza?** Students may start guessing what happened only after asking five different questions.

4 Encourage students to ask each other about other recent activities that do not appear in the list.

5
Com'è strana la vita!

A. In coppia, scrivete due brevi storie: una vera, ma buffa o incredibile di cui uno/a di voi è stato/a protagonista; un'altra completamente inventata, ma anche questa inusuale. Cercate di essere dettagliati e di rispondere alle seguenti domande.

- Cos'è successo?
- Ti ha visto qualcuno?
- Che cosa hai detto?
- Cosa hai fatto dopo?

B. A turno, ogni coppia legge le sue brevi storie alla classe che dovrà indovinare qual è la storia vera e qual è quella falsa.

6
I divertimenti Che fate per divertirvi? Che attività praticate?

A. Fate una lista di cinque cose divertenti che avete fatto il mese scorso.

B. In coppia, domandate al(la) vostro/a compagno/a se ha fatto le attività della vostra lista e scrivete **sì** o **no** accanto a ognuna.

C. In gruppi di quattro, descrivete a turno quello che il/la vostro/a compagno/a ha fatto il mese scorso.

6 As an expansion, ask students to talk about their partner using one of the following reflexive verbs: **stancarsi, stressarsi, rilassarsi, riposarsi, interessarsi, divertirsi, annoiarsi.** Example: **Mary si è stancata perché ha lavorato molto e ha dormito poco.**

INSTRUCTIONAL RESOURCES
Audioscripts, Answer Keys, Lab MP3s, Grammar Presentation Slides
SAM/WebSAM: WB, LM

3.2

The *imperfetto*

- Use the **imperfetto** to talk about what used to happen or to describe ongoing and habitual actions and conditions in the past. The English equivalent of the **imperfetto** is often expressed with *used to* or *would*.

> Da piccoli, **giocavamo** spesso a nascondino.
> *When we were little, we often played (used to play/would play) hide-and-seek.*

- To form the **imperfetto**, remove the final **–re** from the infinitive and add the endings **–vo**, **–vi**, **–va**, **–vamo**, **–vate**, and **–vano**.

tifare	perdere	applaudire
tifavo	perdevo	applaudivo
tifavi	perdevi	applaudivi
tifava	perdeva	applaudiva
tifavamo	perdevamo	applaudivamo
tifavate	perdevate	applaudivate
tifavano	perdevano	applaudivano

- There are few irregularities in the **imperfetto**. Note, however, the irregular forms of **essere** and the special stems for **bere**, **dire**, and **fare**.

essere	ero, eri, era, eravamo, eravate, erano
bere (bev–)	bevevo, bevevi, beveva, bevevamo, bevevate, bevevano
dire (dic–)	dicevo, dicevi, diceva, dicevamo, dicevate, dicevano
fare (fac–)	facevo, facevi, faceva, facevamo, facevate, facevano

- The **imperfetto** is also used to describe or set the scene when narrating a past event. Conditions such as the weather, time, age of persons involved, emotions, and circumstances may all be expressed with the **imperfetto**.

> **Pioveva** a catinelle.　　**Nel 1970, Carla aveva** sei anni.
> *It was raining buckets.*　　*In 1970, Carla was six years old.*

- The **imperfetto** can describe states of mind that continued over an unspecified period of time.

> Mi **sentivo** triste.　　**Volevi** studiare in Italia?
> *I felt sad.*　　*Did you want to study in Italy?*

- Several verbs in the **imperfetto** can be used together to convey simultaneous ongoing activities in the past.

> Il padre **lavava** i piatti mentre i bambini **giocavano** a carte.
> *The father was washing the dishes while the children were playing cards.*
>
> Quando la mamma **cantava**, mia sorella e io **ballavamo** sempre.
> *When mom sang, my sister and I would always dance.*

ATTENZIONE!

When the **imperfetto** conveys ongoing or habitual actions, it is often accompanied by adverbial expressions such as: **mentre, sempre, di solito, spesso, ogni giorno/settimana**, etc., **tutto/a/i/e** + [*period of time*], and **il/la** + [*day of week*]. In Italian, days of the week are masculine except **la domenica**.

La squadra non si allenava la domenica.
The team didn't practice on Sundays.

Da piccola, passavo tutta l'estate dalla nonna.
When I was little, I used to spend the whole summer at my grandmother's.

ATTENZIONE!

Just as it is possible to use **Da quanto tempo** with the present tense to inquire about actions that began in the past but continue into the present, the **imperfetto** can be used with this expression to inquire about actions that began in a more distant past and continued in the more recent past.

Da quanto tempo parlavi il tedesco quando sei andato in Germania per la prima volta?
How long had you been speaking German when you traveled to Germany for the first time?

Lo parlavo da tre anni.
I had been speaking it for three years.

ATTENZIONE!

Verb ending in **–urre, –orre**, and **–arre** use stems derived from Latin roots.

produrre (produc-) → **producevo**
proporre (propon-) → **proponevo**
trarre (tra-) → **traevo**

Pratica e comunicazione

1 🔊

Da piccolo Completa il paragrafo con l'imperfetto dei verbi fra parentesi.

Da piccolo mi (1) ___piaceva___ (piacere) passare l'estate a casa dei nonni, a Lucca.
Di solito (2) ___giocavo___ (giocare) con i miei amici nel parco, oppure (*or*) (3) ___andavo___
(andare) in bicicletta per le strade del centro. Un giorno, mentre (4) ___pedalavo___
(pedalare) e (5) ___guardavo___ (guardare) in alto i tetti rossi delle case lucchesi, sono caduto
e mi sono fatto male al piede. Sono rimasto ingessato (*in a cast*) per un mese intero!
(6) ___Avevo___ (avere) solo sei anni, ma ricordo tutto perfettamente! Quello che
(7) ___preferivo___ (preferire) erano le passeggiate con il nonno quasi ogni domenica.
La mattina la nonna (8) ___preparava___ (preparare) i panini per il pranzo, mentre noi
(9) ___ci mettevamo___ (mettersi) le scarpe da ginnastica. Poi (10) ___cominciavamo___ (cominciare)
la nostra escursione tra i boschi e la natura lungo la Via Francigena.
(11) ___Incontravamo___ (Incontrare) spesso tante persone che (12) ___andavano___ (andare) a caccia
(*hunting*) o (13) ___raccoglievano___ (raccogliere) i funghi. Poi, quando (14) ___era___ (essere)
mezzogiorno, (15) ___ci fermavamo___ (fermarsi) a mangiare sotto un albero. Che bei tempi!

Nota CULTURALE

La **Via Francigena** è un'antica strada medievale che passa per Lucca, collegando° Canterbury a Roma. I pellegrini° che arrivavano a Roma decidevano se fermarsi lì o proseguire fino a Brindisi, dove si imbarcavano° fino in Terra Santa. Oggi i percorsi° della Via Francigena coincidono in parte con strade asfaltate, in parte con affascinanti sentieri tra la natura.

collegando *connecting* **pellegrini** *pilgrims* **si imbarcavano** *embarked* **percorsi** *routes*

2 🧍🧍

Prima e dopo In coppia, confrontate le due immagini e commentatele. Com'era la vita prima e com'è oggi? Rispondete con almeno cinque commenti.

com'era prima   com'è adesso

3 🔊 🧍🧍

Da piccoli

A. Utilizzate gli elementi dati per parlare di voi quando avevate otto anni. Scrivete due frasi per ogni elemento e confrontatevi con il/la compagno/a.

> **Modello**   **abitare**
> Abitavo in un appartamento in centro con i miei genitori e mia sorella.

1. mangiare
2. giocare
3. divertirsi
4. piangere
5. guardare uno spettacolo televisivo
6. praticare uno sport
7. suonare uno strumento musicale
8. avere un animale domestico

B. In gruppi di quattro o cinque, cercate la persona che condivide con voi il maggior numero di caratteristiche. Quando l'avete trovata, spiegate alla classe in cosa siete simili e in cosa differenti.

> **Modello**   Da piccolo io guardavo sempre i Simpson. Anche Jane li guardava.
> Da piccolo io non mangiavo le verdure, invece Jane mangiava tutto!

1 After the activity, have students prepare their own story, beginning with **Da piccolo**, detailing a memory of an important place or person in their lives. Ask for volunteers to share their recollections with the class.

2 For a discussion, write some of the students' comments on the blackboard. Ask students to consider the advantages and disadvantages of living in today's society and of living in the past. Ex: **Nel passato non c'erano così tante automobili: si viveva meglio o peggio? Quali erano i lati positivi di una città senza tante automobili? Quali i lati negativi?**

3 After reading the example, point out that when making a comparison in Italian, the subject of each element is retained. **Anche** is never used at the end of such sentences.

Practice more at **vhlcentral.com**.

INSTRUCTIONAL RESOURCES
Audioscripts, Answer Keys, Lab MP3s, Grammar Presentation Slides
SAM/WebSAM: WB, LM

3.3

The *passato prossimo* vs. the *imperfetto*

- Italian uses both the **passato prossimo** and the **imperfetto** to talk about events in the past. The two tenses have distinct uses, however, and are not interchangeable.

—*All'asilo, poi, **sono diventato** un fenomeno e tutti **riconoscevano** la mia natura.*

- The **passato prossimo** narrates completed events, whereas the **imperfetto** describes ongoing conditions, habitual actions, or the circumstances surrounding such activities, such as the time, weather, and age or emotional state of the people involved.

> **Volevamo** festeggiare il compleanno di Giorgio, così **abbiamo comprato** una torta.
> *We wanted to celebrate Giorgio's birthday, so we bought a cake.*

Uses of the *passato prossimo*

Use the **passato prossimo** in these instances.

- To express completed actions.

> L'allenatrice **ha passato** tre ore in palestra ieri.
> *The trainer spent three hours in the gym yesterday.*

> La sua squadra **ha vinto** la partita sabato scorso.
> *Her team won the game last Saturday.*

- To express the beginning or end of a past action.

> La partita **è cominciata** alle dieci.
> *The game began at ten o'clock.*

> **Ho finito** il libro.
> *I finished the book.*

- To specify the number of times an event took place.

> La Juventus **ha perso** le ultime tre partite.
> *Juventus has lost the last three games.*

> **Hai fatto campeggio** sull'isola due volte?
> *You camped on the island twice?*

- To list a series of past actions.

> **Ho dato** un'occhiata agli ultimi arrivi, poi **ho provato** una gonna.
> *I took a look at the latest fashions, then I tried on a skirt.*

- To indicate a change of state or a reaction.

> Margherita e la sua mamma **si sono stancate**.
> *Margherita and her mom got tired.*

> Dopo l'abbondante cena, non **ho potuto** prendere il dolce.
> *After such a big dinner, I could not have dessert.*

Uses of the *imperfetto*

Use the **imperfetto** in these instances.

- To express ongoing past actions that lack a clear beginning or ending point.

    Andavi in palestra.
    You used to go to the gym.

    Preferivo fare escursionismo.
    I used to prefer hiking.

- To express habitual actions in the past.

    Di solito, non **segnavamo** molti gol.
    Usually, we did not score many goals.

    Da giovane, **praticavo** la scherma.
    When I was young, I used to fence.

- To describe emotional or physical states.

    Leo **era** triste quel giorno.
    Leo was sad that day.

    Mi **faceva** male la schiena.
    My back was hurting.

The *passato prossimo* and the *imperfetto* used together

- The **passato prossimo** and **imperfetto** often appear together, in the same sentence or paragraph, because both are necessary to fully narrate a past event.

- You may find it helpful to think of the **passato prossimo** as the tense that moves a story forward, whereas the **imperfetto** is the tense that fills out the background of the story. The **imperfetto** may also describe what was ongoing when another event took place.

    Ieri io e mio marito **abbiamo fatto** una passeggiata sulla spiaggia. **Erano** le otto di mattina quando **siamo usciti.** Purtroppo (*Unfortunately*) **faceva** brutto tempo; **pioveva**, **tirava** un vento fortissimo e le onde (*waves*) del mare **erano** altissime. All'improvviso **abbiamo visto** un fulmine (*lightening bolt*) tremendo nel cielo! In quel momento **ho avuto** paura, allora **siamo tornati** subito a casa.

Events (passato prossimo)	Details, background (imperfetto)
Abbiamo fatto una passeggiata.	**Erano** le otto di mattina.
...quando **siamo usciti**.	**Faceva** brutto tempo: **pioveva**, **tirava** vento… le onde **erano** altissime.
Abbiamo visto un fulmine.	
Ho avuto paura, allora **siamo tornati**…	

- Note that some verbs carry different meanings in the **passato prossimo** and **imperfetto**.

Verb	Passato prossimo	Imperfetto
conoscere	*to meet*	*to know or be familiar with a person, place, or thing*
sapere	*to find out*	*to know (a fact, how to do something)*

- The verbs **dovere**, **potere**, and **volere** also have different meanings in the **passato prossimo** and **imperfetto**. If the action is completed, use the **passato prossimo**. The **imperfetto** may imply that something was supposed to take place, but for some reason, did not. Compare:

    Abbiamo dovuto fare la fila per comprare un biglietto.
    We had to stand in line to buy a ticket.

    Dovevo comprare i biglietti, ma non l'ho fatto.
    I was supposed to buy the tickets, but I didn't.

ATTENZIONE!

Depending on the tense, certain adverbial expressions may be used to indicate the time frame of a past event or situation. Note these expressions.

Used with the **passato prossimo**:

una volta, in quel momento, all'improvviso, a un tratto *one time, in that moment, suddenly, all of a sudden*

Used with the **imperfetto**:

mentre, sempre, di solito, spesso, ogni giorno/settimana, etc., **tutto/a/i/e** + [*period of time*], and **il/la** + [*day of week*].

TEACHING OPTION Play parts of *Bulli si nasce* with examples of the **passato prossimo** and **imperfetto**. Pass out the script with blank lines for students to fill in the correct past-tense forms, or have them write down the examples they hear.

RIMANDO

Conoscere and **sapere** are not interchangeable. For more information about their uses, see **Strutture 7.4, p. 276.**

RIMANDO

For more information about the use of **dovere**, **potere**, and **volere**, see **Strutture 4.4, p. 150.**

Pratica

1

Una splendida idea! Luisa racconta come ieri ha vinto la noia (*boredom*). Completa il paragrafo coniugando i verbi tra parentesi al passato prossimo o all'imperfetto.

Ieri il tempo (1) ___era___ (essere) brutto. Non (2) ___pioveva___ (piovere), ma (3) ___faceva___ (fare) freddo. (4) ___Mi sentivo___ (sentirsi) un po' triste e così, per provare a cambiare umore, (5) ___ho deciso___ (decidere) di passare il pomeriggio al centro commerciale. (6) ___Sono entrata___ (entrare) in un negozio d'abbigliamento e (7) ___ho provato___ (provare) quindici gonne tutte diverse! La commessa, piuttosto irritata, (8) ___alzava___ (alzare) continuamente gli occhi al cielo. Ovviamente io non (9) ___volevo___ (volere) comprare nulla, ma solo divertirmi come da bambina, quando (10) ___giocavo___ (giocare) con i vestiti della mamma. Alla fine, fingendo di dare un'occhiata agli abiti da sera, (11) ___mi sono avvicinata___ (avvicinarsi) alla porta, (12) ___mi sono messa___ (mettersi) il cappotto e (13) ___ho esclamato___ (esclamare): «Grazie di tutto. Tornerò quando ci saranno i saldi di fine stagione!». È stata una giornata intensa, ma molto divertente!

2

Interruzioni Unisci gli elementi delle quattro colonne e spiega cosa facevano i personaggi quando sono stati interrotti.

Modello I turisti facevano campeggio quando è arrivato un orso.

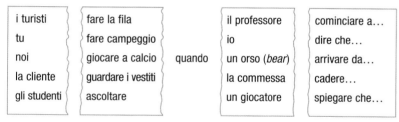

i turisti	fare la fila		il professore	cominciare a…
tu	fare campeggio		io	dire che…
noi	giocare a calcio	quando	un orso (*bear*)	arrivare da…
la cliente	guardare i vestiti		la commessa	cadere…
gli studenti	ascoltare		un giocatore	spiegare che…

3

La vacanze In coppia, guardate le immagini e usate le parole della lista per parlare delle vacanze di Piero e Ida a Taormina l'anno scorso. Usate il passato prossimo e l'imperfetto.

Modello L'anno scorso Piero e Ida sono andati in un'agenzia turistica.
Erano entusiasti…

andare in aereo/barca/taxi/treno	aeroporto	(s)cortese	il giorno dopo
controllare	agenzia turistica	economico/a	mentre
giocare	albergo	entusiasta	ogni giorno
prenotare	camera	lussuoso/a	sempre
	spiaggia	(s)piacevole	un giorno

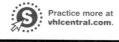
Practice more at vhlcentral.com.

Comunicazione

4 You may want to recap how to express dates in Italian. Then go over the **modello** with a volunteer.

4 Eventi importanti

A. Ecco cinque avvenimenti importanti nella vita di Piero. In coppia, fatevi delle domande per descrivere ogni avvenimento.

Modello —Cosa è successo a Piero nel 1975?

—Il 24 luglio 1975 Piero è nato.

—Dov'era e con chi?

—Era all'ospedale con sua madre.

1984	1990	1991	2009	2010	2013
La mia nascita, 24 luglio	Incontro con il mio migliore amico	Nascita della mia sorellina, 13 maggio	Laurea in ingegneria, 29 giugno	Amore a prima vista con Ida, novembre	Matrimonio, 27 maggio

B. Pensate a cinque date importanti della vostra vita e scrivetele. Poi, in piccoli gruppi, parlatene con i vostri compagni, che vi chiederanno i dettagli di ogni avvenimento.

Modello —Il 26 agosto 2006 è stata una data importante perché ho incontrato il mio fidanzato.

—Dov'eri? Con chi eri? …

5 Una storia

In gruppi di tre o quattro, completate le frasi utilizzando il passato prossimo o l'imperfetto. Poi cambiate l'ordine delle frasi per creare una storia logica.

1. Ogni anno…
2. Di solito…
3. Un giorno…
4. Poco dopo…
5. All'improvviso…
6. Per due ore…

5 After each group has finished its story, ask the students to write a clear, readable draft, eliminating the sentence starters. Collect the stories and pass them out randomly to different groups, instructing them to fill in the blanks using appropriate sentence starters from the list.

6 Interviste

A. In coppia, assumete il ruolo di un giornalista e di una persona celebre di cui conoscete bene la vita. Preparate un'intervista di sei domande con le relative risposte utilizzando il passato prossimo e/o l'imperfetto.

Modello **Giornalista:** Sappiamo che recentemente Lei ha scritto un libro. Cosa ha fatto con i guadagni (*proceeds*) delle vendite?

Celebrità: Volevo comprare una villa, ma li ho donati interamente ad alcune associazioni di beneficenza.

B. Recitate le interviste alla classe. I vostri compagni dovranno indovinare chi è il personaggio intervistato e potranno fare ulteriori domande, se necessario.

INSTRUCTIONAL RESOURCES **3.4**
Audioscripts, Answer Keys, Lab MP3s, Grammar Presentation Slides
SAM/WebSAM: WB, LM

ATTENZIONE!

The **passato remoto** and **passato prossimo** are generally not used together.

Emphasize recognition of **passato remoto** verbs for reading comprehension. Present a reading and ask students to identify the verbs and provide their infinitive forms. As follow up, see if they can generate the other forms of the **passato remoto** verb found in the passage.

In the third person singular, verbs end in an accented form of their characteristic stem vowel, except for the third person singular of **–are** verbs, which replaces **–a** with **–o**. For the forms of the first and second person, and the third person plural, the same endings are used in all conjugations (**–i, –sti, –mmo, –ste, –rono**).

The *passato remoto*

- The **passato remoto**, like the **passato prossimo**, expresses completed past actions. The **passato remoto** usually refers to events of the distant past that do not have a continuing effect in the present.

Passato prossimo
Mia madre **è nata** nel 1939. *My mother was born in 1939.*
Ho scoperto il jazz solo recentemente. *I discovered jazz only recently.*

Passato remoto
Il re **nacque** nel 1546. *The king was born in 1546.*
Chi **scoprì** l'America? *Who discovered America?*

- The **passato remoto** is not commonly used in spoken Italian, although there are regional variations. It is used to some extent in Tuscany and in parts of southern Italy, where it is sometimes used in place of the **passato prossimo**.

- Although, as a student of Italian, you will almost never use the **passato remoto** in conversation, it is essential to recognize its forms because it is frequently used in literature and most magazines and newspapers.

- To form the **passato remoto**, drop the **–re** ending of the infinitive and add the endings indicated in the table below. Note that some **–ere** verbs also have alternate first person singular and third person irregular forms.

parlare → parla–	vendere → vende–	finire → fini–
parlai	vendei/vendetti	finii
parlasti	vendesti	finisti
parlò	vendé/vendette	finì
parlammo	vendemmo	finimmo
parlaste	vendeste	finiste
parlarono	venderono/vendettero	finirono

- Many verbs are irregular in the **passato remoto**. Most of them, however, are irregular only in the first person singular (**io**), and third person singular and plural (**lui/lei, loro**) forms. Because of this pattern, they can be referred to as **1-3-3** verbs. Once you know the first person singular form of these verbs, you can easily derive all the other forms. The verbs are regular in the **tu**, **noi**, and **voi** forms. For example:

lęggere (irregular forms in orange)	
1 lessi	1 leggemmo
2 leggesti	2 leggeste
3 lesse	3 lęssero

- Here is a list of verbs that follow the pattern **1**, **3**, **3**.

avere	ebbi	nascere	nacqui	spegnere	spensi
chiedere	chiesi	perdere	persi	spendere	spesi
chiudere	chiusi	piacere	piacqui	tenere	tenni
conoscere	conobbi	piangere	piansi	uccidere	uccisi
correre	corsi	prendere	presi	vedere	vidi
crescere	crebbi	rimanere	rimasi	venire	venni
decidere	decisi	rispondere	risposi	vincere	vinsi
dipingere	dipinsi	sapere	seppi	vivere	vissi
mettere	misi	scrivere	scrissi	volere	volli

- Some verbs are irregular in all forms of the **passato remoto**.

essere	bere	fare	stare	dire	dare
fui	bevvi	feci	stetti	dissi	diedi/detti
fosti	bevesti	facesti	stesti	dicesti	desti
fu	bevve	fece	stette	disse	diede/dette
fummo	bevemmo	facemmo	stemmo	dicemmo	demmo
foste	beveste	faceste	steste	diceste	deste
furono	bevvero	fecero	stettero	dissero	diedero/dettero

- The **passato remoto** is used in narrations with the **imperfetto** just as the **passato prossimo** is used. The **passato remoto** relates the completed events and moves the action forward; the **imperfetto** is used for descriptions or to express habitual or ongoing actions.

Description (imperfetto)	Events (passato remoto)
C'**era** una volta una fanciulla bellissima che si **chiamava** Cenerentola. *Once upon a time there was a beautiful young girl named Cinderella.*	Il figlio del re **decise** di dare un gran ballo per tutte le fanciulle del regno. *The king's son decided to hold a grand ball for all the young women in the kingdom.*
	La matrigna **prestò** i suoi gioielli alle figlie che **dissero** a Cenerentola: «Resta qui a lavorare!» *The stepmother loaned her jewels to her daughters, who told Cinderella: "Stay here and work!"*
	Cenerentola **arrivò** finalmente e **fece** il suo ingresso nella sala da ballo. *Cinderella finally arrived and made her entrance into the ballroom.*
Era la più bella ed elegante della festa! *She was the most beautiful and elegant one at the party!*	Il principe **fu** colpito dalla sua bellezza e la **invitò** a ballare. *The prince was struck by her beauty and asked her to dance.*

Pratica

1

Che verbo è? Identificate l'infinito di ogni verbo e coniugatelo al passato prossimo.

Modello noi demmo
dare: noi abbiamo dato

1. loro vennero venire: loro sono venuti/e
2. lui nacque nascere: lui è nato
3. voi chiudeste chiudere: voi avete chiuso
4. io lessi leggere: io ho letto
5. lei scrisse scrivere: lei ha scritto

6. tu decidesti decidere: tu hai deciso
7. io persi perdere: io ho perso
8. noi piangemmo piangere: noi abbiamo pianto
9. loro rimasero rimanere: loro sono rimasti/e
10. lui rispose rispondere: lui ha risposto

11. voi uccideste uccidere: voi avete ucciso
12. io vidi vedere: io ho visto
13. tu volesti volere: tu hai voluto
14. lei spense spegnere: lei ha spento
15. lui mise mettere: lui ha messo

2

2 Give students sentences in the **passato remoto** and have them change the verbs to the **passato prossimo**.

Chi l'ha visto? Trasforma le frasi al passato prossimo.

1. Il ragazzo indossò gli sci e partì. Il ragazzo ha indossato gli sci ed è partito.
2. Dopo qualche minuto prese velocità. Dopo qualche minuto ha preso velocità.
3. Vide da lontano un uomo fermo sulla pista (*ski slope*). Ha visto da lontano un uomo fermo sulla pista.
4. Capì di andare troppo veloce. Ha capito di andare troppo veloce.
5. Non riuscì a fermarsi in tempo. Non è riuscito a fermarsi in tempo.
6. L'impatto fu terribile. L'impatto è stato terribile.
7. L'uomo travolto rimase a terra. L'uomo travolto è rimasto a terra.
8. Il ragazzo corse via veloce come il vento. Il ragazzo è corso via veloce come il vento.

3

Raccontiamo una favola! Trasforma i verbi al passato remoto o all'imperfetto, cominciando la storia con **C'era una volta un falegname**....

Un falegname (*carpenter*) di nome Geppetto un bel giorno decide di costruire un burattino. Mentre lavora al suo burattino, sente una voce che dice: «Non mi fare il solletico (*tickle*)!». Geppetto si guarda intorno, ma non vede nessuno. La stessa cosa si ripete altre tre volte. Alla fine Geppetto capisce che la vocina viene proprio dal pezzo di legno (*wood*). Incredibile! Un pezzo di legno che sa parlare! Così Geppetto chiama il pezzo di legno Pinocchio e lo tiene con sé per tutta la vita, come un figlio.

3 Answer: C'era una volta un falegname di nome Geppetto. Un bel giorno decise di costruire un burattino. Mentre lavorava al suo burattino, sentì una voce che disse/diceva: «Non mi fare il solletico!». Geppetto si guardò intorno, ma non vide nessuno. La stessa cosa si ripeté altre tre volte. Alla fine Geppetto capì che la vocina veniva proprio dal pezzo di legno. Incredibile! Un pezzo di legno che sapeva parlare! Così Geppetto chiamò il pezzo di legno Pinocchio e lo tenne con sé per tutta la vita, come un figlio.

Nota
CULTURALE

Le avventure di Pinocchio è un libro scritto da Carlo Collodi nel 1881. Narra le avventure di un burattino bugiardo e disubbidiente che alla fine riesce a diventare buono, trasformandosi in un bambino vero in carne e ossa°. Con il suo film, Walt Disney ha reso Pinocchio famoso in tutto il mondo, insieme agli altri personaggi che popolano il libro.

carne e ossa *flesh and bone*

Comunicazione

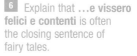

4 **Italiani nella storia** In coppia, create una breve biografia dei quattro italiani rappresentati nelle immagini, mettendo in ordine le informazioni che seguono (tre per ogni persona) e usando il **passato remoto**. Includete i dati biografici con l'anno di nascita e di morte.

Dante Alighieri
(1265–1321)

Leonardo da Vinci
(1452–1519)

Maria Montessori
(1870–1952)

Rita Levi-Montalcini
(1909–2012)

> **Modello** Dante Alighieri nacque nel 1265 e morì nel 1321. Scrisse la *Divina Commedia* in lingua volgare fiorentina.

andare in esilio nel 1302 / non tornare mai più a Firenze

aprire la sua prima scuola nel 1907

dipingere la *Gioconda*

diventare la prima dottoressa italiana nel 1896

essere pittore, scienziato e inventore

laurearsi in medicina / studiare il sistema nervoso

lavorare con i bambini / creare un nuovo metodo di insegnamento

partecipare alla vita politica di Firenze

scrivere la *Divina Commedia* in lingua volgare fiorentina

vincere il premio Nobel per la medicina nel 1986

trasferirsi a Milano / lavorare al suo famoso affresco *L'ultima cena*

vivere e fare ricerca scientifica negli Stati Uniti per trent'anni.

5 **Ti ricordi quando…?** In piccoli gruppi, elencate cinque eventi importanti del mondo dello sport o dello spettacolo accaduti negli ultimi dieci anni e descriveteli usando il passato remoto.

> **Modello** Nel 2006 l'Italia vinse il campionato mondiale di calcio.

6 **…e vissero felici e contenti!** In piccoli gruppi, scegliete l'inizio di una delle due favole e inventatene il proseguimento.

1. C'era una volta un re che aveva tre figli maschi e desiderava ardentemente una figlia. Un giorno incontrò un cervo (*deer*). Stava per colpirlo con una freccia (*arrow*) quando il cervo cominciò a parlare e gli disse: «Se non mi ucciderai, ti prometto che presto avrai una figlia». Allora il re…

2. Chi dice che sui pianeti della nostra galassia non ci sono altre forme di vita, sicuramente non ha mai sentito questa storia. Un afoso (*sultry*) giorno d'agosto il signor Leopoldo camminava per le strade deserte della città quando, a un tratto, vide passare veloce nel cielo un grosso «uovo» luminoso. «Accidenti! Deve essere il caldo…», pensò il signor Leopoldo e si aggiustò il berretto sulla testa…

Sintesi

1

Parliamo In piccoli gruppi, guardate queste foto di persone che praticano sport estremi e rispondete alle domande.

Diving: l'amore per uno sport che mette a rischio la vita: ne vale veramente la pena?

Free-climbing: desiderio di libertà o eccessiva sicurezza di sé?

Alpinismo: sacrificio, fatica e ricompensa finale. Attraverso il corpo si può migliorare anche il proprio carattere?

Parapendio: guardare il mondo dall'alto ci dà la percezione della nostra fragilità umana?

1. Conosci qualcuno di questi sport? Lo hai mai praticato? Perché sì e perché no?
2. Immagina di essere una delle persone nelle foto. Perché hai scelto questo sport? Hai mai avuto paura?
3. Sei mai stato in una situazione pericolosa a causa degli sport? Cosa è successo?
4. Perché la gente in generale sembra attratta da questi sport? La loro popolarità continuerà a crescere?
5. Quali sono gli «effetti collaterali» degli sport estremi? Pensa ad almeno tre cose e discutine con i tuoi compagni.

2

Scriviamo Scrivi una pagina di diario su uno dei seguenti argomenti.

- Descrivi un episodio memorabile che ti è successo mentre praticavi uno sport o passatempo.
- Descrivi un episodio memorabile che è successo mentre guardavi un evento sportivo.

Strategie per la comunicazione

Suggerimenti per scrivere un diario:

- Un diario è di solito un oggetto personale: oltre agli eventi, assicurati di descrivere anche i tuoi sentimenti, le tue reazioni, le tue opinioni, ecc.
- Un diario è per sua natura un testo informale; lo stile è semplice e lineare.
- Cerca di usare un vocabolario familiare e strutture sintattiche semplici.
- Un diario spesso è usato per raccogliere non solo pensieri e ricordi, ma anche buoni propositi per il futuro: termina il tuo testo dicendo cosa hai imparato da quello che è successo.

Preparazione  Vocabulary Tools

Vocabolario della lettura

il calciatore *soccer player*

giocare in casa/ trasferta *to play a home/away game*

leale *loyal*

la maglia *jersey*

il pallone *soccer; ball*

il regolamento *regulations*

la rete *goal; net*

scendere in campo *to join the game*

a squarciagola *at the top of one's voice*

il torneo *tournament*

Vocabolario utile

il calcio di rigore *penalty kick*

il centravanti *center forward*

la difesa *defense*

parare *to save*

pareggiare *to tie*

il portiere *goalkeeper*

tifare (per) *to root for*

Point out that **il calcio** and **il pallone** are synonyms when referring to the sport, although they also mean *kick* and *ball*, respectively.

1

Giochiamo! Utilizza le parole nuove per completare le frasi.

1. Un _____torneo_____ è una serie di partite.
2. Tutti i miei amici _____tifano_____ per il Milan.
3. Il _____portiere_____ ha parato molti rigori (*penalty kicks*).
4. L'allenatore preferisce _giocare in casa_, con tutti gli spettatori che tifano per la sua squadra.
5. Tutta la squadra indossa una _____maglia_____ dello stesso colore.
6. Tutti giocatori devono seguire il _regolamento_.
7. Le squadre _scendono in campo_ per iniziare la partita.
8. Mario è un amico _____leale_____, sincero e generoso.

2

Sondaggio

A. Scopri chi sono i tifosi in classe: domanda ad altri quattro studenti quali sono i loro gusti sportivi. Aggiungi altre due domande.

- Quale sport preferisci guardare alla TV?
- C'è uno sport che vai a vedere allo stadio?
- C'è una squadra che preferisci? Quale?
- C'è un giocatore che ammiri? Chi è?

B. In piccoli gruppi, confrontate i risultati dei vostri sondaggi. Poi scriveteli alla lavagna per determinare quali sono i gusti della vostra classe.

3

Il calcio nel mondo In coppia, fate una lista di tutte le informazioni che avete sul calcio.

- Avete mai giocato a calcio?
- Come funziona il gioco?
- Quali altri sport sono simili al calcio?
- Conoscete qualche giocatore o una squadra in particolare?
- Avete mai guardato una partita importante? Quale?

Nota CULTURALE

Dal 1946 il **Totocalcio** e, più recentemente, il **Totogol** (nato nel 1992) sono **giochi a premi** molto diffusi in Italia. L'obiettivo è quello di pronosticare° i risultati delle partite di calcio settimanali. Per molti italiani compilare la schedina (1 per la squadra che gioca in casa, 2 per la squadra in trasferta e X per il pareggio) è un passatempo e un'occasione per scommettere°. **Fare 13**, cioè indovinare il risultato di tredici partite, è un'espressione entrata nel linguaggio comune che significa «vincere tutto».

pronosticare *predict* **scommettere** *to bet*

2 Assign a couple of students the task of keeping track of the results on the blackboard: **sport alla TV, sport allo stadio,** and **sport da praticare.**

3 After giving the pairs a few minutes to gather the information they remember, you might want to ask a few students to share their information. You could also fill in some gaps and present some further soccer information and/or anecdotes from your personal experience.

RETE!

Reading

«Perché, perché la domenica mi lasci sempre sola per andare a vedere la partita di pallone?» cantava Rita Pavone nel 1962 in una delle classiche canzoni italiane sul calcio, lo sport nazionale. Infatti, la domenica è il giorno in cui ancora oggi si svolgono le partite, seguite alla televisione dalla maggioranza dei tifosi. Molti vanno allo stadio per guardare la squadra del cuore° dal vivo°. Il silenzio dei pomeriggi domenicali è interrotto da grida° entusiaste provenienti da case e appartamenti quando i giocatori segnano un gol e, la sera, dai canti a squarciagola degli autobus pieni di tifosi che rientrano dallo stadio.

Il calcio è uno sport imprevedibile° che combina il gioco di squadra con il talento individuale. Le sorti° della partita possono cambiare da un momento all'altro e nel cuore degli spettatori italiani si alternano disperazione ed estasi nel giro di pochi minuti.

Il calcio è un'industria: dalla vendita dei giornali specializzati, come *La Gazzetta dello Sport*, quotidiano dalle pagine rosa letto avidamente per strada e nei bar, al commercio delle maglie. I giocatori di calcio in Italia sono celebrità, più importanti di attori e musicisti, e guadagnano° milioni di euro all'anno. Le grandi società proprietarie delle squadre vendono e acquistano giocatori: nel giro di pochi giorni un calciatore può trovarsi a giocare contro quelli che l'anno prima erano i suoi più leali compagni. Le migliori venti squadre del calcio italiano competono in Serie A. La stagione è molto lunga e va da settembre a maggio. La squadra che finisce al primo posto vince lo scudetto° mentre le ultime tre classificate retrocedono° in Serie B. La rivalità tra i tifosi è intensa, ma può anche diventare eccessiva e purtroppo negli stadi ci sono stati deplorevoli episodi di violenza o di razzismo. Tra le squadre più antiche e conosciute ci sono il Torino e la Juventus (di Torino), la Roma e la Lazio (di Roma), il Milan e l'Inter (di Milano), il Napoli e la Fiorentina che sono spesso chiamate affettuosamente con il colore delle loro maglie: per esempio «i bianconeri» (la Juventus), «i neroazzuri» (l'Inter) e «i giallorossi» (la Roma).

La passione per il calcio che normalmente divide i tifosi delle varie squadre riesce però a unire un intero paese quando a giocare è la squadra nazionale italiana di calcio.

Anche la squadra nazionale italiana ha un soprannome ispirato al colore delle maglie «gli Azzurri». La nazionale azzurra, formata dai migliori giocatori, gioca nei tornei europei e mondiali, come i Campionati Europei e la Coppa del Mondo. Secondo il regolamento, i giocatori della squadra nazionale devono essere cittadini italiani, al contrario delle squadre di club che possono acquistare calciatori di diverse nazionalità. Finora gli Azzurri hanno vinto quattro campionati del mondo: a Roma nel 1934, a Parigi nel 1938, a Madrid nel 1982 e a Berlino nel 2006. Forza Azzurri! ∎

favorite
live
shouts
unpredictable
outcome
earn
"little shield"
are relegated

I MONDIALI

Dopo la strepitosa vittoria alla Coppa del Mondo di calcio del 2006, gli Azzurri hanno lasciato i tifosi a bocca asciutta per ben tre Mondiali consecutivi—Sudafrica, Brasile e Russia. Infatti, non riuscendo a superare il primo turno°, hanno deluso le speranze dei tifosi italiani che hanno seguito con trepidazione le partite della loro squadra. Nonostante le polemiche° e le delusioni, la passione degli italiani per il calcio rimane inalterata, come la speranza nella ricostruzione di una squadra nazionale che ritornerà presto ai vertici°.

turno *round* **polemiche** *controversy* **vertici** *top*

Analisi

1

Comprensione Abbina ogni frase nella colonna di sinistra con la fine appropriata nella colonna di destra.

1. La domenica negli stadi italiani ___f___
2. Il calcio è ___g___
3. La Coppa del Mondo ___e___
4. I tifosi ___l___
5. Il principale giornale sportivo italiano ___d___
6. I giocatori di calcio italiani sono ___h___
7. Quando un calciatore viene comprato da un'altra squadra ___c___
8. I tifosi cantano ___i___
9. «Il Torino» è ___b___
10. «Gli Azzurri» sono ___a___

a. la squadra nazionale di calcio italiana.
b. la squadra di calcio della città di Torino.
c. può trovarsi a giocare contro la propria ex-squadra.
d. si chiama *La Gazzetta dello Sport.*
e. è il più importante torneo di calcio della Nazionale italiana.
f. si sentono le grida e le canzoni dei tifosi durante la partita.
g. uno sport che combina il gioco di squadra con il talento individuale.
h. celebri come gli attori e i cantanti.
i. a squarciagola.
l. guardano la partita, vanno allo stadio e indossano la maglia dei loro giocatori preferiti.

2

Il tuo sport In coppia, parlate dello sport nazionale del vostro paese. Confrontate le vostre conclusioni con il resto della classe.

- Come sono i tifosi?
- Che effetto ha sulla vita del paese?
- Ha ispirato libri, canzoni o film?
- Ha influenzato l'economia, la politica o la storia nazionale?
- Ha mai causato problemi di traffico?

3

Oltre lo stadio In coppia, esprimete la vostra opinione su eventi legati allo sport che hanno ripercussioni sociali.

	Eventi	Opinione
la violenza nello sport		
il mercato dei giocatori		
lo stipendio delle celebrità sportive		
sport femminili e maschili		
sport amatoriali (*amateur*) e professionistici		

4

Inventiamo una squadra In piccoli gruppi, create la vostra squadra.

- Quale sport pratica la squadra?
- Avete un nome?
- Come sono le vostre maglie?
- Quale slogan volete usare?

Practice more at
vhlcentral.com.

Preparazione  Vocabulary Tools

A proposito dell'autore

Autore satirico, prolifico e versatile, **Stefano Benni** (1947) ha scritto romanzi, racconti, opere teatrali, poesie, articoli ed è anche regista cinematografico. Benni è appassionato di jazz e creatore della *Pluriversità dell'Immaginazione*, un ciclo di conferenze legate all'Associazione culturale Italo Calvino. I generi letterari che predilige (*prefers*) vanno dalla fantascienza al fantastico, dalla fiaba (*fable*) moderna e disincantata alla quotidianità, sempre trattata con umorismo e a volte con un fondo di amarezza (*bitterness*). Benni continua a scrivere e a promuovere attività culturali. I suoi libri sono tradotti in moltissime lingue.

2 Point out that many street players (**artisti di strada**) are actually out-of-work musicians, and sometimes they get discovered playing in the streets, subway stations, coffee houses, etc. Famous street performers include Eric Clapton, Rod Stewart, Bob Dylan, Joni Mitchell, Tracy Chapman, and Jewel, among others. In Italy street artists can even join the **Federazione nazionale artisti di strada** (www.fnas.org) and get assistance and funds for promoting their trade.

Vocabolario della lettura		Vocabolario utile
bastare *to be sufficient*	**il pezzo** *piece*	**la bontà** *goodness*
la classifica *chart*	**gli spiccioli** *small change*	**la coscienza** *conscience*
fatato/a *enchanted*	**lo spinotto** *plug*	**la fiaba/favola** *fairy tale*
fingere *to pretend*	**suonare** *to play*	**la magia** *magic*
la ninnananna *lullaby*	**le zeppe** *wedge shoes*	**la morale** *moral*

1 Definizioni Trova la definizione adatta a ogni parola.

c	1. la favola	a.	la lezione di un racconto
e	2. gli spiccioli	b.	una canzone in rima per dormire
d	3. le zeppe	c.	un racconto di fantasia
a	4. la morale	d.	un tipo di scarpe
f	5. la bontà	e.	pochi soldi in contanti
b	6. la ninnananna	f.	la qualità di essere buoni

2 Preparazione Fate le seguenti domande a un(a) compagno/a.

1. Che tipo di persona sceglie di suonare per la strada?

2. In che modo un suonatore di strada è diverso da un mendicante?

3. Cosa pensi dei suonatori di strada? Di solito dove li incontri? Li trovi bravi? Ti fermi ad ascoltarli? Perché sì o no?

4. Se ti piacciono, dai dei soldi?

5. Suoni uno strumento? Ti verrebbe mai in mente di suonarlo per la strada? Perché sì o perché no?

3 Discussione In coppia, rispondete alle domande.

1. Il racconto che segue è tratto dal libro *Il bar sotto il mare*. Secondo te, che tipo di libro è? Come può esistere un bar sotto il mare?

2. Hai mai letto *Alice nel paese delle meraviglie*? Qual è il principio fondamentale di quel libro?

3. Conosci altre fiabe in inglese in cui il mondo è alla rovescia (*upside-down*)?

4. Immagina di avere un oggetto magico: cos'è e cosa può fare?

Nota CULTURALE

Il bar sotto il mare è una raccolta° di racconti, pubblicata nel 1987. All'inizio della storia il protagonista vede un anziano signore che entra nel mare e scompare° sott'acqua. Lo vuole salvare° e così si ritrova in un fantastico bar sommerso°. Come nel *Decameron* di Boccaccio o *I racconti di Canterbury* di Chaucer, i diversi personaggi del bar raccontano tutti una storia per passare il tempo. La caratteristica comune a tutti è l'elemento assurdo e inaspettato.

raccolta *collection* **scompare** *to disappear* **salvare** *to save* **sommerso** *submerged*

 Practice more at **vhlcentral.com**.

LA CHITARRA *magica*

STEFANO BENNI

Il racconto della ragazza col ciuffo

Ogni ingiustizia ci offende, quando non ci procuri direttamente alcun profitto.

—LUC DE VAUVENARGUES

Audio: Dramatic Reading

C'era un giovane musicista di nome Peter che suonava la chitarra agli angoli delle strade. Racimolava° così i soldi per proseguire° gli studi al Conservatorio: voleva diventare una grande rock star. Ma i soldi non bastavano°, perché faceva molto freddo e in strada c'erano pochi passanti°.

Un giorno, mentre Peter stava suonando «Crossroads» si avvicinò° un vecchio con un mandolino.

—Potresti cedermi° il tuo posto? È sopra un tombino° e ci fa più caldo.

—Certo—disse Peter che era di animo° buono.

—Potresti per favore prestarmi la tua sciarpa°? Ho tanto freddo.

—Certo—disse Peter che era di animo buono.

—Potresti darmi un po' di soldi? Oggi non c'è gente, ho raggranellato° pochi spiccioli e ho fame.

—Certo—disse Peter che eccetera. Aveva solo dieci monete nel cappello e le diede tutte al vecchio.

Allora avvenne° un miracolo: il vecchio si trasformò in un omone° truccato con rimmel° e rossetto°, una lunga criniera° arancione, una palandrana° di lamé e zeppe alte dieci centimetri.

L'omone disse:—Io sono Lucifumandro, il mago degli effetti speciali. Dato che sei stato buono con me ti regalerò una chitarra fatata. Suona da sola qualsiasi° pezzo, basta che tu glielo ordini. Ma ricordati: essa può essere usata solo dai puri di cuore. Guai° al malvagio° che la suonerà! Succederebbero cose orribili!

Ciò detto si udì° nell'aria un tremendo accordo di mi settima° e il mago sparì°. A terra restò una chitarra elettrica a forma di freccia°, con la cassa° di madreperla e le corde d'oro zecchino°. Peter la imbracciò° e disse:

—Suonami «Ehi Joe».

La chitarra si mise a eseguire il pezzo come neanche° Jimi Hendrix, e Peter non dovette far altro che fingere di suonarla. Si fermò moltissima gente e cominciarono a piovere soldini° nel cappello di Peter.

Quando Peter smise di suonare, gli si avvicinò un uomo con un cappotto di caimano°. Disse che era un manager discografico e avrebbe fatto di Peter una rock star. Infatti tre mesi dopo Peter era primo in tutte le classifiche americane italiane francesi e malgasce°. La sua chitarra a freccia era diventata un simbolo per milioni di giovani e la sua tecnica era invidiata da tutti i chitarristi.

Una notte, dopo uno spettacolo trionfale, Peter credendo di essere solo sul palco°, disse alla chitarra di suonargli qualcosa per rilassarsi. La chitarra gli suonò una ninnananna. Ma nascosto° tra le quinte° del teatro c'era il malvagio Black Martin, un chitarrista invidioso del suo successo. Egli scoprì così che la chitarra era magica. Scivolò° alle spalle di Peter e gli infilò° giù per il collo° uno spinotto° a tremila volt, uccidendolo. Poi rubò la chitarra e la dipinse° di rosso.

La sera dopo, gli artisti erano riuniti in concerto per ricordare Peter prematuramente scomparso°. Suonarono Prince, Ponce e Parmentier, Sting, Stingsteen e Stronhaim. Poi salì sul palco il malvagio Black Martin.

Sottovoce ordinò alla chitarra:

—Suonami «Satisfaction».

Sapete cosa accadde°?

La chitarra suonò meglio di tutti i Rolling Stones insieme. Così il malvagio Black Martin diventò una rock star e in breve nessuno ricordò più il buon Peter.

Era una chitarra magica con un difetto di fabbricazione°. ■

Glosses (left and right margins):

- He scraped together
- continue
- were not enough
- passers-by
- approached
- let me have
- manhole cover
- heart
- scarf
- I have scraped together
- took place
- big man
- mascara/lipstick/mane
- long loose coat
- any
- Heaven help
- wicked man
- was heard
- E seven/disappeared
- arrow/body
- pure gold/he slung on his arm
- better than
- coins
- cayman
- Madagascan
- stage
- hidden
- wings
- He slid
- put/neck
- plug
- painted
- dead
- happened
- manufacturing

Many of the musicians Benni mentions are invented. Even though Ponce and Parmentier are actual names, the idea is to create fake foreign-sounding names, to point out, polemically, the Eighties' craze for any music in English. The book was published in 1987.

Analisi

1

Vero o falso? Indica se l'affermazione è **vera** o **falsa**. Dopo, in coppia, correggete le affermazioni false.

Vero	Falso	
☐	☑	1. Peter suona il sassofono.
☑	☐	2. Peter presta la sua sciarpa al vecchio.
☑	☐	3. La chitarra è magica e ha istruzioni precise.
☑	☐	4. La chitarra suona da sola.
☐	☑	5. Black Martin è un amico di Peter.
☐	☑	6. La chitarra funziona secondo le regole dette dal vecchio.

2

Comprensione Rispondi alle domande. Dopo, in coppia, discutete le domande che avete segnato con **d**.

1. Perché il vecchio chiede tante cose a Peter?
   a. perché si sente solo   b. perché è molto curioso
   c. perché Peter è di animo buono   d. perché nelle fiabe ci sono formule ripetitive

2. Che tipo di chitarra gli lascia il mago?
   a. una chitarra classica   b. una chitarra di madreperla con le corde d'oro
   c. una chitarra da concerto rock   d. sia b che c

3. Qual è la magia della chitarra?
   a. suona da sola   b. riconosce le persone buone   c. fa volare
   d. ha le corde d'oro

4. Perché ha successo Peter?
   a. perché ha talento   b. perché i caimani portano fortuna   c. perché suona come Jimi Hendrix   d. perché ha un contratto con una casa discografica

5. Come prende la chitarra Black Martin?
   a. chiede a Peter di prestargliela   b. la trova su una sedia   c. uccide Peter
   d. la ruba mentre Peter dorme

6. Perché fanno un concerto la sera dopo?
   a. perché il mondo dello spettacolo è crudele   b. perché Peter manca a tutti
   c. perché è un'occasione per fare soldi   d. forse tutte e tre le risposte

3

Personaggi

A. Indica le parole dell'elenco che descrivono i personaggi.

affarista	criminale	di talento	generoso	malvagio
assassino	di buon cuore	disonesto	interessato	opportunista

1. Peter   2. Vecchio   3. Manager discografico   4. Black Martin

B. Confronta le tue risposte con un(a) compagno/a e discutete le differenze.

4

Esaminare In coppia, usate la tabella per determinare se *La chitarra magica* segue o non segue la convenzione delle fiabe. Alla fine aggiungete due frasi originali.

Tipico delle fiabe	Segue la convenzione?	NON segue la convenzione?
1. C'è una persona buona che ha un problema.		
2. La persona buona è anche generosa con chi ha bisogno.		
3. Un vecchio insignificante si rivela un mago.		
4. La persona buona ha un beneficio per la sua bontà.		
5. Una persona cattiva cerca di avere lo stesso beneficio.		
6. Il cattivo fa del male al protagonista.		
7. Il bene alla fine trionfa.		
8. Il cattivo è punito.		

5

Cosa pensano? In coppia, improvvisate una conversazione tra Black Martin e Peter, se Peter si svegliasse.

Modello   **Peter:**   Cosa fai?

Black Martin: Niente… passavo di qui…

Peter: Perché hai in mano quello spinotto?

6

Discutere In coppia, rispondete alle domande.

1. Peter è davvero un personaggio totalmente onesto?
2. Qual è il ruolo dell'opportunismo in questa fiaba?
3. Perché il bene non trionfa in questo racconto?
4. Tutte le fiabe hanno una morale più o meno esplicita. Secondo te, hanno una funzione sociale al di là dell'educazione dei bambini?

7

Una conversazione sulle fiabe Conosci il finale originale di queste fiabe? Perché ti piacciono o non ti piacciono? Scegli una fiaba dalla lista e cambia il finale con due compagni.

La sirenetta	Cenerentola	Cappuccetto Rosso
La bella addormentata	(*Cinderella*)	La tua fiaba preferita
Pinocchio	I tre porcellini	

8

Tema Scegli uno dei seguenti argomenti e scrivi una breve composizione.

- Cosa vuole dire la citazione da Vauvenargues all'inizio del racconto? Secondo te, la morale della gente è legata agli interessi personali e cambia secondo la convenienza? Pensa a degli esempi specifici.

- Peter muore ed è dimenticato velocemente. Perché, secondo te, alcuni artisti del mondo dello spettacolo non vengono mai dimenticati? Cosa crea un mito?

- Immagina di dover scrivere una fiaba originale. Qual è la morale della tua fiaba?

Nota CULTURALE

Il formalista russo Vladimir Propp è stato il primo a teorizzare gli elementi base dei racconti folkloristici e di fantasia (le fiabe). Anche se le sue teorie non sono perfette, è vero che ci sono elementi comuni a tutte le fiabe. Questo appare evidente anche nella raccolta *Fiabe italiane* (1956), del famoso scrittore **Italo Calvino**. È importante dire che le fiabe non devono essere sempre a lieto fine. Al contrario, le fiabe hanno una forte struttura morale e il finale rispecchia spesso l'etica del paese d'origine.

6 Ask additional questions:
5. Conosci fiabe in cui l'ordine costituito è rovesciato?
6. È giusto agire secondo coscienza? Perché?
7. Secondo te, esiste davvero la «giustizia poetica», un meccanismo che alla fine punisce i malvagi? Se ci credi, come ti aiuta questa nozione nella vita di tutti i giorni?

7 Point out that in the original stories, the Little Mermaid dies for love and becomes sea foam; the Wolf gets killed in Little Red Riding Hood and in the Three Little Pigs; Pinocchio is extremely undisciplined and rude to both his father and the cricket; etc. All fairy tales have a serious potential for tragedy leading up to the happy ending.

Practice more at vhlcentral.com.

Pratica

La proposizione principale

Il corpo di un saggio si organizza in vari paragrafi nei quali si presentano gli argomenti per difendere la tesi esposta nell'introduzione. Ognuno di questi paragrafi comprende una proposizione principale. Questa proposizione:

- fissa e riassume l'idea principale del paragrafo;
- è utile per il lettore perché offre un'idea chiara sul contenuto del paragrafo;
- è utile per l'autore perché specifica l'informazione che si vuole dare.

1 Before beginning the **Preparazione** activity, review the idea of topic sentences with students. The topic sentence should make the intention of the whole paragraph clear and easy to follow.

1

Preparazione In coppia, leggete il seguente brano e individuate la proposizione principale.

Anna ama studiare l'inglese, ma fino a poco tempo fa aveva sempre paura di fare una brutta figura quando parlava. Anche se è molto timida, un giorno ha fatto una domanda in inglese a uno sconosciuto a New York perché si è persa. Dopo una lunga camminata, Anna ha finalmente trovato la strada giusta per raggiungere il teatro che cercava: per la prima volta si è sentita sicura del suo inglese!

2 Before working on the **Saggio**, have students discuss Americans' attitudes towards their favorite sports.

2

Saggio Scegli uno di questi argomenti e scrivi un saggio.

- Il tuo saggio deve far riferimento a uno o due dei quattro brani di questa lezione contenuti in **Cortometraggio**, **Immagina**, **Cultura** e **Letteratura**.
- Deve includere almeno tre paragrafi per difendere la tua tesi e ogni paragrafo deve contenere una proposizione principale.
- Il saggio deve essere lungo almeno due pagine.

Nel brano (*piece*) Rete! si parla dell'estasi dei tifosi per le vittorie della propria squadra e della disperazione per le sconfitte. Spesso queste scene degenerano e si assiste a veri e propri atti criminali. Che cosa può trasformare un tifoso in un criminale? Che cosa può fare la società per combattere questi fenomeni?

In una realtà quotidiana sempre in movimento, molte persone cercano «sfogo» (*outlet*) nei passatempi. Secondo te, quando questo tempo è ben speso e quando invece diventa tempo perso? In una realtà quotidiana sempre in movimento, molte persone cercano rifugio (*refuge*) dallo stress nei passatempi. Pensi che dedicare del tempo libero a queste attività serva a dare la carica necessaria per affrontare nuovi impegni o sia una distrazione inutile? Secondo te, quando questo tempo è ben speso e quando invece diventa tempo perso?

Have a discussion about how people are influenced by friends, family, or society to become something they are not.

Nel cortometraggio Bulli si nasce, emerge in modo surreale la figura di due genitori che, influenzati dalle regole sociali, spingono il proprio figlio a diventare un «bullo». È giusto forzare la personalità di una persona per adeguarsi alle esigenze della società?

INSTRUCTIONAL RESOURCES
Task-based activities

I passatempi Vocabulary Tools

Lo sport

l'allenatore/allenatrice *coach*
l'alpinismo *mountain climbing*
l'arbitro *referee*
l'automobilismo *car racing*
il calcio *soccer*
il campo di/da gioco *playing field*
il canottaggio *rowing*
il club sportivo *sports club*
l'equitazione *horseback riding*
la gara *race*
il giocatore/la giocatrice *player*
il pareggio *tie*
il pattinaggio (sul ghiaccio) (ice-)skating
il pugilato *boxing*
lo sci (di fondo) *(cross-country) skiing*
la squadra *team*
il/la tifoso/a *fan*

allenarsi *to train*
andare in palestra *to go to the gym*
farsi male *to injure oneself*
scalare *to climb*
segnare (un gol) *to score (a goal)*
vincere/perdere/pareggiare (una partita) *to win/lose/tie (a game)*

Il tempo libero

il biglietto *ticket*
il biliardino *foosball*
il biliardo *billiards*
l'escursionismo *hiking*
il gioco di società *board game*
il gruppo (musicale) *band*
il luna park *amusement park*
la mostra *exhibition*
la prima *opening night*
gli scacchi *chess*
lo spettacolo *show*
il videogioco *videogame*

applaudire *to clap*
fare campeggio *to camp*
fare la fila *to wait in line*
festeggiare *to celebrate*
giocare a nascondino *to play hide-and-seek*

prendere qualcosa da bere/mangiare *to get something to drink/eat*
valere la pena *to be worth it*

buffo/a *funny*
da non perdere *must-see*
tutto esaurito *sold out*

Lo shopping e l'abbigliamento

l'abito da sera *evening dress*
il cappotto *coat*
il centro commerciale *mall*
l'impermeabile *raincoat*
le infradito *flip-flops*
i saldi (di fine stagione) *(end-of-season) sales*
le scarpe da ginnastica/tennis *sneakers*
i tacchi alti *high heels*
il vestito (da uomo/donna) *suit/dress*

cambiare *to exchange*
dare un'occhiata *to take a look*
provare *to try on*

alla moda *fashionable*
firmato/a *designer brand*
passato/a di moda *out-of-style*
raffinato/a *refined*

Cortometraggio

il bullo *bully*
il burattino *puppet*
la coincidenza *coincidence*
l'ecografia *ultrasound*
il fenomeno *phenomenon*
la genetica *genetics*
le lenti a specchio *mirrored lenses*
la merendina *snack*
l'orgoglio *pride*
l'ottico *optician*
il/la quattrocchi *four eyes*
il/la secchione/a *student who studies too hard*
la suora *nun*

improvvisare *to improvise*

sminuire (-isc) *to play down*
competitivo/a *competitive*
prenatale *prenatal*

Cultura

il calciatore *soccer player*
il calcio di rigore *penalty kick*
il centravanti *center forward*
la difesa *defense*
la maglia *jersey*
il pallone *soccer; ball*
il portiere *goalkeeper*
il regolamento *regulations*
la rete *goal; net*
il torneo *tournament*

giocare in casa/trasferta *to play a home/away game*
parare *to save*
pareggiare *to tie*
scendere in campo *to join the game*
tifare (per) *to root for*

leale *loyal*

a squarciagola *at the top of one's voice*

Letteratura

la bontà *goodness*
la classifica *chart*
la coscienza *conscience*
la fiaba/favola *fairy tale*
la magia *magic*
la morale *moral*
la ninnananna *lullaby*
il pezzo *piece*
gli spiccioli *small change*
lo spinotto *plug*
le zeppe *wedge shoes*

bastare *to be sufficient*
fingere *to pretend*
suonare *to play*

fatato/a *enchanted*

Il valore delle idee

La politica, anche se spesso ci appare lontana
e incomprensibile, è un aspetto importante
della società. I governi con i loro rappresentanti
hanno il compito di guidare i cittadini e garantire
i loro bisogni fondamentali come la giustizia e il
bene comune. Ti interessi di politica? Pensi che sia
importante per i giovani avere un'opinione politica
ed esprimerla?

129

154

Destinazione: LOMBARDIA

PREVIEW Have students look at the photo and speculate about what is going on. Ask: **È una dimostrazione politica? È pacifica? Perché le persone protestano? Sei mai stato in una dimostrazione? Quando?**

La giustizia e la politica

 Vocabulary Tools

Le leggi e i diritti

la cittadinanza *citizenship*
la criminalità *crime*
il crimine *felony*
i diritti umani *human rights*
l'emigrazione (f.) *emigration*
la giustizia *justice*
l'immigrazione (f.) *immigration*

la libertà *freedom*
l'uguaglianza *equality*

abusare *to abuse*
approvare/passare una legge
  to pass a law

difendere *to defend*
emigrare *to emigrate*
giudicare *to judge*
imprigionare *to imprison*

analfabeta *illiterate*
colpevole *guilty*
(in)giusto/a *(un)fair*
ineguale *unequal*
innocente *innocent*
(il)legale *(il)legal*
oppresso/a *oppressed*
uguale *equal*

SINONIMI E CONTRARI
la giustizia ≠ l'ingiustizia
l'uguaglianza ≠ la disuguaglianza

VOCABOLARIO SUPPLEMENTARE
l'immigrazione interna *internal immigration*
l'immigrazione clandestina
illegal immigration
l'emigrazione (f.) di massa
mass emigration
l'emigrazione (f.) temporanea
temporary emigration

La politica

l'abuso di potere *abuse of power*
la crudeltà *cruelty*
la democrazia *democracy*
la dittatura *dictatorship*
l'esercito *army*
il governo *government*
la guerra (civile) *(civil) war*
la pace *peace*
il partito politico *political party*

la politica *politics*
la sconfitta *defeat*
la vittoria *victory*

dedicarsi a *to dedicate oneself to*
eleggere *to elect*
governare *to govern*
influenzare *to influence*
vincere/perdere le elezioni
  to win/lose the election
votare *to vote*

conservatore/conservatrice
  conservative
liberale *liberal*
moderato/a *moderate*
pacifico/a *peaceful*
pacifista *pacifist*
potente *powerful*
vittorioso/a *victorious*

Explain that the Italian Armed Forces
include four different branches: **l'Esercito**
(*Army*), **la Marina Militare** (*Navy*),
l'Aeronautica Militare (*Air Force*), and **i
Carabinieri** (*Military Police*). In addition,
La Polizia di Stato (*Civil Police*) patrols

La gente

l'attivista (m., f.) *activist*
l'avvocato (m., f.) *lawyer*
il/la criminale *criminal*
il/la deputato/a *congressman/
congresswoman*
il/la giudice *judge*
la giuria *jury*
il/la ladro/a *thief*

il/la politico/a *politician*
il/la presidente *president*
il/la terrorista *terrorist*
il/la testimone *witness*
la vittima *victim*

La sicurezza e i pericoli

l'arma *weapon*
la minaccia *threat*
la paura *fear*
il pericolo *danger*
lo scandalo *scandal*
la sicurezza *safety*

il terrorismo *terrorism*
la violenza *violence*

combattere *to fight*
promuovere *to promote*
salvare *to save*
spiare *to spy*

highways, railways, and airports, controls
immigration, and maintains public security,
while **la Guardia di Finanza** (*Fraud Squad*)
investigates tax evasion, money laundering,
and drug traffic. Lastly, the **Polizia
Municipale** or **Vigili** (*Local Police*) enforces
traffic and parking regulations.

INSTRUCTIONAL RESOURCES
Audioscripts, Answer Keys, Lab MP3s
SAM/WebSAM: WB, LM

Pratica e comunicazione

1

L'intruso Trova la parola o l'espressione che non c'entra.

1. **I diritti umani**
   a. l'uguaglianza   b. la giustizia
   c. l'abuso di potere d. la libertà

2. **Le professioni**
   a. l'avvocato   b. il pacifista
   c. il giudice   d. il presidente

3. **La politica**
   a. la dittatura   b. la democrazia
   c. il governo   d. la giuria

4. **I pericoli**
   a. il testimone   b. la minaccia
   c. la criminalità   d. il terrorismo

5. **La politica**
   a. conservatore   b. moderato
   c. innocente   d. liberale

6. **Entità governative**
   a. il governo   b. l'attivista
   c. l'esercito   d. il partito politico

Nota CULTURALE

Per i nomi di professione non sempre si ricorre all'uso della desinenza° **–essa** per formare il femminile, quindi è meglio non usare parole come **l'avvocatessa**, **la deputatessa**, **la presidentessa**, ma lasciare invariato il nome maschile e aggiungere il nome della persona, per esempio **l'avvocato Giulia Bongiorno**, **il presidente della Camera dei deputati Laura Boldrini**. Fanno eccezione la **professoressa** e la **dottoressa**, parole comunemente usate.

desinenza *ending*

2

Abbinamenti Collega ogni parola alla sua definizione.

__d__ 1. andare a vivere in un altro paese, soprattutto per motivi di lavoro

__c__ 2. proibito dalla legge

__b__ 3. possibilità di agire (*act*) senza restrizioni

__e__ 4. principio secondo il quale tutti gli uomini hanno gli stessi diritti

__a__ 5. chi opera attivamente all'interno di un'organizzazione

a. attivista
b. la libertà
c. illegale
d. l'emigrazione
e. l'uguaglianza

3

Domande personali In gruppi di tre, fatevi le seguenti domande. Some answers will vary.

1. A quale partito politico ti senti più vicino/a?

2. Hai votato alle ultime elezioni?

3. Chi è il presidente del tuo paese? Ti piace il suo programma politico? Perché?

4. C'è un personaggio politico che ammiri particolarmente? Perché?

5. Secondo te, quali sono i principali problemi del tuo paese?

6. Conosci qualcuno che è immigrato in questo paese? Quali sono stati i problemi principali che ha dovuto affrontare (*face*)?

4

Diritti umani Immagina di essere un attivista per i diritti umani. Discuti i seguenti punti con un(a) compagno/a.

1. Per quale causa ti batti (*fight for*), i diritti umani, l'emigrazione, la giustizia sociale? Perché?

2. Quali problemi combatti? Come cerchi di risolvere questi problemi?

3. Quali mezzi utilizzi per sensibilizzare (*increase awareness in*) l'opinione pubblica su questi problemi?

TEACHING OPTION Have students compare and contrast different types of government and comment on what basic rights a good government must provide. After the discussion, break the class into groups and have them imagine a theoretical government and explain to the class how their system would work.

Practice more at **vhlcentral.com**.

INSTRUCTIONAL RESOURCES
Supersite: Video, Script & Translation
SAM/WebSAM: WB

Preparazione

Vocabolario del cortometraggio

il faro *lighthouse*
inaffidabile *unreliable*
nascosto/a *hidden*
pescare *to fish*
la poppa *stern*

promesso *promised*
la prua *bow*
il punto di riferimento *reference point*
salvo/a *safe*
la spigola *bass (fish)*

Vocabolario utile

il boccaglio *snorkel*
la camera d'aria *inner tube*
il clandestino *illegal immigrant*
la guardia costiera *coast guard*

la maschera *mask*
la muta *wet suit*
naufragare *to sink, wreck*
il naufrago *castaway*
le pinne *flippers*
il subacqueo *scuba diver*

---

1 **Pratica** Completa il dialogo con le parole nuove.

MARCELLO Mimì, vuoi venire a (1) ___pescare___ in barca con me oggi?

MIMÌ Certo! Possiamo andare vicino al vecchio (2) ___faro___! Ho sentito che lì ci sono molti pesci, soprattutto le (3) ___spigole___. È un posto (4) ___nascosto___: non lo conosce nessuno.

MARCELLO Va bene, è un posto molto vicino. Oggi il tempo è (5) ___inaffidabile___. Hai visto quante nuvole? Preferisco non andare troppo lontano se piove.

MIMÌ Sai quali sono i (6) ___punti di riferimento___ per arrivarci? A nord c'è un'isola e a ovest si vede la costa.

MARCELLO Perfetto. Per fare pesca subacquea abbiamo bisogno di indossare la (7) ___muta___; per vedere sott'acqua ci metteremo la (8) ___maschera___; per nuotare più velocemente porteremo le (9) ___pinne___ ai piedi; e per respirare useremo il (10) ___boccaglio___.

Preparazione

2 **A. In coppia, fatevi a turno queste domande.**

1. Sei mai andato/a in barca o in nave? Ti sei divertito/a?
2. Conosci qualcuno che soffre il mal di mare (*seasickness*)?
3. Sai nuotare bene? Come hai imparato? In quali mari, laghi e fiumi hai nuotato?
4. Quanto puoi resistere sott'acqua senza respirare?
5. Hai mai fatto snorkeling o immersioni subacquee? Dove? Che cosa hai visto sott'acqua?
6. Sei mai andato/a a pesca? Qual è il pesce più grande o più strano che hai pescato?

B. Raccontate una delle esperienze dell'altro/a studente(ssa) al resto della classe.

3 **Immigrazione** In coppia, esprimete le vostre opinioni sulle questioni seguenti.

1. In generale, cosa pensi dell'immigrazione?
2. Perché si distingue tra immigrazione legale e illegale?
3. Conosci degli immigrati? Perché? Da quali paesi provengono e da quanto tempo sono nel tuo paese?
4. Hai mai parlato con un clandestino? Perché? In quale lingua?

4 **Clandestinità** In piccoli gruppi, discutete le seguenti domande.

1. Ci sono dei clandestini nel tuo paese?
2. Come arrivano? Per mare, per terra o in aereo?
3. Perché vengono? Che tipo di lavoro fanno?
4. Quali sono le questioni legali legate all'immigrazione clandestina?

4 Circulate among the class answering any questions. When the groups are done with the activity, initiate a class discussion on immigration, covering both the students' personal experiences as well as the experiences of society overall, expanding the topic as needed.

5 **Scelte** In coppia, immaginate d'incontrare per caso un immigrato clandestino. Come vi comportate? Quali scelte fate? Discutetene aiutandovi con questi suggerimenti e spiegate le vostre motivazioni.

- Consegnarlo alle autorità
- Portarlo in un centro di accoglienza
- Portarlo a casa vostra
- Informarvi sulla sua salute
- Informarvi se ci sono altri clandestini nelle vicinanze
- Ignorarlo e avvisare la polizia

6 **Preparazione**

A. In coppia, guardate queste foto e inventate una storia. Usate questo elenco per creare la vostra storia.

- personaggi principali
- inizio della storia
- situazione da risolvere
- conclusione

B. Raccontate la vostra storia e confrontatela con il resto della classe.

Practice more at **vhlcentral.com**.

Video

Trama *Mentre nuota nel Mediterraneo, un pescatore subacqueo siciliano incontra un naufrago africano: tutti e due sono in pericolo di vita.*

MARCELLO Allora, i punti che devi tenere sono questi: la cupola di San Francesco con il Castello di Venere e «Porta Ossuna» che deve diventare bianca. La vedi?

MIMÌ Vai tranquillo, Marcello!

MIMÌ Mi sono addormentato! I punti ho perso! Marcello, sei tu? Guarda che non mi spavento° più!

MARCELLO Mimì? Mimìiiiiiiiii!

MARCELLO Vieni, andiamo al faro… là… al faro… nuotiamo insieme.

NAUFRAGO (*in broken Italian*) Mare entrato nella barca. Nero, non vedere niente. Avere paura, tutti gridare. C'erano delle donne, dei bambini…

Nota
CULTURALE

Mare Nostrum

Il titolo del corto viene da *Mare Nostrum*. È il nome che gli antichi Romani davano al **Mediterraneo** (il nome attuale in latino significa «in mezzo alle terre»). Molti clandestini attraversano questo mare, soprattutto dalle coste settentrionali dell'Africa. Negli ultimi anni, numerose imbarcazioni che trasportavano i clandestini hanno fatto naufragio, con un tragico numero di vittime.

Point out that the castaway is most likely from a French-speaking country in Central or West Africa. He may have reached the coast of Libya or Tunisia by land to then cross the Mediterranean on a raft. Show students a map of the Mediterranean and point out the proximity between Italy and North Africa.

👓 Sullo **SCHERMO**

Mentre guardi il corto, indica l'ordine di questi eventi:

__2__ Marcello prende un pesce con la fiocina (*harpoon*).

__1__ Mimì arriva al porto.

__4__ Marcello incontra il clandestino.

__5__ La guardia costiera si avvicina all'isola.

__3__ Mimì si addormenta.

---

spavento *scare*

Analisi

1 **Comprensione** Scegli la risposta giusta.

1. Cosa fa Marcello sott'acqua?
   (a.) Pesca una spigola.   b. Trova una barca abbandonata.   c. Vede un mostro.

2. Cosa fa Mimì mentre aspetta Marcello?
   a. Guarda i punti di riferimento.   (b.) Si addormenta.   c. Canta una canzone.

3. Mimì è terrorizzato perché _____
   a. ha perso Marcello.   b. vede i cadaveri vicino alla barca.   (c.) a. e b.

4. Cosa è successo all'amico del naufrago?
   (a.) È morto in mare.   b. È tornato a casa.   c. Lo aspetta sull'isola.

5. Il naufrago non è contento dell'arrivo della guardia costiera perché _____
   a. non vuol essere salvato.   b. ha paura di nuotare.
   (c.) ha paura che lo rimandino a casa.

6. Marcello promette al naufrago di _____
   (a.) tornare più tardi a salvarlo con la sua barca.   b. telefonare alla sua famiglia.
   c. tornare più tardi a salvarlo con Mimì.

2 **I personaggi** Associa queste affermazioni con il personaggio giusto. Dopo, in coppia, scrivete quattro nuove affermazioni e scambiatele con un'altra coppia.

<u>f</u> 1. Mimì, puoi andare da Marcello al posto mio?   a. il naufrago

<u>e</u> 2. Speriamo che sia arrivato salvo in Italia!   b. la guardia costiera

<u>b</u> 3. C'è un pescatore subacqueo in pericolo. Salviamolo!   c. Mimì

<u>a</u> 4. Tutti i miei compagni di viaggio sono morti.   d. Marcello

<u>d</u> 5. Dov'è la barca? Mimì, dove sei andato a finire?   e. la famiglia
                                                                    del naufrago
<u>c</u> 6. Pronto, guardia costiera? Non trovo più Marcello!

                                                                 f. Andrea

3 **Analisi** Associa i sentimenti al personaggio e al momento corrispondente nel film. Usa il dizionario per cercare gli aggettivi che non conosci. Dopo, in coppia, aggiungete altri aggettivi per descrivere i personaggi. Some answers will vary.

a. addolorato	c. arrabbiato	e. impaurito	g. speranzoso
b. indaffarato	d. disperato	f. pensieroso	h. stanco

	all'inizio del film	a metà film	alla fine del film
Marcello	b, c	a, d, e, h	f, h
Naufrago	a, d, e, h	a, d, e, h	g, h

4 **Marcello e il naufrago** In coppia, parlate dei personaggi principali del corto.

Marcello	Che tipo è? Cosa fa di professione? Qual è il suo hobby? Tornerà per salvare il naufrago? Perché?
Naufrago	Perché ha affrontato un viaggio così rischioso? Cosa ha lasciato? Cosa spera di trovare? Crede alla promessa che fa Marcello? Perché?

5

Opinioni

A. In coppia, usate la tabella e dite se le affermazioni sono confermate o negate nel film. Poi aggiungete due affermazioni nuove. *Some answers will vary.*

Opinione	Confermata dal film	Negata dal film
1. L'immigrazione è un fenomeno negativo.	☐	☑
2. I clandestini sono pericolosi.	☐	☑
3. I clandestini sono in pericolo.	☑	☐
4. È giusto aiutare le persone in difficoltà.	☑	☐
5. Gli immigrati portano via il lavoro agli italiani.	☐	☑
6. Il Mediterraneo non appartiene soltanto all'Europa.	☑	☐
7. _____	☐	☐
8. _____	☐	☐

B. Adesso proponete le vostre affermazioni al resto della classe: cosa ne pensano gli altri studenti?

6

Riflessione In gruppi di tre, scambiate le vostre opinioni sull'emigrazione e sull'immigrazione.

- Secondo voi, considerando il loro passato di nazione di emigranti, quale dovrebbe essere l'atteggiamento (*attitude*) degli italiani verso l'immigrazione?

- Cosa devono fare gli immigranti per integrarsi nel nuovo paese?

- Cosa deve fare il governo per far fronte alle necessità e ai problemi dei nuovi immigranti?

- Qual è l'atteggiamento del vostro paese verso l'immigrazione regolare e clandestina?

7

Una conversazione In piccoli gruppi, improvvisate un dialogo davanti alla classe su una di queste situazioni.

A

Marcello torna di notte al faro e aiuta il naufrago ad arrivare in Sicilia. Dopo 5 anni, il naufrago riesce a regolarizzarsi (*obtain legal status*). Decide di raccontare a Marcello la buona notizia. Cosa si dicono quando s'incontrano di nuovo?

B

Marcello torna a casa e racconta alla sua famiglia cosa è successo. Cosa ne pensano i suoi familiari? Deve tornare per salvare il naufrago oppure no?

C

Siete una famiglia di immigrati appena arrivati a Milano. Cosa fate il primo giorno in città? Di cosa avete paura? Cosa desiderate di più in quel giorno?

8

Scriviamo Scegli uno di questi argomenti e scrivi una breve composizione usando il vocabolario che hai imparato in questa lezione.

- Commenta la citazione alla fine del film: «Dedicato a tutti coloro che intraprendono un viaggio per conoscersi, migliorarsi e fuggire la sofferenza e vivere in pace su questo piccolo e tormentato pianeta». Chi sono queste persone secondo te?

- Hai un(a) parente o un amico/un'amica che è emigrato/a all'estero? Da dove? Quali difficoltà ha dovuto superare? Quali esperienze positive e negative ti ha raccontato? Cosa pensi della vita e delle idee di questa persona?

- Secondo te, quali sono gli aspetti negativi dell'immigrazione? Quali ne sono invece i benefici sociali ed economici? Qual è il punto di vista del corto?

6 You might suggest that students watch the feature *Quando sei nato non puoi più nasconderti* (2005) by Marco Tullio Giordana. Synopsis: 10-year-old Sandro is the son of a wealthy factory owner. During a cruise in Greece, Sandro is thrown overboard, and picked up by a rickety boat carrying illegal immigrants to Italy. On the boat, Sandro meets two Romanian siblings. The three end up in a waiting facility for illegal immigrants when abandoned by the two Italians in charge.

Nota
CULTURALE

Dalla fine del 1800 agli anni '60 oltre **24 milioni** di italiani sono **emigrati** in diverse parti del mondo, ma soprattutto negli Stati Uniti, in Brasile, in Argentina, nel resto d'Europa e in Australia. Alla fine del 1900 l'Italia è diventata invece meta° di **immigranti**, che adesso sono oltre 5 milioni, ovvero° l'8,4% della popolazione.

meta *destination* **ovvero** *or rather*

6 You might want to bring current articles about immigration in Italy to class, and to discuss the recent Mare Nostrum Operation as well as the concepts of **extracomunitario**, **centro di permanenza temporanea**, **seconde generazioni**, and the **ius soli** debate.

7 Help students adapt and personalize the topics before they start writing so that they become more relevant to their own experience. Encourage them to come up with concrete examples.

Practice more at **vhlcentral.com**.

INSTRUCTIONAL RESOURCES Teaching suggestions; Answer Keys
SAM/WebSAM: WB

IMMAGINA

Milano: capitale del Nord

Milano, capoluogo della regione Lombardia, è una città ricca sotto ogni punto di vista: storia, arte, economia, sport. L'appellativo° **Mediolanum** che i Romani hanno dato alla città descrive la sua collocazione geografica al centro della **pianura Padana**, e oggi questo significato si può estendere al dinamismo cosmopolita di Milano.

A Milano, infatti, è possibile viaggiare in tram o in metropolitana con persone provenienti da° ogni parte del mondo che si trovano nel capoluogo lombardo per turismo e spesso per lavoro. Milano è considerata il «cuore» formativo e professionale del Nord Italia. Le sue numerose e rinomate° università, come la **Bocconi**, il **Politecnico**, la **Cattolica**, la **Bicocca**, sono il motivo per cui migliaia di studenti e lavoratori pendolari° ogni giorno viaggiano da altre città verso Milano.

Economicamente Milano è la città più sviluppata del Nord Italia. Qui hanno la loro sede° la **Borsa valori**°, molte società multinazionali di fama mondiale, aziende del settore pubblicitario, dell'editoria°, del marketing e anche media televisivi.

Per la sua centralità, la posizione geografica di Milano è strategica e permette collegamenti con le maggiori città del Nord-Est e del Nord-Ovest, come **Torino**, **Venezia** e **Genova**, e anche con la catena alpina e i passi doganali°.

Dal punto di vista artistico e storico, Milano possiede dei tesori invidiati° da tutto il mondo: il **Duomo**; il **Teatro alla Scala**; la **Galleria Vittorio Emanuele**, famosa per i negozi esclusivi; il **Castello Sforzesco** del XV secolo; il quartiere dell'**Accademia delle belle arti** di **Brera**; i **Navigli**, canali artificiali iniziati nel XII secolo; e la chiesa di **Santa Maria delle Grazie** con il **Cenacolo Vinciano**°.

Uno dei fiori all'occhiello° della città è l'industria della moda, per cui Milano detiene° un primato mondiale. Qui hanno i loro *atelier*°

Galleria Vittorio Emanuele

MILANO E LA LOMBARDIA

Versace, **Armani**, **Dolce & Gabbana** e molti altri stilisti di fama internazionale.

Milano non è solo istruzione, finanza, arte e moda, ma anche sport. Due delle maggiori società calcistiche° di **Serie A**, l'**Inter** e il **Milan**, rappresentano la città. I rispettivi tifosi, i «nerazzurri» e i «rossoneri» che prendono il nome dal colore delle divise° dei giocatori, affollano lo stadio di **San Siro** e l'incontro° annuale più atteso è il «**derby della Madonnina**». Il derby prende il nome dalla statua che si innalza° sulla guglia° maggiore del Duomo, divenuta il simbolo di Milano.

E per concludere, il nome di Milano occupa un posto importante anche in cucina. Famosi sono, infatti, i suoi piatti tipici come la **cotoletta alla milanese**, il **risotto alla milanese** e il dolce nazionale di Natale: il **panettone**. Scoprire tutto ciò che offre questa meravigliosa città è un'avventura.

In più...

Gli *atelier* degli stilisti più famosi d'Italia e del mondo si trovano nel centro di Milano nel «**Quadrilatero della moda**»: **via Montenapoleone, via della Spiga, corso Venezia e via Manzoni**. Ma anche nel resto della città ci sono negozi d'abbigliamento per tutti i gusti dove si può acquistare un capo° alla moda.

appellativo *name* **provenienti da** *coming from* **rinomate** *renowned* **pendolari** *commuters* **sede** *location* **Borsa valori** *stock market* **editoria** *publishing* **passi doganali** *customs offices* **invidiati** *envied* **Cenacolo Vinciano** *Da Vinci's Last Supper* **fiori all'occhiello** *feathers in its cap* **detiene** *holds* **atelier** *studios* **società calcistiche** *soccer clubs* **divise** *uniforms* **incontro** *match* **si innalza** *rises* **guglia** *spire* **capo** *an item of clothing*

Vero o falso? Indica se ogni frase è **vera** o **falsa**. Correggi le frasi false. Some answers will vary.

1. Milano si trova in mezzo a una pianura. Vero.

2. I pendolari vanno a Milano per turismo. Falso. I pendolari vanno a Milano per lavoro e per studio.

3. A Milano ci sono importanti università. Vero.

4. Milano è una città difficile da raggiungere (*to reach*). Falso. La sua posizione è centrale e permette collegamenti con molte altre città.

5. L'Inter ed il Milan sono squadre di calcio. Vero.

6. La Madonnina si trova all'interno del Duomo. Falso. Si trova sulla guglia del Duomo.

7. Il gorgonzola è un formaggio pronto da mangiare appena prodotto. Falso. Il gorgonzola è pronto dopo 90–110 giorni di stagionatura.

8. Il Lago di Garda è una meta per gli sportivi e gli amanti dell'arte. Vero.

Quanto hai imparato? Rispondi alle domande. Some answers will vary.

1. Qual è il significato antico e moderno dell'appellativo Mediolanum? centralità geografica e centralità socio-culturale

2. Perché Milano è considerata la città economicamente più sviluppata del Nord Italia? Per le industrie, la finanza e la moda.

3. Che cosa sono i Navigli? canali artificiali

4. Qual è l'incontro più atteso tra l'Inter e il Milan? il derby della Madonnina

5. Quali sono le caratteristiche del formaggio gorgonzola? venature verdi-blu, muffe particolari

6. Quali sono le attività che si possono praticare sul Lago di Garda? windsurf, kitesurf

Il gorgonzola Il nome di questo formaggio deriva dalla città in cui è nato, nelle vicinanze di Milano. Le caratteristiche venature° verde-blu dipendono dalla presenza di muffe° aggiunte° agli ingredienti necessari per la sua produzione. Esistono due tipi di gorgonzola: quello «**dolce**», più cremoso, e quello «**piccante**» o «**naturale**», caratterizzato da un gusto più forte. Dopo una stagionatura° tra i 90 e i 110 giorni è pronto da mangiare.

Terra dei laghi La Lombardia è una regione con molti laghi, tra cui il **Lago di Como**, il **Lago Maggiore** e il **Lago di Garda**, il più grande d'Italia. Il Lago di Garda, situato tra la Lombardia e il Veneto, è visitato da moltissimi turisti italiani e stranieri. Diverse ragioni° contribuiscono alla fama di questo lago, tra cui, il **Vittoriale**, che fu la dimora° del poeta **Gabriele D'Annunzio**, e **Sirmione**, famoso centro termale, conosciuto già in epoca romana. Negli ultimi anni la pratica del *windsurf* e del *kitesurf* lungo il lago ha sviluppato un grande interesse tra i giovani appassionati di sport acquatici di tutta l'Europa e del mondo.

Lago di Garda

venature *veins* muffe *molds* aggiunte *added* stagionatura *maturing* ragioni *reasons* dimora *residence*

⌁ **Progetto**

Cremona

Cremona è una città della Lombardia con delle particolarità e delle curiosità legate ai suoi monumenti e alla sua produzione artigianale di dolci e strumenti musicali.

- Cerca informazioni sulla città.

- Scopri quali sono i monumenti e i prodotti artigianali caratteristici di Cremona.

- Raccogli informazioni sui monumenti e sui prodotti.

- Confronta i tuoi risultati con il resto della classe.

GALLERIA DI PERSONE ILLUSTRI

STILISTA
Valentino Garavani (1932–)

Valentino Clemente Ludovico Garavani nasce a Voghera, provincia di Pavia. Frequenta la scuol[a] di figurino (*sketch*) a Milano e a diciassette anni si trasferisce a Parigi per studiare stilismo. Dopo aver lavorato in vari atelier (*workshops*) parigini, torna in Italia e fonda la sua casa di moda a Roma. Nella capitale conosce lo studente di architettura Giancarlo Giammetti che sarà suo compagno per dodici anni, manager, amministratore e sviluppatore del suo marchio. Il successo arriva nel 1962 grazie alla collezione che presenta a Pitti Moda di Firenze. In brevissimo tempo Valentino diventa uno degli stilisti più apprezzati al mondo e le due pagine che *Vogue* gli dedica lo consacrano tra i grandi della moda. I suoi abiti sono da sempre sinonimo di lusso e perfezione manifatturiera. Nel 1998 vende il suo marchio alla casa tedesca HDP, successivamente rilevato (*taken over*) dal Gruppo Marzotto. Nel 2007 Valentino si ritira a vita privata.

LIUTAIO
Antonio Stradivari (1644–1737)

Antonio Stradivari, nato a Cremona nel 1644, è stato uno dei migliori costruttori di strumenti a corde al mondo. Impara il mestiere nella bottega di Nicola Amati, celebre liutaio (*lutist*) cremonese. Nel 1680 acquista una casa in centro e lì apre la propria bottega in cui realizza i suoi violini con l'aiuto dei figli. Durante i suoi settantacinque anni di attività, Stradivari si avvale degli insegnamenti tradizionali della scuola bresciana e cremonese, dei consigli dei grandi violinisti italiani dell'epoca, concentrandosi sulla resa (*performance*) acustica ma anche sul perfezionamento estetico dei suoi strumenti. Stradivari usa come base di partenza i modelli di Amati modificando e migliorando vari aspetti, tra cui la curvatura, lo spessore (*thickness*) e il colore del legno. Stradivari non creò solo violini ma anche arpe, liuti, viole, violoncelli e chitarre, per un totale di 1.100 strumenti musicali. Si stima che 650 di questi siano ancora esistenti. Gli Stradivari oggi hanno un grandissimo valore, il prezzo più alto pagato è stato di 1.790.000 sterline (*pounds*) nel 2006.

PITTORE

Caravaggio (1571–1610)

Michelangelo Merisi, detto Caravaggio, è uno dei più importanti pittori della storia italiana. Nasce a Milano e vive una vita breve fatta di arte, violenza, duelli, grandi successi e devastanti cadute (*lows*). Trasferitosi a Roma nel 1592, Caravaggio frequenta le osterie dei quartieri malfamati (*rough*) e in questi luoghi prende ispirazione per i suoi dipinti che colpiranno (*will strike*) il cardinale del Monte. Il cardinale diventa il suo mecenate e lo introduce nell'ambiente delle committenze. Nel 1599 gli viene commissionato uno dei suoi lavori più celebri, la *Vocazione di San Matteo*. Nonostante la fama Caravaggio continua a frequentare bettole (*taverns*) e a mettersi nei guai (*trouble*). Uccide un uomo e viene condannato alla decapitazione. Inizia così la sua fuga (*escape*) che lo porterà a Napoli, Palermo, Siracusa, Malta. La decapitazione diventa una scena ricorrente nei suoi dipinti, come *Decollazione di San Giovanni Battista* e *Davide con la testa di Golia*. Durante la latitanza (*hiding*), Caravaggio ferisce un cavaliere, i cui sicari (*hit men*) lo feriscono a morte per vendetta (*revenge*). Muore senza sapere che settimane prima il pontefice gli aveva concesso la grazia per i suoi crimini.

CANTANTE

Mina (1940–)

Mina, all'anagrafe (*legally*) Anna Maria Mazzini, è nata nel 1940 a Busto Arsizio. La nonna le infonde l'amore per la musica e a diciotto anni Mina fa la sua prima apparizione al locale *La Bussola* con la canzone *Un'anima pura*. Viene notata da un produttore discografico che le offre un contratto e le fa incidere dischi anche in inglese con lo pseudonimo *Baby Gate*. La sua carriera debutta in televisione nel programma *Musichiere*. Si innamora dell'attore Corrado Pani da cui avrà un figlio. L'attore era già sposato e l'opinione pubblica giudicò duramente la relazione, tanto che Mina venne allontanata dalla televisione. Nel 1964 torna alla ribalta (*stage*) con le canzoni *La città vuota* e *L'uomo per me*. Nel 1970 sposa il giornalista Virgilio Crocco ma il matrimonio finirà presto. Mina si esibisce (*performs*) per l'ultima volta in televisione nel 1974, e per l'ultima volta dal vivo a *La Bussola*, a vent'anni di distanza dal primo spettacolo. Negli anni ha mantenuto il contatto con il pubblico incidendo nuovi album e partecipando a trasmissioni radiofoniche.

Comprensione

Vero o falso? Indica se ogni affermazione è vera o falsa. Correggi le frasi false.

1. Antonio Stradivari costruiva solamente violini.
   Falso. Non creò solo violini ma anche arpe, liuti, viole, violoncelli e chitarre.

2. Stradivari costruisce strumenti musicali per settantacinque anni.
   Vero.

3. Valentino fonda la sua casa di moda a Parigi.
   Falso. La fonda a Roma.

4. Pitti Moda è il trampolino di lancio della carriera di Valentino.
   Vero.

5. Lo stilista di Voghera lavora nella moda fino al 2007.
   Vero.

6. Caravaggio viene condannato alla decapitazione per aver ferito un cavaliere.
   Falso. Viene condannato per aver ucciso un uomo.

7. Il pontefice concede la grazia a Caravaggio.
   Vero.

8. Mina era anche conosciuta come *Baby Gate*.
   Vero.

9. Corrado Pani sposa Mina.
   Falso. Era già sposato con un'altra donna.

10. Negli anni Mina ha mantenuto il contatto con il pubblico.
    Vero.

Scrittura

Scrivi sull'argomento Scegli uno dei seguenti argomenti e scrivi un paragrafo seguendo le indicazioni.

• **Made in Italy** Quali sono i settori trainanti (*leading*) del Made in Italy? Che caratteristiche deve avere un prodotto per essere considerato tale (*as such*)? Scrivi sul marchio dell'Italia nel mondo.

• **Caravaggio** Osserva il dipinto de *La vocazione di San Matteo* dipinto da Caravaggio e descrivi la scena. Cosa ti colpisce di più di questo quadro?

• **La fama** Che cos'è la fama secondo te? Per quale motivo artisti come Mina raggiunto l'apice (*pinnacle*) del successo decidono di ritirarsi a vita privata? Rifletti su questo concetto e spiega che effetti può avere questo fenomeno.

 Practice more at **vhlcentral.com**.

INSTRUCTIONAL RESOURCES
Audioscripts, Answer Keys, Lab MP3s, Grammar Presentation Slides
SAM/WebSAM: WB, LM

4.1

The *trapassato prossimo* and the *trapassato remoto*

*Mimì **aveva** già **perso** i punti quando si è svegliato.*

The *trapassato prossimo*

- The **trapassato prossimo** indicates what someone *had done* or what *had occurred* prior to another past action, event, or state. Like the **passato prossimo** and other compound tenses, the **trapassato prossimo** is formed by combining an auxiliary verb (the **imperfetto** of **essere** or **avere**) with a past participle.

> Abbiamo detto alla polizia che **avevamo visto** i ladri vicino all'edificio.
> *We told the police that we had seen the thieves near the building.*

> **Eravate** già **andati** in tribunale quando l'avvocato ha chiamato.
> *You had already gone to court when the lawyer called.*

The *trapassato prossimo* with *avere*			The *trapassato prossimo* with *essere*	
avevo			ero	andato/a
avevi			eri	caduto/a
aveva	salvato		era	partito/a
avevamo	combattuto		eravamo	andati/e
avevate	finito		eravate	caduti/e
avevano			erano	partiti/e

- You will remember that transitive verbs—those that can take a direct object—require **avere** as their auxiliary. In these cases, the past participle must agree with the direct object pronoun, just as it does with the **passato prossimo**.

> Il presidente **aveva proposto** quelle leggi?
> *Did the president proposed those laws?*

> Sì, e la Camera **le aveva approvate**.
> *Yes, and the House passed them.*

- Intransitive verbs, which take **essere** in compound tenses, often express physical movement, lack of movement, and changes in state. In the **trapassato prossimo** with **essere**, the past participle must agree with the subject of the verb.

> Il giudice sapeva che **la testimone era** già **arrivata**.
> *The judge knew that the witness had already arrived.*

- Reflexive verbs, reciprocal verbs, and the verb **piacere** also require **essere** as their auxiliary in the **trapassato prossimo**. Again, the past participle agrees with the subject of the verb.

> Durante il processo tutti si **erano messi** a piangere perché la sentenza non **era piaciuta**.
> *During the trial, everyone had started to cry because they did not like the verdict.*

- The **trapassato prossimo** expresses past events in relation to one another, indicating what *had already* taken place before something else happened or was going on. It is often used in clauses introduced by **quando**, **dopo che**, **appena**, and **perché** when the verb in the main clause is in the **passato prossimo** or the **imperfetto**. Use the **passato prossimo** to express completed events in the more recent past and the **imperfetto** to describe states of being, conditions, habits, or circumstances in the past. Use the **trapassato prossimo** to express events that occurred before another past point of reference.

trapassato prossimo   passato prossimo   presente

imperfetto

> Il candidato **era** felice perché **aveva vinto** le elezioni.
> *The candidate was happy because he won the election.*

> Dopo che **era entrata** la giuria, il giudice **ha iniziato** il processo.
> *As soon as the jury had entered, the judge began the trial.*

- The adverbs **già**, **(non) ... ancora**, and **(non) ... mai** often accompany a verb in the **trapassato prossimo** because this tense conveys completed events that *already, had not yet,* or *had (n)ever* taken place when another past event occurred or while a past condition existed.

> **Avevo già saputo** i risultati delle elezioni.
> *I had already found out the election results.*

> I politici **non si erano mai dedicati** alla riforma.
> *The politicians had never dedicated themselves to reform.*

The *trapassato remoto*

- The **trapassato remoto** indicates what someone *had done* or what *had occurred* prior to another past action, event, or state *if* that action is expressed with the **passato remoto** instead of with the **passato prossimo**. The **trapassato remoto** is used very rarely in spoken Italian and is found primarily in literary contexts. Compare:

trapassato prossimo + passato prossimo

Dopo che la giuria **era arrivata** a un verdetto, l'avvocato **è entrato**.

After the jury had reached a verdict, the lawyer entered.

trapassato remoto + passato remoto

Dopo che la giuria **fu arrivata** a un verdetto, l'avvocato **entrò**.

After the jury had reached a verdict, the lawyer entered.

- Form the **trapassato remoto** by combining the **passato remoto** of the auxiliary verb with the past participle of the main verb. The agreement rules for compound tenses apply.

The *trapassato remoto* with *avere*	
ebbi	
avesti	
ebbe	**salvato**
	combattuto
avemmo	**finito**
aveste	
ẹbbero	

The *trapassato remoto* with *ẹssere*	
fui	**andato/a**
fosti	**caduto/a**
fu	**partito/a**
fummo	**andati/e**
foste	**caduti/e**
fụrono	**partiti/e**

It may help students to see the **trapassato prossimo** as the "past in the past." Use a timeline to map out a series of past events. Provide simple examples, such as: **Quando sono tornato a casa, la posta era già arrivata**.

Give students additional examples and point out the tense sequencing and the use of conjunctions. Example: **Tra i deputati eletti c'erano pochi moderati perché il partito conservatore aveva vinto le elezioni.**

Remind students to place the adverbs **già**, **mai**, **ancora**, and **più** between the auxiliary verb and the past participle, as with the other compound tenses.

ATTENZIONE!

In English, speakers often use the *simple past* tense to imply the past perfect tense (the **trapassato prossimo**). In Italian, one must use the **trapassato prossimo**.

I politici hanno scritto ai soldati che avevano sconfitto il nemico.
The politicians wrote to the soldiers who defeated (had defeated) the enemy.

RIMANDO

To review the **passato remoto**, see **Strutture 3.4, pp. 106–107**.

Give students additional examples and point out the tense sequencing and the use of conjunctions. Example: **Quando la regina ebbe trovato sua figlia, le diede un bacio e la portò a casa. Non appena l'esercito ebbe sconfitto il nemico, rientrò trionfalmente in patria.**

Pratica

1

Notizie di politica Inserisci i verbi tra parentesi al trapassato prossimo.

1. Il governo voleva fare delle riforme ma i deputati non le _avevano approvate_ (approvare).

2. Anche se il paese era contrario, il governo _aveva inviato_ (inviare) altri militari in missione.

3. L'avvocato _si era battuto_ (battersi) per difendere l'imputato (*accused*) senza riuscire a farlo assolvere (*to acquit*).

4. La polizia si è opposta alla manifestazione anche se i pacifisti l'_avevano organizzata_ (organizzare) secondo le regole.

5. Giovanni _aveva partecipato_ (partecipare) alla protesta nella speranza di aiutare i più deboli.

2

Un pacifista Aldo Capitini, pacifista italiano, racconta come si è avvicinato al movimento pacifista. Completa il brano con i verbi al trapassato prossimo.

I miei genitori mi avevano insegnato che molta gente aveva bisogno di aiuto e io
(1) _avevo provato_ (provare) in vari modi a rendermi utile. Al liceo
(2) _avevo conosciuto_ (conoscere) altri giovani che come me volevano aiutare i più bisognosi. Prima di trasferirmi a Pisa, il nostro gruppo (3) _aveva combattuto_ (combattere) l'ingiustizia e la povertà e (4) _ci eravamo iscritti_ (noi / iscriversi) all'università con l'intenzione di cambiare le cose nel nostro paese. (5) _Ero andato_ (io / andare) all'università per diventare dottore, ma sono diventato avvocato.
(6) _Avevo capito_ (capire) che per aiutare gli oppressi era necessario fare qualcosa di concreto.

3

Notizie Sottolinea i verbi al passato remoto e al trapassato remoto e poi sostituiscili con il passato prossimo e il trapassato prossimo.

> **Modello** La giuria si alzò in piedi dopo che il giudice fu entrato in tribunale.
> La giuria si è alzata in piedi dopo che il giudice era entrato in tribunale.

1. La manifestazione iniziò dopo che furono arrivati tutti i rappresentanti sindacali.
   La manifestazione è iniziata dopo che erano arrivati tutti i rappresentanti sindacali.

2. Capii che non aveva torto dopo che ebbe spiegato le sue ragioni. Ho capito che non aveva torto dopo che aveva spiegato le sue ragioni.

3. I deputati votarono dopo che il presidente ebbe chiuso le discussioni. I deputati hanno votato dopo che il presidente aveva chiuso le discussioni.

4. Applaudimmo dopo che il presidente del Senato ebbe letto il messaggio. Abbiamo applaudito dopo che il presidente del Senato aveva letto il messaggio.

5. Iniziarono i lavori dopo che il governo ebbe allocato i fondi. Hanno iniziato i lavori dopo che il governo aveva allocato i fondi.

4

Causa ed effetto Utilizza il trapassato prossimo per spiegare perché sono accadute (*happened*) queste cose.

> **Modello** La giustizia regnava. La democrazia ha vinto.
> La giustizia regnava perché la democrazia aveva vinto.

1. I cittadini sono diventati più poveri. Il governo non si è accorto dei loro problemi. I cittadini sono diventati più poveri perché il governo non si era accorto dei loro problemi.

2. Il governo è caduto. Il governo non ha ottenuto la fiducia. Il governo è caduto perché non aveva ottenuto la fiducia.

3. Gli studenti hanno manifestato. Il governo ha modificato il sistema scolastico. Gli studenti hanno manifestato perché il governo aveva modificato il sistema scolastico.

4. Abbiamo votato domenica. Abbiamo visto il dibattito politico sabato sera. Abbiamo votato domenica perché avevamo visto il dibattito politico sabato sera.

5. Gli attivisti sono entrati nella sala riunioni. Il sindaco ha finito di parlare. Gli attivisti sono entrati nella sala riunioni perché il sindaco aveva finito di parlare.

Comunicazione

5

Pompei Immagina di essere andato in vacanza in Campania. In coppia, create un dialogo dove a turno vi fate domande sulle vostre vacanze. Utilizzate i verbi suggeriti al trapassato prossimo quando è possibile.

Modello —Dove sei andata in vacanza?

—Sono andata a Pompei; non ero mai stata in vacanza in Campania prima d'ora. Avevo sentito parlare delle rovine, ma non le immaginavo così belle…

andare	finire	piacere
apprezzare	mangiare	preferire
avere l'occasione	passeggiare	vedere
conoscere	permettere	visitare

Nota
CULTURALE

Pompei è un importantissimo centro archeologico vicino a Napoli. In epoca romana Pompei era luogo di villeggiatura dei **patrizi** (nobili romani). Il 24 agosto del 79 d.C. ci fu l'eruzione del **Vesuvio** che ricoprì la città di ceneri° e fango°, causando morte e distruzione. Gli scavi, iniziati a metà del XVIII secolo e non ancora terminati, hanno riportato alla luce le bellezze di questa città.

ceneri *ash* **fango** *mud*

6

Secondo te Cosa pensi dell'attuale governo? È migliore del governo precedente? In coppia, discutete di questi argomenti utilizzando il trapassato prossimo.

Modello —Il governo attuale ha fatto molte cose finora.

—Forse, ma secondo me, il governo precedente era riuscito a migliorare…

- economia
- istruzione
- immigrazione

- ambiente
- relazioni internazionali
- disoccupazione

6 Before assigning this activity, discuss the questions in the direction lines. Then have two students act out the **modello**.

7

Perché? In gruppi di tre, fate una lista di cosa hanno fatto di recente politici o personaggi famosi contemporanei. Utilizzate i verbi suggeriti. Poi, a turno, leggete la lista e commentate.

Modello Il candidato ha perso le elezioni.

Il candidato ha perso le elezioni perché non aveva preparato una campagna elettorale efficace.

approvare una legge	giudicare
dedicarsi a	imprigionare
difendere	influenzare
eleggere	vincere/perdere le elezioni

7 Give students a list of people that they can use as subjects. Example: **il presidente, la senatrice, il ministro per l'educazione, il Dalai Lama, il Papa, l'ambasciatore/ ambasciatrice dell'ONU.**

INSTRUCTIONAL RESOURCES 4.2
Audioscripts, Answer Keys, Lab MP3s, Grammar Presentation Slides
SAM/WebSAM: WB, LM

ATTENZIONE!

A direct object receives the action of a verb and answers the question *what?* or *who(m)?*

Capisco la legge.
Che cosa capisco? – la legge
Avevi visto il ladro?
Chi avevi visto? – il ladro

An indirect object indicates *for whom* or *to whom* an action occurs.

Diamo la bandiera a Franco.
A chi diamo la bandiera?
– a Franco

ATTENZIONE!

In the third person, direct object pronouns have gender and can refer to people, animals, or things. Indirect object pronouns, in contrast, may only refer to people and animals.

Lo vediamo.   **La vediamo.**
We see him/it.   *We see her/it.*

but

Gli parliamo.   **Le parliamo.**
We talk to him. *We talk to her.*

Remind students that direct and indirect object pronouns differ only in the third person. This may also be a good time to remind them that only the direct object pronouns **lo** and **la** may be shortened to **l'**. **Gli** and **le** may not be elided.

While speakers generally attach pronouns to infinitives following **amare**, **desiderare**, **odiare**, and **preferire**, the pronoun may either precede or follow when the main verb is **andare** or **venire**. Example: **Vado/Vengo a prenderla** or **La vado/vengo a prendere**.

Object pronouns

—*Oh, guarda! Vengono a prenderci.*

Direct and indirect object pronouns

- To avoid repetition, use object pronouns to take the place of direct and indirect object nouns.

  I deputati propongono le leggi e la Camera **le** approva. (le = le leggi)
  The congressmen propose the laws and the House approves them.

  Quando vedo l'avvocato, **gli** do i documenti. (gli = all'avvocato)
  When I see the lawyer, I'll give him the documents.

- Object pronouns directly precede a conjugated verb and compound tenses. One exception to this rule is the indirect object pronoun **loro**, which must follow the verb. Note, however, that in contemporary Italian, **gli** is used more than **loro**.

Direct object pronouns		Indirect object pronouns	
mi (m')	ci	mi (m')	ci
ti (t')	vi	ti (t')	vi
lo/la/La/(l')	li/le	gli/le/Le	gli *or* loro

- When using an object pronoun in a *verb + infinitive* construction, drop the final **–e** of the infinitive and attach the pronoun. Verbs commonly used with an infinitive include **amare**, **desiderare**, **odiare**, and **preferire**.

  Claudio desidera combattere la violenza.
  Claudio wants to fight violence.

  Claudio desidera combatter**la**.
  Claudio wants to fight it.

- When an object pronoun is used in a *verb + infinitive* construction with **dovere**, **potere**, or **volere**, the pronoun may be placed either before the conjugated verb or attached to the infinitive, after dropping the final **–e**.

  Il candidato avrebbe potuto difendere i diritti umani.
  The candidate would have been able to defend human rights.

  Il senatore voleva proporre la riforma.
  The senator wanted to propose reform.

  Li avrebbe potuti difendere./Avrebbe potuto difender**li**.
  He would have been able to defend them.

  La voleva proporre./Voleva propor**la**.
  He wanted to propose it.

- When a direct object pronoun precedes a compound verb, the past participle may agree with the pronoun. Agreement is obligatory with the pronouns **lo**, **la**, **li**, and **le**; it is optional with the pronouns **mi**, **ti**, **ci**, and **vi**.

  I candidati hanno promosso **la sicurezza** dei bambini.
  The candidates promoted child safety.

  L'hanno promoss**a**.
  They promoted it.

  Carla, gli attivisti **ti** hanno chiamat**o**?/Carla, gli attivisti **ti** hanno chiamat**a**?
  Carla, did the activists call you?

- Some Italian verbs take an indirect object, whereas their English counterparts take a direct object (e.g. **fare bene/male, fare paura, insegnare, rispondere, somigliare, telefonare**). Conversely, some Italian verbs take a direct object, whereas their English counterparts are followed by *preposition + indirect object* (e.g. **ascoltare, aspettare, cercare, guardare**). Compare:

  Telefoni **a Giorgio**? Sì, **gli** telefono domani.
  Are you calling George? Yes, I'll call him tomorrow.

  Aspettiamo **il giudice**? Sì, **l'**aspettiamo.
  Are we waiting for the judge? Yes, we are waiting for him.

- The neuter pronoun **lo** can replace an entire idea.

  Sai che il governo ha approvato una nuova legge sull'immigrazione?
  Did you know that the government approved a new immigration law?

  Sì, **lo** so.
  Yes, I knew that.

Combined pronouns

- When a sentence contains both direct and indirect object pronouns, they can combine. The indirect object pronoun precedes the direct object pronoun. The pronouns also undergo some changes.

Double object pronouns

indirect object	+ direct object	= double object pronoun
mi		me lo, me la, me li, me le, me ne
ti		te lo, te la, te li, te le, te ne
ci	+ lo, la, li, le, ne	ce lo, ce la, ce li, ce le, ce ne
vi		ve lo, ve la, ve li, ve le, ve ne
gli le (Le)		glielo, gliela, glieli, gliele, gliene

Il politico ha dato i documenti alla segretaria?
Did the politician give the documents to the secretary?

Sì, il politico **glieli** ha dati.
Yes, the politician gave them to her.

L'attivista ti ha dato la bandiera?
Did the activist give you the flag?

No, l'attivista non **me l'**ha data.
No, he didn't give it to me.

- Double object pronouns with **mi**, **ti**, **ci**, and **vi** are written as two words (**me lo, me la**, and so forth). Note the changes in spelling (**mi → me / ti → te / ci → ce / vi → ve**).

ATTENZIONE!

Some object pronouns may elide with the following verb if it begins with a vowel sound. Elision of **mi** and **ti** is less common, while it is frequent with **lo** and **la**. Note that indirect object pronouns and the plural forms **li** and **le** are never elided.

L'avvocato l'ha difeso.
(l'ha = lo + ha)
The lawyer defended him.

RIMANDO

Ne replaces a prepositional phrase or nouns when using certain expressions of quantity. When combined with other pronouns, it always appears last. When **ne** is used with **ci**, the combination becomes **ce ne**. See **Strutture 5.2, pp. 184–185**.

Hai inviato molte lettere al sindaco?
Have you sent many letters to the mayor?

Sì, gliene ho inviate molte.
Yes, I sent him many.

Quante bottiglie di latte ci sono in frigo?
How many bottles of milk are in the fridge?

Ce ne sono due.
There are two.

Remind students that past participle agreement applies also with the direct object pronoun in double pronouns.

- Note that the indirect object pronouns **gli** and **le** (and **Le**) become **glie–** before **lo**, **la**, **li**, and **le**.

    Avete dato i documenti al giudice?
    Did you give the documents to the judge?

    Sì, **glieli** abbiamo dati.
    Yes, we gave them to him.

    Hanno fatto le domande alla testimone?
    Did they ask the witness the questions?

    No, non **gliele** hanno fatte.
    No, they didn't ask her them.

- The indirect object **loro** does not combine with direct object pronouns because it always follows the verb. In current usage **gli** is often used instead of **loro**.

    Ha scritto la lettera di protesta ai senatori.
    He wrote the letter of protest to the senators.

    Gliel'ha scritta. = **L**'ha scritta **loro**.
    He wrote it to them.

- Reflexive pronouns may be combined with direct object pronouns, following the same rules as indirect object pronouns. Note that the reflexive pronoun **si** becomes **se**.

RIMANDO

For information about using the object pronouns with the imperative, see **Strutture 4.3, pp. 146–147.**

Reflexive pronouns with direct object pronouns

reflexive pronoun	+ lo	+ la	+ li	+ le
mi	me lo	me la	me li	me le
ti	te lo	te la	te li	te le
si	se lo	se la	se li	se le
ci	ce lo	ce la	ce li	ce le
vi	ve lo	ve la	ve li	ve le
si	se lo	se la	se li	se le

Mi lavo **le mani.** **Me le** lavo.

- In compound tenses, the past participle of reflexive verbs agrees with the direct object pronoun, not the subject of the verb.

    L'avvocato si è lavato le mani?
    Did the lawyer wash his hands?

    Sì, **se le** è lavate.
    Yes, he washed them.

    Lucia, ti sei messa l'abito da sera?
    Lucia, did you wear an evening gown?

    Sì, **me lo** sono messo.
    Yes, I wore one.

- Direct object pronouns—and combinations of direct and indirect object pronouns—are attached to **ecco**.

    Ecco il caffè per te! Eccotelo!
    Here is the coffee for you! Here it is for you!

    Eccomi!
    Here I am!

Pratica

1

La giornata dell'avvocato Riscrivi le frasi sostituendo le parole sottolineate con i pronomi diretti o indiretti.

1. L'avvocato Rossi parla <u>ai clienti</u>. *L'avvocato Rossi gli parla.*
2. Legge <u>gli appunti sul caso</u>. *Li legge.*
3. Scrive <u>la relazione</u> per il tribunale. *La scrive per il tribunale.*
4. Chiede <u>alla segretaria</u> di mandare un fax. *Le chiede di mandare un fax.*
5. Difende <u>i clienti</u> in tribunale. *Li difende in tribunale.*
6. Telefona <u>ai colleghi</u>. *Gli telefona.*
7. Prepara <u>il controesame</u>. *Lo prepara.*
8. Incontra <u>i collaboratori</u>. *Li incontra.*
9. Manda un messaggio <u>alla fidanzata</u>. *Le manda un messaggio.*
10. Finalmente va a casa e mangia <u>la pizza</u> per cena. *La mangia per cena.*

2

In ufficio Completa le frasi con i pronomi diretti o indiretti.

1. – Signorina Paola, per favore telefoni al signor De Carli.
   – Sì, avvocato, __gli__ telefono subito.
2. – Signor Bianchi, non si dimentichi di portare i documenti in ufficio.
   – Va bene, __li__ porto subito.
3. – Signorina Carmela, deve mandare subito questo fax, è importantissimo!
   – Certamente avvocato, __lo__ mando immediatamente.
4. – Signor Melotti, spedisca le lettere prima della pausa pranzo.
   – Sì avvocato, __le__ spedisco ora.
5. – Signor Varutti, si ricordi di rispondere al signor De Carli.
   – Sì avvocato, __gli__ rispondo subito.
6. – Mi scusi signorina, mi può per cortesia portare il giornale?
   – Certo avvocato, __lo__ porto subito.

3

La scelta Trova la risposta giusta. Fai attenzione agli accordi con il passato prossimo.

1. Sua sorella __gli__ (lo / gli) ha insegnato il tedesco.
2. I politici volevano aiutar__ci__ (ci / ce).
3. La polizia __le__ (le / la) ha telefonato.
4. I vostri amici __vi__ (vi / ve) hanno preparato una festa bellissima.
5. Simona __li__ (gli / li) ha aspettati davanti al bar.
6. Il direttore doveva incontrar__ti__ (ti / te) alle 15.

4

Trasformare Riscrivi le frasi usando i pronomi combinati.

> **Modello**   **La segretaria spedisce le lettere ai clienti.**
>
> Gliele spedisce.

1. Il deputato descrive ai politici i problemi del paese. *Il deputato glieli descrive.*
2. Il presidente mi mostra il nuovo progetto. *Il presidente me lo mostra.*
3. L'avvocato ci spiega il caso. *L'avvocato ce lo spiega.*
4. I ladri rubano i gioielli (*jewelry*) alle vittime. *I ladri glieli rubano.*
5. Gli attivisti portano aiuti agli immigrati. *Gli attivisti glieli portano.*
6. Il sindaco vi illustra le riforme. *Il sindaco ve le illustra.*

5 **Domande** In coppia, preparate a turno delle domande con gli elementi forniti e rispondete usando i pronomi diretti, indiretti o combinati. Some answers will vary.

> **Modello** **Il latte / fare bene**
>
> —Il latte fa bene ai bambini?
>
> —Sì, gli fa bene.

1. La professoressa / insegnare
   La professoressa insegna agli studenti? Sì, insegna loro.
2. Tu / telefonare Telefoni a Giacomo? Sì, gli telefono dopo.
3. Andrea e Marco / cercare Andrea e Marco cercano un lavoro? No, non lo cercano.
4. Tu / ascoltare Ascolti spesso i tuoi CD? Sì, li ascolto tutti i giorni.

5. Voi / rispondere Rispondete a Marina? Sì, le rispondiamo.
6. Alberto / aspettare Alberto aspetta la sua ragazza in biblioteca? Sì, l'aspetta.
7. Laura / guardare Laura guarda i film d'avventura? Sì, li guarda.
8. Carla e Maria / somigliare Carla e Maria somigliano ai loro genitori? Sì, gli somigliano.

6 **La cartolina** Giulia è in vacanza sul Lago Maggiore e manda una cartolina alla sorella. Trova le frasi con i complementi diretti e indiretti e riscrivile con i pronomi. Fai attenzione agli accordi con il passato prossimo.

Cara Elena,

Il Lago Maggiore è proprio come lo immaginavo, circondato da paesi pieni di fascino e di atmosfera. Ti mostrerò le foto al mio ritorno. Mi sono divertita molto, ho visitato l'Isola Bella con i suoi splendidi giardini. Ho comprato una borsa per la mamma e un paio di orecchini per te. Stasera, i miei amici italiani mi portano in un ristorante tipico della zona. Quando torno a casa, manderò un bel regalo ai miei amici ; li voglio ringraziare per la loro ospitalità.

A presto,
Julia

Elena Cargoglio

Via Garibaldi 24

Roma

1. _____te le mostrerò_____
2. _____l'ho visitata_____
3. _____gliel'ho comprata_____
4. _____te l'ho comprato/te li ho comprati_____
5. _____glielo manderò_____

7 **Creare** In coppia, fatevi delle domande a turno, utilizzando gli elementi forniti, e rispondete negativamente.

> **Modello** **testimone / dire / verità / giudice**
>
> —Il testimone ha detto la verità al giudice?
>
> —No, non gliel'ha detta.

1. giudice / farsi la barba Il giudice si è fatto la barba? No, non se l'è fatta.
2. tu / lavarsi / denti Ti sei lavato i denti? No, non me li sono lavati.
3. segretaria / mandare / fax / direttore La segretaria ha mandato il fax al direttore? No, non gliel'ha mandato.
4. voi / volere / offrire / cena / me Mi volete offrire la cena? No, non te la vogliamo offrire./No, non vogliamo offrirtela.
5. ragazzi / scrivere / cartolina / voi I ragazzi vi hanno scritto la cartolina? No, non ce l'hanno scritta.
6. mamma / prestare / macchina / Roberto La mamma ha prestato la macchina a Roberto? No, non gliel'ha prestata.
7. presidente / mettersi / cappello Il presidente si è messo il cappello? No, non se l'è messo.
8. Giovanni / asciugarsi / i capelli Giovanni si è asciugato i capelli? No, non se li è asciugati.

Practice more at
vhlcentral.com.

Comunicazione

8

In aeroporto Guardate il disegno e in coppia fatevi delle domande per capire cosa stanno facendo i personaggi e perché. Utilizzate i pronomi diretti e indiretti e i verbi della lista.

> **Modello** Cosa fa Diana?
>
> Diana legge un libro. Lo legge perché si annoia.

ascoltare	comprare	domandare	mostrare	portare
cercare	dare	leggere	parlare	trovare

Marisa · Signor Fabbri · Giorgio · Signor Collina · Signora Fabbri · Diana · Matteo

9

I premi Tu e due amici avete vinto una strana serie di premi alla lotteria. Usando i pronomi diretti, indiretti o combinati, decidete come dividervi i premi e motivate le vostre decisioni.

> **Modello** **Alessia:** Che belli tutti questi premi! Come ce li dividiamo?
>
> **Silvia:** Tu dovresti prendere il cagnolino e l'aspirapolvere!
>
> **Roberta:** Non, non li voglio. Carlo invece li vuole. Perché non glieli diamo?

un cagnolino	una macchina	una pianta di limoni
una dozzina di uova	un aspirapolvere	un albero di Natale
un asciugacapelli	un ferro da stiro (*iron*)	una bicicletta

10

Secondo te Cosa pensi di queste affermazioni? Scrivi le tue idee e i tuoi commenti. Utilizza almeno otto pronomi diretti e indiretti.

> **Modello** **L'immigrazione illegale causa la criminalità.**
>
> Secondo me, non la causa; la criminalità è causata da…

- L'immigrazione aiuta lo sviluppo economico di un paese.
- Non è necessario conoscere la lingua ufficiale del paese dove si vuole andare a vivere.
- La globalizzazione causa problemi in tutto il mondo.
- I nuovi immigrati fanno i lavori che i cittadini non vogliono fare.
- La sovrappopolazione diminuisce la qualità della vita di un paese.

INSTRUCTIONAL
RESOURCES
Audioscripts, Answer Keys,
Lab MP3s, Grammar
Presentation Slides
SAM/WebSAM: WB, LM

4.3

The imperative

—*Sta'* *attento che c'è corrente! Se scarrocci (*drift*),*
non mi trovi più. **Tieni** *i punti!*

- The imperative mood is used to give a command. Subject pronouns are not usually used.

- The informal imperative forms are used to address people in the **tu**, **noi**, or **voi** forms. Note that the **noi** form expresses *let's* + [*verb*].

Rispetta le leggi!	**Rispettiamo** le leggi!	**Rispettate** le leggi!
Respect the laws!	*Let's respect the laws!*	*Respect the laws!*

Explain that if subject
pronouns are used with the
imperative, they should follow
the verb and that they serve
to provide emphasis.
Parlate voi al testimone!
You talk to the witness!

- The imperative forms of **–are** verbs end in **–a** in the second person singular while the **noi** and **voi** forms are the same as the present indicative forms. The imperative forms of **–ere** and **–ire** verbs are identical to those of the present indicative.

	votare	mettere	partire	finire
tu	**Vota!**	**Metti!**	**Parti!**	**Finisci!**
noi	**Votiamo!**	**Mettiamo!**	**Partiamo!**	**Finiamo!**
voi	**Votate!**	**Mettete!**	**Partite!**	**Finite!**

ATTENZIONE!

It is helpful to remember that the
Lei imperative forms for regular
verbs are the inversion of the
informal **tu** forms.

tu	Lei
Vota!	Voti!
Scrivi!	Scriva!
Finisci!	Finisca!

- To make a command in a formal setting, use the **Lei** and **Loro** forms indicated below. Note, however, that the **voi** form often replaces the **Loro** form in contemporary usage.

votare		mettere		partire		finire	
Voti!	**Votino!**	**Metta!**	**Mettano!**	**Parta!**	**Partano!**	**Finisca!**	**Finiscano!**

It will be helpful for students
to learn the imperative
forms well. When they
reach **Lezione 6**, they will
appreciate finding out that
they already know the forms
of the present subjunctive!

Point out that once students
know the **Lei** form, they must
simply add **–no** to make the
Loro form.

- A number of verbs are irregular in the imperative.

	tu	Lei	noi	voi	Loro
andare (io vado**)**	vai/va'	vada	andiamo	andate	vadano
dire (io dico**)**	dì/di'	dica	diciamo	dite	dicano
tenere (io tengo**)**	tieni	tenga	teniamo	tenete	tengano
venire (io vengo**)**	vieni	venga	veniamo	venite	vengano
uscire (io esco**)**	esci	esca	usciamo	uscite	escano
dare (noi diamo**)**	dai/dà/da'	dia	diamo	date	diano
fare (noi facciamo**)**	fai/fa'	faccia	facciamo	fate	facciano
stare (noi stiamo**)**	stai/sta'	stia	stiamo	state	stiano

ATTENZIONE!

Note that the irregular formal
imperative forms closely resemble
the present indicative stems used
in the first person singular or plural
(**io/noi**). Short forms exist for the
verbs **andare**, **dare**, **dire**, **fare**,
and **stare**.

- The verbs **essere**, **avere**, and **sapere** have irregular imperative forms. Note the similarity of all imperative forms with the present indicative **noi** form.

	tu	Lei	noi	voi	Loro
avere (noi abbiamo)	abbi	abbia	abbiamo	abbiate	ạbbiano
essere (noi siamo)	sịi	sịa	siamo	siate	sịano
sapere (noi sappiamo)	sappi	sappia	sappiamo	sappiate	sạppiano

- For a negative command, use **non** plus the command for all forms except the **tu** form. For the **tu** form, use **non** + [*infinitive*].

<table>
<tr><td>

(voi) Non date i volantini a me!
Don't give me the flyers!

</td><td>

but

</td><td>

(tu) Non dare i volantini a me!
Don't give me the flyers!

</td></tr>
</table>

The imperative with object pronouns

- Imperative verbs are often combined with an object pronoun. All pronouns (except the indirect object pronoun **loro**) attach to the informal (**tu**, **noi**, **voi**) imperative forms, but precede the formal (**Lei**, **Loro**) imperative forms.

Eleggetelo!	**Lo elegga!**
Elect him! (voi)	*Elect him!* (Lei)

- With the short, one-syllable **tu** forms **da'**, **di'**, **fa'**, **sta'**, and **va'**, drop the apostrophe and double the initial consonant of all object pronouns except **gli**.

Da' il libro a me!
Give the book to me!

Dammi il libro!
Give me the book!

Di' a lui la verità!
Tell him the truth!

Digliela!
Tell him!

- With a negative imperative, object pronouns may be placed either before or after the verb. If placed after the negative **tu** form, the infinitive looses the final **–e**.

Non dimenticare le vittime!
Don't forget the victims!

Non le dimenticare!/Non dimenticarle!
Don't forget them!

The imperative of reflexive verbs

- Reflexive pronouns in the imperative follow the same rules as object pronouns. In the informal imperative, they attach to the verb, while in the formal imperative they must precede the verb.

Dedicati alla nostra causa!
Dedicate yourself to our cause! (tu)

Si dedichi alla nostra causa!
Dedicate yourself to our cause! (Lei)

- Reflexive pronouns can be combined with direct object pronouns in the imperative, just as in the indicative. Note that they attach to the imperative verb form.

Chiarisciti le idee!
Think things through!

Chiariscitele!
Think them through!

Si metta gli occhiali!
Put your glasses on!

Se li metta!
Put them on!

ATTENZIONE!

The infinitive often replaces the imperative on street signs, public instructions, and announcements.

Pagare qui.
Pay here.

RIMANDO

To review object pronouns, see **Strutture 4.2, pp. 140–142.**

RIMANDO

To review reflexive verbs, see **Strutture 2.1, pp. 56–57.**

ATTENZIONE!

To make a polite request, use the conditional form of **potere** plus the infinitive.

Mi dica l'ora!
Tell me the time!

Potrebbe dirmi l'ora?
Could you tell me the time?

Pratica

1

Cosa fare? Usa l'imperativo per dare ordini o consigli.

Modello **Dì al tuo fidanzato di telefonarti.**
Telefonami.
Dì a Stefano di andare al teatro con te.
Andiamo al teatro.

Dì a Carlo di:	Dì ai nuovi studenti di:	Dì a Giovanna di:
1. andare in biblioteca *Vai/Va' in biblioteca.*	6. prestare attenzione ai professori *Prestate attenzione ai professori.*	11. andare al cinema con te *Andiamo al cinema.*
2. contare su di te *Conta su di me.*	7. svegliarsi presto *Svegliatevi presto.*	12. bere un caffè con te *Beviamo un caffè.*
3. non uscire spesso *Non uscire spesso.*	8. andare a lezione *Andate a lezione.*	13. ascoltare la musica con te *Ascoltiamo la musica.*
4. dare a te una mano *Dammi una mano.*	9. avere fiducia *Abbiate fiducia.*	14. giocare a tennis con te *Giochiamo a tennis.*
5. aspettare te dopo la lezione *Aspettami* *dopo la lezione.*	10. non uscire la domenica *Non uscite la domenica.*	15. non rimanere a casa con te *Non rimaniamo* *a casa.*

2

Suggerimenti Hai la possibilità di parlare con un politico della tua città; utilizzando l'imperativo formale, dagli dei suggerimenti sui problemi locali.

1. ___*Promuova*___ (Promuovere) riforme per la sicurezza pubblica.

2. ___*Faccia*___ (Fare) rispettare le leggi già esistenti.

3. ___*Risolva*___ (Risolvere) il problema dei parcheggi.

4. _*Non si dedichi*_ (Non dedicarsi) solo ai suoi elettori.

5. ___*Crei*___ (Creare) più spazi verdi.

3

Buoni consigli Quali consigli puoi dare in queste situazioni? Utilizza l'imperativo.
Some answers will vary.

1. I tuoi amici non hanno votato alle ultime elezioni. *Votate alle prossime elezioni.*

2. Il tuo amico non è aggiornato (*up-to-date*) sulla situazione politica del vostro paese. *Leggi più giornali.*

3. I tuoi amici non hanno mai partecipato a una manifestazione pacifista.
Partecipate alla prossima manifestazione.

4. Tu e il tuo amico non avete mai ascoltato un comizio elettorale (*rally*).
Andiamo al prossimo comizio.

5. Il tuo amico legge solo fumetti (*comics*). *Non leggere solo fumetti.*

4

Raccomandazioni Dai dei suggerimenti alle seguenti persone. Usa la forma appropriata dell'imperativo.

1. al tuo professore d'italiano
2. al tuo compagno di stanza
3. al tuo migliore amico
4. al rettore (*dean*) dell'università
5. al tuo compagno di classe
6. al sindaco della tua città

Practice more at
vhlcentral.com.

Comunicazione

5 **Internet** Quali consigli puoi dare a un amico/un'amica per essere più informato/a sull'attualità (*current events*)? In coppia, create una lista di otto raccomandazioni, sia con la forma affermativa che negativa dell'imperativo. Utilizzate i verbi suggeriti e siate creativi.

> **Modello** Naviga su Internet. Ci sono siti web che offrono informazioni di ogni tipo.
> Non leggere solo romanzi di fantascienza.

andare	fare	navigare
ascoltare	interessare	parlare
chiedere	investigare	ricercare
consigliare	leggere	vedere

5 Call on students to write one of their commands on the board. As a variant, have them convert their sentences into commands for the entire class using the **voi** form.

6 **Cosa dicono?** In coppia, inventatevi delle brevi conversazioni per ogni foto. Ricordatevi di utilizzare l'imperativo affermativo e negativo.

1.

3.

2.

4.

6 Ask students to act out their dialogues in small groups. Their classmates can guess which dialogues go with which photos.

7 **Pubblicità** In gruppi di tre, create uno spot pubblicitario per promuovere uno dei prodotti suggeriti. Inventate anche un nome originale per il prodotto. Utilizzate l'imperativo formale e i pronomi diretti e indiretti.

> **Modello** Comprate il nuovo profumo «Fascino», vi renderà più affascinanti e attraenti. Non perdete questa occasione. È il profumo dell'anno!

Yogurt	Automobile
Succo di frutta	Dentifricio
Scarpe da ginnastica	Giornale politico
Cellulare	Crema solare

7 Ask groups to read their advertisements aloud, then have the class discuss whether or not they were convinced to buy the product.

INSTRUCTIONAL RESOURCES 4.4
Audioscripts, Answer Keys, Lab MP3s, Grammar Presentation Slides
SAM/WebSAM: WB, LM

RIMANDO

To review the full conjugation of **dovere**, **potere**, and **volere** in the present tense, see **Strutture 1.4, p. 27.**

ATTENZIONE!

When used alone, the present indicative forms of **volere** means *to want*. Use the conditional form of the verb to make polite requests (using the indicative to make a request can be considered rude).

Voglio un cappuccino.
I want a cappuccino.

Vorrei un cappuccino.
I would like a cappuccino.

When **dovere** is followed by a noun, it means *to owe*, in both a monetary and figurative sense.

Quanto ti devo?
How much do I owe you?

ATTENZIONE!

Dovere, **potere**, and **volere** can be used on their own, sometimes in response to a question containing both the verb and an infinitive.

Francesco, vuoi votare alle elezioni?
Francesco, do you want to vote in the elections?

Sì, voglio. (=Sì, voglio farlo.)
Yes, I want to. (=Yes, I want to do it.)

RIMANDO

To review reflexive verbs, see **Strutture 2.1, pp. 56–57.**

Dovere, potere, and *volere*

● **Dovere**, **potere**, and **volere** are usually followed by an infinitive.

dovere (*need or obligation*)	potere (*ability or permission*)	volere (*willingness*)
Devi studiare.	**Puoi** ballare.	**Vuoi** uscire.
*You **must** study.*	*You **can** dance./You **are able** to dance.*	*You **want** to go out.*

● When **dovere**, **potere**, and **volere** are used with object pronouns and an infinitive, two structures are possible. The pronouns (except **Loro** and **loro**) can be placed either before the conjugated verb or attached to the infinitive (after removing the final –**e**).

L'attivista vuole proteggere le vittime. **Le** vuole proteggere./Vuole protegger**le**.
The activist wants to protect victims. *He wants to protect them.*

● When used in the conditional, **dovere**, **potere**, and **volere** carry the specific meanings of *should*, *could*, and *would like*.

Dovremmo studiare di più. *We should study more.*
Potremmo imparare molto. *We could learn a lot.*
Vorremmo intervistare il sindaco. *We would like to interview the mayor.*

● In compound tenses, when **dovere**, **potere**, and **volere** are used with an infinitive, they can take either **avere** or **essere** as the auxiliary. Use the auxiliary verb that is normally employed with the infinitive. If no infinitive is present, simply use **avere** as the auxiliary verb.

Ho potuto <u>comprare</u> una bandiera. ***but*** **Sono** potuta <u>tornare</u> a casa.
I was able to buy a flag. *I made it back home.*

● Used in the imperfect, **dovere**, **potere**, and **volere** indicate a repeated, habitual, or underlying condition of *needing to*, *being able to*, or *wanting to* do something. In contrast, in the **passato prossimo**, they indicate a specific moment of necessity, success at doing something, or an instance of wanting something.

Non sono uscito perché **dovevo** lavorare.
I didn't go out because I had to work. (I was scheduled to work.)

Non sono uscito perché **ho dovuto** lavorare.
I didn't go out because I had to work. (I had to work this particular day.)

● When **dovere**, **potere**, and **volere** are used with the infinitive of a reflexive verb, the reflexive pronoun can be placed either before the conjugated verb or attached to the infinitive (after removing the final –**e**). Note that it is more common to attach the reflexive pronoun to the infinitive.

Mi voglio dedicare alla causa./Voglio dedicar**mi** alla causa.
I want to dedicate myself to the cause.

Ci possiamo vedere domani./Possiamo veder**ci** domani.
We can see each other tomorrow.

Pratica e comunicazione

1

Consigli Reagisci alle affermazioni. Dai dei suggerimenti con i verbi **dovere**, **potere** e **volere**.

> **Modello** «Non sono contento degli attuali politici».
> Devi **votare alle prossime elezioni per cambiare i politici attuali.**

1. «Francesco non si interessa di politica».
   ____Deve____ (Dovere) dedicarsi di più alla politica.

2. «Noi non abbiamo mai partecipato a una protesta».
   ____Volete____ (Volere) venire con noi la settimana prossima?

3. «Loro non sono membri di un'associazione umanitaria».
   ____Possono____ (Potere) iscriversi alla nostra associazione.

4. «Non ho fiducia nelle istituzioni locali».
   ____Devi____ (Dovere) avere fiducia nei politici che ti rappresentano.

5. «Vorrei contribuire a migliorare la mia città».
   ____Puoi____ (Potere) presentarti alle prossime elezioni.

6. «I giovani non hanno ideali politici».
   ____Devono____ (Dovere) essere più attivi in politica.

2

Lo scorso fine settimana Completa le frasi con la forma giusta dei verbi **dovere**, **potere**, e **volere**. Some answers will vary.

> **Modello** **Volevamo andare alla conferenza ma** abbiamo dovuto accompagnare Laura dal dottore.

1. Dovevi studiare ma ____sei voluto andare alla festa di Paolo____.

2. Non sono potuti venire al cinema perché ____hanno dovuto lavorare____.

3. Marta voleva uscire con gli amici ma ____è dovuta andare con la mamma____.

4. Dovevo incontrare Stefania ma ____sono dovuta uscire con mia zia____.

5. Non siamo potuti partire perché ____abbiamo dovuto portare la macchina dal meccanico____

3

Immagina tre storie In gruppi di tre o quattro persone, immaginate una storia per ogni foto. Includete cosa vogliono, possono e/o devono fare le persone nelle foto.

4

Preparativi I tuoi genitori vengono a trovarti questo fine settimana. Prepara una lista di cosa devi, puoi e vuoi fare per prepararti al loro arrivo.

> **Modello** Per prima cosa devo pulire la casa. Poi devo andare a fare la spesa…

4 Have students share their lists in small groups and discuss who has the most to do, who has the most ambitious plans, etc.

Practice more at **vhlcentral.com**.

Sintesi

1

Parliamo In coppia, discutete dei seguenti argomenti.

La Gazzetta Della Sera

La crisi economica continua!

Ancora uno sbarco di immigrati illegali

Famoso politico arrestato per corruzione

Diminuisce la produzione industriale

1. In che modo si possono risolvere i problemi descritti nei titoli?
2. Quali problemi ti preoccupano di più? Perché?
3. Secondo te, sono stati fatti dei progressi per cercare di risolvere questi problemi?
4. Finalmente hai la possibilità di parlare con un politico. Cosa gli dici? Quali consigli gli dai per risolvere i problemi?
5. Cosa possono o devono fare i cittadini per contribuire a risolverli?

2

Scriviamo Scegli uno dei due argomenti e prepara un discorso di circa una pagina.

- Scrivi un discorso dove esorti (*urge*) i tuoi compagni di classe a diventare politicamente attivi invece che apatici. Suggerisci cose realistiche da fare dove vivi. Fai riferimento ai problemi della tua comunità.

- Scrivi un discorso dove dai il tuo sostegno (*support*) a un politico locale. Spiega perché appoggi (*support*) il politico e il suo partito. Esorta gli ascoltatori a fare qualcosa di concreto per sostenere la campagna elettorale. Fornisci esempi realistici.

Strategie per la comunicazione

Quando ti rivolgi a un pubblico utilizza le seguenti strutture: **Signore e signori, Cittadine e cittadini, Cari elettori,** …
Ricorda di utilizzare l'imperativo per dare consigli e suggerimenti.
Utilizza i verbi che hai imparato in questa lezione: **abusare, approvare una legge, difendere, imprigionare, giudicare, dedicarsi a, eleggere, governare, influenzare, vincere/perdere le elezioni, promuovere, votare.**

Preparazione  Vocabulary Tools

Vocabolario della lettura		Vocabolario utile
il **consiglio** *council*	lo **scambio** *exchange*	l'**accordo** *agreement*
la **crescita** *growth*	il **trattato** *treaty*	la **bandiera** *flag*
la **guerra mondiale** *world war*	la **valuta** *currency*	il **confine** *(national) boundary*
	il **vantaggio** *advantage*	l'**integrazione** *integration*
l'**inno** *anthem*	la **volontà** *willingness*	il **multilinguismo** *multilingualism*
la **potenza** *power*		

1

Da scegliere Completa queste frasi con le parole nuove.

1. Ci sono molti ___vantaggi___ a vivere in una democrazia.
2. La popolazione è aumentata: c'è stata una grande ___crescita___ demografica.
3. Nella prima metà del XX secolo ci sono state due violente ___guerre mondiali___.
4. Prima della partita i giocatori cantano l'___inno___ nazionale.
5. La ___bandiera___ italiana è verde, bianca e rossa.
6. Dopo la guerra le nazioni hanno firmato un ___accordo/trattato___ di pace.
7. In Italia, la ___valuta___ ufficiale è l'euro.
8. Durante la riunione, il ___consiglio___ delle nazioni ha eletto un presidente.

2

Ideali In coppia, leggete il motto dell'Unione Europea e, a turno, rispondete alle domande.

«Unità nella diversità»

1. Secondo te, quale ideale riflette questo motto? Perché?
2. Cosa succede invertendo i due termini: «Diversità nell'unità»? Cambia il significato? Perché?
3. Hai un motto personale? Qual è?
4. Qual è il motto del tuo paese? E della tua università? Quali altri motti conosci? Compila una lista.

3

Inventate Usando le parole della lista, create un nuovo motto nazionale per il vostro paese.

difendere	giustizia	pace	promuovere	vittoria
diritto	libertà	potente	uguaglianza	volontà

4

Feste In piccoli gruppi, rispondete alle domande.

- Quando è la festa nazionale del vostro paese? Perché proprio questa data? In onore di quale evento storico?
- Quando si celebrano altre feste che ricordano eventi storici?

Help students practice new vocabulary by modeling its use.

2 Help students by providing other sample mottos. One famous motto of the US is the Latin **E pluribus unum** (*Out of many, one*). Remind them that many words that end in *–ty* in English in Italian end in **–tà**: **generosità**, **lealtà**, **unità**, and so on.

3 Ask students to share their motto with the class; then ask students to vote for the three best mottos.

4 You might wish to make a timeline on the blackboard, encouraging students to name important historical events, perhaps surrounding WWI and WWII.

Nota **CULTURALE**

L'idea di un'Europa unita risale alle antiche espansioni imperiali dei Romani e, in seguito, di Carlo Magno e di Napoleone. Ma la data storica in cui fu ufficialmente proposta un'istituzione europea sovrannazionale° e democratica fu il **9 Maggio 1950** con la dichiarazione° di **Robert Schuman**, il ministro francese degli affari esteri. Fu un discorso rivoluzionario: secondo Schuman, «La pace mondiale non potrebbe essere salvaguardata senza sforzi creativi all'altezza dei pericoli che ci minacciano». Oggi il **9 maggio** è la festa ufficiale dell'Europa.

sovrannazionale *supranational*
dichiarazione *declaration*

UNITÀ NELLA DIVERSITÀ
L'ITALIA NELL'UNIONE EUROPEA

You might want to share with the students the contributions Italians made to the process of creating the EU, and important figures such as **Altiero Spinelli, Ernesto Rossi**, and **Alcide De Gasperi.** You may also want to mention **il Manifesto di Ventotene** and **i Trattati di Roma.**

L'Europa è un continente formato da 50 nazioni, ognuna con una propria storia, lingue diverse e complesse tradizioni culturali, in alcuni casi incompatibili tra di loro. Anche la geografia montagnosa europea crea delle divisioni che, senza una rete di trasporti internazionale, nel passato sembravano insormontabili. Le differenze tra queste nazioni erano più evidenti delle loro somiglianze tanto che, nel XX secolo, gli antagonismi tra diversi paesi dell'Europa centrale scatenarono° due guerre mondiali che coinvolsero° il resto del mondo.

caused
involved

Come suggerisce il suo motto, l'Unione Europea (UE) promuove l'unità ma allo stesso tempo rispetta la diversità delle nazioni che la formano. Finora° hanno aderito all'Unione Europea 28 paesi. L'UE non è una nazione (come lo sono gli Stati Uniti, per esempio) e non è un'organizzazione internazionale come l'ONU (l'Organizzazione delle Nazioni Unite): l'UE è più simile a un consiglio che decide democraticamente sulle questioni economiche e politiche di interesse comune a tutti i suoi membri.

So far

La Repubblica Italiana è stata una delle nazioni fondatrici dell'Unione Europea, insieme alla Francia, alla Germania, al Belgio, all'Olanda e al Lussemburgo. Oggi, con il suo PIL° (Prodotto Interno Lordo) pari a circa due milioni di miliardi° di dollari, l'Italia è la nona potenza economica mondiale e contribuisce alla stabilità della valuta europea, l'euro (€). La creazione dell'UE permette la libera circolazione dei cittadini dei paesi membri che possono così liberamente trovare lavoro o studiare all'interno dell'unione. L'apertura delle frontiere ha anche aumentato il commercio dell'Italia con

GDP
2.000 trillion

gli altri paesi europei e ha ulteriormente° favorito l'esportazione e la crescita economica del paese. La crescita dell'euro rispetto alle altre valute mondiali è molto positiva non solo per l'Italia, ma per tutti i paesi membri dell'UE.

further

I cambiamenti, soprattutto all'inizio, non sono stati facili. Il processo di adozione dell'euro come nuova valuta ufficiale e l'abbandono della vecchia lira ha portato grandi disagi° ai cittadini italiani. Anche adeguarsi° ai nuovi regolamenti europei per l'industria e il commercio è stato problematico: le nuove norme igieniche, ad esempio, non corrispondevano alle tradizioni artigianali della produzione dei formaggi e di altri prodotti gastronomici. L'improvviso arrivo di un numero inaspettato di immigranti ha causato una vera emergenza e purtroppo anche sentimenti di ostilità nei confronti degli stranieri.

hardships
adapting

Nonostante queste difficoltà, dopo il 1950 e la ricostruzione (favorita dal piano Marshall), l'Europa ha continuato a svilupparsi e a prosperare in pace. Grazie a Internet, ai capillari° collegamenti° aerei e ferroviari e all'apprendimento delle lingue, ogni giorno i cittadini europei sono è in contatto con luoghi e persone in tutto il mondo. Non essendo più legati a un unico territorio nazionale anche la nostra mentalità si sta allargando°. Le singole nazioni europee sono ormai caratterizzate dalla reciproca volontà di scambi e cooperazione. Per il futuro, sia per i cittadini che per gli stati europei, l'applicazione concreta degli ideali di pace, tolleranza e solidarietà dovrà continuare a essere l'obiettivo più importante. ■

extensive/connections
broaden, widen, enlarge

L'inno europeo

«L'Inno alla gioia» è l'adattamento del movimento finale della nona sinfonia composta da Ludwig van Beethoven nel 1824 basata su un poema scritto da Friedrich von Schiller nel 1785. Il poema esprime° idealismo e speranza in un senso di fratellanza° fra gli esseri umani. L'inno è stato adottato per la prima volta dal Consiglio d'Europa nel 1972 dichiarando che «senza parole, con il linguaggio universale della musica, questo inno esprime gli ideali di libertà, pace e solidarietà perseguiti dall'Europa».

esprime *expresses* fratellanza *brotherhood*

Students can listen to the European anthem at europa.eu/abc/symbols/anthem/index_it.htm.

Analisi

1

Comprensione Indica se le affermazioni sono **vere** o **false**. Dopo, in coppia, correggete le affermazioni false.

Vero	Falso	
☐	☑	1. L'Unione Europea è simile alle Nazioni Unite.
☐	☑	2. I paesi europei sono molto simili.
☑	☐	3. L'Unione Europea vuole mantenere la pace.
☑	☐	4. L'Unione Europea non è una nazione come lo sono gli Stati Uniti.
☐	☑	5. Le nazioni fondatrici dell'UE sono cinque.
☑	☐	6. L'entrata nell'UE ha portato molti vantaggi all'Italia.
☑	☐	7. Il 9 maggio è la festa ufficiale dell'Europa.
☐	☑	8. Schiller ha composto la musica per l'inno europeo.

2

L'Italia e l'UE In coppia, rispondete alle domande. Some answers will vary.

1. Per quali ragioni storiche è stata creata l'UE? per evitare la guerra

2. Quali sono i principi di base dell'UE? risolvere democraticamente questioni economiche e politiche di interesse comune a tutti i membri

3. Che cos'è l'UE? un'organizzazione sovrannazionale; un concilio di nazioni europee

4. Come si chiamava la vecchia valuta italiana? lira

5. Quali vantaggi ha comportato (*entailed*) per l'Italia l'entrata nell'UE? Ha reso più facile l'immigrazione che ha contribuito alla crescita economica e demografica del paese; ha permesso la libera circolazione dei cittadini dei paesi membri e ha contribuito alla crescita economica del paese.

6. Quali sono state alcune delle difficoltà che l'Italia ha incontrato dopo l'entrata nell'UE? l'adozione dell'euro, l'adeguamento ai regolamenti europei, l'inaspettato arrivo degli immigranti

3

Opinioni In coppia, confrontate le vostre opinioni.

1. Pensi che la creazione dell'UE sia stata una buona idea? Perché?

2. Quali sono stati, secondo te, gli ostacoli (*obstacles*) più grandi alla fondazione dell'UE? Perché?

3. Si potrebbe creare un'unione simile in un'altra parte del mondo? In quale? Perché? Quali problemi potrebbe risolvere?

4. In che modo l'UE è diversa da altre organizzazioni sovrannazionali come l'ONU o la NAFTA?

5. Pensi che il tuo paese possa un giorno unirsi con degli altri in una comunità simile all'UE? Con quali paesi pensi che sarebbe possibile farlo? Quali sarebbero i vantaggi? E gli svantaggi?

4

Senza frontiere In piccoli gruppi, parlate di come risolvere democraticamente delle gravi dispute o incomprensioni nel mondo in cui viviamo: pensate a degli esempi reali e poi suggerite delle possibili soluzioni.

- **Territorio:** Due nazioni non sono d'accordo sui confini.

- **Commercio:** Una nazione offre prodotti a costi troppo bassi in confronto alle altre.

- **Religione:** Due religioni vorrebbero condividere (*would like to share*) lo stesso luogo sacro.

- **Ideologia:** Due gruppi nella stessa nazione hanno tradizioni e abitudini diverse e vogliono separarsi.

Practice more at **vhlcentral.com.**

Preparazione  Vocabulary Tools

A proposito dell'autrice

Dacia Maraini, scrittrice di romanzi, saggi (*essays*), poesie e opere teatrali, è nata a Fiesole nel 1936. Per il lavoro del padre Dacia ha trascorso l'infanzia in Giappone dove è stata anche internata con i genitori in un campo di prigionia durante la seconda guerra mondiale. In seguito si è trasferita in Sicilia e poi a Roma. Negli anni Sessanta ha pubblicato i primi romanzi e ha incontrato il famoso scrittore Alberto Moravia. Nel 1990 Dacia ha pubblicato *La lunga vita di Marianna Ucrìa* con successo di critica e di pubblico. Nel 1993 ha pubblicato il suo unico romanzo autobiografico, *Bagherìa*.

Vocabolario della lettura	Vocabolario utile
la carrozza *car (train)*	**assaggiare** *to taste*
l'ingordigia *gluttony*	**l'assegno** *check*
il lusso *luxury*	**deporre** *to testify*
la pietanza *dish*	**goloso/a** *food-loving*
rapinare *to rob*	**incassare** *to cash*
sparare *to shoot*	**la rapina** *robbery*
la tovaglia *tablecloth*	**il sapore** *flavor*

1

Definizioni Trova la definizione adatta per ogni parola.

___c___ 1. il lusso   a. portare via illegalmente con violenza o minaccia

___f___ 2. la pietanza   b. la golosità di quelli a cui piace molto mangiare

___e___ 3. la carrozza   c. una spesa superflua o eccessiva

___b___ 4. l'ingordigia   d. telo che si usa per apparecchiare la tavola

___a___ 5. rapinare   e. il vagone del treno

___d___ 6. la tovaglia   f. un piatto o un cibo servito a tavola

2

Preparazione Fate le seguenti domande a un(a) compagno/a.

1. Quale mezzo di trasporto preferisci? Perché?

2. Ti piacerebbe fare un lungo viaggio in treno? Perché sì o no? Dove ti piacerebbe andare?

3. Cosa fai durante un lungo viaggio per passare il tempo? Leggi, ascolti la musica, dormi o parli con gli altri passeggeri?

4. Durante un viaggio hai mai incontrato per caso qualcuno che già conoscevi?

3

Discussione In piccoli gruppi, intervistatevi a vicenda.

In italiano l'espressione «dimmi cosa mangi e ti dirò chi sei» significa che possiamo capire il carattere di una persona dal cibo che mangia.

1. Qual è il tuo cibo preferito? Come riflette la tua personalità?

2. Pensate che le preferenze dei compagni nel gruppo corrispondano al loro carattere? Come e perché?

 Practice more at **vhlcentral.com**.

Nota CULTURALE

Parlare e mangiare

In italiano ci sono moltissimi modi di dire° relativi al cibo che spesso sottolineano l'attività conviviale di sedersi a tavola per mangiare e bere insieme. Spesso si dice che «a tavola non s'invecchia» perché l'allegria di mangiare è un piacere che fa bene e allunga la vita. Gli italiani dicono anche che «l'appetito vien mangiando»: più cose abbiamo, più ne desideriamo. Una delle espressioni usate più comunemente è «parla come mangi», cioè: «parla in modo semplice e spontaneo, non parlare in modo complicato». Naturalmente, il vino ha un posto d'onore tra i proverbi italiani–il più famoso è quasi una prescrizione medica: «buon vino fa buon sangue». Buon appetito a tutti!

modi di dire *sayings*

3 Ask students if they can think of an English expression similar to **dimmi cosa mangi e ti dirò chi sei.** Introduce other Italian idioms related to food (**Buono come il pane, aver sale in zucca, avere una fame da lupo, tutto fumo e niente arrosto,** etc.) Encourage students to discuss similarities and differences between these idioms and expressions in English or other languages.

Dacia Maraini

IL VIAGGIATORE
dalla voce profonda

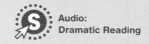

Go over the menu described in the story and bring in pictures
or recipes for some of the regional specialties mentioned.

Il treno correva di notte sotto una pioggia torrenziale. Dall'interno si vedevano i finestrini neri rigati da gocce scintillanti che colavano° *dripped*
5 veloci segnando il vetro per traverso.

Jole Pontormo aveva preso posto al tavolo del vagone ristorante e consultava con attenzione il menú. Le piaceva leggere le descrizioni dei cibi.
10 Fosse stato per lei avrebbe ordinato tutti i piatti, e avrebbe assaggiato un boccone° di ogni pietanza. Ma *bite* si tratteneva per non ingrassare. Da quando suo marito era sparito nelle
15 Americhe, tendeva a mangiare sempre troppo. Le piaceva il cerimoniale che accompagnava i pranzi e le cene. Sapeva che avrebbe speso piú del dovuto per quel pranzo in treno, ma aveva deciso
20 di concedersi quel lusso. Anche se poi l'avrebbe pagato con qualche sacrificio. Seduta in una carrozza di seconda classe non era riuscita a leggere in pace per le chiacchiere della gente.

25 Ora si trovava di fronte a una *carnation* tovaglia bianca, con un garofano° rosso infilato in una bottiglietta trasparente e aveva preso in mano con ingordigia il menú. Un elegante
30 quadernetto di cartoncino giallo decorato di fiori rosa su cui, a caratteri barocchi, in un inchiostro° *ink* azzurro, erano elencate° le specialità *listed* del giorno: *vol-au-vent* ripieni di
35 besciamella e funghi, spaghetti al *hare/pumpkin* sugo di lepre°, cappellacci di zucca°. E poi, a scelta: *vitel tonnè*, manzo al limone di Sorrento, baccalà alla vicentina. Insalate di stagione. Ma
40 quello che piú le piaceva erano i dolci. Col dito seguiva le proposte: *cake* di cioccolata dal cuore fondente. Già ne

percepiva il profumo. Ma la panna dov'era? Senza panna un tortino di cioccolata non è un vero tortino. 45 E poi: involtino° di frutta secca con *roll* crema di fragola, fagottini di mele al profumo di rose, *parfait* di mandorle° *almonds* in nido croccante°. *crunchy*

Jole Pontormo aveva chiuso gli 50 occhi assorbendo gli odori che le parole le suggerivano. Proprio in quel momento sentí una voce maschile che diceva:
«Permette?». 55
Aprí gli occhi sognanti e vide un uomo alto e magro con una borsa in mano che si chinava° con un gesto *was leaning over* cortese, sussiegoso°. […] *haughty*
«Prego!» disse con voce indispettita°. 60 *irritated*

L'uomo, con gesti lenti, si sfilò° *took off* il cappotto e lo appese° al gancio° *hung/hook* sulla parete°. Quindi si sedette con *wall* fare delicato e cauto sulla seggiolina imbottita°: 65 *quilted*
Jole Pontormo alzò lo sguardo sul suo dirimpettaio°. L'uomo era *the man in front of her* vestito con una eleganza un poco impettita°: giacca blu su pantaloni *stuffy* grigi, camicia candida, cravatta a 70 righe verdi e azzurre. Aveva i capelli castani che gli scivolavano° sulla fronte *slid down* ampia e severa. Portava gli occhiali da miope. La bocca era stretta, le labbra sottili e taglienti come di uno abituato 75 a comandare. […]
Il silenzio fu rotto da una voce che a Jole Pontormo parve di conoscere. Ma dove l'aveva sentita? Delle note lontane e stridenti che provenivano da 80 una memoria sepolta°. L'uomo prese a *buried* parlare con un leggero accento veneto, lento e avvolgente°. *enveloping*

«Questo treno che corre nella notte
85 ha qualcosa di misterioso. Non le pare
di essere sospesa nel vuoto fra queste
finestre scure rigate d'argento?».

dumbfounded

Jole Pontormo rimase interdetta°
a fissare il menú. Quel viaggiatore
90 dall'apparenza cosí rigida e severa aveva
una voce profonda e dolce, languida.
Non corrispondeva affatto al corpo
da dirigente d'azienda che aveva visto

slender avanzare con passo slanciato° verso il
95 suo tavolino. Sollevò di nuovo lo sguardo
e vide che in quella faccia anonima e
impenetrabile era spuntato un sorriso

captivating accattivante° e gentile.

«Lei scrive poesie»? gli chiese,
100 ancora sorpresa da quell'attacco
letterario.

«No, commercio in cavalli». […]

«Un commerciante di cavalli? Che
strano... Lei parla come se recitasse
105 una poesia».

«Sono un lettore di poesie infatti».

« Dimmi quello che mangi e ti dirò chi sei. »

Eppure le sembrava di conoscerlo
quest'uomo. Dove aveva sentito quella
voce dal leggero accento veneto?
110 Dove aveva visto quella bocca rigida

closed e serrata°? Quegli occhi duri e decisi?
Quella testa dai capelli lisci, che
tendevano a scivolare continuamente
sulla fronte? E quegli occhiali grandi
115 dalle lenti appena affumicate? Non
riusciva proprio a ricordare.

«Dimmi quello che mangi e ti dirò
chi sei», enunciò lui mandando giú un
sorso° con aria beata°.   *sip/content*

«E noi chi siamo che mangiamo *vol* 120
au vent con crema di funghi?».

«Un uomo e una donna seduti
comodamente al caldo, fra luci seducenti
e un vino squisito nei bicchieri, mentre
fuori la tempesta si accanisce° contro 125 *rages*
i fianchi° del treno e la pioggia cerca di   *sides*
entrare prepotente°. Immagini qualcuno   *overbearing*
che ci vede passare, da fuori, come
un lampo […]

Jole Pontormo lo ascoltava 130
socchiudendo le palpebre. […]

Poi improvvisamente, […] ebbe un
sussulto °. Spalancò gli occhi e guardò   *was startled*
l'uomo con un misto di terrore e di
sbigottimento°.   135 *astonishment*

Le venne in mente il giorno piú
terribile della sua vita. La banca dove
aveva appena ritirato i soldi della
pensione del marito, un irrompere° di   *a sudden entrance*
giovani che imbracciavano mitragliatrici° 140 *machine guns*
e pistole. Ordini secchi. Le casse che si
chiudevano automaticamente, l'allarme
che partiva. Il direttore che urlava mentre
un uomo alto, dai jeans sdruciti° e le   *ripped*
scarpe da ginnastica bianche le puntava 145
una pistola alla tempia. Quell'uomo
parlava, parlava.

Non ha mai ricordato cosa dicesse,
ma parlava con il direttore, dava ordini
brutali... Ricorda a stento° che le aveva 150 *barely*
strappato dalle mani i pochi biglietti
da cento piegati° dentro la ricevuta, e   *folded*
nel farlo l'aveva rabbiosamente spinta°   *pushed*
per terra. Subito dopo si era avventato°   *attacked*
sul direttore costringendolo° a riaprire 155 *forcing him*

risky le casse, e alla fine, quando il direttore aveva fatto un gesto azzardato°, gli aveva sparato sulle gambe senza pietà.

160 Una coincidenza assurda. L'uomo seduto di fronte a lei certamente assomigliava molto a quell'altro, ma non *coincidence* poteva che trattarsi di un caso°. Come poteva, una persona così gentile, così *cultured* colta°, che parlava quasi in versi, [...]
165 No, non poteva essere, la sua memoria la *was decieving her* stava ingannando°. [...]

Intanto erano quasi arrivati. L'uomo – ma come si chiamava? [...] – si infilò il cappotto di cashmere,
170 la aiutò a indossare l'imbottita di *lifted* plastica color fucsia, sollevò° da terra la borsa che appariva davvero pesante e si avviarono ciascuno verso il proprio vagone.
175 «Arrivederci!» disse lei quando si aprirono le porte all'interno della stazione.
«Arrivederci, signora Pontormo!» aveva gridato lui mentre scendeva con *step* 180 un salto dal predellino° e spariva nella folla della stazione. [...]

Come faceva a sapere che si chiamava Pontormo? E improvvisamente le era tornato in mente che l'uomo in banca
185 le aveva strappato dalle mani la ricevuta della pensione del marito con il nome scritto sopra. E ricordava la voce. Era proprio quella voce, anche se il tono era un altro.

190 Ora era sicura che si trattava di lui. Ma dove sarà sparito? E poi perché l'aveva voluta ingannare così perfidamente? [...]

« Un bruto, un ignorante, si vedeva lontano un miglio che era analfabeta, uno cresciuto in mezzo alla strada. »

Ricordò improvvisamente una intervista che aveva dato a un giornale 195 poco dopo il fatto. Al cronista°, che *reporter* le chiedeva cosa pensasse dell'uomo che l'aveva rapinata° e buttata per *had robbed her* terra lussandole° una spalla, aveva *dislocating* risposto: «Un bruto, un ignorante, 200 si vedeva lontano un miglio che era analfabeta°, uno cresciuto in mezzo *illiterate* alla strada». [...] Così aveva detto al giornalista. E ora sapeva con certezza che l'uomo dei cavalli aveva letto 205 quelle parole.

Prese la valigia, scese dal treno e si diresse verso la polizia. Ma cosa avrebbe deposto? Che aveva cenato in treno con l'uomo che un anno prima 210 aveva rapinato la banca vicino casa e l'aveva gettata° per terra strappandole *had thrown her* dalle mani la pensione del marito? Ma se non sapeva nemmeno come si chiamava! [...] Cosa poteva dire? 215 Che quello che aveva creduto un bruto analfabeta era un signore elegante e colto [...]? Era poco, era veramente poco. ∎

Analisi

1 Ask the students to correct the false statements in pairs.

1

Vero o falso? Indica se le affermazioni sono **vere** o **false**.

Vero	Falso		
☑	☐	1.	Jole Pontormo viaggia in treno nel vagone-ristorante.
☐	☑	2.	Il marito di Jole è partito per l'Australia.
☑	☐	3.	Durante il viaggio di Jole c'è una pioggia torrenziale.
☐	☑	4.	L'uomo dalla voce profonda è un poeta.
☐	☑	5.	Jole e l'uomo ordinano il baccalà alla vicentina.
☑	☐	6.	Jole aveva già incontrato l'uomo del treno durante la rapina alla banca.
☑	☐	7.	L'uomo aveva puntato la pistola alla tempia di Jole.
☑	☐	8.	Jole aveva detto al giornalista che l'uomo era un bruto analfabeta.

2

Comprensione del testo Scegli la risposta giusta.

A. Scegli la risposta giusta.

1. Jole è molto sorpresa perché _____.
   a. l'uomo è colto e gentile
   c. la personalità dell'uomo è il contrario di quello che lei ricorda
   b. pensa di aver già incontrato l'uomo del treno
   d. tutt'e tre

2. Leggendo il menù del vagone-ristorante Jole nota che _____.
   a. è uguale tutti i giorni
   c. non include i dolci
   b. elenca alcune pietanze regionali
   d. tutt'e tre

3. In realtà la vera occupazione dell'uomo è _____.
   a. commerciante di cavalli
   c. rapinatore di banche
   b. lettore di poesie
   d. direttore di azienda

4. Durante la rapina in banca, l'uomo _____.
   a. ha sparato alle gambe del direttore
   c. ha rubato i soldi e la ricevuta di Jole
   b. ha lussato la spalla di Jole
   d. tutt'e tre

5. Alla fine del racconto l'uomo salta giù dal treno e _____.
   a. fugge dalla polizia che lo insegue
   c. saluta Jole usando il suo cognome anche se non si sono mai presentati
   b. ruba una fetta di torta perché ha ancora fame
   d. spara al conduttore che lo ha riconosciuto

6. Dopo aver riconosciuto l'uomo Jole decide di _____.
   a. prendere un caffè con panna
   c. andare dalla polizia anche se non sa cosa dire
   b. telefonare al marito per raccontargli la storia
   d. non viaggiare più in treno

3

Personaggi Scegli gli aggettivi che descrivono meglio i due personaggi del racconto.

	Jole	l'uomo
goloso/a		
languido/a		
deciso/a		
indispettito/a		
sbigottito/a		
brutale		
terrorizzato/a		

4

Discussione In piccoli gruppi, rispondete a queste domande usando degli esempi specifici presi dal racconto.

1. Come fa Jole a riconoscere l'uomo sul treno? Cosa le fa capire di averlo già incontrato?
2. Descrivete il contrasto tra l'incontro nel vagone-ristorante e quello precedente durante la rapina nella banca.
3. Cosa pensate che farà Jole dopo la conclusione della storia? Andrà davvero dalla polizia? Cosa racconterà? Le crederanno?
4. Immaginate la vita dell'uomo. Perché era sul treno? Dove stava andando? Aveva intenzione di rapinare un'altra banca o voleva semplicemente cambiare l'opinione che Jole aveva di lui?

5

Opinioni In coppia, rispondete alle domande.

1. Vi è mai capitato di cambiare opinione su un'altra persona? Come e perché? Cosa vi ha fatto capire di esservi sbagliati/e?
2. Durante un viaggio vi è mai successo di incontrare una persona interessante con cui avete fatto una conversazione? Di cosa avete parlato?
3. Avete mai assistito a un crimine? Raccontate la storia.
4. Nel posto in cui abitate, c'è criminalità? Di che tipo? Quale pensate sia la causa del problema? E quale la soluzione?

6

I gialli In piccoli gruppi pensate a romanzi, film e storie poliziesche che parlano di criminali e di investigatori. Quali sono i vostri preferiti? Perché?

7

Scrittura Scegli uno di questi argomenti e scrivi una breve composizione.

- Inventa una storia a sorpresa, in cui alla fine si scopre la vera identità di uno dei personaggi principali.
- Immagina di incontrare una persona famosa durante un viaggio in aereo. Scrivi un dialogo con la vostra conversazione.
- Descrivi una cena in un ristorante di lusso. Com'è l'atmosfera, con i tavoli apparecchiati, i clienti e i camerieri? Descrivi il menù, elencando gli antipasti, le pietanze principali, i contorni e, naturalmente, i dolci.

4 Many interviews and video clips featuring the author of this story can be found by searching for Dacia Maraini on the Rai website.

Show one of the clips in class (e.g. **Dacia Maraini: viaggiare non da turista** to further encourage discussion on travel destinations, readings and approaches. Assign further videochats with Maraini for individual or group presentations.

Nota
CULTURALE
Il giallo

L'origine del termine *giallo* in italiano proviene dalla serie di romanzi *noir* o polizieschi che l'editore Mondadori ha cominciato a pubblicare nel 1929 con una copertina° gialla. È in seguito divenuta una parola di uso comune per indicare tutte le opere letterarie o cinematografiche con storie di criminali e delle indagini° condotte dalla polizia. La presenza di un investigatore carismatico o di criminali molto abili e attraenti° ha catturato molti lettori di questo genere e ispirato anche serie di fumetti°.

copertina *cover* **indagini** *investigations* **attraenti** *alluring* **fumetti** *comic books*

6 To further encourage class discussion, provide examples of the *mystery, police drama,* and *true crime* genres which in Italy are called **gialli**. Ask the students to share novels, authors, movies and series they enjoy reading or watching and introduce popular Italian titles and characters such as Camilleri's Montalbano and series of graphic novels such as **Diabolik** and **Dylan Dog** (which also contain **nero** elements).

 Practice more at **vhlcentral.com.**

Pratica

Preparazione Have students look for examples of essays on the Internet. One good source is the editorial section of online Italian newspapers. Have students bring to class an example of an essay with a good conclusion and write a paragraph analyzing it and explaining its strengths.

La conclusione

L'introduzione e la conclusione sono le due parti della tesi che richiedono maggior lavoro di scrittura. Per questa ragione, sono le due parti che devono essere scritte con maggior attenzione perché costituiscono la struttura della tesi.

Una buona conclusione deve:

- far riferimento alla tesi iniziale e rinforzarla
- sintetizzare i punti principali
- lasciare un'impressione finale chiara
- essere scritta nello stesso registro del resto del saggio

Una buona conclusione non deve:

- limitarsi a ripetere la tesi iniziale
- introdurre nuovi argomenti
- includere argomenti aggiuntivi
- introdurre la tesi per la prima volta

Una buona conclusione può:

- impostare nuove domande
- includere una citazione che sintetizza le idee dello scrittore

1

Preparazione In coppia, rileggete ed esaminate la conclusione di uno dei brani in questa lezione o in quelle precedenti. In base alle caratteristiche che definiscono una buona conclusione, come definireste la conclusione del brano? Quali cambiamenti potrebbero essere fatti?

2

Saggio Scegli uno di questi argomenti e scrivi un saggio.

- Il tuo saggio deve far riferimento ad uno o due dei quattro brani studiati in questa lezione e contenuti in **Cortometraggio**, **Immagina**, **Cultura** e **Letteratura**, oppure studiati nelle lezioni precedenti.

- La parte finale del tuo saggio deve rispettare le caratteristiche di una buona conclusione.

- Il saggio deve essere lungo almeno due pagine.

1. Anche se viviamo in una realtà sempre più multietnica, la diffidenza (*mistrust*) nei confronti dell'«altro» è sempre presente. I confini tra le nazioni sono una necessità che assicura protezione oppure un'imposizione alla libera circolazione delle persone?

2. In un mondo che cambia demograficamente, molti vivono in condizioni di clandestinità e hanno bisogno di aiuto. Secondo te, è giusto aiutare se questo significa non rispettare la legge?

3. La seconda guerra mondiale, con l'Olocausto degli ebrei e di altre minoranze etniche, ha cambiato per sempre il mondo, ma le guerre continuano in varie parti del pianeta. Perché i potenti non sembrano aver imparato dal genocidio di quella guerra a rispettare gli «altri»? Perché si continua a combattere?

La giustizia e la politica

 Vocabulary Tools

Le leggi e i diritti

la cittadinanza *citizenship*
la criminalità *crime*
il crimine *felony*
i diritti umani *human rights*
l'emigrazione (f.) *emigration*
la giustizia *justice*
l'immigrazione (f.) *immigration*
la libertà *freedom*
l'uguaglianza *equality*

abusare *to abuse*
approvare/passare una legge
  to pass a law
difendere *to defend*
emigrare *to emigrate*
giudicare *to judge*
imprigionare *to imprison*

analfabeta *illiterate*
colpevole *guilty*
(in)giusto/a *(un)fair*
ineguale *unequal*
innocente *innocent*
(il)legale *(il)legal*
oppresso/a *oppressed*
uguale *equal*

La politica

l'abuso di potere *abuse of power*
la crudeltà *cruelty*
la democrazia *democracy*
la dittatura *dictatorship*
l'esercito *army*
il governo *government*
la guerra (civile) *(civil) war*
la pace *peace*
il partito politico *political party*
la politica *politics*
la sconfitta *defeat*
la vittoria *victory*

dedicarsi a *to dedicate oneself to*
eleggere *to elect*
governare *to govern*
influenzare *to influence*
vincere/perdere le elezioni *to win/
  lose the election*
votare *to vote*

conservatore/conservatrice
  conservative
liberale *liberal*
moderato/a *moderate*
pacifico/a *peaceful*
pacifista *pacifist*
potente *powerful*
vittorioso/a *victorious*

La gente

l'attivista (m., f.) *activist*
l'avvocato (m., f.) *lawyer*
il/la criminale *criminal*
il/la deputato/a *congressman/
  congresswoman*
il/la giudice *judge*
la giuria *jury*
il/la ladro/a *thief*
il/la politico/a *politician*
il/la presidente *president*
il/la terrorista *terrorist*
il/la testimone *witness*
la vittima *victim*

La sicurezza e i pericoli

l'arma *weapon*
la minaccia *threat*
la paura *fear*
il pericolo *danger*
lo scandalo *scandal*
la sicurezza *safety*
il terrorismo *terrorism*
la violenza *violence*

combattere *to fight*
promuovere *to promote*
salvare *to save*
spiare *to spy*

Cortometraggio

il boccaglio *snorkel*
la camera d'aria *inner tube*
il clandestino *illegal immigrant*
il faro *lighthouse*
la guardia costiera *coast guard*
la maschera *mask*
la muta *wet suit*
il naufrago *castaway*

le pinne *flippers*
la poppa *stern*
la prua *bow*
il punto di riferimento
  reference point
la spigola *bass (fish)*
il subacqueo *scuba diver*

naufragare *to sink, wreck*
pescare *to fish*

inaffidabile *unreliable*
nascosto/a *hidden*
salvo/a *safe*

promesso *promised*

Cultura

l'accordo *agreement*
la bandiera *flag*
il confine *(national) boundary*
il consiglio *council*
la crescita *growth*
la guerra mondiale *world war*
l'inno *anthem*
l'integrazione *integration*
il multilinguismo *multilinguism*
la potenza *power*
lo scambio *exchange*
il trattato *treaty*
la valuta *currency*
il vantaggio *advantage*
la volontà *willingness*

Letteratura

la carrozza *car (train)*
l'assegno *check*
l'ingordigia *gluttony*
il lusso *luxury*
la pietanza *dish*
la rapina *robbery*
il sapore *flavor*
la tovaglia *tablecloth*

assaggiare *to taste*
deporre *to testify*
incassare *to cash*
rapinare *to rob*
sparare *to shoot*

goloso/a *food-loving*

5

Le generazioni in movimento

I legame (*relationship*) tra genitori e figli è indissolubile, anche se con il tempo cambia. Da bambini garantisce sicurezza, protezione ed è determinante nel formare l'identità personale. Poi, durante l'adolescenza, spesso diventa conflittuale. In genere si trasforma in un trampolino da cui prendere il volo per crescere e diventare persone autonome e complete. Ti senti pronto e forte abbastanza per volare? Come giudichi (*judge*) il tuo legame con le generazioni che ti hanno preceduto?

173

196

Destinazione:

SICILIA E SARDEGNA

SARDEGNA

SICILIA

PREVIEW Use the photo on the previous page as a springboard for discussion. Ask students:
1. Le famiglie italiane sono diverse da quelle degli altri paesi? Perché?
2. In Italia danno ai figli solo il cognome del padre. Cosa ne pensi? Porti il cognome di tuo padre, di tua madre o di tutti e due?

Le generazioni in movimento

In famiglia  Vocabulary Tools

I rapporti di parentela

il/la (bis)nonno/a *(great-) grandfather/grandmother*
il/la cugino/a *cousin*
il/la figlio/a (unico/a) *son/daughter; (only) child*
il/la figlioccio/a *godson/goddaughter*
il/la gemello/a *twin*

il genero *son-in-law*
il genitore (single) *(single) parent*
la madrina *godmother*
il marito *husband*
la moglie *wife*
il/la nipote *nephew/niece; grandson/granddaughter*
la nuora *daughter-in-law*
il padrino *godfather*
il/la parente *relative*
la parentela *relatives*
lo/la sposo/a *groom/bride*

il/la suocero/a *father-/mother-in-law*
lo/la zio/a *uncle/aunt*

adottivo/a *adopted*
imparentato/a *related*
lontano/a *distant*
materno/a *maternal*
paterno/a *paternal*

aspettare un figlio *to be expecting (a baby)*
essere incinta *to be pregnant*

INSTRUCTIONAL RESOURCES
Audioscripts, Answer Keys, Lab MP3s
SAM/WebSAM: WB, LM

Le tappe della vita

l'età adulta *adulthood*
la giovinezza *youth*
l'infanzia *childhood*
la maturità *maturity*
la morte *death*
la nascita *birth*
la vecchiaia *old age*

Le generazioni

l'antenato *ancestor*
le radici *roots*
il salto generazionale *generation gap*

il soprannome *nickname*

assomigliare *to resemble*
ereditare *to inherit*
sopravvivere *to survive*

La vita in famiglia

diventare indipendente *to become independent*
educare *to raise*
essere desolato/a *to be sorry*
litigare *to fight*

pentirsi *to regret*
punire (isc) *to punish*
rimproverare *to scold*
sormontare *to overcome*
trasferirsi *to move*
viziare *to spoil*

SINONIMI E CONTRARI
essere desolato/a ←→ essere dispiaciuto/a
il genitore single ←→ monogenitore
(in legal contexts, forms, etc.)
maleducato ≠ educato

La personalità

il carattere *personality*

affiatato/a *close-knit*
amabile *lovable*
autoritario/a *bossy*

codardo/a *coward*
egoista *selfish*
furbo/a *sly*
insopportabile *unbearable*
maleducato/a *bad-mannered*
possessivo/a *possessive*
remissivo/a *submissive*
ribelle *rebellious*

severo/a *strict*
socievole *sociable*
testardo/a *stubborn*
vanitoso/a *vain*
vivace *lively*

Nota CULTURALE

In Italia le famiglie allargate (*extended*) sono una realtà sempre più comune, ma le parole che esprimono questi rapporti di parentela sono percepite come dispregiative (*derogatory*) e quindi sono poco usate.

il patrigno *stepfather*
la matrigna *stepmother*
il figliastro *stepson*
la figliastra *stepdaughter*
il fratellastro *half-brother*
la sorellastra *half-sister*

Pratica e comunicazione

1 **La parentela** Completa le frasi con la forma corretta delle parole nel riquadro.

amabile	litigare	padrino
autoritario	madrina	paterno
carattere	materno	pentirsi

1. Di solito, i miei fratellini gemelli ___litigano___ per i giocattoli.
2. I fratelli di mio padre sono i miei zii ___paterni___.
3. Al battesimo, la ___madrina___ e il ___padrino___ erano molto emozionati.
4. Mio nonno ha un ___carattere___ molto tranquillo. Mia nonna, invece, è un po'___autoritaria___.

1 Have students create sentences with the words not used in this exercise.

2 **Indovinelli** Identifica i membri della famiglia con un aggettivo che descrive la loro personalità utilizzando solo le parole studiate in questa lezione. *Some answers will vary.*

1. Non ho né fratelli né sorelle e non mi piace condividere le mie cose con gli altri.
2. Pretendo (*I expect*) molto dai miei figli: devono essere bravi a scuola, fare sport
   e mangiare frutta e verdura. *un(a) figlio/a unico/a egoista* *una madre severa/un padre severo*
3. L'apparenza è molto importante per me. Mi piace vestire bene e alla moda, ci
   tengo a fare bella figura quando vado a casa della mamma di mia moglie. *un genero vanitoso*
4. Sono il fratello della mamma. Mi piace fare tanti regali ai figli di mia sorella. *uno zio generoso*
5. Sono il figlio della sorella del papà. Sono sempre pieno di vita; mi piace giocare,
   correre e fare scherzi con i figli di mio zio. *un cugino vivace*

2 Have groups of students create an original riddle using new vocabulary. Call on a volunteer from each group to share his or her riddle with the class. Then have the class guess the answer.

3 Have students share their biographies in small groups.

3 **Biografia** Scrivi la biografia di una persona famosa o inventata e utilizza almeno otto parole della lista. Usa la nota culturale come esempio.

amabile	egoista	nonno/a	soprannome
assomigliare	figlio/a	rapporto	trasferirsi
educare	infanzia	socievole	viziare

4 **A pranzo** Descrivete le persone nella foto.

- Quante generazioni sono rappresentate?
- Qual è il loro rapporto di parentela?
- Immaginate com'è la loro vita familiare: I bambini sono rispettosi o viziati? Sono ribelli o educati? Spesso vengono sgridati (*scolded*) o puniti? I genitori sono autoritari o comprensivi?

Nota CULTURALE

Giuseppe Tomasi di Lampedusa (1896–1957) nacque a Palermo il 23 dicembre 1896. Figlio di genitori aristocratici, Giuseppe era molto legato alla madre, mentre con il padre i rapporti erano freddi perché non approvava l'amore di suo figlio per la letteratura. Anche la nonna fu una figura importante nella vita del giovane Giuseppe; fu lei che gli fece leggere i romanzi di **Emilio Salgari**. Dopo la morte della sorella Stefania a causa di una malattia, rimase figlio unico. Nel 1932 sposò **Alessandra Wolf-Stomersee**, figliastra di uno zio. Il suo romanzo più noto è *Il Gattopardo*, libro che divenne ancora più famoso dopo che il regista **Luchino Visconti** lo adattò a un film di grande successo.

4 Have students prepare an oral presentation about their own families, using photographs or other visual aids.

Practice more at vhlcentral.com.

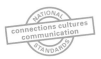

Preparazione

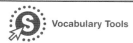

Vocabulary Tools

connections cultures communication NATIONAL STANDARDS

INSTRUCTIONAL RESOURCES
Supersite: Video, Script & Translation
SAM/WebSAM: WB

TEACHING OPTION Along with the verbs in the vocabulary lists, review other relevant reflexive verbs **sposarsi**, **separarsi**, **baciarsi**, **lasciarsi**, **nascondersi**, and others. You might also wish to point out that in Italian **fidanzarsi** (just like **avere un(a) ragazzo/a**) has the more casual meaning of dating and does not necessarily imply engagement.

Vocabolario del cortometraggio

accomodarsi *to make oneself comfortable*
avvicinarsi *to go near*
il/la fidanzato/a *boyfriend/girlfriend*
la lavatrice *washing machine*
l'ordigno *bomb*
il rinforzo *reinforcement*
sorridere *to smile*
stare in fila *to stand in line*
lo zainetto *small backpack*

Vocabolario utile

la bambola *doll*
il banco *(check-in) counter*
la cabina di controllo *cockpit*
i carabinieri *military police*
fare il bucato *to do the laundry*
il nastro trasportatore *luggage carousel*

ESPRESSIONI

fidati di me *trust me*
rompere le scatole *to be a pain in the neck*
senti un po' *hey, listen*
stare insieme *to be together (dating)*

1 **Collegamenti** Completa le frasi.

1. Se chiamiamo i rinforzi _c_
2. Usiamo la lavatrice _a_
3. Quando una persona sorride _d_
4. Un ordigno è _b_
5. I carabinieri _g_
6. I fidanzati _f_
7. All'aeroporto si va al banco _e_
8. Il nastro trasportatore _h_

a. per fare il bucato.
b. una bomba.
c. vuol dire che abbiamo bisogno di aiuto.
d. ha l'aria di essere felice.
e. per fare il check in.
f. sono innamorati.
g. sono la polizia militare italiana.
h. porta i bagagli.

2 Encourage students to share the most unusual stories with the rest of the class.

2 **Sondaggio**

A. Trova qualcuno che da bambino/a...

1. ...aiutava i genitori in casa: cosa faceva?
2. ...si è perso/a: dove?
3. ...andava a scuola a piedi da solo/a: quanti anni aveva?
4. ...ha preso l'aereo o il treno da solo/a: per andare dove?
5. ...faceva il bucato: quanti anni aveva?

B. Confronta i tuoi risultati con gli altri.

3

In viaggio In coppia, parlate delle vostre esperienze di viaggio.

1. Qual è stato il tuo viaggio più interessante? Perché?

2. Hai mai perso il bagaglio? L'hai poi ritrovato?

3. Ti sei mai perso/a in una città che non conoscevi? Cos'è successo?

4. Qual è la cosa più strana che hai visto viaggiando?

5. Ti piace viaggiare in auto, in treno o preferisci l'aereo?

6. Hai mai fatto un viaggio con la tua famiglia? Dove siete andati?

4

Preparativi per il viaggio Stai organizzando un viaggio con un(a) compagno/a. Insieme, decidete dove andare e con chi; poi fate una lista delle cose che volete mettere in valigia.

- Compagni di viaggio
- Mezzi di trasporto
- Destinazione
- Durata
- Luoghi da visitare (monumenti, parchi, spiagge, ecc.)
- Abbigliamento
- Cose indispensabili
- Cose utili
- Cose superflue ma divertenti

4 Have pairs share their lists of travel preferences on the board and encourage the class to find trends. How many pairs chose to go to the beach? To a city? To another country?

5

Immaginiamo

A. Guardate le immagini e inventate una storia.

- Chi è il protagonista? Come si chiama?
- Cosa sta facendo?
- Dove sta andando? Perché?
- Cosa gli succederà?

B. Adesso presentate la vostra storia agli altri studenti.

5 Encourage students to ask/answer questions about their respective stories using **il futuro di probabilità** (See **Strutture 5.3, pp. 188–189**). Example: **Dove andrà il protagonista alla fine della storia? E cosa farà?**

6

Generazioni Parlate della vostra infanzia rispondendo a turno alle domande.

1. I tuoi genitori erano molto protettivi? Perché sì o perché no?

2. Quando eri piccolo/a, c'era un'attività che ti faceva sentire «grande» e indipendente? Quale?

3. Hai mai dovuto prenderti cura di (*take care of*) un fratellino o di una sorellina?

4. Ti ricordi se i tuoi nonni avevano opinioni diverse da quelle dei tuoi genitori?

5. Hai mai cercato di chiedere il permesso di fare qualcosa a un genitore più permissivo dopo che l'altro ti aveva già detto di no?

6. Quanti anni avevi la prima volta che sei uscito/a da solo/a con gli amici? Dove siete andati?

7. Quando avrai dei figli, pensi che li lascerai andare a scuola da soli? Perché?

8. Secondo te, è giusto che i genitori abbiano regole diverse per i figli maschi e le figlie femmine? Perché?

6 Divide the class in two or three groups to debate questions 7 and 8.

Practice more at
vhlcentral.com.

Video

DOVE DORMONO GLI AEREI

(Premio **FACIBA** assegnato dal pubblico)

un film di GIANLUCA ARCHIPINTO produzione PABLO regia di ALESSANDRO FEDERICI. sceneggiatura FRANCESCA COTICONI, LEONARDO ANGELINI, ALESSIO MARIA FEDERICI attori principali ILENIA ROSATI, GABRIELE UNGHERANI, LORENZA INDOVINA, GIANPIERO LUDICA soggetto FRANCESCA COTICONI, ALESSIO MARIA FEDERICI montaggio ANDREA BRIGANTI musiche originali MOKA suono DARIO CALVARI

Trama *Paolo e Alice, due bambini che s'incontrano per caso all'aeroporto di Roma, si allontanano da soli in cerca di avventure.*

Nota
CULTURALE

Come si arriva all'aeroporto di Roma?

Il treno Fiumicino–Termini collega l'aeroporto Leonardo da Vinci con la stazione dei treni Termini al centro di Roma. Il treno più rapido, che non fa fermate intermedie, si chiama «Leonardo Express» e parte ogni mezz'ora nei due sensi°. È un viaggio di circa 31 minuti. Una volta arrivati alla stazione, si possono prendere gli autobus o la metropolitana per spostarsi° nella capitale, oppure un altro treno per raggiungere° altre destinazioni italiane o europee.

sensi *directions* **spostarsi** *move*
raggiungere *reach*

PAPÀ DI ALICE Pronta? Andiamo! Non essere triste. Papà questo weekend ha avuto molto da fare. Ti vengo a trovare presto. Te lo prometto.

PAOLO Mi scusi, le posso rubare il giornale per un paio di minuti?
SIGNORA Prego, prego!

Point out that **aeroporto** is the correct spelling for *airport*. Many people, however, pronounce it **areoporto**.

ALICE Mi chiamo Alice.
PAOLO Io Paolo e mia mamma fa la *hostess*. Sta tornando da Londra.

PAPÀ DI ALICE Dov'è finita? L'ho lasciata qui con un bambino…
IMPIEGATA Non si preoccupi: la cerchiamo subito.
PAPÀ DI ALICE Ma subito, però!

🔊 Sullo SCHERMO

Associa i personaggi con le azioni.

1. Paolo ___e___
2. Il papà di Alice ___b___
3. Alice ___a___
4. La mamma di Paolo ___c___
5. Paolo e Alice ___g___
6. I carabinieri ___d___
7. Il treno ___f___
8. I passeggeri ___l___
9. La mamma di Alice ___h___
10. I bagagli ___i___

a. gioca con le Barbie.
b. è sempre al telefono.
c. torna da Londra.
d. trovano lo zainetto.
e. fa il bucato in lavatrice.
f. parte dalla stazione.
g. si baciano.
h. abita a Parigi.
i. arrivano sul nastro trasportatore.
l. fanno la fila.

ALICE Senti un po', ma tu ce l'hai la fidanzata?
PAOLO No e tu?

MAMMA DI PAOLO Ma dov'è mio figlio?
PAPÀ DI ALICE Non lo so, è sparito° con mia figlia…

sparito *disappeared*

Analisi

1

Vero o falso? Indica se le affermazioni corrispondono alla storia del corto. Dopo, in coppia, correggete le affermazioni false.

Vero	Falso	
☑	☐	1. Alice e Paolo s'incontrano all'aeroporto.
☐	☑	2. Il papà di Alice fa il pilota.
☑	☐	3. Paolo va spesso all'aeroporto ad aspettare la mamma.
☐	☑	4. La signora sul treno è preoccupata perché Paolo è da solo.
☐	☑	5. La mamma di Paolo torna da Parigi.
☑	☐	6. Il papà di Alice è disperato quando non la trova più.
☑	☐	7. L'impiegata aiuta il papà a cercare Alice.
☑	☐	8. Dopo essersi baciati, Alice e Paolo si sentono fidanzati.

2

Comprensione Come si sentono i personaggi?

1. Quando il papà parla al telefono, Alice si sente _____.
   a. ignorata   b. felice   c. indipendente

2. Quando incontra Paolo, Alice è _____.
   a. curiosa   b. allegra   c. sospettosa

3. All'inizio del corto, il papà di Alice è _____.
   a. preoccupato di andare all'aeroporto   b. preoccupato per il suo lavoro
   c. preoccupato per Alice

4. La mamma di Paolo _____.
   a. è avventurosa e vuole ripartire subito   b. è stanca e vuole tornare a casa
   c. non riconosce lo zainetto di Paolo

5. Quando salgono sull'aereo segreto, Paolo e Alice si sentono _____.
   a. liberi   b. abbandonati   c. arrabbiati

6. Quando comincia a giocare con Alice, Paolo non è più _____.
   a. indipendente   b. solo   c. avventuroso

3 Ask students if they think the experience in the airport will make either the parents or the children view their behavior differently. What have the characters learned? How have they changed?

3

Paolo e Alice

A. Descrivi i due protagonisti del corto con le parole più adatte della lista. Some answers will vary.

allegro	avventuroso	gentile	(ir)responsabile	simpatico
arrabbiato	(in)dipendente	preoccupato	serio	triste

Paolo	allegro, avventuroso, gentile, indipendente, simpatico
Alice	arrabbiata, gentile, preoccupata, seria, simpatica, triste

B. In coppia, aggiungete delle altre caratteristiche, gusti, difetti e qualità di Paolo e Alice.

C. Adesso descrivete con le caratteristiche opportune il papà di Alice e la mamma di Paolo, usando le parole del vocabolario e aggiungendone delle altre.

4

Punti di vista

A. In coppia, descrivete come i personaggi vedono la stessa cosa diversamente.

Modello   **il giornale**

Paolo: È importante essere informati! / **Il ragazzo medio:** Che noia!

Oggetto/Situazione	Reazioni			
l'aeroporto	la mamma	Paolo	il papà	Alice
il telefono	il papà	Alice	la signora in treno	il carabiniere
lo zainetto	i carabinieri	l'impiegata	la mamma	il papà
l'aereo	Alice	Paolo	i passeggeri	la hostess
le bambole	Alice	Paolo	gli adulti	tu

B. In coppia, rispondete alle domande.

- Perché le reazioni sono così diverse?
- Con chi ti identifichi di più riguardo a ogni oggetto o situazione? Perché?

5

Opinioni Siete d'accordo o no con queste affermazioni? Rispondete individualmente e poi spiegate le vostre ragioni in coppia.

Affermazione	Sono d'accordo perché...	Non sono d'accordo perché....
I bambini devono imparare a essere indipendenti.		
In una famiglia tutti i membri devono partecipare alle attività domestiche.		
I genitori non devono mai lasciare i loro bambini da soli.		
Bisogna insegnare ai bambini a non parlare con gli sconosciuti.		
La famiglia moderna è diversa dal modello tradizionale del secolo scorso.		
La sicurezza negli aeroporti è eccessiva.		

6

Interpretiamo Improvvisate una conversazione basata su una di queste situazioni e recitatelo davanti alla classe.

A

La mamma di Paolo e il papà di Alice vanno a cena fuori per conoscersi meglio. Si accorgono di avere molto in comune. Di cosa parlano? Che programmi fanno?

B

Una famiglia è all'aeroporto. C'è molta confusione: i genitori si distraggono per un momento e quando si guardano intorno si accorgono che uno dei due bambini non c'è più. Cosa fanno per ritrovarlo?

7

Scriviamo Hai mai incontrato una persona che ti ha mostrato il mondo in maniera diversa o che ti ha fatto capire una cosa molto importante? Racconta l'episodio in uno o due paragrafi.

Practice more at **vhlcentral.com**.

INSTRUCTIONAL RESOURCES
Teaching suggestions; Answer Keys **SAM/WebSAM:** WB

IMMAGINA

SICILIA E SARDEGNA

Due isole che parlano

La **Sicilia** e la **Sardegna** sono le due isole più grandi del **Mediterraneo**, famose per la bellezza delle coste, per le acque cristalline del loro mare e per il clima mite° che permette la crescita° di una vegetazione mediterranea.

Sono regioni con un passato intenso, che ha visto alternarsi° tante dominazioni, le cui testimonianze° sono visibili in molti monumenti.

I templi di **Segesta** e **Agrigento** in Sicilia sono simboli della colonizzazione dei Greci. I mosaici della **Villa romana** di **Piazza Armerina** ci parlano dell'epoca imperiale romana (III-IV secolo d.C.). Numerosi sono anche i segni lasciati da altri popoli come il quartiere arabo della **Kalsa** a Palermo, il **Duomo** normanno di **Monreale** e il **Duomo** aragonese di **Enna**.

Anche la Sardegna è stata a lungo° un luogo di conquiste: Cartaginesi, Romani, Vandali, Arabi, Pisani e altri hanno lasciato le loro tracce°. A Cagliari possiamo ammirare la necropoli cartaginese di **Tuvixeddu**, i resti dell'anfiteatro romano e le chiese in stile romanico di epoca pisana. A **Porto Torres** ci sono rovine° di templi romani, ad **Assemini** ci sono la bellissima chiesa bizantina di San Giovanni e quella di San Pietro in stile gotico. E molti ancora sono i tesori artistici di inestimabile valore in tutte e due le isole.

La mescolanza° di tante culture non è presente soltanto nell'arte e nell'architettura, ma in ogni aspetto della vita siciliana e sarda: dalla cucina, alla musica, alla lingua.

In entrambe° le isole esistono idiomi° originali, il **siculo** e il **sardo**, affascinanti e misteriosi, che si tramandano° da tempi antichissimi. Le popolazioni delle isole lottano° per la sopravvivenza° delle loro lingue, minacciate° in tempi recenti dalla lingua italiana,

Stemma (*coat of arms*) Regione Sicilia

che si è imposta con i mezzi di comunicazione di massa°.

Per contrastare il pericolo di estinzione del siculo e del sardo, negli ultimi anni sono nati movimenti che promuovono la loro riscoperta° e rivalutazione°. La lingua sicula e la lingua sarda oggi hanno dizionari, grammatiche e siti web, oltre a un significativo patrimonio letterario°, musicale e teatrale. Dal 1997 il sardo è lingua ufficiale insieme alla lingua italiana ed è usata nei documenti ufficiali così come nei segnali stradali. Il siculo è oggi parlato da cinque milioni di siciliani in Sicilia e da moltissimi emigrati all'estero. Negli Stati Uniti, in particolare a New York, esiste il **Siculish**, un misto di siciliano e inglese. Insomma, le identità sarda e siciliana sono ancora forti anche quando convivono con l'identità nazionale italiana.

In più...

La Sicilia e le varie isole che la circondano si trovano in una zona con un'intensa attività vulcanica. Ci sono tre vulcani, unici per le loro caratteristiche: l'**Etna**, il vulcano più alto d'Europa, che alterna periodi di inattività a eruzioni; **Vulcano**, che non registra un'eruzione dal 1890; e **Stromboli**, il più attivo dei vulcani europei, che erutta circa ogni ora!

mite *mild* **crescita** *growth* **alternarsi** *alternate; follow one another* **testimonianze** *witnesses* **a lungo** *for a long time* **tracce** *traces* **rovine** *ruins* **mescolanza** *mixture* **entrambe** *both* **idiomi** *languages* **si tramandano** *are handed on* **lottano** *fight* **sopravvivenza** *survival* **minacciate** *threatened* **mezzi...** *mass media* **riscoperta** *rediscovery* **rivalutazione** *revaluation* **patrimonio letterario** *literary heritage*

Palermo Palermo, capoluogo della regione Sicilia, sorge nella **Conca d'Oro**, una pianura sul mar Tirreno circondata da° montagne. La città, fondata dai **Fenici**° nel 735 a.C., è stata conquistata da numerose popolazioni: Romani, Bizantini, Arabi, Normanni e Aragonesi i cui monumenti in stili diversi rendono° unica questa città. Tra i luoghi più caratteristici di Palermo ci sono anche i coloratissimi e profumati mercati della **Vucciria** e di **Ballarò**.

Cucine a confronto La Sicilia e la Sardegna sono rispettivamente le isole più grandi del Mediterraneo. I vari popoli che hanno abitato queste terre le hanno influenzate profondamente, lasciando in eredità profumi° e sapori° che si ritrovano tutt'oggi. Gli amanti dei dolci non resteranno delusi dalla Sicilia, che, con granite°, cassate, cannoli, dolci di mandorla° e fichi° e il cioccolato di Modica, è il paradiso dei golosi. In Sardegna invece si possono gustare° sia sapori più forti, come quello del pecorino sardo, carni di cinghiale° e maiale, che piatti più delicati, come i ravioli culurgiones, la fregola con vongole o pomodoro e il famoso miele° sardo.

circondata da *surrounded by* **Fenici** *Phoenicians* **rendono** *make* **profumi** *aromas* **sapori** *flavors* **granite** *shaved ice* **mandorla** *almond* **fichi** *figs* **gustare** *to savor* **cinghiale** *boar* **miele** *honey*

Vero o falso? Indica se ogni frase è **vera** o **falsa**. Correggi le frasi false. Some answers will vary.

1. La Sicilia e la Sardegna sono le due isole maggiori del mar Mediterraneo. Vero.

2. I Greci e/o i Romani hanno colonizzato le due isole. Vero.

3. Il quartiere della Kalsa si trova in Sardegna. Falso. Si trova a Palermo, in Sicilia.

4. La mescolanza delle culture è visibile solo nell'arte. Falso. È visibile anche nella cucina, nella musica e nella lingua.

5. Televisione e stampa hanno minacciato di estinzione le lingue delle due isole. Vero.

6. La lingua sarda, oggi, è solo orale. Falso. È usata anche come lingua scritta in documenti ufficiali e segnali stradali.

7. Vucciria e Ballarò sono due piazze di Palermo. Falso. Sono due mercati.

8. Gli amanti dei dolci non resteranno delusi dalla Sicilia. Vero.

Quanto hai imparato? Rispondi alle domande.
Some answers will vary.

1. Quali sono le caratteristiche naturali più famose della Sicilia e della Sardegna? belle coste, acque cristalline, clima mite, vegetazione mediterranea

2. Che cosa sono il siculo e il sardo? due lingue originali della Sicilia e della Sardegna

3. Qual è una minaccia per il siculo e per il sardo? L'influenza dell'italiano attraverso i mezzi di comunicazione di massa

4. Quali sono le caratteristiche dei tre vulcani siciliani? L'Etna alterna frequenti periodi di inattività a eruzioni; Vulcano dorme per lunghi periodi ma ha eruzioni violente; Stromboli erutta circa ogni ora.

5. Che cos'è la Conca d'Oro? È il nome della pianura in cui si trova Palermo.

6. Dove si possono gustare sia sapori forti che piatti delicati? in Sardegna

7. Quali sono state alcune dominazioni a Palermo? Fenici, Bizantini, Arabi, Normanni, Aragonesi

8. Quali sono alcuni dolci della Sicilia? granite, cassate, cannoli, dolci di mandorla e fichi, cioccolato di Modica

Progetto

Quali sono le testimonianze degli antichi popoli che hanno abitato in Sicilia e in Sardegna?

- Individua quali popolazioni hanno abitato le due isole e in che epoca.

- Cerca alcuni dei siti archeologici di maggiore interesse sulle due isole.

- Descrivi le loro caratteristiche architettoniche e artistiche.

- Confronta i tuoi risultati con il resto della classe.

GALLERIA DI PERSONE ILLUSTRI

PAROLE COLTE

aderire *to join*
il drammaturgo *playwright*
esordire *to debut*
l'intellettuale *intellectual*
il palcoscenico *stage*

ATTORE, REGISTA
Luigi Lo Cascio (1967–)

Luigi Lo Cascio è uno degli attori di rilievo (*importance*) del panorama cinematografico italiano. Nato a Palermo, Luigi abbandona la facoltà di medicina. Inizia a recitare in un gruppo di teatranti di strada per poi passare ai palcoscenici dei teatri più importanti d'Italia. Il passaggio al cinema avviene quando un

famoso regista italiano lo nota a teatro e gli offre la parte di Peppino Impastato nel film *I cento passi*. L'esordio cinematografico viene premiato con un *David di Donatello* nel 2000. Per Luigi inizia un'intensa carriera nel cinema che lo vedrà recitare in varie pellicole, tra cui *La meglio gioventù*, *Luce dei miei occhi* e *La bestia nel cuore*. Nel 2012 esordisce come regista con il film *La città ideale*, che presenta alla sessantanovesima Mostra internazionale d'arte cinematografica di Venezia.

SCRITTORE, DRAMMATURGO, POETA
Luigi Pirandello (1867–1936)

Luigi Pirandello è stato uno scrittore, drammaturgo e poeta siciliano. Nato in una famiglia benestante (*well-to-do*) originaria della provincia di Agrigento, Pirandello compie i suoi studi universitari a Bonn, in Germania. Sposa la figlia del socio in affari del padre e insieme a lei si trasferisce a Roma nel 1894. Pirandello alterna l'attività di insegnamento scolastica a quella di scrittore e nel 1904 pubblica *Il fu Mattia Pascal*, uno dei suoi libri più famosi. Ma il vero successo Pirandello lo ottiene con le sue opere teatrali, tra cui si ricordano: *Sei personaggi in cerca d'autore*, *Enrico IV* e *Così è (se vi pare)*. Nel corso della sua carriera ne scrive circa quaranta; le tematiche e le innovazioni narrative delle sue opere lo fanno ritenere uno dei maggiori drammaturghi del XX secolo. Nel 1934 viene premiato con il Nobel per la letteratura, diventando une dei sei intellettuali italiani ad aver ricevuto il prestigioso premio.

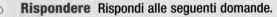

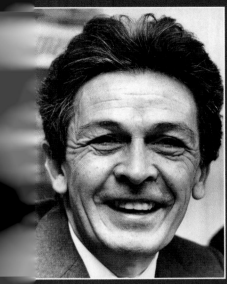

POLITICO
Enrico Berlinguer (1922–1984)

Enrico Berlinguer, nato a Sassari, è stato un politico e leader comunista. Quando ha circa vent'anni aderisce al Partito Comunista Italiano (PCI) e si impegna (*devotes himself*) nella lotta (*struggle*) antifascista. Cinque anni più tardi inizia una vera e propria carriera politica all'interno del PCI per poi diventare segretario generale della Federazione Giovanile Comunista. Negli anni Sessanta entra nella segreteria del PCI e diventa responsabile della sezione esteri. Berlinguer fu un personaggio chiave nel movimento comunista internazionale, aiutò nel processo di distanziamento dall'Unione Sovietica e contribuì a sviluppare un modello politico-ideologico alternativo, chiamato eurocomunismo. Fu segretario generale del partito dal 1972 fino alla sua prematura scomparsa (*passing*) dovuta a un ictus (*stroke*). Il suo funerale è stato il più grande della storia d'Italia, dopo quello di Papa Giovanni Paolo II.

POLITICO, FILOSOFO, GIORNALISTA
Antonio Gramsci (1891–1937)

Antonio Gramsci nasce in un piccolo comune della provincia di Oristano. Considerato uno dei più grandi pensatori del XX secolo, Gramsci ha profondamente influenzato la cultura italiana tra le due guerre mondiali con il suo pensiero politico e con la critica dello stalinismo, proponendo (*proposing*) anche una strategia rivoluzionaria basata su un'indagine (*study*) critica della società, della storia e della cultura moderna. Il suo pensiero politico si basava sull'analisi dei fenomeni sociali e politici internazionali dal Risorgimento in poi. Gramsci fu uno dei fondatori del Partito Comunista Italiano, ne divenne segretario e leader. Nel 1924 fu eletto al parlamento e continuò la sua attività politica antifascista. Nel 1928 Mussolini sciolse (*dissolved*) i partiti politici e Gramsci fu arrestato. Trascorre qualche anno in carcere finché non gli venne concessa la libertà per via delle sue condizioni di salute. Nel 1935 viene trasferito in una clinica dove trascorse gli ultimi anni della sua vita.

Comprensione

Rispondere Rispondi alle seguenti domande.

1. Dove inizia a recitare Luigi Lo Cascio?
   Inizia a recitare in un gruppo di teatranti di strada.

2. Che premio vince grazie al suo primo film?
   Vince il David di Donatello.

3. Qual è il titolo del suo primo film come regista?
   Il titolo è *La città ideale*.

4. Con che cosa Pirandello ottiene il vero successo?
   Il vero successo Pirandello lo ottiene con le sue opere teatrali.

5. Quante opere teatrali scrive Pirandello?
   Ne scrive circa quaranta.

6. Quanti anni ha Berlinguer quando inizia la carriera politica nel PCI?
   Ha circa venticinque anni.

7. Quale fu il contributo di Berlinguer per il movimento comunista internazionale?
   Aiutò nel processo di distanziamento dall'Unione Sovietica e contribuì a sviluppare l'eurocomunismo.

8. Su cosa si basava il pensiero politico di Gramsci?
   Si basava sull'analisi dei fenomeni sociali e politici internazionali dal Risorgimento in poi.

9. Per quale motivo Gramsci ottenne la libertà?
   La ottenne per via delle sue condizioni di salute.

10. Quale partito fondò Gramsci?
    Fondò il Partito Comunista Italiano.

Scrittura

Scrivi sull'argomento Scegli uno dei seguenti argomenti e scrivi un paragrafo seguendo le indicazioni.

- **Cinema o teatro?** Immagina di essere un attore o attrice agli esordi. Ti vengono proposti due importanti ruoli da protagonista, uno per un'opera teatrale e l'altro per il cinema. Quale scegli e perché? Che differenze professionali credi che ci siano tra un attore di teatro e uno del grande schermo?

- **La carriera politica** Hai letto la biografia di due importanti personaggi politici italiani del XX secolo che vengono ricordati e apprezzati a prescindere dal (*regardless of*) loro orientamento politico. Secondo te, quali caratteristiche deve avere un leader politico? Motiva la tua risposta.

- **Il premio Nobel** Il premio Nobel è un'onorificenza mondiale che viene attribuita ogni anno a personaggi che si sono distinti in una delle seguenti categorie: pace, letteratura, medicina, fisica, chimica, economia. A chi assegneresti il premio quest'anno per ognuna delle categorie? Motiva le tue scelte.

 Practice more at **vhlcentral.com**.

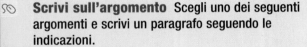

INSTRUCTIONAL RESOURCES **5.1**
Audioscripts, Answer Keys, Lab MP3s, Grammar Presentation Slides
SAM/WebSAM: WB, LM

Review definite articles with students before beginning the discussion of the partitive. Remind them that definite articles are used to refer to specific people or things, with abstract ideas, and with nouns used as the subject of the verb **piacere**.

RIMANDO

To review definite and indefinite articles, see **Strutture 1.2, p. 20**.

To help students practice the various forms of the partitive, call out different food items and ask them to repeat the noun with the appropriate partitive. If you like, make it a contest by dividing the class into two or more teams. Keep score to see which team can get the most correct answers.

Partitives and expressions of quantity

—*Ha fatto **tanti** chilometri.*

Il partitivo

- In English, words like *some, a few, a little, any,* and *several* express an indefinite amount or part of the whole. The Italian equivalent is conveyed by **il partitivo** and expressions of quantity such as **del, un po' di, qualche,** and **alcuni/e**.

- To form the partitive, combine the preposition **di** with the definite article: **del, dello, della, dell', dei, degli, delle**.

  Ho comprato **della pasta**.
  I bought some pasta.

  Metti **dello zucchero** sul tavolo.
  Put some sugar on the table.

  Avete preparato **degli spaghetti**? Gnam!
  Did you make spaghetti? Yum!

  Hanno invitato **delle amiche** alla festa.
  They invited some friends to the party.

- Use **un po' di** (*a little of, a bit of*) with a singular noun that is abstract or that you can measure (but not count).

  Marco mi ha dato **un po' di** carne per il mio cagnolino.
  Marco gave me some meat for my puppy.

  Quando avrò **un po' di** tempo libero, ti telefonerò.
  When I have some free time, I'll call you.

- Use **qualche** with a singular noun, even though it expresses the plural meaning of *some, a few,* or *several*.

  Ti ho preso **qualche** libro. Va bene?
  I picked up some/a few books for you. Is that all right?

  Dove mangiamo stasera? Hai **qualche** idea?
  Where should we eat tonight? Do you have any ideas?

- **Alcuni** and **alcune** are always followed by plural nouns and mean *some* or *a few*.

  Alcune persone sono arrivate in ritardo alla festa.
  A few people arrived late for the party.

  Facciamo **alcuni** acquisti prima di tornare a Spello.
  Let's buy a few things before we go back to Spello.

Point out to students that the partitive is used in negative sentences when a certain quantity is negated. **Non voglio mangiare del pesce.**

- In negative sentences, the partitive is omitted. It may also be omitted in questions and when listing items.

  I vegetariani non mangiano carne.
  Vegetarians don't eat meat.

  Avete figli?
  Do you have children?

  Abbiamo bisogno di cipolle, funghi e pomodori per fare la pizza.
  We need onions, mushrooms, and tomatoes to make the pizza.

Expressions of quantity

- When **molto**, **parecchio**, **poco**, **tanto**, **troppo**, and other expressions of quantity are used as adjectives, they must agree in number and gender with the nouns they modify. Note, however, that the same is not true of **sempre**.

Troppe persone non pensano all'ambiente.
Too many people don't think about the environment.

Ho **molta** fame. Mangiamo!
I'm very hungry. Let's eat!

- When **molto**, **parecchio**, **poco**, **tanto**, **troppo**, and other expressions of quantity are used as adverbs, always use the masculine, singular form.

Riccardo e Giovanni mangiano **troppo**.
Riccardo and Giovanni eat too much.

La storia della Sicilia è **molto** interessante.
The history of Sicily is very interesting.

- Many expressions of quantity are followed by **di**.

un bicchiere di *a glass of*
una bottiglia di *a bottle of*
un chilo di *a kilo of*
un litro di *a liter of*
un paio di *a pair of*

un pezzo di *a piece of*
un po' di *a little (of)*
un sacco di *a lot of/lots of*
una scatola di *a box of*
una tazza di *a cup of*

Mi dia **un chilo di** uva, per favore.
Give me a kilo of grapes, please.

Mio genero ha dato **un pezzo di** cioccolato al figlio.
My son-in-law gave a piece of chocolate to his son.

- The numerical expressions **un milione** and **un miliardo** (and their multiples) are also followed by di.

Te l'ho già detto **un miliardo di** volte!
I've already told you that a billion times!

Tre milioni di persone sono venute alla manifestazione.
Three million people came to the demonstration.

- Note these conversions and equivalencies.

Tabella conversioni - Unità di misura comuni	
1 chilogrammo (kg) = 2,2 libbre	1 chilometro (km) = 0,6 miglia
1 etto = 0,22 libbre	1 metro (m) = 3,28 piedi
1 litro = 1,13 quarto di gallone	1 centimetro (cm) = 0,39 pollici (*inches*)

Numeri – Italia	Numeri – Stati Uniti
milione	*million*
miliardo	*billion*
bilione	*trillion*
biliardo	*quadrillion*

Ask students if they would like a certain food or drink. Tell them to answer "yes" each time. Then ask "**Quanto ne vuoi?**", explaining to them that they must answer with an expression of quantity. (Don't bother explaining **ne** at this point; it will be explained in **Strutture 5.2, pp. 184–185**.)
—Vuoi del caffè?
—Sì (voglio del caffè).
—Quanto ne vuoi?
—Voglio una tazza di/ un litro di/molto caffè.

ATTENZIONE!

Don't forget that the metric system is used in Italy. To buy about two pounds of pasta, for example, ask for **un chilo di pasta**. To buy a little over a pound of something, use **mezzo chilo di...** If you want only a small amount, ask for **un etto di...** or **due etti di...**, 100 or 200 grams, respectively. For liquid measures, **un litro** is somewhat more than a quart.

Pratica

Nota CULTURALE

La **Sardegna** è la seconda isola più grande del Mediterraneo. Grazie al suo clima mite° e alle acque cristalline è diventata dagli anni '60 meta turistica di grande fama. **Porto Rotondo** e **Porto Cervo** (quest'ultimo in **Costa Smeralda**) sono i centri che maggiormente attraggono persone famose da tutto il mondo che arrivano in Sardegna con yacht da favola.

mite *mild*

1 **I preparativi** La famiglia Collina ha organizzato una cena per il prossimo fine settimana e sta ultimando (*finalizing*) i preparativi. Completa la conversazione con i partitivi.

ANDREA Ciao mamma, come va? Tutto pronto per la cena? Chi viene?

MAMMA Vengono (1) _dei_ miei colleghi. Vado a fare la spesa; vuoi venire con me?

ANDREA Va bene, cosa devi comprare?

MAMMA (2) _Degli_ asparagi e (3) _degli_ spinaci per la torta rustica, (4) _del_ formaggio per l'antipasto e (5) _della_ carne.

ANDREA E per dolce, cosa fai?

MAMMA Faccio la torta di mele.

ANDREA Allora prendiamo (6) _delle_ mele e (7) _dello_ zucchero a velo.

MAMMA Sì, hai ragione!

ANDREA E non dimentichiamo qualcosa da bere.

MAMMA Vediamo, dobbiamo prendere (8) _dell'_ acqua gassata, (9) _del_ vino bianco e (10) _dei_ limoni, servono sempre!

2 **Sardegna** Elena è in vacanza in Sardegna. Completa l'e-mail con il partitivo e le espressioni di quantità. Some answers will vary.

Da:	Elena <elena73@email.it>
A:	Lucia <lucia.partemi@email.it>
Oggetto:	Saluti dalla Sardegna

Cara mamma,
la Sardegna è stupenda! Ho passato (1) _alcuni_ giorni a Porto Cervo. Ci sono (2) _delle_ spiagge bellissime e (3) _dei_ locali (4) _molto_ alla moda, dove è facile incontrare (5) _molte_ persone famose. (6) _Qualche_ giorno fa, siamo andati a fare un giro in macchina e abbiamo visto (7) _delle_ ville meravigliose e al porto c'erano (8) _tanti_ yacht (9) _molto_ grandi! Ci siamo divertiti (10) _tanto_.
Baci e abbracci,
Elena

3 **Immagina** In coppia, completate la prima frase con il partitivo e poi finite la seconda frase usando le espressioni di quantità indicate e la vostra immaginazione. Some answers will vary.

> una bottiglia di | un pezzo di | un po' di | qualche | tanto

1. Mi piace mangiare _del_ pesce. Oggi preferisco comprare _un po' di carne_.
2. Durante il volo leggiamo _delle_ riviste o _qualche libro_. Ho comprato soltanto _qualche rivista_.
3. Mi sono dimenticato di prendere _dello_ spumante. Però ho comprato _una bottiglia di aranciata_.
4. Nel mio giardino voglio piantare _degli_ alberi e anche _tanti fiori_.
5. Sono a dieta. Devo mangiare _della_ frutta, non posso mangiare _un pezzo di formaggio_.

 Practice more at **vhlcentral.com**.

Comunicazione

4 **La festa** Gli invitati stanno per arrivare e volete essere sicuri che tutto sia pronto. Con un(a) compagno/a, a turno create delle domande e delle risposte usando le parole nelle tre colonne.

> **Modello** —Ci sono degli stuzzichini (*appetizers*)?
>
> —Certo! Ci sono delle bruschette al pomodoro.

Hai messo	degli	tovaglioli sul tavolo
Ci sono	del	stuzzichini
Hai preparato	dei	spumante
Hai	della	frutta
C'è	delle	verdure per contorno
Hai portato	dello	?

5 **Prodotti** In coppia, per ogni prodotto, dite la quantità che acquistate o che tenete in casa e perché. Utilizzate le espressioni di quantità.

| caffè | pomodori | latte | verdura | vino |
| carne | formaggio | pasta | succo di frutta | zucchero |

> **Modello** —Di solito tengo sempre molte bottiglie di acqua gassata in frigo; non mi piace bere l'acqua del rubinetto (*tap*).
>
> —Io invece non bevo l'acqua gassata, ma compro sempre alcune lattine (*cans*) di aranciata.

6 **Al supermercato** Sei andato/a a trovare un amico a Taormina e vuoi preparargli uno dei tuoi piatti preferiti. In coppia, create una conversazione dove parlate di cosa hai bisogno per preparare quel piatto. Utilizzate il partitivo e le espressioni di quantità dove possibile.

> **Modello** —Oggi voglio cucinarti un piatto tipico della mia zona, gli spaghetti alla carbonara.
>
> —Devi comprare dei pomodori?
>
> —No, devo prendere della pancetta.

7 **Cosa ne pensi?** Le famiglie di oggi hanno molti problemi. Quali sono i più ricorrenti? Cosa bisogna fare, secondo te, per risolverli? In coppia, elencate (*list*) sei problemi e trovate delle possibili soluzioni. Utilizzate le parole relative alla famiglia che avete imparato in questa lezione e le espressioni di quantità come **tanto**, **molto**, **poco**, **troppo**, **parecchio** e **alcuni/e**.

> **Modello** —Il rapporto tra genitori e figli è molto problematico.
>
> —Sì, bisogna educare i figli a rispettare i genitori.

Nota CULTURALE

Taormina è una delle mete turistiche più famose della Sicilia dove ogni anno arrivano turisti da tutto il mondo. Tra i monumenti principali c'è il **Teatro Antico** dove si svolgono i maggiori eventi culturali come il **Taormina Film Fest,** rassegna° cinematografica che si svolge° all'interno della manifestazione culturale **Taormina Arte.**

rassegna *festival* **si svolge** *takes place*

6 Have a few pairs act out their conversations for the class.

INSTRUCTIONAL RESOURCES `5.2`
Audioscripts, Answer Keys, Lab MP3s, Grammar Presentation Slides
SAM/WebSAM: WB, LM

RIMANDO

To review reflexive pronouns, see **Strutture 2.1, pp. 56–57.**

To review direct and indirect object pronouns, see **Strutture 4.2, pp. 140–142.**

Let students know they should use **lì** or **là** to express the idea of *there* when a location has not been previously mentioned.
Mettete le carote lì.
Put the carrots there.

ATTENZIONE!

Ci is frequently used with verbs such as **andare, venire, stare, rimanere, restare,** and **essere** because they often are followed by a prepositional phrase indicating location.

ATTENZIONE!

When **ci** is used with a direct object pronoun, a reflexive pronoun, or **ne**, the pronoun precedes **ci** in some cases and follows it in others. The correct forms are **mi ci, ti ci, vi ci, ci si, ce lo, ce l', ce la, ce li, ce le, ce ne.** The form **vi ci** is used to avoid the awkward form **ci ci.** Note that **ci** changes to **ce** before **lo, la, l', li, le** and **ne.**

Avete messo il rossetto nel cassetto?
Did you put the lipstick in the drawer?

Sì, ce l'abbiamo messo.
Yes, we put it there.

Remind students that with the verbs **dovere, potere,** and **volere, ci** and **ne** can precede the conjugated verb or attach to the infinitive.

Ci and *ne*

Uses of ci

- You have already learned that **ci** is used as a reflexive and reciprocal pronoun meaning *ourselves* or *each other* and as a direct and indirect object pronoun meaning *us* or *to us*. **Ci** also has other meanings and uses.

- **Ci** can refer to a location. It often replaces a prepositional phrase introduced by **a**, **su**, or **in**.

  Vai **in discoteca** stasera?
  Are you going to the club tonight?

  Sì, **ci** vado con Roberto.
  Yes, I'm going there with Roberto.

  Hanno messo i cibi **sul tavolo**?
  Did they put the food on the table?

  No, **ci** hanno messo le bottiglie.
  No, they put the bottles there.

- **Ci** can replace **da** + [*noun/pronoun*] to mean *someone's house* or *someone's place*.

  Venite **da me** domenica?
  Are you coming to my place Sunday?

  Sì, **ci** veniamo.
  Yes, we're coming.

  Quando vai **dal dentista**?
  When are you going to the dentist?

  Ci vado martedì prossimo.
  I'm going there next Tuesday.

- **Ci** often replaces a phrase introduced by **a** or **su** after verbs such as **riuscire (a)**, **pensare (a)**, **credere (in/a)**, and **contare (su)**.

  Possiamo contare sul **suo aiuto**?
  Can we count on his help?

  Sì, **ci** potete contare.
  Yes, you can count on it.

  È riuscita a **mangiare tutti gli gnocchi**?
  Did she manage to eat all the gnocchi?

  No, non **ci** è riuscita.
  No, she couldn't do it.

- **Ci** precedes a conjugated verb and the formal imperative, but follows and is attached to infinitives and informal imperatives. Drop the **–e** of the infinitive before attaching **ci**.

  Ecco la mia borsa. Metti**ci** le chiavi.
  Here's my purse. Put the keys in it.

  Devo andare a Perugia, ma non desidero restar**ci**.
  I have to go to Perugia, but I don't want to stay there.

- Verbs such as **avercela (con)** (*to have it in for someone*), **farcela** (*to manage*), **tenerci** (*to care for something*), **sentirci** (*to be able to hear*), **vederci** (*to be able to see*), **volerci** and **metterci** have idiomatic meanings that are not related to location. **Volerci**, used only in the third person, refers to how long it takes to do something, and **metterci**, conjugated in all forms, refers to how long it takes a particular person to do something.

  Non so perché lui **ce l'ha** con me.
  I don't know why he has it in for me.

  Quanto tempo **ci vuole** per andare a Roma?
  How long does it take to get to Rome?

  Penso di **farcela**; anzi, **ci tengo**!
  I think I can get it done; in fact, it means a lot to me!

  Ci hanno messo un'ora per finire il giallo.
  It took them an hour to finish the detective story.

  La mia bisnonna ha cento anni. Non **ci sente** e non **ci vede** più.
  My great-grandmother is one hundred years old. She can't hear or see anything anymore.

Uses of **ne**

- **Ne** replaces nouns that are introduced by the partitive. The partitive article is deleted along with the noun that is being replaced.

  Ho trovato del limoncello al supermercato. **Ne** vuoi?
  I bought some limoncello at the supermarket. Do you want some?

  Mia madre mi dà spesso delle caramelle, ma non **ne** dà a mia sorella.
  My mother often gives me candies, but she doesn't give my sister any.

- **Ne** also replaces a noun or phrase introduced by an expression of quantity or a number. The number or quantity remains in the sentence even after the noun or phrase is replaced. Note that in this instance **ne** means *of it* or *of them*, which often is not expressed in English.

  Quanti amici hai?
  How many friends do you have?

  Ne ho tanti!
  I have a lot (of them)!

  Mi compri un gelato?
  Will you buy me an ice cream?

  Certo, te **ne** compro due se vuoi!
  Of course, I'll buy you two (of them) if you want!

- **Ne** is used to replace a phrase introduced by a preposition. **Ne** typically replaces **di** + [*a person or thing*], **di** + [*an infinitive*] or **da** + [*a place*].

  Hai paura **dei serpenti**?
  Are you afraid of snakes?

  Io, sì, **ne** ho molta paura.
  I am, I'm really afraid of them.

  Avete voglia **di andare in trattoria**?
  Do you feel like going to the trattoria?

  Sì, **ne** abbiamo voglia.
  Yes, we feel like it.

  Sono tornati **dalla spiaggia**. **Ne sono tornati** stanchi ma felici.
  They came back from the beach. They came back (from there) tired but happy.

- When **ne** replaces a noun or a partitive and is used with a verb in a compound tense, the past participle agrees in number and gender with the noun that **ne** replaces. There is no agreement when **ne** replaces a prepositional phrase.

  Quante magliette hai comprato al mercato di Sant'Ambrogio? **Ne ho comprate** tre.
  How many T-shirts did you buy at the Sant'Ambrogio market? I bought three (of them).

  Berenice ha preso **degli asparagi e ne ha dati** un po' a Matteo.
  Berenice took some asparagus and gave some to Matteo.

- **Ne** precedes a conjugated verb and the formal imperative, but follows and is attached to infinitives and informal imperatives. Drop the **–e** of the infinitive before attaching **ne**.

  Cerco un'orologio per mia moglie. Dove posso comprar**ne** uno?
  I'm looking for a watch for my wife. Where can I buy one?

  Non mangiate tutto il pollo! Dat**e**ne a vostra sorella!
  Don't eat all the chicken! Give some to your sister!

- When using the various forms of **tutto**, you must use the appropriate direct object pronoun instead of **ne**.

  L'ha mangiato tutto!
  He ate the whole thing!/He ate all of it!

ATTENZIONE!

Ne is used idiomatically with certain expressions and verbs. **Andarsene**, *to go away*, and the phrase **che ne dici (di)...?**, *what do you think (of)...?* are two examples. You may also use **ne** when asking what the date is.

Non voglio più vederti! Vattene!
I don't want to see you anymore. Go away!

Che ne dici di fare una passeggiata con me?
What do you think of taking a walk with me?

Quanti ne abbiamo oggi?
What's today's date?

RIMANDO

To review the partitives and expressions of quantity, see **Strutture 5.1, pp. 180–181**.

ATTENZIONE!

When **ne** is combined with other pronouns, it comes last. Also, remember to change **ci** to **ce** when combined with **ne**. See the combined pronouns chart on **p. 142**.

ATTENZIONE!

Pensare may be followed by the preposition **a** or **di**. Both are translated *to think about* in English. However, with **a**, the verb has a meaning of *to consider something* whereas **di** suggests an opinion. Note how **ne** and **ci** can be used with **pensare** in these instances.

Cosa pensi del mio motorino? Che ne pensi?
What do you think of my scooter? What do you think of it?

Pensi ai tuoi guai?
Do you think about your problems?

Sì, ci penso ogni giorno.
Yes, I think about them every day.

Pratica

1 Have students check each other's work. Then have pairs act out the conversation.

1 Progetti Sara e Mauro si incontrano e parlano dei loro progetti per l'estate. Completa il dialogo con **ci** e **ne**.

MAURO Ciao Sara, come va?

SARA Bene, e tu?

MAURO Sto organizzando un viaggio a Pantelleria.

SARA (1) _Ne_ ho sentito parlare molto bene. Perché (2) _ci_ vai?

MAURO Ho sempre voluto (3) andar_ci_ perché i miei nonni materni vengono da lì e me (4) _ne_ parlano spesso.

SARA Ah, che bello! Loro (5) _ci_ tornano spesso?

MAURO No, purtroppo è da tanto tempo che non (6) _ci_ tornano perché il viaggio è troppo lungo, però (7) _ci_ pensano sempre.

SARA Quanto tempo (8) _ci_ vuole per arrivare a Pantelleria?

MAURO Penso che (9) _ci_ metterò sei ore.

SARA Hai tanti parenti a Pantelleria?

MAURO Sì, (10) _ne_ ho tanti, i miei zii e i miei cugini ancora (11) _ci_ vivono. Che (12) _ne_ dici, hai voglia di partire con me?

SARA Certo!

TEACHING OPTION
To help students practice answering questions with **ci**, tell them about places you have gone and what you did there. Then ask them "E tu?" and require them to answer with **ci**.
—**Sono andata al mare e ho visto un delfino. E tu?**
—**Anch'io ci sono andato/ Non ci sono mai andato.**

TEACHING OPTION
To elicit responses using **ne**, ask students questions about their family, pets, and possessions. Ask how many brothers and sisters they have, if they have a cat or dog, how many books they have in their room, etc. You may want to ask and answer the first couple of questions to model **ne** for them.
—**Quanti fratelli hai? Io ne ho due. E tu?**
—**Marco ha fratelli? Quanti ne ha?**

2 Quanti/e ce ne sono? Utilizza la statistica relativa alla Sicilia e scrivi una frase con i pronomi **ci** e **ne** per indicare la quantità delle cose citate.

> **Modello** **Abitanti in Sicilia (5.000.000 circa):**
> Ce ne sono cinque milioni circa.

1. Isole minori (17): _Ce ne sono diciassette._
2. Vulcani attivi (3): _Ce ne sono tre._
3. Laghi (1): _Ce n'è uno._
4. Riserve marine (6): _Ce ne sono sei._
5. Festival internazionali (2): _Ce ne sono due._

Teatro Antico di Taormina

3 La nostra società In coppia, scrivete delle frasi in base ai suggerimenti forniti.

Some answers will vary.

> **Modello** **Restare a casa il sabato sera.**
> Non ci resto mai!

1. Andare a trovare i nonni. Ci vado...
2. Avere paura della morte. Ne ho paura...
3. Parlare dell'infanzia. Ne parlo...
4. Pensare alla vecchiaia. Ci penso...
5. Contare sull'aiuto dei tuoi genitori. Ci conto...
6. Mangiare schifezze (*junk food*). Ne mangio...

 Practice more at **vhlcentral.com.**

Comunicazione

4

In giro per il mondo In coppia, chiedetevi quali paesi avete già visitato, cosa avete visto, quando ci siete andati e se ci tornerete.

> **Modello** —Sei mai stato in Irlanda?
>
> —Sì, ci sono stato, è bellissima!
>
> —Ah sì? E quando ci sei andato?
>
> —Ci sono andato due anni fa....

5

Ricetta Un(a) tuo/a amico/a ti ha dato la ricetta per preparare il tiramisù, ma tu non sei sicuro/a di aver capito bene. Gli/Le fai delle domande sulla ricetta e lui/lei risponde usando **ci** e **ne**.

TIRAMISÙ

Ingredienti 5 uova, 5 cucchiai di zucchero, 500 gr. di mascarpone, 1 pacchetto di biscotti Pavesini o Savoiardi, caffè, liquore, cacao.

Procedimento Preparare il caffè. Separare gli albumi (*egg whites*) dai tuorli (*yolk*), lavorare i tuorli con lo zucchero, aggiungere il mascarpone e mescolare bene. Montare a neve (*beat until stiff*) gli albumi e aggiungerli delicatamente al composto. Bagnare i biscotti nel caffè zuccherato, al quale si può aggiungere il liquore.

Mettere i biscotti in una pirofila (*pan*) e coprirli con metà della crema. Ripetere lo stesso procedimento per il secondo strato e mettere in frigo per 2 ore. Spolverizzare (*Sprinkle*) con del cacao prima di servire.

> **Modello** —Grazie per la ricetta, ma non sono sicura di aver capito bene.
>
> —Dimmi pure.
>
> —Quanto caffè devo preparare?
>
> —Ne devi preparare un po'.

6

Sondaggio

A. Fai ai tuoi compagni le seguenti domande. Per ogni domanda trova un(a) compagno/a che risponde **sì** e uno/a che risponde **no** e annota le risposte nella tabella. Usa **ci** e **ne** nelle risposte.

> **Modello** —Ti piace andare in montagna per le vacanze?
>
> —Sì, mi piace andarci.

Trova qualcuno che...	Nome	Sì	No
...ha paura del futuro.	_____	☐	☐
...ha delle incertezze.	_____	☐	☐
...discute di politica.	_____	☐	☐
...pensa ai problemi ambientali.	_____	☐	☐
...crede al destino.	_____	☐	☐
...fa dei pettegolezzi.	_____	☐	☐
...spera di superare tutti gli esami.	_____	☐	☐
...va in palestra tutti i giorni.	_____	☐	☐
...riesce a studiare con la TV accesa.	_____	☐	☐
...beve troppo caffè.	_____	☐	☐

B. A turno, condividete con la classe quello che avete imparato sui vostri compagni.

4 Have volunteers point out different places they have visited on a world map or globe. Review with the class the names of various countries.

TEACHING OPTION Show students pictures of different objects and/ or people. Ask them what they see and how many there are. Example: **Vedi turisti davanti alla chiesa? Quanti ce ne sono? Ne vedi venti? Molti? Troppi?**

5 You can turn this into a discrete activity in which students need to fill in the blanks with **ne** and **ci**.
—**Quanto caffè devo preparare?**
—(1) _Ne_ **devi preparare un po' per inzuppare i biscotti.**
—**Allora basta una caffettiera?**
—**Sì, (2) _ne_ basta una!**
—**Ma tu (3) _ci_ metti sempre il liquore?**
—**Io veramente (4) _ci_ metto solo il caffè; non mi piacciono i liquori.**
—**E quanti biscotti (5) _ci_ vogliono?**
—**Beh, un pacco da mezzo kg è sufficiente, comunque dipende da te; se vuoi (6) _ci_ puoi mettere più biscotti.**

6 Before assigning this activity, have students go through the list and note whether they should use **ci** or **ne** to talk about each item. Then have them indicate the part that **ci** or **ne** will replace. (**1. ne; del futuro 2. ne; delle incertezze 3. ne; di politica 4. ci; ai problemi... 5. ci; al destino 6. ne; dei pettegolezzi 7. ci; di superare... 8. ci; in palestra 9. ci; a studiare 10. ne; caffè**)

INSTRUCTIONAL RESOURCES
Audioscripts, Answer Keys, Lab MP3s, Grammar Presentation Slides
SAM/WebSAM: WB, LM

5.3

The future

Il futuro semplice

- To form the simple future (**il futuro semplice**), drop the final **–e** of the infinitive and add the future ending. For **–are** verbs, change the **–a–** of the infinitive ending to **–e–**.

cantare	prendere	dormire	capire
canterò	prenderò	dormirò	capirò
canterai	prenderai	dormirai	capirai
canterà	prenderà	dormirà	capirà
canteremo	prenderemo	dormiremo	capiremo
canterete	prenderete	dormirete	capirete
canteranno	prenderanno	dormiranno	capiranno

> Domani, **dormiremo** dodici ore!
> *Tomorrow we will sleep twelve hours!*

> Chi **canterà** al teatro domani?
> *Who's going to sing at the theater tomorrow?*

- To maintain the hard sound, insert an **–h–** after the **–c–** or **–g–** of verbs ending in **–care** and **–gare**.

> Lui **pagherà** i biglietti e io **pagherò** l'albergo.
> *He will pay for the tickets and I will pay for the hotel.*

> Non **dimenticheranno** mai la nascita del loro figlio.
> *They will never forget the birth of their son.*

- Drop the **–i–** of the stem of verbs ending in **–ciare**, **–giare** and **–sciare**.

> **Comincerete** a fare i compiti alle tre.
> *You will start your homework at three.*

> Mio marito non mi **lascerà** mai.
> *My husband will never leave me.*

- Some verbs have irregular stems in the simple future. The verbs **dare**, **fare**, and **stare** retain the **–a–** of the infinitive in their future stem: **dar–**, **far–**, **star–**. The future stem of **essere** is **sar–**.

> **Starai** a casa stanotte?
> *Are you staying in tonight?*

> Un giorno **sarete** meno egoisti.
> *One day you will be less selfish.*

- Irregular verbs drop the characteristic vowel of the infinitive before adding the future endings.

andare	andr–	dovere	dovr–	vedere	vedr–
avere	avr–	potere	potr–	vivere	vivr–
cadere	cadr–	sapere	sapr–		

> Mia nonna **vivrà** con mia zia quando **andremo** in Francia.
> *My grandmother will live with my aunt when we go to France.*

- Some verbs have irregular future stems that end in **–rr–**.

bere	berr–	tenere	terr–
parere	parr–	venire	verr–
rimanere	rimarr–	volere	vorr–

> Mia nipote **rimarrà** con la nostra famiglia quest'estate.
> *My niece will stay with our family this summer.*

To help students learn to recognize the two future tenses when they hear them, read some sentences with the present, simple future, and future perfect aloud. Ask students to hold up one hand when they hear the simple future, two hands when they hear the future perfect, and to keep their hands flat on their desks or to clap when they hear the present tense.

- The simple future is used to express actions that will happen in the future.

Finirò gli studi nel 2020.
I will graduate in 2020.

Secondo me, la vecchiaia **sarà** molto divertente.
I think old age will be really fun.

- The simple future may be used to express probability or speculation.

Quanti anni **avrà** quella signora?
How old do you think that lady is?

Avrà 80 anni.
She must be 80.

- The simple future may be used to express a polite command.

Pulirai la tua camera, poi **andrai** al supermercato.
(You will) clean your room, then go to the supermarket.

- After **se**, **quando**, **dopo che**, **(non) appena**, and other expressions of time, use the simple future for the main verb and for the verb in the dependent clause, if the action takes place in the future. In English, the verb in the dependent clause is usually in the present tense.

Quando **arriveremo**, **metteremo** le valige in camera.
When we get there, we'll put the bags in the room.

Se **avrà** tempo, **andrà** a comprare il formaggio.
If he/she has time, he/she will go buy the cheese.

Il futuro anteriore

- The future perfect (**il futuro anteriore**) is used to express an action that *will have taken place* by a particular time in the future. **Il futuro anteriore** is formed with the future tense of the auxiliary verb **avere** or **essere** plus the past participle of the main verb.

finire	arrivare	alzarsi
avrò **finito**	sarò **arrivato/a**	mi sarò **alzato/a**
avrai **finito**	sarai **arrivato/a**	ti sarai **alzato/a**
avrà **finito**	sarà **arrivato/a**	si sarà **alzato/a**
avremo **finito**	saremo **arrivati/e**	ci saremo **alzati/e**
avrete **finito**	sarete **arrivati/e**	vi sarete **alzati/e**
avranno **finito**	saranno **arrivati/e**	si saranno **alzati/e**

- The future perfect is almost always used with the simple future to indicate that one action will have taken place before another in the future. The future perfect is often introduced by the expressions **quando**, **se**, **dopo che**, **(non) appena**, etc.

Quando **avrò preparato** il minestrone, mangeremo.
When I finish the soup, we'll eat.

Dopo che **ci saremo alzati**, ci vestiremo.
After we get up, we will get dressed.

- **Il futuro anteriore** may be used to express probability in the past. In English, the same concept is expressed by the use of *must have* plus the past participle or by the word *probably* and the simple past tense.

Saranno già **usciti**.
They must have already gone out.

Avrà stampato la tesi all'università.
He probably printed his thesis at school.

ATTENZIONE!
The simple future may be used for "on-the-spot" decisions, statements of concession or predictions.
Piove. Non uscirò, guarderò un DVD a casa.
It's raining. I'm not going out, I'll watch a DVD at home.

ATTENZIONE!
Some words that are often used with the future are **il/la prossimo/a** + [expressions of time] and, **fra/tra** + [expressions of time].
Il prossimo anno, comprerò una casa per la mamma.
Next year, I will buy a house for my mom.
Credo che fra alcuni minuti pioverà.
I think it will rain in a few minutes.

RIMANDO
To study hypothetical statements with **se**, see **Strutture 9.3, pp. 360–361.**

ATTENZIONE!
With the future perfect, as with other compound tenses, you must follow the rules for past participle agreement, the choice of the auxiliary verb, and word order (with negation and adverbs).
Dopo che Gianna sarà uscita, telefonerò a suo fratello.
After Gianna has gone out, I will call her brother.

ATTENZIONE!
In spoken Italian, the **futuro anteriore** is often replaced by the simple future. Example:
Quando farà la torta di spinaci, la metterà sul tavolo.
Quando avrà fatto la torta di spinaci, la metterà sul tavolo.

Pratica

1 Remind students to watch for irregular verbs as they complete the activity.

1

Oroscopo cinese Leggi le previsioni dell'oroscopo cinese per il segno del gallo. Metti i verbi al futuro semplice.

LAVORO (1) _Sarà_ (essere) un anno importante per il lavoro. All'inizio (2) _avrai_ (tu / avere) qualche delusione ma se (3) _terrai_ (tenere) duro, dopo l'estate (4) _ti rifarai_ (rifarsi) e (5) _otterrai_ (ottenere) grandi soddisfazioni.

SOLDI La tua situazione finanziaria (6) _migliorerà_ (migliorare), i tuoi investimenti (7) _daranno_ (dare) frutto e così (8) _potrai_ (tu / potere) fare un acquisto importante.

Gallo: 1945-1957-1969-1981-1993-2014

SALUTE Non (9) _avrai_ (tu / avere) grossi problemi di salute ma (10) _dovrai_ (dovere) seguire un'alimentazione sana e questo ti (11) _farà_ (fare) sentire pieno/a d'energia.

AMORE Questo è l'anno in cui i tuoi sogni (12) _si realizzeranno_ (realizzarsi): (13) _incontrerai_ (tu / incontrare) una persona importante che ti (14) _renderà_ (rendere) felice e (15) _starete_ (voi / stare) insieme per tutta la vita.

2

I preparativi Il signor Mancini e la sua famiglia partono domani per l'isola della Maddalena. Completa le frasi con i verbi al futuro anteriore.

Finalmente domani mattina si parte per le vacanze, ma dovremo fare tutto in fretta (*in a hurry*) senza perdere tempo. Dopo che (1) _ci saremo svegliati_ (svegliarsi) e (2) _avremo fatto colazione_ (fare colazione), ci vestiremo. Appena i ragazzi (3) _si saranno preparati_ (prepararsi), prenderanno le loro valige e le porteranno in macchina. Nel frattempo, mia moglie (4) _avrà finito_ (finire) di sistemare la casa e io (5) _avrò controllato_ (controllare) i biglietti. Non appena tutti (6) _saranno saliti_ (salire) in macchina, partiremo per l'aeroporto.

3 On the board, list the infinitives of several verbs that have irregular past participles. Have students work in pairs to write a new dialogue using the future perfect and five verbs from the list.

3

Conversazione Marco si lamenta di suo fratello Francesco perché fa sempre tante promesse e non le mantiene mai. In coppia, completate la conversazione usando il futuro semplice o il futuro anteriore poi leggetela ad alta voce per controllare le risposte. Some answers will vary.

MARCO Dove sono i CD che ti ho dato tanto tempo fa?

FRANCESCO Non so più dove li ho messi. Te li ridarò appena li (1) _avrò trovati_.

MARCO Questa camera è un disastro!

FRANCESCO (2) _La pulirò_ dopo che sarò tornato dalla festa.

MARCO Guarda che il frigo è vuoto, e toccava a te fare la spesa!

FRANCESCO Hai ragione, andrò al supermercato non appena (3) _avrò finito di guardare la TV_.

MARCO E quando pensi di restituirmi i soldi che ti ho prestato?

FRANCESCO Che noia, te li restituirò dopo che (4) _saranno arrivati i soldi di mamma e papà_.

MARCO E guarda tutti i piatti nel lavandino!

FRANCESCO Ma dai, (5) _li laverò_ appena avrò finito di fare tutte le cose che mi hai chiesto!

Comunicazione

4 **Progetti** Come passerai l'estate? In coppia, fatevi a turno queste domande.

- Dove andrai in vacanza?

- Passerai l'estate con la tua famiglia?

- Ti sarai riposato per la fine dell'estate?

- Avrai guadagnato abbastanza soldi prima dell'inizio delle lezioni?

5 **Come sarà?** Tutto cambia con il tempo. In coppia, discutete di come cambieranno i seguenti elementi. In ogni caso, indicate l'anno.

le case	la religione
la cucina	la televisione
la medicina	l'umanità
i mezzi di trasporto	la vecchiaia
i rapporti umani	la vita in famiglia

6 **Nel 2030** In gruppi di tre, dite come sarà cambiata la vostra vita nel 2030. Poi, spiegate al resto della classe quello che sarà cambiato nella vita dei vostri compagni.

> **Modello** —Io e i miei genitori avremo imparato a capirci meglio nel 2030.

- la carriera

- il rapporto con i vostri amici

- il rapporto con i vostri genitori

- i passatempi

- la vostra situazione economica

- i vostri gusti

- ?

7 **Tra 20 anni** In piccoli gruppi, fate una lista di almeno cinque persone famose e immaginate come saranno tra 20 anni e cosa avranno fatto.

8 **Situazioni** In coppia, scegliete uno dei seguenti temi e inventate una conversazione utilizzando il futuro semplice e il futuro anteriore.

- Una mamma e un(a) figlio/a che sta per sposarsi parlano di come sarà diversa la vita dopo il matrimonio.

- Un papà e un(a) figlio/a che vuole cambiare lavoro parlano di cosa farà il/la ragazzo/a per cercare un nuovo lavoro e per avere una brillante carriera.

- Un nonno e un(a) nipote, che si trasferisce in un'altra città, parlano di cosa farà il/la ragazzo/a per iniziare la sua nuova vita.

- Due compagni di università parlano di cosa faranno dopo la laurea (*graduation*).

5 Tell students to describe what each item in the list will be like in a particular year in the future. Example: **La televisione avrà mille canali nel 2057**.

6 Have students use their ideas for this activity to write a short, futuristic story that explains what will or won't have happened in their lives in the next twenty years.

7 Model the activity by citing an example and briefly talking about it as a class.

8 Have volunteers perform their conversations for the class. For listening comprehension, ask students to write down the verbs used in the future and future perfect tenses.

INSTRUCTIONAL RESOURCES 5.4
Audioscripts, Answer Keys, Lab MP3s, Grammar Presentation Slides
SAM/WebSAM: WB, LM

ATTENZIONE!

Some common adverbial expressions consist of two or more words.

Ogni tanto mia nuora fa un salto da noi.
Every once in a while my daughter-in-law drops by for a visit.

Di solito ai nonni piace viziare i nipoti.
Grandparents usually like to spoil their grandchildren.

ATTENZIONE!

Some exceptions to this rule are:
altro → altrimenti
benevolo → benevolmente
leggero → leggermente
violento → violentemente

Remind students that adverbs modify verbs, adjectives, or other adverbs, but adjectives modify only nouns. Adverbs are invariable, but adjectives agree with the nouns they modify.

ATTENZIONE!

Adverbs usually follow the verb. However, they may precede a verb for emphasis.

Non tornerò mai in questo ristorante.
I will never come back to this restaurant.

Mai tornerò in questo ristorante!
Never will I return to this restaurant!

Sometimes the placement of an adverb can change the meaning of the sentence.

Le piace molto mangiare con gli amici.
She really likes eating with her friends.

Le piace mangiare molto con gli amici.
She likes to eat a lot with her friends.

Adverbs

—*Sinceramente a me fa un po' schifo.*

- Adverbs provide information about location, time, manner, quantity, and frequency. Adverbs modify verbs, adjectives, or other adverbs. They are invariable.

  Carla è **molto** bella ma si veste **male**.
  Carla is very pretty, but she dresses badly.

  Arrivano **puntualmente** a lezione.
  They are on time for class.

- Most adverbs are formed by adding **–mente** to the feminine singular form of an adjective.

  lenta > **lentamente**   veloce > **velocemente**

- Adjectives that end in **–le** or **–re** drop the final **–e** before adding **–mente**, unless a consonant precedes that ending.

  normale > **normalmente**
  speciale > **specialmente** *but* mediocre > **mediocremente**

- **Bene** and **male** are the adverbs that correspond to the adjectives **buono** and **cattivo**.

- Some adverbs have exactly the same form as the corresponding adjective.

  Chi va **piano** va **sano** e va **lontano**.
  Slow and steady wins the race.

  Il papà single che abita sopra lavora **sodo**.
  The single dad that lives upstairs works hard.

- Some common adverbs have their own form: **spesso**, **insieme**, **così**, **volentieri**, etc.

  Andrò **volentieri**!
  I will go with pleasure!

  Carla fa **spesso** stupidaggini.
  Carla often does foolish things.

- In sentences with compound tenses, common, short adverbs such as **già**, **ancora**, **più**, **mai**, **sempre**, and **spesso** are usually placed after the auxiliary verb.

  Avete **già** finito di traslocare?
  Have you already finished moving?

  In Italia siamo **spesso** andati al mercato.
  In Italy we went often to the market.

- Adverbs that express time or location often come at the beginning or end of a sentence, or they may follow the past participle in compound tenses.

  Il volo è partito **tardi**.
  The flight left late.

  Qui si parla italiano.
  Italian is spoken here.

- An adverb precedes the adjective or adverb that it modifies.

  Ecco un cliente **molto** soddisfatto.
  There's a very satisfied customer.

  Oggi lavoro **proprio** bene.
  Today I'm working really well.

Pratica e comunicazione

1 **Gli avverbi** Per ogni aggettivo scrivi il corrispondente avverbio.

1. gentile ___gentilmente___
2. vero ___veramente___
3. sincero ___sinceramente___
4. facile ___facilmente___
5. recente ___recentemente___
6. particolare ___particolarmente___
7. buono ___bene___
8. cattivo ___male___
9. leggero ___leggermente___
10. molto ___molto___

1 Have pairs ad-lib a short conversation that uses as many of these adjectives and adverbs as possible.

2 **In che modo?** Riscrivi le frasi con l'avverbio al posto giusto.

1. Isabella torna a casa. (rapidamente) Isabella torna a casa rapidamente.
2. Giovanni cucina la pizza. (bene) Giovanni cucina bene la pizza.
3. I nonni sono arrivati. (già) I nonni sono già arrivati.
4. La signora ha aiutato la vecchietta. (gentilmente) La signora ha gentilmente aiutato la vecchietta.
5. Le ragazze sono simpatiche. (molto) Le ragazze sono molto simpatiche.
6. Il bambino dorme. (tranquillamente) Il bambino dorme tranquillamente.

3 **La famiglia Stipa** In coppia, dite a turno in che modo fanno le loro attività i membri della famiglia Stipa. Some answers will vary.

> **Modello** Vittorio è tornato dall'università. È orgoglioso dei suoi voti.
> Mostra orgogliosamente i suoi voti.

1. La signora Stipa è in fila allo sportello. È paziente. Aspetta pazientemente il suo turno.
2. Laura è a casa. È nervosa. Aspetta nervosamente una telefonata.
3. I signori Stipa vanno a una festa. Sono eleganti. Sono vestiti elegantemente.
4. Il signor Stipa ascolta il figlio. È attento. Ascolta attentamente il discorso.
5. I ragazzi escono da casa. Sono veloci. Escono da casa velocemente.

3 Have students list errands around town and say how they run them. Example: **Fare la spesa: Faccio la spesa regolarmente.**

4 **Sondaggio** Intervista alcuni tuoi compagni di classe. Con che frequenza fanno le seguenti cose? Aggiungi altre due attività. Confronta i tuoi risultati con il resto della classe.

> **Modello** andare al cinema
> —Vai spesso al cinema?
> —No, ci vado raramente.

	Sempre	Spesso	Qualche volta	Raramente	Mai
1. andare a un concerto					
2. visitare un museo il fine settimana					
3. partecipare a una gara sportiva					
4. annoiarsi il sabato sera					
5. utilizzare i mezzi pubblici					
6. cucinare per gli amici					

4 Compile the results of the survey to determine which activity or occurrence is most/least common among students.

 Practice more at **vhlcentral.com**.

1 Have students share their answers with the class. Encourage class discussion.

Sintesi

1 **Foto di famiglia** In gruppi di tre, rispondete alle seguenti domande.

1. Che cosa vedete nelle due foto?
2. Chi ha fatto le due foto? In quale occasione?
3. Quale delle due situazioni vi è più familiare? Perché?
4. Quali saranno le attività delle persone nelle foto?
5. Le due foto rispecchiano (*reflect*) una situazione tipica degli Stati Uniti, o piuttosto una italiana? Perché?
6. Secondo voi, quale delle due situazioni sarà quella più comune negli anni futuri?

2 After students have finished the activity, have them exchange papers to peer edit.

2 **Scriviamo** Scegli uno dei seguenti argomenti e scrivi un tema di circa una pagina.

● Come sarà la tua famiglia quando avrai l'età dei tuoi genitori? Sarai sposato/a? Avrai figli? Tu e il/la tuo/a compagno/a lavorerete entrambi fuori casa? Cosa farete spesso e cosa farete raramente come famiglia? Sarai in contatto con la tua famiglia acquisita (*in-laws*)?

● Immagina come sarà tra quindici anni la vita dei componenti della famiglia ritratta nella foto a sinistra. La loro vita sarà simile alla vita che vivono ora? In che modo? Come sarà cambiata?

Point out the difference between **anche** and **inoltre**. **Anche** (*also, too, as well*) should be placed in front of the phrase or word to which it refers. **Inoltre** (*furthermore, besides, in addition, moreover*) should be used instead of **anche** when referring to a whole sentence or phrase. Examples: **Anch'io desidero ballare con Giusy**. (*I, too, want to dance with Giusy.*) **Desidero ballare anche con Giusy**. (*I want to dance with Giusy, too.*) **Sono in ritardo. Inoltre, ho lasciato il regalo a casa!** (*I'm running late. In addition, I left the gift at home.*)

> ### Strategie per la comunicazione
>
> **Quando ti prepari a scrivere un tema, ricordati di utilizzare gli avverbi per rendere più chiaro e vivace quello che scrivi.**
>
> ● Usa gli avverbi di tempo, come **spesso**, **mai**, **già**, ecc., per dire con quale frequenza fai alcune cose.
>
> ● Usa gli avverbi di modo, come **bene**, **male**, **velocemente**, ecc., per dire in che modo fai le cose.
>
> ● Usa gli avverbi di quantità, come **molto**, **poco**, **troppo**, **di più**, **di meno**, ecc., per dire in che misura fai qualcosa.

Preparazione  Vocabulary Tools

Vocabolario della lettura

abbiente *affluent*
le abitazioni *housing*
il fenomeno *phenomenon*
il mammone *mama's boy*
il vitto e l'alloggio *room and board*
  (lit. *food and lodging*)

Vocabolario utile

assumersi una responsabilità
  to assume responsibility
autosufficiente *self-sufficient*
di prima necessità *absolutely necessary*
il nucleo familiare *family unit*
prendere l'iniziativa *to take initiative*
rimandare *to postpone*
il ruolo *role*

1 Lessico Trova un sinonimo per ogni parola.

1. cibo ___vitto___
2. iniziare ___prendere l'iniziativa___
3. indipendente ___autosufficiente___
4. ricco ___abbiente___
5. essenziale ___di prima necessità___
6. genitori e figli ___il nucleo familiare___
7. case ___abitazioni/alloggi___
8. ritardare ___rimandare___

2 La mia famiglia Rispondete alle domande individualmente e poi confrontate insieme le risposte.

1. Che età avevi quando hai cominciato a frequentare l'università? Sei rimasto/a a casa o ti sei trasferito/a?
2. Secondo te, dopo l'università abiterai da solo/a o resterai in famiglia?
3. I tuoi genitori saranno d'accordo?
4. A quale età pensi che i tuoi genitori ti considererebbero troppo grande per abitare con loro?
5. Hai dei fratelli o delle sorelle maggiori che non abitano più a casa? Da quanto tempo? Sono sposati?
6. Hai un parente che ha più di 30 anni e che abita con i genitori?
7. Quanti anni avevano i tuoi nonni quando si sono sposati?
8. Hai intenzione di sposarti? A quale età?
9. Secondo te, cosa significa essere indipendenti?

3 Ipotesi Leggete il titolo e guardate le immagini della lettura nella pagina seguente; poi rispondete insieme alle domande.

- Chi sono le persone nell'immagine? Dove sono e cosa fanno?
- Quale sarà l'argomento della lettura?
- Che cosa sapete sull'argomento? Fate una lista delle informazioni.
- Perché, secondo voi, «vivere con la mamma» è un fenomeno culturale tipicamente italiano?

Nota CULTURALE

L'amore degli italiani per la mamma si manifesta anche con la musica. Le arie più famose sono certamente «**Mamma**» (Bixio e di Stefano) del 1941 e «**Addio alla madre**» dall'opera lirica *Cavalleria Rusticana* (Mascagni) del 1889. Molto amate sono anche le più recenti «**Viva la mamma**», canzone pop di Edoardo Bennato (1989), e «**Portami a ballare**», con la quale Luca Barbarossa ha vinto il Festival di Sanremo, il più importante concorso musicale in Italia, nel 1992.

VIVERE CON LA MAMMA

A quale età è comune lasciare la casa dei genitori e andare a vivere da soli? In Italia questa domanda ha una risposta diversa da quelle tipiche in altri paesi. È infatti una delle caratteristiche più specifiche degli italiani quella di restare in famiglia fino ad un'età più avanzata. Il fenomeno dei «mammoni» o «bamboccioni» si riferisce ai figli che vivono con i genitori fino a trent'anni e passa°. *and beyond*

Secondo gli ultimi dati ISTAT 8,6 milioni i giovani tra i 18 e i 35 anni vivono ancora in casa con i genitori. Si tratta del 68,1% dei giovani non sposati. Spesso questo si attribuisce alla disoccupazione e ai prezzi molto alti delle abitazioni, specialmente in città, ma in realtà non si tratta solo di fattori economici ma anche di tradizioni culturali. Alcuni sociologi pensano che questo fenomeno sia il risultato di una società consumista: restando a casa i giovani non devono preoccuparsi di pagare vitto e alloggio e hanno più denaro° a disposizione. Se vogliono, possono mettere da parte lo stipendio° per potere un giorno comprare un appartamento. A differenza del Nord America, in Italia le case dello studente non sono comuni, e molti giovani, terminate le scuole superiori, restano a casa mentre frequentano i corsi all'università. Le difficoltà a trovare lavoro dopo gli studi prolungano la permanenza. Con la disoccupazione e la mancanza° di alloggi, molti giovani italiani non hanno i mezzi finanziari per andare a vivere da soli. *money* *salary* *lack*

I dati indicano che il fenomeno è prevalente tra i figli maschi, che sono circa sei milioni, quasi due milioni in più a confronto con le giovani donne. E il numero dei mammoni continua a crescere: la maggioranza resta a casa fino al matrimonio,

La festa del papà

Il 19 marzo, il giorno della festa di san Giuseppe, in Italia si festeggiano tutti i papà. Per l'occasione si mangiano i deliziosi bignè o zeppole di san  Giuseppe (che in ogni regione hanno ricette e nomi un po' diversi): delle paste fritte, ripiene° di crema e spolverate° di zucchero a velo°.

ripiene *filled* **spolverate** *dusted* **zucchero a velo** *powdered sugar*

che in Italia avviene° abbastanza tardi (oltre ai trent'anni) ed è in declino (secondo i risultati dell'ISTAT). *happens*

In generale le donne italiane si separano dai genitori prima degli uomini e quelle che rinunciano° alla vita indipendente lo fanno per poter risparmiare° prima del matrimonio. *give up* *to save*

Quali sono le conseguenze del mammismo sulla società italiana?

La convivenza con un marito mammone che si sente ancora legato° a sua madre e che si sente figlio prima che genitore può essere molto difficile. Alcuni ricercatori attribuiscono la crescita dei divorzi in Italia al progressivo aumento dei mammoni. I genitori italiani, ormai° anziani, continuano ad assumersi le responsabilità dei figli adulti e a sentirsi in dovere di mettersi a loro completa disposizione. E poi ci sono le questioni più difficili da capire: si può diventare adulti senza separarsi dai genitori? Ci si può formare un'identità individuale senza essere indipendenti? La riluttanza a tagliare° il cordone ombelicale può portare anche a rimandare le scelte importanti della vita, inclusa quella di diventare genitori, una categoria in diminuzione nella penisola. Ma il vantaggio di restare vicino all'amore incondizionato dei genitori rimane una forte tentazione per i giovani italiani. ■ *tied* *already* *to cut*

> I genitori italiani, ormai anziani, continuano ad assumersi le responsabilità dei figli adulti e a sentirsi in dovere di mettersi a loro completa disposizione.

Analisi

1

Comprensione Indica se le affermazioni sono **vere** o **false**. Dopo, in coppia, correggete le affermazioni false.

Vero	Falso	
☐	☑	1. La famiglia italiana non è unita.
☑	☐	2. Ai genitori italiani piace prendersi cura dei figli.
☑	☐	3. Ai figli italiani piace la sicurezza della famiglia.
☐	☑	4. Restare a casa con i genitori rende i figli indipendenti.
☑	☐	5. I matrimoni in Italia stanno diminuendo.
☑	☐	6. Le cause del mammismo includono l'alto costo delle abitazioni.

2

Opinioni A turno rispondete alle domande.

1. Quali sono le caratteristiche del mammone italiano?
2. Quali sono i risultati dell'indagine ISTAT?
3. Perché i figli e i genitori italiani hanno difficoltà a separarsi?
4. Quali sono le conseguenze del fenomeno dei mammoni nella società italiana?
5. Quali sono i vantaggi e gli svantaggi di abitare con i genitori anche da adulti?
6. Come si può definire un mammone nel tuo paese? Conosci qualcuno?
7. Qual è la tua opinione sui mammoni?
8. Abiteresti con i tuoi genitori oppure vicino a loro dopo l'università? Perché?

TEACHING OPTION
Rai International has compiled and explained other common stereotypes about Italians regarding musical and artistic aptitude, pasta consumption, religion, terrorism, mafia, and soccer. If you'd like to share and discuss them with your students, they can be found at http://www.italiano.rai.it/

3

Un'altra opinione Leggete il paragrafo e rispondete alle domande.

I genitori traggono beneficio dalla compagnia e dai servizi che i figli possono offrire e soprattutto, secondo la ricerca, dall'opportunità di costringere° i figli a osservare le loro regole. Mentre, quindi, per i genitori la situazione risulta vantaggiosa, al contrario i giovani si trovano con le ali tarpate°, sono spesso disoccupati°, viaggiano di meno e faticano a mettere su famiglia°. «Il prezzo che i giovani italiani si trovano a pagare è una scarsa indipendenza e, a lungo termine, poca soddisfazione nella vita. In conclusione, riteniamo che i genitori italiani si sforzino molto per farsi amare dalla loro prole°, ma in un certo senso comprano questo amore in cambio dell'indipendenza dei figli», hanno concluso i ricercatori.

(Fonte: Il Corriere della Sera, 3 febbraio 2006)

costringere to force **le ali tarpate** clipped wings **disoccupati** unemployed **faticano a...** find it hard to start a family **la prole** offspring

1. Come è diversa l'opinione espressa nell'articolo rispetto a quella della lettura?
2. Chi è responsabile del mammismo, secondo l'articolo?
3. Quali sono i vantaggi di tenere i figli in casa per i genitori?
4. Secondo te, il mammismo è un fenomeno temporaneo o a lungo termine?

4

Situazioni In gruppi di tre, improvvisate una conversazione basata su una di queste situazioni e recitatelo per gli altri studenti.

A

A Roma uno/a studente(ssa) di 18 anni deve spiegare ai suoi genitori molto protettivi che vuole frequentare l'università di Bologna e che vuole abitare con degli amici. I suoi genitori preferiscono che frequenti l'università vicino a casa e che abiti con loro.

B

A New York uno/a studente(ssa) che ha appena finito l'università vuole tornare ad abitare con i suoi genitori prima di decidere cosa fare del proprio futuro, ma loro non sono d'accordo. Preferirebbero che il/la figlio/a cominciasse subito a lavorare e che fosse indipendente.

Practice more at vhlcentral.com.

Preparazione

 Vocabulary Tools

A proposito dell'autrice

Elsa Morante (1912–1985) è una delle maggiori scrittrici italiane del XX secolo. *La storia* (1974) è il suo libro più importante, iniziato nel 1943 quando si era rifugiata in un paesino vicino a Roma con il marito, il famoso scrittore Alberto Moravia. Finita la guerra, la casa della coppia a Roma divenne il ritrovo del mondo intellettuale romano di sinistra. I racconti, le fiabe e i romanzi della Morante sono un inno (*hymn*) alla vita, anche quando la guerra cerca di distruggere le cose più belle.

Vocabolario della lettura		Vocabolario utile
l'anima *soul*	la palpebra *eyelid*	l'estraneo/a *stranger*
bussare *to knock*	la pelliccia *fur*	il fantasma *ghost*
dare retta *to pay attention*	rubare *to steal*	l'ingenuità *naïveté*
la dentiera *denture*	il sangue *blood*	invecchiare *to age*
la gengiva *gum*	sordo/a *deaf*	il miracolo *miracle*
il legno *wood*	spettinare *to ruffle hair*	strano/a *strange*

Teach students common expressions with the word **anima**. Examples:
con tutta l'anima *with all one's heart*
buon'anima *may he/she rest in peace/God rest his/her soul*
l'anima della festa *the life of the party*
rompere l'anima a qualcuno *to drive somebody mad*

1

Definizioni Trovate la definizione adatta ad ogni parola.

_c_ 1. la dentiera   a. parte immortale dell'uomo
_e_ 2. l'ingenuità   b. liquido che scorre nelle vene
_b_ 3. il sangue   c. dentatura artificiale
_f_ 4. il fantasma   d. che non sente
_d_ 5. sordo   e. l'essere ingenuo; candore
_h_ 6. la gengiva   f. apparizione soprannaturale
_a_ 7. l'anima   g. battere alla porta per farsi aprire
_g_ 8. bussare   h. parte carnosa che copre la base dei denti

2

Preparazione In coppia, fatevi le seguenti domande.

1. Quando eri piccolo passavi del tempo con i nonni? Ti piaceva stare con loro?
2. È importante che i bambini passino del tempo con i nonni? Perché?
3. Secondo te, per un bambino è meglio stare con un nonno o con una baby-sitter? Perché?
4. Ti ricordi una storia divertente che ti è successa quando eri con uno dei tuoi nonni?
5. Da piccolo/a inventavi storie fantastiche per spiegare cose che non capivi?

3

Discussione In piccoli gruppi, discutete queste domande.

1. Invecchiare fa paura? Puoi fare un esempio di metodi che la gente usa per cercare di esorcizzare (*exorcise*) la paura di invecchiare?
2. I bambini spesso si trovano in situazioni pericolose e non lo sanno. Ti ricordi di essere mai stato/a in una situazione pericolosa senza saperlo? Che cosa è successo?

Nota CULTURALE

Il romanzo° più famoso della Morante, **La storia**, dopo una breve carrellata° storica che va dal 1900 al 1940, è un grande affresco degli anni della seconda guerra mondiale. Il carattere popolare e poetico dello stile narrativo dell'autrice rendono *La storia* uno dei più importanti romanzi storici del Novecento°.

romanzo *novel* **carrellata** *overview*
Novecento *twentieth century*

 Practice more at vhlcentral.com.

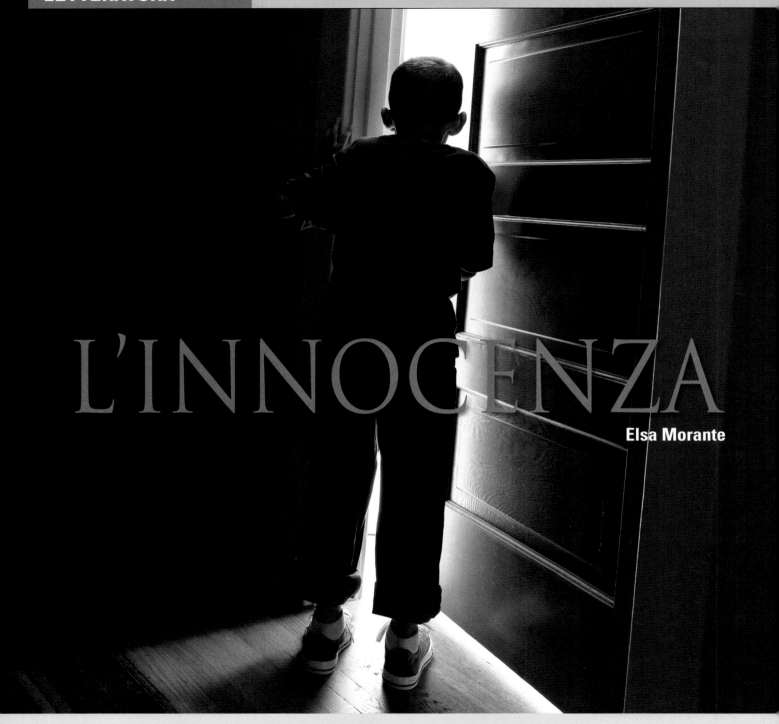

L'INNOCENZA

Elsa Morante

wise
decrepit

fault
happen 5
won't fall

countless/drained

C erto non è saggio° lasciare in casa, soli, una nonna decrepita° e un nipote che appena incomincia a cambiare i denti. La colpa° di ciò che può accadere° non ricadrà° su loro due, ma sugli altri.

Il piccolo Camillo era rimasto in casa solo con la nonna. Questa nonna era sorda, e gli anni innumerevoli° l'avevano succhiata° fino a ridurla° quasi un piccolo scheletro di legno. Non solo, ma per tenere insieme quei suoi quattro ossicini° di legna, ella era costretta° a fasciarsi stretta stretta sotto le sottane°, come un fantolino°. La sua testa minuscola e rotonda, quasi nuda° di capelli, dondolava°, e le palpebre grige rimanevano sempre abbassate°. Non era, lei, una di quelle nonne che raccontano favole: se ne

10 reduce her

little bones
forced
skirts/baby
15 deprived
bobbed
lowered

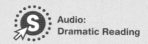

curled up/high chair
back of a chair/mumbling 20
slipped
trembling gums
stool

door
yelled

broth soup

slurring

shook

ran 40

purple-ish/curls

white
listlessly

Come in

hall
50

except

ruffled up

storm
distract her

60

showed off

stuttered
hoarse/crossed 65
boldly

stava tutta rannicchiata° nel seggiolone° dall'alto schienale°, borbottando° tra sé parole che sdrucciolavano° tra le sue gengive tremolanti°. E il nipote, tranquillo, seduto sullo sgabello°, ricontava le pietre del pavimento (giacché da poco aveva imparato a contare).

Mentre così passavano il tempo, si udì bussare forte all'uscio°. Camillo eccitato strillò°:

—Nonna, bussano!—

—Ma no, no, non è l'ora della minestrina° —borbottò la nonna che, come si è detto, era sorda.

—Macché, nonna, ho detto che bussano! —strillò più forte il bambino.

—La vuoi col brodo o col latte? —chiese biascicando° la nonna.

Allora Camillo scosse° il capo con rassegnazione, e, saltato giù dallo sgabello, corse° ad aprire. Fu stupefatto al vedere una grande e bellissima signora con una pelliccia violacea°, con riccioli° scuri intorno al viso ovale e malato, le dita lunghe e candide° intrecciate con languore°. —È permesso? —chiese la signora, con una voce pigra, che pareva il suono dell'organo. E Camillo, inesperto com'era, disse:

—Accomodatevi°.

La signora si sedette in anticamera°, e il suo corpo, mezzo nudo sotto la pelliccia, pareva di statua; senonché° la faccia non era di statua, era di donna triste e pazza, e ogni tanto, per aumentare quell'apparenza, ella si scompigliava° tutti i capelli. Così spettinata, sembrava un nero temporale°. Camillo pensò che fosse suo dovere distrarla°, e incominciò a raccontarle della nonna:

— Mia nonna, —disse, —ha gli orecchi sbagliati e non capisce niente. Se dico «due» capisce «uno» (avendo imparato da poco a contare, egli faceva sfoggio° di esempi numerici).

—Le nonne diventano così —balbettò° la signora con voce rauca°. E accavallò° sfacciatamente° le gambe nude.

—Mia nonna non ha sangue, —aggiunse in fretta Camillo, —è come

una formica°. Mia nonna non ha denti per mangiare. Anch'io da piccolo ero così, ma adesso no. Guardi qui c'è un buchettino° vuoto, ma presto spunterà° il dente nuovo.

—Foglie, fiori e denti spuntano, —sentenziò° la visitatrice con aria severa, fissandolo con occhi rabbuiati°.

—Mia nonna non esce mai di casa, —proseguì Camillo in tono saccente°, —non cammina, è come una sedia, come… come il muro. Ma ogni tanto parla, e nessuno le dà retta. Mia nonna ha novantacinque anni.

—Novantacinque primavere e basta, —corresse la signora. E detto questo si spettinò con furia ed ebbe una specie di singhiozzo°.

—Primavera è una stagione, —esclamò Camillo, fiero° della propria dottrina°. —Quand'io sarò grande, comprerò una dentiera per la nonna, coi denti d'oro, e pure un carretto col ciuco° per portarla a spasso°.

—Ah, ah, ah! Innocente! Innocente! —gridò la signora balzando in piedi con una risata sfrontata° e terribile.

—Addio, mio bell'innocente. Me ne vado.

—Non aspetti? —chiese Camillo deluso.

—Ah, ah, ah, me ne vado, —ripeté la signora, e Camillo si accorse che uscendo ella raccoglieva un non so che da un angolo e se lo nascondeva nel pugno°, sotto la pelliccia; gli parve qualcosa come una bambolina di legno.

—Che hai rubato? —le gridò rincorrendola° sulla scala. Ma quella, coi capelli al vento, sempre ridendo orribilmente se ne andò, e pareva tuono quando dilegua°.

Camillo furibondo° ritornò dalla nonna, e la trovò addormentata. Questo sonno durò in eterno. Soltanto adesso, fattosi grande°, Camillo ha capito ogni cosa. L'oggetto misterioso rubato da quella signora, e da lui creduto una bambolina di legno, era invece l'anima della nonna. Infatti quella bellissima signora, che lui stesso aveva lasciato entrare per innocenza, era la Morte. ■

ant

70

empty little space
will appear

pronounced
75 *darkened*

know-it-all

80

sob

85

proud/knowledge

buggy with a donkey
90 *take her around*

shameless laugh

95

100
fist

105 *running after her*

fade away
furious
110

all grown up

115

Analisi

1

Comprensione Scegli quale frase è vera in ogni coppia.

1. (a.) La nonna di Camillo è sorda.   b. La nonna di Camillo è muta.

2. a. Camillo vuole mangiare la minestrina col latte.
   (b.) Camillo vuole dire che qualcuno bussa alla porta.

3. a. Alla porta c'è una signora bellissima che Camillo conosce.
   (b.) Alla porta c'è una signora che Camillo fa accomodare anche se non la conosce.

4. (a.) La signora si spettina e sembra una pazza (*crazy woman*).
   b. La signora ha la faccia di una statua.

5. (a.) Camillo dice che anche lui non aveva denti come la nonna.
   b. Camillo dice che i denti spuntano (*begin to grow*) come i fiori.

6. (a.) La signora è divertita dall'ingenuità di Camillo.
   b. La signora prende in giro Camillo.

2

Interpretazione Scegli una risposta e poi, con un(a) compagno/a, discuti perché ti sembra giusta.

1. Camillo è _____.
   a. un bambino che può già stare da solo in casa   (b.) un bambino che non va ancora a scuola   c. un bambino che ha già perso tutti i denti da latte   d. un fantolino (*baby*)

2. La signora _____.
   a. è una pazza scappata dal manicomio (*mental home*)   b. è un'amica della nonna   c. vende delle bambole   (d.) è un po' strana e dà risposte criptiche

3. Camillo è un bambino _____.
   (a.) socievole che cerca di intrattenere come un grande
   b. timido che ha paura degli sconosciuti   c. antipatico
   d. che ha fame e non ha voglia di parlare

4. La signora _____.
   a. entra nelle case dove ci sono vecchi per rubare   b. è la mamma di Camillo e vuole portarlo via   c. fa collezione di bamboline e ne trova una rara in casa di Camillo   (d.) è la Morte che Camillo si immagina bellissima e pallida

5. La nonna _____.
   a. dorme tranquilla mentre Camillo parla con la signora   (b.) muore perché Camillo lascia entrare la signora   c. cucina la minestrina che Camillo voleva mangiare   d. muore perché la signora ruba la sua bambolina preferita

3

3 This is a good exercise to make students learn new adjectives. You will have to give the definition of quite a few of the ones listed. A follow-up activity could be asking them whether they agree with the adjectives given and how else they would describe the characters listed. Ask them to come up with at least one new adjective and see what kind of general ideas emerge about the characters.

Personaggi Scegli gli aggettivi che descrivono meglio i tre personaggi. Usa il dizionario per cercare gli aggettivi che non conosci. Some answers will vary.

a. attraente	f. ingenuo	m. saccente	r. sorpreso
b. loquace	g. fiducioso	n. fragile	s. criptico
c. sordo	h. stanco	o. vecchio	t. silenzioso
d. lento	i. misterioso	p. bizzarro	u. indifeso
e. provocante	l. curioso	q. ladro	v. ospitale

● Camillo
  b, f, g, l, m, r, v

● la nonna
  c, d, h, n, o, t, u

● la signora
  a, e, i, p, q, s

4

Discussione In coppia, rispondete a queste domande.

1. Secondo te, per quale causa muore la nonna?
2. La nonna del racconto è proprio così o è come sembrava a Camillo bambino?
3. La signora, secondo te, è vera o immaginaria?
4. Immagina che Camillo non apra la porta: come cambia la storia?
5. Perché Camillo crede che la signora abbia rubato proprio una bambolina? Qual è il significato della bambolina?

5

Opinioni In coppia, rispondete a queste domande.

1. Com'eri tu da bambino/a? Eri fiducioso/a o diffidente?
2. C'erano delle regole che dovevi seguire anche quando non c'era con te un adulto? Quali? Menzionane due.
3. Ti sei mai trovato in situazioni in cui eri più responsabile dell'adulto che era con te?
4. Hai paura della vecchiaia e della morte? Perché?
5. Come t'immagini la morte?
6. Il racconto finisce con Camillo adulto che capisce un episodio del passato modificato dalla sua fantasia di bambino. Conosci altre storie, romanzi, film che hanno la stessa struttura (un adulto che guarda al passato)?

6

Inventa una storia! In gruppi di tre o quattro, inventate delle soluzioni alternative al finale descritto nel racconto.

- I genitori di Camillo arrivano mentre sta parlando con la signora. La vedono anche loro o è solo immaginata da Camillo? Se la vedono, cosa succede? Diventano anche loro vittime?

- Cambia il carattere dei tre personaggi: Camillo è molto timido, la morte è un vecchio, la nonna non è sorda. Come cambiano le dinamiche tra i tre?

- La nonna in realtà non è sorda! È un super-eroe che aspettava la morte per sconfiggerla (*defeat her*). Immagina una storia completamente inventata: super-eroe, alieno, figura religiosa; immagina una nonna combattiva. Come reagisce Camillo quando vede che la nonna è fortissima?

6 Students should have a lot of freedom with this exercise. The idea is to see how they can change the outcome and perhaps even the spirit of the story. While they work in small groups, walk around and provide extra vocabulary. The planning phase should not last longer than 15-20 minutes. Have students act out their remakes in class.

7

Generazioni a confronto Come si comportano generazioni diverse?

A. In gruppi di tre, parlate di come si comportano di solito i bambini e i vecchi che conoscete nelle seguenti situazioni.

compleanni	nascita di un nuovo bambino
Giorno del Ringraziamento	Natale
matrimoni	traslochi (*moves*)
funerali	vacanze

B. Come si comportano gli adolescenti e gli adulti? Trovi che abbiano delle reazioni totalmente diverse?

8

Tema Scrivi due paragrafi e racconta un episodio della tua infanzia con uno dei tuoi nonni o con una persona anziana che sia stata importante per te.

Practice more at **vhlcentral.com**.

Pratica

Tipi e struttura di un saggio

Nelle lezioni precedenti è stato esaminato il saggio di tipo argomentativo che difende una tesi. Altri tipi di saggio possono essere:

- **Informativo** Si dichiara un tema. Si deve essere obiettivi e non presentare opinioni personali. Si devono offrire informazioni e contesto necessari perché il lettore possa capire.

- **Persuasivo** Il fine è convincere il lettore della posizione dell'autore su un tema. Si devono presentare argomenti a favore e contrari, e dimostrare che la posizione dell'autore è corretta.

- **Narrativo** Si racconta una storia o un episodio. È necessario usare una sequenza logica che descriva l'accaduto dall'inizio alla fine.

Il tipo di saggio e la sua lunghezza dipendono dall'intenzione dell'autore e dal tipo di pubblico. Ecco un modello per un tipico saggio di cinque paragrafi:

- **Primo paragrafo:** Introduzione/Tesi (in un saggio lungo nell'introduzione si possono anticipare le proposizioni principali);

- **Secondo paragrafo:** Prima proposizione principale e argomenti;

- **Terzo paragrafo:** Seconda proposizione principale e argomenti;

- **Quarto paragrafo:** Terza proposizione principale e argomenti;

- **Quinto paragrafo:** Ricapitolazione/Conclusione.

1 **Preparazione** In coppia, scrivete tre o quattro frasi di tipo informativo, persuasivo e narrativo partendo da questa affermazione: «Imparare l'italiano è difficile ma importante».

- Prima di scrivere, scegli e dichiara il tipo di saggio a cui lavorerai: informativo, persuasivo o narrativo.

- Il saggio deve far riferimento ad almeno due dei quattro brani studiati in questa lezione e nelle precedenti lezioni e contenuti in **Cortometraggio**, **Immagina**, **Cultura** e **Letteratura**.

- Il saggio deve svolgersi in cinque paragrafi, come suggerito nel modello.

- Il saggio deve essere lungo almeno due pagine.

2 **Saggio** Scegli uno di questi argomenti e scrivi un saggio.

> I bambini ricorrono al mondo della fantasia quando giocano e anche quando sono di fronte a situazioni nuove che non capiscono. Gli adulti devono incoraggiare questa fantasia o cercare di mostrare loro la realtà?

> Responsabilizzare i bambini li aiuta a diventare adulti migliori o bambini a metà?

> Si finisce mai di essere genitori? Si finisce mai di essere bambini?

Brainstorm with students the different kinds of informative, narrative, and persuasive essays they might encounter. Examples:
- *How-to essays vs. descriptive essays about a topic*
- *Dramatic narratives vs. humurous anecdotes*
- *Newspaper ads that look like an article vs. editorials on a political issue.*

Quickly review with students each of the key elements listed in the model essay structure.

In famiglia Vocabulary Tools

I rapporti di parentela

il/la (bis)nonno/a *(great-) grandfather/grandmother*
il/la cugino/a *cousin*
il/la figlio/a (unico/a) *son/daughter; (only) child*
il/la figlioccio/a *godson/goddaughter*
il/la gemello/a *twin*
il genero *son-in-law*
il genitore (single) *(single) parent*
la madrina *godmother*
il marito *husband*
la moglie *wife*
il/la nipote *nephew/niece; grandson/granddaughter*
la nuora *daughter-in-law*
il padrino *godfather*
il/la parente *relative*
la parentela *relatives*
lo/la sposo/a *groom/bride*
il/la suocero/a *father-/mother-in-law*
lo/la zio/a *uncle/aunt*

adottivo/a *adopted*
imparentato/a *related*
lontano/a *distant*
materno/a *maternal*
paterno/a *paternal*

aspettare un figlio *to be expecting (a baby)*
essere incinta *to be pregnant*

Le tappe della vita

l'età adulta *adulthood*
la giovinezza *youth*
l'infanzia *childhood*
la maturità *maturity*
la morte *death*
la nascita *birth*
la vecchiaia *old age*

Le generazioni

l'antenato *ancestor*
le radici *roots*
il salto generazionale *generation gap*
il soprannome *nickname*

assomigliare *to resemble*
ereditare *to inherit*
sopravvivere *to survive*

La vita in famiglia

diventare indipendente *to become independent*
educare *to raise*
essere desolato/a *to be sorry*
litigare *to fight*
pentirsi *to regret*
punire (isc) *to punish*
rimproverare *to scold*
sormontare *to overcome*
trasferirsi *to move*
viziare *to spoil*

La personalità

il carattere *personality*

affiatato/a *close-knit*
amabile *lovable*
autoritario/a *bossy*
codardo/a *coward*
egoista *selfish*
furbo/a *sly*
insopportabile *unbearable*
maleducato/a *bad-mannered*
possessivo/a *possessive*
remissivo/a *submissive*
ribelle *rebellious*
severo/a *strict*
socievole *sociable*
testardo/a *stubborn*
vanitoso/a *vain*
vivace *lively*

Cortometraggio

la bambola *doll*
il banco *(check in) counter*
la cabina di controllo *cockpit*
i carabinieri *military police*
il/la fidanzato/a *boyfriend/girlfriend*
la lavatrice *washing machine*
il nastro trasportatore *luggage carousel*
l'ordigno *bomb*

il rinforzo *reinforcement*
lo zainetto *small backpack*

accomodarsi *to make oneself comfortable*
avvicinarsi *to go near*
fare il bucato *to do the laundry*
sorridere *to smile*
stare in fila *to stand in line*

Cultura

le abitazioni *housing*
il fenomeno *phenomenon*
il mammone *mama's boy*
il nucleo familiare *family unit*
il ruolo *role*
il vitto e l'alloggio *room and board (lit. food and lodging)*

assumersi una responsabilità *to assume responsibility*
prendere l'iniziativa *to take initiative*
rimandare *to postpone*

abbiente *affluent*
autosufficiente *self-sufficient*
di prima necessità *absolutely necessary*

Letteratura

l'anima *soul*
la dentiera *denture*
l'estraneo/a *stranger*
il fantasma *ghost*
la gengiva *gum*
l'ingenuità *naïveté*
il legno *wood*
il miracolo *miracle*
la palpebra *eyelid*
la pelliccia *fur*
il sangue *blood*

bussare *to knock*
dare retta *to pay attention*
invecchiare *to age*
rubare *to steal*
spettinare *to ruffle hair*

sordo/a *deaf*
strano/a *strange*

La società che si evolve

V iviamo in un mondo in cui culture ed etnie si incontrano e si mescolano, ma non sempre con tolleranza e in armonia. Troppo spesso l'«altro» e il «diverso» ci fanno paura. Quali passi si possono fare per promuovere l'integrazione e superare (*overcome*) le divergenze (*differences*)? Come possiamo creare un mondo in cui la convivenza (*sharing*) delle differenze favorisca l'arricchimento (*enrichment*) culturale delle persone?

213

240

Destinazione:
L'ITALIA MERIDIONALE

MOLISE

PUGLIA

CAMPANIA

BASILICATA

CALABRIA

PREVIEW Invite students to observe the photo on the previous page. Ask: **Pensi che questa sia una foto contemporanea, scattata in Italia in questi anni? Perché sì e perché no? Pensi che le persone ritratte in questa foto appartengano alla stessa comunità o classe sociale? Questa foto potrebbe rappresentare una sezione della società italiana di 40 anni fa? Perché sì e perché no?**

Società e cambiamenti Vocabulary Tools

I cambiamenti

adattarsi *to adapt*
adeguarsi *to adjust*
appartenere *to belong to*
arricchirsi *to become rich*

aumentare *to increase*
conformarsi *to conform*
diminuire *to decrease*
impoverirsi *to become poor*
ottenere *to obtain*

pianificare *to plan*
realizzare *to achieve*
stabilirsi *to settle*
tutelare *to protect; to defend*

INSTRUCTIONAL RESOURCES
Audioscripts, Answer Keys, Lab MP3s
SAM/WebSAM: WB, LM

SINONIMI E CONTRARI
fedele ←→ credente
il maltrattamento ←→ l'offesa
musulmano ←→ islamico
tutelare ←→ difendere
l'integrazione ≠ l'emarginazione

Point out that **credere a qualcuno** means *to believe what someone says* while **credere in qualcuno/Dio** means *to trust someone/ to believe in God.*
While **cattolico**, **musulmano**, and **protestante** work both as nouns and as adjectives, **ebreo** is a noun (*Jew*) that can be used as an adjective (*Jewish*) only when referring to a person (**un bambino ebreo**). The adjective **ebraico** is used in other instances (**la religione ebraica**).

Le tendenze sociali

la (s)comparsa *(dis)appearance*
la diversità *diversity*

la globalizzazione *globalization*
l'integrazione *integration*
la lingua madre *native language*
la (sovrap)popolazione
(over)population
(il)lo (sotto)sviluppo
(under)development
il tasso di natalità *birthrate*
il tenore di vita *standard of living*

(anti)conformista *(non)conformist*
multilingue *multilingual*

I problemi e le soluzioni

il caos *chaos*
la comprensione *understanding*

il conflitto di classe *class conflict*
il dialogo *dialogue*
l'incertezza *uncertainty*
il maltrattamento *abuse*
la polemica *controversy*
la povertà *poverty*
il razzismo *racism*
la volontà *will(power)*

lamentare/lamentarsi *to regret*
lottare *to fight*
manifestare *to demonstrate*
reclamare *to complain, to protest; to claim*
superare *to overcome*
tirare avanti *to go forth*

Le convinzioni religiose

la cattedrale *cathedral*

la chiesa *church*
Dio *God*
la fede *faith*
il/la fedele *believer*
la libertà di culto *freedom of worship*
la moschea *mosque*
il papa *pope*
il prete *priest*
il rabbino *rabbi*
la sinagoga *synagogue*
il/la santo/a *saint*

credere *to believe*
pregare *to pray*

agnostico/a *agnostic*
ateo/a *atheistic*
cattolico/a *Catholic*
ebreo/a *Jewish*
musulmano/a *Muslim*
protestante *Protestant*

Nota
CULTURALE

In Italia, specialmente nel Sud, **l'onomastico** (*name day*), il giorno associato al santo da cui la persona ha preso il nome, è un evento importante in cui gli italiani dicono **Auguri!** proprio come per il compleanno.

Pratica e comunicazione

1

Sinonimi e contrari Collega ogni parola al suo sinonimo o al suo contrario.

Sinonimi

1. miscredente _____ateo_____
2. poliglotta _____multilingue_____
3. adattarsi _____adeguarsi_____
4. programmare _____pianificare_____

Contrari

5. emarginazione _____integrazione_____
6. uguaglianza _____diversità_____
7. certezza _____incertezza_____
8. arricchirsi _____impoverirsi_____

Nota
CULTURALE
Secondo un recente studio condotto dal CESNUR (Centro Studi Nuove Religioni), in Italia si contano oggi circa 600 confessioni religiose. Pur rimanendo un paese a maggioranza cattolica, l'Italia si sta aprendo infatti a nuove fedi e nuove culture. In particolare e in ordine di importanza numerica, al fianco dei **cattolici** si contano oggi in Italia molti **cristiani ortodossi**, **protestanti**, **ebrei**, **testimoni di Geova**, **musulmani**, **Bahai**, **induisti**, **buddisti**, **sikh**, **radhasoami** e fedeli di altre religioni di origine orientale.

(FONTE: cesnur.org)

2

Una domenica in Vaticano Completa la conversazione con le parole della lista.

| ateo | fede | libertà di culto | pregare |
| cattolici | fedeli | papa | sinagoga |

NICOLA Ecco! Questa è la basilica di San Pietro!

JOHN Ma quanta gente! Come mai?

NICOLA Perché è domenica. Ogni domenica a mezzogiorno il (1) _____papa_____ si affaccia al balcone della basilica e recita l'Angelus insieme ai (2) _____fedeli_____.

JOHN Tutta questa gente è venuta qui per (3) _____pregare_____? A proposito, è vero che gli italiani sono poco aperti alle religioni diverse da quella cattolica?

NICOLA Ma no; a Roma c'è anche la Grande Moschea, il centro islamico più grande d'Europa! Abbiamo anche una bellissima (4) _____sinagoga_____ ebraica. Nonostante i (5) _____cattolici_____ siano la maggioranza, in Italia c'è (6) _____libertà di culto_____ e quindi anche altre religioni possono professare la propria (7) _____fede_____.

JOHN Mi sembra giusto! Io sono un intellettuale (8) _____ateo_____ e penso che sia opportuno dare spazio a tutti.

NICOLA Sono d'accordo. Ma è importante conoscere i monumenti cattolici per capire il patrimonio storico, culturale e artistico dell'Italia.

2 Explain that the **Angelus** is a devotion of the Catholic Church said in the morning, at noon, and in the evening. Every Sunday at noon the Pope gives a short talk from a balcony of Saint Peter's Church to the people gathered in San Peter's Square. After the talk, the Pope recites the **Angelus** with the crowd.

2 Mention that **come mai?** is just another way to say **perché?**

3 Monitor the groups while they work on their stories, then ask volunteers from each group to read their story to the class.

4 Ask students if they think the situation on Earth is more similar to that of planet B612 or planet H724. Encourage them to point out similarities and differences. Discuss possible solutions to the problems that have been identified on the two planets.

3

Definizioni In gruppi di tre o quattro, definite le parole della lista. Poi, componete una storia utilizzandone almeno sei.

| impoverirsi | reclamare | la sovrappopolazione | il tenore di vita |
| incertezza | il sottosviluppo | superare | tirare avanti |

4

Nel 3215 Siete nel 3215. Molti abitanti del pianeta B612 si trasferiscono su H724, dove cominciano una nuova vita. Immaginate di essere due inviati speciali de *La gazzetta dello spazio* e descrivete, in due brevi articoli, le situazioni che hanno portato all'emigrazione dal pianeta B612 e le nuove condizioni di vita su H724.

Modello **Articolo 1:** La vita su B612 è diventata insostenibile….

Articolo 2: La vita su H724 comincia faticosamente ma si presenta ricca di nuove opportunità….

 Practice more at **vhlcentral.com**.

Preparazione Vocabulary Tools

INSTRUCTIONAL RESOURCES
Supersite: Video, Script & Translation
SAM/WebSAM: WB

To help students understand some of the references in the film, point out that **Linate** is the Milan airport, **l'impepata di cozze** is a traditional Neapolitan dish of mussels, and that **via Montenapoleone** is a famous street in Milan. You might want to review Italian regions and islands with a map. Mention the inhabitants of different cities/regions, such as **i calabresi, i siciliani, i romani, i torinesi**, and remind students that there are often enormous linguistic and cultural differences among Italians, sometimes even between neighboring towns.

Vocabolario del cortometraggio	Vocabolario utile
il capitone *large eel*	**il dialetto** *dialect*
la corriera *long-distance bus*	**l'incomprensione** *lack of understanding*
l'estero *foreign countries*	**meridionale** *southern*
il ferroviere *railway employee*	**il pregiudizio** *prejudice*
il maltempo *bad weather*	**il proverbio** *proverb*
il panettone *Christmas bread*	**il realismo** *realism*
il tassista *taxi driver*	**settentrionale** *northern*
la vigilia *eve*	**lo stereotipo** *stereotype*
	la tradizione *tradition*
	l'umorismo *humor*

ESPRESSIONI

ammazzare il tempo *to kill time*
Che fretta c'è? *Why rush?*
Che peccato! *What a shame!*
farsi i fatti propri *to mind one's business*
mangiare in bianco *to eat light*
più o meno *more or less*
Sono stufo/a! *I've had enough!*
Vuoi/Vuole favorire? *Would you like some (food or drink)?*

1

Definizioni Abbina ogni parola con la sua definizione.

1. La vigilia di Natale è ___e___ a. quando le persone non si capiscono bene.
2. Il tassista ___g___ b. è un tipo di autobus per viaggi più lunghi.
3. L'incomprensione si crea ___a___ c. è un tipo di pesce che si mangia a Natale.
4. Il capitone ___c___ d. sono le regioni del Nord Italia.
5. La corriera ___b___ e. la sera prima del giorno di Natale.
6. Il senso dell'umorismo ___f___ f. può aiutarci a ridere anche nelle situazioni difficili.
7. Un pregiudizio ___h___ g. guida il taxi.
8. Il Meridione ___i___ h. è un'opinione ostile e precostituita.
9. Il Settentrione ___d___ i. è la zona del Sud Italia.

2 Tell students that **il panettone**, literally *big bread*, is a Christmas dessert with candied fruit and sometimes nuts and chocolate. **La colomba**, which means *dove*, is a traditional Easter cake covered with sugar and almonds.

2

Feste e tradizioni Guardate queste immagini di dolci tradizionali in Italia: li riconoscete? Come si chiamano? Quali sono i dolci che mangiate durante le feste? E per il vostro compleanno?

3

Intervista

A. Domanda agli altri studenti se si sono mai trovati nelle seguenti situazioni, come hanno reagito e cosa hanno imparato dall'esperienza. Prendete appunti mentre ascoltate.

Hai mai avuto questa esperienza?	Descrivi la situazione	Racconta la tua reazione	Cosa hai imparato?
viaggiare con una persona difficile			
parlare con qualcuno con cui non eri d'accordo			
trovarti in una città poco ospitale			
avere una conversazione molto interessante con una persona che non conoscevi			
imparare una lezione quando non te l'aspettavi			
sentirti vittima di uno stereotipo			
assaggiare un piatto che non ti è piaciuto per niente			

B. Dopo aver fatto le interviste, raccontate gli episodi più interessanti al resto della classe.

4

Opinioni Rispondete alle domande individualmente e poi commentate le risposte insieme.

1. Ci sono differenze culturali tra le diverse regioni del tuo paese?
2. Quante lingue diverse si parlano nel tuo paese? E nella tua comunità?
3. Secondo te, alcuni stereotipi corrispondono almeno in parte alla realtà?
4. Pensi che il clima e la posizione geografica possano influenzare le persone?
5. Qual è la tua festa preferita? Come la celebri? Segui delle tradizioni speciali?

5

I personaggi In coppia, immaginate il carattere e la vita di questi due italiani.

- Come sarà la loro personalità?
- Dove abiteranno?
- Cosa faranno di professione? E nel tempo libero?
- Come sarà la loro famiglia?
- Cosa preferiranno mangiare e bere?
- Cosa guarderanno alla televisione?

 Practice more at **vhlcentral.com**.

LACREME NAPULITANE

Menzione speciale
**Clermont Ferrand
Film Festival**

una produzione di **FRANCESCO SATTA** e **CASA CIRCONDARIALE** sceneggiatura e regia **FRANCESCO SATTA** direttore di produzione **IGOR BELLINELLO.** attori principali **ANTONIO ALLOCA, DARIO OPPIDO, ADAM SELO, LYSANDRA CORIDON, DAVID WHITE, MARCO MANFREDI** montaggio **ANDREA MAGUOLO** fotografia **MICHELE D'ATTANASIO**

Trama *Un milanese e un napoletano attraversano l'Italia sullo stesso treno ma con due prospettive completamente diverse.*

RADIO …il maltempo divide in due l'Italia: mentre al Sud gli italiani si godono° una tiepida vigilia di Natale, al Nord le temperature sono in discesa° e la neve blocca i passi alpini e appenninici. Si prevedono perciò gravi disagi° per chi viaggia, con aeroporti chiusi e ritardi nella circolazione dei treni…

MILANESE Ferroviere, scusi, va a Milano?
FERROVIERE Chi, io? No.
MILANESE Non Lei, il treno.
FERROVIERE Più o meno.

NAPOLETANO Treni italiani sempre in ritardo!
DONNA INGLESE *What did he say?*
UOMO INGLESE *I don't know, but it's all so picturesque!*

NAPOLETANO Finalmente si parte! Pure voi, dotto', andate a Milano?
MILANESE Io… sarei già a casa da un pezzo, se non mi avessero chiuso Linate per la neve.
NAPOLETANO E che fretta c'è di arrivare a Milano? Dotto', non vi offendete, ma a me Milano non mi piace proprio. No. È brutta, è triste… insomma, non mi piace, anche se i milanesi dicono di no.

NAPOLETANO Scusate se mi permetto… Volete favorire?
MILANESE No, grazie: ho già il mio pranzo.
NAPOLETANO Senza complimenti…
MILANESE No, grazie.

godersi *to enjoy* **in discesa** *going down* **disagi** *inconveniences*

NAPOLETANO Ma perché non vi tagliate 'sti capelli? Siete ridicolo!
MILANESE Adesso basta! Io intanto non sono ridicolo! E poi basta! E prima il capitone, e poi le canzoni, e poi cosa c'è stato ancora? Ma io sono stufo! Lei si deve fare i fatti suoi!

🎬 Sullo SCHERMO

Riordina la sequenza di questi eventi.

7	**a.**	Il napoletano è da solo per la strada.
2	**b.**	Il milanese sale sul treno.
6	**c.**	Il milanese e il napoletano prendono il taxi a Milano.
1	**d.**	Il milanese prende il taxi a Napoli.
4	**e.**	Il milanese e il napoletano arrivano a Piacenza.
5	**f.**	Il milanese e il napoletano salgono sulla corriera.
3	**g.**	Il capitone spaventa i turisti.
8	**h.**	Il ciclista ha un incidente.
9	**i.**	Il napoletano e il milanese fanno amicizia.

Analisi

Comprensione Scegli la risposta giusta.

1. Che giorno è?
   a. È una giornata lavorativa.   (b.) È la vigilia di Natale.   c. È il giorno di Natale.

2. Il milanese non prende l'aereo...
   a. perché non c'è un aeroporto a Napoli.   (b.) a causa del maltempo.
   c. perché il treno è più veloce.

3. Quando il napoletano canta, gli altri passeggeri...
   a. applaudono tutti, incluso il milanese.   (b.) applaudono, ma il milanese è irritato.
   c. sono irritati, ma il milanese applaude.

4. Mentre il treno attraversa l'Italia dai finestrini...
   a. si vedono delle città italiane.   b. si vedono le stazioni delle città italiane.
   (c.) si vedono delle fotografie di città italiane.

5. Nella stazione di quale città i passeggeri scendono dal treno e prendono la corriera?
   (a.) A Piacenza.   b. A Pisa.   c. A Padova.

6. Il napoletano rimane per strada e non va a casa della figlia perché...
   a. si è dimenticato l'indirizzo a Napoli e non sa trovare la casa.
   (b.) non parla con la figlia da molto tempo e non conosce il suo indirizzo.
   c. la sua unica figlia è morta molti anni prima.

Interpretazione Scegli la frase corretta tra le due. Poi, con un(a) compagno/a confrontate e spiegate le vostre risposte.

1. (a.) Secondo il napoletano, i milanesi hanno il cuore di pietra.
   b. Secondo il milanese, i napoletani hanno sempre fretta.

2. (a.) Secondo il milanese, i napoletani sono incivili e lenti.
   b. Secondo il milanese, i napoletani sono freddi.

3. a. I protagonisti litigano sempre perché sono ostinati.
   (b.) I protagonisti litigano sempre perché sono incompatibili.

4. a. I protagonisti usano il **Lei** quando si parlano.
   (b.) Il napoletano usa il **Voi** e il milanese il **Lei**.

5. (a.) I protagonisti sono caricature culturali delle loro città.
   b. I protagonisti rappresentano bene le loro rispettive città.

Stereotipi

A. Fate una lista degli stereotipi sui napoletani e i milanesi suggeriti nel corto.

a. apprezzano i rapporti umani	e. hanno una cucina poco interessante	i. sono razionali
b. apprezzano il lavoro	f. hanno un'ottima cucina	l. sono passionali
c. sono emotivi	g. parlano molto	m. sono freddi
d. hanno il cuore di pietra	h. parlano poco	n. sono sentimentali

Napoletani: a, c, f, g, l, n	**Milanesi:** b, d, e, h, i, m

B. In coppia, scegliete due stereotipi dalla parte A. Spiegate in che modo avviene (*happens*) il contrario nel corto; poi condividete le vostre risposte con il resto della classe.

4

Critica In coppia, rispondete alle domande. Some answers will vary.

1. Che ruolo hanno i turisti inglesi nel film? Come sono rappresentati?

2. Come sono gli effetti speciali nel film?

3. Com'è la struttura del film? Come sono le scene all'inizio e alla fine?

4. Come interpretate la fine del film? Perché si vede il set con le telecamere, le luci e la macchina per la neve?

5. Come definiresti questo film a qualcun altro? Ironico? Malinconico? Realistico? Umoristico? Perché? Ti ricorda altri film?

5

I rapporti umani Qual è la reazione del tassista quando vede l'incidente? Qual è la reazione del milanese? Cosa rivelano dei loro caratteri? Ci sono altri esempi di reazioni nel film? Come avresti reagito tu nelle stesse situazioni?

MILANESE Cos'è successo?
TASSISTA Va' (*Look*) lì lo *stupid* con la bicicletta!
MILANESE Eh, ma si sarà fatto male!
TASSISTA Si sarà fatto male, però noi dobbiamo fare tutto il giro adesso!

6

Opinioni In piccoli gruppi, esprimete le vostre opinioni rispondendo alle domande.

1. Sei veloce a formarti un'opinione sulle persone che incontri per la prima volta?

2. Hai mai cambiato la tua prima impressione su una persona quando hai avuto l'opportunità di conoscerla meglio?

3. Pensi che il tuo ambiente ti dia la possibilità di conoscere una varietà di persone diverse?

4. Credi che Internet e la televisione peggiorino o migliorino la nostra conoscenza del mondo e degli altri? Secondo te, quale effetto hanno sugli stereotipi?

7

Incontro In coppia, scegliete una situazione e improvvisate una conversazione fra due persone con opinioni e gusti diversi. Usate le parole e le espressioni nella lista.

| chiacchierare | (non) essere d'accordo | insistere | spiegare |

A

In aereo un(a) giovane è seduto/a vicino a una persona simpatica ma che vuole assolutamente parlare. Il/La giovane spiega che ha appena finito gli esami e vuole semplicemente dormire, perché è stanchissimo/a.

B

Un(a) turista sta prendendo un caffè in un bar di Roma e incontra una persona italiana piena di pregiudizi sulla nazionalità del(la) turista. Dopo aver ascoltato, il/la turista cerca gentilmente di convincere l'italiano/a che si tratta solo di stereotipi che non corrispondono alla realtà e spiega quali sono alcuni dei pregiudizi sugli italiani.

 Practice more at **vhlcentral.com**.

---

4 These are some possible answers to questions 1 to 4:
1. Anche i turisti sono degli stereotipi: pensano che gli italiani siano «pittoreschi» e sorridono anche quando non capiscono quello che si dice.
2. Sono volutamente falsi, stereotipati.
3. La struttura del film è simmetrica: tutti gli elementi sono presentati come opposti (l'inizio e la fine; il sud e il nord; il sole e la neve; il napoletano e il milanese, ecc.). La fine rispecchia l'inizio del film.
4. Forse la fine collega la finzione della cinematografia alla falsità degli stereotipi e dei pregiudizi.

TEACHING OPTION Write some proverbs or sayings about Italian cities:
• Vedi Napoli e poi muori.
• Tutte le strade portano a Roma.
• Milano la grande, Venezia la ricca, Genova la superba, Bologna la grassa, Firenze la bella, Padova la dotta, Ravenna l'antica, Roma la santa.
Then, ask students:
1. Qual è il significato di questi proverbi?
2. Secondo voi, come sono nati? Ci sono forse delle ragioni storiche?
3. Pensando a quello che sapete sulle città italiane, siete d'accordo con il significato dei proverbi?
4. Ci sono dei proverbi simili sulla vostra città o paese?

If necessary, provide students with English explanations:
• You have to see Naples at least once in your life.
• All roads lead to Rome.
• Milan is great, Venice is rich, Genoa is haughty, Bologna is fat, Florence is beautiful, Padova is learned, Ravenna is ancient, and Rome is blessed.

INSTRUCTIONAL RESOURCES: Teaching suggestions; Answer Keys
SAM/WebSAM: WB

IMMAGINA

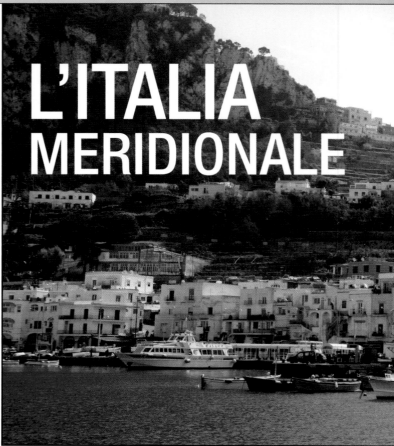

L'ITALIA MERIDIONALE

Tra storia e natura

Prima dell'unificazione d'Italia, conclusa nel 1861, le regioni del Sud Italia, tra cui **Campania**, **Molise**, **Basilicata**, **Puglia** e **Calabria**, per secoli sono state storicamente accomunate°. I Greci le hanno colonizzate dall'VIII secolo a.C.; dal III secolo a.C. i Romani le hanno invase°; in seguito, dinastie provenienti dal Nord Europa, dalla Spagna e dalla Francia hanno esercitato la loro dominazione unendo le regioni nei **Regni di Napoli** e **di Sicilia**.

Oggi, ciò che continua ad accomunare queste regioni è la bellezza del territorio e delle coste unita a un incomparabile patrimonio° artistico, storico e culturale.

I litorali° offrono scenari straordinari. La tortuosa° e suggestiva **Costiera Amalfitana**, in Campania, è una finestra sulle isole di **Capri** e **Ischia**. Le insenature° e le grotte° delle coste pugliesi, in particolare quelle del **Gargano**, sono altrettanto caratteristiche; da qui si può raggiungere la riserva marina delle **Isole Tremiti**. Non meno spettacolari sono le coste della Calabria o della Basilicata, dove le acque dell'**Adriatico** e quelle dello **Ionio** si incontrano, dando al mare colori unici.

L'entroterra° si presenta spesso con colline coperte di vigneti° e di oliveti° che producono oli e vini eccellenti; le aree più interne sono sempre montagnose, con vette° anche molto elevate.

Viaggiare attraverso l'Italia meridionale significa anche visitare città di origini antiche e siti archeologici grandiosi.

In Molise ci sono numerose necropoli arcaiche, i resti romani di **Sepino** e quelli di un vasto villaggio nei pressi di **Isernia**, in cui è stato scoperto l'*Homo Aeserniensis*. In Basilicata, nel centro storico di **Matera**, ci sono i «**Sassi**», abitazioni antiche scavate nella roccia calcarea° e, sulla costa, i resti delle colonie greche di **Metaponto**, dove si può ammirare il superbo tempio dorico di **Hera**.

In Puglia ci sono tesori artistici come la fortezza medievale

Napoli

di **Castel del Monte** o gli edifici barocchi di **Lecce**, senza dimenticare i misteriosi **trulli**. In Calabria, esempi dell'intervento dei Greci e di altri popoli sono visibili nelle mura greche di **Reggio Calabria**, nelle statue dei

Bronzi di Riace o nel **Castello Aragonese**. Risalendo verso nord, in Campania si incontrano i resti della città greca di **Paestum**, e quelli di **Pompei** ed **Ercolano**, città romane scomparse dopo l'eruzione del Vesuvio nel 79 d.C.

Napoli, capoluogo della Campania, è una gemma che brilla° non solo per la luce riflessa dalle acque del golfo, ma anche per il prestigioso patrimonio artistico. **Castel dell'Ovo**, il **Duomo di San Gennaro**, la **Certosa di San Martino** sono solo alcuni esempi della prestigiosa architettura napoletana. Ma Napoli è unica anche per i vicoli ombrosi° e gli angoli caratteristici dei quartieri **Spagnoli** del centro storico.

Viaggiare attraverso il Sud Italia, insomma, significa immergersi in profumi, sapori e colori che non hanno eguali al mondo; città dalle origini antiche ci raccontano la loro storia attraverso monumenti che evocano emozioni uniche.

In più...

Tra l'VIII ed il III secolo a.C., mercanti, agricoltori°, allevatori° e artigiani° greci iniziano un processo di colonizzazione del Sud Italia. Le regioni interessate sono: Puglia, Basilicata, Calabria, Campania e Sicilia. La colonizzazione ha un carattere commerciale e il successo è tale che° i Greci iniziano a fondare città che impreziosiscono° con la loro arte. Queste regioni hanno preso il nome di **Magna Grecia**.

accomunate *associated* **invase** *invaded* **patrimonio** *heritage* **litorali** *coastline* **tortuosa** *winding* **insenature** *inlets* **grotte** *caves* **entroterra** *inland* **vigneti** *vineyards* **oliveti** *olive groves* **vette** *peaks* **roccia calcarea** *limestone* **brilla** *shines* **vicoli ombrosi** *dark alleyways* **agricoltori** *farmers* **allevatori** *stockbreeders* **artigiani** *craftsmen* **è tale che** *it is such that* **impreziosiscono** *embellish*

Pompei Nel 79 d.C., il **Vesuvio** eruttò° seppellendo° la città romana di **Pompei** con lapilli e cenere° che coprirono° interamente gli edifici e immobilizzarono per sempre persone e animali. Dopo molto tempo, nel XVIII secolo sono stati riportati alla luce° i primi resti della città sepolta°. Passeggiando per le sue strade lastricate° è possibile ammirare templi, basiliche, anfiteatri, botteghe° e ville con bellissimi mosaici e affreschi che ci raccontano la vita quotidiana di una città in cui il tempo si è fermato. Pompei è uno dei siti archeologici più visitati del mondo.

La pizza napoletana Preparare un pane con farina, acqua e lievito° era un costume molto comune tra le antiche popolazioni delle coste del Mediterraneo, ma l'idea di condire° il tutto con la *pummarola*, il pomodoro, è un'idea napoletana. La vera pizza napoletana, la stessa dal XVIII secolo, ha un impasto° leggero che si cuoce brevemente in un forno molto caldo. Aggiungete **pomodoro**, **mozzarella fresca** e qualche foglia° di **basilico** profumato e otterrete il piatto più buono del mondo!

eruttò *erupted* **seppellendo** *burying* **lapilli e cenere** *lapillus and ashes* **coprirono** *covered* **riportati alla luce** *brought to light* **sepolta** *buried* **lastricate** *paved* **botteghe** *shops* **lievito** *yeast* **condire** *to season* **impasto** *dough* **foglia** *leaf*

Vero o falso? Indica se ogni frase è **vera** o **falsa**. Correggi le frasi false. Some answers will vary.

1. Le regioni del Sud hanno formato il Regno di Napoli e di Sicilia. Vero.
2. Il Gargano si trova in Campania. Falso. Si trova in Puglia.
3. Il Molise è una regione montuosa. Vero.
4. I «Sassi» si trovano in Molise. Falso. Si trovano in Basilicata.
5. Paestum era una città romana. Falso. Era una città greca.
6. Napoli è il capoluogo della Campania. Vero.
7. Pompei è stata sepolta dalla lava del Vesuvio. Falso. È stata sepolta dalle ceneri e dai lapilli.
8. La ricetta della pizza napoletana è la stessa dal XVIII secolo. Vero.

Quanto hai imparato? Rispondi alle domande. Some answers will vary.

1. Quali sono le caratteristiche naturali delle regioni del Sud Italia? coste suggestive, entroterra collinoso e montuoso in alcune regioni
2. Che cosa si produce sulle colline delle regioni del Sud? olio e vino
3. Che cosa sono i «Sassi» di Matera? abitazioni scavate nella roccia
4. A che epoca risale la fortezza di Castel del Monte? al Medioevo
5. Dove si trovano le città romane di Pompei ed Ercolano? in Campania
6. In che parte di Napoli si trovano i quartieri Spagnoli? al centro della città
7. Quali sono le caratteristiche dell'impasto della pizza napoletana? L'impasto è leggero, deve cuocere per poco tempo in un forno molto caldo.
8. Che cosa è possibile vedere a Pompei? templi, basiliche, botteghe, ville, mosaici e altro

Progetto

La musica napoletana affonda le sue radici nel folklore locale, nei ritmi mediterranei ed ha strumenti caratteristici.

- Cerca informazioni su alcune delle canzoni più famose del repertorio napoletano.
- Cerca informazioni sugli strumenti della musica napoletana.
- Cerca anche informazioni su due artisti di oggi che continuano la tradizione musicale napoletana.
- Confronta i tuoi risultati con il resto della classe.

GALLERIA DI PERSONE ILLUSTRI

STILISTA
Gianni Versace (1946–1997)

Gianni Versace è stato un stilista e imprenditore (*entrepreneur*) italiano. Nato a Reggio Calabria, inizia la sua carriera nel mondo della moda sin da giovane, lavorando nell'atelier della madre. A venticinque anni si trasferisce a Milano per lavorare come disegnatore di abiti e sei anni più tardi presenta la prima collezione firmata con il suo nome. Il successo non tarda ad arrivare e Versace inizia collaborazioni con famosi fotografi e con il teatro, disegnando gli abiti di scena di balletti milanesi. Versace diventa un'icona della moda italiana nel mondo, lavora a vari progetti con cantanti come Madonna ed Elton John, e le modelle più in voga del momento appaiono nelle sue campagne pubblicitarie e in passerella con le sue creazioni. Nel 1997 Versace viene assassinato con due colpi (*shots*) di pistola sugli scalini della sua villa a Miami Beach.

GIORNALISTA, SCRITTORE
Roberto Saviano (1979–)

Roberto Saviano è un acclamato giornalista e scrittore nato a Napoli. Dopo una laurea in Filosofia inizia la sua carriera giornalistica che ha come soggetto la Camorra, cioè il crimine organizzato della Campania, e i fenomeni criminali del capoluogo campano. Nel 2006 l'autore pubblica il suo primo successo editoriale, *Gomorra*. Saviano scrive

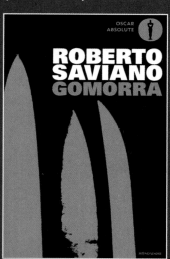

il romanzo in prima persona, raccontando dei luoghi in cui è cresciuto e di come la criminalità organizzata opera e viene protetta dalla popolazione locale. Dal libro, che vende oltre dieci milioni di copie in tutto il mondo, vengono tratti uno spettacolo teatrale, un film e una serie televisiva. Poco dopo l'uscita di *Gomorra*, Saviano viene messo sotto scorta a seguito di minacce di morte da parte dei cartelli camorristici del clan dei Casalesi. Oggi Saviano vive all'estero, collabora con varie università, giornali e si dedica alla scrittura di nuovi libri.

ATTORE

Rodolfo Valentino (1895–1926)

Rodolfo Alfonso Pietro Filiberto Raffaello Guglielmi, meglio conosciuto come Rodolfo Valentino, è stato uno dei più grandi divi del cinema muto americano. Nato a Castellaneta, in provincia di Taranto, in Puglia, Rodolfo è un giovane irrequieto (*restless*) che, dopo aver studiato danza a Parigi, salpa per l'America a soli diciotto anni con l'eredità lasciatagli dal padre. Arriva a New York nel 1913, in poco tempo sperpera tutto il denaro ricevuto e inizia a lavorare come cameriere, giardiniere e ballerino in un night club. Lascia New York per Hollywood e a meno di un anno dal suo arrivo debutta nel cinema con *My Official Wife* di James Young. Recita in altre pellicole ma il grande successo arriva con *I quattro cavalieri dell'Apocalisse* e *Lo sceicco* che manda in visibilio il pubblico femminile. All'apice della sua carriera il giovane Rodolfo Valentino viene stroncato (*struck down*) da un'ulcera gastrica e muore a New York a soli trentuno anni.

REGISTA

Paolo Sorrentino (1970–)

Paolo Sorrentino è un pluripremiato regista originario di Napoli. Muove i primi passi nel mondo del cinema a venticinque anni come ispettore di produzione (*set manager*), aiuto-regista e successivamente sceneggiatore (*scriptwriter*). Nel 2001 esordisce come regista con il lungometraggio (*feature film*) *L'uomo in più* vincendo numerosi riconoscimenti. Sette anni più tardi produce il suo primo film, *Il divo*, che presenta al Festival di Cannes aggiudicandosi (*winning*) il Premio della giuria. Il successo internazionale continua con il suo primo film in lingua inglese *This Must Be the Place* e prosegue con *La grande bellezza*, che, oltre a quattro European Film Awards, un Golden Globe e il Premio BAFTA, si aggiudica nel 2014 l'Oscar per il miglior film straniero. I successi continuano con il secondo film in lingua inglese, *Youth*, e la prima serie televisiva da lui scritta e diretta, *The Young Pope*.

Comprensione

Completare Completa le seguenti frasi.

1. Roberto Saviano è un ___giornalista___ e ___scrittore___.

2. *Gomorra* è scritto in ___prima___ persona.

3. Dopo l'uscita del suo primo libro, Roberto Saviano riceve ___minacce di morte___.

4. Gianni Versace disegnava abiti di scena per il ___teatro___.

5. Versace viene assassinato a ___Miami Beach___.

6. Rodolfo Valentino è molto amato dal ___pubblico___ femminile.

7. ___My Official Wife___ è il primo film in cui recita Rodolfo Valentino.

8. Valentino muore a causa di ___un'ulcera gastrica___.

9. Paolo Sorrentino è nato a ___Napoli___.

10. *La grande bellezza* ha ricevuto numerosi premi tra cui l'Oscar ___per il miglior film straniero___.

Scrittura

Scrivi sull'argomento Scegli uno dei seguenti argomenti e scrivi un paragrafo seguendo le indicazioni.

- **Da giornalista a scrittore** Molti scrittori come Roberto Saviano iniziano la loro carriera nel mondo del giornalismo. Conosci altri scrittori che hanno seguito lo stesso percorso? Quali sono, secondo te, i motivi per cui alcuni giornalisti diventano scrittori?

- **Il cinema muto** Prova a immaginare quali sono state le sfide (*challenges*) dei registi e gli attori che negli anni Venti hanno dato vita al cinema muto. Spiega quali qualità doveva avere un buon attore e come doveva essere pensato e diretto un film.

- **Roberto Saviano** Sei l'autore di *Gomorra* e stai partecipando a un'intervista radiofonica. Il presentatore ti chiede di spiegargli come si vive sotto scorta. Racconta come sono le tue giornate, quali limitazioni hai e cosa ti manca della vita che avevi prima del tuo *best seller*.

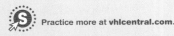

Practice more at **vhlcentral.com.**

INSTRUCTIONAL RESOURCES 6.1
Audioscripts, Answer Keys, Lab MP3s, Grammar Presentation Slides
SAM/WebSAM: WB, LM

Remind students that *would* may be translated by either the imperfect or the conditional, depending on the context.
Quando avevo cinque anni, giocavo con il mio cagnolino.
When I was five, I would (used to) play with my little dog.
Se avessi il tempo, giocherei con il mio cagnolino.
If I had the time, I would play with my little dog.

RIMANDO

The conditional forms of **dovere**, **potere**, and **volere** are translated as *should*, *could*, and *would like*, respectively. They are often used to soften a request or when giving advice.

Maria, dovresti mangiare di meno.
Maria, you should eat less.

Potresti darmi una mano?
Could you give me a hand?

Vorreste venire a parlare con il mio rabbino?
Would you like to come talk to my rabbi?

To review **dovere**, **potere**, and **volere**, see **Strutture 4.4, p. 150**.

ATTENZIONE!

Use these irregular future stems for the conditional also.
andare: andr–
avere: avr–
cadere: cadr–
dovere: dovr–
essere: sar–
fare: far–
potere: potr–
sapere: sapr–
venire: verr–
volere: vorr–

The conditional

The conditional mood expresses a statement that might be contrary to reality, a desire or a preference, or a polite request. In Italian, as in English, there are two conditional tenses, **il condizionale presente** (*the present conditional*) and **il condizionale passato** (*the past conditional*). They often correspond to *would* or *would have* in English.

—*E poi io a Napoli devo andarci perché sono obbligato ad andarci per lavoro. Altrimenti **starei** a casa mia, ma molto volentieri.*

The present conditional

- The present conditional of regular verbs is formed using the same stem as the future. Drop the last –**e** of the infinitive and add the endings –**ei**, –**esti**, –**ebbe**, –**emmo**, –**este**, and –**ebbero**. Regular –**are** verbs also change –**a**– to –**e**– to form the future or conditional stem.

The present conditional of regular verbs		
lottare	**credere**	**finire**
lotterei	**cred**erei	**fin**irei
lotteresti	**cred**eresti	**fin**iresti
lotterebbe	**cred**erebbe	**fin**irebbe
lotteremmo	**cred**eremmo	**fin**iremmo
lottereste	**cred**ereste	**fin**ireste
lotterebbero	**cred**erebbero	**fin**irebbero

- Verbs ending in –**care** and –**gare** show the same spelling changes as the future stem; an –**h**– is inserted to keep the hard sound of the verb.

  pregare → pregherei, pregheresti, pregherebbe, pregheremmo, preghereste, pregherebbero

  pianificare → pianificherei, pianificheresti, pianificherebbe, pianificheremmo, pianifichereste, pianificherebbero

- Verbs ending in –**ciare** and –**giare** show the same spelling changes as the future stem: the –**i**– of the stem is dropped.

  cominciare → comincerei, cominceresti, comincerebbe, cominceremmo, comincereste, comincerebbero

  mangiare → mangerei, mangeresti, mangerebbe, mangeremmo, mangereste, mangerebbero

- Verbs that have irregular stems in the future are also irregular in the conditional.

  Vorremmo combattere il razzismo.
  We would like to fight racism.

  Vivresti in un paese straniero?
  Would you ever live in a foreign country?

- The present conditional is used to express possibility or probability under certain conditions. It is also used to express uncertainty.

Un iPad **sarebbe** il regalo perfetto per Matteo.
An iPad would be the perfect gift for Matteo.

Non so se lo **farebbero** di nuovo.
I don't know if they would do that again.

- The present conditional is also used to express wishes, desires, or polite requests.

Ci **piacerebbe** frequentare una scuola multilingue.
We would like to attend a multilingual school.

Mi **potrebbe** spiegare il vocabolario?
Could you explain the vocabulary to me?

The past conditional

- The past conditional expresses an action that *would have occurred* in the past.

Il condizionale

Senza la nebbia, **vedremmo** il cartello.
Without the fog, we would see the sign.

Il condizionale passato

Senza la nebbia, **avremmo visto** il cartello.
Without the fog, we would have seen the sign.

- The past conditional is formed using the conditional form of the auxiliary **avere** or **essere** plus the past participle of the verb. Follow the same rules for agreement of the past participle that you use for the **passato prossimo** and other compound tenses.

The past conditional

ottenere	venire	arricchirsi
avrei ottenuto	sarei venuto/a	mi sarei arricchito/a
avresti ottenuto	saresti venuto/a	ti saresti arricchito/a
avrebbe ottenuto	sarebbe venuto/a	si sarebbe arricchito/a
avremmo ottenuto	saremmo venuti/e	ci saremmo arricchiti/e
avreste ottenuto	sareste venuti/e	vi sareste arricchiti/e
avrebbero ottenuto	sarebbero venuti/e	si sarebbero arricchiti/e

- The past conditional, corresponding to *would have* + [*verb*], is used in a manner similar to the present conditional. It expresses opinions and preferences in the past.

Giovanni non **sarebbe** mai **venuto** senza di te.
Giovanni would never have come without you.

Chi **avrebbe previsto** gli effetti della globalizzazione?
Who would have predicted the effects of globalization?

- The past conditional forms of **dovere**, **potere**, and **volere** are translated as *should have*, *could have*, and *would have liked*, respectively.

Avrebbero potuto pagare.
They could have paid.

Sarei voluto andare alla cattedrale con lei.
I would have liked to go to the cathedral with her.

Avreste dovuto chiederlo al prete.
You should have asked the priest for it.

RIMANDO

The conditional is also used in hypothetical statements. See **Strutture 9.3, pp. 360–361**.

Remind students that the placement of pronouns, negations, short adverbs, etc., in the past conditional is the same as in other compound tenses, including the **passato prossimo**. Example: **L'avrebbe comprato./Secondo me, tu avresti già finito**.

TEACHING OPTION
Ask students to imagine a new version of a well-known story, explaining what would *not* have happened. Example: **Riccioli d'Oro (*Goldilocks*) non avrebbe bevuto il latte dei tre Orsi, avrebbe bevuto una Coca-Cola!**

RIMANDO

The past conditional may also be used with indirect discourse. However, use the present conditional in English to translate it.

Ha detto che l'avresti fatto tu.
He said that you would do it.

You will learn about indirect discourse in **Strutture 10.3, pp. 400–401**.

RIMANDO

To review **dovere**, **potere**, and **volere**, see **Strutture 4.4, p. 150**.

Pratica

1

I nuovi studenti Il professor Antonio Rossi la professoressa Elena Bacci parlano di Fatima ed Amir, due nuovi studenti da poco arrivati in Italia. Completa la conversazione coniugando i verbi al condizionale presente.

ANTONIO Buongiorno, Elena. Hai già conosciuto i nostri nuovi studenti, Fatima e Amir? Io vorrei conoscerli, ma non parlano molto bene l'italiano.

ELENA Sì, è vero. Credo che (1) __dovremmo__ (dovere) aiutarli a inserirsi (*fit in*). Credo che così (2) __si adatterebbero__ (adattarsi) più facilmente.

ANTONIO Che strategie (3) __adotteresti__ (adottare) tu?

ELENA Non so, probabilmente (4) __pianificherei__ (pianificare) un percorso di conoscenza reciproca, cominciando con dei giochi di ruolo che (5) __arricchirebbero__ (arricchire) anche gli studenti italiani e (6) __faciliterebbero__ (facilitare) il confronto fra le due culture.

ANTONIO Mi sembra una buona idea.

ELENA Poi (7) __organizzerei__ (organizzare) delle lezioni di lingua.

ANTONIO In questo modo, però, i ragazzi (8) __perderebbero__ (perdere) familiarità con la loro lingua madre...

ELENA (9) __Suggerirei__ (suggerire) una lezione in lingua madre almeno una volta a settimana.

2

Vacanze... che stress! Giorgio, Antonio e Manuela sono andati in vacanza insieme, ma erano spesso in disaccordo. Ecco cosa racconta Giorgio. Completa le frasi coniugando i verbi al condizionale passato.

1. Antonio ha visitato le rovine romane di Pompei ma io __avrei visitato__ la Costiera Amalfitana.

2. Antonio ha mangiato una sfogliatella mentre io e Manuela __avremmo mangiato__ un babà al rum.

3. Antonio ha visitato la Campania ed è andato sul Vesuvio in macchina. Io, invece __sarei andato__ in seggiovia (*chair lift*).

4. Io sono andato in Sicilia e ho comprato le panelle al mercato di Ballarò, mentre Antonio __avrebbe comprato__ il pesce alla Vucciria.

5. Io sono andato in Puglia e ho visto i trulli di Alberobello, mentre Antonio e Manuela __avrebbero visto__ più volentieri il centro storico di Lecce.

Nota
CULTURALE

Napoli è famosa per vari prodotti alimentari tra i quali la **pizza**, il **babà** (soffice dolce imbevuto di rum), la **pastiera** (una torta pasquale fatta di germe di grano) e il **caffè**.

3

I casi della vita In piccoli gruppi, discutete cosa fareste in queste situazioni? Usate i verbi nella lista per formulare le vostre risposte.

andare dal meccanico	chiamare la polizia	prendere l'autobus
andare all'ufficio oggetti smarriti (*lost and found*)	chiedere aiuto	raccogliere
avere paura	fare finta di niente	scappare

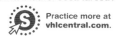

Comunicazione

4 Explain that the title of the activity is inspired by an old Italian saying: **dimmi con chi vai e ti dirò chi sei**, meaning that it is possible to judge what a person is like by looking at his/her friends.

4

Dimmi dove vai e ti dirò chi sei!

A. Scegli un luogo da visitare tra queste due proposte e discuti la tua scelta con un(a) compagno/a, rispondendo alle domande.

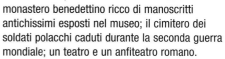

Montecassino:
Per chi ama la montagna, la pace e la tranquillità.

Attrattive: l'Abbazia di Montecassino, un antico monastero benedettino ricco di manoscritti antichissimi esposti nel museo; il cimitero dei soldati polacchi caduti durante la seconda guerra mondiale; un teatro e un anfiteatro romano.

Nelle vicinanze: il parco nazionale d'Abruzzo; la catena montuosa delle Mainarde, punto naturalistico e faunistico di grande importanza.

Specialità culinarie: salsicce e pasta fatta in casa.

Tempo libero: passeggiate tranquille lungo la via principale della cittadina o nel parco comunale, lungo il fiume Gari.

A cosa stare attenti: durante l'inverno ogni mattina la cittadina è immersa nella nebbia, che diminuisce la visibilità per chi guida.

Costiera Amalfitana:
Per chi ama il mare, il sole e l'architettura araba.

Attrattive: le chiese e i chiostri hanno affascinanti forme e decorazioni arabe; un'antica cartiera trasformata in un originale museo ricorda ai turisti l'antica tradizione della città come produttrice di carta secondo tecniche importate dai paesi arabi e poi perfezionate dagli amalfitani; prodotti artigianali in ceramica.

Nelle vicinanze: Napoli, Sorrento, Capri, Ischia.

Specialità culinarie: limoncello, pizza.

Tempo libero: romantiche passeggiate in riva al mare, ma anche molti pub e ristoranti.

A cosa stare attenti: il traffico è intenso e molto caotico; le strade sono strette e a strapiombo (*overhanging*) sul mare.

4 As an expansion, invite students who chose the same destination to work together to create an ad with ideas and proposals from every student in the group. Suggest possible titles to advertise the destination: **Vorresti trascorrere una vacanza tranquilla e rilassante? Ti piacerebbe arricchire la tua cultura e goderti la vita notturna allo stesso tempo?**

- Dove andresti? Perché?
- Chi sarebbe il/la tuo/a compagno/a di viaggio?
- Che luoghi in particolare visiteresti?
- Quanto tempo vorresti rimanere?
- Quanti soldi porteresti e cosa faresti con questi soldi?
- Cosa non dovresti fare e perché?

B. In gruppi di quattro, presentate ai compagni il vostro programma di viaggio e decidete qual è, tra tutti, il più interessante.

5

Microfono aperto Siete due giornalisti: pensate a una domanda che vorreste fare ad ognuno dei personaggi qui elencati usando il condizionale presente. Sono personaggi importanti: ricordatevi di usare il formale!

5 Ask pairs of students to exchange their written questions and invent replies for them by pretending to be the people in the list. Then ask the volunteers to act out their interviews while the class votes on the funniest/ wittiest/most believable.

Roberto Benigni	**Bill Gates**	**Sophia Loren**
Andrea Bocelli	**Barack e Michelle Obama**	**Sarah Palin**
Il papa	**Steven Spielberg**	**Angelina Jolie e Brad Pitt**

6

Avete rimpianti? C'è qualcosa che avete fatto nella vostra vita ma che non avreste dovuto fare? O qualcosa che non avete fatto ma che avreste potuto o voluto fare? A gruppi di tre, usate il condizionale passato di **dovere, potere** e **volere** per parlare dei vostri rimpianti.

Modello Sarei potuto diventare un grande musicista, ma ho deciso di smettere di suonare il pianoforte.

6 Remind students that the auxiliary verb for **dovere, potere,** and **volere** depends on the verb that follows (**sarei potuto andare** vs. **avrei potuto visitare**).

INSTRUCTIONAL RESOURCES 6.2
Audioscripts, Answer Keys, Lab MP3s, Grammar Presentation Slides
SAM/WebSAM: WB, LM

RIMANDO

To review negative commands, see **Strutture 4.3, pp. 146–147.**

Negation

- There are many ways to express negation (**la negazione**) in Italian. The simplest way is to place the word **non** before a verb (or an object pronoun and a verb).

    Lorenzo **non** esce con noi stasera perché è impegnato.
    Lorenzo is not going out with us tonight because he is busy.

- Many other expressions that begin with **non** can be used to make sentences negative. **Non** is placed in front of the verb and is followed by another word after the verb. Unlike in English, more than one negative expression can be used in the same sentence.

    Allora, **non** faccio più **niente**!
    Fine, then I won't do anything else!

    Claudia **non** dice **mai niente** a **nessuno**.
    Claudia never says anything to anyone.

- Note where the different negative expressions are placed in the sentences shown in the chart. **Non** precedes the auxiliary verb in compound tenses, and, depending on the negative expression, the other element follows either the auxiliary verb or the past participle.

Remind students that the negative expressions **ancora**, **mai**, **mica**, and **più** are placed between the auxiliary verbs **avere** and **essere** and the past participle in compound tenses. Example: **Non avevano mai discusso della sovrappopolazione della regione.**

TEACHING OPTION
Provide students with some affirmative phrases or questions and ask them to provide the negative forms or responses. Ex.: **Abbiamo già visto il film *New Moon.* → Non abbiamo ancora… Sei mai andato/a a Roma? → Non sono mai/ancora andato/a… Tutti hanno voglia di uscire. → Nessuno ha voglia … Tutto era facile quando ero piccolo/a. → Niente era facile…**

Negative expressions	
non… affatto *not at all*	**Non** mi piace **affatto** il ristorante Da Valerio. *I don't like Da Valerio at all.*
non… ancora *not yet*	Lucia, **non** hai **ancora** trovato un divano per il soggiorno? *Lucia, haven't you found a sofa for the living room yet?*
non… mai *never*	**Non** ho **mai** ascoltato la musica di Zucchero. *I've never heard Zucchero's music.*
non… mica *not in the least,* *not a bit, not at all*	Giusy **non** è **mica** stanca. *Giusy isn't tired at all.*
non… né… né *neither… nor*	I poveri **non** hanno **né** soldi **né** cibo. *The poor have neither money nor food.*
non… neanche **… nemmeno** **… neppure** *not even*	Marcella **non** ha comprato **neanche** un regalo di Natale. *Marcella didn't even buy one Christmas present.* **Non** ci ha detto **neppure** una parola. *She has not even said a word to us.*
non… nessuno *not… anyone, no one,* *nobody*	**Non** abbiamo visto **nessuno** davanti alla moschea. *We didn't see anyone in front of the mosque.*
non… nessun/o/a *not… a single, not… any*	**Non** aveva **nessuna** voglia di vederlo. *She didn't want to see him at all.*
non… niente/nulla *nothing, not… anything*	**Non** faccio **niente** di speciale stasera. *I'm not doing anything special tonight.*
non… più *no longer, not anymore,* *no more*	Barbara **non** esce **più** con il suo fidanzato italiano. *Barbara isn't going out with her Italian boyfriend anymore.*

—*Io **non** ho figli, e **nemmeno** i nipotini.*

- When a negative expression is the subject of the sentence, **non** must be omitted.

  Nessuno capisce bene il conflitto di classe.
  No one really understands class conflict.

  Niente cambierà le idee del Papa.
  Nothing will change the Pope's ideas.

  Né Giancarlo **né** Domenico potrebbero accompagnarmi.
  Neither Giancarlo nor Domenico could go with me.

- **Nessuno** may be used as an adjective. When it is, the forms follow the pattern of the indefinite article **un**.

  Nessuna ragazza è venuta alla festa!
  Not a single girl came to the party!

  Davide non pratica **nessuno** sport.
  Davide doesn't play any sports.

- The pronouns **niente**, **nulla**, and **nessuno** are considered masculine and singular for agreement purposes.

  Nessuno si è **stabilito** in quella parte della città.
  No one settled in that part of town.

  Nulla sarebbe **piaciuto** ai nipoti di Tommaso.
  Nothing would have pleased Tommaso's grandchildren.

- Use **niente/nulla di** plus an adjective but **niente/nulla da** plus an infinitive.

  Non c'era **niente di** interessante al cinema.
  There wasn't anything interesting at the movies.

  Ho già guardato nel frigo—non c'è **nulla da** mangiare!
  I already looked in the fridge—there's nothing to eat!

*Non c'è **niente da** fare! È tutto finito!*

- **Alcuno/a** can be used instead of **nessuno/a** in negative sentences. In this case, always use the singular form.

  Mi ha licenziato senza **alcuna/nessuna** spiegazione.
  They fired me without any explanation.

  Non c'è **alcun/nessun** problema.
  There's no problem.

Pratica

1

Disaccordi politici Immagina di essere un membro del Parlamento. Un esponente (*representative*) di un partito politico opposto al tuo si vanta (*boasts*) del proprio programma politico. Completa le frasi usando le espressioni suggerite tra parentesi.

Modello
—**Questa nuova legge risolverà tutti i problemi del paese.** (non... nessuno)
—**Non è vero,** questa nuova legge non risolverà nessun problema del paese.

1. —Questa nuova legge porterà vantaggi per tutti. (non... nessuno)
   —Non è vero, <u>questa nuova legge non porterà vantaggi per nessuno.</u>

2. —In questo modo le persone più povere saranno sempre tutelate (*protected*). (non... mai)
   —Non è vero, <u>in questo modo le persone povere non saranno mai tutelate.</u>

3. —Tutti i cittadini apprezzano la legge che sto per proporre. (nessun)
   —Non è vero, <u>nessun cittadino apprezza la legge che stai/sta per proporre.</u>

4. —La maggioranza del Parlamento ha già dato la sua approvazione. (non... ancora)
   —Non è vero, <u>la maggioranza del Parlamento non ha ancora dato la sua approvazione.</u>

5. —I giovani mi amano moltissimo! (non... affatto)
   —Non è vero, <u>i giovani non ti/La amano affatto.</u>

6. —La popolazione mi eleggerà ancora! (non... più)
   —Non è vero, <u>la popolazione non ti/La eleggerà più.</u>

2

Opinioni contrarie Stai assistendo a una conferenza sulla situazione sociale in Italia oggi, ma non sei affatto d'accordo con quello che afferma il relatore (*speaker*). Some answers will vary.

Modello
Ho sempre lottato contro il maltrattamento dei bambini.
No, Lei non ha mai lottato contro il maltrattamento dei bambini.

1. Ho sempre manifestato contro il razzismo. No, Lei non ha mai manifestato contro il razzismo.

2. Tutti pensano che la globalizzazione sia inevitabile. No, nessuno pensa che la globalizzazione sia inevitabile.

3. Il tasso di natalità in Italia quest'anno è già sceso dell'1% rispetto all'anno scorso. No, il tasso di natalità in Italia quest'anno non è ancora sceso dell'1% rispetto all'anno scorso.

4. La polizia ha registrato ancora casi di razzismo in città. No, la polizia non ha più registrato casi di razzismo in città.

5. Oggigiorno i giovani hanno tutto. No, oggigiorno i giovani non hanno niente.

6. L'Italia ha completamente superato le difficoltà legate all'integrazione delle comunità straniere. No, l'Italia non ha superato affatto le difficoltà legate all'integrazione delle comunità straniere.

3

Conversazioni In coppia, immaginate quali dialoghi hanno provocato queste reazioni.

Modello
—Ragazzi! Ho un'idea straordinaria per il weekend. Invece di andare al mare, potremmo visitare il museo di scienze naturali!
—Non interessa a nessuno!

Non lo farò mai!

Niente te lo impedirà!

No, non più.

Non dovrei né vederlo né parlargli!

Non interessa a nessuno!

Non ha ancora terminato gli studi all'università.

Practice more at **vhlcentral.com.**

Comunicazione

4

Noi e gli altri In coppia, ponetevi queste domande a turno. Rispondete utilizzando il più possibile le espressioni negative che avete imparato. Poi discutete delle vostre rispettive opinioni.

>**Modello** —Sei mai stato in un tribunale?
>
>—No, non sono mai stato in un tribunale.

Gli ideali

Sei un anticonformista? Perché pensi di esserlo o non esserlo?

Conosci persone che lo sono?

Secondo te, perché è giusto/sbagliato conformarsi alla società intorno a noi?

I problemi e le soluzioni

Hai mai avuto problemi di comprensione con qualcuno? In che occasione?

Hai mai reclamato un tuo diritto? Quale?

Hai mai lottato per una causa? Quale?

La religione

Hai mai visitato una chiesa/moschea/sinagoga?

Ti mette a disagio (*make uncomfortable*) parlare di religione con altre persone? Perché?

5

Le opinioni dell'esperto In coppia, immaginate di essere esperti sociologi e utilizzate le espressioni negative della colonna a destra per creare sei frasi sugli argomenti suggeriti nella colonna di sinistra.

>**Modello** A causa della globalizzazione, alcuni oggetti non sono più prodotti in un unico paese.

5 Have students read their sentences to the class without mentioning the noun from the column on the left. The others can guess what the missing word is.

la globalizzazione	la sovrappopolazione	non... più	non... ancora
il sottosviluppo	la diversità	non... niente	non... affatto
il tenore di vita	il razzismo	non... mai	non... né... né

6

Generazioni a confronto In coppia, immaginate una conversazione tra un papà e un figlio adolescente su uno di questi argomenti. Usate delle espressioni negative. Le vostre tesi devono essere convincenti!

6 Ask students to act out their dialogues for the class. Whose is most convincing?

- Il papà pensa che sia giusto vestirsi bene per un colloquio di lavoro, ma il figlio, anticonformista, non è d'accordo.

- Il papà pensa che non si debbano mai abbandonare le proprie tradizioni, mentre il figlio crede nel dialogo e nel confronto tra culture diverse.

- Il papà difende i valori tradizionali della religione, ma il figlio non è d'accordo.

INSTRUCTIONAL
RESOURCES
Audioscripts, Answer
Keys, Lab MP3s, Grammar
Presentation Slides
SAM/WebSAM: WB, LM

6.3

The subjunctive: impersonal expressions; will and emotion

- The subjunctive (**il congiuntivo**), is a grammatical mood that exists in both English and Italian to express attitudes or feelings such as opinion, happiness, fear, willingness, desire, obligation, necessity, or doubt.

The present subjunctive

- The present subjunctive of regular verbs is formed by adding the subjunctive endings to the stem. For verbs conjugated like **finire**, insert –**isc**– as you would in the present indicative.

The present subjunctive

	ascoltare	prendere	dormire	finire
che io	ascolti	prenda	dorma	finisca
che tu	ascolti	prenda	dorma	finisca
che lui/lei/Lei	ascolti	prenda	dorma	finisca
che noi	ascoltiamo	prendiamo	dormiamo	finiamo
che voi	ascoltiate	prendiate	dormiate	finiate
che loro	ascoltino	prendano	dormano	finiscano

- Verbs like **cercare** and **pagare** maintain the hard sound of the infinitive by inserting –**h**– between the stem and endings of all forms of the present subjunctive.

   cercare: cerchi, cerchi, cerchi, cerchiamo, cerchiate, cerchino
   pagare: paghi, paghi, paghi, paghiamo, paghiate, paghino

- Many verbs that are irregular in the indicative are also irregular in the subjunctive.

andare	vada, vada, vada, andiamo, andiate, vadano
avere	abbia, abbia, abbia, abbiamo, abbiate, abbiano
bere	beva, beva, beva, beviamo, beviate, bevano
dare	dia, dia, dia, diamo, diate, diano
dire	dica, dica, dica, diciamo, diciate, dicano
essere	sia, sia, sia, siamo, siate, siano
fare	faccia, faccia, faccia, facciamo, facciate, facciano
potere	possa, possa, possa, possiamo, possiate, possano
rimanere	rimanga, rimanga, rimanga, rimaniamo, rimaniate, rimangano
sapere	sappia, sappia, sappia, sappiamo, sappiate, sappiano
stare	stia, stia, stia, stiamo, stiate, stiano
uscire	esca, esca, esca, usciamo, usciate, escano
venire	venga, venga, venga, veniamo, veniate, vengano
volere	voglia, voglia, voglia, vogliamo, vogliate, vogliano

Subjunctive with impersonal expressions, will, and emotion

- The subjunctive is generally used in dependent clauses introduced by **che**, where the subjects of the main and dependent clauses are different. The verb or verb phrase in the main clause triggers the use of the subjunctive in the clause.

MAIN CLAUSE	CONJUNCTION	DEPENDENT CLAUSE
È possibile	che	Giorgio vada alla manifestazione.
It's possible	*that*	*Giorgio is going to the demonstration.*

- Use the subjunctive in clauses introduced by impersonal expressions that state an opinion.

Impersonal expressions followed by the subjunctive

è bene/male che... *it is good/bad that...*	**è probabile che...** *it is likely that...*
è difficile che... *it is difficult/unlikely that...*	**è strano che...** *it is strange that...*
è importante che... *it is important that...*	**può darsi che...** *it is possible that...*
è possibile che... *it is (not) possible that...*	**si dice che...** *it is said/they say that...*

È strano che Salvatore vada alla sinagoga: è cattolico!
It's strange that Salvatore is going to the synagogue; he's Catholic!

Può darsi che il telefonino sia spento.
It's possible that his cell phone is off.

- Use the subjunctive in subordinate clauses when the verb in the main clause expresses opinion, will or emotion.

Expressions of will	Expressions of emotion and opinion
desiderare... *to desire...*	**avere paura...** *to be afraid...*
esigere... *to require...*	**credere...** *to believe...*
insistere... *to insist...*	**dispiacere...** *to be sorry...*
permettere... *to allow...*	**essere +** *[emotion]*
preferire... *to prefer...*	**felice/contento/a...** *to be happy...*
	sorpreso/a... *to be surprised...*
suggerire... *to suggest...*	**pensare...** *to think...*
volere... *to want...*	**piacere...** *to be pleased, to like...*
	ritenere... *to believe, to maintain...*
	sperare... *to hope...*
	temere... *to fear, to be afraid...*

Desiderano che Chiara gli dica la verità.
They want Chiara to tell him the truth.

Temo che questo libro non sia più disponibile.
I'm afraid this book is no longer available.

ATTENZIONE!

Some additional impersonal expressions followed by **che** and the subjunctive include:

bisogna	**(è un) peccato**
è facile/	**è (im)possibile**
difficile	**è raro/strano**
è giusto	**è (in)utile**
è incredibile	**occorre**
è meglio	**pare**
è necessario	**sembra**
è ora	**vale la pena**

ATTENZIONE!

Not all clauses introduced by **che** require use of the subjunctive. Verbs and expressions indicating certainty or fact are followed by the indicative.

Sanno che Rita viene domani.
They know that Rita is coming tomorrow.

È vero che Massimo fa lo scrittore.
It's true that Massimo is a writer.

ATTENZIONE!

If the subject of the main clause and the dependent clause is the same, use an infinitive instead of the subjunctive in the dependent clause.

Gianni vuole che tu finisca la lettera.
Gianni wants you to finish the letter.

Gianni vuole finire la lettera.
Gianni wants to finish the letter.

RIMANDO

To learn about the use of infinitive constructions, see **Strutture 8.1, pp. 306–307**.

RIMANDO

To learn about other uses of the subjunctive, see **Strutture 7.3, pp. 272–273** and **Strutture 9.4, p. 364**.

To learn about tense sequencing, see **Strutture 9.1, pp. 350–352**.

Pratica

Le vacanze Completa l'e-mail che Laura ha scritto a Manuele. Usa il congiuntivo presente.

> Carissimo Manuele,
> sono davvero felice che tu (1) ___sia___ (essere) qui da noi, nel Matese, e che ci
> (2) ___rimanga___ (rimanere) per un'intera settimana, così almeno potremo vederci!
> È probabile che tu non (3) ___voglia___ (volere) uscire stasera e che invece (4) ___preferisca___ (preferire)
> rimanere in albergo a riposare. Ma spero che almeno un giorno tu (5) ___venga___ (venire) con
> me a percorrere «il sentiero delle quindici vette». La nostra zona non è molto vivace, ma è
> affascinante per i suoi scenari naturali.
> Desidero davvero che tu (6) ___veda___ (vedere) i laghi e le conche (*basins*) naturali di
> queste montagne e che tu (7) ___beva___ (bere) l'acqua delle nostre sorgenti (*springs*).
> Spero che tu (8) ___abbia___ (avere) voglia di camminare e che (9) ___faccia___ (fare) bel tempo,
> così potremo goderci la bellezza di queste zone. Ora ti lascio. È possibile che domani
> mattina io e Giorgio (10) ___passiamo___ (passare) in albergo per salutarti.
> A presto,
> Laura.

Difendiamo la natura Gli effetti dello sviluppo sono devastanti per gli ecosistemi. Combinate elementi delle tre colonne per creare delle frasi complete. Dopo aggiungete tre frasi originali.

È bello che	gli animali	aumenti ancora nella mia città
Sembra che	allo zoo	diminuisca sempre di più
Non voglio che	i giovani	maltrattino gli animali
Non credo che	l'inquinamento	manifestino per la difesa dell'ambiente
È impossibile che	il numero di foche (*seals*) nel mondo	si adeguino (*adapt*) al nuovo clima

I coinquilini Giorgio e Alberto hanno deciso di frequentare l'Università di Lingue Orientali a Napoli. Per potersi pagare gli studi, però, dovranno condividere l'appartamento. Cosa pensate che debbano fare Giorgio e Alberto per adeguarsi l'uno all'altro? Suggerite delle soluzioni usando le espressioni della lista.

bisogna che	è necessario che
è difficile che	(non) è possibile che
è meglio che	può darsi che

Giorgio

Alberto

Comunicazione

4 **Opinioni** In coppia, impostate una discussione su cosa sarebbe giusto fare per migliorare la società.

> **Modello** —È bene che gli immigrati imparino a parlare la lingua del paese ospite.
>
> —Sì, ma è importante che non perdano le proprie tradizioni culturali.

- bisogna che
- è bene che
- è giusto che
- è importante che
- penso che
- ritengo che

- abitudini
- lingua
- periferia
- religione
- scuola
- tenore di vita

4 Have each pair add two more words/expressions to the list and create additional statements. Have the rest of the class respond with other priorities.

5 **Annunci** In coppia, leggete gli annunci e immaginate di essere voi le persone che li hanno pubblicati; quindi continuate con la stesura (*draft*) dell'annuncio, usando quanto più possibile il congiuntivo presente. Poi presentate i vostri annunci completi alla classe.

> **Modello** **Annuncio 1:** È importante che la ragazza abiti in casa con noi.
>
> **Annuncio 2:** Occorre che il batterista abbia tempo libero il fine settimana.

Cercasi baby-sitter per famiglia con quattro figli

Cercasi batterista (drummer) per una rock band!

5 Ask students to act out a conversation between the writer of an announcement and the newspaper employee responsible for classified ads. The employee should ask for more detailed information that is not specified in the announcement. Example: —È meglio che la baby-sitter sia una persona giovane o matura? —Preferisco che sia giovane ed energica, ma che sappia anche essere severa.

6 **Per un mondo migliore** In gruppi di tre, provate a immaginare una conversazione fra due ragazzi che manifestano in piazza e il sindaco della città, che risponde in maniera pratica ai loro desideri.

> **Modello:** **Ragazza:** Vogliamo che i quartieri siano più sicuri!
>
> **Ragazzo:** È importante che la gente cammini per strada senza paura!
>
> **Sindaco:** Sì, sono d'accordo. Ma per fare questo, bisogna che tutti rispettino le leggi.

La società che si evolve

INSTRUCTIONAL RESOURCES **6.4**
Audioscripts, Answer Keys, Lab MP3s, Grammar Presentation Slides
SAM/WebSAM: WB, LM

Suffixes

—*L'importante è che lei non mi canti più quelle* **canzonacce** *napoletane, perché io veramente non le sopporto.*

- Suffixes (**i suffissi**) are added to many Italian nouns and adjectives to denote affection, size, poor quality, ugliness, or other traits. As in English, adding a suffix can reflect the speaker's feelings about a particular noun or the adjective used to describe it. For example, the two words, *dog*, **cane**, and *doggie*, **cagnolino**, demonstrate a difference that reflects the speaker's perception (a *doggie* is cuter or more dear to the speaker than a *dog*).

- Italian is very rich in its choice and variety of suffixes. English tends to rely on adjectives to convey shades of meaning. An Italian might say «**Che ragazzaccio!**» whereas an English speaker would probably say "*What a bad boy!*"

- Some suffixes are associated with diminutives (smallness, cuteness, affection).

–ino/a/i/e	un tavolo	un tavol**ino**	*a small table*
–etto/a/i/e	un pezzo	un pezz**etto**	*a little piece*
–ello/a/i/e	una fontana	una fontan**ella**	*a little fountain*
–olo/a/i/e	un figlio	un figli**olo**	*a little boy*
–uccio/a/i/e	una femmina	una femmin**uccia**	*a baby girl*
–uzzo/a/i/e	una vịa	una viụ**zza**	*a little street*

- Some suffixes indicate exaggeration or large size.

–one/a/i/e	un naso	un nas**one**	*a big nose; big-nosed person*
	una minestra	un minestr**one**	*a big, hearty soup*

- Some suffixes are pejorative, denoting ugliness, poor quality, or nastiness.

–accio/a/i/e	una parola	una parol**accia**	*a swear word*
–astro/a/i/e	un poeta	un poet**astro**	*a really bad poet*
–uccio/a/i/e	una casa	una cas**uccia**	*a small, unassuming house*

- Some suffixes may also be added to adjectives and adverbs.

pigro → pigr**one**	bello → bell**ino**	bene → ben**ino**

ATTENZIONE!

Be very careful when using suffixes and try to use only those you have learned from native speakers or teachers. Adding them to words you are not sure of can lead to misunderstandings or even trouble if you are not absolutely certain of the meaning of the word that you have coined! For example, **cagnolino** means *doggie* but **canino** means *canine tooth*, and **un mulo**, a mule, is not related to **un mulino**, a mill.

ATTENZIONE!

Note that more than one suffix can be added to the same noun. For example, **una casa → una cas-ett-ina**.

ATTENZIONE!

Sometimes a noun changes gender when a suffix is added. For example, **una cucina**, *a kitchen*, becomes **un cucinino**, *a kitchenette*; **una finestra**, *a window*, becomes **un finestrino**, *a car window*; and **una minestra**, *broth*, becomes **un minestrone**, *a hearty soup*.

Pratica e comunicazione

1 **Suffissi** Scegli la parola adeguata per completare ogni frase.

1. Paolo! Mamma mia come sei cresciuto! Sei diventato davvero un __ragazzone__ (ragazzone / ragazzino).

2. Uffa! Piove anche oggi! È proprio un __tempaccio__ (tempuccio / tempaccio).

3. Oh no! Un __topolino__ (topone / topolino) si è nascosto sotto il frigorifero!

4. Eugenio, ho letto un articolo su di te sul giornale di ieri! Complimenti! Sei diventato un __professorone__ (professorone / professoruccio)!

5. Mario, per cortesia, metti questi fiori sul __tavolino__ (tavolaccio / tavolino) davanti alla televisione.

6. Ho comperato una simpatica __borsetta__ (borsetta / borsaccia) per il mio vestito viola.

7. No, Sandra. Non ho voglia di parlare di Paolo. È una __storiaccia__ (storiella / storiaccia).

2 **Una parola per ogni occasione** Inventate una frase per descrivere ogni foto usando il vocabolario nel riquadro.

Modello —Michele è proprio un tenerone! Bacia Maria ogni volta che torna a casa!...

amicona	incidentaccio
bestiaccia	ragazzaccio
cagnolino	pigrone
caratteraccio	simpaticone
dormiglione	tenerone

3 **Storie** In coppia, inventate una storia buffa con almeno sei parole scelte tra quelle nella lista.

angolino	nasone
cagnolino	ragazzino
finestrella	stradina
librone	vecchietto
macchinona	ventaccio

1 Tell the students that **Topolino** means Micky Mouse in Italian, **Paperino** is Donald Duck, and **Paperon de' Paperoni** is Scrooge McDuck.

1 Point out that **tavolinetto** may be a synonym for **tavolino**, that **borsettina** is a synonym for **borsetta**, and that **macchinuccia/macchinina** are as acceptable as **macchinetta**.

2 Ask volunteers to share captions with the rest of the class.

3 Have students share their stories and vote on the funniest one.

Practice more at **vhlcentral.com**.

Sintesi

1

Parliamo In coppia, leggete l'articolo e rispondete alle domande.

ITALIA O ITALIE?

Le differenze tra l'Italia del nord e l'Italia del sud esistono da sempre per motivi storici e geografici.

A causa della sua posizione geografica, nel corso dei secoli l'Italia è stata conquistata (*conquered*) da varie popolazioni: l'Italia settentrionale dai popoli dell'attuale Nord Europa, l'Italia meridionale principalmente dai popoli arabi e spagnoli, arrivati nella penisola via mare.

Per questo motivo, l'Italia è stata frammentata in tanti piccoli regni (*kingdoms*) fino al 1861, quando l'impresa (*venture*) di Garibaldi ha portato a compimento (*achieved*) l'unità politica della penisola, che diventò Regno d'Italia.

Dopo l'unificazione, il centro del potere, in Piemonte, era però geograficamente lontano e culturalmente distante dal Sud e dai suoi problemi: un'economia povera basata su pratiche agricole molto antiquate.

Ancora oggi, a chi visita la penisola italiana da nord a sud, sembra che l'Italia abbia due anime diverse: una più ordinata, disciplinata, privata e fredda (il Nord) e una più confusionaria, chiassosa (*loud*), ribelle, amichevole e solare (il Sud).

Ma «non è tutto oro quello che luccica (*glitters*)», e nel clima di abbandono successivo all'unificazione, nel Sud è nata la mafia, una sorta di anti-stato che interveniva là dove lo stato era assente. Purtroppo, oggi la mafia è presente ovunque nel paese, anche nella realtà industriale del Nord Italia.

Continuando una tradizione cominciata subito dopo la seconda guerra mondiale, ancora oggi i giovani del Sud emigrano verso le città del Nord in cerca di lavoro. Il tasso di disoccupazione al Sud supera, infatti, il 17% della popolazione, il doppio rispetto al Nord, nonostante il tasso di istruzione sia più alto al Sud!

Resta, dunque, un'Italia a due velocità.

1. L'articolo parla di «due anime» dell'Italia. Sei d'accordo o ti sembra che non abbia senso fare queste generalizzazioni? Quali sono, secondo te, i fattori che determinano la cultura di un popolo?

2. Per introdurre l'argomento della mafia nell'articolo è usato un antico proverbio. Cosa pensi che significhi?

3. Pensi che le migrazioni interne (nord-sud, est-ovest) possano creare degli scontri culturali? Ti sembra possibile l'idea che spostarsi all'interno di uno stesso paese sia come trasferirsi in un paese straniero? Fai alcuni esempi.

4. Hai mai sperimentato uno shock culturale? Racconta.

Strategie per la comunicazione
Suggerimenti per esprimere reazioni e opinioni personali

Che + aggettivo
• Che bello sarebbe vivere al Sud!

Quanto/Come + frase
• Quanto mi piacerebbe vivere al Nord!

• Come ha ragione l'autore dell'articolo!

2

Scriviamo Scrivi un tema di una pagina rispondendo a una delle seguenti domande e usando le strutture grammaticali che hai imparato in questa lezione.

• Ti piacerebbe di più vivere nel Sud o nel Nord Italia? Perché?

• Ti trasferiresti mai in un luogo con una cultura e uno stile di vita molto diversi dai tuoi? Perché sì o perché no?

• Hai mai avuto occasione di sperimentare la diversità regionale e culturale del tuo paese? Quando? Come?

Preparazione  Vocabulary Tools

Vocabolario della lettura

avvenire *to happen*
la carta geografica *map*
distinguere *to distinguish*
il dominio *domination*
le fondamenta *foundations*
il Medioevo *Middle Ages*

la provincia *province*
il regno *kingdom*
il Rinascimento *Renaissance*
il Risorgimento *Resurgence*
lo statista *statesman*
tracciare *to trace*

Vocabolario utile

l'autonomia *autonomy*
la costituzione *constitution*
il nazionalismo *nationalism*
il parlamento *parliament*

SINONIMI
la carta geografica =
la cartina

1

Vocabolario Inserisci le parole nuove nelle frasi.

1. Per costruire una casa bisogna cominciare dalle ___fondamenta___.
2. La ___Costituzione___ è il documento che contiene le leggi di un paese.
3. L'unificazione d'Italia ___avvenne/è avvenuta___ nel 1861.
4. Le principesse delle fiabe (*fairy-tales*) spesso abitano in un ___regno___ magico.
5. Un sinonimo di indipendenza è ___autonomia___.
6. Quando viaggio porto una ___carta geografica___ del paese che visito.
7. Per governare bene una nazione c'è bisogno di ___statisti___ esperti.
8. L'Italia si ___distingue___ per la sua forma a stivale (*boot*).

TEACHING OPTION
Bring a large map to class and have a discussion of regional traditions, cuisines, and dialects. Break the class into groups and assign a region to each. Ask the groups to prepare a brief presentation on one interesting aspect, city, dish, etc. for the next class.

2

La cartina geografica Ricordate la geografia italiana? In coppia, segnate i nomi delle regioni sulla cartina.

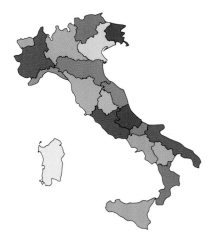

- Abruzzo
- Basilicata
- Calabria
- Campania
- Emilia-Romagna
- Friuli-Venezia Giulia
- Lazio
- Lombardia
- Liguria
- Marche

- Molise
- Piemonte
- Puglia
- Sardegna
- Sicilia
- Toscana
- Trentino-Alto Adige
- Umbria
- Valle d'Aosta
- Veneto

3

Tradizioni regionali In piccoli gruppi, parlate degli aspetti tipici della città o della regione in cui abitate.

- Ci sono feste, piatti speciali, dialetti, monumenti o altre tradizioni della vostra zona che sono diverse rispetto a quelle nazionali? Quali?

- Quali sono le origini di queste tradizioni? Provengono da eventi storici?

- Cosa pensa il resto del paese delle vostre tradizioni?

Nota CULTURALE

«Fatta l'Italia bisogna fare gli italiani». Questa celebre frase attribuita a **Massimo D'Azeglio** (ma da alcuni attribuita a **Ferdinando Martini**) rifletteva le difficoltà degli inizi del **Regno d'Italia**. Era un paese con 22 milioni di abitanti, molti dei quali analfabeti°, un'economia debole° basata sull'agricoltura e una forte divisione tra il Nord ed il Sud. Oltre a risolvere i problemi pratici, il nuovo governo doveva anche incoraggiare° lo sviluppo di un'identità nazionale ancora inesistente.

analfabeti *illiterate* **debole** *weak* **incoraggiare** *to encourage*

L'unità d'Italia
identità regionale e nazionale

L'Italia prima dell'unificazione

Line 30: Give students additional details about the integration process. Mention the dates that other regions in Italy unified (**Toscana**, 1858; **Lombardia**, 1859; **Marche**, 1860, etc.). Mention that students might find some ambiguity if they research these dates, as unification was a long process with many complex benchmarks, and different historians recognize different events as the formal moments of integration.

Reading

rather

L'identità nazionale italiana non si è sviluppata su fondamenta politiche, economiche o religiose ma bensì° sul concetto di una cultura, cioè di una lingua e letteratura comuni a partire da Dante Alighieri in poi. Già sapete che l'Italia ha venti regioni. Ma sapevate che molte delle regioni italiane corrispondono agli antichi regni e ai territori delle dominazioni straniere che, dopo le invasioni barbariche e la dissoluzione dell'Impero Romano, hanno diviso politicamente e geograficamente il paese?

E sapevate che l'Italia è un paese più giovane degli Stati Uniti?

Confrontando le carte geografiche della penisola dal Medioevo a oggi si possono tracciare le ragioni storiche per le differenze culturali e linguistiche che distinguono ogni regione e, in molti casi, ogni provincia italiana. L'unificazione ufficiale della nazione è relativamente recente: risale° al 1861, durante l'epoca storica chiamata Risorgimento.

dates back

Le prime regioni unificate nel 1861 furono la Sicilia e gran parte dell'Italia meridionale (il Regno delle due Sicilie, dei Borbone), con la Sardegna e il Piemonte (il Regno di Sardegna, dei Savoia) sotto il nome di Regno d'Italia, governato dalla casa reale Savoia. Nel 1870 furono incluse Roma e gran parte del Lazio (quello che rimaneva dello Stato Pontificio governato dal papa). La sede della capitale italiana fu spostata° da Torino a Firenze nel 1865 e infine a Roma nel 1871. Il Friuli e parte del Veneto (dell'Impero Austriaco) furono annessi° nel 1866. Il resto del Veneto, il Trentino-Alto Adige e la Venezia Giulia, a loro volta sotto il dominio austriaco, diventarono italiani soltanto dopo la prima guerra mondiale. Il passaggio da monarchia a repubblica parlamentare avvenne nel 1946, dopo il famoso referendum del 2 giugno, giorno

moved

annexed

> **Confrontando le carte geografiche dal Medioevo ad oggi si possono tracciare le ragioni storiche per le differenze culturali e linguistiche.**

in cui, ancora oggi, ogni anno si celebra la Festa della Repubblica.

Durante il lungo processo dell'unificazione italiana ci furono molte dominazioni e guerre su tutto il territorio. Già nel Rinascimento scrittori come Niccolò Machiavelli e Francesco Guicciardini invocavano la presa di coscienza di un'identità nazionale mentre l'Italia era al centro delle guerre tra la Francia e la Spagna. In seguito°, gli ideali del movimento liberale repubblicano italiano ed europeo di statisti come Giuseppe Mazzini, Camillo Benso, conte di Cavour, e del generale Giuseppe Garibaldi resero° possibile l'unificazione politica.

Later

made

Il processo di unificazione è stato lento e difficile: oltre ai molti dialetti e idiomi regionali parlati dagli italiani, alcune regioni sono ufficialmente bilingui, come il Trentino-Alto Adige (italiano e tedesco), la Valle d'Aosta (italiano e francese) e il Friuli (italiano e sloveno). Le guerre mondiali e la ripresa economica del dopoguerra hanno contribuito a rafforzare il patriottismo di molti italiani. Dalla metà del XX secolo in poi, una delle forze unificanti della lingua e della cultura italiana è stata la televisione. Il senso d'identità regionale è ancora molto forte: gli italiani sono legati sentimentalmente alle loro antiche radici, fatte di storia, lingue e tradizioni. ∎

Giuseppe Garibaldi

Giuseppe Garibaldi (1807–1882) è una delle figure più carismatiche ed amate del Risorgimento italiano. È considerato un eroe nazionale e padre dell'unità d'Italia, che contribuì a realizzare con l'esercito dei Mille formato da giovani idealisti volontari. Garibaldi, con il suo esercito di italiani, oltre all'unificazione d'Italia ha partecipato anche alle guerre d'indipendenza del Brasile e dell'Uruguay.

Analisi

Comprensione

A. Indica se l'affermazione è **vera** o **falsa**.

Vero	Falso	
☐	☑	1. Le regioni italiane sono molto simili.
☑	☐	2. Il processo di unificazione dell'Italia è stato lungo e difficile.
☐	☑	3. Il Piemonte e la Sardegna facevano parte della Francia.
☑	☐	4. All'inizio, l'Italia unita si chiamava Regno d'Italia.
☑	☐	5. Il Lazio era governato dal Papa.
☐	☑	6. Garibaldi ha partecipato alla guerra d'indipendenza argentina.
☐	☑	7. Roma è sempre stata la capitale d'Italia.
☑	☐	8. Il 2 giugno si celebra l'anniversario della Repubblica Italiana.

B. In coppia, correggete le affermazioni false.

2

Opinioni In coppia, confrontate le vostre opinioni rispondendo alle domande.

1. Secondo voi, quali sono stati i vantaggi dell'unificazione d'Italia? E gli svantaggi?
2. Quale pensate che sia stato il ruolo dei dialetti e dell'italiano nel creare un senso d'identità regionale e nazionale?
3. Pensate che i dialetti italiani possano sparire nel futuro? Perché?
4. Conoscete altri paesi in cui coesistono lingue diverse? Quali?
5. In quali altri paesi è stata necessaria una guerra o una rivoluzione per ottenere l'indipendenza o l'unità?
6. Quali sono gli elementi più importanti per gli abitanti di un paese per sentirsi uniti? Cosa significa per un paese essere unito?

3

Ideali In piccoli gruppi, analizzate questo motto italiano.

«Unità, uguaglianza e umanità»

- A quale altro motto nazionale assomiglia (*is similar to*) quello italiano?
- A cosa corrispondono i tre ideali del motto? Potete tracciarne (*trace*) le ragioni storiche?
- Quali altri valori o ideali avrebbe potuto includere il motto?
- Questo motto italiano può essere utilizzato anche per il tuo paese? Perché?
- Secondo voi, cosa vuol dire essere patriottici?

4

Dibattito Dividete la classe in squadre per dibattere le seguenti questioni.

- È importante conservare le diverse identità regionali.
- Le diverse identità regionali costituiscono un problema.
- È più importante creare un'identità nazionale che conservare le differenze regionali.
- L'identità nazionale deve includere le differenze regionali.

Practice more at vhlcentral.com.

Preparazione Vocabulary Tools

A proposito dell'autore

Dario Fo (Sangiano, Varese 1926–Milano 2016) è stato attore, commediografo, capocomico, scenografo e pittore. Nel 1997, ha vinto il Premio Nobel per la letteratura, sorprendendo il mondo intellettuale italiano e internazionale. Da sempre autore controverso e coraggioso, Fo è famoso in tutto il mondo per il suo teatro politico, attento ai problemi sociali. Sposato per quasi sessant'anni con l'attrice teatrale Franca Rame, Fo e la moglie, deceduta nel 2013, sono stati una delle coppie più interessanti del mondo dello spettacolo; hanno sempre lottato per i diritti civili, anche pagando di persona con arresti, minacce, querele e aggressioni personali.

Point out that **ospizio** is somewhat of a false cognate. It refers to a nursing home and does not have the connotation of terminal illness that the English word *hospice* does.

Mention that the "politically correct" term for **vecchio** is **anziano**. There is not a great deal of consensus on this term, though, and some people find it more insulting.

Vocabolario della lettura

aggrapparsi *to hold on to*
andarsene *to leave (to go away from it)*
buttare di sotto *to throw down*
il delitto *crime*
disfarsi *to get rid of*
farcela *to make it (to work it out)*
fregarsene (di) *not to care (about)*
incosciente *irresponsible*
l'incoscienza *recklessness*
laggiù/lassù *down/up there*
mollare *to let go*
l'ospizio *nursing home*
penare *to suffer*
scommettere *to bet*
spingere *to push*

Vocabolario utile

il buon senso *common sense*
dissentire (da, su) *to disagree*
l'empatia *empathy*
fare una manifestazione *to demonstrate*
mobilitare *to mobilize*
l'opinione pubblica *public opinion*
risolvere *to solve*

1

Definizioni Collega ogni parola alla sua definizione.

_b_ 1. fregarsene   a. soffrire

_e_ 2. l'opinione pubblica   b. credere che una cosa non sia abbastanza importante

_c_ 3. scommettere   c. mettere dei soldi in gioco

_f_ 4. aggrapparsi   d. atto grave che offende i diritti dei cittadini

_h_ 5. disfarsi   e. quello che pensano molte persone

_g_ 6. laggiù   f. tenere forte

_a_ 7. penare   g. in basso

_d_ 8. il delitto   h. buttare via

2

Discussione In coppia, fatevi queste domande.

1. Quale pensi che sia la responsabilità della società nei confronti dei suoi elementi più deboli (vecchi, bambini, disabili, ecc.)? Questi sono problemi individuali o collettivi?

2. Chi si deve occupare delle persone anziane? E dei bambini?

3. Secondo te, i vecchi sono tristi? Si può imparare qualcosa da loro?

4. I vecchi dovrebbero stare con la famiglia o da soli, secondo te? Cosa pensi di quei villaggi abitati solo da vecchietti?

5. Ci sono dei problemi per cui è giusto protestare e fare manifestazioni di massa? Fai alcuni esempi. Hai mai manifestato contro qualcosa?

Nota CULTURALE

Una volta in Italia solo i vecchi senza famiglia o gravemente malati finivano in **ospizio** o in **case di riposo**°. Ora che la struttura familiare è sempre più nucleare, con coppie in cui entrambi° lavorano, è sempre più difficile occuparsi dei propri vecchi. Dario Fo già ne parlava ironicamente nel 1980, denunciando° lo squallore e il degrado° degli ospizi, in cui i vecchi si lasciavano morire di tristezza. Il teatro di Fo ha sempre denunciato le carenze° della società e della politica, e spesso ha contribuito a generare dibattiti° che hanno portato a cambiamenti nelle leggi.

case di riposo *retirement homes* **entrambi** *both* **denunciando** *denouncing* **degrado** *degradation* **carenze** *shortcomings* **dibattiti** *debates*

 Practice more at **vhlcentral.com**.

IL PROBLEMA

Scena: fondo° prospettico di una grande strada cittadina. Un gruppo di persone sta guardando per aria° verso i piani superiori della casa di fronte. S'avvicina un giovanotto in bicicletta, si ferma.

   backdrop

   upward

GIOVANOTTO Che sta succedendo?

DONNA CON LA BORSA DELLA SPESA Non vede? Buttano giù un vecchio.

GIOVANOTTO Un vecchio?! Da dove?

DONNA Da lassù, guardi bene: due, tre, quattro, dal quinto piano.
5 Eccolo! Vede, lo spingono!

GIOVANOTTO Ma perché lo vogliono buttare di sotto? Che ha fatto?

UOMO CON UN PACCO SOTTO IL BRACCIO Niente, ha fatto! Che discorsi. Stai a vedere che adesso, per buttare giù un vecchio, bisogna aspettare che abbia fatto qualcosa di illegale. Staremmo freschi°!

   We'd be finished

10 **DONNA CON LA BORSA DELLA SPESA** Sì, d'accordo. Ma devo dire che non è certo uno spettacolo edificante! Ormai sta diventando uno sconcio°! Con tutti questi vecchi buttati giù sulla strada... almeno avvertissero quelli che passano sotto!

   scandal

GIOVANOTTO Ma dico, lo stanno buttando giù davvero quello?! Ma
15 è ignobile! Incivile! Ma chi sono quegli energumeni° che lo spingono?

   big burly men

UOMO CON UN CAPPELLO A LOBBIA° IN TESTA Chi lo sa? Forse inquilini del palazzo o gente del quartiere. Certo, ha ragione lei, è incivile. Dovrebbe pensarci l'amministrazione, mica costringere i cittadini a fare da sé. Ma quelli del comune se ne fregano, figurati°!
20 ... Buoni solo a farci pagare le tasse!

   homburg hat

   just think

GIOVANOTTO Ma la polizia che fa? Non interviene?

DONNA Sì, ce n'è uno... un agente, là sotto, sul marciapiede, che tiene lontano i curiosi e i passanti, perché non gli
25 caschi° in testa il vecchio.

   fall

UOMO COL PACCHETTO Non ce la fanno. Guardate come s'è aggrappato alla balaustra°, quel vecchietto, accidenti°, com'è arzillo°!

   railing

   damn/lively

30 **ALTRO UOMO** È incredibile come sono attaccati° alla vita!

   attached

> Ma la polizia
> che fa?
> Non interviene?

Illustrazioni di Dario Fo

GIUDIZIO : gioco di'equilibrio.

DEI VECCHI

UOMO CON LOBBIA È naturale. Più sono anziani-decrepiti e più desiderano stare al mondo, amano la vita, hanno il doppio istinto di conservazione!

35 *Passa un venditore ambulante*

AMBULANTE Cannocchiali°, binocoli anche tridimensionali, a colori. Godetevi° più da vicino la caduta del vecchio. Approfittate°, li diamo anche in affitto. Sconti speciali, ricchi premi.

ALTRO UOMO Ne dia uno a me, prego. Quant'è?

40 **DONNA** Ma guarda come è caparbio°, quel vecchietto! Non molla proprio.

GIOVANOTTO Ma scusate, davvero non capisco! È un delitto, un fatto criminale e voi state tutti qui a guardare, non fate niente?

UOMO CON LOBBIA E che dovremmo fare se sono d'accordo i suoi?

45 **GIOVANOTTO** I suoi chi?

UOMO CON LOBBIA I suoi parenti, dal momento che hanno firmato la carta di delibera°.

GIOVANOTTO Delibera a che?

DONNA Come a che? Ma dove vive giovanotto?
50 La delibera per il vecchio da buttare. Lei non è di queste parti, vero?

spyglasses

Enjoy/Take advantage

obstinate

release

Io dico che è indegno, i vecchi sono esseri umani!

UOMO COL PACCHETTO Ma che fa quella donna?

ALTRO UOMO Quale?

UOMO COL PACCHETTO Ma come, ha il binocolo e non la vede?
55 Là, guardi bene. S'è affacciata° una donna dalla finestra accanto°, *leaned out/adjacent*
ha afferrato° il vecchio per le braccia, lo vuole tirare su! *grabbed*

DONNA Sarà qualche parente stretto, succede... all'ultimo
momento si sarà lasciata prendere dalla pietà.

UOMO CON LOBBIA Ma che pietà, questa è incoscienza!

60 **DONNA** Eh, forse lei non può capire, anch'io quando mi hanno
buttato di sotto il mio vecchio ho avuto un momento, come
dire... insomma, è sempre uno del tuo sangue, dopotutto! Poi
ho ragionato. Ecco! L'hanno portata via, finalmente, povera
donna! Guardate il vecchio, s'è aggrappato al cornicione°... *ledge*
65 non ce la fa più!

UOMO CON IL PACCHETTO Io scommetto che invece quello ce la
fa ancora, quello si salva!

UOMO CON LOBBIA Scommette? Quanto scommette?

UOMO CON IL PACCHETTO Cinquemila.

70 **UOMO CON LOBBIA** D'accordo. Ci sto! Ci metto cinquemila che
fra due minuti è di sotto.

UOMO CON IL PACCHETTO Scommessa andata.

DONNA Ma non vi vergognate, voi due? Scommettere su
certe tragedie?

75 **ALTRO UOMO** Però, almeno dovrebbero evitare che i ragazzini se
ne stiano ad assistere a certi spettacoli, andiamo! Date un'occhiata
laggiù, ce ne saranno una decina° e anche piccoli. *about ten*

DONNA Ma che razza° di genitori hanno? Ma come fanno a non *kind*
capire che certi fatti, ai minori poi, lasciano uno shock magari per
80 tutta la vita!

GIOVANOTTO (*grida verso l'alto*) Bravo, bravo nonno! Guardate, ce
l'ha fatta! È riuscito a scivolare° lungo la grondaia° e s'è calato° *to slide/gutter/dropped*
sul terrazzo di sotto... Forza nonno!

DONNA Ah, bravo, e ci fa il tifo pure! Che razza di incosciente!

85 **GIOVANOTTO** Perché scusi?

UOMO CON LA LOBBIA Ma per favore, se ne vada di qui!

ALTRO UOMO Ma che crede, di essere allo stadio!? Crede che noi si
sia qui a divertirci? Si soffre più di lei, sa?

GIOVANOTTO Soffrite? Non direi, state qui a guardare e basta!

90 **DONNA** Noi non guardiamo, assistiamo°, che è ben altra cosa! *we attend*

GIOVANOTTO Sì, ma insomma lasciate fare!

DONNA Invece lei applaude, da incosciente, lo incita! Ma non
capisce che se i vecchi cominciano a ribellarsi, rifiutano° di farsi *they refuse*
buttare dalla finestra, è la fine, il disordine, l'anarchia!

95 **UOMO CON LA LOBBIA** (*al giovanotto*) Sbaglio o lei è uno di quei
fanatici del comitato antinucleare per la difesa della natura e per
la difesa dei vecchi da defenestrare°? *to be thrown out of the window*

**Abbiamo deciso
che i nostri anziani
ci sono di peso?
Che non possiamo
più né curarli
né aiutarli?**

Explain to students that the
illustration below is actually a
rendition of the play's action
drawn by the author himself.

GIOVANOTTO Io non sono di nessun comitato. Io dico che
è indegno°, i vecchi sono esseri umani! °outrageous

100 **DONNA** Ecco! Ecco che si è scoperto°, il solito sbandieratore° °come out/flag waver
patetico dei diritti umani, di quelli che vogliono distribuire l'eroina
gratis ai giovani e nello stesso tempo vorrebbero veder ripristinati° °reinstated
quegli ignobili ricoveri° per vecchi, dove si sbattono° a crepare° di °nursing home/are thrown/to die
malinconia i nostri poveri anziani ridotti a larve, mangiati dalla
105 solitudine, e qualche volta anche dalle formiche...

UOMO CON IL PACCHETTO Sa cos'è lei, caro giovanotto? Lei, in verità,
è un conservatore ipocrita, un reazionario!

ALTRO UOMO Stai a vedere che dopo tutte le battaglie disperate che
abbiamo portato avanti°, per anni e anni, per arrivare a chiuderle, °we have carried on
110 quelle galere° infami, adesso dovremmo sopportare° ancora certi °prisons/endure
discorsi ipocriti-populisti!?

GIOVANOTTO Ipocriti-populisti? Ma che discorsi, e su che cosa?

DONNA Sui vecchi, caro giovanotto. Sui nostri vecchi! Bisogna avere
coraggio delle proprie scelte, non fare i demagogici. Abbiamo deciso
115 che i nostri anziani ci sono di peso°? Che non possiamo più né curarli °are a burden for us
né aiutarli? Se non sono generali, con le pensioni non sopravvivono.
Che non ci resta più tempo per occuparci di loro? E allora, invece di
disfarcene da veri criminali, abbandonandoli in quelle puzzolenti° °stinking
galere, che sono gli ospizi, meglio, molto più onesto e civile,
120 prenderci la responsabilità di buttarli!

UOMO COL BINOCOLO Attenti. Ecco, l'hanno riacciuffato°. °have caught
Lo buttano!

CORO L'hanno buttato!

DONNA Povero vecchio ha finito di penare.

125 **VIGILE** Avanti, circolare. Su andate a casa, sgomberare°! °leave

UOMO CON LA LOBBIA Scusi signore, le mie cinquemila! Ho vinto
la scommessa!

UOMO CON IL PACCHETTO Ma mi faccia il piacere, lei non ha vinto un
bel niente°! È andata pari e patta°! °nothing at all/We're even

130 **UOMO COL BINOCOLO** Attenzione! Ne stanno buttando un altro.

DONNA Dove?

UOMO COL BINOCOLO Là, da quella parte, quarto piano!
La seconda finestra.

VIGILE Eh no, adesso esagerano, mica posso continuare a tenere
135 bloccato il traffico per ore e ore!

DONNA Certo, dovrebbero mettere degli orari, alla mattina presto e
al massimo per due o tre giorni fissi alla settimana... se no, è il caos!
Ma scusi signor vigile, non c'era quella proposta dell'Assessore° alla °council member
viabilità°, di radunare° tutti i vecchi da buttare, e portarli allo stadio °road and traffic conditions/gather
140 la domenica, e fare una cosa di massa prima della partita?

VIGILE Sì, ma quelli del totocalcio° si sono opposti! Volevano gestirlo °soccer pools
in proprio°! ■ °to administer it themselves

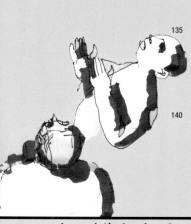

1 Make sure that the central ideas of the play are clear. The first point is not that old people should be killed, but that leaving them to die alone in substandard nursing homes is not an acceptable solution. This farce is not meant to provide a solution, but to provoke and make people be responsible. The second point is that crowd mentality is capable of endorsing even the most unethical behavior; rather than going with the flow, individuals must always be prepared to evaluate moral issues on their own and be ready to dissent.

1 Ask students:
Perché il pubblico rimprovera il giovanotto? Cosa pensa la donna delle case di riposo?

3 Give students additional adjectives: **seccato, compassionevole, perplesso, scioccato.**

This is a good exercise to make students learn new adjectives. You will have to give the definition of some of the words listed. A follow-up activity could be asking students whether they agree with the adjectives given and how else they would describe the characters listed.

Analisi

Comprensione Scegli la frase vera tra le due.

1. a. Il giovanotto si ferma a chiedere perché la folla guarda per aria.
   b. Il giovanotto in bicicletta crede che ci sia una festa in città.

2. a. Stanno buttando un vecchio di sotto.
   b. Stanno guardando un vecchio alla finestra.

3. a. La polizia non interviene.
   b. La polizia regola il traffico sotto la finestra.

4. a. Un venditore ambulante vende gelati.
   b. Un venditore ambulante vende binocoli.

5. a. Il giovanotto è perplesso perché è un fatto criminale.
   b. Il giovanotto è perplesso perché il vecchio ha fatto qualcosa di illegale.

6. a. Due uomini scommettono su come finirà la vicenda (*event*).
   b. Due uomini scommettono cinquemila volte.

Interpretazione Scegli la risposta giusta.

1. Il giovanotto è _____.
   a. sconvolto (*upset*) da quello che vede   b. indifferente e imparziale
   c. incuriosito e divertito da quello che vede
   d. d'accordo e incita a defenestrare

2. La gente _____.
   a. è indifferente e distratta   b. sa che l'amministrazione paga i cittadini
   c. non capisce perché il giovanotto non conosca le leggi
   d. ha paura che la balaustra cada

3. Secondo l'uomo con la lobbia, incitare il vecchio a salvarsi è _____.
   a. da incoscienti   b. umano   c. un fatto criminale   d. una cosa da stadio

4. La donna è convinta che _____.
   a. le scelte sono solo coraggiose   b. senza coraggio non si sceglie
   c. bisogna fare delle scelte ed avere coraggio
   d. bisogna avere il coraggio delle proprie scelte

5. La scena ha un finale _____.
   a. moderato   b. ironico   c. ragionevole   d. felice

Personaggi Scegli gli aggettivi nella lista che meglio descrivono le seguenti persone.
Usa il dizionario per cercare gli aggettivi che non conosci. Some answers will vary.

a. sorpreso	e. curioso	i. attento	o. chiacchierone
b. approfittatore	f. indignato	l. imbroglione	p. incredulo
c. legalitario	g. logico	m. arrabbiato	q. opportunista
d. professionale	h. spazientito	n. onesto	r. rigido

- il giovanotto a, f, p
- l'ambulante b, q
- la donna a, c, g, h, m, n, o, r
- l'uomo col pacchetto a, e, h, i, l, o, r
- il vigile d, h

4

Tu cosa ne pensi? In coppia, rispondete alle seguenti domande.

1. Secondo te, è giusto pensare che i vecchi debbano avere un posto marginale nella società? Cosa si dovrebbe fare per prendersi cura delle persone anziane?

2. Come sarebbe un mondo senza vecchi? Descrivilo.

3. Ci sono paesi (l'Italia e il Giappone per esempio) in cui il tasso di natalità è bassissimo. Con una popolazione tanto vecchia, quali strutture dovrebbero esserci in una società per rendere la vita migliore per tutti?

4. Nella tua regione, che strutture ci sono per la terza età (*for seniors*)? Cosa manca secondo te?

5. È efficace discutere di problemi seri mostrando una soluzione ironica e grottesca? Qual è l'effetto di questo espediente (*device*) narrativo?

As a curiosity, you can tell students that in Italy there is a **Partito dei Pensionati** (a political party made up of retirees that defends the interests of senior citizens).

5

Reality show! In piccoli gruppi, immaginate di essere il conduttore e i partecipanti di un *reality show* che discute un problema sociale. Immaginate una soluzione ragionevole e una totalmente grottesca. Potete usare qualunque formato di *reality* che volete.

5 Students can also be divided into "tribes" as on *Survivor*, where they will vote off the least desirable solution to the problem. Students can debate any problem they perceive as important, including issues on campus or in their daily lives.

6

Discussione

A. In gruppi di tre, scegliete un argomento di discussione sociale che mobilita (*mobilizes*) l'opinione pubblica. Cercate di pensare ai diversi punti di vista su questi argomenti e stendete una lista al riguardo. Quale pensate sia il punto di vista predominante nel vostro paese?

l'assistenza medica per tutti	l'immigrazione la pubblica istruzione	la libertà di culto la pena di morte	la povertà ?

B. Paragonate il vostro parere all'opinione predominante su questi argomenti. Ci sono dei ragionamenti riguardo ai quali «dissentite»? Perché? Fate qualcosa per andare controcorrente?

7

Andare controcorrente Dario Fo ha sempre lottato attivamente contro le ingiustizie, pagando in prima persona. Secondo te, quanto può contare la voce di un singolo individuo per mobilitare l'opinione pubblica, cambiare leggi, regole, istituzioni? In gruppi di quattro, pensate a personaggi famosi della storia che hanno cambiato il corso delle cose nell'arte, nella scienza, nella religione, nella cultura, nella politica, nell'ambiente, ecc. e fate una lista. Poi confrontatela con quella degli altri gruppi.

- Chi sono?
- Come hanno lottato?
- Hanno avuto successo?
- Hanno subìto (*suffered*) delle conseguenze?
- Con chi vi identificate di più?

8

Tema Pensa a come tu risolveresti il problema dell'invecchiamento. Nella tua utopia, cosa succederebbe una volta passati i sessantacinque anni? Scrivi almeno due paragrafi.

 Practice more at **vhlcentral.com**.

Pratica

La confutazione

Nella **Lezione 1 (p. 40)**, si presentano strategie per scrivere argomenti in difesa di una tesi. Una strategia è la confutazione, che consiste nel difendere il nostro punto di vista in forma indiretta esaminando il punto di vista opposto. Invece di usare argomenti che difendono la sua tesi, l'autore dimostra le debolezze (*weaknesses*) della tesi opposta. In un buon saggio, la confutazione deve essere usata solo in combinazione con altri tipi di argomenti. Non deve mai essere l'unico argomento utilizzato. Una buona confutazione:

- non deve essere un attacco contro il punto di vista opposto.

- deve essere basata su una prova o, nel caso di un'opinione personale, deve essere basata su un ragionamento logico che l'autore può esprimere con un linguaggio obiettivo.

Modello

- **Tesi:** Anche in un mondo in cui l'inglese è la lingua franca, soprattutto in rete, imparare una lingua straniera come l'italiano offre grandi vantaggi.

- **Tesi contraria:** Imparare una lingua straniera «minore» come l'italiano non è importante e non è competitivo in un mondo in cui l'inglese è spesso la lingua franca in rete.

- **Proposizione principale:** Ci sono coloro che argomentano che imparare una lingua come l'italiano sia inutile e non serva. Senza dubbio queste sono affermazioni eccessive e affrettate.

- **Esempio di confutazione:** Secondo i dati più recenti, l'italiano è la quarta lingua straniera più studiata nel mondo. Inoltre, ci sono molti studi che sostengono l'utilità di Internet nell'apprendimento delle lingue straniere, compreso l'italiano.

1

Preparazione In coppia scegliete e rileggete alcuni brani delle lezioni precedenti. Qual è la tesi opposta? Quali argomenti si possono usare per respingere (*reject*) la tesi opposta?

2

Saggio Scegli uno di questi argomenti e scrivi un saggio.

- Il saggio deve far riferimento ad almeno due dei quattro brani studiati in questa lezione e nelle precedenti lezioni contenuti in **Cortometraggio**, **Immagina**, **Cultura** e **Letteratura**.

- Il tuo saggio deve includere almeno due esempi di confutazione.

- Il saggio deve essere lungo almeno due pagine.

> Le divisioni politiche del passato possono aiutarci a costruire un mondo unito nel presente?

> Lo stile di vita moderno aiuta a colmare le divisioni (*fill in the gaps*) culturali radicate (*rooted*) nella storia e nella geografia di una nazione?

> Si può «andare controcorrente»? Quali sono i vantaggi o gli svantaggi?

Società e cambiamenti

INSTRUCTIONAL RESOURCES
Task-based activities

 Vocabulary Tools

I cambiamenti

adattarsi *to adapt*
adeguarsi *to adjust*
appartenere *to belong to*
arricchirsi *to become rich*
aumentare *to increase*
conformarsi *to conform*
diminuire *to decrease*
impoverirsi *to become poor*
ottenere *to obtain*
pianificare *to plan*
realizzare *to achieve*
stabilirsi *to settle*
tutelare *to protect; to defend*

Le tendenze sociali

la (s)comparsa *(dis)appearance*
la diversità *diversity*
la globalizzazione *globalization*
l'integrazione *integration*
la lingua madre *native language*
la (sovrap)popolazione
  (over)population
(il)lo (sotto)sviluppo
  (under)development
il tasso di natalità *birthrate*
il tenore di vita *standard of living*

(anti)conformista *(non)conformist*
multilingue *multilingual*

I problemi e le soluzioni

il caos *chaos*
la comprensione *understanding*
il conflitto di classe *class conflict*
il dialogo *dialogue*
l'incertezza *uncertainty*
il maltrattamento *abuse*
la polemica *controversy*
la povertà *poverty*
il razzismo *racism*
la volontà *will(power)*

lamentare/lamentarsi *to regret*
lottare *to fight*
manifestare *to demonstrate*
reclamare *to complain, to protest;*
  to claim

superare *to overcome*
tirare avanti *to go forth*

Le convinzioni religiose

la cattedrale *cathedral*
la chiesa *church*
Dio *God*
la fede *faith*
il/la fedele *believer*
la libertà di culto *freedom of worship*
la moschea *mosque*
il papa *pope*
il prete *priest*
il rabbino *rabbi*
la sinagoga *synagogue*
il/la santo/a *saint*

credere *to believe*
pregare *to pray*

agnostico/a *agnostic*
ateo/a *atheistic*
cattolico/a *Catholic*
ebreo/a *Jewish*
musulmano/a *Muslim*
protestante *Protestant*

Cortometraggio

il capitone *large eel*
la corriera *long-distance bus*
il dialetto *dialect*
l'estero *foreign countries*
il ferroviere *railway employee*
l'incomprensione *lack*
  of understanding
il maltempo *bad weather*
il panettone *Christmas bread*
il pregiudizio *prejudice*
il proverbio *proverb*
il realismo *realism*
lo stereotipo *stereotype*
il tassista *taxi driver*
la tradizione *tradition*
l'umorismo *humor*
la vigilia *eve*

meridionale *southern*
settentrionale *northern*

Cultura

l'autonomia *autonomy*
la carta geografica *map*
la costituzione *constitution*
il dominio *domination*
le fondamenta *foundations*
il Medioevo *Middle Ages*
il nazionalismo *nationalism*
il parlamento *parliament*
la provincia *province*
il regno *kingdom*
il Rinascimento *Renaissance*
il Risorgimento *Resurgence*
lo statista *statesman*

avvenire *to happen*
distinguere *to distinguish*
tracciare *to trace*

Letteratura

il buon senso *common sense*
il delitto *crime*
l'empatia *empathy*
l'incoscienza *recklessness*
l'opinione pubblica *public opinion*
l'ospizio *nursing home*

aggrapparsi *to hold on to*
andarsene *to leave (to go away*
  from it)
buttare di sotto *to throw down*
disfarsi *to get rid of*
dissentire (da, su) *to disagree*
farcela *to make it (to work it out)*
fare una manifestazione
  to demonstrate
fregarsene (di) *not to care (about)*
mobilitare *to mobilize*
mollare *to let go*
penare *to suffer*
risolvere *to solve*
scommettere *to bet*
spingere *to push*

incosciente *irresponsible*

laggiù/lassù *down/up there*

Le scienze e la tecnologia

La ricerca scientifica e il progresso tecnologico per molti aspetti migliorano la qualità di vita e facilitano i rapporti tra le persone. Ma è sempre così? La tecnologia avvicina (*brings closer*) le persone e semplifica la vita o ci isola e ci separa dagli altri? Che rapporto avete con le scienze e la tecnologia? Potreste vivere senza gli oggetti tecnologici che fanno ormai parte della vostra quotidianità?

255

280

Destinazione:
IL TRIVENETO

FRIULI-VENEZIA GIULIA
TRENTINO-ALTO ADIGE
VENETO

PREVIEW Ask students to look at the photo on the previous page. Ask: **La tecnologia può provocare dei cambiamenti sociali? Quali sono gli effetti positivi e negativi della tecnologia?**

Il progresso e la ricerca  Vocabulary Tools

Gli scienziati

l'astronauta *astronaut*
l'astronomo/a *astronomer*

il/la biologo/a *biologist*
il/la (bio)chimico/a *(bio)chemist*
il/la fisico/a (nucleare) *(nuclear) physicist*
il/la geologo/a *geologist*
il/la matematico/a *mathematician*
il/la ricercatore/ ricercatrice *researcher*
lo/la zoologo/a *zoologist*

La ricerca scientifica

il brevetto *patent*
il DNA *DNA*

l'esperimento *experiment*
il gene *gene*
la ricerca *research*

la scoperta *discovery*
lo scopo *aim; goal*
lo sviluppo *development*
il vaccino *vaccine*

dimostrare *to prove*
guarire (-isc-) *to cure; to heal*

notevole *remarkable*

La tecnologia

la banca dati *database*
il codice *code*
il dispositivo *device*
l'elettronica *electronics*
l'informatica *computer science*
l'ingegneria *engineering*
l'intelligenza artificiale *artificial intelligence (A.I.)*
la nanotecnologia *nanotechnology*
la rete (senza fili) *(wireless) network*
la robotica *robotics*

il segnale (analogico/digitale) *(analog/digital) signal*
le telecomunicazioni *telecommunications*
la trasmissione *broadcast*

Il mondo digitale

la chiavetta USB *flash drive*
la chiocciola *@ symbol*
il computer (da tavolo/portatile) *(desktop/laptop) computer*
l'indirizzo e-mail *e-mail address*
il lettore CD/DVD/MP3 *CD/DVD/MP3 player*
il libro elettronico *e-book*
l'SMS (m.) *text message*

aggiornare *to update*
allegare *to attach*
cancellare *to erase*
copiare *to copy*
incollare *to paste*
masterizzare *to burn*
navigare su Internet/sulla rete *to browse/to surf the Internet/Web*
salvare *to save*
scaricare *to download*

Problemi e sfide

la cellula staminale *stem cell*
il codice deontologico *code of conduct*
il furto d'identità *identity theft*
l'inquinamento *pollution*

la sfida *challenge*

clonare *to clone*
riciclare *to recycle*

controverso/a *controversial*
etico/a *ethical*
giusto/a *right*
(im)morale *(un)ethical*
sbagliato/a *wrong*

SINONIMI
lo scopo ⟷ il fine

The word **ricerca** in its singular form may mean both *search* and *academic research*, while in its plural form it only means *searches*. Example: **Ho vinto una borsa di studio per fare ricerca all'estero./La polizia ha iniziato le ricerche in tutta la città.**

Chiocciola in Italian means *snail*.

Point out that many English words about computing enter into Italian, like **mouse**, **smartphone**, **desktop**, **file**, **software**, and **e-mail**, while other words are taken from English and adapted to Italian grammar, like **chattare** and **cliccare**.

Point out that **guarire** means *to cure/ heal* when it is used transitively. Used intransitively, it means *to recover*. Example: **Sono guarito dal raffreddore.**

INSTRUCTIONAL RESOURCES
Audioscripts, Answer Keys, Lab MP3s
SAM/WebSAM: WB, LM

Pratica e comunicazione

1 **Associazioni** Trova la parola della colonna di destra che è associata ai termini della colonna di sinistra.

_b_ 1. il codice, la banca dati, Internet   a. l'ingegneria

_e_ 2. il DNA, il vaccino, la malattia   b. l'informatica

_c_ 3. l'intelligenza artificiale, il codice, il dispositivo   c. la robotica

_a_ 4. i progetti, la matematica, la fisica   d. lo sviluppo

_f_ 5. la rete, il segnale, la trasmissione   e. la medicina

_d_ 6. il progresso, la scoperta, la ricerca   f. le telecomunicazioni

2 **Che bisogna fare per...?** Completa le frasi con la parola appropriata.

1. Per ricevere dei messaggi elettronici bisogna avere un _indirizzo e-mail/computer_.

2. Per navigare sulla rete quando sei in spiaggia devi avere un _computer portatile/uno smartphone_

3. Per aggiornare l'antivirus puoi _scaricare_ l'ultima versione da Internet.

4. Per non perdere i documenti devi _salvare_ tutto su una chiavetta USB.

5. Per non riempire troppo la casella di posta elettronica bisogna _cancellare_ i messaggi inutili.

6. Per inviare un documento via Internet bisogna _allegare_ il file al messaggio.

7. Per vedere un film su DVD bisogna avere un _lettore DVD_.

8. Se non vuoi telefonarmi, puoi inviarmi un _SMS_ sul cellulare.

3 **Chi è?** Leggi le frasi e individua gli scienziati descritti. Aggiungi l'articolo corrispondente.

1. Mario esamina la struttura, la composizione e il cambiamento delle rocce (*rocks*). Fa _il geologo_.

2. Carlo studia la storia, l'evoluzione e i comportamenti degli animali. Fa _lo zoologo_.

3. Marcella studia la composizione della materia e fa esperimenti in laboratorio. Fa _la chimica_.

4. Antonio è specializzato nello studio della struttura e delle funzioni degli organismi viventi e della loro interazione con l'ambiente. Fa _il biologo_.

4 **Questioni di attualità** Sembra che la scienza e il progresso oggi non abbiano e non debbano avere limiti. Qual è la tua opinione sui seguenti temi?

A. Contrassegna con una X le affermazioni con cui sei d'accordo e preparati a spiegare le tue opinioni con una o due frasi.

☐ 1. La clonazione umana è uno strumento importante per combattere molte malattie genetiche.

☐ 2. È immorale provare ad avere un figlio a ogni costo! Ci sono tanti bambini senza genitori: perché non adottarli?

☐ 3. I vantaggi apportati dalla tecnologia informatica sono maggiori degli svantaggi.

☐ 4. La tecnologia oggi ha semplificato molto il lavoro dell'uomo.

B. Confronta le tue risposte con quelle di un(a) compagno/a e preparate insieme un riassunto spiegando le vostre differenze o similarità.

2 Have pairs of students write sentences for other related vocabulary words, such as **chiocciola** and **navigare**.

3 Ask pairs of students to come up with two more sentences to read to their classmates, who can guess the scientists described.

4 Start a discussion with the class about each topic. Invite students that share the same point of view to explain their reasons, then ask students with opposite opinions to respond. List the students' points of view in two columns titled **perché sì** and **perché no** on the blackboard.

Practice more at vhlcentral.com.

INSTRUCTIONAL
RESOURCES
Supersite: Video, Script &
Translation
SAM/WebSAM: WB

Have students read the
vocabulary lists and
hypothesize about the
subject matter of the
short film.

Preparazione  Vocabulary Tools

Vocabolario del cortometraggio

il/la benzinaio/a *gas station attendant*

bollente *boiling hot*

dividere *to share*

l'intervento *operation*

mettere sotto *to run over*

sgranchirsi *to stretch out*

soffrire *to suffer*

Vocabolario utile

l'angoscia *anguish*

l'attesa *wait*

il distributore automatico *beverage dispenser*

la gratitudine *gratitude*

la preoccupazione *worry*

lo sbadiglio *yawn*

lo scoraggiamento *discouragement*

ESPRESSIONI

avere il silenzioso *to have the ringer off*

chissà *who knows?*

essere forte *to be strong*

fare presto *to hurry*

fare tardi *to be late*

mangiarsi le unghie *to bite one's nails*

tagliare la strada *to cut off*

Occhio! *Watch out!*

1 Remind students to
conjugate verbs using the
appropriate tenses.

1 **Un incidente drammatico** Anna è testimone di un incidente. Usa le parole delle liste qui sopra per completare la storia.

Una mattina d'estate, mentre Anna era scesa dalla macchina per (1) __sgranchirsi__ mentre il (2) __benzinaio__ metteva il pieno di benzina, ha visto un incidente: una macchina è impazzita e ha (3) __messo__ sotto un ciclista. Anna ha gridato: (4) «__Occhio!__», ma il guidatore stava facendo uno (5) __sbadiglio__, non l'ha sentita e ha (6) __tagliato la strada__ al ciclista. Il caffè (7) __bollente__ che Anna aveva appena preso a un (8) __distributore automatico__ le si è rovesciato addosso. Ha subito chiamato un'ambulanza, sperando che un chirurgo potesse salvare il ciclista con un (9) __intervento__. I minuti di (10) __attesa__ dell'ambulanza sono sembrati infiniti, nell' (11) __angoscia__ che il ciclista morisse. Per fortuna l'ambulanza ha (12) __fatto presto__ e la (13) __preoccupazione__ di Anna non è durata a lungo: i paramedici hanno stabilizzato le condizioni del ciclista che non è morto. L'autista distratto, sotto shock dopo l'incidente, ha espresso la sua (14) __gratitudine__ a Anna per essere stata (15) __forte__ mentre lui si mangiava (16) __le unghie__.

2 As a follow-up, have
pairs create and act out a
skit in which they use six
words or expressions from
the **Cortometraggio**
vocabulary.

2 **Completate** Completa ogni frase con la parola o l'espressione appropriata dalle liste qui sopra.

1. Vuoi __dividere__ un panino con me?

2. Non ho sentito il telefono perché __avevo il silenzioso__.

3. Ceniamo alle 8: non __fare tardi__!

4. Prendi un'aspirina: è inutile __soffrire__.

5. Passerai gli esami: non farti prendere dallo __scoraggiamento__. Studia!

3

Domande In coppia, fatevi le seguenti domande.

1. Sei mai stato preoccupato/a per un intervento di qualcuno? Chi?

2. Hai mai visto o avuto un incidente? Conosci qualcuno che è stato vittima di un incidente?

3. In caso di malattia, secondo te, causa più angoscia l'attesa di sapere o il sapere cosa ha una persona?

4. Secondo te, che qualità deve avere un buon chirurgo?

4

Sondaggio In piccoli gruppi, chiedete ai vostri compagni se sono d'accordo o no con le seguenti affermazioni e perché. Poi condividete le vostre opinioni con la classe.

1. Il razzismo e i pregiudizi sono sentimenti naturali.

2. Tutti dovrebbero essere donatori di organi.

3. La preoccupazione per una persona cara fa venire fuori il peggio di noi.

4. Non bisogna avere paura di informarsi, rivedere i propri pregiudizi e cambiare idea.

5

Espansione In gruppi di tre o quattro, discutete i seguenti temi.

1. Cosa faresti se ti trovassi di fronte a un episodio di razzismo? Reagiresti o staresti zitto? Fai un esempio concreto.

2. Doneresti un organo (non vitale) a un familiare o a un amico? Per esempio?

3. La sofferenza unisce o divide coppie, amici, famiglie? In che modo?

6

Descriviamo In coppia, descrivete accuratamente le seguenti immagini.

A. Descrivete tutto di questa immagine: il luogo (geometrie, colori, divisioni vere o immaginarie, dove sono le due coppie), le persone (aspetto fisico, vestiti, atteggiamento (*attitude*), cosa fanno lì).

B. Immagina chi sono questi quattro personaggi. Descrivine il carattere e lo stato d'animo (*mood*). Sono tutti amici? Si sono appena incontrati? Cosa si dicono? Immaginate un dialogo di quattro battute (*lines*) per coppia.

3 As a warm-up, ask students: **Che tipo sei? Ansioso/a o calmo/a? Sai essere forte in circostanze estreme o vai nel panico? Ti proccupi di cose che non puoi controllare?**

4 Ask these follow-up questions: **Sei sicuro/a di non avere mai avuto pregiudizi? Anche su cosa banali? Quali sono i pro e i contro di donare organi dopo morti? Ci sono considerazioni religiose da considerare?**

6 After students have completed the **Preparazione** activities and watched the short film, have them compare their predictions with what actually happens in the film.

Practice more at
vhlcentral.com.

Video

Mattia Riccio e Roberto Gentile
presentano

Stanza 8

DAVIDE	FRANCESCA	SONNY	ASHAI	GIANNI
LO COCO	**ANTONUCCI**	**SAMPSON OLUMATI**	**LOMBARDO AROP**	**ROSATO**

Diretto da **Mattia Riccio**

sceneggiatura MATTIA RICCIO aiuto regia ROBERTO GENTILE
direttore della fotografia MATTIA BERNABEI edizione LUDOVICA BARTOLO
suono STEFANO SAVINO e MASSIMO SAVINO macchinista ADRIANO AGOSTINACCHIO
trucco MARTINA MORO montaggio MATTIA RICCIO musiche NICOLO' SALVATORE
prodotto da MATTIA RICCIO e ROBERTO GENTILE

si ringrazia

Trama *Due coppie aspettano con ansia fuori da una sala operatoria in un ospedale. Il finale a sorpresa ribalta° i pregiudizi.*

Nota CULTURALE

Numero di stranieri residenti in Italia

Dalla fine della seconda guerra mondiale a oggi il numero degli stranieri legalmente residenti in Italia è aumentato esponenzialmente, specialmente negli ultimi quarant'anni. Secondo i dati forniti dall'ISTAT (Istituto Nazionale di Statistica), al primo gennaio 2018 sono 5.144.440, pari al° 8,4% della popolazione. Gli immigrati normalmente fanno i lavori umili° che gli italiani non vogliono più fare e che non possono essere fatti da robot (prendersi cura° delle persone anziane, pulire le case degli altri, etc.). Pagano regolarmente le tasse° e contribuiscono alla crescita° del paese. In Italia come altrove°, sono oggetto di manipolazioni politiche che tendono ad accusarli tutti di essere criminali, dando luogo° a generalizzazioni pericolose.

pari al *equal to* **umili** *humble* **prendersi cura** *take care* **tasse** *taxes* **crescita** *growth* **altrove** *elsewhere* **dando luogo** *giving rise*

MARCO Anna, adesso calmati, sto arrivando. Mi hai sentito?
ANNA Sì. Ti aspetto.

MARCO Ma che? Sei impazzito?

TEACHING OPTION Have students read the **Nota culturale**, then ask: **Sai quanti sono gli immigrati legali negli Stati Uniti? Che lavori fanno? E gli illegali? Quanti sono e che lavori fanno loro? Cosa vuol dire dichiarare una città «santuario»? Conosci esempi?**

ANNA Che c'è? Li conosci?
MARCO Per poco non lo mettevo sotto quello lì. E chissà se non facevo bene.

MARCO Spero solo di non dovere dividerla con uno di loro.

EXPANSION Have students research the concept of sanctuary city.

ANNA Marco, basta! Smettila! Io ho capito che sei nervoso ma non vedi che stanno soffrendo anche loro?
MARCO Ma io rispetto il loro dolore. Dico solo che non potrebbero andare a soffrire al paese loro?

CHIRURGO L'intervento è riuscito alla perfezione. Le prossime ore ovviamente saranno le più delicate, ma abbiamo tutto sotto controllo.

Sullo SCHERMO

Mentre guardi il corto, completa queste frasi.

1. Il film comincia ___d___.
2. Marco quasi mette sotto ___b___.
3. Il figlio della coppia è ___a___.
4. I genitori non sanno ___e___.
5. Il padre porta ___f___.
6. La coppia di immigrati chiede ___c___.

a. in sala operatoria
b. un ciclista perché distratto dal telefono
c. di loro figlio
d. al telefono su schermo buio (*dark*)
e. in che stanza sarà il figlio
f. un tè alla madre

ribalta *reverses*

Analisi

1

Comprensione Scegli la risposta giusta.

1. Marco fa in fretta e guarda il telefonino perché _____.
   a. la moglie lo aspetta   b. la cugina lo aspetta   c. deve parlare con un chirurgo

2. Marco è ostile perché _____.
   a. crede che l'immigrato volesse farsi uccidere in bici   b. è nervoso per l'operazione della moglie   c. è razzista senza sapere bene perché lo è

3. Anna è _____.
   a. intollerante quanto il marito   b. più tollerante del marito   c. gentile ma solo in superficie

4. La coppia di immigrati è _____.
   a. molto nervosa   b. rilassata e tranquilla   c. cordiale e comunicativa

5. Anna accetta un _____.
   a. caffè   b. un tè   c. un succo di frutta

6. Il chirurgo dice che l'intervento _____.
   a. non è riuscito e devono aspettare mezz'ora   b. è andato benissimo e il figlio verrà portato in stanza in una mezz'ora   c. non è finito e tra mezz'ora il figlio riceverà un cuore

7. Nella stanza 8 ci sarà il ragazzo che ha _____.
   a. donato il cuore con i suoi genitori   b. donato il cuore con i genitori di chi lo ha ricevuto   c. ricevuto il cuore e i genitori anche di chi lo ha donato

8. Marco cambia il suo atteggiamento (*attitude*) perché il figlio della coppia di immigrati _____.
   a. era simpatico   b. è in classe col loro   c. ha salvato la vita del suo

2 Ask pairs to share their descriptions. Have them write their lists on the board to form one larger list. Then ask if there is anything to add to the portrayal of each character.

2

I protagonisti In coppia, indicate quali sono gli aggettivi che descrivono la personalità e i sentimenti dei seguenti personaggi. Secondo voi, perché la coppia di immigrati non ha nomi? Cosa vuol dire all'interno del cortometraggio?

Personaggio	Aggettivi descrittivi
Marco	
Anna	
Immigrato	
Immigrata	
Chirurgo	

3

Analisi In coppia, fatevi le seguenti domande e scambiatevi opinioni. Poi condividetele con il resto della classe.

1. Secondo te, Marco è sempre stato razzista? Cosa vuol dire per lui essere razzista? Conosce degli africani, degli indiani, degli albanesi, etc.? Cosa lo rende ostile? Dei fatti concreti o delle dicerie (*hearsay*)?

2. Perché Anna non è come il marito? Cosa la rende più tollerante? Perché sembra essere subito in sintonia (*harmony*) con la signora immigrata?

3. Perché la coppia di immigrati è così nervosa? Secondo te, perché sono così preoccupati di come andrà l'intervento in cui il cuore del figlio morto viene dato a qualcun altro?

4. Perché il chirurgo svela (*reveals*) l'identità di donatori e riceventi? Il regista alla fine scrive che è un'opera di fantasia perché la legge italiana tutela la privacy. Perché pensi che decida di far finire così il suo film?

4

Dialogo In gruppi di tre o quattro, immaginate come potrebbe continuare la conversazione tra Marco e Anna e la coppia di genitori immigrati, magari date loro dei nomi, dopo che hanno capito di essere uniti dal cuore di un figlio.

5

Espansione Immaginate ora un dialogo dal significato opposto, in cui una coppia (o tutte e due) si arrabbia perché non vuole ricevere il cuore di un immigrato o dare il cuore a un italiano. Puoi immaginare uno scenario in cui il razzismo esplode?

6

Situazioni estreme In gruppi di tre o quattro, immaginate ora che si verifichi (*happens*) una di queste due situazioni. Come finirebbe il film?

A. Marco, distratto dal telefonino, mette sotto la macchina il signore in bicicletta. Si può salvare solo trapiantadogli un rene (*kidney*). Marco e il signore hanno lo stesso gruppo sanguigno. Cosa fa Marco?

B. Il figlio di Marco e Anna, muore in sala operatoria. Nella tristezza generale, Marco e Anna apprendono che il cuore era del figlio della coppia di immigrati. Come reagiscono?

7

Scriviamo Scegli uno di questi argomenti e scrivi uno o due paragrafi usando il vocabolario di questa lezione.

● Descrivi una situazione in cui hai dovuto mettere da parte i tuoi pregiudizi.

● Quali sono le implicazioni etiche dei trapianti (*transplants*)? Sei a favore o contro? Perché?

● Hai vissuto una situazione estrema che ti ha fatto cambiare idea su qualcosa o qualcuno?

3 Ask students if they can imagine a time in history when a situation like the one described in the film would have caused a scandal. You might also mention the ethical or religious issues caused by using animal valves in transplants.

3 Encourage pairs to search for the true motivations behind the characters' actions. List all responses on the board.

4 After students have discussed their scenarios, have them perform the conversations for the class. Then have students rate each group of performers on a scale from 1 to 5. The ratings should take into account creativity, use of new expressions, and coherence of the new ending.

5 Ask students which one of the two conversations was more difficult to write or perform. Ask them to explain why.

 Practice more at vhlcentral.com.

INSTRUCTIONAL RESOURCES: Teaching suggestions; Answer Keys
SAM/WebSAM: WB

IMMAGINA IL TRIVENETO

Dove l'Italia incontra l'Europa

La parte nord orientale dell'Italia è conosciuta come **Triveneto** e comprende° le regioni **Veneto**, **Trentino-Alto Adige** e **Friuli-Venezia Giulia**. Questo è un territorio in cui la cultura italiana si incontra e si mescola° con quella germanica e con quella slava: ciò rende° il Triveneto particolarmente affascinante.

Il confine nord orientale è incorniciato° dalle Alpi, che nella parte centrale della regione diventano **Dolomiti**, e appaiono come alte torri° con rocce dai riflessi arancioni e rosa. Molte stazioni sciistiche° prestigiose, tra cui **Cortina d'Ampezzo** in Veneto e i centri della **Val di Fiemme** e della **Val di Fassa** in Trentino-Alto Adige, accolgono gli appassionati di sport invernali. La **Pianura Padana** si estende a sud e qui è attraversata da grandi fiumi come l'**Adige**, il **Tagliamento** e il **Po**, con il suo grande delta. Lungo la costa orientale si trovano località balneari° ben note°, come **Lignano Sabbiadoro** e **Iesolo**.

Il **Veneto** possiede un incomparabile patrimonio artistico. **Venezia**, costruita sulla laguna, è famosa in tutto il mondo per le sue **calli**°, **i canali** e gli splendidi monumenti. Il cuore della città è **piazza San Marco**, con la basilica di San Marco, grande esempio di architettura bizantina, e l'alto campanile. A **Verona** l'**Arena**, oggi sede di importanti eventi musicali, è un anfiteatro di epoca romana in ottimo stato di conservazione; di grande interesse sono anche il **ponte scaligero** e i tanti palazzi e monumenti costruiti quando la famiglia della **Scala** era al potere. Una meta° classica è la **casa di Giulietta** che fa da sfondo° alla sfortunata storia d'amore shakespeariana. **Vicenza** è nota per i capolavori dell'architetto **Andrea Palladio**, mentre **Padova** preserva alcuni degli affreschi più belli di **Giotto** nella cappella degli **Scrovegni**, oltre all'imponente basilica di **Sant'Antonio**.

Il **Trentino-Alto Adige** è una terra di incontro tra la cultura italiana e quella tedesca, entrambe presenti nell'architettura delle case, nelle lingue e persino° nella tradizione gastronomica. A **Bolzano** e in tutto l'Alto Adige, a nord, si parlano italiano e tedesco; le abitazioni hanno un inconfondibile stile austriaco e lo **strudel di mele** e la **torta Sacher** sono una costante sui menù! **Trento** e la sua provincia, nel sud della regione, hanno uno stile più italiano.

L'atmosfera multiculturale si respira anche in **Friuli-Venezia Giulia**, in particolare nelle zone di confine con la Slovenia, dove la presenza italiana e quella slava convivono da secoli e dove è presente una popolazione di lingua slovena. **Trieste**, capoluogo regionale, con il suo porto è stata ed è una finestra tra Oriente e Occidente. Il famoso **Caffè San Marco**, nel secolo scorso, era frequentato da intellettuali internazionali del calibro° di **James Joyce**, **Italo Svevo** e **Umberto Saba**.

Il Triveneto è una meta consigliata per chi ama le bellezze classiche dell'Italia arricchite da una buona dose di internazionalità.

In più...

Il fascino di Venezia è inalterato° in ogni stagione dell'anno: deriva dal riflesso di motivi architettonici, di monumenti e di luci nei canali e nelle acque della laguna. Se visitate Venezia in inverno, fatelo durante il famoso **Carnevale**, periodo in cui la città si trasforma in un teatro all'aperto e le calli sono frequentate da personaggi in maschere e costumi straordinari.

comprende *includes* **si mescola** *mixes* **rende** *makes* **incorniciato** *framed* **torri** *towers* **stazioni sciistiche** *ski resorts* **località balneari** *seaside resorts* **ben note** *well-known* **calli** *narrow streets in Venice* **meta** *destination* **sfondo** *background* **persino** *even* **calibro** *caliber* **inalterato** *unchanged*

Vero o falso? Indica se ogni frase è **vera** o **falsa.** Correggi le frasi false. Some answers will vary.

1. Il Triveneto è un'area nel Nord-Est della penisola italiana. Vero.

2. Le Dolomiti si trovano in tutte le regioni del Triveneto. Falso. Si trovano nella parte nord orientale.

3. Andrea Palladio era un architetto veneto. Vero.

4. In Trentino-Alto Adige non si parla italiano. Falso. Si parla italiano e anche tedesco.

5. Il Friuli-Venezia Giulia confina con la Slovenia. Vero.

6. Trieste era una città frequentata da personaggi della società intellettuale. Vero.

7. Gli italiani che abitano in Slovenia e Croazia sono la maggior parte della popolazione. Falso. Sono delle minoranze, il 7% della popolazione.

8. Una tempesta colpisce la scialuppa di Pietro Querini. Vero.

Quanto hai imparato? Rispondi alle domande. Some answers will vary.

1. Quali sono alcune caratteristiche culturali del Triveneto? la presenza di diverse lingue e tradizioni, l'incontro di culture diverse

2. In quale parte del Triveneto è possibile praticare sport invernali? sulle Dolomiti, nel Trentino-Alto Adige e nel Veneto

3. Quali sono le differenze tra l'Alto Adige ed il Trentino? L'Alto Adige ha una cultura prevalentemente tedesca. Il Trentino ha una cultura prevalentemente italiana.

4. Perché il Friuli-Venezia Giulia è considerato una regione multiculturale? Confina con la Slovenia, Trieste è dove l'Oriente e l'Occidente si incontrano.

5. Perché in alcune città della Slovenia e della Croazia si parla italiano? vicinanza geografica, vicende storiche comuni, presenza di minoranze etniche italiane

6. Con che cosa riparte Pietro Querini per Venezia? Riparte con un carico di stoccafisso.

L'italiano in Slovenia e Croazia A causa della vicinanza geografica e delle comuni vicende° storiche, in **Slovenia** e nella **regione istriana** della **Croazia** ci sono minoranze etniche° italiane, circa il 7% dell'intera popolazione. Queste minoranze parlano la lingua italiana che diventa seconda lingua ufficiale dopo lo sloveno o il croato. La Regione istriana di lingua italiana occupa la parte più occidentale della penisola omonima° mentre l'italiano in **Slovenia** è parlato nei comuni di **Capodistria**, **Istria** e **Pirano**.

Pola, Croazia

La storia del baccalà Nel 1492 il mercante veneziano **Pietro Querini** si trova al largo della Norvegia, quando una tempesta colpisce la sua scialuppa°. Querini trova rifugio sull'isola di Rost dove, accolto dalla popolazione locale, mangia per la prima volta un pesce a lui sconosciuto°. Questo pesce viene mangiato fresco, essiccato° o salato e Querini riparte per Venezia con un carico di stoccafisso°. I nobili non apprezzarono quel pesce duro che chiameranno **baccalà**. Lo stoccafisso entrerà ufficialmente nella cucina italiana durante il Concilio di Trento, quando viene sancito° l'obbligo di duecento giorni di astinenza dalla carne.

vicende *events* minoranze etniche *ethnic minorities* omonima *homonymous* scialuppa *lifeboat* sconosciuto *unknown* essiccato *dried* stoccafisso *dried cod* sancito *decreed*

Progetto

Un viaggio tra i castelli del Triveneto ti farà vivere la vita degli imperatori, dei re e delle regine.

- Ricerca almeno tre castelli nel Triveneto, uno per ogni regione.
- Per ogni castello dai informazioni sulla famiglia che lo abitava.
- Cerca anche informazioni sullo stato attuale del castello (a chi appartiene, come viene usato, ecc.).
- Presenta il tuo lavoro alla classe.

GALLERIA DI PERSONE ILLUSTRI

ARCHITETTO
Andrea Palladio (1508–1580)

Andrea Palladio è stato un celebre architetto del Rinascimento italiano. Nato a Padova e cittadino della Repubblica di Venezia, Palladio inizia a tredici anni l'apprendistato di scalpellino (*stonecutter*) per poi passare alla bottega (*workshop*) di uno dei più importanti scultori di Vicenza. L'incontro e l'amicizia con il poeta e umanista Giangiorgio Trissino cambieranno la vita di Palladio che grazie a lui avrà accesso a una formazione classica. L'amico lo porta più volte a Roma dove osserva dal vivo le architetture, studia i materiali e conosce i grandi del suo tempo come Michelangelo. Palladio diventa presto un architetto di successo, richiestissimo dalle nobili famiglie del Veneto che gli commissionano grandi ville diventate oggi patrimonio UNESCO. Oltre a (*In addition to*) celebri opere come il Teatro Olimpico, lascia ai posteri *I quattro libri di architettura*, che influenzeranno profondamente l'architettura occidentale.

VIAGGIATORE
Marco Polo (1254–1324)

Marco Polo nasce a Venezia. A diciassette anni con il padre e lo zio, commercianti di pietre preziose, intraprende un viaggio in Asia percorrendo (*following*) la Via della seta e attraversando tutto il continente asiatico fino a raggiungere (*to reach*) la Cina. Marco trascorre (*spends*) circa venticinque anni in Oriente e, spinto (*motivated*) dalla sua curiosità e da presunti incarichi (*assignments*) del Kubilai Khan, fa numerosi viaggi. Il racconto delle sue avventure è raccolto (*collected*) nel libro *Il Milione*, dove Marco Polo sostiene di aver portato in Europa, oltre a (*as well as*) oggetti favolosi,gli spaghetti e il gelato. Le descrizioni dell'Asia contenute nel libro hanno ispirato Cristoforo Colombo che restò per sempre convito di aver raggiunto la Cina.

SCRITTORE

Italo Svevo (1861–1928)

Italo Svevo, pseudonimo di Ettore Schmitz, è stato uno scrittore italiano ed esponente della cultura mitteleuropea. Mentre lavorava in banca, coltivò la passione per la letteratura scrivendo saggi e articoli di critica letteraria e teatrale in vari quotidiani (*newspapers*) di Trieste, la sua città natale. Quando pubblicò il suo primo romanzo, *Una vita*, non ebbe molto successo ma decise di continuare a scrivere. James Joyce, suo insegnante di inglese alla Berlitz School di Trieste, lo incoraggiò a scrivere un terzo romanzo ma anche questo non colpì il pubblico. Grazie all'opera, *La coscienza di Zeno*, Svevo ebbe successo all'estero. Il suo stile influenzato dalla lettura dei classici italiani e francesi, dai filosofi dell'Ottocento e dalla psicoanalisi, venne capito e valorizzato in Italia molti anni più tardi. Lo scrittore triestino morì in un incidente automobilistico nel 1928.

IMPRENDITORE

Luciano Benetton (1935–)

Luciano Benetton è un imprenditore (*entrepreneur*) nato a Treviso che, insieme ai fratelli Giuliana, Gilberto e Carlo, ha lanciato nel 1965 la Benetton Group. La società è oggi presente in 120 paesi del mondo con oltre 6.000 punti vendita (*retail outlets*). Sotto la guida di Luciano, l'azienda entra nella Formula 1 fondando la *Benetton Formula*. Negli anni Ottanta e Novanta la Benetton lanciò la carriera del pilota Michael Schumacher, il quale vinse ventisette Gran Premi su 260 gare (*races*) e due mondiali piloti. Luciano Benetton è anche il padre del progetto culturale no profit *Imago Mundi*, una collezione di arte contemporanea formata da migliaia (*thousands*) di opere create da artisti di tutto il mondo.

Comprensione

Completare Completa le seguenti frasi.

1. Il padre e lo zio di Marco Polo erano ___commercianti di pietre preziose___.

2. Marco Polo ___trascorre___ circa venticinque anni in Oriente.

3. ___Il Milione___ è il nome del libro in cui sono raccolte le storie delle avventure di Marco Polo.

4. Palladio era molto richiesto ___dalle nobili famiglie del Veneto___.

5. Le ville create da Palladio sono oggi ___patrimonio UNESCO___.

6. ___Una vita___ è il primo romanzo pubblicato da Italo Svevo.

7. Italo Svevo ha avuto James Joyce come ___insegnante___ di inglese.

8. *La coscienza di Zeno* ebbe ___successo___ all'estero.

9. Luciano Benetton ___è nato___ a Treviso.

10. *Imago Mundi* è un ___progetto culturale___ no profit.

Scrittura

Scrivi sull'argomento Scegli uno dei seguenti argomenti e scrivi un paragrafo seguendo le indicazioni.

- **Critica letteraria** Immagina di essere uno scrittore. Hai da poco pubblicato il tuo primo romanzo e nonostante le vendite siano positive, alcuni importanti critici letterari hanno giudicato il tuo lavoro malamente. Come reagisci? Cosa dovrebbe interessare di più a uno scrittore? Il piacere del pubblico e le vendite o il giudizio dei critici?

- **Tirocinio da Benetton** Hai deciso di inviare la tua candidatura per un tirocinio estivo da Benetton. L'annuncio è rivolto (*directed*) a studenti anglofoni che studiano italiano. Spiega in una lettera per quale motivo studi italiano e perché sei interessato/a a questo tirocinio.

- **Patrimonio UNESCO** La Convenzione del patrimonio mondiale ha il compito di identificare e mantenere nella lista i siti che hanno eccezionale importanza culturale o naturale. Proponi all'UNESCO di preservare un sito d'importanza storica o artistica presente nel tuo stato e spiega perché.

 Practice more at **vhlcentral.com**.

INSTRUCTIONAL RESOURCES 7.1
Audioscripts, Answer Keys, Lab MP3s, Grammar Presentation Slides
SAM/WebSAM: WB, LM

Comparatives and superlatives

- The comparative form is used to compare qualities in people, things, concepts, or actions. Comparisons express three kinds of relationships: inferiority, equality, and superiority. These relationships are conveyed by structures containing the words **meno**, **così** or **tanto**, and **più**.

Il mio computer è **meno** veloce **del** tuo.
*My computer is slower (*lit. *less fast) than yours.*

Il mio computer è **più** veloce **del** tuo.
My computer is faster than yours.

Il mio computer è (**così**) veloce **come** il tuo./Il mio computer è (**tanto**) veloce **quanto** il tuo.
My computer is as fast as yours.

Comparisons of equality

- To express equality (**uguaglianza**) when comparing adjectives or adverbs, use (**così**) + [*adjective or adverb*] + **come**. You may also use (**tanto**) + [*adjective or adverb*] + **quanto**. **Così** and **tanto** are often omitted.

Also give students examples with adverbs.
I francesi si vestono (così) bene come gli italiani.
I francesi si vestono (tanto) bene quanto gli italiani.

Le vacanze sono (**così**) piacevoli **come** necessarie.
Le vacanze sono (**tanto**) piacevoli **quanto** necessarie.
Vacations are as fun as they are necessary.

- When comparing nouns, use **tanto** + [*noun*] + **quanto**... to express *as much/many as*. When **tanto** and **quanto** precede a noun, they should agree in gender and number with the noun.

Ho letto **tanti** libri **quante** riviste.
I read as many books as magazines.

Ci sono **tante** bambine **quanti** bambini.
There are as many girls as boys.

Comparisons of inequality

- To express comparisons of inequality—indicating inferiority (**minoranza**) or superiority (**maggioranza**)—use **meno**... **di** and **più**... **di** or **meno**... **che** and **più**... **che**. The choice of structure depends on the type of comparison that is made.

- Use **meno**... **di** and **più**... **di** to compare two nouns or pronouns (people or things) in terms of a single quality (adjective or adverb) or action (verb).

Two nouns (**scienziato** and **Franco**)	+	one adjective (**etico**)	Quello scienziato è **più** meticoloso **di** Franco. *That scientist is more meticulous than Franco.*
Two nouns (**Claudio** and **Maria**)	+	one verb (**scrive articoli**)	Claudio scrive **meno** articoli **di** Maria. *Claudio writes fewer articles than Maria does.*

To help students decide between **di** and **che**, give them pairs of sentences and ask them to join them in a single sentence using a comparative. Example:
Mario parla molto./Luigi parla moltissimo. →
Luigi parla più di Mario.
Tu studi tre lingue./Io studio due lingue. →
Tu studi più lingue di me.
Il film è molto sperimentale./Il film è poco interessante →
Il film è più sperimentale che interessante.

- Use **meno**... **che** and **più**... **che** to compare two qualities or attributes of a single noun. Use it also to compare two adverbs or two objects with respect to a single verb.

One noun + (**idee**)	two adjectives (**originali** and **convenzionali**)	Le idee di Claudio sono **più** originali **che** convenzionali. *Claudio's ideas are more original than they are conventional.*
One verb + (**Bevo**)	two objects (**caffè** and **tè**)	Bevo **più** caffè **che** tè. *I drink more coffee than tea.*
One verb + (**Piove**)	two adverbs (**adesso** and **stamattina**)	Piove **meno** adesso **che** stamattina. *It's raining less now than (it was) this morning.*

- Use **meno … che** and **più … che** before prepositions and infinitives.

> Viaggiamo **meno** in treno **che** in aereo.
> *We travel less by train than by plane.*

> È **più** importante bere **che** mangiare?
> *Is it more important to drink than to eat?*

Relative superlative

- The relative superlative indicates that a person or thing is *the most* or *the least* of a particular group. To form the relative superlative of adjectives, use this structure: [*definite article*] + **più/meno** + [*adjective*] + **di** (or sometimes **in** or **tra**). To form the relative superlative of adverbs, omit the definite article, unless **possibile** is used after the adverb.

> Quale materia è **la meno** difficile **tra** quelle scientifiche?
> *Of all the science subjects, which is the least difficult?*

> Quale automobile è **la più** veloce **di** tutte?
> *Which car is the fastest of all?*

> Piero lavora **più duramente** di tutti.
> *Piero works harder than anyone.*

> Ti chiamo **il più presto** possibile!
> *I'll call you as soon as possible!*

- The superlative may precede or follow the noun. The article is not repeated when it follows the noun.

> Quello zoologo è **il più famoso del** mondo. (superlative precedes noun)
> Quello è **lo** zoologo **più** famoso **del** mondo. (superlative follows noun)

- When the relative superlative is followed by a conjugated verb, the verb is usually in the subjunctive mood.

> *Guerra e pace* è il libro più lungo che io **abbia letto**.
> *War and Peace is the longest book I have read.*

—*Le prossime ore ovviamente saranno quelle **più** delicate.*

Absolute superlative

- The absolute superlative conveys the highest possible degree of an adjective or adverb.

- The absolute superlative of an adjective is most commonly expressed by dropping the final vowel of the masculine plural form and adding **–issimo/a/i/e**.

> La risposta è **semplicissima**.
> *The answer is very simple.*

> L'inquinamento è un problema **gravissimo**.
> *Pollution is an extremely serious problem.*

- The absolute superlative of adverbs that end in a vowel follows a similar pattern: add **–issimo** after dropping the final vowel. However, if an adverb ends in **–mente**, form the feminine superlative adjective first and add **–mente**.

> Il tecnico è arrivato **tardissimo**.
> *The technician arrived very late.*

> Il computer funziona **rapidissimamente**.
> *The computer is very fast.*

To practice structures requiring **di** or **che**, first ask students to compare two famous actors based on various qualities. All of these sentences should require **di**. Next, ask them to talk about only *one* actor and describe his or her qualities. These sentences should elicit use of **che**. Example: **Roberto Benigni ha più talento di Seth Rogen./Roberto Benigni è più famoso in Italia che negli Stati Uniti. Roberto Benigni è più comico che drammatico.**

ATTENZIONE!

In a relative phrase introduced by *more/less… than what*, use **più/meno… di quello che, di ciò che/di quanto** followed by the subjunctive.

I computer sono più facili da usare di quello che pensiate.
Computers are easier to use than you think.

L'esperimento ha dimostrato meno di quanto sperassimo.
The experiment proved less than we had hoped.

ATTENZIONE!

To express *one of the most/least… in/of*, use the indefinite article + **di** + **più/meno… di**.

L'Italia è uno dei più affascinanti paesi del mondo.
Italy is one of the most fascinating countries in the world.

Fra plus the definite article is sometimes used instead of **uno/a di**.

Il computer è fra le invenzioni più importanti del Novecento.
The computer is one of the most important inventions of the twentieth century.

RIMANDO

The subjunctive in superlative statements is presented in **Strutture 9.4, p. 364.**

- An alternative way to form the absolute superlative of adjectives is to place **molto** or another adverb, such as **assai**, **bene**, **estremamente**, and **incredibilmente**, before the adjective.

> È un lavoro **estremamente difficile**.
> *It's an extremely difficult job.*

> Avere un portatile è **assai conveniente**.
> *Having a laptop is very convenient.*

- The absolute superlative of an adjective or adverb can also be formed with a prefix. The most common of these prefixes are **arci–**, **iper–**, **stra–**, **super–**, and **ultra–**.

> Alcuni politici sono **ultraconservatori**.
> *Some politicians are extremely conservative.*

> Quel portatile è **ipermoderno**.
> *That laptop is very modern.*

Irregular comparatives and superlatives

- Some adjectives have both regular and irregular comparative and superlative forms.

	comparative	relative superlative	absolute superlative
buono	più buono/**migliore**	il più buono/**il migliore**	buonissimo/**ottimo**
cattivo	più cattivo/**peggiore**	il più cattivo/**il peggiore**	cattivissimo/**pessimo**
grande	più grande/**maggiore**	il più grande/**il maggiore**	grandissimo/**massimo**
piccolo	più piccolo/**minore**	il più piccolo/**il minore**	piccolissimo/**minimo**
alto	più alto/**superiore**	il più alto/**il superiore**	altissimo/**supremo**
basso	più basso/**inferiore**	il più basso/**l'inferiore**	bassissimo/**infimo**

- In general, the irregular form is used when comparing figurative or abstract qualities, while the regular form is used to compare physical qualities. When speaking of siblings' ages, for example, or describing figuratively the importance of a historical figure, use **maggiore** and **minore**.

> Francesco ha due sorelle **minori**.
> *Francesco has two younger sisters.*

> Questo libro è **più piccolo** di quello.
> *This book is smaller than that one.*

> Conosci le opere dei poeti **minori** del Medioevo?
> *Are you familiar with the works of the minor poets of the Middle Ages?*

- Some adverbs have irregular comparative and superlative forms. In the relative superlative, omit the article unless **possibile** is used.

	comparative	relative superlative	absolute superlative
bene	meglio	(il) meglio	benissimo
male	peggio	(il) peggio	malissimo
molto	più, di più	(il) più	moltissimo
poco	meno, di meno	(il) meno	pochissimo

> Franco canta **meglio** di tutti.
> *Franco sings better than everyone.*

> Lavoro **il più** possibile.
> *I work as much as possible.*

> Mi piace l'informatica, ma mi piace **di più** il giornalismo.
> *I like computer science, but I like journalism more.*

Pratica

1

Paragoni Completa le frasi inserendo **come, quanto, di, di + articolo** o **che**.

1. Una macchina elettrica inquina (*pollutes*) meno ___di___ una macchina ibrida.

2. Il vaccino contro la tubercolosi è più importante ___della___ scoperta di una cura per altre malattie meno diffuse.

3. Il mio portatile è più pratico ___che___ bello.

4. Oggi i ricercatori guadagnano meno ___di___ un impiegato di banca.

5. La fisica nucleare è tanto difficile ___quanto___ la chimica.

6. È più facile distruggere un atomo ___che___ un pregiudizio.

2

Il mondo di oggi Completa le frasi logicamente usando i comparativi. Some answers will vary.

1. La rete senza fili è ___più___ pratica ___del___ collegamento via cavo (*wire*). (+)

2. Mandare un SMS è ___più___ facile ___che___ scrivere un'e-mail.

3. La clonazione umana è un argomento ___così/tanto___ attuale ___come/quanto___ controverso. (=)

4. Una lettera cartacea (*paper*) è sicuramente ___meno___ veloce ___di___ un'e-mail. (–)

5. È ___meno___ costoso allegare un documento ___che___ inviare un fax. (–)

6. Il computer non è ancora ___così/tanto___ diffuso ___come/quanto___ la televisione. (=)

7. Il furto d'identità è un crimine ___meno___ diffuso ___del___ furto di oggetti. (–)

8. Il problema dell'inquinamento è ___più___ sentito in città ___che___ in campagna. (+)

3

Opinioni diverse Cambiate le seguenti frasi trasformando i comparativi di uguaglianza in comparativi di maggioranza o minoranza. Some answers will vary.

> **Modello**   **Il treno oggi è comodo tanto quanto l'automobile.**
>
>   Il treno oggi è più comodo dell'automobile.

1. Il dottor Bisi usa la posta elettronica tanto quanto me.   Il dottor Bisi usa la posta elettronica più/meno di me.

2. Negli Stati Uniti i centri di ricerca sono buoni tanto quanto in Italia.   Negli Stati Uniti i centri di ricerca sono migliori/peggiori che in Italia.

3. Ci sono tante automobili a Roma quante ce ne sono a New York.   Ci sono più/meno automobili a Roma che a New York.

4. Le energie rinnovabili sono tanto costose quanto importanti per l'ambiente.   Le energie rinnovabili sono più/meno costose che importanti per l'ambiente.

5. Il professore di astronomia è più anziano di quello di biologia, ma parla inglese bene come lui.   Il professore di astronomia è più anziano di quello di biologia, ma parla inglese meglio/peggio di lui.

4

Classifiche In coppia, usate il superlativo relativo per formare delle frasi con le parole della lista. Dopo trasformate le frasi usando il comparativo di maggioranza o di minoranza.

> **Modello**   La radio è il mezzo di comunicazione più antico fra quelli oggi esistenti. La radio è più antica della televisione./La televisione è meno antica della radio.

la radio	il mezzo di comunicazione	celebre	di tutte
l'inquinamento	problema	urgente	fra quelli oggi esistenti
la fisica nucleare	l'argomento	antico	dei nostri tempi
la clonazione	astronomo	controverso	del mondo industrializzato
Galileo Galilei	scienza	difficile	nella storia dell'umanità

4 Suggested answers:
La radio è il mezzo di comunicazione più antico fra quelli oggi esistenti.
L'inquinamento è il problema più urgente del mondo industrializzato.
La fisica nucleare è la scienza più difficile di tutte.
La clonazione è l'argomento più controverso dei nostri tempi.
Galileo Galilei è l'astronomo più celebre nella storia dell'umanità.

5

L'evoluzione delle cose In coppia, guardate le due immagini e fate dei paragoni usando aggettivi, avverbi e verbi al comparativo o al superlativo.

6 Have students ask each other questions that elicit comparatives and additional superlatives. Example: **Il pranzo al ristorante è stato migliore del film o peggiore?**

6

Incontri Immaginate di essere andati a un appuntamento al buio (*blind date*). In coppia, usate il superlativo relativo e il superlativo assoluto per parlare del vostro incontro. Aiutatevi con le parole della lista.

> **Modello** È stato l'incontro più emozionante della mia vita!
>
> Abbiamo passato una giornata divertentissima!

casa	conversazione	macchina
cellulare	film	passeggiata
conto	gelato	ristorante

7

Sondaggi In coppia, osservate i dati riportati nella tabella su alcune delle città più importanti dell'Italia centrale e meridionale. Fatevi domande sui dati aiutandovi con le espressioni della lista.

> **Modello** In quali città ci sono più uomini che donne? Qual è la città meno popolata?

> Quale città è la più / meno...?
> In quali città ci sono più / meno... che...?
> Quale città ha il maggior / minor numero di...?
> Qual è la città con il più alto / basso numero di...?

Città	Popolazione	Uomini	Donne
Roma	2.638.842	1.241.870	1.396.972
Napoli	959.052	454.660	504.392
Palermo	654.987	311.874	343.113
Bari	313.213	149.338	163.875
Reggio Calabria	180.686	86.426	94.260

 Practice more at **vhlcentral.com**.

Comunicazione

8 **Più o meno** In coppia, paragonate a turno gli elementi della lista.

> **Modello** —Lo schermo del mio computer è di 17 pollici (*inches*).
> —Il mio è di 15 pollici. Il tuo è più grande del mio.
> —Sì, il mio schermo è il più grande dei due.

- il vostro cellulare
- il vostro lettore MP3
- la vostra casella di posta elettronica
- il vostro sito web preferito
- la vostra connessione Internet

- il vostro programma televisivo preferito
- la vostra macchina fotografica
- la vostra rete sociale preferita
- la vostra materia preferita
- ?

9 **La vita di tutti i giorni** In gruppi di tre, discutete alcuni aspetti della vita quotidiana che sono stati migliorati dai progressi tecnologici. Come era la vostra vita prima dell'arrivo di queste tecnologie? Come è la vostra vita oggi? Usate i comparativi e i superlativi.

9 As an expansion, have students interview older generations in their family to see how certain technological advances affected their lives. Then have a class discussion based on what students found out.

10 **La scoperta più importante**

A. In coppia, selezionate quelle che, secondo voi, sono le tre scoperte più importanti per l'umanità e discutete il perché.

1492: Cristoforo Colombo, navigatore italiano, cercando di dimostrare che la Terra era rotonda e pensando di arrivare in India, ha «scoperto» l'America.

1500: Leonardo da Vinci, pittore, scultore, architetto, ingegnere, anatomista, letterato, musicista e inventore italiano, scrive il *Trattato delli Uccelli*, in cui studia l'anatomia degli uccelli e la resistenza dell'aria. Poi studia la caduta dei corpi e progetta il primo esempio di paracadute.

1600: Galileo Galilei, fisico, filosofo, astronomo e matematico italiano, scopre che le macchie lunari sono le ombre delle montagne della luna proiettate dalla luce del sole. Questa scoperta confuta la teoria di Aristotele secondo cui tutti i corpi celesti, esclusa la Terra, sono lisci, perfetti e incorruttibili.

inizio 1800: Alessandro Volta, fisico italiano, inventa la «pila» (*battery*), il primo generatore di energia elettrica. Grazie alla pila, è stato possibile trasmettere i segnali attraverso il telegrafo elettrico.

1830 circa: Louis Daguerre, artista e chimico francese, inventa il «dagherrotipo», il primo esempio di fotografia della storia.

1895: Guglielmo Marconi, fisico italiano, inventa un sistema di telegrafia senza fili via onde radio. Questa invenzione ha portato allo sviluppo dei moderni metodi di telecomunicazione come la televisione, la radio, il telefono cellulare, i telecomandi e, in generale, di tutti i sistemi che utilizzano le comunicazioni senza fili.

1928: Alexander Fleming, biologo britannico, scopre la penicillina, una sostanza in grado di combattere numerose malattie infettive come la polmonite, la tubercolosi, la meningite e il tifo.

2008: Alcuni astronomi canadesi e francesi scoprono la «materia oscura» dell'Universo: tutti i pianeti, le stelle e gli oltre 120 miliardi di galassie costituiscono solo il 4% della materia esistente. Il resto, il 96%, non si sa cosa sia, è «oscuro». Il 70% di questa «oscurità» è «energia oscura», il 26% è materia oscura.

B. In gruppi di quattro, discutete le scelte che avete fatto e fate domande sulle scelte dell'altra coppia. Usate dei comparativi e dei superlativi. Alla fine della conversazione, il gruppo deve elencare tre scoperte giudicate le più importanti.

INSTRUCTIONAL RESOURCES
Audioscripts, Answer Keys, Lab MP3s, Grammar Presentation Slides
SAM/WebSAM: WB, LM

7.2

Relative pronouns

- Relative pronouns unite two ideas containing a common element into a single complex sentence, eliminating repetition of the common element. A complex sentence contains a main clause and a dependent (or relative) clause, introduced by a relative pronoun. The noun represented by the relative pronoun is called the *antecedent*. The most common Italian relative pronouns are **che** and **cui**.

- In the example below, the common element, or antecedent, is **il lettore DVD**. In the complex sentence, the relative pronoun **che** refers to this antecedent.

Hanno comprato un lettore DVD.		Il lettore DVD funziona bene.		Il lettore DVD **che** hanno comprato funziona bene.
They bought a DVD player.	+	*The DVD player works well.*	⟩	*The DVD player that they bought works well.*

Che vs. *cui*

- **Che** corresponds to *who, whom, that,* and *which.* **Cui** corresponds to *whom, that, which,* and—when preceded by a definite article—*whose.*

- Use **che** as the direct object or the subject of a relative clause.

  La rete **che** installeranno sarà velocissima.
  The network that they're installing will be very fast.

  È un ricercatore **che** si occupa di genetica.
  He is a researcher who studies genetics.

- Use **cui** to replace the object of a preposition. Preceded by the preposition **a**, **cui** functions as an indirect object.

  Il sistema operativo **di cui** ci ha parlato è distribuito con licenza libera.
  The operating system he told us about is free to use.

  Il tecnico **a cui** ho scritto non mi ha risposto.
  The technician I wrote to didn't reply to me.

- With a definite article, **cui** indicates possession (the equivalent of *whose*). The article used agrees with the noun to which it refers.

  Lo scienziato, **le cui** teorie hanno raggiunto una grande fama, terrà una conferenza domani.
  The scientist, whose theories garnered much attention, will give a lecture tomorrow.

  Non ci fidiamo dei vaccini **la cui** efficacia non è ancora dimostrata.
  We don't trust vaccines whose effectiveness has not yet been proven.

- You can also use **in cui** or **che** to indicate *when*.

  Agosto è un mese **in cui** gli italiani lavorano pochissimo.
  August is a month when Italians work very little.

  Il giorno **che** ti ho visto, stavo proprio male.
  The day (when/that) I saw you, I was really sick.

Sidebar

ATTENZIONE!

In English, relative pronouns are often omitted. In Italian, relative pronouns must always be stated explicitly.

Il portatile che ho comprato pesa pochissimo.
The laptop (that) I bought weighs very little.

ATTENZIONE!

Il che corresponds to *which* and refers to an entire idea or sentence.

Si è rotto il mio portatile, il che mi crea tanti problemi!
My laptop broke, which is causing me lots of problems!
(il che = Il mio portatile si è rotto.)

Because *who* (subject pronoun) and *whom* (object pronoun) are often confused in English, discuss with students the different translations of **che** depending on whether it refers to a subject or an object. Example: **L'amico che invito alla festa si chiama Tom** (*The friend whom I am inviting to the party is named Tom.*) vs. **C'è un ricercatore qui che sappia leggere il francese?** (*Is there a researcher here who can read French?*)

ATTENZIONE!

Here are some set phrases that use **cui** after a preposition.

la ragione/il motivo per cui
the reason why

la maniera/il modo in cui
the way in which

Non capisco il motivo per cui mi hanno licenziato!
I don't understand the reason why they fired me!

Il/la quale, i/le quali

- In place of **che** and **cui**, it is also possible to use a form of **quale** preceded by the definite article. **Quale** agrees in number and gender with the antecedent. Use **il/la quale** and **i/le quali** when **che** or **cui** could result in ambiguity.

> Discutiamolo con l'amica di Marco, **che** si specializza in informatica.
> *Let's discuss it with the friend of Marco's, who is majoring in computer science. (ambiguous: **che** could refer to **l'amica** or to **Marco**)*

> Discutiamolo con l'amica di Marco, **la quale** si specializza in informatica.
> *Let's discuss it with Marco's friend, who is majoring in computer science. (clear: **la quale** must refer to **l'amica**)*

Chi

- The pronoun **chi** can be used as a relative pronoun corresponding to *he/she who, people who, one who, those who,* or *whoever.* It is never preceded by an antecedent. **Chi** is always singular in form, although it can refer to a single unspecified person or to a group of people. **Chi** must always be used with a third person (masculine) singular verb.

> **Chi** naviga su Internet spesso spreca tempo prezioso.
> *People who surf the web often waste precious time.*

> **Chi** è andato via, si è perso il meglio.
> *Those who left, missed the best (part).*

- **Chi** is heard frequently in proverbs.

> **Chi** dorme non piglia pesci.
> *The early bird gets the worm.*
> (Lit. *He who sleeps catches no fish.*)

> **Chi** la vuole cotta, **chi** la vuole cruda.
> *Different strokes for different folks.*
> (Lit. *Some want it cooked, some want it raw.*)

> **Chi** cerca trova.
> *Seek and you shall find.*

> Ride bene **chi** ride ultimo.
> *He who laughs last laughs longest.*

Other relative pronouns

- There exist a number of other relative pronouns. Those referring only to things are followed by singular verbs and modifiers, while those indicating people (or people and things) require plural forms. They are summarized in the chart below:

pronoun	meaning	refers to things	refers to people
quello che, quel che, ciò che, quanto	that which, that, what	✓	
tutto quello che, tutto quel che, tutto ciò che, tutto quanto	everything that, all that	✓	
tutti quelli che, tutti quanti, quanti	everyone, all who, all that	✓	✓

> La guida spiega **tutto ciò che** dovete sapere su Roma.
> *The guidebook explains everything that you need to know about Rome.*

> **Tutti quelli che** erano alla fiera della tecnologia hanno scoperto tante novità.
> *Everyone who was at the technology fair learned many new things.*

Pratica

Nota CULTURALE

L'**Arberia** comprende circa 54 isole linguistiche, situate soprattutto nel Sud Italia, solitamente in zone montuose. Le regioni in cui le comunità arbereshe sono più numerose sono l'Abruzzo, la Basilicata, la Campania, il Molise, la Puglia, la Calabria e la Sicilia. La Pasqua, nei centri arbereshe ancora legati al rito greco-bizantino, è una festa molto partecipata, in cui si mescolano sacro e profano.

1 **Un mondo digitale** Scegli il pronome relativo giusto per completare la frase.

1. Purtroppo non ho ricevuto l'SMS __che__ (cui / che) mi hai mandato.
2. Ho allegato all'e-mail il documento di __cui__ (che / cui) parli.
3. Stefano ha un cellulare con __il quale__ (il quale / che) può navigare su Internet.
4. Il computer __che__ (cui / che) funziona meglio è quello con la tastiera (*keyboard*) nera.
5. Piero, __il quale__ (cui / il quale) è sempre informatissimo, ha scaricato un programma per modificare le foto.
6. La stampante __che__ (che / cui) ho comprato ha bisogno di una nuova cartuccia (*cartridge*).

2 **Realtà (quasi) sconosciute** Completa il testo dell'e-mail usando le parole della lista.

che	le quali	per cui	che
con cui	che	i quali	in cui

Da:	Aldo <aldobianchi@libero.it>
A:	Marco <marcosipini@libero.it>
Oggetto:	Vieni a trovarmi?

Caro Marco,
hai mai sentito parlare di una regione culturale (1) __che__ si chiama «Arberia»? È un'area geografica del Sud Italia (2) __in cui__ nel 1400 emigrarono numerose comunità di albanesi (3) __le quali__ diedero origine a diversi paesi. La lingua (4) __con cui/con la quale__ gli abitanti dell'arbereshe comunicano è «l'arbereshe», (5) __che__ è un miscuglio (*mix*) di antichi dialetti albanesi con contaminazioni di italiano. I membri di queste comunità, (6) __i quali__ sono cittadini italiani a tutti gli effetti, conservano anche le proprie tradizioni, le proprie festività e soprattutto la propria cucina. La ragione (7) __per cui__ ti dico queste cose è che nel mio paese domenica si celebrerà la Pasqua (*Easter*) arbereshe e la sera ci sarà un concerto di un gruppo musicale (8) __che__ canta in arbereshe. Vieni a trovarmi! Sarà interessantissimo!

3 **Ogni progresso è un successo?** Collega le due frasi usando i pronomi relativi.

Modello Alcuni rifiuti (*waste*) sono tossici. In questi rifiuti c'è il mercurio.
Alcuni rifiuti che contengono il mercurio sono tossici.

1. L'inquinamento è un grave problema. Tutti dobbiamo sentirci responsabili di questo problema. L'inquinamento, di cui tutti dobbiamo sentirci responsabili, è un grave problema.
2. Alcune cellule sono chiamate «staminali». Queste cellule sono capaci di trasformarsi in qualsiasi altro tipo di cellula. Le cellule che sono capaci di trasformarsi in qualsiasi altro tipo di cellula si chiamano «staminali».
3. La persona ha commesso un furto d'identità. È entrata nel sito Internet con il tuo nome. La persona che è entrata nel sito Internet con il tuo nome ha commesso un furto d'identità.
4. I medici hanno un codice deontologico. Essi devono attenersi a questo codice. I medici hanno un codice deontologico a cui devono attenersi.
5. La manipolazione genetica pone un problema etico. Tu parli della manipolazione genetica con entusiasmo. La manipolazione genetica, di cui tu parli con entusiasmo, pone un problema etico.

 Practice more at **vhlcentral.com**.

Comunicazione

4

Cultura generale

A. In coppia, scrivete una o due frasi per ogni città della lista usando i pronomi relativi in tutte le loro varietà.

Modello	**Firenze**
	Firenze è una città che ha accolto molti artisti. Chi va a Firenze per la prima volta, deve visitare la Galleria degli Uffizi.

1. New York   3. Tokyo   5. Las Vegas   7. Parigi
2. Napoli   4. Roma   6. Pompei   8. ?

B. Leggete le vostre frasi alla classe. Vince la coppia che ha usato la maggiore varietà di pronomi e li ha usati correttamente.

5

I vostri compagni In piccoli gruppi, scrivete nella tabella i nomi di alcuni dei vostri compagni di classe. Per ciascuno/a scrivete poi una frase per descriverlo/a usando i pronomi relativi. Infine, confrontate le vostre frasi con il resto della classe.

Valeria	Valeria è la compagna con cui studio prima degli esami.

6

Curiosità In coppia, fatevi delle domande aiutandovi con le parole della lista. Rispondete usando i pronomi relativi.

Modello	—A chi scrivi il maggior numero di e-mail?
	—La persona a cui scrivo il maggior numero di e-mail è il mio ragazzo.

A chi	chattare
Per chi	dare / ricevere messaggi personali
Con chi	ricevere / mandare il maggior numero di SMS
Chi	trovare / cercare informazioni sul web
Da chi	imparare a usare il computer
Di chi	conoscere la tua password

7

Ricordi In piccoli gruppi, commentate i vostri primi ricordi d'infanzia aiutandovi con le parole della lista. Cercate di usare i pronomi relativi sia nelle domande che nelle risposte.

Modello	—Chi è la persona che ricordi meglio?
	—Mio nonno, con cui giocavo ai pirati!

- il/la mio/a migliore amico/a
- la mia prima vacanza
- la mia casa
- il mio primo giocattolo

INSTRUCTIONAL RESOURCES **7.3**
Audioscripts, Answer Keys, Lab MP3s, Grammar Presentation Slides
SAM/WebSAM: WB, LM

RIMANDO

To review the subjunctive with impersonal expressions and verbs of will and emotion, see **Strutture 6.3, pp. 228–229**.

The subjunctive with indefinite expressions and with superlative statements is covered in **Strutture 9.4, p. 364**.

ATTENZIONE!

Remember to use the indicative after expressions of certainty. The verb **sapere** is always followed by the indicative, as is **essere certo (chiaro/evidente/ovvio/vero/sicuro)**. In contrast, **non sapere** and **non essere sicuro** are followed by the subjunctive.

Sappiamo che Giorgio ricicla molto. (indicative)
We know that Giorgio recycles a lot.

È chiaro che la gente non ricicla abbastanza. (indicative)
It's clear that people don't recycle enough.

Non sono sicura che tu dica la verità. (subjunctive)
I am not sure that you are telling the truth.

ATTENZIONE!

Note that **perché** has two meanings. When expressing *because*, it is followed by the indicative. When it means *so that*, with an expression of purpose, it is followed by the subjunctive.

Studio informatica perché mi piace. (indicative)
I am studying computer science because I like it.

Ti parla lentamente perché tu possa capire. (subjunctive)
He speaks slowly so that you can understand.

The subjunctive with expressions of doubt and conjunctions; the past subjunctive

—*Ci vorrà almeno un'altra mezz'ora **prima che** lo **portino** su dalla sala operatoria.*

- Use the subjunctive in subordinate clauses that are introduced by a verb expressing doubt or uncertainty.

    Dubito che **arrivino** in tempo.
    I doubt that they will arrive on time.

    Pare che lui **sia** un fisico.
    It seems that he is a physicist.

- These verbs and expressions of doubt or uncertainty are typically followed by the subjunctive.

dubitare che	*to doubt that*	**può darsi che**	*it's possible that*
è (im)possibile che	*it's (im)possible that*	**non è sicuro che**	*it's not certain that*
è (im)probabile che	*it's (un)likely that*	**non sapere che**	*to not know that*
immaginare che	*to imagine that*	**supporre che**	*to suppose that*
pare che	*it seems that*		

- With verbs expressing doubt or uncertainty, use the subjunctive only when there is a change in subject. When the subject of both clauses is the same, use an infinitive preceded by the preposition **di**.

different subjects	same subject
Dubito **che** il tecnico mi **richiami** presto.	Dubito **di finire** il lavoro presto.
I doubt the technician calls me back soon.	*I doubt that I will finish work soon.*

- Use the subjunctive after these conjunctions, which indicate a limitation or condition placed upon the verb in the independent clause. Note that many can be used interchangeably.

provided that	**a condizione che, a patto che**
although	**benché, nonostante, sebbene, malgrado**
unless	**a meno che, salvo che**
so that	**affinché, perché**
as long as	**purché**
in the case that	**nel caso che**
before	**prima che**
without	**senza che**

- When the subject of the two clauses is the same, **prima che**, **affinché/perché**, and **senza che** are replaced with **prima di**, **per**, and **senza**, and they are followed by the infinitive.

<table>
<tr><td>different subjects</td><td>same subject</td></tr>
</table>

Stampo il documento **affinché** tu e Paolo possiate discuterlo.
I'll print the document so that you and Paolo can discuss it.

Stampo il documento **per** poterlo leggere meglio.
I'll print the document so that I can read it better.

Fate l'esercizio **prima che** la lezione finisca!
Do the exercise before class ends!

Fate l'esercizio **prima di** andare via!
Do the exercise before leaving!

Puliamo **senza che** la mamma ce lo chieda.
Let's clean up without mom asking us (to do it).

Puliamo **senza** stancarci troppo.
Let's clean up without tiring ourselves too much.

The past subjunctive

- When the verb in the main clause is in the present (or sometimes future) tense, and the action of the subordinate clause took place before the action of the main clause, use the past subjunctive.

È probabile che il capo **abbia inviato** quel messaggio.
It's likely that the boss sent that message.

Sembra che il senatore **si sia opposto** alla legge sugli animali in pericolo d'estinzione.
It seems that the senator opposed the law on endangered animals.

- The past subjunctive is formed like the **passato prossimo** of the indicative, except that the auxiliary verb is in the present subjunctive. Verbs that take **avere** in the **passato prossimo** of the indicative are conjugated with **avere** in the past subjunctive.

	salvare	**ricevere**	**finire**
che io	abbia salvato	abbia ricevuto	abbia finito
che tu	abbia salvato	abbia ricevuto	abbia finito
che lui/lei	abbia salvato	abbia ricevuto	abbia finito
che noi	abbiamo salvato	abbiamo ricevuto	abbiamo finito
che voi	abbiate salvato	abbiate ricevuto	abbiate finito
che loro	abbiano salvato	abbiano ricevuto	abbiano finito

- Verbs that take **essere** in the **passato prossimo** of the indicative are conjugated with **essere** in the past subjunctive. Remember that past participles must agree with the subject of these verbs.

	andare	**mettersi**	**partire**
che io	sia andato/a	mi sia messo/a	sia partito/a
che tu	sia andato/a	ti sia messo/a	sia partito/a
che lui/lei	sia andato/a	si sia messo/a	sia partito/a
che noi	siamo andati/e	ci siamo messi/e	siamo partiti/e
che voi	siate andati/e	vi siate messi/e	siate partiti/e
che loro	siano andati/e	si siano messi/e	siano partiti/e

Students may need to be reminded only to use the subjunctive—past or present—when the mood is required by a particular verb or expression in the independent clause. It may be useful to ask students to complete a variety of sentences introduced by **Sembra che** and **Sappiamo che** followed by a past tense. Example: **Sembra che la classe abbia capito gli esempi./Sappiamo che Marco ha capito**.

Students are likely to get ahead of themselves and try to use the past subjunctive after independent verbs in the past. Stress for now that the past subjunctive can only be used when introduced by a main clause in the present, future, or imperative.

Point out to students that the conjugations for first, second, and third person singular are the same.

Pratica

1 Have students use expressions of doubt and uncertainty to write two more sentences, one with the present subjunctive and one with the past subjunctive.

1

Due approcci differenti Piero ha problemi con il suo computer e Attilio lo aiuta a cercare di capire cosa succede. Piero, però, preferisce le soluzioni veloci. Completa il dialogo con il congiuntivo presente o passato del verbo tra parentesi.

PIERO Non capisco cosa (1) ___succeda___ (succedere) al mio computer: pare che non (2) ___voglia___ (volere) spegnersi...

ATTILIO Hai provato a resettarlo?

PIERO Sì, ma sembra che il problema non (3) ___sia andato___ (andare) via.

ATTILIO È possibile che (4) ___abbia preso___ (prendere) un virus. Hai un buon antivirus?

PIERO Ho un antivirus, ma non so se (5) ___sia___ (essere) abbastanza efficace. L'ho scaricato dal web gratuitamente.

ATTILIO Prova a chiamare un tecnico. Può darsi che ti (6) ___consigli___ (consigliare) di formattare il disco e reinstallare il sistema operativo. In questo caso suppongo che tu (7) ___debba___ (dovere) fare una copia di back-up di tutti i documenti.

PIERO No, Attilio. Sono sicuro che non è nulla di così grave. Guarda, facciamo così!

ATTILIO Ma che fai? Hai staccato la spina (*unplugged*) senza spegnere il computer? Beh, ora dubito davvero che tu (8) ___possa___ (potere) riaccenderlo!

2 Have students write Piero's reply to Attilio. In his answer, Piero should also describe what followed after he unplugged his computer, how he feels about travelling, and what means of transportation he prefers.

2

Una vita da pendolare I «pendolari» sono le persone che ogni giorno prendono un mezzo di trasporto per andare al lavoro. Attilio è uno di loro. Leggi la sua e-mail e completa il testo usando il verbo tra parentesi al congiuntivo (presente o passato) o all'indicativo (presente o passato prossimo).

Da:	Attilio <attilio.gandolfo@email.it>
A:	Piero <piero.piso@email.it>
Oggetto:	Una vita da pendolare

Ciao Piero!
Come va con il tuo computer? Immagino che tu non lo (1) ___abbia rovinato___ (rovinare) definitivamente... Oggi ho cominciato con il mio nuovo lavoro. Bolzano è un po' lontana, ma con il Frecciargento si viaggia benissimo. In ogni posto c'è una presa (*socket*) a cui posso collegare il portatile! È chiaro che il biglietto (2) ___costa___ (costare) di più, ma non sono sicuro che sui treni più economici (3) ___ci siano___ (esserci) queste comodità. Inoltre, è sicuro che il Frecciargento (4) ___arriva___ (arrivare) sempre puntuale! Suppongo che anche alcuni autobus (5) ___facciano___ (fare) servizio tra Trento e Bolzano, ma io preferisco il treno: è più largo e più comodo. So che (6) ___hai___ (avere) molte cose da fare in questo periodo, ma spero che tu (7) ___venga___ (venire) a trovarmi uno di questi giorni. Cerca di evitare i giorni festivi perché dubito che tu (8) ___riesca___ (riuscire) a trovare posto.
Fatti sentire. A presto, Attilio.

Nota
CULTURALE

Il **treno** in Italia è un mezzo di trasporto molto popolare. Ci sono vari tipi di treni che offrono servizi diversi a costi, ovviamente, diversi. I treni regionali mettono in comunicazione le città di una stessa regione e sono i più economici. Gli Intercity coprono invece lunghe distanze. Nei treni Intercity c'è una carrozza ristorante e la possibilità di comprare snack e bibite e si può viaggiare sia in prima che in seconda classe, ma di solito non c'è una grande differenza fra le due. Le Frecce (Frecciarossa, Frecciargento e Frecciabianca) sono i treni più costosi ma anche i più veloci. Con un treno Frecciarossa possiamo viaggiare da Roma a Milano in circa tre ore.

 Practice more at **vhlcentral.com**.

Comunicazione

3

Io sono così! A turno, completate le frasi usando il congiuntivo o l'infinito, secondo le vostre necessità. Se volete, potete cambiare le frasi per adattare il significato alla vostra reale personalità.

1. Io controllo la mia e-mail due volte al giorno. Vado in vacanza solo a patto che...
2. Ho comprato una macchina fotografica digitale per/affinché...
3. Amo le cose programmate in anticipo. Non parto mai prima di/prima che...
4. Mi piace essere bene informata. Non esprimo mai giudizi sulla bioetica senza/ senza che...
5. Di solito evito di prendere medicine a meno che non...
6. Sono contraria ai rifiuti tossici benché...

4

Consigli Alfredo detesta le scienze, ma vuole diventare un astronauta. In coppia, utlizzate gli elementi della lista per dirgli quello che pensate della sua scelta.

> **Modello** —È possibile che tu diventi un astronauta, ma devi migliorare i tuoi voti in matematica.
>
> —Puoi diventare un astronauta a condizione che tu faccia i compiti di matematica ogni giorno.

a condizione che	è vero che
affinché	è sicuro che
credere	pensare
(non) è possibile che	perché
benché	tutti sanno che

5

Ipotesi sul futuro A gruppi di tre, immaginate come sarà il mondo nel 2050 e nel 2100. Utilizzate il più possibile le espressioni che reggono (*take*) il congiuntivo e presentate le vostre idee alla classe.

> **Modello** È poco probabile che le nazioni smettano di fare guerre.

- la società
- la tecnologia
- le relazioni internazionali
- la conquista dello spazio

6

Notizia straordinaria!

A. Il telegiornale ha annunciato la scoperta di forme di vita su un nuovo pianeta della galassia. In piccoli gruppi, provate a immaginare come sono e come vivono gli abitanti di questo pianeta. Parlate dei punti elencati nella lista.

- aspetto fisico
- società
- sviluppo tecnologico
- comunicazione
- attività
- cibo

B. Ecco che i primi uomini sbarcano sul nuovo pianeta per studiare la nuova specie vivente. Descrivete in sei frasi le interazioni fra gli umani e gli alieni, basandovi sulla realtà che avete descritto sopra e usando le seguenti parole: **a condizione che, affinché, perché, a meno che non, malgrado, benché, nonostante.**

> **Modello** Gli alieni non si spaventano, malgrado non abbiano mai visto esseri umani prima di adesso.

3 Have pairs of students write two sentences about a famous person or someone the whole class will know. Each pair will share their sentences with the rest of the class, who can guess the person's identity.

4 As a variant, have students think of a time when they or someone they know wanted to do something unrealistic. Have pairs discuss advice they received or gave others using as many expressions of doubt as appropriate.

5 Have students add at least two more topics to the list and share them with the class.

6 Have students use two more expressions on their own.

INSTRUCTIONAL RESOURCES 7.4
Audioscripts, Answer Keys, Lab MP3s, Grammar Presentation Slides
SAM/WebSAM: WB, LM

Conoscere and *sapere*

—Non **sappiamo** ancora che stanza ci è stata assegnata.

- **Conoscere** and **sapere** both mean *to know*, but they are used in different contexts. **Conoscere** is a regular verb, while **sapere** has irregular forms.

conoscere		sapere	
conosco	conosciamo	so	sappiamo
conosci	conoscete	sai	sapete
conosce	conoscono	sa	sanno

- **Conoscere** means *to know* or *to be familiar with* a person, place, or thing.

> **Conosco** un ottimo ristorante in centro.
> *I know an excellent restaurant downtown.*

> **Conoscete** il dottor Ruspoli?
> *Do you know Dr. Ruspoli?*

- **Conoscere** in the **passato prossimo** means *met* (for the first time).

> Ieri **abbiamo conosciuto** il professore di biologia.
> *We met the biology professor yesterday.*

> **Ho conosciuto** mio marito nel 1964.
> *I met my husband in 1964.*

- **Sapere** means *to know* (a fact), or *to know how* (to do something). To indicate an ability, use the infinitive after a conjugated form of **sapere**.

> **Sapete** quando è stato inventato il computer?
> *Do you know when the computer was invented?*

> Mio padre **sa** parlare tedesco.
> *My father knows how to speak German.*

- **Sapere** in the **passato prossimo** means *found out*.

> Che bella notizia! **Abbiamo saputo** che Laura e Marco si sposano!
> *What great news! We found out that Laura and Marco are getting married!*

- In the **imperfetto**, **conoscere** and **sapere** have the same meanings as they do in the present tense, but these meanings are conveyed in a past, descriptive framework.

> Prima di viaggiare in Italia, John non **conosceva** la polenta.
> *Before he went to Italy, John wasn't familiar with polenta.*

> Tua nonna **sapeva** parlare italiano?
> *Did your grandmother know how to speak Italian?*

ATTENZIONE!

Note that in the present tense, the conjugation of **sapere** closely resembles that of **avere**.

SAPERE/AVERE

so/ho
sai/hai
sa/ha
sappiamo/abbiamo
sapete/avete
sanno/hanno

ATTENZIONE!

Note that **sapere** is commonly used in the phrase **Non lo so**, where the generic pronoun **lo** refers to an idea or concept.

Dov'è il tuo quaderno?
Where is your notebook?

Non lo so.
I don't know.

ATTENZIONE!

Remember that **sapere che**, which conveys certainty, should be followed by a subordinate clause in the indicative. In contrast, **non sapere se**, which conveys uncertainty, should be followed by the subjunctive.

Sanno che il codice è giusto.
They know it's the right code.

Non sanno se il codice sia giusto.
They do not know if it's the right code.

Pratica e comunicazione

1

Interessi in comune Catia e Massimo si sono conosciuti via Internet. Hanno scoperto di fare ricerca entrambi a Bolzano, così hanno deciso di incontrarsi. Completa il dialogo inserendo **conoscere** o **sapere** nella forma appropriata.

CATIA Ciao, Massimo! Finalmente ti (1) _conosco_ di persona!

MASSIMO Ciao! Che piacere!

CATIA Da quanto tempo sei qui a Bolzano?

MASSIMO Da poco, una settimana. Non ho avuto il tempo di (2) _conoscere_ nessuno...

CATIA Io qui ho tanti amici, ma fanno ricerca in campi diversi dal mio. Spesso non (3) _so_ di cosa parlare con loro.

MASSIMO Non (4) _sapevo_ che tu cercassi un amico con cui parlare di lavoro!

CATIA Beh... (5) _Conoscevo_ una persona con cui uscivo spesso, un linguista anche lui, ma alla fine mi ha confessato che era stanco di parlare di grammatica e sintassi con me e non (6) _sapeva_ come dirmelo. Pensi che sia un problema?

MASSIMO Non so... non (7) _ho conosciuto_ mai nessuno che amasse tanto parlare di lavoro... Possiamo provare ad andare da qualche parte e poi vediamo...

CATIA Ma certo! Che ne dici di andare in centro domani pomeriggio? (8) _Ho saputo_ che hai aperto un nuovo istituto di rieducazione linguistica!

2

Collegamenti Con un(a) compagno/a, costruisci le frasi unendo le parole delle colonne.

io	conoscere	parlare italiano
tu	non conoscere	una persona celebre
il mio professore di italiano	sapere	navigare su Internet
mio nonno	non sapere	accendere il computer
il/la mio/a compagno/a di stanza		un tecnico bravo ed economico
i miei genitori		chi ha inventato il telefono
io e il/la mio/a compagno/a		una persona creativa
?		?

3

Ricordi e novità I verbi **sapere** e **conoscere** all'imperfetto indicano ricordi, mentre al passato prossimo indicano azioni complete, eventi nuovi che sono entrati improvvisamente nella nostra vita. In coppia, fai domande al(la) tuo/a compagno/a.

I ricordi

- quali sono tre cose che sapeva fare quando aveva otto anni

- quali sono tre cose che non sapeva fare due anni fa e che sa fare adesso

- quali persone conosceva bene quando aveva cinque anni

- quali storie conosceva prima di cominciare a leggere

Le novità

- quali sono tre cose che ha saputo recentemente su alcuni suoi amici

- a che età ha saputo che Babbo Natale non esiste

- quante persone ha conosciuto questo semestre

- dove ha conosciuto il/la suo/a migliore amico/a

1 Have students continue the conversation between Catia and Massimo. Ask them to use **sapere** and **conoscere** both in the **presente** and in the **passato prossimo**.

2 Have students make statements of their own using the four verb possibilities.

Practice more at **vhlcentral.com**.

Sintesi

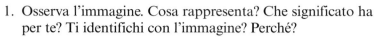

1

Parliamo In coppia, rispondete alle domande riflettendo sui vari punti.

1. Osserva l'immagine. Cosa rappresenta? Che significato ha per te? Ti identifichi con l'immagine? Perché?

2. Vai in vacanza per quindici giorni in un posto in cui non è possibile usare Internet: ti senti più nervoso/a o più tranquillo/a del solito? Perché?

3. Quando non sai come arrivare in un posto, che fai?

4. Devi depositare un assegno (*check*) di diecimila dollari. Preferisci usare il bancomat (*ATM*) o andare in banca? Perché?

5. È possibile che l'uomo moderno dipenda troppo dalla tecnologia. In che modo? Fai degli esempi.

6. Pensi che la tecnologia influenzi la capacità degli uomini di interagire tra di loro? In che modo?

7. Credi che gli uomini oggi comunichino meglio o peggio di cinquanta anni fa?

8. Grazie alla tecnologia (SMS, chat, e-mail) noi oggi scriviamo più spesso dei nostri genitori. Pensi che la tecnologia abbia migliorato le capacità linguistiche dei giovani di oggi?

Strategie per la comunicazione

- Per esprimere *either... or...* usa **o... o...**

  Quando esco durante il week-end porto con me **o** il cellulare **o** il portatile, ma non tutti e due.

- Per esprime *both... and...* usa **sia... che...** (più comune) o **sia... sia...** (meno comune e quindi più elegante).

  Io parlo con i miei amici **sia** in chat **che** al telefono.
  Io credo di avere bisogno **sia** del computer **sia** del cellulare.

  Per esprimere *neither... nor...* usa **né... né...**

  Quando sono in vacanza non voglio **né** computer **né** televisione.

2

Scriviamo Scegli uno di questi titoli e scrivi una composizione di una pagina.

- Credi che la tecnologia porti sempre a un progresso, o ci sono cose che la tecnologia non può sostituire? Usa questi oggetti come esempi.

  - macchina fotografica tradizionale/macchina digitale

  - carta/e-mail

  - un piccolo regalo consegnato di persona/una cartolina di auguri elettronica

- Immagina di avere gli oggetti elencati nella lista, ma di dovere rinunciare a tre di loro. Quali scegli? Che cambiamento ci sarà nella tua vita senza questi oggetti? Qual è l'oggetto più importante della lista per te?

| bancomat | computer da tavolo | lavastoviglie | macchina fotografica |
| bicicletta | computer portatile | macchina | televisore |

Preparazione
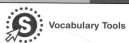 Vocabulary Tools

Vocabolario della lettura

l'allagamento *flooding*
l'alluvione *flood*
le calli *Venetian streets*
i campi *Venetian squares*
la marea *tide*

la passerella *footbridge*
i pollici *inches* (lit. *thumbs*)
prevedere *to predict*
il riscaldamento globale *global warming*
sommerso/a *submerged*

Vocabolario utile

i canali *canals*
l'impatto ambientale *environmental impact*
il traghetto *ferry*
il vaporetto *motor boat (used for public transportation in Venice)*

1

Il mare Completa il paragrafo con le parole nuove.

I navigatori esperti conoscono abbastanza astronomia per (1) _prevedere_ i movimenti marini. Per esempio, seguendo le fasi della luna possono determinare quando ci saranno le alte e le basse (2) _maree_. Anche i veneziani seguono attentamente il mare: la loro città è spesso vittima di (3) _allagamenti_ e corre il rischio di venire un giorno completamente (4) _sommersa_ dall'acqua. Venezia è costruita su una laguna. Per muoversi, i suoi abitanti devono usare ponti e mezzi di trasporto come i (5) _vaporetti/traghetti_. Se la marea è alta, bisogna installare delle (6) _passerelle_ per poter camminare sopra al livello dell'acqua.

2

Città particolari In coppia, rispondete a turno alle domande.

1. Qual è la città (antica o moderna) più diversa dalle altre, secondo te? Perché?
2. Descrivi questa città: quali sono le sue caratteristiche speciali?
3. Come vivono gli abitanti della città? Come hanno risolto i problemi particolari del loro ambiente?
4. C'è un modo innovativo per eliminare i problemi tipici della città come l'inquinamento o il traffico? Quale?
5. Conosci delle città famose la cui storia sia legata al mare o a qualche fiume? Quali sono i vantaggi o gli svantaggi di una simile posizione geografica?

3

Venezia In coppia, guardate la cartina a pagina 281 e rispondete alle domande.

1. Cosa sapete su Venezia? Perché è famosa?
2. Quali sono i punti d'entrata dell'acqua marina nella laguna?
3. Come si potrebbe fermare l'entrata dell'acqua per prevenire un allagamento?
4. Pensate che sia importante salvare Venezia prima che venga sommersa? Perché?

Point out that **vaporetti**, as the name suggests, used to be steam boats.

TEACHING OPTION Ask students to write sentences using the new vocabulary.

1 Show images of Venice, including bridges, **calli**, **vaporetti**, and **acqua alta** to the class to further illustrate the new vocabulary.

2 As a follow up question, ask: **Conosci delle città costruite sull'acqua? Quali?** Besides Venice, other cities partly/completely built on water and with an extensive system of canals are: Amsterdam (Netherlands), St. Petersburg (Russia), Miami and Ft. Lauderdale (FL), and the Gold Coast in Queensland (Australia).

3 Use a map to help students identify the main water inlets of **Lido**, **Malamocco** and **Chioggia**, and the different islands (**Murano**, **Burano**, etc.) as well as areas on land (e.g. **Mestre**) that form the city of Venice.

Nota CULTURALE

Considerata una delle più belle città del mondo, **Venezia** fa parte del «patrimonio dell'umanità» protetto dall'UNESCO. Le sue ricchezze artistiche e architettoniche rendono Venezia la città italiana con il più alto numero di turisti (secondo l'ISTAT). Anticamente, gli abitanti della terraferma si rifugiarono sulla laguna per sfuggire alle varie invasioni barbariche, soprattutto quelle dei Longobardi e degli Unni. Da piccola comunità, Venezia divenne in pochi secoli uno dei principali porti per il commercio con l'Oriente, e una repubblica che controllava gran parte del Mediterraneo orientale.

Venezia
sommersa o salvata?

Venezia, la romantica città-laguna con i suoi canali, ponti e gondole, è da sempre minacciata° di essere sommersa dall'Adriatico. La sua posizione geografica così unica, sospesa° tra terra e mare, la rende infatti vulnerabile agli allagamenti o all'«acqua alta». I veneziani chiamano così l'alta marea, che insieme al vento più forte in autunno e in primavera, provoca gravi allagamenti e alluvioni nella zona urbana. Anche indossando le galosce, camminare e attraversare le calli e i campi veneziani diventa difficile e in molti casi pericoloso. Durante gli allagamenti il passaggio è interdetto° anche alle barche: con l'acqua alta sopra ai 93 cm (36 pollici) non possono più passare sotto i ponti!

Gli scienziati prevedono che, a causa del riscaldamento globale, il livello del mare si alzerà notevolmente, aggravando perciò° i problemi di Venezia. La Serenissima (uno dei soprannomi della città) ha già fatto molto per proteggere il proprio patrimonio° artistico e storico dagli allagamenti e ha dei nuovi progetti per il futuro.

Quando il livello dell'acqua comincia a salire, la città usa uno speciale sistema di comunicazione per avvertire gli abitanti molto velocemente, permettendogli di prepararsi prima possibile. Nei periodi di allagamento più lunghi, viene installata una rete di passerelle, alte fino a 120 cm (47 pollici) che permettono di camminare nelle calli principali della città.

Venezia è stata storicamente una città di mercanti, navigatori e viaggiatori. Attualmente, per la minaccia dell'acqua, è diventata anche una città di innovatori.

Per risolvere il fenomeno dell'acqua alta, dal 2003 si sta realizzando il rivoluzionario progetto MO.S.E. (modulo sperimentale elettromeccanico), basato su un principio di Archimede. Delle barriere mobili bloccheranno l'accesso dell'acqua marina nella laguna alle tre bocche di porto del Lido, di Malamocco e di Chioggia. La necessità di questo progetto nacque nel 1966, dopo un'alluvione che sommerse la città di Venezia sotto 193 cm (74 pollici) d'acqua.

Il MO.S.E. è una soluzione molto innovativa, nata da ricerche, prove e analisi basate su modelli matematici e fisici. Proprio perché costituisce un nuovissimo sistema, gli ingegneri e gli architetti coinvolti nel progetto hanno considerato molte opzioni diverse in altre parti della laguna con barriere di vari tipi. Ma, dopo un'analisi comparativa, hanno deciso di implementare questa soluzione, l'unica che rende possibile l'isolamento temporaneo della laguna dal mare. Un prototipo costruito nel canale di Treporti, vicino alla bocca di porto Lido, ha permesso di osservare e perfezionare il funzionamento del sistema e dei materiali in condizioni reali.

I successi tecnologici nella protezione della città hanno però portato alla luce importanti questioni sull'equilibrio ambientale° della laguna e del mare Adriatico. Il progetto MO.S.E. è stato criticato dagli ambientalisti che si preoccupano dell'impatto delle barriere artificiali sull'ecosistema marino. Nonostante le proteste la costruzione continua e il sistema sarà completato entro il 2020. Riuscirà il MO.S.E. salvare Venezia dalle alluvioni? ■

threatened
suspended
forbidden
therefore
heritage
environmental

Laguna di Venezia
Venezia
Porto di Lido
Golfo di Venezia
Laguna di Venezia
Porto di Malamocco
Porto di Chioggia

Analisi

1 Ask students to correct the false statements.

Comprensione Indica se le affermazioni sono **vere** o **false**. Dopo, in coppia, correggete le affermazioni false.

Vero	Falso	
☑	☐	1. Venezia è costruita sulla laguna.
☑	☐	2. Le cause principali dell'acqua alta sono il mare e il vento.
☑	☐	3. Se il livello dell'acqua si alza troppo a Venezia le barche non possono passare sotto i ponti.
☑	☐	4. La Serenissima è uno dei soprannomi di Venezia.
☑	☐	5. Il riscaldamento globale potrebbe aggravare i problemi di Venezia.
☐	☑	6. Piazza San Marco non si allaga mai.
☐	☑	7. Il progetto MO.S.E. è stato abbandonato.
☐	☑	8. Gli ambientalisti appoggiano il progetto MO.S.E.
☐	☑	9. Gli allagamenti minacciano l'ecosistema marino.

2 Divide the class in two teams: **gli ingegneri** and **gli ambientalisti**. Give the teams a few minutes to come up with a list of points, then ask students to debate the two sides of the Venice issue.

Il fronte «NO MOSE» Leggete il paragrafo e rispondete alle domande.

> Nel corso degli anni i movimenti ambientalisti e alcune forze politiche hanno contestato° il progetto MO.S.E tanto per **l'impatto sull'equilibrio idrogeologico e il delicato ecosistema lagunare**, quanto per gli altissimi costi di costruzione e della futura manutenzione° del sistema. Nel corso della costruzione il fronte «NO MOSE» ha anche evidenziato alcuni difetti strutturali dell'opera e la possibile inefficacia del sistema a fronteggiare il previsto aumento del livello del mare. Si è richiesto di esaminare **proposte alternative con soluzioni meno costose e a minore impatto ambientale**. Diversi ricorsi° sono stati presentati a livello nazionale italiano e anche all'Unione Europea.
>
> **hanno contestato** *protested against* **manutenzione** *maintenance* **ricorsi** *legal appeals*

1. Quali sono le preoccupazioni degli ambientalisti? Perché sono contrari al progetto MO.S.E.?
2. Che cosa hanno evidenziato i critici del MO.S.E.?
3. A chi hanno presentato ricorso?

3 Discuss the similar problems of the bridge between **Messina** and **Reggio Calabria**—another long-term project riddled with environmental, political, and cultural debates. You might also want to discuss the Hoover Dam, the Suez Canal, the Golden Gate Bridge, and other engineering feats.

Opinioni In coppia, fatevi a turno queste domande.
1. È più importante l'ambiente o l'arte?
2. Si può trovare un compromesso per salvare sia Venezia che l'habitat marino?
3. Pensi che la tecnologia possa risolvere i problemi ambientali o solo causarne dei nuovi?
4. È giusto salvare le città antiche o ci sono dei progetti più importanti da risolvere con la tecnologia?
5. Quali sono i problemi globali che si potrebbero risolvere con la tecnologia?

 Practice more at **vhlcentral.com**.

Preparazione Vocabulary Tools

A proposito dell'autore

Emilio Salgari (Verona, 1862–1911) è l'autore italiano di libri d'avventura per ragazzi per eccellenza. Spesso ignorato dalla critica «seria», Salgari ha avuto un enorme impatto sulla cultura popolare del ventesimo secolo. I suoi numerosissimi romanzi hanno influenzato registi cinematografici come Sergio Leone e Federico Fellini; la serie televisiva tratta dal suo romanzo *Sandokan, la tigre della Malesia* è stata vista da oltre 80 milioni di telespettatori a settimana in tutta Europa. Salgari non ha mai viaggiato fuori d'Italia, ma i suoi romanzi hanno spaziato con la fantasia dal Far West americano, all'India, alle Bermude, all'Asia.

Vocabolario della lettura		Vocabolario utile
il bue (i buoi) *ox (oxen)*	**il pompiere** *firefighter*	**abituarsi** *to get used to*
coltivare *to grow*	**predire** *to predict*	**l'arma** *weapon*
esaurirsi *to run out*	**scomparire** *to disappear*	**l'energia pulita** *clean energy*
la mandria *herd*		**il/la marziano/a** *Martian*
il pascolo *pasture*	**stupire** *to surprise*	**fantascientifico/a** *futuristic*
	la truppa *troop*	**il ritrovato** *discovery*

1

Definizioni Trovate la definizione adatta a ogni parola.

c	1. il marziano	a. una scoperta scientifica o tecnica
f	2. la mandria	b. oggetto utilizzato per difendersi o per combattere
a	3. il ritrovato	c. un abitante di Marte
b	4. l'arma	d. fare una profezia
d	5. predire	e. non essere più disponibile (*available*)
e	6. esaurirsi	f. un gruppo di animali a quattro zampe

2

Preparazione In coppia, fatevi a turno le seguenti domande.

1. Ti piace la fantascienza? Perché sì o perché no?
2. Da bambino immaginavi mai di viaggiare nel futuro? Come te lo immaginavi?
3. Cosa volevi che esistesse nel futuro?
4. Conosci altri romanzi che parlano dei problemi e dei vantaggi del progresso, anche a livello politico?

3

Discussione Progresso o perdita di piaceri? In coppia, rispondete alle domande.

1. Secondo voi, il progresso è sempre una cosa positiva?
2. Quali sono dei ritrovati della tecnica che hanno migliorato la vita dell'uomo e quali la hanno peggiorata? Date almeno due esempi per ognuno.
3. La qualità della vita dipende dalla produttività o da quanto il proprio lavoro permette di godersi la vita?
4. Si vive per lavorare o si lavora per vivere?

 Practice more at **vhlcentral.com**.

2 For item 4, some examples are Orwell's *1984* and Huxley's *Brave New World*. Science fiction in general deals with utopias and dystopias as a way to comment on the current political situation. Like most science fiction writers, Salgari has a critical (and prophetic) vision of the future: he points out in his novel the dangers of pollution, speed, fast-paced life, and chemically synthesized food.

LE MERAVIGLIE DEL DUEMILA

(FRAMMENTO)

Emilio Salgari

Il dottor Holker aveva detto la verità°. Il brodo° era squisitissimo, ma nessuna pietanza° era di carne di bue, di maiale° e di montone°. Solo dei pesci: tutti gli altri piatti si componevano° di vegetali, fra cui molti che erano assolutamente sconosciuti° a Toby ed a Brandok.

In compenso il vino era così eccellente che né l'uno né l'altro mai ne avevano gustato° di simile.

«Signor Holker,» disse Brandok, che mangiava con un appetito invidiabile°, come se si fosse svegliato solo da dieci o dodici ore «siete vegetariano voi?»

«Perché mi fate questa domanda?» chiese il lontano pronipote° del dottore.

«Ai nostri tempi si parlava molto di vegetarianismo, specialmente in Germania ed in Inghilterra. Si vede che quella cucina ha fatto dei progressi.»

«Perché non trovate delle bistecche°?»

«Sì, e mi stupisce come i moderni americani abbiano rinunciato alle succose° bistecche ed ai sanguinanti° roast beef.»

«Sono piatti diventati un po' rari, oggi, mio caro, e pel° semplice motivo che i buoi ed i montoni sono quasi scomparsi.»

«Ah!»

«Ve ne stupite?»

«Molto.»

«Mio caro signore, la popolazione del globo in questi cento anni è enormemente cresciuta, e non esistono più praterie° per nutrire° le grandi mandrie che esistevano ai vostri tempi. Tutti i terreni disponibili sono ora coltivati intensivamente per chiedere al suolo° tutto quello che può dare. Se così non si fosse fatto, a quest'ora la popolazione del globo sarebbe alle prese° colla° fame. I grandi pascoli

truth
broth
dish/pork
ram
were made of 5

unknown

had tasted 10

enviable

15

great-grandson

20

steaks

succulent
raw (lit. bloody)

25
for the (lit. per il)

30

prairies
feed

35

soil

40 *would have to deal/ with the (lit. con la)*

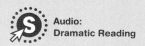

dell'Argentina e i nostri del Far-West non esistono più, ed i buoi ed i montoni a poco a poco sono quasi scomparsi, *non rendendo°* le praterie in proporzione all'estensione. *D'altronde°* non abbiamo più bisogno di carne al giorno d'oggi. I nostri chimici, in una semplice *pillola°* dal peso di qualche grammo, fanno concentrare tutti gli elementi che prima si *potevano ricavare°* da una buona *libbra°* di ottimo bue.»

not yielding
on the other hand 45

pill

could be found/
pound 50

«E l'agricoltura come va senza buoi?»

«*Anticaglie°*» disse Holker. «I nostri *campagnoli°* non fanno uso *che°* di macchine *mosse°* dall'elettricità.»

Old stuff
peasants/only use
moved 55

«*Sicché°* non vi sono più neanche cavalli?»

Therefore

«A che cosa potrebbero servire? Ce ne sono ancora alcuni, conservati più per curiosità che per altro.»

60

«E gli eserciti non ne fanno più uso?» chiese il dottor Toby. «Ai nostri tempi tutte le nazioni ne avevano dei reggimenti.»

«E che cosa ne facevano?» chiese Holker, con aria ironica.

65

«Se ne servivano nelle guerre.»

«Eserciti! *Cavalleria°*! Chi se ne ricorda ora?»

Cavalry

«Non vi sono più eserciti?» chiesero ad una voce Toby e Brandok.

70

«Da sessant'anni sono scomparsi, dopo che la guerra ha ucciso la guerra, l'ultima battaglia combattuta per mare e per terra fra le nazioni americane ed europee è stata terribile, *spaventevole°*, ed è costata milioni di vite umane, senza *vantaggio°* né per le une né per le altre *potenze°*. Il massacro è stato *tale°* da decidere le diverse nazioni del mondo ad abolire per sempre le guerre. E poi non sarebbero più possibili. Oggi noi *possediamo°* degli esplosivi capaci di far *saltare°* una città di qualche milione di abitanti; delle macchine che *sollevano°* delle montagne; possiamo *sprigionare°*, colla semplice *pressione°* del dito, una *scintilla°* elettrica trasmissibile a centinaia di *miglia°* di distanza e far *scoppiare°* qualsiasi deposito di *polvere°*. Una

frightening 75

advantage
powers/such

80

we have
that can blow up

lift 85

release
pressure
spark
miles/blow up
(gun) powder 90

guerra, al giorno *d'oggi°*, *segnerebbe°* la fine dell'umanità. La scienza ha vinto *ormai°* su tutto e su tutti.»

today/would mark

nowadays

«*Eppure°* quest'oggi, appena svegliato, mi fu comunicata dal vostro giornale una notizia che *smentirebbe°* quello che avete detto ora, mio caro nipote» disse Toby.

And yet

95

would run counter

«Ah sì! La distruzione di *Cadice°* da parte degli anarchici. *Bazzecole°*! Ormai questi *bricconi irrequieti°* saranno stati completamente distrutti dai pompieri di Malaga e di Alicante.»

Cadiz (Spanish city)
Trifles
100 *restless scoundrels*

«Dai pompieri?»

«Non abbiamo altre truppe al giorno d'oggi, e vi assicuro che sanno mantenere l'ordine in tutte le città e *sedare°* qualunque tumulto. Mettono in *batteria°* alcune pompe e *rovesciano°* sui *sediziosi°* torrenti d'acqua *elettrizzata°* al massimo *grado°*. Ogni *goccia°* *fulmina°*, e l'affare è *sbrigato°* presto.»

105

quell
they line up
they pour/rioters
electrified
110 *at the utmost level/*
drop/electrifies/
the deal is done

«Un mezzo un po' brutale, signor Holker, e anche inumano.»

«Se non si facesse così, le nazioni si *vedrebbero costrette°* ad avere delle truppe per mantenere l'ordine. E del *resto°* siamo in troppi in questo mondo, e se non troviamo il mezzo d'invadere qualche pianeta, non so come se la *caveranno°* i nostri pronipoti fra altri cent'anni, a meno che non tornino, come i nostri antenati, all'*antropofagia°*. La produzione della terra e dei mari non basterebbe a nutrire tutti, e questo è il *grave°* problema che *turba°* e preoccupa gli scienziati. Ah! se si potesse dar la *scalata°* a Marte che ha invece una popolazione così scarsa e tante terre ancora *incolte°*!»

115 *would be forced*
on the other hand

will manage

120

cannibalism

serious
125 *upsets*
climb

uncultivated

«Come lo sapete voi?» chiese Toby, facendo un gesto di stupore.

130

«Dagli stessi *martiani°*» rispose Holker.

Martians

«Dagli abitanti di quel pianeta!» esclamò Brandok.

«Ah, dimenticavo che ai vostri tempi non si era trovato ancora un mezzo per *mettersi in relazione°* con quei bravi martiani.»

135

to communicate

«*Scherzate°*?»

Are you kidding?

«Ve lo dico sul serio, mio caro signor Brandok.»

140

«Voi comunicate con loro?»

«Ho anzi un carissimo amico lassù che mi dà spesso sue notizie.»

«Come avete fatto a mettervi in 145 relazione coi martiani?»

«Ve lo dirò più tardi, quando avrete visitato la stazione elettrica di Brooklyn. Eh! Sono già° quarant'anni che siamo in relazione coi martiani.»

already

150 «È incredibile!» esclamò il dottor Toby. «Quali meravigliose scoperte avete fatto voi in questi cent'anni!»

«Molte che vi faranno assai° stupire, zio. Appena vi sarete completamente rimessi°, vi proporrò° di fare una corsa attraverso il mondo. In sette giorni saremo nuovamente a casa.»

a lot

rested/propose 155

«Il giro del mondo in 160 una settimana!...»

«È naturale che ciò vi stupisca. Ai vostri tempi s'impiegavano° quarantacinque o cinquanta giorni, se non m'inganno°.»

it took

I am not mistaken 165

«E ci sembrava d'aver raggiunto° la massima velocità.»

to have reached

«Delle tartarughe°» disse Holker, ridendo. «Poi faremo anche una corsa al 170 polo nord a visitare quella colonia.»

turtles

«Si va anche al polo, ora?»

«Bah!... è una semplice passeggiata.»

«Avete trovato il mezzo di distruggere° i ghiacci° che lo circondano°?...»

to destroy

ice/surround

not at all 175

«Niente affatto°, anzi io credo che le calotte di ghiaccio° che avvolgono° i due confini della terra siano diventate più enormi di quello che erano cent'anni fa; eppure noi abbiamo° trovato egualmente° 180 il mezzo di andare a visitarli e anche a popolarli°. Vi abbiamo relegati là...»

icecaps/surround

yet/in any case

to populate them

whistle/escaped

Un sibilo° acuto che sfuggì da un foro° aperto sopra una mensola° che si trovava in un angolo della stanza, 185 gl'interruppe la frase.

hole/shelf

«Ah, ecco la mia corrispondenza che arriva» disse Holker, alzandosi.

«Un'altra meraviglia!» esclamarono Toby e Brandok alzandosi.

190 «Una cosa semplicissima» rispose

Holker. «Guardate, amici miei.»

Premette° un bottone al disotto° d'un quadro che rappresentava una battaglia navale. La figura scomparve, innalzandosi entro due scanalature°, e 195 lasciando un vano° d'un mezzo metro quadrato°. Dentro v'era° un cilindro di metallo coperto di numeri segnati° in nero, lungo sessanta o settanta centimetri, con una circonferenza di 200 trenta o quaranta.

He pushed/underneath

grooves

compartment

square/c'era

marked

«Il mio numero d'abbonamento° postale è il 1987» disse Holker. «Eccolo qui, e in un piccolo scompartimento° sono state collocate° le mie 205 lettere.»

subscription

compartment

have been placed

Mise un dito sul numero, s'aprì uno sportellino° e trasse° la sua corrispondenza, poi fece ridiscendere° il quadro e 210 premette un altro bottone.

flap/extracted

lowered

«Ecco il cilindro ripartito°» disse. «Va a distribuire la corrispondenza agli inquilini° della casa.»

sent again

tenants

215

«Come è giunto° qui quel cilindro?» chiese Brandok.

has arrived

«Per mezzo d'un tubo comunicante° coll'ufficio postale più vicino, e rimorchiato° da una piccola macchina elettrica.» 220

communicating

towed

«E come si ferma?»

«Dietro il quadro vi è uno strumento destinato ad interrompere la corrente elettrica. Appena il cilindro vi passa sopra, si ferma e non riparte se io prima non riattivo 225 la corrente premendo quel bottone.»

«Vi è un cilindro per ogni casa?»

«Sì, signor Brandok; devo avvertirvi che le abitazioni moderne hanno venti o venticinque piani e che contengono dalle 230 cinquecento alle mille famiglie.»

«La popolazione d'uno dei nostri antichi sobborghi°» disse il dottore. «Non ci sono dunque° più case piccole?»

suburbs

therefore

«Il terreno è troppo prezioso oggidì°, 235 e quel lusso° è stato bandito°. Non si può sottrarre° spazio all'agricoltura. Ma comincia a far buio°; sarebbe tempo d'illuminare° il mio salotto. Ai vostri tempi che cosa si accendeva alla sera?» 240

nowadays

luxury/has been banned

take away

to get dark

light up

«Quali meravigliose scoperte avete fatto voi in questi cent'anni!»

«Gas, petrolio, luce elettrica» disse Brandok.

«Povera gente» disse Holker. «E come doveva costar cara allora l'illuminazione!»

245 «Certo, signor Holker» disse Brandok. «Ora invece?»

free «Abbiamo quasi gratis° la luce ed il calore.»

hung/iron pole Dal soffitto pendeva° un'asta di ferro°
ball 250 che finiva in una palla°, composta d'un metallo azzurro.

Il signor Holker l'aprì facendola
soon scorrere sopra l'asta e tosto° una luce brillante, simile a quella che mandavano
255 un tempo le lampade elettriche, si
emanated/flooding sprigionò°, inondando° il salotto.

Ciò che la produceva era una
little ball/barely pallottolina° appena° visibile che si
stuck trovava infissa° sotto la sfera, e la luce che
transmitted/gave off 260 tramandava°, espandeva° un dolce calore assai superiore a quello del gas.

«Che cos'è?» chiesero ad una voce Brandok e Toby.

small piece «Un semplice pezzetto° di radium»
265 rispose Holker.

«Il radium!» esclamarono [...]

«Si conosceva ai vostri tempi?»

«L'avevano già scoperto» rispose Toby. «Ma non si usava ancora a causa
270 dell'enorme suo costo. Un grammo non si poteva avere a meno di tre o quattromila lire. E poi non s'era potuto trovare ancora il modo di applicarlo, come avete fatto ora voi. Tutti però gli predicevano un
275 grande avvenire.»

«Quello che non hanno potuto fare i chimici del 1900 l'hanno fatto quelli del Duemila» disse Holker. «Quel pezzetto lì non vale che un dollaro e brucia° sempre,
burns
280 senza mai consumarsi. È il fuoco eterno.»

«Meraviglioso metallo!...»

«Sì, meraviglioso, perché oltre a darci la
has dethroned luce, ci dà anche il calore. Ha detronizzato°
coal il carbon fossile°, la luce elettrica, il gas, il
stoves/chimneys 285 petrolio, le stufe° ed i camini°.»

«Sicché anche le vie sono illuminate con lampade a radium?» chiese Toby.

plants/factories «E anche gli stabilimenti°, le officine° e così via.»

«E nelle miniere° di carbone non si 290 *mines* lavora più?»

«A che cosa servirebbe il carbone? Poi cominciavano già ad esaurirsi.»

«La forza necessaria per far agire° *work* le macchine degli stabilimenti, chi ve la 295 dà ora?»

«L'elettricità trasportata ormai a distanze enormi. Le nostre cascate° del *falls* Niagara, per esempio, fanno lavorare delle macchine che si trovano a mille miglia° 300 *miles* di distanza. Se noi volessimo, potremmo dare di quelle forze° anche all'Europa, *those resources* mandandole attraverso l'Atlantico. Ma anche laggiù hanno costruito° delle *have built* cascate sui loro fiumi e non hanno più 305 bisogno di noi.»

«Amico James,» disse Toby «ti penti° *are you sorry* d'aver dormito cent'anni per poter vedere le meraviglie del Duemila?»

«Oh no!» esclamò vivamente il giovane. 310

«Credevi di veder il mondo così progredito°?» *advanced*

«Non mi aspettavo tanto.»

«E il tuo spleen?»

«Non lo provo più, tuttavia... non 315 senti nulla tu?»

«Sì, un'agitazione° strana, un'irritazione *anxiety* inesplicabile del sistema nervoso» disse Toby. «Mi sembra che i muscoli ballino sotto la mia pelle.» 320

«Anche a me» disse Brandok.

«Sapete da che cosa deriva?» chiese Holker.

«Non saprei indovinarlo°» rispose Toby. *guess it*

«Dall'immensa tensione elettrica che 325 regna° ormai in tutte le città del mondo *reigns* ed a cui voi non siete ancora abituati. Cent'anni fa l'elettricità non aveva ancora raggiunto° un grande sviluppo, *had not reached yet* mentre ora l'atmosfera ed il suolo ne 330 sono saturi. [...] E per oggi basta. Andate a riposare e domani mattina faremo una corsa attraverso Nuova York sul mio Condor.»

«È un'automobile?» chiese Brandok. 335

«Sì, ma di nuovo genere°» rispose *kind* Holker, con un sorriso. «Cominceremo così il nostro viaggio attraverso il mondo.» ■

Analisi

1

Invenzioni Scegli quale invenzione è presente nella lettura.

		SÌ	NO			SÌ	NO
1.	pillole di vitamine e proteine	☑	☐	7. truppe antropofaghe (*cannibalistic*)		☐	☑
2.	macchine elettriche per coltivare i campi	☑	☐	8. mezzi di comunicazione con Marte		☑	☐
3.	buoi meccanici	☐	☑	9. oro (*gold*) per illuminare		☐	☑
4.	eserciti virtuali	☐	☑	10. sistema postale ultra-rapido		☑	☐
5.	pillole per essere intelligenti	☐	☑	11. edifici molto alti		☑	☐
6.	acqua fulminante	☑	☐	12. cascate radioattive		☐	☑

2

Comprensione Scegli una risposta e poi, in coppia, dite perché le altre sono sbagliate.

1. Toby e Brandok sono due _____.
   a. personaggi dell'anno 2003   ⓑ personaggi dell'anno 1903
   c. carnivori che non apprezzano la verdura   d. marziani

2. Le praterie non esistono perché _____.
   a. tutti i terreni sono coltivati con soia   b. non ci sono più mandrie di buoi
   c. i buoi hanno mangiato i montoni   ⓓ ci sono troppe persone sulla Terra

3. Le guerre non ci sono più perché _____.
   a. i cavalli sono morti   b. gli eserciti hanno sterminato le persone
   ⓒ una guerra ora ucciderebbe tutti   d. gli esplosivi sono nascosti nelle montagne

4. I pompieri usano l'acqua per _____.
   a. spegnere gli incendi   ⓑ dare la scossa (*electrify*) alle persone
   c. diluire il vino   d. lavarsi

5. Il giro del mondo si può fare _____.
   ⓐ in una settimana   b. in quarantacinque giorni
   c. solo con gli amici   d. solo passando da un polo

6. La posta arriva _____.
   a. portata dal postino   b. con un cavallo molto veloce
   ⓒ elettronicamente attraverso dei tubi   d. in un cilindro di plastica

3

Profezie Indica quali elementi della storia di Salgari si sono avverati (*came true*) e poi con un(a) compagno/a discuti in che modo l'autore è profetico. Cosa oggi è esattamente come lo descrive l'autore (A), cosa esiste in maniera un po' diversa (B) e cosa non esiste o non è successo (C)? È meglio o peggio quello che immagina Salgari? Dai esempi concreti.

Some answers will vary.

		A	B	C			A	B	C
1.	estinzione di specie animali	☑	☐	☐	10. viaggi nello spazio		☑	☐	☐
2.	vegetarianismo	☐	☑	☐	11. comunicazione con i marziani		☐	☐	☑
3.	edifici sempre più alti	☑	☐	☐	12. macchine volanti		☑	☐	☐
4.	mono-coltivazioni agricole	☐	☑	☐	13. energie alternative		☑	☐	☐
5.	assenza (*absence*) di eserciti	☐	☐	☑	14. energia pulita		☐	☐	☑
6.	assenza di guerre	☐	☐	☑	15. mezzi di trasporto iper-veloci		☐	☑	☐
7.	forze dell'ordine molto repressive	☑	☐	☐	16. aumento dei ghiacci polari		☐	☐	☑
8.	una guerra per l'estinzione dell'uomo	☐	☑	☐	17. posta veloce		☐	☑	☐
9.	armi troppo potenti	☑	☐	☐	18. inquinamento atmosferico		☑	☐	☐

4

Viaggi nel tempo In coppia, fatevi le seguenti domande.

1. Se potessi viaggiare nel tempo, dove vorresti andare e perché?

2. Con chi vorresti viaggiare nel tempo? Preferiresti avere un(a) compagno/a di viaggio o andare da solo/a? Perché?

3. Se viaggiassi nel futuro, quali avanzamenti della scienza, della medicina, e della tecnica vorresti trovare? Elencane almeno due.

4. Se viaggiassi nel futuro, cosa vorresti non trovare più?

5. Se una guerra apocalittica distruggesse quasi tutto, cosa vorresti salvare?

5

Risveglio tra un secolo In piccoli gruppi, immaginate di dormire per cento anni: come sarà il ventiduesimo secolo? Fate una lista di almeno sei invenzioni, scoperte, o disastri che ci saranno in un futuro non troppo lontano ma che comunque non appartiene alla vostra vita attuale.

Il ventiduesimo secolo: invenzioni, scoperte e disastri

5 Ask students to also explain how they traveled into the future. At the end, you could poll groups and see if they had similar ideas. It could be potions, herbs, cryogenics, etc.

6

Reazioni In piccoli gruppi, rispondete alle seguenti domande e pensate a cosa vuol dire viaggiare nel tempo.

1. Quali sono le implicazioni etiche ed emotive di un viaggio come quello descritto nel romanzo?

2. Il modo di comportarsi è sempre lo stesso attraverso i secoli?

3. Pensate a un viaggio che comincia nell'antica Roma (o nel medioevo) e che arriva al ventiduesimo secolo in tre o quattro tappe (*stages*). Come cambia il mondo?

4. Chi viaggia può mantenere un comportamento neutrale? Pensate, per esempio, a come sarebbe sconvolto (*upset*) un uomo del medioevo dall'assenza di meditazione e di vita religiosa o dalla presenza di donne sul posto di lavoro.

7

Tema Sei uno dei due personaggi del libro (Toby o Brandok): scrivi due paragrafi e descrivi com'è il *Condor*.

- Che tipo di veicolo è? Di che colore?

- A che velocità va? Quanti posti ha? Sono posti tradizionali?

- Come si muove nel traffico?

Practice more at
vhlcentral.com.

Pratica

Confutazioni parziali

Nella **Lezione 6** (p. 246) abbiamo fatto riferimento alla confutazione come strategia argomentativa. È possibile però, che il disaccordo con il punto di vista opposto sia solo parziale.

Una strategia molto comune nei saggi argomentativi consiste nel non accettare l'idea opposta facendo allo stesso tempo alcune concessioni, vale a dire riconoscere la validità di alcuni aspetti del punto di vista contrario.

Esistono alcuni elementi verbali che indicano l'utilizzo di questa strategia. Tra questi ricordiamo le congiunzioni: **sebbene**, **nonostante**, **senza dubbio**, **malgrado**, **e così via**.

Modello

- Sebbene sia d'accordo con il punto di vista degli ambientalisti sui rischi ambientali del progetto MO.S.E., credo che la loro critica sia eccessiva. In primo luogo…
- Lo scrittore esprime un punto di vista affascinante sul mondo del futuro, ma poco obiettivo perché…

1 **Preparazione** A coppie, rileggete le affermazioni dell'**Attività 4, p. 251**. Scrivete delle confutazioni parziali usando alcune delle congiunzioni suggerite.

2 **Saggio** Scegli uno di questi argomenti e scrivi un saggio.

- Il saggio deve far riferimento ad almeno due dei quattro brani studiati in questa lezione o nelle precedenti lezioni e contenuti in **Cortometraggio**, **Immagina**, **Cultura** e **Letteratura**.
- Il tuo saggio deve contenere almeno due confutazioni parziali di idee contrarie.
- Il saggio deve essere lungo almeno due pagine.

> Esiste, secondo te, una soglia (*threshold*) etica che la scienza e la tecnologia non devono oltrepassare?

> Al giorno d'oggi, la tecnologia serve all'uomo o l'uomo è servo della tecnologia?

> Con tutte le scoperte scientifiche e con l'uomo esploratore dell'universo, c'è ancora spazio per la fantasia?

> Nonostante il cortometraggio dimostri cosa può succedere quando la tecnologia viene a mancare, non possiamo dimenticare gli aspetti positivi del progresso tecnologico…

INSTRUCTIONAL RESOURCES
Task-based activities

Il progresso e la ricerca

 Vocabulary Tools

Gli scienziati

l'**astronauta** *astronaut*
l'**astronomo/a** *astronomer*
il/la **biologo/a** *biologist*
il/la **(bio)chimico/a** *(bio)chemist*
il/la **fisico/a (nucleare)**
  (nuclear) physicist
il/la **geologo/a** *geologist*
il/la **matematico/a** *mathematician*
il/la **ricercatore/**
  ricercatrice *researcher*
lo/la **zoologo/a** *zoologist*

La ricerca scientifica

il **brevetto** *patent*
il **DNA** *DNA*
l'**esperimento** *experiment*
il **gene** *gene*
la **ricerca** *research*
la **scoperta** *discovery*
lo **scopo** *aim; goal*
lo **sviluppo** *development*
il **vaccino** *vaccine*

dimostrare *to prove*
guarire (-isc-) *to cure; to heal*

notevole *remarkable*

La tecnologia

la **banca dati** *database*
il **codice** *code*
il **dispositivo** *device*
l'**elettronica** *electronics*
l'**informatica** *computer science*
l'**ingegneria** *engineering*
l'**intelligenza artificiale**
  artificial intelligence (A.I.)
la **nanotecnologia** *nanotechnology*
la **rete (senza fili)**
  (wireless) network
la **robotica** *robotics*
il **segnale (analogico/digitale)**
  (analog/digital) signal
le **telecomunicazioni**
  telecommunications
la **trasmissione** *broadcast*

Il mondo digitale

la **chiavetta USB** *flash drive*
la **chiocciola** *@ symbol*
il **computer (da tavolo/portatile)**
  (desktop/laptop) computer
l'**indirizzo e-mail** *e-mail address*
il **lettore CD/DVD/MP3**
  CD/DVD/MP3 player
il **libro elettronico** *e-book*
l'**SMS (m.)** *text message*

aggiornare *to update*
allegare *to attach*
cancellare *to erase*
copiare *to copy*
incollare *to paste*
masterizzare *to burn*
navigare su Internet/sulla rete
  to browse/to surf the Internet/Web
salvare *to save*
scaricare *to download*

Problemi e sfide

la **cellula staminale** *stem cell*
il **codice deontologico** *code of
  conduct*
il **furto d'identità** *identity theft*
l'**inquinamento** *pollution*
la **sfida** *challenge*

clonare *to clone*
riciclare *to recycle*

controverso/a *controversial*
etico/a *ethical*
giusto/a *right*
(im)morale *(un)ethical*
sbagliato/a *wrong*

Cortometraggio

l'**angoscia** *anguish*
l'**attesa** *wait*
il/la **benzinaio/a** *gas station
  attendant*
il **distributore**
  automatico *beverage dispenser*
la **gratitudine** *gratitude*
l'**intervento** *operation*
la **preoccupazione** *worry*

lo **sbadiglio** *yawn*
lo **scoraggiamento** *discouragement*

dividere *to share*
mettere sotto *to run over*
sgranchirsi *to stretch out*
soffrire *to suffer*

bollente *boiling hot*

Cultura

l'**allagamento** *flooding*
l'**alluvione** *flood*
le **calli** *Venetian streets*
i **campi** *Venetian squares*
i **canali** *canals*
l'**impatto ambientale**
  environmental impact
la **marea** *tide*
la **passerella** *footbridge*
i **pollici** *inches* (lit. *thumbs*)
il **riscaldamento globale**
  global warming
il **traghetto** *ferry*
il **vaporetto** *motor boat (used for
  public transportation in Venice)*

prevedere *to predict*

sommerso/a *submerged*

Letteratura

l'**arma** *weapon*
il **bue (i buoi)** *ox (oxen)*
l'**energia pulita** *clean energy*
la **mandria** *herd*
il/la **marziano/a** *Martian*
il **pascolo** *pasture, grazing land*
il **pompiere** *fireman*
il **ritrovato** *discovery*
la **truppa** *troop*

abituarsi *to get used to*
coltivare *to grow*
esaurirsi *to run out*
predire *to predict*
scomparire *to disappear*
stupire *to surprise*

fantascientifico/a *futuristic*

Le ricchezze culturali e storiche

Viviamo in una società che guarda costantemente verso il futuro e il progresso in tutti i campi del sapere. Ma ci fermiamo mai a riflettere su come tutto questo sia possibile? Guardiamo mai indietro alla storia, alle donne e agli uomini che con fatica (*hard work*) e spesso controcorrente hanno fatto compiere (*complete*) passi da gigante all'umanità? Facciamo abbastanza per preservare la loro memoria e l'eredità che ci hanno lasciato? Che ruolo ha la storia nella nostra vita quotidiana? I grandi del passato ci ispirano o ci intimidiscono? Ora la storia siamo noi: che passato lasceremo alle generazioni future?

299

324

Destinazione: EMILIA-ROMAGNA

PREVIEW Have groups of students discuss the following question from the text on the preceding page: **Facciamo abbastanza per preservare la loro memoria e l'eredità che ci hanno lasciato?** Have them think of important cultural and historical figures from the second half of the 20th century and suggest what they would do to preserve their memory for posterity.

Le ricchezze culturali e storiche

Le arti e la storia  Vocabulary Tools

La storia

la battaglia *battle*
la civiltà *civilization*
il decennio *decade*
l'età *age; era*
l'imperatore/imperatrice *emperor/empress*
il re/la regina *king/queen*
il regime *regime*

il regno *kingdom*
la schiavitù *slavery*
il secolo *century*

abitare *to inhabit*
abolire *to abolish*
arrendersi *to surrender*
colonizzare *to colonize*
conquistare *to conquer*
dirigere *to lead*
espellere *to expel*
invadere *to invade*
liberare *to liberate*
opprimere *to oppress*
rovesciare *to overthrow*
sconfiggere *to defeat*
stabilirsi *to settle*

democratico/a *democratic*
fascista *fascist*
monarchico/a *monarchic*
(prei)storico/a *(pre)historic*

a.C. (avanti Cristo) *BC*
d.C. (dopo Cristo) *AD*

La letteratura

la biografia *biography*
il diritto d'autore *copyright*
il genere *genre*
il giallo *thriller*
il narratore *narrator*
la novella *short novel*
il personaggio *character*
la poesia *poetry*
la prosa *prose*
la rima *rhyme*
il romanzo *novel*
la strofa *stanza*
la trama *plot*
il verso *line (of poetry)*

censurare *to censor*

svolgersi *to take place*

classico/a *classic*
oggettivo/a *objective*
premiato/a *award-winning*
realistico/a *realistic*
satirico/a *satirical*
soggettivo/a *subjective*
tragico/a *tragic*
umoristico/a *humorous*

SINONIMI E CONTRARI
svolgersi ⟷ avere luogo
opprimere ⟷ perseguitare

Point out that the noun **obiettivo** means *aim* or *target*, while **oggettivo** is an impartial judgement.

Point out that **pittura** is the activity or the material, while **dipinto** is the work of art.

INSTRUCTIONAL RESOURCES
Audioscripts, Answer Keys, Lab MP3s
SAM/WebSAM: WB, LM

L'arte

l'acquerello *watercolor*
l'autoritratto *self-portrait*
le belle arti *fine arts*
il dipinto *painting*
la natura morta *still life*

l'opera *work (of art); opera*
l'orchestra sinfonica/da camera *symphony/chamber orchestra*
il pennello *paintbrush*
la pittura *paint; painting*
la pittura a olio/pastello *oil/pastel painting*
il quadro *painting; picture*
la scultura *sculpture*

dipingere *to paint*
scolpire *to sculpt*

d'avanguardia *avant-garde*
estetico/a *aesthetic*

Gli artisti

l'artigiano/a *artisan*
il/la drammaturgo/a *playwright*

il pittore/la pittrice *painter*
il/la saggista *essayist*
lo scultore/la scultrice *sculptor*

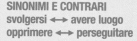

Pratica e comunicazione

1 **Il regno di Romolo** Completa il brano con le parole giuste.

Secondo la leggenda, la (1) ___civiltà___ (età / civiltà) romana risale (*dates back*) all'VIII (2) ___secolo___ (secolo / decennio) a.C. con la fondazione di Roma avvenuta il 21 aprile 753 (3) ___a.C.___ (a.C. / d.C.). Romolo e Remo (4) ___si stabilirono___ (si stabilirono / invasero) vicino al fiume Tevere e fondarono una città. Romolo uccise Remo, chiamò la città Roma e ne divenne il primo (5) ___re___ (monarchico / re). Poiché nella città (6) ___abitavano___ (abitavano / colonizzavano) solo uomini, i romani combatterono una (7) ___battaglia___ (schiavitù / battaglia) con i vicini Sabini per rapire (*abduct*) le loro donne. Il (8) ___regno___ (secolo / regno) di Romolo durò 37 anni, quasi 4 (9) ___decenni___ (decenni / secoli), durante i quali (10) ___conquistò___ (conquistò / abitò) i territori vicini.

2 **Il fascismo** Completa la conversazione tra nonno e nipote con le parole della lista.

abolirono	dirigeva	liberarono	regime
democratica	invasero	opprimeva	si arrese

NIPOTE Nonno, cosa ricordi del (1) ___regime___ fascista?

NONNO Ricordo tante cose, in particolare che Benito Mussolini (2) ___dirigeva___ il governo da dittatore.

NIPOTE Che cosa succedeva a chi era contrario?

NONNO Beh, il governo fascista (3) ___opprimeva___ ogni tipo di opposizione.

NIPOTE L'Italia combatté durante la seconda guerra mondiale, ma quando (4) ___si arrese___?

NONNO Il 3 settembre 1943, dopo che ebbe firmato l'armistizio.

NIPOTE E poi che successe?

NONNO I tedeschi (5) ___invasero___ la penisola.

NIPOTE Fino a quando durò l'occupazione tedesca?

NONNO Il 25 aprile 1945 gli Alleati e le formazioni partigiane (6) ___liberarono___ l'Italia.

NIPOTE Cosa successe dopo la liberazione?

NONNO Con un referendum popolare gli italiani (7) ___abolirono___ la monarchia e il 2 giugno 1946 nacque la repubblica (8) ___democratica___ italiana.

3 **L'arte** Pensate alla vostra opera d'arte preferita e a turno descrivetela con almeno quattro frasi. Tenete in considerazione l'autore, lo stile e la tecnica usata.

Modello La mia opera d'arte preferita è la Pietà di Michelangelo. È una scultura di marmo…

4 **Libri** In piccoli gruppi, parlate dell'ultimo libro che avete letto. Considerate queste domande.

1. Qual è il titolo?
2. Chi è l'autore?
3. Che genere di libro è?
4. Dove e quando si svolge la storia?
5. Qual è la trama?
6. Chi è il narratore?
7. Chi sono i personaggi principali?
8. Consiglieresti questo libro? Perché?

3 For an expansion activity, ask students to research and present an Italian work of art of their choice to the class.

Practice more at **vhlcentral.com**.

Preparazione  Vocabulary Tools

Vocabolario del cortometraggio	Vocabolario utile
fucilare *to execute*	**il/la connazionale** *compatriot*
il ricevimento *reception*	**la crostata** *pie*
la sartoria *tailor's shop*	**incinta** *pregnant*
la Sua/vostra signora (*form.*) *your wife*	**ingrassare** *to gain weight*
la spia *spy*	**l'invito** *invitation*
la stoffa *fabric*	**il metro** *tape measure*
il taglio *cut*	**il/la partigiano/a** *partisan*
tedesco/a *German*	**la Resistenza** *The Resistance*

ESPRESSIONI

Che ci fai qui? *What are you doing here?*
Come mi sta? *How does it look (on me)?*
È la morte sua. *It's the perfect pairing.*
il mi babbo *my father*
Mi raccomando. *Make sure that you do it.*

1

Vero o Falso? Decidi se la frase è **vera** o **falsa**.

1. Quando si è incinta, si ingrassa. *Vero.*
2. Per andare a un ricevimento esclusivo c'è bisogno di un invito. *Vero.*
3. Si può fucilare qualcuno con un coltello. *Falso.*
4. Chi dice «mi raccomando» vuole ottenere una raccomandazione. *Falso.*
5. La marmellata sulla crostata è la morte sua. *Vero.*
6. I partigiani hanno combattuto nella Resistenza. *Vero.*
7. Per farmi fare un vestito su misura non ho bisogno di andare in sartoria. *Falso.*
8. Babbo è un altro modo per dire papà. *Vero.*

2

Lessico Completa ogni frase con la parola o l'espressione appropriata.

1. _____Mi raccomando_____, copriti bene e non prendere freddo in montagna.
2. Una _____spia_____ tradisce i suoi connazionali.
3. Se vuole, può portare _____la Sua signora_____ al ricevimento.
4. Secondo te, _____come mi sta_____ questo vestito? Preferisci l'altro?
5. Per prendere le misure per fare un vestito ci vuole _____un metro_____.
6. In Germania si parla _____tedesco_____.

3

Inchiesta In coppia contrastate gli elementi a favore (**Pro**) della collaborazione con le forze di occupazione durante una guerra e gli elementi negativi (**Contro**). Riempite la lista e poi discutete con tutta la classe le opinioni contrastanti.

Pro	Contro

4

Espansione In gruppi di tre o quattro discutete i seguenti temi.

1. Ti offriresti volontario nell'esercito del tuo paese? Perché?
2. C'è una differenza tra quello che può fare un uomo e quello che può fare una donna in guerra?
3. Sai di guerre che si stanno svolgendo ora? Dove?
4. Se potessi aiutare una causa in un modo tangibile, cosa faresti?
5. Perderesti il rispetto per un(a) amico/a o familiare che si unisse al nemico per salvarsi? Perché?

5

Descriviamo Come sono i personaggi di questo film?

A. In piccoli gruppi, guardate le immagini del film e descrivete l'aspetto fisico e la personalità dei personaggi. Poi immaginate che ruolo hanno nel film. Descrivete anche l'ambiente.

B. Dalle foto, qual è lo stato sociale di questi personaggi? A che tempi è ambientato il cortometraggio? Immaginate la storia associata a queste quattro immagini.

6

Intervista In coppia, fatevi a turno le seguenti domande.

1. Sei mai stato/a a un ricevimento formale? Quando?
2. Ti faresti fare un vestito su misura? Per quale occasione?
3. Hai mai visto un film di guerra (presente, passata o futuristica)? È un genere di film che ti piace? Perché sì o perché no?

3 Ask: **Preferiresti avere un ruolo di comando o seguire ordini? Preferiresti fare qualcosa di pratico o partecipare a strategie di guerra?**

4 Ask students to come up with sci-fi scenarios for wars in the future. Ask how they would contribute to the war effort and how they think they would behave in ethically charged situations like cooperating with the enemy.

5 Ask students to look at the images and think of at least three words they do not know per image, then provide the corresponding Italian terms (e.g., **macchina da cucire, lampadina, ritratto, salone**).

5 As an expansion activity, after students have watched the film and completed the **Preparazione** activities, have them compare their predictions with what actually happens in the film.

 Practice more at **vhlcentral.com.**

Video

TEACHING OPTION Have students read the Nota culturale, then ask them what they know about World War II. Explain that Italy had a king, Vittorio Emanuele III, and also a Prime Minister, Benito Mussolini, who exercised more power than the king. In 1946 Italy abolished the monarchy altogether.

Trama *Paolino è un sarto del paesino di San Miniato, in Toscana, durante l'occupazione tedesca nel 1944. Collabora coi tedeschi ed è prediletto dall'ufficiale Rudolf Schmidt, che gli chiede di fargli un vestito per un ricevimento ufficiale.*

SCHMIDT Servono° ancora? Mi vede ingrassato?
PAOLINO No, no, no, no. Voi siete in grande forma. È che io… il vestito sarà perfetto, voglio essere molto preciso.
SCHMIDT Stavo scherzando. Fate pure°.

PAOLINO E questo?
LUCIA E questo è il futuro, Paolino. E tu? Marisa come sta?
PAOLINO Tutti bene, grazie a Dio.

SCHMIDT È il sarto dei tedeschi. I pantaloni sono perfetti.
PAOLINO Grazie, ufficiale, ma aspettate di indossare° la giacca. Vedrete…

PAOLINO Nonostante° quello che si sente su questi tedeschi almeno Schmidt mi dà il lavoro.
MARISA Il sarto dei tedeschi….
PAOLINO Oh, Marisa, se non era per lui, noi neanche si mangiava.
MARISA Quelli ammazzano la gente per strada.

SCHMIDT La più insospettabile° delle traditrici: una lavandaia°. Bene, bene. Stai tranquilla, ti restano ancora un po' di ore da vivere. Prima, però, mi devi raccontare un po' di cose.

SCHMIDT Allora, Paolino, come mi sta?
PAOLINO Avevate proprio ragione… è la morte Sua°.

EXPANSION Ask students to research some of the topics mentioned in the **Nota Culturale**, particularly one of the following: **l'armistizio**, **Badoglio** e **Vittorio Emanuele III**, **Mussolini**, **la Repubblica di Salò**, **l'avanzata alleata**, **la Liberazione**, **il movimento partigiano**.

Servono *Are they needed* **Fate pure** *Go ahead* **Nonostante** *Notwithstanding* **insospettabile** *innocent-looking* **lavandaia** *washerwoman* **indossare** *to wear* **è la morte Sua** *it's the perfect pairing (lit., it's your death)*

Nota CULTURALE

L'occupazione tedesca

Durante la seconda guerra mondiale, l'Italia ha fatto parte dell'Asse° Roma-Tokio-Berlino fino al settembre 1943, quando è stato firmato in Sicilia l'armistizio con le forze alleate. La notizia è stata data alla radio, prima dal generale Eisenhower, comandante in capo delle forze alleate, e poi dal maresciallo Pietro Badoglio, capo del governo italiano nominato dal re Vittorio Emanuele III, dopo la caduta di Mussolini. Gli alleati hanno occupato il sud d'Italia mentre i tedeschi hanno occupato il nord. I tedeschi hanno imposto Mussolini a capo della Repubblica Sociale Italiana, detta anche «Repubblica di Salò.» L'avanzata° delle forze Alleate verso il nord ha preso vari mesi, fino alla Liberazione il 25 aprile 1945. Senza l'aiuto dei Partigiani gli Alleati non sarebbero riusciti a sconfiggere° i tedeschi.

Asse *Axis* **avanzata** *advance* **sconfiggere** *to defeat*

Sullo SCHERMO

Indica l'ordine delle seguenti scene.

_5_ **a.** Paolino va a trovare Mauro tra i partigiani.

_2_ **b.** Paolino si rende conto che Lucia è incinta.

_1_ **c.** L'ufficiale Schmidt chiede a Paolino di fargli un vestito.

_3_ **d.** Marisa disprezza (*despises*) la posizione politica del marito.

_6_ **e.** L'ufficiale Schmidt è contento del suo vestito nuovo ma avrà una sorpresa.

_4_ **f.** Paolino e sua moglie vedono l'esecuzione di Lucia.

Analisi

1

Comprensione Indica se l'affermazione è **vera** o **falsa**. Dopo, in coppia, correggete le affermazioni false.

1. Il sarto è felice quando l'ufficiale Rudolf Schmidt gli chiede di fargli un vestito. Falso. È spaventato.
2. L'ufficiale Schmidt dà a Paolino delle sigarette. Vero.
3. Lucia è incinta. Vero.
4. Tutti sanno del ricevimento. Falso. L'ufficiale si raccomanda di non farlo sapere.
5. Lucia viene fucilata subito. Falso. Prima viene torturata.
6. Lucia è una lavandaia. Vero.
7. I soldati tedeschi lasciano passare Paolino. Vero.
8. I partigiani accolgono bene Paolino. Falso. Pensano che sia una spia dei tedeschi.
9. Paolino dice a Mauro che se non consegna il vestito entro sera ammazzano sua moglie. Vero.
10. Rudolf Schmidt fa bene a fidarsi di Paolino. Falso. Paolino lo ammazza.

2

Personaggi In coppia decidete se i personaggi vogliono davvero realizzare le loro intenzioni. Ci sono zone d'ombra (*gray areas*)? Ci sono personaggi che sono ambivalenti? Discutete.

Intenzione	Realizzata o no? Cosa vorrebbe davvero?
1. L'ufficiale tedesco vuole che Paolino sia felice di collaborare.	
2. Paolino vuole fare ciò che è meglio per la sua famiglia.	
3. Lucia vuole che Paolino aiuti lei e Mauro.	
4. Mauro vuole che Paolino si unisca alla Resistenza.	
5. Marisa vuole che suo marito, Paolino, sia meno codardo (*coward*).	
6. Paolino vuole diventare partigiano.	

Interpretazioni In coppia, rispondete alle domande.

1. Qual è l'evento che fa cambiare atteggiamento (*attitude*) a Paolino nei confronti dell'ufficiale Schmidt? Cosa gli fa pensare che forse non è «una brava persona»?
2. Come credete che si senta la moglie di Paolino quando decide di andare da Mauro a dirgli che Lucia è stata fucilata? Cosa credete che speri?
3. Perché Paolino ha sempre collaborato coi tedeschi?
4. Cosa succede a Paolino dopo aver ucciso l'ufficiale Schmidt? Cosa succede a sua moglie?

4

Temi

A. In copia indicate in che modo i seguenti elementi visivi (*visual*) sono importanti e perché.

Elementi visivi	1. In che modo? 2. Perché?
gli stivali	1. 2.
il vestito	1. 2.
il papillon	1. 2.
il fucile	1. 2.
le sigarette	1. 2.
l'uniforme	1. 2.

B. In coppia, rispondete alle domande.

1. Quali sono i temi del cortometraggio?

2. Hai visto o conosci film che mostrano gli effetti della guerra sulla popolazione civile? Per esempio?

3. Cosa pensi dei personaggi nella storia? Credi che sia moralmente riprovevole (*reproachable*) aiutare i nemici della patria o pensi che salvarsi la vita sia un istinto più forte delle ideologie? Tu cosa faresti?

4. C'è un proverbio che dice che «tutto è permesso in guerra e in amore». È vero? Perché?

5

Situazioni In piccoli gruppi, improvvisate un dialogo davanti alla classe su una di queste situazioni.

A	B
Immaginate che Paolino e Marisa si salvino alla fine. Come riescono a sfuggire (*escape*) ai tedeschi? Dove vanno? Cosa fanno?	Immaginate la fine dopo che Paolino ha ucciso Schmidt: cosa fanno i tedeschi? Cosa succede?

6

Scriviamo In uno o due paragrafi, descrivi una situazione difficile in cui hai dovuto scegliere tra ciò che era eticamente giusto e un interesse personale.

4 Explain that a **papillon**, the French word for *butterfly*, is a bowtie. Like many words in Italian, it was borrowed from French (c.f., **omelette**, **crêpe**, **champagne**), which in turn has borrowed words from Italian.

4 As an expansion activity, ask students for examples of English words borrowed from Italian or French.

Practice more at **vhlcentral.com**.

INSTRUCTIONAL RESOURCES: Teaching suggestions; Answer Keys
SAM/WebSAM: WB

IMMAGINA EMILIA

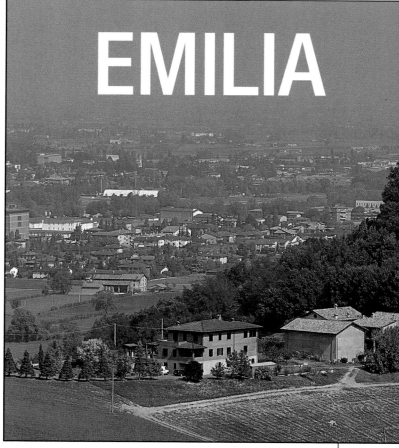

Una regione da... mangiare!

L'Emilia-Romagna, situata nell'Italia settentrionale, è una delle regioni più grandi e più ricche della penisola. Grazie ai numerosi prodotti agricoli e all'allevamento del bestiame°, l'industria alimentare è fiorente°. Conoscere meglio alcuni prodotti enogastronomici° tipici può diventare «un'appetitosa variante» per un itinerario attraverso la regione.

Il **Parmigiano Reggiano**, un formaggio prodotto sin dal Medioevo, è tipico dell'Emilia-Romagna ed è apprezzato in tutto il mondo. Si produce a **Parma**, **Reggio Emilia**, **Modena** e **Bologna**. Ottenuto dal latte di mucca°, il Parmigiano Reggiano è un formaggio ricco di valori nutritivi e non contiene né conservanti° né additivi. È un prodotto a **Denominazione di origine protetta (D.O.P.)** e solo il formaggio prodotto secondo specifiche regole può usare il marchio ufficiale di Parmigiano Reggiano. Oltre al Parmigiano, l'Emilia-Romagna dà i natali° anche al **Grana Padano**. Il Grana ha una consistenza più «granulosa» del Parmigiano e può essere messo sul mercato dopo 15 mesi di stagionatura° contro i 18–24 mesi o, a volte, anche tre anni del Parmigiano.

La cucina dell'Emilia-Romagna è anche nota per la **pasta ripiena°** che varia nella forma e nel ripieno, come **tortellini**, **tortelloni**, **agnolotti**, **cappelletti** e **ravioli**, che vengono generalmente serviti con un sugo° o in brodo°.

Anche i salumi° sono tipici della regione. Primo tra tutti il **Prosciutto di Parma** che, insieme al Parmigiano Reggiano, è forse il prodotto emiliano-romagnolo più conosciuto al mondo. Si produce in un'area limitata e ha come caratteristiche l'assenza di conservanti e la minima componente di grasso° nella carne. La stagionatura del prosciutto varia, a seconda del peso, dai 10 ai 30 mesi.

La città di **Bologna** è storicamente legata alla **mortadella** che in molte parti d'Italia e all'estero si chiama infatti «la Bologna» o «*baloney*». La mortadella di Bologna si ottiene con carni di suino tritate°, pezzetti di grasso, sale e pepe, insaccati° e poi cotti in stufe° ad aria secca.

La provincia di **Piacenza** è nota anche per la **pancetta°** e la **coppa°**, prodotte con carni suine°. Limitato nella produzione è il **culatello di Zibello**, che si ottiene dalla carne della coscia° di suino salata, insaccata e stagionata per 10 mesi.

Formaggi e salumi possono essere accompagnati da vini locali eccellenti come il **Lambrusco** e il **Sangiovese** e anche dal famoso **aceto balsamico di Modena**, prodotto con vino o mosto° e invecchiato in botti° di legno. Insomma, l'Emilia-Romagna può soddisfare ogni tipo di palato!

In più...

L'azienda **Ferrari**, con sede a **Maranello** in Emilia-Romagna, produce e vende automobili sportive di alta classe e gestisce° anche la **Scuderia Ferrari**, che compete nelle gare di **Formula Uno**. Queste magnifiche autovetture° si distinguono per lo stile che è affidato a designer famosi come **Giugiaro**, **Pininfarina**, **Scaglietti**, **Bertone** e **Vignola**. Il colore rosso delle macchine da corsa è stato scelto negli anni Venti per rappresentare l'Italia nelle gare.

allevamento... *animal farming* **fiorente** *flourishing* **enogastronomici** *food- and wine-related* **mucca** *cow* **conservanti** *preservatives* **natali** *birth* **stagionatura** *ripening; aging* **pasta ripiena** *filled pasta* **sugo** *sauce* **brodo** *broth* **salumi** *cold cuts* **grasso** *fat* **carni...tritate** *minced pork meat* **insaccati** *wrapped* **cotti in stufe** *cooked on stoves* **pancetta** *unsmoked bacon* **coppa** *pork loaf* **carni suine** *pork* **coscia** *thigh, leg* **mosto** *must* **botti** *barrels* **gestisce** *manages* **autovetture** *automobiles*

ROMAGNA

Vero o falso? Indica se ogni frase è **vera** o **falsa**. Correggi le frasi false. Some answers will vary.

1. In Emilia-Romagna l'agricoltura è molto sviluppata. Vero.

2. La produzione del Parmigiano Reggiano è cominciata nel secolo scorso. Falso. È cominciata nel Medioevo.

3. Il Parmigiano Reggiano deve stagionare per molti mesi. Vero.

4. In provincia di Piacenza si producono soltanto formaggi. Falso. Si producono anche la pancetta e la coppa.

5. Il Lambrusco e il Sangiovese sono aceti balsamici. Falso. Sono vini.

6. La pasta ripiena si serve generalmente con un sugo o in brodo. Vero.

7. Nella Repubblica di San Marino si parla italiano. Vero.

8. La lavorazione del mosaico è usata solo nelle opere antiche. Falso. Oggi si realizzano opere contemporanee con il mosaico.

Quanto hai imparato? Rispondi alle domande. Some answers will vary.

1. Quali sono alcune differenze tra il Parmigiano Reggiano e il Grana Padano? La produzione del Parmigiano è iniziata prima; il Grana ha una consistenza più granulosa; la stagionatura del Parmigiano è più lunga di quella del Grana.

2. Quali sono le caratteristiche nutrizionali del Prosciutto di Parma? Non ha conservanti e ha pochi grassi.

3. Quali sono alcuni degli ingredienti della mortadella di Bologna? carne di suino tritata, grasso, sale e pepe

4. Che tipo di autovetture produce l'azienda Ferrari? Produce automobili sportive di alta classe e autovetture da corsa.

5. Su che cosa si basa l'economia di San Marino? Si basa sul turismo e sulle attività finanziarie.

6. Quando è nata la Repubblica di San Marino? nel Medioevo

7. Qual è l'origine dell'arte del mosaico dell'Emilia-Romagna? l'arte bizantina

8. Chi produce oggetti lavorati con il mosaico? artigiani e industrie

La Serenissima Repubblica di San Marino Tra l'Emilia-Romagna e le Marche si trova la piccola **Repubblica di San Marino**, che conserva la sua identità dal Medioevo. San Marino è divisa in nove castelli, con cui si indicano i comuni, e la capitale è **Città di San Marino**. La lingua ufficiale è l'italiano e abbastanza diffuso è anche un dialetto romagnolo. L'economia della Repubblica di San Marino si basa principalmente sul turismo e su attività finanziarie. San Marino ha relazioni diplomatiche con molti paesi ed ha 15 ambasciate° all'estero.

I mosaici ieri e oggi L'Emilia-Romagna, e in particolare la città di **Ravenna**, custodiscono° un patrimonio musivo° unico al mondo. Per gli appassionati del mosaico, Ravenna con i capolavori del **Mausoleo di Galla Placidia**, del **Battistero degli Ariani** e della chiesa di **San Vitale**, è una tappa da non perdere.

 La tradizione dell'arte del mosaico affonda le radici° nell'arte bizantina ma si è consolidata nella regione e ancora oggi è un importante aspetto dell'economia. Infatti, ci sono molti artigiani° e industrie che producono preziose creazioni in mosaico per usi contemporanei.

ambasciate *embassies* custodiscono *preserve* musivo *works in mosaic*
affonda le radici *has roots in* artigiani *craftsmen*

Progetto

I tortellini sono uno dei piatti tipici della cucina emiliano-romagnola.

• Fai una ricerca sull'origine e la storia dei tortellini.

• Cerca qualche fatto curioso che riguarda questo piatto.

• Cerca una ricetta per cucinare i tortellini. Qual è un sugo (*sauce*) tradizionale per condirli (*seasoning them*)?

• Confronta i tuoi risultati con il resto della classe.

GALLERIA DI PERSONE ILLUSTRI

PAROLE COLTE

affinare *to perfect*
esibirsi *to perform*
la messa in scena *staging*
il patrimonio *assets*
il repertorio *repertory*

CANTANTE LIRICO

Luciano Pavarotti (1935–2007)

Luciano Pavarotti è stato un tenore italiano molto apprezzato
tutto il mondo. Il cantante modenese è considerato uno dei di
tenori più grandi di tutti i tempi e viene ricordato anche per il
suo impegno nel sociale. La popolarità arriva nel 1961 quand
grazie all'interpretazione di Rodolfo ne La Bohème di Puccini,
vince un importante concorso (*competition*) internazionale e
diventa popolare in patria. Il ruolo di Rodolfo rimarrà quello pi
rappresentativo nel repertorio del tenore, tanto da considerarl
una sorta di suo alter ego sul palco (*stage*). Qualche anno più
tardi Pavarotti conquista l'Inghilterra, inizia a incidere i primi
dischi e a esibirsi (*to perform*) anche in America. Il tenore
colleziona un successo dietro l'altro e si esibirà con i più gra
artisti del mondo nelle più prestigiose location. Pavarotti si spe
(*passed away*) nel 2007 a Modena.

STILISTA

Giorgio Armani (1934–)

Giorgio Armani è uno dei più celebri stilisti italiani.
Dopo aver lavorato al grande magazzino la Rinasce
lo stilista piacentino disegna linee per alcune azien
finché nel 1975 decide finalmente di creare un mar
(*brand*) personale. Lo stile inconfondibile di Armani
che si ispira al cinema americano in bianco e nero,
conquista le passerelle (*fashion runways*) di tutto il
mondo grazie a tagli nitidi (*clean lines*) e una palett
colori freddi come il grigio, il beige e il rappresenta
blu Armani. Alla linea principale si aggiungono Arma
collezioni, Emporio Armani, Armani Exchange, Arma
Jeans, Armani Junior e Armani Casa. Nel 2015 Forb
ha valutato il patrimonio di Giorgio Armani in circa
7,6 miliardi di dollari.

MUSICISTA
Giuseppe Verdi (1813–1901)

Giuseppe Verdi è stato un compositore protagonista del teatro musicale italiano dell'Ottocento. Verdi, universalmente ritenuto uno dei più grandi compositori lirici, compone le sue prime opere per la Scala di Milano; tra queste il celeberrimo *Nabucco*, che debuttò nel 1842 e i cui cori, come il «Va, pensiero», diventarono successi strepitosi (*resounding*). Seguirono altre opere eccezionali come la cosiddetta trilogia popolare: *Rigoletto, Il trovatore* e *La traviata*. Oltre alla carriera musicale partecipò alla vita politica appoggiando (*supporting*) il movimento risorgimentale che voleva l'Unità d'Italia, diventando successivamente un simbolo artistico che univa il Paese. Oggi le opere di Verdi vengono messe in scena in tutto il mondo e sono sempre ai primi posti delle opere più eseguite (*performed*).

ARTISTA CINEMATOGRAFICO
Carlo Rambaldi (1925–2012)

Carlo Rambaldi è stato un effettista e artista italiano famoso in tutto il mondo per le sue opere in campo cinematografico. Rambaldi inizia a frequentare gli ambienti cinematografici italiani verso la metà degli anni Cinquanta realizzando effetti speciali per grandi registi come Pier Paolo Pasolini e Dario Argento. Grazie alla grande produzione cinematografica americana ha la possibilità di affinare le sue abilità nella creazione di effetti speciali. Vince tre Oscar per i migliori effetti speciali grazie alle produzioni hollywoodiane di *King Kong* di John Guillermin, *Alien* di Ridley Scott ed *E.T. l'extraterrestre* di Steven Spielberg. Per quest'ultimo crea il protagonista alieno che sarà considerato da tutti il suo capolavoro.

Comprensione

Rispondere Rispondi alle domande.

1. Che tipo di cantante è stato Pavarotti?
   È stato tenore.

2. Qual è il ruolo più caratteristico del repertorio di Pavarotti?
   Il ruolo di Rodolfo ne *La Bohème* è il ruolo più caratteristico del suo repertorio.

3. Dov'è nato Pavarotti?
   È nato a Modena.

4. Dove lavora Giorgio Armani prima di diventare stilista?
   Lavora alla Rinascente.

5. Quali sono i colori caratteristici dello stile di Armani?
   Sono i colori freddi come il grigio, il beige e il blu Armani.

6. A cosa si ispira il suo stile?
   Si ispira al cinema americano in bianco e nero.

7. Il «Va, pensiero» è un coro composto da Verdi per quale opera lirica?
   È composto per *Nabucco*.

8. Quali opere costituiscono la trilogia popolare di Verdi?
   Rigoletto, Il trovatore e *La traviata* costituiscono la trilogia popolare di Verdi.

9. Quando inizia a frequentare il mondo del cinema Carlo Rambaldi?
   Inizia a frequentarlo verso la metà degli anni '50.

10. Quanti e che tipo di Oscar vince Rambaldi?
    Vince tre Oscar per i migliori effetti speciali.

Scrittura

Scrivi sull'argomento Scegli uno dei seguenti argomenti e scrivi un paragrafo seguendo le indicazioni.

- **Cantanti lirici** L'Italia è la patria della musica lirica e tutt'oggi nei teatri più prestigiosi del mondo cantanti lirici di ogni nazionalità cantano in italiano. Cosa sai della vita dei cantanti lirici? Hai idea di quanto si allenino? Immagina come si svolge la giornata di un artista lirico.

- **I personaggi della moda italiana** Giorgio Armani è uno degli stilisti italiani più apprezzati in tutto il mondo. Qual è il tuo stilista italiano preferito? Descrivi lo stile della casa di moda e spiega cosa ti piace di quel marchio.

- **Gli effetti speciali** Gli effetti speciali sono una parte fondamentale dei film. Le tecniche utilizzate nel cinema degli ultimi anni sono talmente (*so*) perfette che si fatica a credere (*it's hard to believe*) che ci sia della finzione (*illusion*). Quali sono gli esempi di effetti speciali meglio riusciti? Spiega le tue scelte.

 Practice more at **vhlcentral.com**.

INSTRUCTIONAL RESOURCES
Audioscripts, Answer Keys, Lab MP3s, Grammar Presentation Slides
SAM/WebSAM: WB, LM

8.1

To help students practice both forms of the infinitive, ask them to provide either the past or present infinitive of a verb form that you call out. For example, you say **avere fatto** and students reply **fare**. Conversely, if you say **dire**, students reply **avere detto**. Be sure to provide verbs that take **essere** as well as **avere** for the past infinitive.

ATTENZIONE!

The auxiliary verbs **essere** and **avere** often drop the final –e when used in past infinitive construction.

RIMANDO

To review object pronouns, see **Strutture 4.2, pp. 140–142.**

Uses of the infinitive

The present and past infinitive

The infinitive has two forms in Italian: the present and the past. You are already very familiar with the present infinitive, the equivalent of *to* + [*verb*] in English. The past infinitive is formed with the infinitive of **avere** or **essere** + the past participle of the main verb. When the past infinitive is formed with **essere**, the past participle must agree with the subject.

present infinitive	past infinitive
abitare (*to live*)	**avere abitato** (*to have lived*)
credere (*to believe*)	**avere creduto** (*to have believed*)
dormire (*to sleep*)	**avere dormito** (*to have slept*)
cadere (*to fall*)	**essere caduto/a/i/e** (*to have fallen*)
lavarsi (*to wash up*)	**essersi lavato/a/i/e** (*to have washed up*)

Dopo **aver mangiato**, Gianni si alzò e si lavò le mani.
After eating, Gianni got up and washed his hands.

Penso di **aver guardato** tutti i quadri.
I think that I have seen all the paintings.

Dopo **essere arrivati** al convegno, i saggisti si sono messi a chiacchierare.
Once they arrived at the convention, the essayists started to chat.

Speriamo di **esserci** ben spiegati.
We hope that we made ourselves clear.

- Object and reflexive pronouns are attached to the infinitive after the final –e has been dropped. The past participle of a past infinitive must agree in number and gender with the pronoun. The past participle of the past infinitive of a reflexive verb agrees in number and gender with the subject.

  Finirlo in anticipo sarebbe ideale.
  Finishing it early would be ideal.

  Dopo **averli comprati**, Luca ha messo i quadri nella macchina.
  After he bought them, Luca put the pictures in the car.

  Sono contenta di **essermi divertita** alla festa.
  I'm glad I had a good time at the party.

Uses of the infinitive

- In Italian, an infinitive may be used as a noun, even as the subject of a sentence or clause. When used as nouns, infinitives are masculine and are often preceded by a definite article. The English equivalent is expressed with a gerund (a verb form ending in –*ing*).

  Il dire è una cosa, **il fare** è un'altra.
  Saying is one thing, doing is another. (Easier said than done.)

  Non pensavo che **parlare** lingue straniere fosse **necessario**.
  I did not think that speaking foreign languages was necessary.

- The infinitive is often used to give commands or instructions, especially in signs, directions, notices, and recipes.

> **Per cortesia, lasciare** la porta aperta.
> *Please leave the door open.*

> **Girare** a destra, poi **continuare** dritto.
> *Turn right, then stay straight.*

> **Selezionare** il numero e **premere** il bottone «Next».
> *Select your number and push the "Next" button.*

> **Salare, pepare, coprire** e **far** cuocere a fiamma bassa.
> *Salt, pepper, cover, and let cook at a low temperature.*

RIMANDO

To review the use of the infinitive for negative **tu** commands, see **Strutture 4.3, pp. 146–147.**

- The infinitive directly follows modal verbs such as **potere**, **volere**, and **dovere** when the subject of both verbs is the same. It also follows verbs like **desiderare**, **piacere**, **preferire**, and **sapere** when there is no change of subject.

RIMANDO

To review **dovere**, **potere**, and **volere**, see **Strutture 4.4., pp. 150.**

—*Devo finire questi pantaloni entro mezzogiorno.*

> **Voglio dare** le tele a Leonardo.
> *I want to give the canvases to Leonardo.*

> **Dobbiamo studiare**; non possiamo **uscire**.
> *We have to study; we can't go out.*

> Mi **piace andare** all'opera.
> *I like going to the opera.*

> **Preferirebbe studiare** arte in Italia.
> *He would prefer to study art in Italy.*

- Sometimes a conjugated verb is followed by the prepositions **a** or **di** + [*infinitive*]. You must memorize which verbs require prepositions or look them up in a reference book or table.

> **Spero di tornare** in Italia quest'estate.
> *I hope to go back to Italy this summer.*

> **Cominciano a capire** le rime.
> *They are starting to understand the rhymes.*

ATTENZIONE!

Other common prepositions that introduce infinitives are **invece di**, **per**, **prima di**, and **senza**. **Per** expresses purpose.

Invece di andare al museo, facciamo una passeggiata.
Instead of going to the museum, let's take a walk.

Ti ho scritto per invitarti alla mostra.
I wrote to you (in order to) to invite you to the exhibition.

- Infinitives are used after impersonal expressions when the sentence has no explicit subject.

> Bisogna **rispettare** i diritti d'autore.
> *It is necessary to respect copyrights.*

> È bene **arrivare** in anticipo.
> *It's good to arrive early.*

> Non è possibile **dimenticare** i momenti vissuti con te.
> *It's impossible to forget the time spent with you.*

> Basta **firmare** qui.
> *It is sufficient to sign here.*

RIMANDO

As you have learned, the subjunctive is used after impersonal expressions when the subjects of the main clause and the dependent clause differ. See **Strutture 6.3, pp. 228–229** and **Strutture 7.3, pp. 272–273.**

- The past infinitive is generally used after the word **dopo** or another verb. It expresses an action completed before the action of the main verb.

> Dopo **avere sconfitto** Vercingetorige nella battaglia di Alesia, Cesare lo portò a Roma.
> *After having defeated Vercingetorix at the battle of Alesia, Caesar took him to Rome.*

> Sono contento di **essere nato** nelle Marche.
> *I'm glad I was born in Marche.*

RIMANDO

You will learn about the use of infinitives after **fare**, **lasciare**, and verbs of perception in **Strutture 10.4, pp. 404–405.**

Pratica

1

Situazioni Riscrivi le frasi sostituendo le parole sottolineate con l'infinito presente e fai tutte le modifiche necessarie.

> **Modello** La vita in Italia era difficile durante la seconda guerra mondiale.
>
> Vivere in Italia era difficile durante la seconda guerra mondiale.

1. L'abolizione di quella legge è stata necessaria. Abolire quella legge è stato necessario.
2. La colonizzazione di quel paese è stata uno sbaglio. Colonizzare quel paese è stato uno sbaglio.
3. La conquista dello spazio è possibile. Conquistare lo spazio è possibile.
4. L'invasione di altre nazioni è condannata dalle Nazioni Unite. Invadere altre nazioni è condannato dalle Nazioni Unite.
5. La liberazione degli ostaggi è stata un successo. Liberare gli ostaggi è stato un successo.
6. L'oppressione delle minoranze è ingiusta. Opprimere le minoranze è ingiusto.

2

I promessi sposi Completa il breve riassunto del romanzo *I promessi sposi* con i verbi all'infinito presente e passato.

Renzo e Lucia sono due giovani semplici che desiderano (1) __sposarsi__ (sposarsi) e vanno da don Abbondio, il prete del paese. Ma don Abbondio si rifiuta di (2) __celebrare__ (celebrare) il matrimonio dopo (3) __essere stato__ (essere) minacciato dai bravi (*henchmen*) di don Rodrigo, il signorotto del paese che si è innamorato di Lucia. Padre Cristoforo, dopo (4) __aver parlato__ (parlare) con Lucia, va da don Rodrigo per (5) __convincerlo__ (convincere / lui) a (6) __lasciarla__ (lasciare / lei) in pace. Dopo (7) __aver tentato__ (tentare) un matrimonio a sorpresa, Lucia si rifugia in un convento a Monza e Renzo va a Milano per (8) __cercare__ (cercare) giustizia. L'Innominato, un uomo potente a cui don Rodrigo ha chiesto aiuto, dopo (9) __aver rapito__ (rapire) (*kidnap*) Lucia, decide di (10) __liberarla__ (liberare / lei). Renzo si trova coinvolto nelle rivolte popolari causate della carestia (*famine*) e fugge a Bergamo. Torna a Milano a (11) __cercare__ (cercare) Lucia e dopo (12) __averla ritrovata__ (ritrovare / lei) tornano al loro paese. Dopo (13) __aver affrontato__ (affrontare) la peste (*the plague*), finalmente Renzo e Lucia si possono (14) __sposare__ (sposare).

3

Cosa è successo dopo? Completate le frasi con i verbi all'infinito passato per dire cosa avete fatto ieri tu e altre persone. Dopo, aggiungete altre due frasi.

> **Modello** Dopo essermi svegliato, mi sono alzato e ho fatto la doccia.

1. Dopo _____, il mio compagno di appartamento è uscito con gli amici.
2. Dopo _____, i miei genitori sono andati a riposare.
3. Dopo _____, io e i miei amici abbiamo guardato un film.
4. Dopo _____, la mia amica Silvana è andata al supermercato.
5. Dopo _____, ho letto un libro.
6. Dopo _____, sono andato/a all'università.
7. _____.
8. _____.

 Practice more at **vhlcentral.com**.

Comunicazione

4

Consigli In coppia, preparate almeno due consigli per foto usando le espressioni suggerite. Condivideteli poi con la classe.

bisogna	è importante	è possibile
basta	non è necessario	non è possibile
è bene	è meglio	

Modello **Non supererò mai l'esame di storia! Non riesco a memorizzare tutto!**

Non è possibile memorizzare tutto. È meglio cercare di capire i concetti e fare dei collegamenti!

Mi alleno sette giorni alla settimana, ma non diventerò mai una maratoneta!

Non andrò a dormire fino a quando non avrò finito di scrivere la tesina.

Non sarò mai bravo come Totti. Dovrei lasciar perdere il calcio!

Mi arrendo. Proprio non gli piaccio! (*I give up. He just doesn't like me!*)

5

I segnali In coppia, preparate dei segnali (*signs*) da mettere nei posti suggeriti. Usate l'infinito presente.

Modello **in cucina**

Lavarsi le mani prima di iniziare a cucinare. Pulire gli utensili che si usano. Mettere sempre tutto a posto.

- nel parcheggio del campus
- nella biblioteca
- nel parco
- nello spogliatoio (*locker room*) della palestra
- nella mensa universitaria
- nel collegio universitario

6

Quando...? In coppia, chiedetevi a turno quando farete le seguenti cose. Utilizzate la struttura **prima di** + [*infinito*] o **dopo** + [*infinito*] per rispondere.

Modello —Quando studierai oggi?

—Studierò prima di preparare la cena./Studierò dopo aver preparato la cena.

1. preparare la cena
2. fare la spesa
3. guardare la TV
4. andare in palestra
5. uscire con gli amici
6. usare il computer

6 Have students ask each other questions about the future. Example: **Farai un Master? Sì, farò un Master dopo aver finito l'università.**

INSTRUCTIONAL RESOURCES 8.2
Audioscripts, Answer Keys, Lab MP3s, Grammar Presentation Slides
SAM/WebSAM: WB, LM

ATTENZIONE!

Disjunctive pronouns are used in comparisons after words such as **come**, **quanto**, or **di**.

Maria cerca un bel ragazzo come te.
Maria is looking for a handsome boyfriend like you.

Lei preferisce quel ragazzo americano perché è più ricco di me.
She prefers that American boy because he is richer than I am.

ATTENZIONE!

Da solo/a/i/e is often used instead of **da** + [*disjunctive pronoun*] to show that something is done without help.

Noi abbiamo studiato la poesia classica da soli.
We studied classic poetry (all) by ourselves/on our own.

To reinforce different pronoun forms, ask students questions with the preposition **con** followed by a name or a personal pronoun. Have students respond with **con** and a disjunctive pronoun. Example:
—**Vai al mercato con Patrizia?**
—**Sì, con lei.**

RIMANDO

To review preposition and article contractions, see **Strutture 1.2, p. 20.**

Disjunctive pronouns; prepositions

Disjunctive pronouns

—*Paolino, ho un messaggio per* **te**.

- Disjunctive pronouns, **i pronomi tonici**, are also known as *stressed pronouns* because they are used to emphasize or clarify the object of a verb. They are also frequently used as objects of prepositions. Unlike other Italian pronouns, they are placed in the same position in a sentence as their English equivalents, after a verb or a preposition.

singular	me	te	lui	lei	Lei	sé
	me	*you*	*him*	*her*	*you* (formal)	*himself/herself/oneself/ yourself* (formal)
plural	noi	voi	loro	Loro	sé	
	us	*you*	*them*	*you* (formal)	*themselves/yourselves* (formal)	

Ceniamo con **loro** stasera.
We are having dinner with them tonight.

Guardo **lui**, non **lei**.
I am looking at him, not her.

- **Sé** only has a reflexive meaning; **me**, **te**, **noi**, and **voi** can also have a reflexive meaning.

Sergio preferisce fare tutto da **sé**.
Sergio wants to do everything (by) himself.

Ti piace parlare di **te**, non è vero?
You like talking about yourself, don't you?

- For extra emphasis, the adjective **stesso** is used with disjunctive pronouns. It must agree in number and gender with the stressed pronoun.

Quando osservo quella pittrice al lavoro, vedo **me** stessa.
When I watch that painter at work, I see myself.

Non fatelo per **me**, fatelo per **voi** stessi.
Don't do it for me, do it for yourselves.

- Disjunctive pronouns are also used with certain brief exclamations.

Beata **lei**!
Lucky her!

Maledetto **te**!
Curse you!

Povero **me**!
Poor me!

Prepositions

Prepositions have different meanings and functions in Italian and English. It is important not to translate them literally. The most common Italian prepositions are **a**, **con**, **da**, **di**, **in**, **per**, and **su**. As you know, some of these can be combined with the definite article.

Dobbiamo andare **dal** dottore alle tre.
We have to go to the doctor's office at three.

All'inizio, tutti hanno riso **del** pittore.
At first, everyone laughed at the painter.

- Italian prepositions have varied functions and indicate diverse relationships. It is useful to sort prepositions into categories based on their function.

Geographical names	**a**	Vado a Roma.	*I am going to Rome.*
	da	Viene da Spello.	*She is coming from Spello.*
	di	Sono di Lucca.	*They are from Lucca.*
	in	Abita in Italia.	*He lives in Italy.*
Time	**a**	A che ora parti?	*What time are you leaving?*
	da	Studio dalle otto alle nove.	*I study from eight to nine.*
	di	Di notte non si lavora.	*You don't work at night.*
	in	In autunno fa freddo.	*It's cold in autumn.*
	per	Abbiamo parlato per due ore.	*We talked for two hours.*
Dates	**a**	A maggio vado in campagna.	*In May, I go to the countryside.*
	di	D'inverno, sciamo.	*In the winter we go skiing.*
	in	Nel 2006 gli Azzurri hanno vinto.	*In 2006, the Azzurri won.*
Manner or means	**a**	Ci vado a piedi.	*I'm going there on foot.*
	con	Lavora con gioia.	*He works with joy.*
	di	La ringrazia di cuore.	*He thanks her with all his heart.*
	in	Arrivano in treno.	*They are arriving by train.*
	per	Lo spedisco per posta.	*I send it by mail.*
Description/Material	**a**	È un vestito a righe.	*It's a striped dress.*
	da	Dov'è il ferro da stiro?	*Where is the iron?*
	di	Porta una sciarpa di seta.	*She is wearing a silk scarf.*
	in	Avevo una statua in legno.	*I had a wooden sculpture.*
Purpose	**a**	È destinato a trionfare.	*He is destined to succeed.*
	da	Ti aspetto nella sala da pranzo.	*I'll wait for you in the dining room.*
	in	Si è svolta una manifestazione in memoria dei soldati.	*There was a demonstration in memory of the soldiers.*
	per	Combatte per l'uguaglianza.	*He fights for equality.*
Place/Location	**a**	Si trova all'angolo.	*It's on the corner.*
	da	Vado dal dottore.	*I'm going to the doctor's.*
	in	In aula ci sono venti studenti.	*There are twenty students in the classroom.*
	per	Cammino per il parco.	*I walk in/around the park.*
	su	Sul tavolo c'è un coltello.	*There is a knife on the table.*
Possession/ Authorship	**di**	Il libro è di Marco. La *Pietà* di Michelangelo	*The book belongs to Marco.* La *Pietà* by Michelangelo
Cause	**per**	Non vado per la neve.	*I'm not going because of the snow.*
Instrument	**con**	Lo taglio con le forbici.	*I cut it with the scissors.*
Company	**con**	Vieni con me!	*Come with me!*

Remind students that there are many more prepositions than the ones listed here, and that they will need to learn their usage on a case-by-case basis. You may wish to share some of the compound or prepositional phrases such as **a sinistra, a destra, davanti a, in cima a, in fondo a, lontano da, vicino a,** etc., with them.

ATTENZIONE!

Other common prepositions are:

contro *against*
dietro *behind*
dopo *after*
durante *during*
fra/tra *between/among, in (time)*
lungo *along*
mediante *by means of*
oltre *beyond*
presso *near, with*
salvo *except (for)*
senza *without*
sotto *under*
tranne *except*

Parto fra/tra due giorni.
I am leaving in two days.

ATTENZIONE!

Common expressions with **in** include:

in montagna
in campagna
in centro
in classe
in biblioteca

ATTENZIONE!

Many prepositions are followed by **di** when used with a disjunctive pronoun. They include **contro, dietro, dopo, fra, presso, senza, sopra, sotto,** and **su.**

Mia sorella conta su di me.
My sister counts on me.

Le mie cugine vivono con i loro amici; vivranno presso di loro fino ad agosto.
My cousins are living with their friends; they will live with them until August.

Mio fratello ha un appartamento in via Firenze; sotto di lui abita una ragazza greca.
My brother has an apartment on Via Firenze; a Greek girl lives downstairs from him.

Il drammaturgo non è ancora qui; parliamo fra di noi nel frattempo.
They playwright isn't here yet; let's talk among ourselves in the meantime.

Pratica

1

Sostituire Sostituisci le parole sottolineate con i pronomi tonici giusti.

1. Sono andato alla festa con <u>Annamaria</u>. lei
2. Chi viene con <u>te e tuo fratello</u>? voi
3. Abbiamo fatto la prenotazione per <u>Luigi</u>. lui
4. Questa cartolina è per <u>me e mia sorella</u>. noi
5. La nonna è con <u>i bambini</u>. loro
6. Sofia è egocentrica (*self-centered*), ama sempre parlare di <u>Sofia</u>. sé

2

Opzioni Scegli la preposizione giusta.

1. Dante era (di/ da) Firenze ma fu sepolto (*buried*) (in /a) Ravenna.
2. Le città (di/ a) Pompei ed Ercolano furono distrutte (dell' / dall')eruzione del Vesuvio.
3. Gli Etruschi vivevano (a /in) città indipendenti, circondate (da/ di) grosse mura.
4. La *Gioconda* è uno (dei/ di) quadri più famosi (del/ in) mondo.
5. Dario Fo è stato il vincitore (del/ dal) Premio Nobel (nella /per la) Letteratura (in /nel) 1997.
6. La Fontana dei Fiumi di Bernini è (con /di) marmo.

3 Have students write a brief postcard to a person of their choice, modelled on the one in this activity. Have them include at least six geographical prepositions.

3

Bologna Completa la cartolina con le preposizioni giuste.

Ciao Mauro,

finalmente sono (1) __in__ Italia. Sono arrivata (2) __a__ Bologna (3) __in__ Emilia-Romagna ieri sera. Sono venuta (4) __in__ treno, e il viaggio è stato molto interessante perché ho potuto vedere tutta la campagna emiliana. Il mio albergo è (5) __in__ centro, non troppo lontano (6) __dalla__ stazione e vicino c'è una fermata (7) __dell'__ autobus. Bologna non è una città molto grande e quindi si può girare (8) __a__ piedi. Stasera vado (9) __da__ Guido (10) __per__ cena; non vedo l'ora di rivederlo. Poi (11) __tra/fra__ due giorni partirò (12) __per__ Parma e (13) __tra/fra__ una settimana sarò (14) __a__ casa. A presto,

Giulia

Mauro Stipa

Via Nazionale, 31

16100 Genova

4 Tell students to come up more options.

4

Destinazioni In coppia, e usando i suggerimenti dati, create delle frasi per dire dove e quando volete andare in vacanza in Italia. Condividete le vostre frasi con la classe.

Modello Voglio andare a Siena a marzo.

Preposizioni	Luoghi	Preposizioni	Quando
a	montagna	a	2 settimane
al	Siena	a/in	luglio
ad	campagna	da…a	giugno…settembre
in	lago	di	autunno
nelle	Marche	fra	marzo
	Lombardia	in	estate
	mare		mattina
	Ascoli Piceno		mezzogiorno

Comunicazione

5 **La festa** Nel disegno ci sono varie situazioni d'incontro tra persone. Descrivi quello che vedi, usando il maggior numero di preposizioni possibile.

5 Have students share their description with the rest of the class. Who has incorporated the most prepositions into the description? Whose description is most imaginative?

6 **La vostra famiglia** In coppia, parlate della vostra famiglia usando le preposizioni della lista e i pronomi tonici.

Modello Mia madre è sempre occupata, allora spesso faccio io la spesa per lei di mattina.

a	di	sotto
con	in	su
da	per	tra/fra

7 **Sogni** Girando per la classe, domandate a sei compagni/e in quale città sognano di vivere e perché. Raccogliete le informazioni su un foglio di carta e poi condividetele con la classe. Non dimenticate di usare le preposizioni giuste.

7 Review geographical names and/or refer students to the map in front of the book.

Nome	Città	Nazione	Motivo
Silvia	a Boston	negli Stati Uniti	per studiare

Modello —In quale città sogni di vivere e perché?

—Sogno di vivere a Boston, negli Stati Uniti, per studiare.

8 **Il giro del mondo** In coppia, create un giro del mondo fantastico. Dite dove andate, in quale città, in quale paese, quando partite, a che ora, in che giorno e in quale stagione. Utilizzate le preposizioni giuste. Presentate il vostro itinerario alla classe e rispondete alle domande che vi fanno.

Modello Partiamo da Siena, in Italia, in Europa, alle 8 di mattina del 2 giugno, in primavera e arriviamo a Pisa. Dopo Pisa...

INSTRUCTIONAL RESOURCES   8.3
Audioscripts, Answer Keys, Lab MP3s, Grammar Presentation Slides
SAM/WebSAM: WB, LM

RIMANDO

To review preposition and article contractions, see **Strutture 1.2, p. 20**.

To review prepositions, see **Strutture 8.2, pp. 310–311**.

ATTENZIONE!

You are already familiar with a number of verbs and impersonal expressions that are followed directly by an infinitive in Italian.

Il protagonista desidera colonizzare la luna.
The protagonist wants to colonize the Moon.

Sarà possibile farlo nel 2020 d.C.
It will be possible to do it in 2020 AD.

Point out the overlap between this table and the previous one.

To have students practice verbs followed by prepositions, do a stand-up drill. Each student will give a verb and its appropriate preposition, then the next student will give a sentence using that verb. If both are correct, they may sit down; if not, they remain standing and wait for another turn.

Verbs followed by prepositions

- Many verbs and expressions require the use of a preposition to introduce an infinitive, a noun, or pronoun. You must learn which verbs require prepositions through practice and/or by checking them in a dictionary.

> **Avevo voglia di parlargli** prima di partire.
> *I wanted to talk to him before I left.*

> **Andiamo a vedere** Massimo stasera.
> *Let's go visit Massimo tonight.*

- The following verbs and expressions require the preposition **a** before an infinitive.

abituarsi a *to get used to*	**invitare a** *to invite*
andare a *to go*	**mandare a** *to send*
cominciare a *to begin to*	**mẹttersi a** *to start to*
continuare a *to continue to*	**obbligare a** *to oblige, to compel*
decịdersi a *to make up one's mind to*	**pensare a** *to think about*
ẹssere attento/a a *to be careful*	**persuadere a** *to persuade to*
ẹssere pronto/a a *to be ready to*	**preparare a** *to prepare to*
ẹssere ụltimo/a a *to be last*	**provare a** *to try to*
fare meglio a *to be better off*	**rinunciare a** *to give up*
giocare a *to play*	**riuscire a** *to manage to*
imparare a *to learn to*	**servire a** *to be good for*
incoraggiare a *to encourage to*	**venire a** *to come*
insegnare a *to teach*	**volerci a** *to take, require*

> **Siete pronti a** vedere la mostra d'arte moderna?
> *Are you ready to see the modern art exhibit?*

- The following verbs and expressions take the preposition **a** before a noun or pronoun.

assịstere a *to attend*	**interessarsi a** *to be interested in*
assomigliare a *to resemble*	**partecipare a** *to participate in*
crẹdere a *to believe in*	**pensare a** *to think about*
dare nọia a *to bother*	**rinunciare a** *to give up*
fare attenzione a *to pay attention to*	**servire a** *to be good for*
fare vedere a *to show*	**strịngere la mano a** *to shake hands with*
giocare a *to play*	**tenere a** *to care about*

> I miei fratelli **giocano a** calcio ogni giorno.
> *My brothers play soccer every day.*

- Note that the preposition may be separated from the verb by an adverb; the preposition immediately precedes the infinitive, noun, or pronoun.

> **Pensiamo** spesso **al** nostro futuro.
> *We often think about our future.*

> **Ci vuole** un'ora **a** trovare un parcheggio a Roma.
> *It takes an hour to find a parking lot in Rome.*

- The following verbs and expressions require the preposition **di** before an infinitive.

accorgersi di *to notice*	**chiedere di** *to ask*
aspettare di *to wait*	**consigliare di** *to advise*
avere bisogno di *to need*	**decidere di** *to decide to*
avere fretta di *to be in a hurry*	**dimenticarsi di** *to forget to*
avere paura di *to be afraid of*	**finire di** *to finish*
avere ragione di *to have reason*	**occuparsi di** *to take care of*
avere torto di *to be wrong*	**pensare di** *to plan to*
avere vergogna di *to be ashamed of*	**preoccuparsi di** *to worry about*
avere voglia di *to feel like*	**promettere di** *to promise to*
cercare di *to try*	**ricordarsi di** *to remember*
cessare di *to stop*	**trattarsi di** *to be about*

- The following verbs and expressions require the preposition **di** before a noun or pronoun.

accorgersi di *to notice*	**parlare di** *to talk about*
avere bisogno di *to need*	**preoccuparsi di** *to worry about*
coprire di *to cover with*	**rendersi conto di** *to realize*
dimenticarsi di *to forget*	**ricordarsi di** *to remember*
discutere di *to discuss*	**ridere di** *to laugh at*
fidarsi di *to trust*	**riempire di** *to fill with*
innamorarsi di *to fall in love with*	**ringraziare di** *to thank for*
interessarsi di *to be interested in*	**soffrire di** *to suffer from*
lamentarsi di *to complain about*	**trattare di** *to deal with*
occuparsi di *to take care of*	**vivere di** *to live on*

- The following verbs require the preposition **da** before a noun or pronoun.

allontanarsi da *to distance oneself*	**partire da** *to leave from*
dipendere da *to depend on*	**uscire da** *to leave*
divorziare da *to divorce (someone)*	**venire da** *to come from*

- Certain verbs in Italian change meaning according to the preposition that follows. Some common ones are **decidere di/decidersi a, finire di/finire per,** and **pensare a/pensare di.**

Betta **pensa** sempre **ai** personaggi delle sue novelle prima di scrivere.
Betta always thinks about the characters in her short novels before writing.

Lei **pensa di** andare in Toscana.
She's planning to go to Tuscany.

Cosa **pensi del** suo romanzo?
What do you think of her novel?

Finiremo di studiare alle 15.00.
We will finish studying at 3:00.

Tutti **finiranno per** capirla.
Everyone will understand it in the end.

Si è **deciso a** cercare un altro lavoro.
He made up his mind to find another job.

Ha **deciso di** diventare ingegnere.
She has decided to become an engineer.

Give students the following examples: **Patrizia e Marco pensano di costruire una casa in Sardegna./ Ti consiglio di smettere di fumare.** Then have students provide additional examples. Point out the overlap between this table and the next one.

ATTENZIONE!

There are verbs in Italian that take a preposition, but do not take a preposition in English.

Mi sono dimenticata di comprare il latte!
I forgot to buy the milk!

Cerco di comprare un libro sull'arte preistorica.
I'm trying to buy a book on prehistoric art.

Point out that there are also Italian verbs that do not take a preposition where the English equivalent does, for example: **ascoltare, aspettare, cercare, chiedere, guardare, pagare,** and **sognare.**
Che cosa ascolti: un CD di Andrea Bocelli o un CD dei Black Eyed Peas?

ATTENZIONE!

Uscire takes **di** instead of **da** as a preposition in the expression **uscire di casa** (*to leave home*).

ATTENZIONE!

Several verbs are followed by the preposition **su.**

contare su *to count on*
giurare su *to swear on*
riflettere su *to reflect on, to ponder*
scommettere su *to bet on*

Give students additional examples to illustrate how the meaning changes.
Finirò di scrivere il saggio verso mezzanotte./Finirò per scrivere il saggio verso mezzanotte.

Pratica

1

L'università Completa il seguente paragrafo con le preposizioni semplici o le preposizioni articolate. Dove non sono necessarie, metti una X.

Nel XII secolo cominciò (1) __ad__ aumentare il numero di persone che volevano (2) __X__ dedicarsi agli studi superiori. Fino a quel momento la chiesa si era occupata (3) __dell'__ istruzione ma ora le città avevano bisogno (4) __di__ più scuole. Cominciarono (5) __a__ formarsi gruppi di studenti e di maestri. Gli studenti invitavano i maestri (6) __a__ insegnare e i maestri incoraggiavano (7) __a__ studiare. La prima università fu quella di Bologna nel 1088, dove gli studenti si interessavano soprattutto (8) __alla__ giurisprudenza (*law*). Sull'esempio di Bologna nacquero altre università come quella di Parigi o di Oxford.

2 Sample answers:
1. Marta s'interessa alla pittura a olio.
2. Noi pensiamo alla mostra di domani.
3. Tu rifletti sull'importanza dell'arte.
4. Io desidero visitare molti musei.
5. Voi vi occupate di restaurare vecchi dipinti.
6. Il successo dell'esposizione dipende da noi.
7. Eleonora e Sofia preferiscono scolpire piuttosto che dipingere.
8. Il professore d'arte invita a creare opere artistiche.

2

Preferenze Inventa delle frasi utilizzando gli elementi di ogni colonna. Non dimenticare di aggiungere le preposizioni se necessario.

> **Modello** **Marco / decidere / andare alla mostra**
> Marco ha deciso di andare alla mostra.

tu	interessarsi	l'importanza dell'arte
noi	pensare	visitare molti musei
Marta	riflettere	pittura a olio
io	desiderare	noi
il professore d'arte	occuparsi	mostra di domani
voi	invitare	creare opere artistiche
il successo dell'esposizione	preferire	scolpire piuttosto che dipingere
Eleonora e Sofia	dipendere	restaurare vecchi dipinti

3 Have students come up with additional statements of their own.

3

Completare Completa le frasi con la preposizione giusta e un nome o pronome. Condividile poi con la classe.

> **Modello** **Io assomiglio...**
> Io assomiglio alla nonna.

1. Io e i miei amici ci lamentiamo _____.
2. Gli studenti di questa università vivono _____.
3. La mia migliore amica si preoccupa _____.
4. Io rido _____.
5. Secondo me, la maleducazione dà noia _____.
6. Mio cugino Matteo vuole stringere la mano _____.
7. Noi abbiamo assistito _____.
8. I miei amici giocano _____.
9. Ho deciso _____.
10. I miei amici non si fidano _____.

 Practice more at **vhlcentral.com**.

Comunicazione

4

Have students compare their answers with the rest of the class.

4

Al parco Diverse persone al parco sono impegnate in varie attività.

A. In coppia, guardate il disegno e fatevi delle domande su cosa vedete. Usate i verbi suggeriti seguiti dalle preposizioni giuste.

aspettare	avere voglia	consigliare	giocare	provare
assomigliare	chiedere	fare vedere	pensare	ridere

B. Aggiungete dei dettagli alla descrizione che avete fatto. Immaginate che cosa è successo prima e dopo quello che vedete nel disegno. Usate i verbi seguiti dalle preposizioni.

5

Intervista In coppia, usate i verbi della lista per creare delle domande da farvi a turno. Poi condividete le risposte con la classe.

5

Have students come up with additional questions to ask.

> **Modello** **incoraggiare**
>
> Cosa ti incoraggiano a fare i tuoi genitori?

aspettare	fidarsi
avere bisogno	obbligare
contare	partecipare
credere	preparare

6

La storia In coppia, scegliete un titolo e inventate una storia usando almeno dieci verbi dalla lista seguiti dalle preposizioni giuste, se necessarie.

andare	avere voglia	fare attenzione	preoccuparsi
assomigliare	consigliare	mandare	servire
avere bisogno	decidere	mettersi	tenere
avere fretta	decidersi	pensare	uscire
avere paura	desiderare	persuadere	volere

- Un'estate da non dimenticare
- E così sono diventato artista
- La mia notte al museo
- Il mio viaggio nel passato

INSTRUCTIONAL RESOURCES
Audioscripts, Answer Keys, Lab MP3s, Grammar Presentation Slides
SAM/WebSAM: WB, LM

8.4

Gerunds and participles

Gerunds

- The Italian gerund is the equivalent of the English verb form ending in –*ing*. It is used to describe an action that is or was in progress.

  > **Piangendo**, ha letto la sua poesia per le amiche.
  > *Crying, she read her poem for her friends.*

  > **Guardando** le sculture, abbiamo scoperto un Modigliani.
  > *Looking at the sculptures, we discovered one by Modigliani.*

- To form the present gerund, add **–ando** to the stem of **–are** verbs and **–endo** to the stem of **–ere** and **–ire** verbs.

conquistare	conquistando
dirigere	dirigendo
abolire	abolendo

- Some verbs form the gerund based on an archaic infinitive:

bere	(bevere)	bevendo
dire	(dicere)	dicendo
fare	(facere)	facendo
tradurre	(traducere)	traducendo
porre	(ponere)	ponendo

- The gerund may be used to introduce a dependent clause if the subject of the gerund and the dependent clause is the same. The gerund can provide information about how something is done, what will happen if someone does something, or the outcome that results from the action of the gerund.

  > **Gesticolando**, Marco spiegò la sua teoria.
  > *Gesturing, Marco explained his theory.*

  > **Ascoltando** la canzone, Patrizia e Paolo si divertono molto.
  > *While listening to the song, Patrizia and Paolo are having a lot of fun.*

  > **Studiando** il regno di Carlomagno, imparerai la storia francese.
  > *By studying Charlemagne's reign, you will learn French history.*

- If the gerund is used to express a condition leading to the action of the main clause, the subject of the two clauses can be different.

  > Tempo **permettendo**, andremo a vedere il castello per la lezione di educazione civica.
  > *Weather permitting, we will go see the castle for our civic education class.*

- Use the present, imperfect, or future tense of the verb **stare** + [*gerund*] to indicate an action in progress. The progressive forms are not used as frequently in Italian as they are in English.

  > –Piero, cosa **stai facendo**?
  > –*Piero, what are you doing?*

  > –**Sto scrivendo** un'e-mail, mamma.
  > –*I am writing an e-mail, Mom.*

  > Il re **stava parlando** con i suoi cavalieri quando la regina è entrata.
  > *The king was (in the process of) talking to his knights when the queen came in.*

ATTENZIONE!

In some instances, an infinitive must be used in Italian where a gerund is used in English. In Italian, the gerund can never be used as the subject or direct object of a sentence.

Imparare l'italiano non è semplice.
Learning Italian isn't easy.

Mi piace nuotare.
I like swimming.

Erano occupati a scrivere gialli.
They were busy writing thrillers.

Hai passato ore a leggere un romanzo.
You spent hours reading a novel.

Share the saying **Sbagliando s'impara** and its usual translation (*practice makes perfect*), then ask students for a more literal translation (*one learns by making mistakes*). Point out the use of "by" in the more literal translation.

ATTENZIONE!

Object pronouns precede the conjugated verb **stare** + [*infinitive*].

Gli sto spiegando il quadro di Botticelli.
I'm explaining Botticelli's painting to him.

To provide practice of the various forms of the gerund, *act out an action, and have students guess what you are doing.* Some examples: writing on the board (**sta scrivendo**), drinking a beverage (**sta bevendo**), singing (**sta cantando**), dancing (**sta ballando**), eating something (**sta mangiando**), translating a word or phrase (**sta traducendo**), reading aloud (**sta leggendo**), leaving (**sta partendo**), etc. Be sure to include varied regular verbs, irregular verbs, and gerunds that come from archaic roots.

- The past gerund is used to express an action that happened before the action of the main clause. To form the past gerund, use the gerund of **avere** or **essere** + the past participle. The past participle of a verb conjugated with **essere** must agree in number and gender with its subject.

fare ➤ avendo fatto   arrivare ➤ essendo arrivato/a/i/e

Avendo visto l'acquerello, hanno deciso di comprarlo.
Having seen the watercolor, they decided to buy it.

Essendo arrivata in ritardo alla mostra, non ha visto l'autoritratto di Van Gogh.
Having arrived late at the exposition, she didn't see Van Gogh's self-portrait.

- Reflexive and object pronouns are attached to the gerund. Used with the past gerund, the pronouns attach to **avendo** or **essendo**. The past participle agrees in number and gender with direct object pronouns.

Mettendola nella scatola di cartone, l'artigiano proteggerà la sua opera.
By putting it in a cardboard box, the artisan will protect his work of art.

Essendomi seduta in aula, ho visto che gli altri studenti non erano ancora arrivati.
Having sat down in the classroom, I saw that the other students hadn't arrived yet.

Participles

- There are two forms of the Italian participle: present and past. To form the present participle, add **–ante** to the stem of **–are** verbs and **–ente** to the stem of **–ere** and **–ire** verbs.

abitare ➤ abitante *(inhabitant)*
opprimere ➤ opprimente *(oppressive)*
seguire ➤ seguente *(following)*

- The present participle is often used as an adjective or noun. When used as an adjective, the participle agrees in number and gender with the noun it modifies. The present participle can replace a relative clause in some instances.

I **seguenti** studenti devono andare in aula alle 8.00.
The following students must go to the classroom at 8 o'clock.

Lo scultore ha fatto una statua **rappresentante** (che rappresenta) la primavera.
The sculptor made a statue representing (that represents) spring.

- Past participles may also be used as adjectives or nouns. When used as adjectives, past participles agree in number and gender with the nouns they modify.

Quei pittori non sono ben **conosciuti**.   La natura morta non è ancora **finita**.
Those painters aren't well known.   *The still life isn't finished yet.*

Il nuovo **arrivato** mi ha domandato di accompagnarlo all'appartamento.
The newcomer asked me to accompany him to the apartment.

- The past participle can replace a clause beginning with **dopo che** or **quando** + [past action].

Quando aveva finito la strofa, il poeta ha sorriso.   **Dopo che era tornata** a casa, si è seduta.
When he had finished the stanza, the poet smiled.   *After returning home, she sat down.*

Finita la strofa, il poeta ha sorriso.   **Tornata** a casa, si è seduta.
Having finished the stanza, the poet smiled.   *Having returned home, she sat down.*

ATTENZIONE!

Remember that a reflexive pronoun used with a gerund must correspond to the subject of the sentence.

Telefonandoci con Skype, non ci perderemo di vista.
By calling each other with Skype, we won't lose touch.

RIMANDO

To review the formation of the past participle, see **Strutture 3.1, pp. 96–97.**

Let students know that some present participles of **–ire** verbs are irregular. Example: **dormire→dormiente, salire→saliente, soffrire→sofferente.**

ATTENZIONE!

Object and reflexive pronouns are attached to the past participle. The past participle agrees with a direct object.

Finita la strofa, il poeta ha chiuso il quaderno.
Having finished the stanza, the poet closed the notebook.

Finitala, il poeta ha chiuso il quaderno.
Having finished it, the poet closed the notebook.

Pratica

1 After students have completed this activity, have them substitute object pronouns in the gerund phrases.

Give students additional items:
6. Quando hanno sconfitto il nemico, hanno ristabilito la democrazia. (Sconfiggendo il nemico, hanno ristabilito la democrazia)
7. Se segui i consigli del professore, riuscirai a fare un bell'autoritratto. (Seguendo i consigli del professore, riuscirai a fare un bell'autoritratto)
8. Quando hanno vinto la battaglia, hanno conquistato la regione. (Vincendo la battaglia hanno conquistato la regione.)

2 Answers:
1. Avendo liberato il paese, hanno introdotto le loro leggi.
2. Avendo realizzato un quadro bellissimo, era stato premiato dalla giuria.
3. Essendosi stabiliti al confine, hanno assimilato le tradizioni dei vicini.
4. Essendo partiti presto, non hanno incontrato la scultrice.
5. Avendo abolito la schiavitù, era diventato il re più popolare.

2 After students have completed this activity, have them substitute object pronouns in the gerund phrases.

1

Conseguenze Riscrivi le frasi usando il gerundio.

Modello **Quando ha letto la biografia di Mussolini, ha imparato molto sul dittatore e sul periodo fascista.**

Leggendo la biografia di Mussolini, ha imparato molto sul dittatore e sul periodo fascista.

1. Quando ho guardato il *David*, ho capito la grandezza di Michelangelo. *Guardando il David, ho capito la grandezza di Michelangelo.*
2. Mentre restauravamo una chiesa, abbiamo scoperto un affresco di Giotto. *Restaurando una chiesa, abbiamo scoperto un affresco di Giotto.*
3. Mentre curiosava (*looked around*) in un negozio di libri, Piero ha scoperto un giallo molto interessante. *Curiosando in un negozio di libri, Piero ha scoperto un giallo molto interessante.*
4. Poiché ha scritto molti romanzi è diventato famoso. *Scrivendo molti romanzi è diventato famoso.*
5. Quando ho analizzato le poesie di Giacomo Leopardi, sono rimasta affascinata dal suo stile. *Analizzando le poesie di Giacomo Leopardi, sono rimasta affascinata dal suo stile.*

2

Risultati Forma delle frasi usando il gerundio passato.

Modello **vedere l'acquerello / hanno deciso di comprarlo.**

Avendo visto l'acquerello, hanno deciso di comprarlo.

- liberare il paese / hanno introdotto le loro leggi.
- realizzare un quadro bellissimo / era stato premiato dalla giuria.
- stabilirsi al confine / hanno assimilato le tradizioni dei vicini.
- andare via presto / non hanno incontrato la scultrice.
- abolire la schiavitù / era diventato il re più popolare.

3

Arte Completa il brano con il participio presente dei verbi della lista.

assistere	insegnare	passare	studiare
imbarazzare	interessare	splendere	

Per Laura era un giorno molto (1) _interessante_: avrebbe realizzato il suo primo acquerello. C'erano molti (2) _studenti_ d'arte a lezione, ma l'(3) _assistente_ le aveva assicurato che seguendo i consigli dell'(4) _insegnante_, avrebbe fatto un quadro bellissimo. Si sistemarono per strada con i loro fogli, alcuni (5) _passanti_ si fermarono a guardare ed era una situazione (6) _imbarazzante_ per Laura, che si vergognava perché lei non era una studentessa d'arte esperta. Era una giornata (7) _splendente_ e Laura si lasciò guidare dalle sue emozioni e alla fine realizzò un'opera stupenda.

4

Cosa hai fatto? Rispondi alle domande utilizzando il participio passato. *Some answers will vary.*

Modello **Cosa hai fatto dopo che... hai guardato il film?**

Guardato il film, sono andato/a a letto.

Cosa hai fatto dopo che...
- sei arrivato/a a casa?
  Arrivato/a a casa, ho controllato la posta elettronica.
- hai parcheggiato la macchina?
  Parcheggiata la macchina, sono andato/a in centro.
- sono partiti i tuoi amici?
  Partiti i miei amici, sono andato/a a dormire.
- hai finito di studiare?
  Finito di studiare, ho guardato un film.
- hai mangiato gli spaghetti?
  Mangiati gli spaghetti, ho ordinato una bistecca.
- sei tornato/a dalle vacanze?
  Tornato/a dalle vacanze, sono andato/a a lavorare.

Comunicazione

5

Cosa fanno? In coppia, dite cosa sta accadendo nei disegni usando il gerundio presente.

> **Modello**   Guardando la partita, Andrea si è annoiato.

6

Intervista In coppia, fatevi almeno sei domande su cosa stavate facendo ieri in determinati momenti della giornata. Rispondete usando **stare** + [*gerundio*].

> **Modello**   —Cosa stavi facendo ieri alle quattro del pomeriggio?
> —Stavo studiando.

7

E dopo? In coppia, completate le frasi usando il gerundio passato e il participio passato.

> **Modello**   **Massimo stava dipingendo un quadro...**
> Avendo dipinto abbastanza, è uscito con gli amici.
> Finito il quadro, è uscito con gli amici.

1. Giovanna stava leggendo un libro...
2. Paolo e Francesca stavano preparando la cena...
3. Carlo stava scrivendo un romanzo...
4. Giovanni aveva appena chiuso la porta di casa...
5. Maria aveva preso il treno...
6. I compagni avevano finito di studiare...
7. Noi sentivamo degli strani rumori sul tetto della casa...

8

Rimini In coppia, fatevi a turno delle domande usando gli indizi che seguono. Rispondete usando il gerundio o il participio passato.

> **Modello**   **come trovare un albergo non troppo costoso**
> —Come posso trovare un albergo non troppo costoso?
> —Andando all'ufficio del turismo, puoi trovare molte informazioni sugli alberghi.

- dove trovare un ristorante tipico della zona
- come noleggiare una macchina per visitare le colline dell'Emilia-Romagna
- come trovare una spiaggia dove affittare un ombrellone (*beach umbrella*) e due sdraio (*deckchairs*)
- dove comprare prodotti tipici della zona
- come trovare un locale dove passare una serata divertente
- dove trovare un posto per fare un po' di sport

Sintesi

1

Parliamo In piccoli gruppi, guardate la foto e rispondete alle domande.

1. Cosa vedete nella foto?
2. Dopo aver guardato la foto, a cosa pensate?
3. Riuscite a spiegare lo scopo e le intenzioni dell'autore?
4. Vi piace? Perché sì o perché no?
5. Vi piacerebbe vedere questo monumento dal vivo? Perché?
6. Assomiglia a qualcosa nella vostra città? Che cosa?

Strategie per la comunicazione
Quando descrivi opere d'arte, ricordati di spiegare:
• il tipo di opera: una scultura, un dipinto, una fotografia, un edificio
• la tecnica usata: pittura a olio, pittura a pastello, acquerello, affresco
• lo stile: classico, moderno, d'avanguardia

2

Scriviamo Scegli uno dei seguenti argomenti e scrivi un tema di circa una pagina usando le strutture grammaticali che hai imparato in questa lezione.

• Scegli una scultura, un edificio o un sito storico che rappresenta la tua zona e/o la tua cultura. Se possibile inserisci una foto. Descrivi e valuta l'opera e poi spiega perché l'hai scelta. Dì qual è il suo significato storico o artistico. Spiega cosa significa per te o per la tua comunità.

• La città dove vivi ha ricevuto dei fondi per acquistare un'opera d'arte da esporre pubblicamente. Prepara una proposta per il consiglio comunale. Indica che tipo di opera dovrebbe essere commissionata: una scultura, un dipinto, un monumento o un edificio. Pensa chi dovrebbe essere l'autore. Descrivi l'opera in generale e indica dove andrà messa. Rifletti su quale sarà il suo scopo e pensa a come migliorerà la città. Cerca di prevedere come reagirà la comunità o come utilizzerà quest'opera.

Preparazione 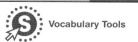 Vocabulary Tools

Vocabolario della lettura		Vocabolario utile
l'affresco *fresco*	**il martello** *hammer*	**la composizione** *composition*
l'apprendista *apprentice*	**il/la mecenate** *patron*	**il Neoplatonismo** *Neoplatonism*
la bottega *shop*	**il pigmento** *pigment*	**la mostra** *exhibit*
la commissione *commission*	**lo schizzo** *sketch*	**il paesaggio** *landscape*
il marmo *marble*		**l'Umanęsimo** *Humanism*

1

Lessico Completa le frasi.

1. Il ___pigmento___ è una sostanza colorata.
2. I giovani che imparano un'arte o un mestiere (*trade*) si chiamano ___apprendisti___.
3. Al museo c'era una ___mostra___ speciale sugli impressionisti.
4. Un ___affresco___ è un tipo di dipinto.
5. Un disegno molto veloce si chiama ___schizzo___.
6. Una ___commissione___ è un progetto che devi completare.

2

Le arti Rispondete a turno alle domande.

1. Ti piace visitare i musei? Di che tipo?
2. C'è un'opera d'arte in uno spazio pubblico che ti piace? Che tipo di opera è? Chi è l'artista? Perché ti piace?
3. Se tu potessi commissionare un'opera d'arte, quale sarebbe (un quadro, una scultura, ecc.)? Quale artista sceglieresti? Lo stile sarebbe classico o moderno? Una volta finita, dove metteresti l'opera d'arte?
4. È importante conoscere la biografia di un artista, scrittore o musicista per capire la sua opera?
5. Prima di scegliere un film o un libro leggi le recensioni (*reviews*)?
6. Quali musicisti ascolti? Hai dei gusti simili ai tuoi amici?

3

La pittura Guardate l'immagine e rispondete alle domande.

1. Com'è la composizione? Descrivetela.
2. Chi sono i personaggi?
3. Qual è il colore dominante?
4. Cosa pensi del disegno?
5. Perché è considerato un capolavoro (*masterpiece*), secondo te?
6. Che reazioni provoca quest'opera in te?

---

2 Encourage students to share their personal preferences with the rest of the class.

3 Ask students to define what constitutes a work of art by discussing controversial exhibits in recent times. What was considered controversial ten years ago may be in the mainstream today. Encourage students to come up with examples and to think about how future generations might view what we consider edgy today.

Nota CULTURALE

Rivale di **Michelangelo** nella geniale innovazione sia delle arti che delle scienze, anche **Leonardo** (1452–1519) era toscano. Autore della **Gioconda** (chiamata anche la **Monna Lisa**) e dell'**Ultima cena** (l'affresco dell'ultima cena di Gesù con gli apostoli), Leonardo è anche famoso per innumerevoli invenzioni meccaniche, tra cui una macchina volante che potrebbe essere considerata il primo aeroplano. Per Leonardo, oltre a dipingere la realtà fisica, l'artista deve presentare i «moti mentali» (i pensieri e le emozioni) dei suoi soggetti.

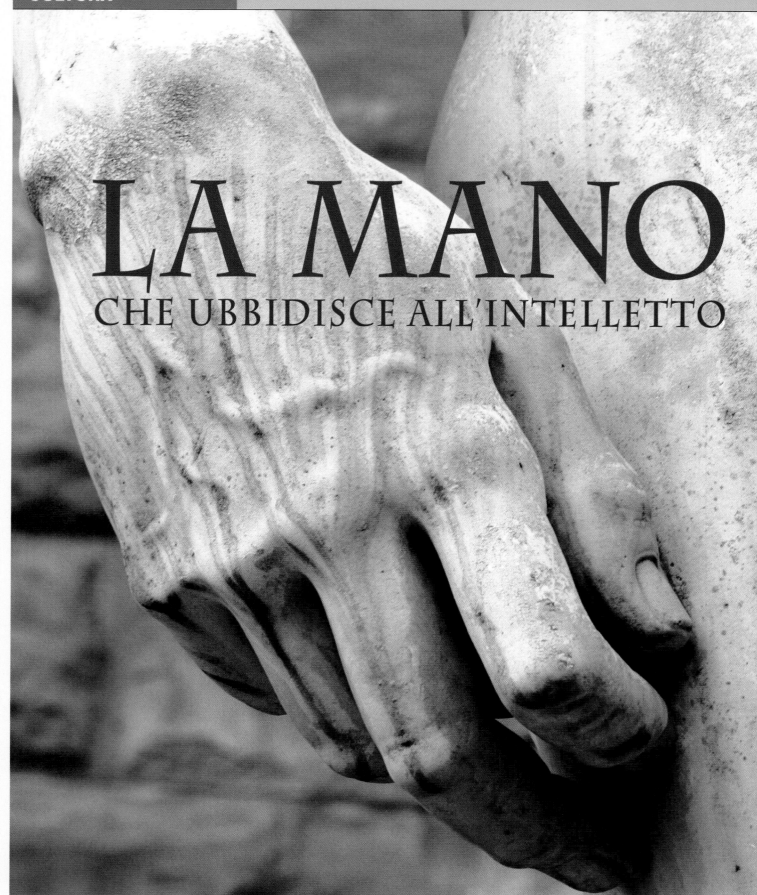

LA MANO
CHE UBBIDISCE ALL'INTELLETTO

Reading

Introduce the concept of the **presente storico** by using the cultural reading to illustrate its use.

Il nome di Michelangelo Buonarroti è sinonimo di genio creativo. L'artista rinascimentale nasce il 6 marzo del 1475 a Caprese, una città toscana in provincia d'Arezzo, e la famiglia sceglie di chiamarlo con il nome di un arcangelo: in seguito, la sua arte gli porterà il soprannome° di «Divino». Il padre, poverissimo, lo manda a lavorare già a quattordici anni come apprendista nella bottega del pittore Ghirlandaio a Firenze. Il giovane dimostra° subito delle forti

nickname

shows

La leggenda narra che l'artista stesso, impressionato dal realismo del Mosè che aveva appena completato, gli abbia scagliato un martello contro il ginocchio chiedendogli: «Perché non parli?»

---

attitudini artistiche: Lorenzo de' Medici, riconoscendo il suo grande talento, gli commissiona diverse opere quando è ancora giovanissimo. Michelangelo va ad abitare nel palazzo mediceo, dove incontra molti tra i personaggi più eminenti della cultura del tempo, come il poeta Angelo Poliziano e i filosofi Marsilio Ficino e Pico della Mirandola, uomini che influenzarono la sua pittura con le loro teorie.

Seguendo mecenati e commissioni, Michelangelo si trasferisce prima a Venezia, poi a Bologna dove studia letteratura e in seguito a Roma, dove scolpisce la *Pietà* da un unico blocco di marmo di Carrara, che diventa il suo materiale preferito. Lo usa infatti anche per il *David* (lavoro che dura ben tre anni) e per tutte le sue più celebri sculture. Le figure di Michelangelo sono così morbide° da apparire vive: la leggenda narra che l'artista stesso, impressionato dal realismo del Mosè° che aveva appena completato, gli abbia scagliato° un martello contro il ginocchio° chiedendogli: «Perché non parli?»

smooth

Moses

hurled/knee

Papa Giulio II gli commissiona molte opere, tra le quali l'affresco sul soffitto della Cappella Sistina, da molti considerato il suo capolavoro°. Anche il papa successivo, Clemente VII, gli chiede di continuare il suo lavoro nella cappella, dove Michelangelo dipinge il *Giudizio universale* che, pur ispirando molta ammirazione, scandalizza tante persone dell'epoca per via della nudità delle figure. L'artista ha un rapporto tormentato con la religione cattolica che traspare nelle sue rappresentazioni bibliche.

masterpiece

Come architetto, Michelangelo intraprende progetti monumentali, quali la biblioteca Laurentina, e disegna la cupola più famosa del mondo, quella della basilica di San Pietro al Vaticano.

Oltre ad eccellere nella pittura, scultura e architettura, Michelangelo è anche poeta. Durante l'arco della sua vita scrive centinaia di importanti sonetti, influenzati da Dante e Petrarca. Il poeta americano Ralph Waldo Emerson li traduce in inglese nell'Ottocento. Quando Michelangelo muore, nel 1564, con il suo testamento° (citato dal famoso biografo Giorgio Vasari) lascia «l'anima sua nelle mani di Dio, il suo corpo alla terra, e la roba° ai parenti più prossimi». Al mondo lascia un'eredità artistica impossibile da descrivere o quantificare. Anche recentemente sono stati ritrovati schizzi di sua mano; le opere esistenti, quelle mai finite, insieme all'influenza che ha avuto su artisti successivi rendono Michelangelo uno dei personaggi più emblematici del mondo occidentale. ∎

will

belongings

Ingredienti per la pittura

Le ricette per i colori erano spesso segrete. Nelle botteghe gli apprendisti preparavano le pitture usando pigmenti che si compravano in farmacia. Alcuni materiali, come il lapislazuli, una pietra semi-preziosa, erano costosi come l'oro e l'argento. I mecenati volevano il proprio prestigio personale riflesso non solo dalla fama dell'artista ma anche dalla ricchezza dei materiali usati nelle opere che commissionavano.

Analisi

1

Comprensione Indica se le affermazioni sono **vere** o **false**. Dopo, in coppia, correggete le affermazioni false.

Vero	Falso	
☑	☐	1. Il *Giudizio universale* è un affresco.
☑	☐	2. Michelangelo è stato l'apprendista del Ghirlandaio.
☐	☑	3. Michelangelo ha studiato pittura a Bologna.
☑	☐	4. Le sculture di Michelangelo sono di marmo di Carrara.
☐	☑	5. La cupola della basilica di San Pietro è stata progettata da Leonardo.
☐	☑	6. Le poesie di Michelangelo hanno ispirato Dante.
☑	☐	7. I sonetti di Michelangelo sono stati tradotti in inglese.
☐	☑	8. Michelangelo lascia le sue proprietà alla Chiesa.

2 Ask students to refer to specific artists/styles/works in their comments and to debate each statement.

2

Opinioni In piccoli gruppi, parlate delle vostre reazioni alle seguenti affermazioni.

> Tutti gli studenti devono seguire un corso di storia dell'arte.

> La depressione, il tormento e anche le malattie mentali possono essere fonte di creatività.

> L'arte moderna è molto difficile da capire perché è astratta.

> Capire l'espressione artistica di un paese è importante come studiare la sua storia.

> La vera arte deve essere controversa.

> Per avere successo gli artisti hanno bisogno di mecenati.

3 Ask students to exchange questions with other groups and to then reply as the artist.

3

Intervista Scegliete uno degli argomenti.

- Dovete intervistare un artista, musicista, scrittore o architetto del passato. Scrivete insieme delle domande da fargli.

- Quale artista contemporaneo ha oggi il talento e l'influenza che Michelangelo ha avuto durante il suo tempo? In che modo sono simili?

4

Scrittura Descrivi un'opera artistica, musicale o letteraria che adori o che detesti e spiega perché. Includi:

- lo stile
- la composizione
- il tema
- i colori

 Practice more at **vhlcentral.com**.

Preparazione  Vocabulary Tools

A proposito dell'autore

Gianrico Carofiglio (Bari, 1960), prima di dedicarsi alla scrittura, è stato magistrato (*judge*) e Senatore della Repubblica Italiana. La sua familiarità con procedure investigative lo ha ispirato a creare la figura (*character*) dell'avvocato Guido Guerrieri, eroe atipico motivato da un senso etico nel mondo farraginoso (*chaotic*) della giustizia italiana. Oltre ai cinque romanzi «dell'avvocato Guerrieri» dal 2002 ad oggi, Carofiglio ha pubblicato otto altri romanzi, raccolte di racconti, saggi, sceneggiature e un romanzo a fumetti (*graphic novel*). Ha ricevuto numerosi premi, ha venduto oltre cinque milioni di copie ed è stato tradotto in ventotto lingue. Gli uomini di Carofiglio cercano di fare la cosa giusta. È la loro umanità e imperfezione che determina il loro successo.

Vocabolario della lettura

a buon mercato *cheap*
adatto/a *suitable*
aspettarsi *to expect*
capitare *to happen*
la caserma *barracks*
cogliere in fallo *to catch out*
il disagio *discomfort*

fuori posto *out of place*
l'informativa *report*
l'interrogatorio *interrogation*
il particolare *detail*
rivolgersi *to address*
il verbale *police report*
vigile *alert*

Vocabolario utile

l'assassinio *assassination*
l'investigazione *investigation*
omicida *homicidal*
la precisione *precision*
lo scambio di idee *exchange of opinions*

1

Definizioni Trova la definizione adatta a ogni parola.

f	1. l'interrogatorio	a. il posto dove vivono e lavorano i militari
h	2. il verbale	b. per pochi soldi
j	3. l'investigazione	c. un elemento piccolo ma importante
g	4. il disagio	d. uno scritto divulgativo
a	5. la caserma	e. un tipo di omicidio
d	6. l'informativa	f. le domande fatte a un testimone o a un sospettato
c	7. il particolare	g. l'essere in imbarazzo e sentirsi fuori posto
e	8. l'assassinio	h. l'insieme dei fatti scritti durante un interrogatorio
i	9. essere adatto	i. non essere fuori posto
b	10. a buon mercato	j. la ricerca della verità

2

Discussione In piccoli gruppi, discutete questi argomenti.

1. La precisione linguistica è importante. Se non si hanno le parole giuste per esprimersi, sentimenti, sensazioni o fatti esistono lo stesso? Perché?

2. In italiano si può mantenere rispetto e distanza usando il **lei** invece del **tu**. In inglese come si fa? È giusto chiamare le persone che non si conoscono bene o con cui c'è un rapporto di lavoro per nome? Perché?

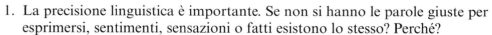 Practice more at **vhlcentral.com**.

2 Provide examples of what linguistic differences reveal about culture. For instance, English tends to avoid passive constructions, which abound in Italian. What does that say about different worldviews?

Explain that the *Carabinieri* are a branch of the Italian armed
forces as well as police, performing civil and military duties
alike since pre-unification 1814.

L'ESTATE
FREDDA

(frammento)   Gianrico Carofiglio

Subtleties

marshal

female lawyer

mafioso being investigated

police report/prompted

betrays

They remained silent/both

Tell students that
Giuseppe Fenoglio
(1922–1963) was
a partisan,
translator from
English, writer,
and playwright.
He was author,
among other things,
of *Una questione
privata* and *Il
partigiano Johnny*.
It is no coincidence
that Carofiglio
chose the name
of a writer for a
marshal who thinks
and writes well.

Che dialogo stravagante,
pensò Fenoglio. Sottigliezze°
linguistiche fra un capitano e
un maresciallo° dei carabinieri
a margine dell'interrogatorio di un
mafioso pluriomicida. Cronache di un
mondo parallelo.

—Ma a parte la dottoressa° e
Lopez°, —riprese Fenoglio dopo la
sua rapida digressione privata, —non
ci vuole niente, in generale, perché una
verbalizzazione° troppo formale, mossa°
dalle ragioni di cui parlava Calvino,
tradisca° il senso di quello che ha detto il
teste o l'indagato.

Tacquero° entrambi° per un poco.

—Non è frequente l'opportunità
di fare conversazioni del genere, in una
caserma, —disse il capitano.

—In effetti no, —rispose Fenoglio.

—Da bambino facevo un gioco.
Sceglievo una parola e la ripetevo ad
alta voce tante volte, fino a quando non
perdeva il suo significato e diventava solo
una sequenza di lettere.

—Anch'io lo facevo, —disse Fenoglio.

—Sì, credo sia piuttosto comune.

Qualche volta mi capita di farlo anche
adesso. È interessante —fa pure un po'
paura— verificare quanto sia fragile
il legame° fra le cose e le parole. Il
mondo si regge° sul collegamento° fra le
parole e le cose e questo collegamento
può essere infranto° in due minuti con
un gioco da bambini. Mi sono sempre
detto: deve significare qualcosa,
qualcosa di importante. Ma non sono
mai riuscito a capire cosa.

tie

stands/link

shattered

> ## "—Non è frequente l'opportunità di fare conversazioni del genere, in una caserma."

La lingua è una convenzione, un
patto° implicito fra le persone. Nessuna
legge di natura dice che a un certo
oggetto corrisponde una certa sequenza
di segni°—lettere e vocali. Questo

pact

signs

The dialogue preceding this excerpt is about the absurdity and abstruseness of the language used in Italian
police reports as well as about Italo Calvino, who wrote a parody of the language of police reports. For Calvino,
the "semantic terror" that ensues from reading words that have little to do with the way people actually speak
is how a writer asserts his or her superiority. Calvino calls it **antilingua**.

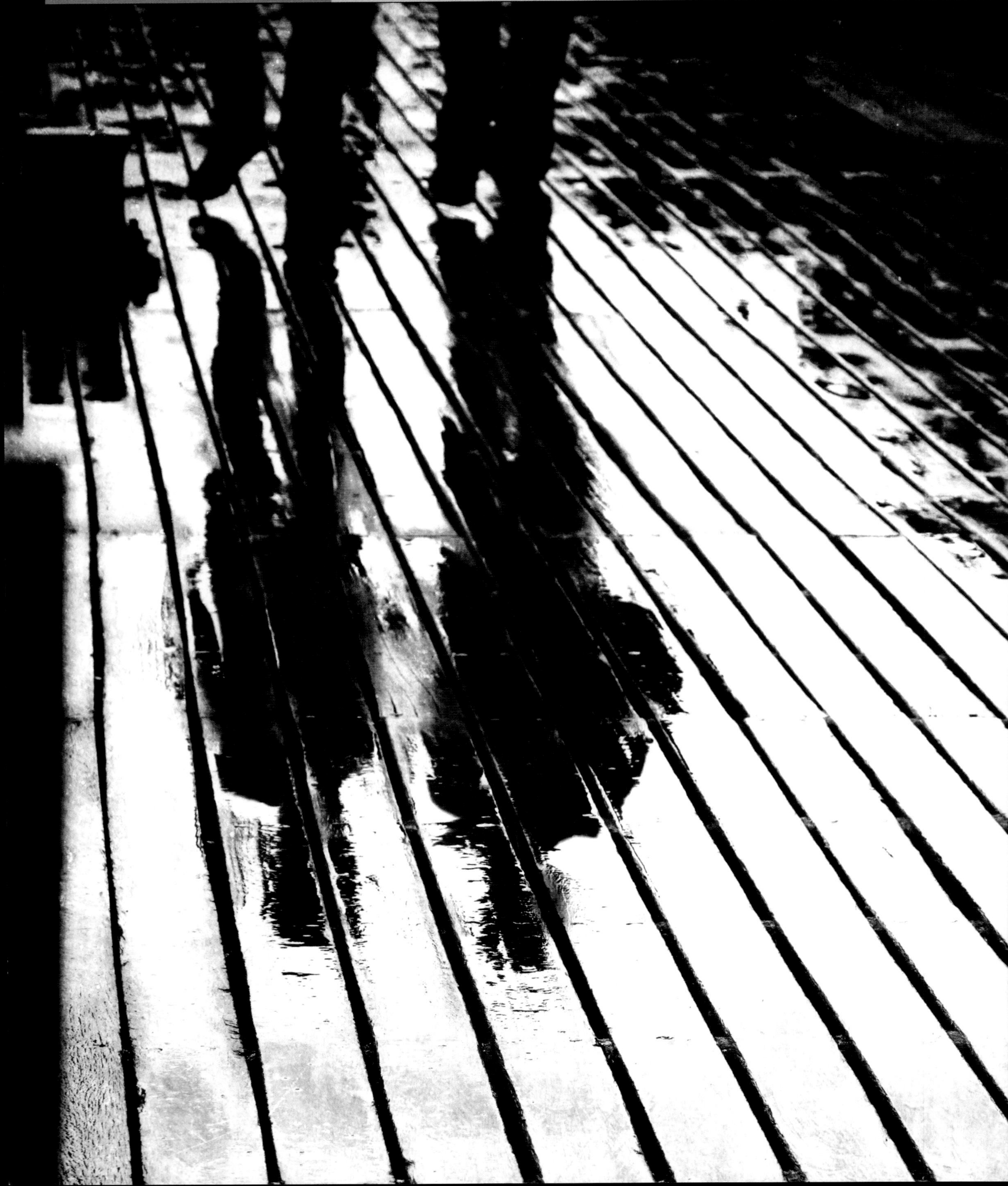

again/wine glass

è l'aspetto affascinante e un po'
45 pauroso della questione. Fenoglio
pensò queste cose, ma non le disse.
Dopo una lunga pausa e dopo aver di
nuovo° vuotato il calice° fu il capitano a
parlare ancora.

50   —Non credo che sarò un ufficiale dei
carabinieri per tutta la vita. Mi ci sono
trovato, ma sin dall'inizio ho pensato di
non essere adatto.

    —Forse questa è filosofia a buon
55 mercato, ma io credo che certi lavori
dovrebbero essere fatti da *quelli che
non si sentono adatti*, per usare la sua
espressione. Sentirsi un po' fuori posto

it makes

aiuta, rende° più vigili. Uno che si
60 sente *molto adatto*, per esempio,
non nota l'assurdità del modo in
cui scriviamo i verbali. Non nota i
particolari importanti.

    —Non avevo mai pensato alla cosa
65 in questi termini. —Neanch'io. È un'idea
che mi è venuta parlando. —Quanti anni
ha, maresciallo? —Quarantuno.

    —Io ne ho trentacinque. Da ragazzo
pensavo che a quest'età sarei stato un
70 famoso attore di teatro. Lei?

novelist

    —Pensavo che avrei voluto
scrivere. Giornalista o romanziere° era
indifferente nella mia immaginazione.
L'idea era che mi sarei guadagnato
75 da vivere scrivendo, in un modo
o nell'altro.

nodded

    Valente annuì°, come se quella
fosse esattamente la risposta che si
era aspettato.

In some ways 80

    —Per certi versi° è quello che fa.
Le sue informative sono le migliori
che abbia mai letto.

    Fenoglio era sempre stato a
disagio con i complimenti. Non

sapeva cosa dire e sentiva il bisogno di 85
cambiare discorso.

    —Posso farle una domanda, signor
capitano? —Certo. —Dà del lei a tutti
i subalterni, anche ai carabinieri di
vent'anni. Perché? Il capitano sorrise, 90
come un ragazzino colto in fallo.

It makes me
personnel
conceited

    —Mi rende° antipatico, vero? Il
personale° pensa che voglia mantenere
le distanze, che sia superbo°, lo so. Ma
voglio raccontarle un aneddoto. Una 95
volta, quando ero bambino, andai
con i miei genitori a far visita a dei
loro amici. Erano proprietari terrieri°,

landowners
large farm

avevano una masseria° e figli più grandi
di me: il maggiore poteva avere sedici 100
anni. A un certo punto sentii questo
ragazzo che dava del tu —e impartiva
degli ordini— a un vecchio contadino,
che invece si rivolgeva a lui con il voi.
Non ho mai dimenticato il senso di 105
disagio che mi diede quella scena. Forse
è per via di questo episodio che non mi

"La lingua è una convenzione, un patto implicito fra le persone."

riesce di dare del tu se non posso dire
al mio interlocutore di fare lo stesso
con me. E credo lei converrà° che non 110 *will agree*
sarebbe una buona idea se dicessi a
tutto il personale che possono dare del
tu al capitano.

    —No, in effetti non sarebbe una buona
idea, —rispose Fenoglio sorridendo. ■ 115

Analisi

1

Comprensione Scegli quale frase è vera in ogni coppia di opzioni.

1. a. Una parola ripetuta tante volte perde significato.
   b. Non importa quante volte si ripete una parola, il significato è sempre lo stesso.

2. a. La lingua è una cosa fissa.
   b. La lingua è una convenzione.

3. a. È meglio non sentirsi adatti che essere troppo sicuri di sè.
   b. È importante avere certezze assolute nella polizia.

4. a. Il maresciallo da giovane pensava di diventare scrittore.
   b. Il maresciallo da giovane pensava di diventare attore.

5. a. Il Maresciallo Fenoglio ama i complimenti.
   b. Il Maresciallo Fenoglio è a disagio con i complimenti.

6. a. Il capitano preferisce dare del lei ai subalterni per una questione di rispetto.
   b. Il capitano preferisce dare del lei ai subalterni perché è antipatico.

2

Opzioni Scegli una risposta e poi con un(a) compagno/a discuti perché ti sembra giusta.

1. Fenoglio è _____.
   a. un maresciallo non comune
   b. il tipico militare di carriera
   c. una persona che dà giudizi definitivi
   d. uno che dice parole senza senso

2. Il gioco da bambino del capitano è _____.
   a. ripetere una parola ad alta voce
   b. ripetere una sequenza di lettere
   c. ripetere una parola finché perde significato
   d. ripetere parole senza significato

3. Il Maresciallo Fenoglio _____.
   a. scrive che la lingua è una convenzione
   b. pensa che la lingua sia una convenzione
   c. pensa che a un oggetto corrisponda un segno
   d. dice che le parole sono affascinanti

4. Fenoglio crede che _____.
   a. sentirsi fuori posto sia un errore
   b. sentirsi fuori posto sia un'assurdità
   c. tutti notino come i verbali siano scritti in modo assurdo
   d. sia meglio sentirsi a disagio per essere buoni carabinieri

5. Il capitano _____.
   a. si è sentito a disagio perché un ragazzino ha insultato un vecchio
   b. si è sentito a disagio perché uno poco più grande di lui ha trattato male un sottoposto (*subordinate*)
   c. avrebbe voluto essere come il ragazzo di sedici anni
   d. avrebbe dato del tu al contadino anche lui

3 **I protagonisti** In coppia, decidete se le seguenti affermazioni sono verosimili. Perché sì o perché no?

1. Il Maresciallo Fenoglio è sorpreso dall'apertura mentale del Capitano Valente. Sì.
2. Il Capitano Valente è nostalgico della sua infanzia. No.
3. Il Maresciallo Fenoglio è più arguto (*sharp*) di quello che fa vedere. Sì.
4. Il Capitano Valente vorrebbe ancora fare l'attore. No.
5. Il Maresciallo Fenoglio ha usato le sue doti analitiche di scrittore nel suo lavoro attuale. Sì.

3 Have pairs discuss their opinions and write one sentence per item to explain why the statement is true or false; then have them share their sentences with the class. Encourage students to go beyond a simple interpretation.

4 **Opinioni** Scambia opinioni con un(a) compagno/a di classe.

1. Secondo te, è possibile avere conversazioni informali in un ambiente di lavoro rigido come quello di una caserma? Puoi immaginare una conversazione simile in un posto dove lavori tu? Per esempio? Quali sono i vantaggi e gli svantaggi di parlare di cose non di lavoro al lavoro?

2. Secondo te, è vero che sentirsi fuori posto aiuta ad essere più vigili, più attenti al lavoro che si fa, come dice il Maresciallo Fenoglio? In che modo? Puoi pensare a un esempio specifico? O credi invece che sia meglio sapere tutto? Perché?

3. Preferisci che un professore ti chiami per nome o per cognome? Perché?

4. È giusto mantenere le distanze dai colleghi sul lavoro? Cosa pensi, per esempio, di relazioni romantiche al lavoro? Sono una buona idea o no? Perché?

4 As a follow-up, have students do an Internet search on **relazioni sul posto di lavoro**, and have them write or talk about the pros and cons expressed on one or two websites. Encourage students to contribute their own opinions.

5 **Inventa una lingua** In piccoli gruppi, scrivete un dialogo in cui usate una parola diversa da quella convenzionalmente associata a un concetto e poi chiedete al resto della classe di indovinare (*guess*) che parola è.

> **Modello**   Usate **tazza** al posto di **mela**.
>
> —Mi piacciono molto le tazze rosse.
> —Come le Fuji? Io preferisco quelle verdi. Sono più aspre (*tart*).
> —Ci sono molte tazze gialle, per esempio le Golden Delicious che sono sempre buone da mangiare.

5 Make sure that students understand from this activity that language is a convention.

6 **Come continua?** In gruppi di tre, scegliete una possibile continuazione delle pagine che avete letto tra queste proposte, e scrivete una storia da leggere poi al resto della classe.

1. Il maresciallo e il capitano diventano amici e finiscono per darsi del tu, ma mai davanti ad altri colleghi.
2. Il capitano decide che non è adatto alla carriera militare e cambia mestiere.
3. Il maresciallo si mette a scrivere libri e diventa famoso.

6 After students have finished the activity, remind them that Option 3 is what happened to Carofiglio.

7 **Tema** Scegli una di queste due situazioni e scrivi un tema di almeno tre paragrafi.

- Hai trovato un lavoro per guadagnarti da vivere. In qualche modo non ti senti adatto/a e per questo metti molta cura in tutto quello che fai. Che lavoro è? Puoi descrivere quali sono le tue mansioni (*duties*)?

- Sei al lavoro e vedi un tuo superiore trattare con condiscendenza un sottoposto. Spiega cosa succede. Come reagisci? C'è qualcosa che puoi fare? O dire qualcosa ti espone al rischio di perdere il lavoro?

Practice more at **vhlcentral.com**.

Pratica

Revisione e correzione

Per scrivere un buon saggio, è necessario imparare a revisionare e correggere il proprio lavoro. Alla fine della prima stesura, usa le domande di seguito come guida per revisionare il tuo saggio e apportare tutti i cambiamenti necessari:

- **Contenuto** Hai risposto al tema assegnato? Mancano esempi o argomenti? Ci sono parti che si ripetono o che non sono pertinenti?

- **Organizzazione** L'organizzazione è chiara? Hai incluso una buona introduzione e una buona conclusione? Esiste una connessione logica tra i paragrafi?

- **Ortografia e grammatica** I verbi sono coniugati correttamente? C'è concordanza tra aggettivi e sostantivi? Ci sono errori di ortografia? Leggi ogni frase due volte e controlla minuziosamente. Assicurati che il tuo linguaggio sia preciso e specifico.

Pensa al tuo saggio come se lo avesse scritto un'altra persona. Ti convince? Ci sono dei problemi? Quali? Osservando le tue idee obbiettivamente, riesci ad anticipare le reazioni dei tuoi lettori?

1 **Preparazione** In coppia, rivedete i commenti del vostro insegnante sui saggi che avete scritto finora. A quali delle precedenti tre categorie dovete prestare più attenzione?

2 **Saggio** Scegli uno di questi argomenti e scrivi un saggio.

- Il tuo saggio deve far riferimento ad almeno due dei quattro brani studiati in questa lezione e nelle precedenti lezioni e contenuti in **Cortometraggio**, **Immagina**, **Cultura** e **Letteratura**.

- Il saggio deve essere lungo almeno due pagine.

- Quando finisci, revisiona e correggi il tuo saggio seguendo le indicazioni elencate per il contenuto, l'organizzazione, l'ortografia e la grammatica e i suggerimenti che troverai nei **Punti per la revisione dei saggi** a pagina A-1.

> Ci sono molti esempi di artisti famosi che hanno avuto una vita fuori dal comune. Bisogna essere «diversi» e non convenzionali per essere dei bravi artisti? Che cosa fa di una persona un artista?

> L'arte è solo qualcosa da ammirare nei musei, oppure può avere un effetto nella vita di tutti i giorni? Come?

> Potrebbero esserci un Leonardo da Vinci o un Michelangelo ai nostri giorni? In quali campi esprimerebbero la loro genialità? Come verrebbero giudicati dalla società?

> Che ruolo ha la storia nella nostra vita quotidiana? È importante guardare indietro alla storia o dobbiamo concentrarci sul presente?

Le arti e la storia

 Vocabulary Tools

La storia

la battaglia *battle*
la civiltà *civilization*
il decennio *decade*
l'età *age; era*
l'imperatore/imperatrice *emperor/empress*
il re/la regina *king/queen*
il regime *regime*
il regno *kingdom*
la schiavitù *slavery*
il secolo *century*

abitare *to inhabit*
abolire *to abolish*
arrendersi *to surrender*
colonizzare *to colonize*
conquistare *to conquer*
dirigere *to lead*
espellere *to expel*
invadere *to invade*
liberare *to liberate*
opprimere *to oppress*
rovesciare *to overthrow*
sconfiggere *to defeat*
stabilirsi *to settle*

democratico/a *democratic*
fascista *fascist*
monarchico/a *monarchic*
(prei)storico/a *(pre)historic*

a.C. (avanti Cristo) *BC*
d.C. (dopo Cristo) *AD*

La letteratura

la biografia *biography*
il diritto d'autore *copyright*
il genere *genre*
il giallo *thriller*
il narratore *narrator*
la novella *short novel*
il personaggio *character*
la poesia *poetry*
la prosa *prose*
la rima *rhyme*
il romanzo *novel*
la strofa *stanza*
la trama *plot*
il verso *line (of poetry)*

censurare *to censor*
svolgersi *to take place*

classico/a *classic*
oggettivo/a *objective*
premiato/a *award-winning*
realistico/a *realistic*
satirico/a *satirical*
soggettivo/a *subjective*
tragico/a *tragic*
umoristico/a *humorous*

L'arte

l'acquerello *watercolor*
l'autoritratto *self-portrait*
le belle arti *fine arts*
il dipinto *painting*
la natura morta *still life*
l'opera *work (of art); opera*
l'orchestra sinfonica/da camera *symphony/chamber orchestra*
il pennello *paintbrush*
la pittura *paint; painting*
la pittura a olio/pastello *oil/pastel painting*
il quadro *painting; picture*
la scultura *sculpture*

dipingere *to paint*
scolpire *to sculpt*

d'avanguardia *avant-garde*
estetico/a *aesthetic*

Gli artisti

l'artigiano/a *artisan*
il/la drammaturgo/a *playwright*
il pittore/la pittrice *painter*
il/la saggista *essayist*
lo scultore/la scultrice *sculptor*

Cortometraggio

il/la connazionale *compatriot*
la crostata *pie*
l'invito *invitation*
il metro *tape measure*
il/la partigiano/a *partisan*
la Resistenza *The Resistance*
il ricevimento *reception*
la sartoria *tailor's shop*

la Sua/vostra signora (*form.*) *your wife*
la spia *spy*
la stoffa *fabric*
il taglio *cut*

fucilare *to execute*
ingrassare *to gain weight*

incinta *pregnant*
tedesco/a *German*

Cultura

l'affresco *fresco*
l'apprendista *apprentice*
la bottega *shop*
la commissione *commission*
la composizione *composition*
il marmo *marble*
il martello *hammer*
il/la mecenate *patron*
la mostra *exhibit*
il Neoplatonismo *Neoplatonism*
il paesaggio *landscape*
il pigmento *pigment*
lo schizzo *sketch*
l'Umanesimo *Humanism*

Letteratura

l'assassinio *assassination*
la caserma *barracks*
il disagio *discomfort*
l'informativa *report*
l'interrogatorio *interrogation*
l'investigazione *investigation*
il particolare *detail*
la precisione *precision*
lo scambio di idee *exchange of opinions*
il verbale *police report*

aspettarsi *to expect*
capitare *to happen*
cogliere in fallo *to catch out*
rivolgersi *to address*

a buon mercato *cheap*
adatto/a *suitable*
fuori posto *out of place*
omicida *homicidal*
vigile *alert*

L'influenza dei media

Radio, giornali, televisione, Internet, social media, contribuiscono alla diffusione dell'informazione e, in molti casi, influenzano la conoscenza globale. Oggi abbiamo accesso completo all'informazione in casa e fuori, a ogni ora del giorno e della notte. Che uso ne facciamo? Siamo in grado di (*in a position to*) controllare l'enorme quantità di informazioni che ci arriva o ne siamo vittime passive? I mezzi di comunicazione ci mostrano una realtà vera o in qualche modo distorta?

342

368

Destinazione: LIGURIA

PREVIEW Have students reflect on the photo on the previous page and engage them in a discussion about the influence of media. Ask: **Guardate la TV? Ascoltate la radio? O preferite navigare su Internet? Come è cambiata la vita delle persone con la disponibilità** (*availability*) **di tanti mezzi di comunicazione?**

Media e cultura  Vocabulary Tools

Cinema, radio e televisione

l'adattamento *adaptation*
i cartoni animati *cartoons*
la colonna sonora *soundtrack*
il documentario *documentary*
il doppiaggio *dubbing*
gli effetti speciali *special effects*
l'intervista *interview*

la puntata *episode*
lo schermo *screen*
il sottotitolo *subtitle*
la (stazione) radio *radio (station)*

la televisione satellitare
  satellite TV
la televisione via cavo *cable TV*

filmare *to film*
registrare *to record*
trasmettere *to broadcast*
uscire *to be released*

SINONIMI E CONTRARI
filmare ←→ riprendere, girare
l'inviato/a speciale ←→ il/la corrispondente
editore/editrice ←→ casa editrice

Point out that **editore/editrice** means *publisher*, and not *editor* (**redattore/redattrice**). Point out that **filmare** and **riprendere** are used in expressions like: **filmare/riprendere una scena, un'attrice, un episodio, ecc.** When the word **film** appears in the sentence, **girare** is preferred: **Il film è stato girato a Cinecittà.**

I media

l'attualità *current events*
la censura *censorship*
il giornale radio *radio news*
la notizia *news story*
il notiziario *news program*
la pubblicità *commercial; advertisement*
il sondaggio *opinion poll*
il telegiornale *TV news*

essere aggiornato/a *to be up-to-date*
informarsi *to get/stay informed*

in differita *pre-recorded*
in diretta *live*
influente *influential*
(im)parziale *(im)partial; (un)biased*

La gente dei media

l'ascoltatore/ascoltatrice
  (radio) listener
l'attore/attrice *actor/actress*
il/la cronista *reporter*
l'editore/editrice *publisher*
il/la giornalista *journalist*
l'inviato/a speciale *correspondent*
il/la redattore/redattrice *editor*
il/la telespettatore/telespettatrice
  television viewer

Schermo may be used metaphorically as well. **Il grande schermo** means *movie theatre*, while **il piccolo schermo** is *television*. The English expression *starring* is usually given in Italian by a simple preposition: **con**. Example: **Ho visto un bellissimo film con Monica Bellucci.**

La stampa

il comunicato stampa *press release*
la cronaca (locale/sportiva)
  (local/sports) news
il fumetto *comic strip*
il giornale *newspaper*
la libertà di stampa *freedom of the press*
il mensile *monthly magazine*
l'oroscopo *horoscope*
la rivista *magazine*
la rubrica (di cultura
  e società) *(lifestyle) section*
il settimanale
  weekly magazine
la vignetta *cartoon*

fare un abbonamento *to subscribe*

La cultura popolare

il carnevale *carnival; Mardi Gras*

Ferragosto *August 15 (holiday); August vacation*
i festeggiamenti *festivities*
il folclore *folklore*
la Pasquetta *Easter Monday*
il patrimonio culturale
  cultural heritage
il/la santo/a patrono/a *patron saint*
l'usanza *custom*

festeggiare *to celebrate*

INSTRUCTIONAL RESOURCES
Audioscripts, Answer Keys, Lab MP3s
SAM/WebSAM: WB, LM

Uscire usually refers to the release of a film, newspaper, or magazine. **La settimana prossima uscirà l'ultimo film del noto regista...** Point out that **un'intervista** is usually carried out by a journalist, while a job interview is **un colloquio di lavoro**.

Pratica e comunicazione

1 **Relazioni** Completa le relazioni scegliendo la parola opportuna dal vocabolario.

1. la radio : l'ascoltatore :: la televisione : _il telespettatore_

2. il libro : la traduzione :: il film : _il doppiaggio/il sottotitolo_

3. la televisione : il canale :: la radio : _la stazione radio_

4. l'imparzialità : la libertà di stampa :: la parzialità : _la censura_

5. il film : il produttore :: la rivista : _l'editore_

6. adulti : il telegiornale :: bambini : _i cartoni animati_

1 Ask pairs of students to create two additional analogies using the new vocabulary. Then have them share them with the rest of the class.

2 **Discussioni... festive!** Carlo ha deciso di trascorrere il pomeriggio del 15 agosto a casa. Stefania, invece, ha altre idee. Completa il dialogo con le parole della lista.

| Ferragosto | festeggiare | patrimonio culturale |
| festeggiamenti | folclore | usanza |

CARLO Accidenti! Non c'è niente di interessante in televisione! Su nessun canale!

STEFANIA Ma certo! A (1) _Ferragosto_ gli italiani non stanno a casa! Non vedi che la città è deserta e i negozi sono chiusi? Sono tutti fuori!

CARLO Mi rifiuto di viaggiare a Ferragosto: tutto costa di più, c'è traffico in autostrada e fa un gran caldo... Preferisco andare ai (2) _festeggiamenti_ in paese questa sera.

STEFANIA E la processione? Dovremmo andarci, è un'antica (3) _usanza_ del nostro paese...

CARLO Grazie, ma preferisco (4) _festeggiare_ stasera in piazza con un bel piatto di carne alla brace (*grilled*). Anche questo è parte del (5) _patrimonio culturale_ del nostro paese. Risale (*It dates back*) ai Romani...

STEFANIA Sei il solito materialista!

CARLO E tu sei poco esperta di (6) _folclore_: certe tradizioni sono antichissime! Informati!

2 Have pairs of students write and perform a mini-dialogue related to a national holiday they celebrate.

Nota CULTURALE

Quasi tutte le maggiori festività italiane hanno avuto origine in epoca pagana e sono poi state assimilate dal cristianesimo. **Pasqua** è la risurrezione di Cristo, ma era anche una remota celebrazione della rinascita della natura. Il giorno di **Pasquetta**, inserito nel calendario per prolungare la festa di Pasqua, è dedicato a un tradizionale picnic all'aperto, un giorno di festa insieme a parenti o amici. Anche **Ferragosto**, che oggi celebra l'assunzione in cielo di Maria, segnava in epoca romana la fine dei lavori agricoli con balli, canti e cibo per tutti. A causa del caldo, anche questo giorno è tradizionalmente dedicato ad una gita al mare o in montagna in cerca di refrigerio°.

in cerca di refrigerio *relief from the heat*

3 **Secondo te** Rispondi al questionario. Poi, in coppia, confrontate le vostre risposte e supportatele con degli esempi.

	Sì	No
1. Oggi informarsi è più facile che nel passato.	☐	☐
2. Grazie ai mass media, oggi la gente conosce meglio il mondo.	☐	☐
3. La libertà di stampa è un'utopia.	☐	☐
4. Ci sono più notizie imparziali su Internet che sui giornali.	☐	☐
5. Nei mass media le immagini influenzano più delle parole.	☐	☐
6. Per informarsi bisogna guardare la televisione piuttosto che leggere i giornali.	☐	☐

3 Ask students to share with the class the episodes and real events that they used to support their opinions.

4 **I miei gusti** In coppia, conversate sui seguenti argomenti.

• se ascoltate la radio e, se sì, quali programmi o quali stazioni preferite

• se leggete regolarmente o se siete abbonati a giornali, riviste o fumetti

• quale rubrica preferite in un giornale o se preferite invece leggere l'oroscopo o le vignette

• se avete un cronista, un presentatore o un attore preferito e perché vi piace

4 Encourage students to add questions of their own.

Practice more at vhlcentral.com.

INSTRUCTIONAL
RESOURCES
Supersite: Video, Script &
Translation
SAM/WebSAM: WB

Preparazione Vocabulary Tools

Vocabolario del cortometraggio	
bruciare *to burn*	
capitare *to happen*	
chattare *to chat online*	
contare *to be important*	
il colpo di fulmine *lightning strike*	
la lavanderia *dry cleaner*	
la tacca *cellular reception bar*	

Vocabolario utile	
il calcetto *foosball*	
il campo *cellular reception, field*	
l'elettricista *electrician*	
fare/comporre un numero *to dial a number*	
il prefisso *area code*	
la probabilità *probability*	
squillare *to ring*	
il telefonino *cell phone*	
il temporale *storm*	

ESPRESSIONI

a caso *by chance, randomly*

Appunto! *exactly!*

in un attimo *in an instant*

sbagliare numero *to get the wrong number*

1

Pratica Associa le parole con la definizione nelle due colonne.

h	1. il calcetto	a.	è un momento molto breve
e	2. il telefonino	b.	brucia
g	3. la lavanderia	c.	installa e aggiusta i sistemi elettrici
a	4. l'attimo	d.	succede durante un temporale
f	5. il numero di telefono	e.	squilla
b	6. il fuoco	f.	ha un prefisso
d	7. il colpo di fulmine	g.	è dove si lavano i vestiti
c	8. l'elettricista	h.	è il calcio in miniatura

2

2 Before starting the
activity, make sure
students understand that
the title of the film refers
to the American actress
Sharon Stone.

2 Encourage students
to report each other's
preferences to the rest
of the class.

Le celebrità Rispondi alle domande e commenta le risposte con un/a compagno/a.

1. Chi è la tua celebrità preferita? (della TV, del cinema, dello sport, della musica, ecc.)
2. C'è un altro personaggio che ammiri che non è una star famosa? Chi è?
3. Ti interessa la vita personale dei personaggi famosi?
4. Come ti tieni informato? Leggi i giornali scandalistici?
5. Perché, secondo te, alla gente piace seguire la vita privata delle persone famose?
6. Hai mai incontrato una persona famosa? Chi? In quale circostanza?
7. Hai mai chiesto un autografo? A chi?

3

Sondaggio Intervistate i vostri compagni e trovate qualcuno che abbia fatto le seguenti cose. Alla fine del sondaggio presentate i risultati alla classe.

Attività	Nome del(la) compagno/a
Ha visto un film con Sharon Stone. Quale?	
Appartiene a un fan club. Di chi?	
Legge i giornali scandalistici. Quali? In quali circostanze li legge?	
Ha cercato di trovare il numero di telefono o l'e-mail di una persona famosa. Chi?	
Segue delle celebrità su Twitter. Chi?	
È stato/a in fila per molte ore per comprare dei biglietti o incontrare una celebrità. In quale circostanza?	

3 Have students walk around the classroom asking each other the survey questions. Poll students to determine which celebrities/TV shows/sports events are the most popular in the class.

4

Il caso e la fama In gruppi di tre studenti discutete le seguenti affermazioni e spiegate le vostre opinioni con degli esempi specifici.

Affermazione	D'accordo Sì/No	Perché
Il caso ha una parte importante nella vita delle persone comuni e di quelle famose.		
I colpi di fulmine non durano mai.		
Incontrarsi e innamorarsi è un destino.		
Con la fama si perde la privacy.		

5

I personaggi e la storia

A. In coppia, descrivete le caratteristiche fisiche e le personalità di questi personaggi del corto.

B. Pensate al possibile rapporto tra i personaggi ritratti sopra e immaginate la storia.

Practice more at vhlcentral.com.

Premio **Solinas** in collaborazione con Gratta e Vinci, 2010

Finalista di **Talenti in Corso**, 2011

Il numero di
SHARON

Regia, Soggetto e Sceneggiatura ROBERTO GAGNOR, **Cast** GLEN BLACKHALL, MASSIMO DE LORENZO e ELENA RADONICICH **Fotografia** STEFANO PALOMBI **Montaggio** DESIDERIA RAYNER

Trama *Andrea, chattando, si innamora di Lisa. C'è un blackout e Andrea resta con un numero di cellulare incompleto: per ritrovare Lisa decide di provare le mille combinazioni possibili.*

ANDREA La rete dei cellulari in Italia copre circa il 98% del paese. Io vivo qui: nel 2% dove non c'è una tacca neanche a pagarla.

ANDREA Sapete cos'è una chat casuale? Io una sera ci ho trovato Lisa...

LISA No, ... Un pochino. È che mi ha lasciato il mio ragazzo.

ANDREA Fatto sta che ci mettiamo a parlare. Lei è bellisima anche con gli occhi rossi e io vorrei darle un bacio e dirle che passerà tutto.

ANDREA Sarà che qui non vedo molta gente. Sarà che mi innamoro in un attimo. Sarà che mi stava dando il suo numero di telefono.
LISA 3-4-9 64-39-...
ANDREA No!

ETTORE Mille?
ANDREA Sì. Mancano tre cifre del numero. Dieci per dieci per dieci, mille combinazioni possibili.

TEACHING OPTION Encourage students to discuss possible reasons for the differences and similarities in cell phone use in specific countries: Economic growth? Educational levels? National production of cell phones and other electronic devices?

Sullo SCHERMO

Indica se le affermazioni sono **vere** o **false**.

V **1.** Nel paese di Andrea non c'è campo cellulare.

V **2.** Andrea usa il computer per comunicare.

F **3.** Lisa e Andrea si incontrano per strada.

F **4.** Lisa sta piangendo perché ha perso il lavoro.

V **5.** Il temporale interrompe l'elettricità.

V **6.** Andrea ha solo parte del numero di cellulare di Lisa.

Analisi

1 Comprensione Completa le frasi.

1. La zona di Andrea non ha __e__
2. Per incontrare delle ragazze __g__
3. Lisa __a__
4. Mentre Andrea e Lisa chattano __h__
5. Il temporale __b__
6. Andrea cerca di __d__
7. La probabilità __c__
8. Mentre Andrea sta componendo il suo numero __f__

a. è stata lasciata dal fidanzato.
b. causa un blackout.
c. di completare il numero è una su mille.
d. chiamare Lisa.
e. campo cellulare.
f. Lisa entra nel bar.
g. Andrea chatta sul computer.
h. c'è un temporale.

2 Analisi Scegli la risposta giusta.

1. Nel bar di Ettore si gioca a _____.
   a. carte   b. calcetto   c. tombola

2. All'inizio del film Andrea si sente _____.
   a. solo   b. innamorato   c. allegro

3. Per Andrea e Lisa l'incontro in chat è _____.
   a. una probabilità   b. un errore   c. un colpo di fulmine

4. Andrea va al bar per _____.
   a. usare il telefono fisso   b. bere il caffè   c. parlare con gli amici

5. Gli ospiti del bar che ascoltano le telefonate di Andrea sono _____.
   a. annoiati   b. curiosi   c. scioccati

6. Andrea trova il numero di Lisa _____.
   a. sistematicamente   b. casualmente   c. disperatamente

7. Ettore riesce a trovare il numero di _____.
   a. Andrea   b. Lisa   c. Sharon Stone

8. Di professione Lisa è _____.
   a. un'attrice   b. un'elettricista   c. un'insegnante

3 Opinioni In coppia rispondete a turno alle domande.

1. Cosa pensi delle chat? Le usi spesso?
2. Come preferisci comunicare? A voce o scrivendo un'e-mail o un SMS?
3. Puoi immaginare la tua vita senza il telefonino? Perché? Come lo usi?
4. A quale persona famosa ti piacerebbe telefonare? Cosa le/gli diresti?
5. Qual è il modo migliore di incontrare persone nuove?
6. Cosa avresti fatto al posto di Andrea dopo il blackout?

3 Ask students to share their preferences with the rest of the class.

4

Al telefono Rispondi alle domande e confronta le tue risposte con quelle di un/a compagno/a.

1. Usi il video con Skype o FaceTime? Con chi e perché?
2. Ricevi spesso chiamate di persone che hanno sbagliato numero? Come reagisci?
3. Hai mai mandato un SMS a una persona sbagliata? A chi?
4. Ci sono dei momenti in cui non rispondi al telefono? Perché?
5. C'è qualcuno, un amico o un parente, che ti chiama troppo spesso? Cosa fai?
6. Dimentichi mai il cellulare a casa? Come ti senti quando non ce l'hai con te?

4 Set up a video call with an Italian native speaker. Have the students prepare questions to ask in advance.

5

Discussione In gruppi di tre rispondete alle domande.

1. Pensate che Andrea e Lisa saranno felici insieme?
2. Come sarà la loro vita futura?
3. Quale personaggio nel film è il più fortunato? Perché?
4. Hai mai avuto un colpo di fulmine? Descrivilo.

6

Scenette In piccoli gruppi improvvisate dei dialoghi basati su una di queste situazioni e poi recitateli davanti alla classe.

Situazione 1

Mentre lavora nel suo bar Ettore ha trovato il numero di Sharon Stone. Che cosa le dirà quando lei risponderà al telefono? Immaginate la conversazione e la reazione dei clienti del bar che stanno ascoltando.

Situazione 2

Una delle persone chiamate da Andrea sta cucinando e si sente solo/a. Anche se Andrea continua a scusarsi e cerca di riattaccare il telefono, l'altro/a insiste a chiacchierare e a raccontargli la sua vita. Riuscirà Andrea a concludere la conversazione?

7

Scriviamo Scegli uno di questi argomenti e discutilo in una breve composizione.

- Come sono cambiati i mezzi di comunicazione da quando sei nato/a? Come li usi tu? Pensi che le persone adesso comunichino meglio o peggio di prima?

- Scrivi un'e-mail (o una lettera) a un personaggio contemporaneo (o del passato) con cui hai sempre desiderato scambiare delle idee.

- Come comunicheremo tra 20 anni secondo te? Immagina e descrivi le tecnologie future per la comunicazione.

Practice more at
vhlcentral.com.

INSTRUCTIONAL RESOURCES: Teaching suggestions; Answer Keys
SAM/WebSAM: WB

IMMAGINA

I patrimoni dell'umanità

La **Liguria** è una regione del Nord-Ovest d'Italia, situata tra le Alpi, gli Appennini e il mar Ligure. Il litorale° è conosciuto come **Riviera di Ponente** e **Riviera di Levante** con **Genova**, il capoluogo, quasi nel mezzo. Nel 1997 e nel 2006 l'UNESCO ha riconosciuto alla Liguria due siti come patrimonio dell'umanità°. Il primo comprende° **Porto Venere**, le **Cinque Terre** e le **isole del** golfo di **La Spezia**. Il secondo riguarda il centro storico di Genova, in particolare la **Strada Nuova** e i **palazzi dei Rolli**.

Porto Venere è un borgo° ben conservato° con angoli molto pittoreschi e un considerevole patrimonio architettonico.

I cinque borghi che costituiscono le Cinque Terre sono noti in tutto il mondo per la loro bellezza suggestiva e romantica. **Riomaggiore**, **Manarola**, **Vernazza**, **Corniglia** e **Monterosso al Mare** si ergono° su colline a strapiombo° sul mare. Un sentiero° collega i cinque borghi e il tratto° tra Riomaggiore e Manarola è conosciuto come la «Via dell'Amore» con magnifici panorami del mare e delle colline. Ogni borgo è caratteristico per le case colorate, i «carrugi» —le tipiche stradine della Liguria— e per le colline su cui i contadini hanno costruito terrazzamenti° che coltivano con vigneti e oliveti. Purtroppo nel 2011 e nel 2012 le Cinque Terre sono state colpite da violenti alluvioni° e gravi frane°.

Andando nel centro storico di Genova, in **via Garibaldi**, conosciuta durante il Rinascimento come **Strada Nuova**, possiamo ammirare il secondo sito UNESCO. Lungo questa strada le famiglie nobili della città costruirono palazzi iscritti° ai ***Rolli degli alloggiamenti pubblici di Genova*** per accogliere° personaggi importanti o visite di Stato. La costruzione e la disposizione di questi palazzi rappresenta il primo esempio di architettura urbana in Europa, emulato in seguito in molte parti del mondo. Passeggiando per le strade e visitando i palazzi, il turista ha l'opportunità di scoprire una Genova antica. Durante il '500 ed il '600, Genova conobbe un periodo di grande splendore che le è valso° l'appellativo la «Superba°». Tra gli edifici della Strada Nuova, **Palazzo Tobia Pallavicini** conserva la magnifica **Galleria d'oro** in stile rococò; **Palazzo Nicolosio Lomellini** ha il bellissimo ninfeo° all'ingresso; ricordiamo anche il **Palazzo Rosso** e il **Palazzo Bianco**, dal colore delle loro facciate°, in cui sono conservate collezioni d'arte europea; **Palazzo Tursi**, infine, è oggi la sede della municipalità di Genova.

La Liguria, insomma, promette di soddisfare sia gli appassionati della natura che gli amanti della storia e dell'architettura.

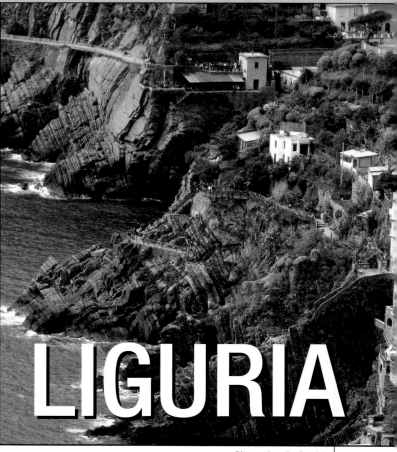

Riomaggiore (La Spezia)

Palazzo Tursi

In più...

Vernazza è l'unico borgo delle Cinque Terre dotato di un piccolo porto naturale su cui si trovano i resti° del Castello dei Doria con la torre di avvistamento. Al centro del borgo, pieno di vicoli stretti, portici e archi, sorge° la chiesa di Santa Margherita d'Antiochia, in stile gotico-ligure, con un campanile a pianta ottagonale°. Le colline che circondano Vernazza sono coltivate a vigneti e producono il passito° Schiacchetrà.

litorale *coastline* **patrimonio dell'umanità** *human heritage* **comprende** *includes* **borgo** *village* **ben conservato** *well-preserved* **si ergono** *stand up* **colline a strapiombo** *hills overhanging* **sentiero** *path* **tratto** *section* **terrazzamenti** *terraces* **alluvioni** *floods* **frane** *landslides* **iscritti** *registered* **accogliere** *welcome* **le è valso** *earned it* **la Superba** *the Proud* **ninfeo** *ornamental; fountain* **facciate** *façades* **resti** *remains* **sorge** *it is located* **pianta ottagonale** *octagonal plan* **passito** *wine made from raisins*

Vero o falso? Indica se ogni frase è **vera** o **falsa**. Correggi le frasi false. Some answers will vary.

1. Genova si trova a metà tra la Riviera di Levante e la Riviera di Ponente. Vero.

2. I «carrugi» sono abitazioni colorate. Falso.

3. La «Via dell'Amore» è un'autostrada della Liguria. Falso.
   È un sentiero in collina che collega Riomaggiore e Manarola nelle Cinque Terre.

4. I terrazzamenti sono balconi delle case dei borghi liguri.
   Falso. Sono «terrazze» per coltivare in collina.

5. I palazzi dei Rolli furono costruiti da famiglie aristocratiche. Vero.

6. Il Castello di Vernazza si vede dal porto. Vero.

7. Al Festival di Sanremo gli artisti devono cantare canzoni nuove. Vero.

8. Slow Food è un movimento internazionale. Vero.

Quanto hai imparato? Rispondi alle domande.
Some answers will vary.

1. Quali sono alcune caratteristiche dei siti UNESCO della Liguria? bellezza del paesaggio, beni architettonici e artistici

2. Quali sono le coltivazioni tipiche dei terrazzamenti liguri? I vigneti e gli oliveti.

3. Quali sono alcuni elementi comuni ai borghi delle Cinque Terre? case colorate, strade strette, magnifici panorami, una bellezza romantica e suggestiva

4. Perché sono importanti i palazzi dei Rolli da un punto di vista architettonico? Sono il primo esempio di architettura urbana.

5. Che cos'è il Festival di Sanremo? È una gara musicale tra cantanti.

6. Che obiettivo ha il movimento Slow Food? educazione al gusto, difesa della biodiversità e interazione tra i produttori e consumatori

Il Festival della canzone italiana Il **Festival di Sanremo** si svolge° ogni anno, dal 1951, nell'omonima cittadina ligure, tra la fine di febbraio e i primi giorni di marzo. La manifestazione è una gara° tra cantanti che interpretano, in prima assoluta°, una canzone di autori italiani. Di solito gareggiano° due gruppi di cantanti, quelli già famosi e i giovani, cioè cantanti poco conosciuti o nuovi al pubblico. Le canzoni sono votate da giurie° di esperti o giurie popolari.

Slow Food è un movimento internazionale nato in Italia nel 1986. Fondato dal gastronomo e sociologo **Carlo Petrini**, il movimento nasce in risposta al dilagare° del *fast food* e riassume° nel suo motto, «buono, pulito e giusto», i tre obiettivi principali e la missione di Slow Food: l'educazione al gusto, la difesa della biodiversità e l'interazione tra i produttori e consumatori. Slow Food promuove il diritto a vivere il cibo e l'enogastronomia come un piacere, nel rispetto di chi produce, dell'ambiente e del territorio. Oggi l'associazione opera in più di 150 paesi attraverso iniziative locali e internazionali.

si svolge *takes place* **gara** *competition* **prima assoluta** *for the very first time* **gareggiano** *compete* **giurie** *juries* **dilagare** *flood* **riassume** *summarizes*

Progetto

La Liguria ha dato i natali a famosi personaggi della cultura italiana, tra cui lo scrittore **Edmondo De Amicis** e il critico letterario **Carlo Bo**.

- Cerca informazioni su uno dei due personaggi menzionati o un ligure famoso a tua scelta.

- Scrivi una breve presentazione biografica e una presentazione su uno dei loro lavori. Includi delle riflessioni personali.

- Confronta il tuo lavoro con il resto della classe.

GALLERIA DI PERSONE ILLUSTRI

VIOLINISTA, COMPOSITORE

Niccolò Paganini (1782–1840)

Niccolò Paganini è considerato uno dei più grandi violinisti dell'Ottocento e fra i più importanti esponenti (*figures*) della musica romantica. Padre della moderna tecnica violinistica, viene ricordato per la maestria esecutiva, le ineguagliabili doti compositive e le fondamentali innovazioni. Nato a Genova, Paganini studiò violino nella città natale e successivamente a Parma. A soli quindici anni iniziò una brillante carriera concertistica in Italia e poi in tutta Europa. Tra le sue opere più celebri si ricordano i *24 Capricci per Violino solo op. 1*, i *6 Concerti per violino e orchestra* e numerose partiture per chitarra. A causa della figura emaciata e dell'unione di «genio e sregolatezza (*recklessness*)», Paganini è stato spesso accusato dai critici di aver stipulato un patto con Satana. Morì a soli cinquantasette anni e, a causa dei supposti collegamenti con il diavolo, lo Stato della Chiesa approvò la sepoltura (*burial*) solo sette anni dopo.

PAROLE COLTE

la dote *talent*
incidere un album *to record an album*
la maestria *mastery*
la partitura *music score*
il/la redattore/redattrice *journalist, editor*

POETA

Eugenio Montale (1896–1981)

Eugenio Montale è stato uno dei massimi poeti italiani del Novecento e premio Nobel per la letteratura nel 1975. Il tema principale della poetica di Montale è il «male di vivere», la crisi del rapporto tra l'uomo contemporaneo e il reale. Nato a Genova, segue studi tecnici, studia lingue straniere e si dedica alla letteratura da autodidatta (*self-taught*) leggendo i testi di Dante, Petrarca, Boccaccio e D'Annunzio. Intorno ai trent'anni si trasferisce a Firenze dove lavora prima come redattore per una casa editrice e poi direttore della Biblioteca del Gabinetto Vieusseux da cui viene allontanato per essersi rifiutato di prendere la tessera (*membership*) del partito fascista. Nel 1948 si trasferisce a Milano dove intraprende l'attività giornalistica diventando

redattore per il *Corriere della Sera*. Tra le sue opere si ricordano: *Ossi di seppia*, (Cuttlefish Bones) *Le occasioni, La bufera* (storm) e altro.

ARCHITETTO
Renzo Piano (1937–)

Renzo Piano è nato a Genova-Pegli nel 1937. Ha studiato in Italia e all'estero e da oltre trent'anni è uno degli architetti più famosi nel mondo. Il suo stile si distingue (*stands out*) per i materiali altamente tecnologici e un design pulito e lineare. Tra i progetti più famosi ricordiamo la ristrutturazione (*renovation*) del centro storico e del porto di Genova, l'auditorium della musica di Roma, l'aeroporto internazionale di Osaka ed il palazzo del New York Times. Renzo Piano è anche fondatore del Renzo Piano Building Workshop, con sedi (*offices*) a Genova e a Parigi, che offre tirocini (*internships*) per giovani architetti.

L'architetto genovese è stato il primo italiano ad apparire nella Time 100, l'elenco delle 100 personalità più influenti del mondo secondo la rivista *Time*, nel 2006.

CANTAUTORE
Fabrizio De André (1940–1999)

Nato a Genova nel 1940, è stato uno dei cantautori italiani più amati e celebrati di sempre. De André è stato anche scrittore e attivista politico, si è sempre schierato (*sided*) con gli ultimi e i ribelli, coloro che vogliono cambiare il mondo ma falliscono (*fail*). In quasi quarant'anni di carriera il cantautore genovese ha inciso quattordici album oltre a numerosi singoli. Tra le sue canzoni più celebri si ricordano: *La guerra di Piero, Bocca di Rosa, Don Raffaè, Via del campo*. Le sue canzoni raccontano

le vicende (*stories*) di prostitute, emarginati, ribelli e vengono considerate da molti critici delle vere e proprie poesie. Insieme a Gino Paoli, Luigi Tenco e altri è stato uno degli esponenti della Scuola genovese, un nucleo di artisti che negli anni Settanta ha rilanciato la musica leggera italiana.

Comprensione

Rispondere Rispondi alle seguenti domande.

1. Per cosa viene ricordato Paganini? Viene ricordato per la maestria esecutiva, le ineguagliabili doti compositive e le fondamentali innovazioni.
2. Per quale motivo Paganini è stato accusato di aver stipulato un patto con Satana? È stato accusato a causa della figura emaciata e dell'unione di «genio e sregolatezza».
3. Perché il cadavere di Paganini venne sepolto sette anni dopo la sua morte? Venne sepolto sette anni dopo la sua morte a causa dei supposti collegamenti con il diavolo.
4. Quale importante premio vinse Eugenio Montale? Vinse il premio Nobel per la letteratura.
5. Qual è il tema principale della poetica di Montale? Il suo tema principale è il «male di vivere».
6. Che ruolo ricopre (*holds*) Montale al *Corriere della Sera*? Ricopre il ruolo di redattore.
7. Per che cosa si distingue lo stile dell'architetto Renzo Piano? Si distingue per i materiali altamente tecnologici e un design pulito e lineare.
8. In che elenco lo ha inserito la rivista *Time*? Lo ha inserito nell'elenco delle 100 personalità più influenti del mondo.
9. Quanti album ha inciso De André? Ha inciso quattordici album.
10. Chi sono i personaggi delle canzoni di De André? Sono prostitute, emarginati e ribelli.

Scrittura

Scrivi sull'argomento Scegli uno dei seguenti argomenti e scrivi un paragrafo seguendo le indicazioni.

- **Renzo Piano** Immagina di essere Renzo Piano, di aver appena appreso di essere stato incluso nella Time 100 e di dover rilasciare un commento per la stampa. Cosa diresti?

- **Essere autodidatta** Molti artisti come Paganini hanno avuto una formazione autodidatta. Immagina di dover imparare da zero a suonare uno strumento musicale. Come ti organizzeresti? Dove cercheresti le informazioni necessarie per imparare?

- **Professione cantautore** La categoria artistica del cantautore ha avuto il suo apice (*height*) durante la seconda metà del Novecento in Italia. Quali sono i cantautori più famosi e celebri del tuo paese oggi? Cosa differenzia un cantautore da un cantante?

 Practice more at **vhlcentral.com**.

INSTRUCTIONAL RESOURCES **9.1**
Audioscripts, Answer Keys, Lab MP3s, Grammar Presentation Slides
SAM/WebSAM: WB, LM

RIMANDO

To review the formation and uses of the present subjunctive, see **Strutture 6.3, pp. 228–229** and **Strutture 7.3, pp. 272–273**.

Additional uses of the subjunctive are presented in **Strutture 9.4, p. 364**.

ATTENZIONE!

Like the imperfect indicative, the imperfect subjunctive can convey several different meanings. These depend on the time relationship between the independent and dependent clauses and the writer's or speaker's intentions.

Nostra madre pensava che bevessimo troppo caffè.
Our mother thought we were drinking/used to drink/drank too much coffee.

ATTENZIONE!

As in the imperfect indicative, in the imperfect subjunctive, the verbs **bere**, **dire**, and **fare** retain their Latin stems **beve–**, **dice–**, and **face–**, to which the imperfect subjunctive endings are added.

Non credevamo che bevessero molto tè.
We didn't think they drank a lot of tea.

Era probabile che il cronista dicesse la verità.
It was likely that the reporter was telling the truth.

Era necessario che ogni lettore facesse un abbonamento alla rivista.
Each reader had to subscribe to the magazine.

The imperfect subjunctive and the past perfect subjunctive; tense sequencing

*Sembrava impossibile che Andrea **potesse** trovare la giusta combinazione di numeri.*

The imperfect subjunctive

- Use the imperfect subjunctive (**congiuntivo imperfetto**) when the verb in the independent clause is in a past tense or the conditional and requires the subjunctive, and the action in the dependent clause occurs at the same time or after the action in the independent clause.

Speravo che **trasmettessero** la conferenza stampa in diretta.
I was hoping they would broadcast the press conference live.

Marco e Sabrina pensarono che la vignetta **fosse** offensiva.
Marco and Sabrina thought the cartoon was offensive.

Vorremmo che il giornale **pubblicasse** quell'intervista.
We'd like the newspaper to publish that interview.

Sarebbe bello se l'intervista **durasse** più di cinque minuti.
It would be nice if the interview lasted more than five minutes.

- To form the imperfect subjunctive, use the same stems as for the imperfect indicative and add the endings shown, which are identical for all three conjugations. Remember that in the imperfect **–are**, **–ere**, and **–ire** verbs all maintain their characteristic vowel.

filmare > filma–	scrivere > scrive–	uscire > usci–
filma**ssi**	scrive**ssi**	usci**ssi**
filma**ssi**	scrive**ssi**	usci**ssi**
filma**sse**	scrive**sse**	usci**sse**
filma**ssimo**	scrive**ssimo**	usci**ssimo**
filma**ste**	scrive**ste**	usci**ste**
filma**ssero**	scrive**ssero**	usci**ssero**

Non credevo che **filmaste** la prima puntata oggi.
I didn't think you were filming the first episode today.

Speravamo che il nuovo film **uscisse** entro febbraio.
We were hoping that the new movie would come out by February.

Ci piacerebbe che quel canale **mettesse** in onda meno cartoni animati.
We wish that channel would show fewer cartoons.

Vorrei che la televisione pubblica **offrisse** più programmi educativi.
I wish public television offered more educational programs.

- The verbs **dare**, **essere**, and **stare** have entirely irregular forms, as shown below.

dare	dessi, dessi, desse, dęssimo, deste, dęssero
essere	fossi, fossi, fosse, fossimo, foste, fossero
stare	stessi, stessi, stesse, stęssimo, steste, stęssero

Speravo che mi **dessero** più soldi.
I hoped they would give me more money.

Non sembrava che quell'uomo **fosse** un attore.
It didn't seem like that man was an actor.

Sarebbe meglio che non **steste** a casa tutto il giorno a guardare la TV.
It would be better if you didn't stay at home all day watching TV.

- Verbs ending in **–rre** use the same stems for both the imperfect indicative and the imperfect subjunctive. They take the imperfect subjunctive endings used for **–ere** verbs.

infinitive	**porre**	**condurre**	**tradurre**	**trarre**
stem	**pon–**	**conduc–**	**traduc–**	**tra–**
imperfect subjunctive	**ponessi**, ecc....	**conducessi**, ecc....	**traducessi**, ecc....	**traessi**, ecc....

The past perfect subjunctive

- Use the past perfect subjunctive (**congiuntivo trapassato**) when the verb in the independent clause is in a past tense or the conditional and requires the subjunctive, and the action in the dependent clause occurs prior to the action in the independent clause.

Sembrava che il cronista **avesse condotto** un'inchiesta in profondità.
It seemed like the reporter had carried out an extensive investigation.

Speravo che il mensile **fosse** già **arrivato** in edicola.
I was hoping that the magazine had already made it to the newsstands.

- To form the past perfect subjunctive, use the imperfect subjunctive form of **essere** or **avere** plus the past participle of the verb. Remember that the past participle of verbs conjugated with **essere** agrees with the subject in number and gender.

festeggiare		partire		informarsi	
avessi		fossi		mi fossi	
avessi		fossi	partito/a	ti fossi	informato/a
avesse	festeggiato	fosse		si fosse	
avęssimo		fǫssimo		ci fǫssimo	
aveste		foste	partiti/e	vi foste	informati/e
avęssero		fǫssero		si fǫssero	

Mia sorella sperava che il paese non **avesse** ancora **festeggiato** il santo patrono.
My sister hoped that the town hadn't celebrated the patron saint yet.

Avremmo voluto che la conferenza stampa **fosse stata** più lunga.
We would have liked the press conference to go on longer.

ATTENZIONE!

The adverbs **già**, **più**, **ancora** and **mai** are often used with the past perfect indicative and the past perfect subjunctive. Remember that these adverbs are usually placed between the auxillary verb (**essere** or **avere**) and the past participle.

Non avevo ancora letto la rivista.
I hadn't read the magazine yet.

Pensavi che io avessi già letto la rivista.
You thought that I had already read the magazine.

Tense sequencing

- Italian follows specific rules regarding the tense of a subjunctive verb in a dependent clause. These rules take into account the tense of the verb in the independent clause and the time relationship between the two clauses. There are two general sequences: one for sentences whose independent clause is in the present, future, or imperative, and another for sentences in the past or conditional.

Independent clause	Dependent clause	The action of the verb in the dependent clause occurs…
Present, future, imperative	present subjunctive	at the same time or later than the action of the independent clause
	past subjunctive	prior to the action of the independent clause
Past, conditional	imperfect subjunctive	at the same time or later than the action of the independent clause
	past perfect subjunctive	prior to the action of the independent clause

Dubito che la rivista **esca** in anticipo.
I doubt the magazine comes out early.

Pensava che i biglietti **fossero** esauriti.
She thought that the tickets were sold out.

Credete che l'attore **sia nato** in Danimarca?
Do you think the actor was born in Denmark?

Ero deluso che il film **fosse cominciato**.
I was disappointed that the movie had started.

- The examples below demonstrate that a dependent verb can express an action that is (a) after, (b) contemporaneous with, or (c) prior to the action expressed by the main verb.

Sequence for independent verbs in present, future, or imperative

after (posteriorità)	contemporaneous (contemporaneità)	prior (anteriorità)
Penso che **arrivino** domani.	Penso che **arrivino** oggi.	Penso che **siano arrivati** ieri.
I think they are arriving (will arrive) tomorrow.	*I think they're arriving today.*	*I think they arrived yesterday.*
Penseranno che tu **capisca**.	Penseranno che tu **capisca**.	Penseranno che tu **abbia capito**.
They will think that you (will) understand.	*They will think that you understand.*	*They will think that you understood.*
Non credere che **arrivi** in orario!	Non credere che **arrivi** in orario!	Non credere che **sia arrivato** in orario!
Don't think that he's going to arrive on time!	*Don't think that he arrives on time!*	*Don't think that he arrived on time!*

Sequence for independent verbs in past tenses or conditional

after (posteriorità)	contemporaneous (contemporaneità)	prior (anteriorità)
Pensavo che **arrivassero** il giorno dopo.	Pensavo che **arrivassero** quel giorno stesso.	Pensavo che **fossero arrivati** il giorno prima.
I thought they were arriving the next day.	*I thought they were arriving that same day.*	*I thought that they had arrived the day before.*
Vorrebbe che **veniste**.	Vorrebbe che **veniste**.	Vorrebbe che **foste venuti**.
He would like you all to come. (sometime in the future)	*He would like you all to come. (at that same time)*	*He would have liked for you to have come.*

ATTENZIONE!

The imperfect or past perfect subjunctive is required after the expression **come se** (*as if*).

Carlo canta come se nessuno lo sentisse.
Carlo sings as if no one were listening to him.

Ci guardava come se ci fossimo già conosciuti.
He was looking at us as if we had already met.

ATTENZIONE!

Note that the imperfect subjunctive can be used after independent clauses in the present, future, or imperative to express a habitual action or to describe a condition in the past.

Non credo che leggessero il giornale ogni giorno.
I don't think they read the paper every day.

Dubito che piovesse quando sono arrivati.
I doubt that it was raining when they arrived.

Pratica

1

Animali e cartoni animati! Secondo alcuni psicologi, gli animali che prima facevano paura ora suscitano (*provoke*) nei bambini sensazioni completamente diverse grazie ad alcuni cartoni animati. Completa le frasi scegliendo fra il congiuntivo presente e il congiuntivo imperfetto.

1. Alcuni bambini oggi credono che il leone ____sia____ (sia / fosse) un animale simpatico e socievole.
2. I miei genitori da piccoli pensavano che i maiali non ___avessero___ (abbiano / avessero) un'intelligenza.
3. Mi dispiace che alcune persone ___mangino___ (mangino / mangiassero) i conigli.
4. Mi sembra che il cavallo ___occupi___ (occupi / occupasse) ruoli importanti in molti film e cartoni animati attuali.
5. Da bambino non volevo che gli animali ___morissero___ (muoiano / morissero) nei film.
6. Molti bambini sperano che il proprio cane ___abbia___ (abbia / avesse) le qualità di un eroe della TV.

2

Lingua e comunicazione Leggi il paragrafo e completalo usando il congiuntivo imperfetto o il congiuntivo trapassato.

Ieri sera sono tornata a casa; era vuota e ho pensato che Franco (1) ___fosse andato___ (andare) al cinema con il suo amico Stefano, appassionato di Neorealismo, e che (2) ___si fosse dimenticato___ (dimenticarsi) di dirmelo. Così ho letto un articolo sulla storia della televisione. Quando è nata la Rai, nel 1954, nessuno si aspettava che la TV (3) ___riuscisse___ (riuscire) a entrare anche nelle case in cui si parlava dialetto e che (4) ___potesse___ (potere) contribuire alla diffusione di una lingua nazionale. Anche Dante Alighieri sperava che gli italiani (5) ___parlassero___ (parlare) una lingua unitaria, ma chi poteva immaginare che il suo sogno si sarebbe concretizzato grazie a uno strumento così poco poetico? Quando Franco è tornato, gli ho chiesto che mi (6) ___raccontasse___ (raccontare) del film. Mi ha detto che non era sicuro che gli (7) ___fosse piaciuto___ (piacere) perché gli attori parlavano in dialetto ed era difficile capirli. Il regista, Luchino Visconti, riteneva che il cinema (8) ___avesse escluso___ (escludere) il popolo dalla storia, per questo voleva che i suoi attori (9) ___fossero___ (essere) spontanei. Un vero artista va sempre controcorrente, no?

3

Il Festival di Sanremo Leggete il paragrafo e riscrivetelo al passato coniugando i verbi sottolineati al modo e al tempo adeguato, come nel modello.

Modello Non <u>ricordo</u> quale canzone <u>abbia vinto</u> nel 2009.

Non ricordavo quale canzone avesse vinto nel 2009.

Il Festival di Sanremo

Alcuni (1) <u>dicono</u> che il Festival di Sanremo (2) <u>sia</u> il Festival della canzone italiana più seguito. Altri (3) <u>pensano</u> che al Festival si (4) <u>ascolti</u> solo musica banale e commerciale. Io (5) <u>credo</u> che solo alcune canzoni del Festival si (6) <u>distinguano</u> per originalità di testi e musica. Non (7) <u>so</u> quale cantante (8) <u>abbia vinto</u> per più volte, ma (9) <u>credo</u> che (10) <u>sia stato</u> Domenico Modugno. Non mi (11) <u>meraviglia</u> che gli italiani (12) <u>abbiano votato</u> per Modugno, e mi (13) <u>fa</u> piacere che lo (14) <u>considerino</u> ancora un grande artista. (15) <u>Sembra</u> che le sue canzoni non (16) <u>invecchino</u> mai!

1. dicevano, 2. fosse, 3. pensavano, 4. ascoltasse, 5. credevo, 6. distinguessero, 7. sapevo, 8. avesse vinto, 9. credevo, 10. fosse stato, 11. meravigliava, 12. avessero votato, 13. faceva, 14. considerassero, 15. Sembrava, 16. invecchiassero

---

1 Before the students start this activity, have them discuss animal characters from cartoons they know and review names for animals in Italian, including: **leone** (*lion*), **coniglio** (*rabbit*), and **cavallo** (*horse*).

Nota
CULTURALE

Luchino Visconti è uno dei più importanti registi cinematografici e teatrali italiani del XX secolo. Oltre ad essere un esponente del cinema neorealista (vedi nota a pagina 367) Visconti ha diretto anche numerosi film a carattere storico ed è famoso per le meticolose ricostruzioni sceniche. La sua produzione cinematografica ha ricevuto molti riconoscimenti tra cui un Leone d'oro, il premio principale alla Mostra del Cinema di Venezia, un festival cinematografico internazionale che dal 1932 si tiene ogni estate al Lido di Venezia.

3 Refer students to the paragraph about the festival on p. 347.

3 As an expansion, ask students to search the Web for Italian songs presented at the latest edition of the Festival. Ask them to listen to some of them and get ready for a discussion next class.

4

Chi l'avrebbe immaginato! Completa l'e-mail che Paolo scrive ad Alfredo raccontandogli tutte le cose interessanti che ha scoperto oggi alla lezione di storia del cinema. Attenzione, devi scegliere tu il tempo del congiuntivo appropriato: presente, passato, imperfetto o trapassato.

Ciao Alfredo,
mi dispiace che tu non (1) __sia venuto__ (venire) oggi alla prima lezione del corso di cinema. Non avrei mai pensato che (2) __fosse__ (essere) così interessante! Io ho sempre creduto che il doppiaggio (3) __fosse nato__ (nascere) dalla pigrizia (*laziness*) di qualche italiano che non voleva leggere i sottotitoli, ma non sapevo che proprio le case di produzione americane (4)__avessero incentivato__(incentivare) il doppiaggio per distribuire i film in Europa! Pare che questa necessità (5) __si sia presentata__ (presentarsi) già nel 1929, quando lo stesso film ha cominciato a essere girato più volte in diverse lingue! Sembra che alcuni attori (6) __si limitassero__ (limitarsi) a muovere la bocca, mentre altri attori madrelingua parlavano al loro posto. I registi, però, volevano che almeno gli attori principali (7) __recitassero__ (recitare) in tutte le lingue e che (8) __leggessero__ (leggere) la trascrizione fonetica delle parole su dei cartelli posizionati dietro le videocamere! Ti immagini? È un peccato che molte di queste versioni in italiano (9)__siano andate perdute__(andare perdute): sarebbe divertente guardarle oggi! Spero che tu (10) __venga__ (venire) mercoledì prossimo, perché ne vale davvero la pena!
Un saluto, Paolo.

5 As an expansion, have pairs of students add detail to the three sentences they find most interesting. Example: **Non pensavo che solo i personaggi italo-americani conservassero un accento regionale. Questo significa che Tony De Vito in italiano è sempre un siciliano!**

5

Il doppiaggio Leggete le frasi e commentatele usando il congiuntivo imperfetto.
Some answers will vary.

Modello **L'arte del doppiaggio richiede che i doppiatori parlino un italiano senza accenti regionali.**

Non immaginavo che i doppiatori parlassero senza accento.

1. È ormai accettato che solo i personaggi italo-americani conservino nel doppiaggio un accento regionale, solitamente siciliano.
Non pensavo che __solo i personaggi italo-americani conservassero un accento regionale__.

2. Tutti concordano con il fatto che un buon doppiaggio debba rispettare il senso della frase originale e il movimento delle labbra dell'attore.
Non avevo mai considerato il fatto che __un buon doppiaggio dovesse rispettare il senso della frase e il movimento delle labbra dell'attore__.

3. La sincronizzazione dei tempi richiede che la frase doppiata sia sempre un po' diversa da quella originale.
Non credevo che __la frase doppiata fosse sempre un po' diversa da quella originale__.

4. Chi ama il doppiaggio pensa che i sottotitoli affatichino (*tire*) lo spettatore distraendolo dall'immagine.
Non ho mai ritenuto che __i sottotitoli affaticassero lo spettatore__.

5. Pare che alcuni paesi dell'Est Europa preferiscano il «lettore», un attore che legge le battute degli attori, mentre le voci originali si possono sentire in sottofondo, a un volume più basso.
Non avrei mai pensato che __i paesi dell'Est Europa preferissero il lettore__.

6. Si ritiene che l'Italia e la Germania abbiano la più lunga e migliore tradizione di doppiaggio.
Non avrei mai detto che __l'Italia e la Germania avessero la più lunga e migliore tradizione di doppiaggio__.

Nota
CULTURALE

L'Italia è una delle nazioni che più utilizza il **doppiaggio**. I principali centri di doppiaggio si trovano a Roma, dove si doppia fin dal 1933, e, a partire dagli anni Settanta, a Milano. A volte un doppiatore segue un attore per tutta la sua carriera. Così, per gli italiani, Al Pacino, Sylvester Stallone, Dustin Hoffman, Robert De Niro e Peter Falk hanno tutti la voce di Ferruccio Amendola, che li ha doppiati in ogni loro film fino alla sua scomparsa. È probabile che anche questi attori si sentano intimamente legati alla figura di Ferruccio,e forse è per questo che hanno tutti partecipato ai suoi funerali, nel 2001.

S Practice more at **vhlcentral.com**.

Comunicazione

6 **I genitori sono tutti uguali!** Scrivi sei frasi spiegando cosa i tuoi genitori speravano che tu facessi o non facessi una volta iscritto/a all'università. Poi confronta le tue frasi con quelle del(la) tuo/a compagno/a e trova le similarità.

> **Modello** I miei genitori speravano/volevano/desideravano che io avessi molti amici.

7 **Riflettere** In coppia e a turno, completate le frasi con il tempo giusto del congiuntivo. Poi riflettete: avete avuto esperienze simili? Avete speranze diverse?

1. Da piccolo/a la sera, a letto, avevo paura che…
2. Quando giocavo con gli altri bambini non volevo che…
3. Ho sempre sperato che i miei amici…
4. Non avrei mai immaginato che in così pochi anni…
5. Mi piacerebbe che i ragazzi della mia età…
6. Non vorrei mai che i bambini di oggi…

8 **Vacanze italiane** Ecco le foto delle vostre vacanze in Italia con alcuni amici. In coppia, descrivi ogni immagine con almeno due frasi, aiutandoti con le espressioni suggerite.

> **Modello** È stato necessario che Riccardo bevesse anche il caffè di Emily per rimanere sveglio.

È stato necessario che…	Io avevo paura che…
È stato necessario che…	
Gli amici volevano che…	Noi speravamo che…
Bisognava che…	Sembrava che…

9 **Situazioni di vita** Leggete le seguenti situazioni e provate a commentarle suggerendo una soluzione. Aiutatevi con le espressioni della lista.

| Sarebbe stato/Sarebbe meglio che… | È bene/male che… | Pensiamo che… |
| È possibile/impossibile che… | È consigliabile che… | Pare che… |

1. Una sera Monica esce e, in un pub, trova Sandro, il ragazzo della sua amica Roberta. Non ci sarebbe niente di male, ma Monica ha appena parlato al telefono con Roberta, la quale le ha detto che Sandro è a casa con l'influenza!

2. È febbraio, fa freddo, ma Luigi è contento: oggi stesso parte per Santo Domingo! È all'aeroporto, in fila per il check in, quando improvvisamente si rende conto di aver scambiato la sua valigia con quella del fratello, partito per la Norvegia.

INSTRUCTIONAL
RESOURCES
Audioscripts, Answer Keys,
Lab MP3s, Grammar
Presentation Slides
SAM/WebSAM: WB, LM

9.2

Indefinite adjectives and pronouns

- Indefinite adjectives and pronouns are used to speak about unspecified people or things and to indicate general quantities. The English equivalents include *someone, something, no one, nothing, everyone, everything, whoever, whatever, none, some, a few, each, any, every,* and *all.* Some Italian indefinites function only as adjectives or only as pronouns, while others can function as both adjectives and pronouns.

Indefinite Adjectives	Indefinite Pronouns
Qualche attore inizia la carriera in teatro. *Some actors begin their careers in the theater.*	**Alcuni** iniziano la carriera in teatro. *Some begin their careers in the theater.*
Pochi giornalisti lavoravano all'estero. *Few journalists were working abroad.*	**Pochi** lavoravano all'estero. *Few were working abroad.*

Indefinite Adjectives

- An indefinite adjective modifies a noun. Some indefinite adjectives are singular and invariable, even though a plural meaning may be implied. Other adjectives change according to the noun they modify.

singular invariable		singular variable		plural	
ogni	*every, all*	tutto/a	*every, all*	alcuni/e	*some, a few*
qualche	*some, a few*	nessuno/a	*no, not any*	tutti/e	*every, all*
qualunque, qualsiasi	*any, whatever, whichever*	ciascuno/a	*each*		

> **Qualunque** giornale leggeranno, gli studenti saranno aggiornati sulle notizie del mondo.
> *Whatever newspaper they read, the students will be updated on world news.*

> **Alcune** riviste pubblicano anche vignette.   Non esiste **nessuna** radio libera qui.
> *Some magazines also print cartoons.*   *There is no independent radio station here.*

- Note that some indefinite words are synonymous. Remember, however, that the words **qualche** and **ogni** require singular forms, even if they indicate a plural meaning.

qualche + [*singular noun*]   =   **alcune** + [*plural noun*]
Compriamo **qualche** rivist**a**.   Compriamo **alcune** rivist**e**.
Let's buy a few magazines.

ogni + [*singular noun*]   =   **tutti** + [*plural noun*]
Ogni giornalista scrive bene.   **Tutti** i giornalisti scrivono bene.
All journalists write well.

- The form **alcuno/a** is used with the negative **non** to indicate *no* + [*noun*] + *whatsoever.*

> **Non** pone **alcun** rischio alla salute.
> *It poses no health risks whatsoever.*

ATTENZIONE!

Note that the words **nessuno, alcuno,** and **ciascuno** employ the same forms as the indefinite article (**un, un', uno, una**).

Non vi è nessun dubbio.
There is no doubt.

Si licenzia senza alcuna ragione?
She is resigning for no reason?

ATTENZIONE!

The expressions **tutto questo** and **tutto quello** refer broadly to a concept or fact and correspond to *all this/all that/everything.*

Hai capito tutto quello che ti ho detto?
Did you understand everything I told you?

ATTENZIONE!

Remember that **qualche** is always singular and invariable, even though the English translation is plural.

Guardo la TV solo qualche volta. Preferisco leggere.
I only watch TV once in a while. I prefer to read.

Abbiamo qualche domanda.
We have a few questions.

ATTENZIONE!

Note that the adjective **tutto/a/i/e** requires the definite article (**il/lo/l'/la/i/gli/le**).

Non conosco tutte le usanze degli italiani.
I am not familiar with all the customs of Italians.

Non guardare la TV tutto il giorno!
Don't watch TV all day!

Indefinite pronouns

—*Qualcuno pensa che sia un destino trovare l'anima gemella.*

- An indefinite pronoun replaces a noun and stands alone. Their forms are summarized below. Note that **tutto** and **niente** refer to things, while **tutti/e** and **nessuno** refer to people.

singular invariable		singular variable		plural	
chiunque	*anyone, whoever*	qualcuno/a	*someone*	alcuni/e	*some, a few*
		ognuno/a	*everyone*	tutti/e	*everyone*
niente, nulla	*nothing*	nessuno/a	*no one, not anyone*		
qualcosa	*something*				
tutto	*everything*	ciascuno/a	*each*		

Niente è impossibile.
Nothing is impossible.

Nessuno riesce a capire.
No one is able to understand.

Chiunque può venire al concerto. L'ingresso è libero.
Anyone can come to the concert. Admission is free.

I giornalisti lavorano tanto, **alcuni** anche la domenica.
Journalists work a lot; some even (work) on Sundays.

- **Qualcosa**, **nulla**, and **niente** are considered masculine singular. When used with an adjective, they are followed by **di**. When used with an infinitive, they are followed by **da**.

È successo **qualcosa**?
Did something happen?

Non è **cambiato niente**.
Nothing has changed.

Avete mangiato **qualcosa di buono**?
Did you eat something good?

Non hai trovato **niente da guardare** alla TV?
You didn't find anything to watch on TV?

Indefinite adjectives and pronouns

- As you may have noticed from the above tables, several indefinite words can function as either an adjective or a pronoun. When a noun is stated, use the adjectival form and make it agree with the noun. To replace a noun, use the pronoun alone.

indefinite word	adjective	pronoun
tutto/a/i/e	Vediamo **tutti i film**. *We see all the films.*	**Tutti** sono interessanti. *They're all interesting.*
alcuni/e	Guardo **alcune telenovele**. *I watch some soap operas.*	Me ne piacciono **alcune**. *I like some (of them).*
nessuno/a	Non ami **nessuno sport**? *You don't like any sports?*	Non te ne piace **nessuno**? *You don't like any (of them)?*
ciascuno/a	**Ciascun giornalista** scrive un articolo. *Each journalist writes an article.*	**Ciascuno** scrive un articolo. *Each one writes an article.*

It may be helpful to play a game of *generalization* and *specification*. Provide students with a generic statement such as **Tutti gli studenti sono sportivi** and ask them to restrict the statement to **Alcuni studenti sono sportivi**. The same game can be played to isolate singular and plural forms. Provide a sentence utilizing an indefinite plural form. Ask students to provide a grammatically singular equivalent. For example, **Alcune riviste pubblicano interviste** can be changed to **Qualche rivista pubblica interviste**.

RIMANDO

To review negation, see **Strutture 6.2, pp. 224–225.**

ATTENZIONE!

Some indefinites may function as adverbs, and are invariable when they do so. These adverbs are **molto, parecchio, poco, tanto, troppo**.

ATTENZIONE!

Other words that act like the ones in the chart on the left are **altro, certo, diverso, molto, parecchio, poco, tanto, troppo,** and **vario**.

Abbiamo comprato **parecchi** DVD di Charlie Chaplin. (indefinite adjective)
We bought a lot of Charlie Chaplin DVDs.

Parecchi dimostrano il suo indiscutibile talento. (indefinite pronoun)
Many (of them) reveal his indisputable talent.

Pratica

1 Tell the students that on Halloween night, in 1938, Orson Welles starred in a radio adaptation of *The War of the Worlds*, by H.G. Wells on a CBS network. The broadcast caused panic but launched Welles' career.

1 Have pairs of students write and perform a dialogue featuring an unusual news report. Tell them to use as many indefinite adjectives and pronouns as possible.

1

Strane notizie alla radio Sonia e Paolo stanno ascoltando la radio ma, improvvisamente, il programma viene interrotto… Completa il dialogo con le parole della lista.

alcune	nessun	niente	qualche	qualcuno	tutti
alcune	nessuna	niente	qualcosa	tutte	tutto

PRESENTATORE Buona sera a (1) __tutti__. Interrompiamo il nostro programma per dirvi che alle 19.40 il prof. Boschi dell'Università di Genova ha osservato (2) __alcune__ esplosioni di gas incandescente che dal pianeta Marte si dirigono verso la Terra! Continuiamo ora con il nostro programma...

SONIA Hai sentito, Paolo? Speriamo che non sia (3) __niente__ di serio! Forse dovremmo ascoltare (4) __qualche__ giornale radio.

PAOLO Non intendo ascoltare (5) __nessun__ giornale radio a quest'ora. Ho solo bisogno di rilassarmi. Vuoi (6) __qualcosa__ da bere?

SONIA No, grazie, non voglio (7) __niente__. Vorrei solo che (8) __qualcuno__ mi dicesse cosa sta succedendo...

PRESENTATORE Scusateci ancora per l'interruzione, ma questa è un'emergenza. (9) __Alcune__ persone ci hanno raccontato di un'astronave cilindrica che è appena atterrata nella campagna fuori Genova. (10) __Tutte__ le abitazioni nei dintorni sono state evacuate. Vi preghiamo di rimanere nelle vostre case e di non uscire per (11) __nessuna__ ragione!

SONIA Paolo! Che facciamo? Ci uccideranno!

PAOLO Sonia! Ma non hai ancora capito? È l'adattamento di *La Guerra dei Mondi*, il romanzo di H.G. Wells! Ma credi proprio a (12) __tutto__!

Nota
CULTURALE

La città di **Savona** è situata nella **Riviera delle Palme**, che va dalla cittadina di Varazze fino ad Andora. A Savona, la notte prima di Ferragosto, c'è la «posa a mare dei lumini»: al tramonto il mare è illuminato da migliaia di lumini galleggianti°. I fondali di Savona, ricchi di relitti° di navi antiche, sono oggi un interessante parco archeologico per gli amanti degli sport subacquei. **La Fortezza del Priamar** è la prigione che ha ospitato Giuseppe Mazzini, famoso patriota italiano che ha contribuito all'unificazione d'Italia nel diciannovesimo secolo.

lumini galleggianti *floating lights*
relitti *wrecks*

2

Noi e i media Sostituisci gli aggettivi indefiniti sottolineati con un pronome indefinito e fai le modifiche necessarie. Some answers will vary.

Modello <u>Alcune persone</u> sono contrarie ad avere la televisione in casa.

Alcuni sono contrari ad avere la televisione in casa.

1. <u>Molte persone</u> credono alle cose che sentono in televisione. Molti...
2. Non <u>tutte le cose</u> che sono scritte sui giornali sono vere. Non tutto quello che...
3. <u>Qualunque persona</u> vorrebbe andare in televisione per diventare famoso. Chiunque vorrebbe...
4. Quando guardo la televisione non voglio vedere <u>nessun programma</u> scandalistico. ...niente di scandalistico.
5. <u>Ogni telespettatore</u> vorrebbe incontrare il proprio attore preferito. Ognuno vorrebbe...

3

Le vacanze Per le vacanze, un tuo amico vorrebbe andare a Savona, ma tu non sei d'accordo. Contraddici ogni sua affermazione usando un aggettivo o un pronome indefinito.

Modello Ci sarebbe tanto da fare a Savona.

Non, non ci sarebbe niente da fare a Savona.

1. Il 14 di agosto vanno tutti a Savona per vedere la «posa a mare dei lumini». No, il 14 di agosto nessuno va a Savona per vedere la posa a mare dei lumini.
2. Tutti gli esperti conoscono la grotta (*cave*) di Borgio Verezzi. No, nessun esperto conosce la grotta di Borgio Verezzi.
3. C'è molto da vedere all'interno della Fortezza del Priamar. No, non c'è niente da vedere all'interno della Fortezza del Priamar.
4. Ci sono vari spettacoli interessanti durante l'estate nella Riviera delle Palme. No, non c'è niente di interessante durante l'estate nella Riviera delle Palme.
5. Alcuni sentieri partono da Savona e si arrampicano sulle montagne della costa. No, nessun sentiero parte da Savona e si arrampica sulle montagne della costa.

Practice more at vhlcentral.com.

Comunicazione

4

Si parte! Che tipo di persona sei? Ti piace andare all'avventura o programmare tutto in anticipo? Preferisci rischiare a occhi chiusi o informarti bene prima di prendere una decisione? Rispondi alle domande, poi, con un(a) compagno/a, confrontate e discutete le vostre risposte.

1. **Prima di visitare un paese straniero...**
   a. vado in biblioteca e studio tutta la storia del posto fin dalle origini.
   b. raccolgo qualche informazione sommaria su Internet circa i vari aspetti del luogo: sociale, economico, storico e naturale.
   c. non studio niente prima e lascio che tutto sia una sorpresa.

2. **Quando viene il momento di preparare le valigie...**
   a. porto con me tutto quello di cui potrei avere bisogno, incluso il mangiare.
   b. non metto in valigia niente che non sia indispensabile e mi adatto.
   c. mi informo prima su dove poter comprare tutte le comodità a cui sono abituato/a.

3. **Quando arrivo in una città...**
   a. ho già un itinerario dettagliato di tutti i posti che voglio vedere.

   b. vado all'ufficio turistico e chiedo informazioni sul posto e qualche consiglio su cosa vedere.
   c. comincio a camminare in qualsiasi direzione e mi faccio guidare dal caso.

4. **Mentre visito i vari luoghi...**
   a. mi piace parlare con chiunque e per questo studio un po' la lingua prima di partire.
   b. di solito non parlo con nessuno oltre ai miei compagni di viaggio.
   c. vorrei parlare con qualcuno del posto, ma di solito non conosco la lingua.

5. **Quando sono in un ristorante...**
   a. scelgo solo alcuni piatti specifici: quelli che conosco.
   b. provo a ordinare qualunque piatto abbia un nome incomprensibile.
   c. chiedo al cameriere di consigliarmi alcuni piatti tipici.

5

Racconti di viaggio

A. In coppia, preparate sei domande su alcune esperienze di viaggio usando le parole della lista come nel modello.

> **Modello** Hai mai fatto qualcosa che non ti aspettavi di fare?

niente	qualcosa	tutti
qualche	qualcuno	tutto

B. In gruppi di quattro, fatevi le domande e rispondete raccontando le vostre esperienze.

6

Cosa succede? Riccardo e Emily sono in gita. Fanno e vedono cose molto divertenti. A un certo punto, succede qualcosa. Qualcosa di buffo, di strano, di tragico o di romantico? Decidetelo voi! Guardate le immagini e scrivete una storia usando almeno otto aggettivi o pronomi indefiniti.

INSTRUCTIONAL
RESOURCES **9.3**
Audioscripts, Answer Keys,
Lab MP3s, Grammar
Presentation Slides
SAM/WebSAM: WB, LM

RIMANDO

To review the verb tenses used in hypothetical statements, see

**The imperative, p. 146;
The future, p. 188;
The conditional, p. 220;
The imperfect subjunctive and the past perfect subjunctive, p. 350.**

ATTENZIONE!

Note that when the future is used in the **se** clause, the main clause is also often in the future. It is also permissible, however, to use the present tense in the main clause.

**Se registrerai il programma, lo guarderemo più tardi.
(fut. + fut.)
Se registrerai il programma, lo guardiamo più tardi.
(fut. + pres.)**
If you record the program, we will watch it later.

ATTENZIONE!

It is possible to reverse the order of the clauses in a hypothetical statement.

I tuoi amici verrebbero alla festa se li invitassimo?
Would your friends come to the party if we invited them?

Hypothetical statements

- Hypothetical statements enable us to state what might occur if something else happens. Hypothetical statements contain two parts: a subordinate clause introduced by **se** (*if*) that expresses a condition or possibility, and an independent clause that expresses the result.

> Se **vieni** a Roma la prossima settimana, **chiamami**!
> *If you come to Rome next week, call me!*

> Se **avessimo** tempo, **guarderemmo** tutte le puntate.
> *If we had the time, we would watch all the episodes.*

- Italian grammar allows for three types of **se** clauses, depending on an event's probability: (a) when the condition is likely or real, (b) when the condition is unlikely but possible, and (c) when the condition is impossible. The verb tense and mood convey these levels of probability.

Hypothetical Statements

likely or real condition	unlikely but possible condition	impossible condition
Se + **indicative**	*Se* + **imperfect subjunctive**	*Se* + **past perfect subjunctive**
Se **leggi** il giornale, **ti tieni** aggiornato sulla politica.	Se **vivessi** in Italia, **capirei** meglio la politica del paese.	Se **fossi nato** in Italia, **potrei** votare alle elezioni.
If you read the paper, you stay up to date on politics.	*If I lived in Italy, I would understand the country's politics better.*	*If I had been born in Italy, I could vote in the elections.*

- To state hypothetically what is possible or real, use the indicative in the **se** clause and the indicative or the imperative in the independent clause. Often the same mood and tense are used in both clauses, but other combinations are possible.

Tense combination *Se* clause, main clause	Examples
presente + presente	Se **parli** lentamente, **capisco** meglio. *If you speak slowly, I understand better.*
passato prossimo + presente	Se **hai** già **letto** il libro, me lo **puoi** prestare? *If you have finished reading the book, can you loan it to me?*
passato prossimo + imperativo	Se **avete guardato** il DVD, **riportatelo** in biblioteca. *If you have watched the DVD, bring it back to the library.*
passato prossimo + futuro	Se non **ha** ancora **finito** l'articolo, lo **finirà** presto. *If she hasn't finished the article yet, she will finish it soon.*
passato prossimo + imperfetto	Se **hanno mangiato** tutto, **avevano** molta fame. *If they ate everything, they were very hungry.*
futuro + futuro	Se **avrai** voglia, **potrai** venire a trovarmi. *If you want to, you'll be able to visit me.*
imperfetto + imperfetto	Se **andavo** al cinema, **guardavo** solo film comici. *If I went to the movies, I only watched comedies.*

- Only in the case of *likely* or *real* hypothetical statements, you may note that a synonymous meaning could be derived by substituting **quando** for **se**.

  Se avrò i soldi comprerò una macchina sportiva.
  If I have the money, I will buy a sports car.

  Quando avrò i soldi comprerò una macchina sportiva.
  When I have the money, I will buy a sports car.

- To state hypothetically what may be unlikely but possible, use the imperfect subjunctive in the **se** clause, and the present or past conditional in the result clause.

  Se **credessero** all'oroscopo, lo **leggerebbero** ogni giorno.
  If they believed in the horoscope, they would read it every day.

  Se mi **informassi**, **avrei capito** meglio la conferenza stampa.
  If I kept myself informed, I would have understood the press conference better.

Se Andrea **avesse** il numero di Lisa le **potrebbe** telefonare.

- To state a hypothesis about the past, a condition that could not change or is contrary to fact, use the **past perfect subjunctive** in the **se** clause, and the present or past conditional in the result clause. The conditional present expresses the potential current outcome if something in the past had occurred.

  Se **avesse letto** il libro, **capirebbe** meglio il film.
  If he had read the book, he would understand the film better. (**now** – conditional present)

  Se **avesse letto** il libro, gli **sarebbe piaciuto**.
  If he had read the book, he would have liked it. (**then** – past conditional)

Se **avessi studiato** di più, adesso non **avrei** problemi a scuola!

ATTENZIONE!

Remember to use the conditional mood only in the main clause, never in the **se** clause.

Se avesse più soldi, Claudio comprerebbe una casa al mare.
If he had more money, Claudio would buy a house by the sea.

Provide students with a **se** clause and ask them to complete the statement logically. Move from likely to possible to impossible situations.
Se capite gli esempi…
Se finiremo tutti gli esercizi…
Se avessimo più tempo…
Se ci fosse lezione anche la domenica…

ATTENZIONE!

Occasionally, in spoken Italian, you may notice that the word **se** is omitted.

Certo, avessi tempo, rileggerei quel libro!
Sure, if I had the time, I would reread that book!

Pratica

1 Have volunteers read their answers to the class and explain their choices.

1 Ask students to add two more lines to the dialogues using two **se** clause construction with the indicative.

Nota CULTURALE

La **mimosa** è il fiore simbolo della festa della donna, che in Italia si celebra l'8 marzo. La Liguria con il suo clima temperato favorisce la fioritura della mimosa. Per non far passare inosservata la fioritura di un fiore così simbolico, la prima domenica di febbraio si festeggia a Pieve Ligure l'inizio della primavera con la Festa della Mimosa.

2 Ask the students to provide two more questions for their partners.

1 **La festa della mimosa** Luisa invita Miriam alla Festa della Mimosa, a Pieve Ligure. Completa il dialogo inserendo la forma corretta del verbo nel tempo indicativo.

LUISA Ciao Miriam! Vieni anche tu oggi alla Festa della Mimosa?

MIRIAM Dipende, se (1) _trovo/troverò_ (trovare) chi mi accompagna, vengo volentieri.

LUISA Se prendi la macchina, (2) _ricordati_ (ricordarsi) che il centro è chiuso al traffico per tutta la giornata.

MIRIAM Potrei venire in treno, ma la stazione è lontana.

LUISA Se vieni in treno, (3) _puoi/potrai_ (potere) prendere la navetta (*shuttle bus*) alla stazione e arrivare in centro.

MIRIAM A che ora comincia la festa?

LUISA Il prete benedirà le mimose a mezzogiorno, se tutto (4) _procede/ procederà_ (procedere) secondo il programma.

MIRIAM Sinceramente, mi interessa di più l'aspetto folcloristico...

LUISA Allora vieni il pomeriggio! Se (5) _prendi/ prenderai_ (prendere) il treno subito dopo pranzo, farai in tempo a vedere la sfilata (*parade*) dei carri e dei quadri fioriti.

MIRIAM Bene! Invito anche Luca! Se (6) _avrà finito_ (finire) gli esami, forse vorrà rilassarsi un po'...

LUISA Va bene. Se arrivi prima, (7) _chiamami_ (chiamarmi). Possiamo mangiare insieme agli stand gastronomici. Ciao!

Pro o contro?

A. Sei pro o contro il modo in cui i mezzi di comunicazione di massa vengono usati? Completate il questionario usando il condizionale semplice nella prima opzione e quello composto nella seconda.

1. Se Internet non esistesse...
   a. le persone _si sentirebbero_ (sentirsi) più sole.
   b. i rapporti interpersonali _sarebbero rimasti_ (rimanere) come una volta: umani e non virtuali!

2. Se la televisione trasmettesse più programmi educativi...
   a. il livello della cultura _si alzerebbe_ (alzarsi).
   b. la maggior parte dei telespettatori _si sarebbe lamentata_ (lamentarsi) già da tempo.

3. Se la televisione non esistesse...
   a. le persone _leggerebbero_ (leggere) di più.
   b. la popolazione _sarebbe stata esclusa_ (essere esclusa) dall'informazione.

4. Se tu avessi un'antenna parabolica...
   a. la _useresti_ (usare) per guardare canali stranieri e familiarizzarti con nuove lingue.
   b. _avresti trovato_ (trovare) già il tuo canale preferito per guardare solo quello!

5. Se i giornali e le riviste fossero tutte on-line...
   a. _risparmierebbero_ (risparmiare —*to save*) molta carta.
   b. tutti noi _avremmo perso_ (perdere) ormai il gusto di leggere il giornale al bar, sul treno o con gli amici.

6. Se non esistesse il doppiaggio...
   a. _sarebbe_ (essere) più facile imparare altre lingue.
   b. i buoni film non _sarebbero circolati_ (circolare) così diffusamente.

B. In coppia, rispondete al questionario discutendo sulle risposte.

Comunicazione

3 **Consigli sulla TV** In coppia, parlate delle vostre reazioni in determinate circostanze. Completate le frasi suggerite, scegliendo con attenzione i modi e i tempi da usare.

> **Modello** ...metto il volume al massimo.
>
> Se qualcuno mi disturba mentre guardo la TV, metto il volume al massimo.

1. Se io dovessi decidere dove mettere il televisore in casa…
2. Se qualcuno cambiasse canale mentre sto guardando un programma che mi interessa...
3. Se guardo la TV insieme a un'altra persona...
4. ...proverei a vivere senza.
5. ...uso i tappi per le orecchie (*earplugs*).
6. ...avrei comprato un televisore con le cuffie (*headphones*).

4 **Cosa fareste voi?** Guardate le immagini e dite cosa fareste in queste circostanze. Siate creativi!

> **Modello** Se io diventassi un'attrice famosa, chiederei a tutta la famiglia di guardare i miei film!

 **1.**   **2.**  **3.**

 **4.**  **5.**

5 **Se fossi** Prova a immaginare come sarebbe la tua vita se tu fossi uno dei seguenti personaggi.

> **Modello** **Scarlett Johansson**
>
> Se fossi Scarlett Johansson, girerei un film in Italia…

- Robert De Niro
- Justin Timberlake
- Roberto Benigni
- Lindsay Lohan
- Mike Myers
- Leonardo Di Caprio

6 **Rimpianti (*Regrets*)** Scrivi quattro frasi su alcune cose che avresti fatto diversamente la scorsa estate. Quindi spiega le tue frasi ai tuoi compagni, in gruppi di tre o quattro.

> **Modello** Se avessi saputo quanto era difficile trovare lavoro, avrei cominciato prima a cercarne uno.

3 Ask students to add three sentences about how different people behave when they are watching TV or reading a book or newspaper.

4 As a warm-up, have students look at the five illustrations and note vocabulary which they will use in their answers. Write useful words on the blackboard, such as: **vicini di casa**, **ascensore**, **coccodrillo**, **isola**, **squalo**.

4 Sample answers:
1. Se i miei vicini fossero rumorosi, andrei a chiedergli di essere più silenziosi.
2. Se io non potessi uscire dall'ascensore, andrei in panico.
3. Se il mio coinquilino venisse a casa con un coccodrillo, gli chiederei di portarlo allo zoo.
4. Se rimanessi solo su un'isola deserta, mi annoierei molto.
5. Se uno squalo mi seguisse, nuoterei più velocemente.

5 Write **Se io fossi** on the board and ask students to use the prompt to write sentences about other famous people, both contemporary and from the past.

INSTRUCTIONAL RESOURCES 9.4
Audioscripts, Answer Keys, Lab MP3s, Grammar Presentation Slides
SAM/WebSAM: WB, LM

RIMANDO

Previous presentations related to the subjunctive include the following.

The subjunctive: impersonal expressions; will and emotion, **Strutture 6.3, pp. 228–229**.

The subjunctive with expressions of doubt and conjunctions; the past subjunctive, **Strutture 7.3, pp. 272–273**.

RIMANDO

To review comparatives and superlatives, see **Strutture 7.1, pp. 262–263**.

ATTENZIONE!

Note that the word order in sentences containing a relative superlative can vary. Remember also that the forms of some adjectives (such as **bello** and **buono**) change depending on their position in the sentence.

Il Pantheon è l'edificio più bello che esista.
Il Pantheon è il più bell'edificio che esista.
The Pantheon is the most beautiful building there is.

Other uses of the subjunctive

- You have already learned to use the subjunctive mood in dependent clauses following expressions of opinion, doubt, will, and emotion. You will recall that the indicative mood, in contrast, conveys facts and other objective information.

- Italian also requires the use of the subjunctive in several other instances, in which the subjunctive is not triggered by a particular verb in an independent clause (such as **pensare che**, **dubitare che**, **sperare che**). Rather, it is required because of restrictive or limiting words (indefinites, negatives, and superlatives) that trigger its use in a relative clause.

- Use the subjunctive in relative clauses introduced by the indefinite words **qualunque** and **qualsiasi** (*whichever/whatever*), **chiunque** (*whoever*), **comunque** (*however*), and **dovunque** (*wherever*).

  Qualunque cosa **succeda**, non dimenticarti di me!
  Whatever happens, don't forget me!

  Non rispondo al telefono, **chiunque chiami**.
  I'm not answering the phone, no matter who calls.

  Comunque vadano le cose, non disperare!
  However things go, don't despair!

  Dovunque traslochiate, vi verrò a trovare.
  No matter where you move, I will visit you.

- Use the subjunctive in relative clauses that speak of something or someone that is unknown or does not yet exist. For example, the subjunctive is used after the indefinite article (**un, uno, un', una**) + [*noun*] and after the indefinite pronouns **qualcuno** and **qualcosa**.

  Dobbiamo trovare **un articolo** che **appoggi** le nostre idee.
  We need to find an article that supports our ideas.

  Conosci **qualcuno** che **possa** darci una mano?
  Do you know anyone who can give us a hand?

- Use the subjunctive when speaking of someone or something unknown or nonexistent, for example, after the negative expressions (**non**)... **nulla/niente/nessuno**.

  Di quel museo, non c'è **nulla** che mi **piaccia**.
  There is nothing about that museum that I like.

  Non conosciamo **nessuno** che **possa** aiutarci.
  We don't know anyone who can help us.

- Use the subjunctive after the relative superlative (**il più... che, il meno... che, il migliore... che, il peggiore... che**).

  Novecento è **il** film **più lungo** che io **abbia** mai **visto**!
  1900 *is the longest film I have ever seen!*

- The subjunctive is often used after the restrictive adjectives **unico**, **solo**, **primo**, and **ultimo** in combination with the definite article.

  La Strada è **l'unico** film di Fellini che **abbiate visto**.
  La Strada *is the only film by Fellini that you have seen.*

  I cartoni animati sono **i primi** programmi che io **abbia visto**.
  Cartoons are the first shows I watched.

Pratica e comunicazione

1 **Al Genova Comics** Jennifer, studentessa americana in Italia, incontra per la prima volta Paolo al Genova Comics: forse può consigliarle quale fumetto comprare per suo fratello... Completa la conversazione inserendo i verbi al congiuntivo o all'indicativo.

JENNIFER Ciao! Puoi aiutarmi, per favore? Cerco un fumetto per mio fratello... qualcosa di tipicamente italiano, ma fuori dagli stereotipi. Puoi consigliarmi qualcosa?

PAOLO Diabolik, senza dubbio! Ovunque tu (1) __vada__ (andare), il suo stand è sempre pieno di gente: significa che è il più amato!

JENNIFER Diabolik... non lo conosco, ma chiunque lui (2) __sia__ (essere), ha un nome davvero inquietante!

PAOLO Diabolik è «il re del terrore»! Non c'è nessuno in Italia che non lo (3) __conosca__ (conoscere).

JENNIFER Cosa fa nella vita questo... Diabolik?

PAOLO Il ladro. Chiunque (4) __abbia__ (avere) denaro o (5) __nasconda__ (nascondere) gioielli è una sua possibile vittima.

JENNIFER Una specie di Robin Hood moderno!

PAOLO Non proprio... Diabolik non dà niente ai poveri. Tiene per sé tutto quello che (6) __ruba__ (rubare).

JENNIFER E tu sei d'accordo con tutto quello che lui (7) __fa__ (fare)?

PAOLO Certo che no! Ma Diabolik è un personaggio assolutamente innovativo per i suoi tempi! La sua amante, Eva Kant, è una donna forte, astuta (*smart*) e sempre fedele. Chiunque (8) __dica__ (dire) di essere un fan di Diabolik, in realtà è un fan di Eva Kant.

2 **Confronti** Confronta i tuoi gusti con quelli di un(a) compagno/a usando il congiuntivo presente o passato come nell'esempio.

Modello **il miglior film**

«Gli Intoccabili» è il miglior film che io abbia mai visto.

1. la rivista più interessante
2. il fumetto più divertente
3. il cartone animato più comico
4. il programma meno commerciale
5. il personaggio più misterioso
6. il giornalista più polemico
7. il peggior telefilm
8. l'opinionista più critico

3 **Quest'anno a Ferragosto** Guardate le immagini e decidete come passare il prossimo Ferragosto. Scrivete poi almeno due frasi al superlativo per ogni immagine e spiegate perché l'avete, o non l'avete, scelta. Aiutatevi con le parole della lista.

Modello Non farò più trekking perché è la cosa meno entusiasmante che io abbia mai fatto.

1 Ask pairs of students to write a similar dialogue about the main character of a cartoon strip they like and then read it to the class. While reading, the name of the character could be omitted so that the rest of the class guesses who he/she is.

Nota
CULTURALE

Genova Comics è il festival internazionale che ogni anno propone fumetti e musica di ogni epoca, formato e genere. Al festival, un posto speciale è occupato dalle edizioni di *Diabolik, il «re del terrore»*, inventato nel 1962 dalle sorelle Giussani in formato tascabile° per i pendolari° che ogni giorno prendevano il treno per andare al lavoro. Figura decisamente controversa, Diabolik non era certo un esempio morale, mentre la sua amante, Eva Kant, era l'opposto dello stereotipo della donna remissiva propagandato da stampa e televisione fin ad allora. Inizialmente attaccato dalla critica, Diabolik vanta oggi un fan club molto numeroso per la bellezza dei disegni, il fascino dei personaggi e la storia d'amore assolutamente sincera ed onesta fra il protagonista ed Eva.

formato tascabile *pocket format*
pendolari *commuters*

2 Have students share their answers with the class and make lists on the blackboard showing the most interesting magazines, the most amusing comic strips, etc.

 Practice more at vhlcentral.com.

Sintesi

Parliamo In piccoli gruppi, esaminate il sondaggio e discutete degli argomenti proposti dalle domande.

Il rapporto Agcom sul consumo di informazione da parte degli italiani nel 2018

- Telegiornali: 68,8%
- Informazioni sul web (da pc o mobile): 41,8%
- Radio: 24,6%
- Carta stampata: 17,1%

fonte: www.agcom.it/

---

1. Qual è il mezzo di informazione più usato dagli italiani? Pensi che sia una fonte valida oppure no? Perché?
2. Quale pensi sia il futuro della stampa?
3. Tra i mezzi di informazione elencati, qual è il migliore che tu possa consigliare a un(a) amico/a?
4. Secondo te, qual è il mezzo d'informazione più diffuso tra i giovani?

Strategie per la comunicazione

Espressioni utili...

...per esprimere le proprie opinioni:

Secondo me/i sondaggi... (+ indicativo)

Personalmente penso/credo/ritengo che... (+ congiuntivo)

Sono assolutamente contrario/a a...

Sono d'accordo con...

...per esprimere punti di vista diversi:

Da un lato..., dall'altro…

Sono d'accordo con..., tuttavia...

Anche se... (+ indicativo)

Nonostante... (+ congiuntivo)

...per indicare i risultati di un sondaggio:

La maggior parte di... (+ verbo al singolare)

La maggioranza/minoranza di...

Scriviamo Scegli uno di questi argomenti e scrivi una breve composizione.

- Descrivi il tuo rapporto con la televisione. La usi? Come? Quando? Quanto? Trovi che sia giusto parlare di un «uso buono» e un «uso cattivo» della televisione, o pensi che questo sia un atteggiamento moralistico che limita la libertà dell'individuo?

- Descrivi come, in un paese ideale, i cittadini risponderebbero alle domande del sondaggio. Avrebbero un atteggiamento (*attitude*) diverso nei confronti dei mezzi di informazione? Perché? Come si potrebbe creare una società con un maggiore spirito critico? Se tu avessi la possibilità di pianificare la programmazione televisiva del tuo paese, come la struttureresti?

- Descrivi come accedono alle fonti di informazione i tuoi coetanei. Pensi che la tua sia una generazione ben informata? Perché sì o no? Quali sono i vantaggi e gli svantaggi, secondo te, delle fonti di informazione in tempo reale?

Preparazione  Vocabulary Tools

Vocabolario della lettura	Vocabolario utile
il **capolavoro** *masterpiece*	il **critico (cinematografico)** *(film) critic*
il/la **cineasta** *filmmaker*	**giallo** *mystery*
il **copione** *script*	**premiato/a** *award-winning*
il **culmine** *height* (fig.)	la **rassegna** *festival*
girare *to film*	la **recensione** *review*
onirico/a *dream-like*	**rosa** *romance*
il/la **regista** *director*	**sperimentale** *experimental*
la **sceneggiatura** *screenplay*	
il **volto** *face*	

1

Significati Collega le parole con le loro definizioni.

<u>c</u> 1. capolavoro   a. copia del testo di un'opera drammatica

<u>e</u> 2. cineasta   b. filmare

<u>a</u> 3. copione   c. opera più importante

<u>b</u> 4. girare   d. testo teatrale o cinematografico

<u>f</u> 5. volto   e. professionista del cinema

<u>d</u> 6. sceneggiatura   f. faccia

2

Generi

A. In coppia, inserite dei titoli di film in ogni categoria.

- Film d'azione/Thriller
- Commedia
- Film neorealista
- Film giallo (storie poliziesche, di detective, misteriose)
- Film rosa (storie d'amore)
- Film dell'orrore
- Western
- Commedia all'italiana
- Spaghetti western

B. Confrontate le vostre risposte con quelle di un'altra coppia.

3

Gusti In coppia, rispondete alle domande.

1. Vai spesso al cinema?
2. Quale genere di film preferisci? Quale non andresti mai a vedere? Perché?
3. Quali attori hanno vinto il premio Oscar quest'anno? Secondo te, se lo meritavano o no?
4. Quando vai al cinema vedi spesso film stranieri? Preferisci i film doppiati o quelli con i sottotitoli? Perché?
5. Cosa ti viene in mente quando pensi al cinema italiano? Quali film, attori, registi, produttori italiani conosci?
6. Hai mai visto un film di Federico Fellini? Quale? Cosa ne pensi?

Review other relevant film vocabulary from the beginning of the lesson as needed for class discussion.

Ask students if they know how a **commedia all'italiana** differs from other comedies. Use examples and video clips from films such as Pietro Germi's **Divorzio all'italiana** (for which the term was coined) and others to illustrate this particular genre and its ties to **neorealismo**. In the same vein, encourage a discussion on the differences and similarities between Hollywood westerns and Italian spaghetti westerns. You might also wish to explain how colors came to describe genres in Italian literature and cinema.

Nota CULTURALE

Il movimento **neorealista** è nato durante la seconda guerra mondiale con la resistenza antifascista ed è continuato durante gli anni '50. È un periodo durante il quale gli intellettuali italiani cercavano un nuovo modo di descrivere il mondo con un forte senso di impegno sociale e politico. Nel cinema, i creatori del neorealismo sono registi che usavano attori non professionisti e narravano storie di vita quotidiana: i più celebri sono **Roberto Rossellini, Luchino Visconti, Michelangelo Antonioni** e **Vittorio de Sica**.

Federico Fellini
IL 'MAESTRO' DEI SOGNI

Reading

In quarant'anni di carriera—dal 1950 al 1990—il regista Federico Fellini (1920–1993) ha girato ventiquattro film e cambiato il volto del cinema mondiale. Con il loro «realismo magico», i suoi film costituiscono per molti aspetti uno sviluppo del neorealismo italiano ma anche l'espressione di un particolarissimo immaginario allo stesso tempo autobiografico e universale.

Il più conosciuto tra i registi italiani, vincitore di cinque Oscar e innumerevoli altri premi internazionali, da giovane aveva aspirazioni molto diverse: voleva fare il fumettista° e il giornalista e non immaginava che un giorno sarebbe diventato un celebre cineasta. Già dai tempi in cui era ancora studente al liceo, il giovane Federico aveva cominciato a pubblicare vignette satiriche su giornali e riviste.

Ad appena 19 anni, si è trasferito a Roma promettendo ai genitori di studiare giurisprudenza° all'università, ma iniziando invece a collaborare con giornali e con la principale rivista umoristica del tempo, il *Marc'Aurelio*, disegnando e scrivendo una serie di rubriche intitolate «Le storielle di Federico». A Roma ha cominciato anche a frequentare il mondo del teatro di varietà (chiamato anche l'avanspettacolo) e del cinema, ambiente in cui ha conosciuto personaggi e attori famosi che lo hanno incoraggiato a scrivere copioni e sceneggiature.

Nel 1945 il grande regista Roberto Rossellini lo ha invitato a scrivere con lui la sceneggiatura di *Roma città aperta* e, l'anno successivo, quella di *Paisà*. È l'inizio di una collaborazione storica e dell'entrata del giovane Fellini nel grande cinema. Il primo film di cui ha curato completamente la regia è *Lo sceicco bianco* del 1952, che però non è stato accolto bene né dal pubblico né dalla critica. Il successo e i premi però sono cominciati ad arrivare molto presto: già l'anno successivo il film *I vitelloni* ha vinto il Leone d'argento alla prestigiosa Mostra

Margin glosses:
cartoonist° (line 15)
law° (line 23)

Il cinema contemporaneo in Italia

Dopo un periodo di crisi alla fine del Novecento, il cinema italiano del Duemila ha cominciato a riprendersi. I grandi registi contemporanei come Nanni Moretti, Matteo Garrone, Gianni Amelio e Marco Tullio Giordana e Paolo Sorrentino sono molto diversi tra di loro stilisticamente; i loro film trattano gli aspetti più complessi dell'Italia di oggi. Da vedere sono: *Lamerica* (Amelio 1994), *Caro Diario* (Moretti 1993), *Quando sei nato non puoi più nasconderti* (Giordana 2005), *Gomorra* (Garrone 2008) e *La grande bellezza* (Sorrentino 2013).

del cinema di Venezia. Nel 1942, mentre scriveva anche per la radio, Federico ha incontrato l'attrice Giulietta Masina, sua futura moglie e indimenticabile interprete dei film *La strada* (1956), *Giulietta degli spiriti* (1965) ed altri capolavori cinematografici felliniani.

La seconda fase del cinema del Fellini maturo ha continuato a ricevere applausi e premi, ma ha causato anche scandalo nella società italiana del tempo con film come *La dolce vita* (1960): una delle scene più controverse in cui l'attrice Anita Ekberg entra nella fontana di Trevi è oggi leggendaria. Ma il culmine del cinema felliniano è certamente il rivoluzionario *8 ½* (1963), la storia onirica e interiore di un regista, interpretato da Marcello Mastroianni (uno dei protagonisti preferiti di Fellini), sul set di un film che non finisce mai. Come il cinema di Fellini stesso, è un mondo in cui l'immaginazione permette la coesistenza di realtà in apparenza opposte, come tristezza e umorismo, personaggi insieme poetici e grotteschi, nostalgia e e ironia. ■

Fellini dopo *8 ½*

Dopo il successo internazionale di *8 ½*, i film più ricordati di Fellini sono: *Roma* (1972), *Amarcord* (1973), *E la nave va* (1983) e *Ginger e Fred* (1986).

Analisi

1

Analisi Indica se queste affermazioni sono **vere** o **false**. Poi, in coppia, correggete le affermazioni false.

Vero	Falso	
☐	☑	1. Fellini ha inventato il neorealismo.
☑	☐	2. I genitori di Fellini volevano che studiasse giurisprudenza.
☑	☐	3. Prima di diventare regista Fellini voleva fare il giornalista.
☐	☑	4. Fellini non ha mai lavorato per la radio.
☑	☐	5. Roberto Rossellini è stato uno dei mentori di Fellini.
☑	☐	6. Molti film di Fellini hanno degli elementi onirici.

2

Dibattito In piccoli gruppi, rispondete alle domande.

1. Com'è il cinema di Hollywood paragonato a quello italiano?

2. Quali cineasti americani sono contemporanei di Fellini? Che tipo di cinema hanno creato? Il loro stile è cambiato con il passare degli anni o è rimasto simile?

3. Quali registi contemporanei parlano di problemi sociali?

4. Quali film recenti hanno causato dei dibattiti o degli scandali?

5. Vi piacciono i film fatti solo per divertire o cercate di vedere quelli che hanno un messaggio più complesso? Pensate che ci sia spazio per tutti e due i generi?

3 Ask students to consider collaborations from different genres, countries, etc. Some suggestions: Aerosmith and Run DMC; Merce Cunningham and John Cage; Eros Ramazzotti and Tina Turner; Andy Warhol and Jean-Michel Basquiat; Salvador Dalí and Luis Buñuel.

3

Collaborazioni Sappiamo che Fellini ha scritto delle sceneggiature per Rossellini e poi, una volta divenuto regista, ha spesso usato gli stessi attori, come Giulietta Masina e Marcello Mastroianni. Quali altre celebri collaborazioni tra artisti vi vengono in mente?

4

Citazioni Leggete e commentate queste celebri frasi di Fellini.

«Sono un artigiano che non ha niente da dire, ma sa come dirlo.»

«Sono un grande bugiardo.»

«Il cinema non ha bisogno della grande idea.»

«Faccio un film alla stessa maniera in cui vivo un sogno.»

- Pensate che Fellini non avesse davvero niente da dire?

- Che cosa intende, secondo voi, per «bugiardo»?

- Quali sono gli elementi di un film eccezionale? Che cos'è una «grande idea»?

- In che modo un film può essere come un sogno?

- Quali sono le qualità di un bravo regista? Perché?

- Che cosa costituisce una trama avvincente (*enthralling*)?

- Quale mezzo sceglieresti per raccontare la tua autobiografia? Un film o un romanzo?

5

Scrittura Scegli uno dei seguenti argomenti e scrivi una breve composizione.

- Proponi un'idea per un film a un produttore italiano. Qual è la storia principale? Dov'è ambientato? Perché avrà successo?

- Guarda un film di Fellini e scrivi una breve recensione. Descrivi i personaggi, racconta la trama e riassumi gli elementi che ti hanno sorpreso.

Practice more at vhlcentral.com.

Preparazione  Vocabulary Tools

A proposito dell'autrice

La scrittrice **Natalia Ginzburg** (Palermo 1916–Roma 1991), nata Levi, è una delle figure più importanti della letteratura italiana del Novecento. Cresciuta a Torino, ha iniziato a scrivere da giovane. Per le leggi razziali anche contro gli ebrei (*Jews*) e per essere antifascisti, Natalia e il marito Leone Ginzburg hanno passato tre anni al confino (*internal exile*) in un piccolo paese dell'Abruzzo. Leone è morto torturato in prigione a Roma nel 1944. Dopo la guerra Natalia ha continuato a dedicarsi alla letteratura e ha lavorato come redattrice (*editor in chief*) della casa editrice Einaudi. Nel 1962 ha pubblicato la raccolta *Le piccole virtù* e nel 1963 ha vinto il Premio Strega con *Lessico famigliare*, che ha ottenuto un forte consenso di critica e pubblico. Natalia si è anche impegnata (*engaged*) in attività politiche e sociali.

Vocabolario della lettura

i baffi *moustache*
la carta topografica *city map*
il golf *sweater*
infilarsi *to slip on (clothing)*

la multa *traffic ticket*
sdegnarsi *to become indignant*
lo sforzo *effort*
vagare *to roam, to wander*

Vocabolario utile

l'affinità di coppia *compatibility*
il coniuge *spouse*
i gusti *tastes, preferences*
il rapporto *relationship*

Nota CULTURALE

Prima del regime fascista che Mussolini instaurò nel 1922, gli ebrei vivevano integrati con il resto della popolazione italiana. La comunità ebraica italiana (specialmente a Roma) era la più antica d'Europa. Nel 1938, dopo essersi alleato con la Germania di Hitler, il regime fascista introdusse le «leggi razziali», principalmente antisemite, che continuarono durante l'occupazione tedesca fino al 1944. Molti italiani erano contrari alla discriminazione verso i propri connazionali e cercarono di aiutarli: come ha scritto la studiosa ebrea tedesca Hannah Arendt: «L'Italia era uno dei pochi paesi d'Europa dove ogni misura antisemita era decisamente impopolare».

---

1 Definizioni Trovate la definizione adatta per ogni parola.

_e_ 1. la carta topografica   a. avere idee e gusti simili
_d_ 2. il coniuge   b. i peli sopra il labbro e intorno alla bocca
_b_ 3. i baffi   c. un maglione
_f_ 4. uno sforzo   d. il marito o la moglie
_a_ 5. affinità   e. un disegno con le vie di una città
_c_ 6. un golf   f. un impiego di energia fisica o mentale

2 Preparazione Fatevi le seguenti domande a vicenda.

1. Pensi che esista la coppia ideale? Com'è? Usa degli esempi (una coppia famosa, i tuoi genitori, ecc.).
2. È importante avere una certa affinità di carattere e di gusti per andare d'accordo? Perché?
3. Quali attività non ti interessano ma ogni tanto devi fare con sforzo per far contenta un'altra persona (il/la tuo/a ragazzo/a, i tuoi amici o parenti)?
4. Hai mai litigato con qualcuno per differenze di gusti? Perché?

3 Il matrimonio Rispondete insieme alle seguenti domande.

1. Quali sono gli elementi fondamentali per una vita di coppia felice? Fate una lista.
2. Come si possono risolvere le differenze tra coniugi?
3. Con quale tipo di persona non potresti mai andare d'accordo? Perché no?
4. Secondo voi, è vero il detto che «gli opposti si attraggono»?

2 Encourage students to share their responses with rest of the class.

 Practice more at vhlcentral.com.

NATALIA GINZBURG

Lui e io

Tutt'e due amiamo
il cinematografo;
e siamo disposti a
vedere, in qualsiasi
momento della
giornata, qualsiasi
specie di film.

Audio:
Dramatic Reading

*L*ui ha sempre caldo; io sempre freddo. D'estate, quando è veramente caldo, non fa che lamentarsi del gran caldo che ha. Si sdegna se vede che m'infilo, la sera, un golf.

Lui sa parlare bene alcune lingue; io non ne parlo bene nessuna. Lui riesce a parlare, in qualche suo modo, anche le lingue che non sa.

Lui ha un grande senso dell'orientamento; io nessuno. Nelle città straniere, dopo un giorno, lui si muove leggero come una farfalla°. Io mi sperdo nella mia propria città; devo chiedere indicazioni per ritornare alla mia propria casa. Lui odia chiedere indicazioni; quando andiamo per città sconosciute, in automobile, non vuole che chiediamo indicazioni e mi ordina di guardare la pianta topografica. Io non so guardare le piante topografiche, m'imbroglio° su quei cerchiolini° rossi, e si arrabbia.

Lui ama il teatro, la pittura, e la musica: soprattutto la musica. Io non capisco niente di musica, m'importa molto poco della pittura, e m'annoio a teatro. Amo e capisco una cosa sola al mondo, ed è la poesia.

Lui ama i musei, e io ci vado con sforzo, con uno spiacevole senso di dovere e fatica.

Lui ama le biblioteche, e io le odio.

Lui ama i viaggi, le città straniere e sconosciute, i ristoranti. Io resterei sempre a casa, non mi muoverei mai.

Lo seguo, tuttavia, in molti viaggi. Lo seguo nei musei, nelle chiese, all'opera. Lo seguo anche ai concerti, e mi addormento. Siccome conosce dei direttori d'orchestra, dei cantanti, gli piace andare, dopo lo spettacolo, a congratularsi con loro. Lo seguo per i lunghi corridoi che portano ai camerini° dei cantanti, lo ascolto parlare con persone vestite da cardinali e da re.

Non è timido; e io sono timida. Qualche volta, però, l'ho visto timido.

Coi poliziotti, quando s'avvicinano alla nostra macchina armati di taccuino° e matita.

Con quelli diventa timido, sentendosi in torto.

E anche non sentendosi in torto. Credo che nutra rispetto per l'autorità costituita.

Io, l'autorità costituita, la temo, e lui no. Lui ne ha rispetto. È diverso.

Io, se vedo un poliziotto avvicinarsi per darci la multa, penso subito che vorrà portarmi in prigione. Lui, alla prigione, non pensa; ma diventa, per rispetto, timido e gentile.

Per questo, per il suo rispetto verso l'autorità costituita, ci siamo, al tempo del processo Montesi, litigati fino al delirio.

> **Lui ama il teatro,
> la pittura, e la musica.
> Io non capisco niente di
> musica, m'importa molto
> poco della pittura,
> e m'annoio a teatro.**

A lui piacciono le tagliatelle, l'abbacchio°, le ciliege°, il vino rosso. A me piace il minestrone, il pancotto°, la frittata, gli erbaggi°.

Suole° dirmi che non capisco niente, nelle cose da mangiare; e che sono come certi robusti fratacchioni°, che divorano zuppe di erbe nell'ombra dei loro conventi; e lui, lui è un raffinato, dal palato sensibile. Al ristorante, s'informa a lungo sui vini; se ne fa portare due o tre bottiglie, le osserva e riflette, carezzandosi la barba pian piano.

In Inghilterra, vi sono certi ristoranti dove il cameriere usa questo piccolo cerimoniale: versare al cliente qualche dito di vino nel bicchiere, perché senta se è di suo gusto. Lui odiava questo piccolo cerimoniale; e ogni volta impediva al cameriere di compierlo, togliendogli di

butterfly

I get confused
little circles

dressing rooms

notepad

lamb roast

cherries

soup with bread

vegetables

He is in the habit of

fat friars

85 mano la bottiglia. Io lo rimproveravo, facendogli osservare che a ognuno dev'essere consentito° di assolvere alle proprie incombenze°.

permitted
tasks

Così, al cinematografo, non vuol mai 90 che la maschera° lo accompagni al posto. Gli dà subito la mancia, ma fugge in posti sempre diversi da quelli che la maschera, col lume, gli viene indicando.

usher

Al cinematografo, vuole stare 95 vicinissimo allo schermo. Se andiamo con amici, e questi cercano, come la maggior parte della gente, un posto lontano dallo schermo, lui si rifugia, solo, in una delle prime file. Io ci vedo bene, 100 indifferentemente, da vicino e da lontano; ma essendo con amici, resto insieme a loro, per gentilezza; e tuttavia soffro, perché può essere che lui, nel suo posto a due palmi dallo schermo°, siccome non mi son seduta 105 al suo fianco, sia offeso con me.

screen

Tutt'e due amiamo il cinematografo.

Tutt'e due amiamo il cinematografo; e siamo disposti a vedere, in qualsiasi momento della giornata, qualsiasi specie di film. Ma lui conosce la storia 110 del cinematografo in ogni minimo particolare; ricorda registi e attori, anche i più antichi, da gran tempo dimenticati e scomparsi; ed è pronto a fare chilometri per andare a cercare, nelle più lontane 115 periferie, vecchissimi film del tempo del muto°, dove comparirà magari per pochi secondi un attore caro alle sue più remote memorie d'infanzia. Ricordo, a Londra, il pomeriggio d'una domenica; davano in un 120 lontano sobborgo sui limiti della campagna un film sulla Rivoluzione francese, un film del '30, che lui aveva visto da bambino, e dove appariva per qualche attimo un'attrice famosa a quel tempo. Siamo 125 andati in macchina alla ricerca di quella

silent movies

lontanissima strada; pioveva, c'era nebbia, abbiamo vagato ore e ore per sobborghi tutti uguali, tra schiere° grigie di piccole case, grondaie°, lampioni e cancelli°; avevo sulle ginocchia la pianta topografica, 130 non riuscivo a leggerla e lui s'arrabbiava; infine, abbiamo trovato il cinematografo, ci siamo seduti in una sala del tutto deserta. Ma dopo un quarto d'ora, lui già voleva andar via, subito dopo la breve comparsa 135 dell'attrice che gli stava a cuore; io invece volevo, dopo tanta strada, vedere come finiva il film. Non ricordo se sia prevalsa° la sua o la mia volontà; forse, la sua, e ce ne siamo andati dopo un quarto d'ora; anche 140 perché era tardi, e benché fossimo usciti nel primo pomeriggio, ormai era venuta l'ora di cena. Ma pregandolo io di raccontarmi come si concludeva la storia, non ottenevo nessuna risposta che m'appagasse°; perché, 145 lui diceva, la storia non aveva nessuna importanza, e la sola cosa che contava erano quei pochi istanti, il profilo, il gesto, i riccioli° di quell'attrice.

rows
gutters/gates

had prevailed

satisfied me

curls

Io non mi ricordo mai i nomi degli 150 attori; e siccome sono poco fisionomista, riconosco a volte con difficoltà anche i più famosi. Questo lo irrita moltissimo; gli chiedo chi sia quello o quell'altro, suscitando il suo sdegno; « non mi dirai — 155 dice - non mi dirai che non hai riconosciuto William Holden! » Effettivamente, non ho riconosciuto William Holden.

E tuttavia, amo anch'io il cinematografo; ma pur andandoci da tanti anni, 160 non ho saputo farmene una cultura. Lui se ne è fatto, invece, una cultura: si è fatto una cultura di tutto quello che ha attratto la sua curiosità; e io non ho saputo farmi una cultura di nulla, nemmeno delle cose che ho 165 più amato nella mia vita: esse sono rimaste in me come immagini sparse, alimentando sì la mia vita di memorie e di commozione ma senza colmare° il vuoto, il deserto della mia cultura. 170

fill

[...]

Era, da ragazzo, bello, magro, esile°, non aveva allora la barba, ma lunghi e morbidi baffi; e rassomigliava all'attore

slight

Robert Donat. Era così quasi vent'anni
175 fa, quando l'ho conosciuto; e portava,
ricordo, certi camiciotti scozzesi, di
flanella, eleganti. Mi ha accompagnato,
ricordo, una sera, alla pensione dove
allora abitavo; abbiamo camminato
180 insieme per via Nazionale. Io mi sentivo
già molto vecchia, carica di esperienza
e d'errori; e lui mi sembrava un ragazzo,
lontano da me mille secoli. Cosa ci siamo
detti quella sera, per via Nazionale, non
185 lo so ricordare; niente d'importante,
suppongo; era lontana da me mille
secoli l'idea che dovessimo diventare,
un giorno, marito e moglie. Poi ci siamo
persi di vista; e quando ci siamo di nuovo
190 incontrati, non rassomigliava più a Robert
Donat, ma piuttosto a Balzac. Quando
ci siamo di nuovo incontrati, aveva
sempre quei camiciotti scozzesi, ma ora
garments sembravano, addosso a lui, indumenti°
195 per una spedizione polare; aveva ora
crumpled la barba, e in testa lo sbertucciato°
cappelluccio di lana; e tutto in lui faceva
pensare a una prossima partenza per il
Polo Nord. Perché, pur avendo sempre
200 tanto caldo, sovente usa vestirsi come
se fosse circondato di neve, di ghiaccio
e di orsi bianchi; o anche invece si veste

come un piantatore di caffè nel Brasile;
ma sempre si veste diverso da tutta
l'altra gente.   205

Se gli ricordo quell'antica nostra
passeggiata per via Nazionale, dice di
ricordare, ma io so che mente° e non ricorda   *is lying*
nulla; e io a volte mi chiedo se eravamo
noi, quelle due persone, quasi vent'anni fa 210
per via Nazionale; due persone che hanno

> **Era lontana da me
> mille secoli l'idea che
> dovessimo diventare, un
> giorno, marito e moglie.**

conversato così gentilmente, urbanamente,
nel solo che tramontava; che hanno
parlato forse un po' di tutto, e di nulla;
due amabili conversatori, due giovani   215
intellettuali a passeggio; così giovani, così
educati, così distratti, così disposti a dare
l'uno dell'altra un giudizio distrattamente
benevolo; così disposti a congedarsi° l'uno   *say goodbye*
dall'altra per sempre, quel tramonto, a 220
quell'angolo di strada. ■

1

2

3

Nota
CULTURALE

Il processo Montesi

Nel 1953 tutti i giornali parlavano della misteriosa morte di una giovane ragazza, Wilma Montesi, trovata su una spiaggia vicino a Roma. Il caso, le lunghe indagini° e il processo che seguì, crearono un grande fenomeno mediatico, che durò quattro anni, coinvolgendo° persone famose e figure politiche. Il mistero non è ancora stato risolto.

indagini *investigations*
coinvolgendo *involving*

Analisi

Vero o falso? Indica se le affermazioni sono **vere** o **false**.

Vero	Falso	
☑	☐	1. Lui ama le biblioteche, e lei le odia.
☑	☐	2. Lei ama la poesia, ma non la musica.
☐	☑	3. Lui si veste con abiti pesanti perché ha sempre freddo.
☑	☐	4. Sia lui che lei si divertono ad andare al cinema.
☐	☑	5. Quando era giovane lui era molto robusto e grasso.
☐	☑	6. I due protagonisti sono sposati da vent'anni.
☑	☐	7. Lui e lei hanno litigato a proposito del processo Montesi.
☑	☐	8. A lui piace assaggiare il vino quando va nei risoranti.

Comprensione Completa le frasi scegliendo la risposta giusta.

1. Quando lui e lei sono andati a Londra hanno cercato _____.
   a. William Holden
   b.) un cinema in un sobborgo
   c. un vino francese

2. Dopo i concerti lei lo accompagna _____.
   a.) nei camerini dei cantanti
   b. in biblioteca
   c. nella cantina del direttore d'orchestra

3. Al ristorante lui ordina _____.
   a. minestrone e frittata
   b. zuppa e erbaggi
   c.) abbacchio e vino rosso

4. Quando guida lui non vuole _____.
   a. consultare la carta topografica
   b.) chiedere indicazioni
   c. parlare con lei

5. Adesso lui si veste come _____.
   a.) un piantatore di caffè del Brasile
   b. un esploratore al Polo Nord
   c. un poliziotto

6. Quando vanno al cinema _____.
   a. lei dorme
   b. lui si offende
   c.) sono contenti tutti e due

Interpretazione In coppia, rispondete alle seguenti domande.

1. Come pensate che sia il rapporto tra lui e lei? Perché?
2. Lui e lei vi ricordano un'altra coppia che conoscete? In che modo?
3. Qual è il tono usato dalla narratrice? Arrabbiato? Ironico? Dolce?
4. Cosa pensate che direbbe «lui» descrivendo «lei»?

4 **Lui e lei** In coppia, abbinate gli aggettivi con il personaggio che descrivono.

	LUI	LEI
timido/a		
impaurito/a dall'autorità		
distratto/a		
intellettuale		
socievole		
informato/a sul mondo del cinema		
paziente		

4 Have students suggest additional adjectives that describe each of the two characters.

5 **Discussione** In piccoli gruppi, rispondete alle seguenti domande.

1. Quali sono le differenze principali tra lui e lei?
2. Pensate che lui e lei abbiano delle cose in comune? Quali?
3. Credete che la narratrice dica sempre la verità o che usi anche una dose di ironia nelle sue descrizioni? Perché?
4. Che cosa hanno fatto lui e lei quando sono andati a Londra?
5. Quale è stato il litigio più serio tra i due protagonisti? Potete immaginare perché?
6. Secondo voi, perché lei segue lui a teatro, alle feste e ai concerti anche se non le piacciono per niente?

5 The story *Lui e io* was originally published in 1962. Have students explore how relationships have changed since this story was written.

6 **Dialogo** In coppia, ricostruite il dialogo tra lui e lei che la narratrice non ricorda:

«Mi ha accompagnato, ricordo, una sera, alla pensione dove allora abitavo; abbiamo camminato insieme per via Nazionale. Io mi sentivo già molto vecchia, carica di esperienza e d'errori; e lui mi sembrava un ragazzo, lontano da me mille secoli. Cosa ci siamo detti quella sera, per via Nazionale, non lo so ricordare; niente d'importante, suppongo; era lontana da me mille secoli l'idea che dovessimo diventare, un giorno, marito e moglie».

LEI: _____

LUI: _____

6 Ask pairs to perform their dialogues for the class.

7 **Tema** Scegli uno dei seguenti argomenti e scrivi una breve composizione.

● Scrivi un'e-mail al/la tuo/a compagno/a vero/a o ideale, illustrando i tuoi gusti, le tue attività preferite e quelle che pensi possano essere delle differenze tra di voi.

● Come pensi che sarai tra vent'anni? Dove abiterai? Che lavoro farai? Sarai sposato/a? Immagina se e come cambierai con il passare del tempo.

Practice more at
vhlcentral.com.

Pratica

Preparazione Tell the students that breaches in logic can occur within sentences (as shown in the example of **2 Preparazione**) as well as between paragraphs. They should look carefully at transitions between their paragraphs to make sure that they flow logically from one to the next.

Generalizzazioni e mancanza di continuità

Due problemi comuni nella stesura (*drafting*) di un saggio sono le generalizzazioni e la mancanza (*lack*) di continuità. Una generalizzazione non tiene in considerazione tutte le possibili eccezioni che il lettore potrebbe notare. La mancanza di continuità esiste quando mancano dei passaggi logici in quello che stiamo scrivendo. Per evitare questi problemi, leggi ogni paragrafo e ogni frase con queste domande in mente:

- **Quello che sto dicendo è vero in ogni caso?** Se noti delle eccezioni, devi prenderle in considerazione per non incorrere in un'altra generalizzazione.

- **Quello che ho scritto può essere considerato come un passaggio che segue logicamente il precedente?** Se la transizione non è chiara, si devono organizzare le idee in una sequenza logica per evitare la mancanza di continuità.

1

Preparazione Scrivi una frase che presenti una generalizzazione o un esempio di mancanza di continuità. Mostrala ad un(a) compagno/a e chiedigli/le di correggerla.

Modello

Generalizzazione: Guardare la televisione è una perdita di tempo.

Correzione: Sebbene alcuni programmi siano informativi, la maggior parte presenta contenuti futili. Inoltre, passare troppo tempo davanti alla TV isola le persone ed è uno spreco (*waste*) di tempo che potrebbe essere utilizzato in maniera più produttiva.

Mancanza di continuità: Alla fine abbiamo deciso di non comprare un computer da tavolo.

Correzione: Volevamo comprare un computer da tavolo, ma i computer portatili non costano molto e, in realtà, non abbiamo abbastanza spazio per un computer da tavolo e tutti i suoi accessori.

- Il saggio deve far riferimento ad almeno due dei quattro brani studiati in questa lezione e nelle precedenti lezioni e contenuti in **Cortometraggio**, **Immagina**, **Cultura** e **Letteratura**.

- Revisiona il tuo saggio. Cerca esempi di generalizzazione o mancanza di continuità e fai le necessarie correzioni.

- Il saggio deve essere lungo almeno due pagine.

2 Saggio Preview some of the topics. Ask students how they get their information: TV, Internet, newspapers, etc., and how often. Ask them if they ever read or watch foreign mass media. How does foreign media compare to domestic media?

2

Saggio Scegli uno di questi argomenti e scrivi un saggio.

I mezzi di comunicazione possono raccontarci la realtà in modo vero (notizie, documentari e reality show), oppure immaginario (letteratura, film e fiction). Secondo voi, realtà e immaginario possono mescolarsi e confondersi? L'immaginario può influenzare la realtà?

Molti programmi alla TV, in particolare i reality show, sembrano voler stimolare il pettegolezzo e l'intromissione nella vita degli altri. Perché piacciono alle persone?

La grande quantità di informazione aiuta a sviluppare un pensiero critico o inibisce la mente?

Media e cultura Vocabulary Tools

INSTRUCTIONAL RESOURCES
Task-based activities

Cinema, radio e televisione

l'adattamento *adaptation*
i cartoni animati *cartoons*
la colonna sonora *soundtrack*
il documentario *documentary*
il doppiaggio *dubbing*
gli effetti speciali *special effects*
l'intervista *interview*
la puntata *episode*
lo schermo *screen*
il sottotitolo *subtitle*
la (stazione) radio *radio (station)*
la televisione satellitare *satellite TV*
la televisione via cavo *cable TV*

filmare *to film*
registrare *to record*
trasmettere *to broadcast*
uscire *to be released*

I media

l'attualità *current events*
la censura *censorship*
il giornale radio *radio news*
la notizia *news story*
il notiziario *news program*
la pubblicità *commercial; advertisement*
il sondaggio *opinion poll*
il telegiornale *TV news*

essere aggiornato/a *to be, up-to-date*
informarsi *to get/stay informed*

in differita *pre-recorded*
in diretta *live*
influente *influential*
(im)parziale *(im)partial; (un)biased*

La gente dei media

l'ascoltatore/ascoltatrice *(radio) listener*
l'attore/attrice *actor/actress*
il/la cronista *reporter*
l'editore/editrice *publisher*
il/la giornalista *journalist*

l'inviato/a speciale *correspondent*
il/la redattore/redattrice *editor*
il/la telespettatore/telespettatrice *television viewer*

La stampa

il comunicato stampa *press release*
la cronaca (locale/sportiva) *(local/sports) news*
il fumetto *comic strip*
il giornale *newspaper*
la libertà di stampa *freedom of the press*
il mensile *monthly magazine*
l'oroscopo *horoscope*
la rivista *magazine*
la rubrica (di cultura e società) *(lifestyle) section*
il settimanale *weekly magazine*
la vignetta *cartoon*

fare un abbonamento *to subscribe*

La cultura popolare

il carnevale *carnival; Mardi Gras*
Ferragosto *August 15 (holiday); August vacation*
i festeggiamenti *festivities*
il folclore *folklore*
la Pasquetta *Easter Monday*
il patrimonio culturale *cultural heritage*
il/la santo/a patrono/a *patron saint*
l'usanza *custom*

festeggiare *to celebrate*

Cortometraggio

il calcetto *foosball*
il campo *cellular reception, field*
il colpo di fulmine *lightning strike*
l'elettricista *electrician*
la lavanderia *dry cleaner*
il prefisso *area code*
la probabilità *probability*
la tacca *cellular reception bar*
il telefonino *cell phone*
il temporale *storm*

bruciare *to burn*
capitare *to happen*
chattare *to chat online*
contare *to be important*
fare/comporre un numero *to dial a number*
squillare *to ring*

Cultura

il capolavoro *masterpiece*
il/la cineasta *filmmaker*
il copione *script*
il critico (cinematografico) *(film) critic*
il culmine *height (fig.)*
la rassegna *festival*
la recensione *review*
il/la regista *director*
la sceneggiatura *screenplay*
il volto *face*

girare *to film*

giallo *mystery*
onirico/a *dream-like*
premiato/a *award-winning*
rosa *romance*
sperimentale *experimental*

Letteratura

l'affinità di coppia *compatibility*
i baffi *moustache*
la carta topografica *city map*
il coniuge *spouse*
il golf *sweater*
i gusti *tastes, preferences*
la multa *traffic ticket*
il rapporto *relationship*
lo sforzo *effort*

infilarsi *to slip on (clothing)*
sdegnarsi *to become indignant*
vagare *to roam, to wander*

Prospettive lavorative

Il lavoro è un mezzo per soddisfare non solo dei bisogni materiali. La gratificazione di essere ricompensati per ciò che abbiamo realizzato con impegno e dignità non ha eguali. In una realtà competitiva come quella di oggi, bisogna però fare attenzione a non lasciare che il lavoro prenda il sopravvento, alienandoci dai veri valori della vita. Qual è la tua visione del lavoro? Come pensi di presentarti nel mondo del lavoro? Come è possibile bilanciare vita lavorativa, vita personale e famiglia?

387

410

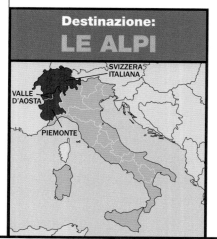

Destinazione:
LE ALPI

SVIZZERA ITALIANA
VALLE D'AOSTA
PIEMONTE

PREVIEW Point to the photo on the previous page and ask students: **Come vi preparereste per un colloquio? Quale sarà la vostra strategia per cercare il primo lavoro dopo l'università?**

Il lavoro e le finanze  Vocabulary Tools

La ricerca di lavoro

l'agenzia di collocamento
  job agency
la carriera *career*
il colloquio di lavoro *job interview*
il curriculum (vitae) *résumé*
l'esperienza (professionale)
  (professional) experience
la formazione *education; training*
l'intervistatore/intervistatrice
  interviewer
il mestiere *occupation; trade*
il posto/la posizione *job*
le qualifiche *qualifications*

lo/la stagista *intern*
___
fare domanda (per un lavoro)
  to apply (for a job)
impiegare *to employ*

La gente al lavoro

il capo *boss*
il/la consulente *consultant*
il/la contabile *accountant*
il direttore/la direttrice *manager*
il/la dirigente *executive*

l'impiegato/a *employee*
il/la proprietario/a *owner*

il/la segretario/a *secretary*

Al lavoro

il/la collega *colleague*

la ditta/l'azienda *company*
le ferie *holidays*
il lavoro a orario normale/ridotto
  full-/part-time job
l'orario di lavoro *work hours*
la promozione *promotion*
lo sciopero *strike*
il sindacato *labor union*
lo stipendio (minimo)
  (minimum) wage
l'ufficio *office*
___
andare in pensione *to retire*
guadagnare *to earn*
dare le dimissioni *to quit*
dirigere *to manage*
fare lo straordinario
  to work overtime

licenziare *to fire*

SINONIMI
dare le dimissioni ←→ dimettersi
il dirigente ←→ il responsabile
fare un prelievo ←→ prelevare ←→
ritirare denaro
fare un deposito ←→ depositare ←→
versare denaro
il bancomat ←→ lo sportello automatico
il lavoro a orario normale ←→ il lavoro
a tempo pieno
il lavoro a orario ridotto ←→ il lavoro
a tempo parziale/il lavoro part-time

Tell students that there are two ways to
indicate what a person's job is. They can
use **fare il/la** + *profession* or **essere** +
profession. Example: **Faccio l'ingegnere/
Sono ingegnere**.

INSTRUCTIONAL RESOURCES
Audioscripts, Answer Keys, Lab MP3s
SAM/WebSAM: WB, LM

Le finanze

la bancarotta *bankruptcy*
il bancomat *ATM*

la borsa *stock exchange*
la carta di credito *credit card*
la cifra *figure, number*
il conto (corrente)
  (checking) account
la crisi economica *economic crisis*
il debito *debt*
il mercato immobiliare
  real estate market

il prestito *loan*
la recessione *recession*
la ricevuta/lo scontrino *receipt*
il risparmio *savings*
lo sportello *window; counter*
la tassa *tax*
il tasso (d'interesse) *(interest) rate*
___
approfittare *to take advantage of*
aprire/chiudere un conto *to open/
  close an account*
avere dei debiti *to be in debt*
cambiare un assegno *to cash
  a check*
depositare/versare *to deposit*
fare un mutuo *to take out
  a mortgage*
fare un prelievo/deposito *to make
  a withdrawal/deposit*
investire *to invest*
risparmiare *to save*
___
a breve/lungo termine *short-/long-term*
finanziario/a *financial*
prospero/a *successful*

Pratica e comunicazione

1

In banca Alcune persone vanno in banca per vari motivi e l'impiegato dice loro dove andare e con chi parlare. Completa con le parole della lista.

assegno	colloquio	direttore	prelievo
bancomat	depositare	fare un mutuo	prestito

1. —Salve, ho risposto all'annuncio di lavoro, sono qui per il ___colloquio___.
   —Prego, vada nell'ufficio del ___direttore___.

2. —Scusi, devo ritirare dei soldi, ma non voglio fare la fila allo sportello.
   —Allora le consiglio di utilizzare il ___bancomat___.

3. —Buongiorno, la mia fidanzata e io vogliamo comprare una casa, ma non abbiamo abbastanza soldi, quindi siamo venuti a ___fare un mutuo___.
   —Per chiedere un ___prestito___ andate nell'ufficio in fondo al corridoio.

4. —Mi scusi, devo cambiare questo ___assegno___, ___depositare___ la somma sul mio conto corrente e poi voglio fare un ___prelievo___.
   —Non si preoccupi, può fare tutto allo sportello A.

2

I mestieri Indovina che lavoro fanno queste persone. Ricorda di aggiungere l'articolo corrispondente.

1. Sono un professionista che dà informazioni e consigli alle persone su argomenti di mia competenza. ___il/la consulente___

2. Tengo la contabilità dell'azienda in cui lavoro. ___il/la contabile___

3. Sono il capo della ditta, decido io le strategie da seguire. ___il dirigente___

4. Possiedo (*I own*) una ditta. ___il/la proprietario/a___

5. Lavoro in ufficio, prendo gli appuntamenti per il capo, scrivo lettere ed e-mail e rispondo al telefono. ___il/la segretario/a___

3

Colloquio In coppia, parlate del lavoro dei vostri sogni rispondendo alle seguenti domande.

1. Qual è il lavoro dei tuoi sogni? Perché?
2. Dove vorresti lavorare e perché?
3. Che lavoro volevi fare quando eri più giovane? È lo stesso di oggi o hai cambiato idea?
4. Qual è il tuo orario di lavoro ideale?
5. Secondo te, qual è lo stipendio adeguato al lavoro che vuoi fare?
6. Quanti giorni di ferie deve avere chi svolge il lavoro che hai scelto?

4

Soluzioni Marco e Stefania cercano lavoro per motivi diversi. In coppia, discutete dei seguenti problemi e poi date dei consigli per risolverli.

Marco: Dopo tanti anni di lavoro nella stessa ditta, a causa della crisi economica, sono stato licenziato. Mia moglie non lavora perché deve badare (*take care of*) ai nostri due figli; io devo pagare il mutuo e alla mia età è difficile trovare lavoro. Anche se ho molta esperienza, tutte le aziende preferiscono assumere un giovane.

Stefania: Finalmente mi sono laureata! È ora di mandare il mio curriculum all'agenzia di collocamento per cercare un lavoro. Io voglio trovare un lavoro adatto alle mie capacità, alla mia formazione e che mi faccia guadagnare tanto.

1 Have pairs of students act out the mini-dialogues after they have completed them.

2 Have students come up with additional job descriptions to present to their classmates. They should then guess which profession is being described.

3 Have students add questions of their own to the list.

3 Have students summarize what they have learned about their partners and compare their results with other groups. Ask: **Ci sono studenti che hanno le stesse aspirazioni/ambizioni?**

4 Before you begin the activity, brainstorm with the class types of advice students might give.

Practice more at **vhlcentral.com**.

INSTRUCTIONAL RESOURCES
Supersite: Video, Script & Translation
SAM/WebSAM: WB

Point out that both **assumere** and **promuovere** have irregular past participles: **assunto** and **promosso**.

SINONIMO
il fioraio/il fiorista

Preparazione

Vocabolario del cortometraggio

affidare *to entrust*
assumere *to hire*
la direzione *management*
disoccupato/a *unemployed*
l'impegno *commitment*
rinunciare *to give up*
il/la socio/a *(business) partner*

Vocabolario utile

l'annuncio (di lavoro) *(job) ad*
la casalinga *housewife*
il fioraio *florist*
gli occhiali da sole *sunglasses*
la piscina *swimming pool*
promuovere *to promote*
lo sguardo *gaze*
la società *firm; society*

ESPRESSIONI

ce la mettiamo tutta *we'll do our best*
peccato! *what a shame!*
pentirsi amaramente *to bitterly regret*
senz'altro *surely*

1

Il mondo del lavoro Inserisci le parole più adatte.

1. Ieri, mentre leggevo gli ___annunci___ di lavoro su Internet, ne ho visto uno molto interessante.
2. L'azienda sta crescendo e abbiamo deciso di ___assumere___ molti nuovi impiegati.
3. Purtroppo sono ___disoccupato/a___ e non lavoro da due mesi.
4. Oggi è il compleanno di una collega: sono andata dal ___fioraio___ per comprarle un mazzo (*bunch*) di rose.
5. Per festeggiare l'inizio dell'estate siamo andati tutti a nuotare in ___piscina___ dopo il lavoro.
6. Mia madre non ha mai lavorato fuori casa. Ha sempre fatto la ___casalinga___.

2 Encourage students to browse other job postings at www.corriere.it. You might also ask them to respond to an ad by writing an application letter and preparing a résumé in Italian.

2

Annunci Leggete gli annunci e rispondete alle domande.

Direttore di un negozio di cosmetici: il/la candidato/a ideale deve avere esperienza nel settore e capacità organizzative del punto vendita. Indispensabile: passione per l'estetica e la cosmesi. In Toscana.

Responsabile commerciale: Società internazionale cerca esperta per lancio di campagne marketing. Si richiede: laurea in economia e commercio, disponibilità a viaggiare in Italia e all'estero.

Agente immobiliare: Agenzia esclusiva cerca agente esperto/a per vendita di castelli e ville. Richiediamo: conoscenza dell'inglese e del tedesco; alta professionalità; interesse per l'architettura.

- Quale annuncio ti sembra più interessante? Perché?
- Come risponderesti? Che altra documentazione manderesti?

3 Professioni

A. In coppia, completate la tabella. Quali sono le professioni tradizionalmente più diffuse (*widespread*) tra le donne? E tra gli uomini?

Professione	Più donne	Più uomini
1.		
2.		
3.		
4.		
5.		
6.		
7.		
8.		

B. Rispondete alle domande.

1. Secondo voi, per quali ragioni alcune professioni sono più «maschili» e altre più «femminili»?
2. Quali professioni state considerando per il vostro futuro? Perché?
3. Le vostre scelte sono tradizionali (come nella tabella) o no?
4. Pensate che la vostra vita professionale cambierà quando avrete dei figli? Perché sì o perché no?

4 Al lavoro In piccoli gruppi, rispondete alle domande.

1. Come hai trovato il tuo primo lavoro?
2. Hai mai cercato lavoro leggendo gli annunci?
3. Sei mai stato/a promosso/a?
4. Conosci qualcuno che è stato licenziato? Secondo te, le ragioni erano giuste o ingiuste?
5. Hai mai dato le dimissioni? Perché hai lasciato quel lavoro?
6. Qual è la decisione più difficile che tu abbia dovuto prendere riguardo al lavoro?

4 If some students have never had a job, ask these additional questions: **Vorresti lavorare d'estate? Vorresti lavorare mentre studi o preferiresti cominciare a lavorare dopo aver finito di studiare? I tuoi genitori hanno dovuto lavorare mentre studiavano?**

5 Cosa succederà? In coppia, guardate queste immagini e inventate delle possibili situazioni.

- Com'è il rapporto tra i personaggi?
- Qual è la storia?

 Practice more at **vhlcentral.com**.

Video

Trama *Cosa succede quando in una coppia una persona viene promossa e l'altra licenziata? Quali sono i problemi che il lavoro può causare in famiglia?*

DIRETTORE Ho il piacevole compito di informarLa che, dopo attente valutazioni (e non poche discussioni), abbiamo deciso di affidare a Lei la direzione del settore marketing.

MARINA Che è successo?
PAOLO Mi hanno licenziato.
MARINA Ma se ti hanno assunto neanche un anno fa…

MARINA Paolo, dobbiamo parlare di una cosa che è successa oggi.
PAOLO No, scusa, sono stanco. Possiamo parlarne in un altro momento?

PAOLO E tu che sei così brava non lo capisci? Sei un'egoista, ecco che cosa sei!

DIRETTORE Capisco. Va bene: Lei sa senz'altro cos'è meglio per la sua vita. Peccato!

MARINA Paolo!!!

Sullo SCHERMO

Indica se queste affermazioni sono **vere** o **false**.

V 1. Marina telefona alla mamma.
V 2. Marina ha due bambini.
F 3. Marina è una casalinga.
V 4. La mamma di Marina non è contenta che la figlia lavori.
F 5. Paolo viene promosso.
F 6. Paolo cucina per festeggiare la promozione.

Analisi

1

Comprensione Completa le frasi.

1. Marina ha ___b___   a. è stato licenziato.
2. Mentre guida, Marina ___f___   b. una bella notizia.
3. Il direttore ___d___   c. spiano Marina dalla macchina.
4. Paolo torna a casa e dice che ___a___   d. vuole promuovere Marina.
5. I bambini di Marina ___e___   e. dormono dalla nonna.
6. Il direttore e suo marito ___c___   f. parla al telefono con la mamma.

2 Ask students to share their statements with the rest of the class.

2

A scelta Trova l'affermazione corretta. Dopo aggiungine altre due e scambiale con un(a) compagno/a.

1. (a.) Il direttore si identifica con Marina.
   b. Il direttore è gelosa di Marina.

2. a. Paolo è stato licenziato per colpa sua.
   (b.) Paolo è stato licenziato perché era un nuovo assunto.

3. a. Paolo si arrabbia con Marina.
   (b.) Marina ha paura che Paolo si arrabbi con lei.

4. (a.) La baby-sitter è stanca perché i bambini piangono.
   b. La baby-sitter è un'irresponsabile.

5. (a.) Il direttore ha un lavoro e una famiglia.
   b. Il direttore ha un nuovo marito.

6. a. Alla fine Marina rinuncia alla promozione.
   (b.) Alla fine Marina accetta la promozione.

7. a. _____
   b. _____

8. a. _____
   b. _____

3 Encourage students to read their conversations out loud, with emotion.

3

Dialogo Immaginate la conversazione tra Marina e Paolo mentre passeggiano nel parco.

MARINA _____
_____

PAOLO _____
_____

MARINA _____

PAOLO _____

MARINA _____

PAOLO _____

MARINA _____

PAOLO _____

MARINA Sei sicuro?

PAOLO No, ma ce la metteremo tutta. E poi vedremo.

TEACHING OPTION To introduce the topics for discussion, ask students: **Com'è cambiato il ruolo delle donne nel XX secolo? E quello degli uomini? Quante famiglie conosci in cui il papà resta a casa con i bambini e la mamma lavora fuori casa? E quante in cui i genitori fanno a turno per occuparsi dei figli? Qual è il ruolo delle/dei baby-sitter e degli asili nido?**

4 Punti di vista

4 Poll the class about their opinions.

A. In piccoli gruppi, discutete cosa vogliono dire i commenti dei personaggi.

Mamma di Marina: «O la mamma o la carriera.»	**Paolo:** «Voglio dormire per 12 ore e svegliarmi su un altro pianeta.»	**Marina:** «I miei problemi familiari sono molto gravi.»	**Il direttore:** «Il nostro peggior nemico siamo noi stessi.»

B. In piccoli gruppi, rispondete alle domande.

- Siete d'accordo con alcune opinioni dei personaggi? Quali?
- Quali sono i commenti con i quali non siete d'accordo? Perché?

5 Situazioni alternative In coppia, pensate a cosa succederebbe se...

5 Remind students that **sia... che...** means *both... and...*

- Paolo avesse ricevuto la promozione e Marina fosse stata licenziata.
- sia Paolo che Marina avessero ricevuto una promozione.
- fossero stati licenziati tutti e due.
- il direttore incontrasse la madre di Marina.
- la baby-sitter lasciasse il lavoro.

6 Analisi In coppia, rispondete alle domande.

1. Immaginate la vita di Paolo disoccupato. Come è cambiata la sua routine? Che cosa gli manca? Che cosa gli piace fare adesso che ha più tempo?
2. Quali aspetti della vita moderna mostra questo film? Pensate che abbia un messaggio particolare? Quale? (È stato prodotto dalla Camera di Commercio di Firenze.)
3. Come facevano i vostri nonni e i vostri genitori per bilanciare la vita personale e quella familiare? Pensate che la vostra vita sarà molto diversa dalla loro? In che modo?
4. Qual è il lavoro ideale per conciliare serenamente carriera e vita familiare? È giusto desiderare tutte e due?

7 Scenette In piccoli gruppi, improvvisate una conversazione basata su una di queste situazioni e poi recitatela davanti alla classe.

A

Come sarà la vita di Paolo e Marina tra due anni? Marina e sua madre ne parlano.

B

Ad un colloquio di lavoro due dirigenti parlano con una ragazza che si è appena laureata. All'inizio c'è molta tensione, ma poi i dirigenti le fanno una bellissima offerta.

8 Scriviamo Immagina di essere licenziato/a dopo molti anni di lavoro. Non hai più un lavoro, ma i tuoi datori di lavoro (*employers*) ti hanno dato una liquidazione (*severance pay*) molto alta. Che cosa faresti in questa situazione? Investiresti i soldi o li spenderesti? Come? Fonderesti una nuova azienda o compagnia? Di che tipo? Racconta cosa faresti in uno o due paragrafi.

Practice more at **vhlcentral.com**.

INSTRUCTIONAL RESOURCES: Teaching suggestions; Answer Keys
SAM/WebSAM: WB

IMMAGINA LE ALPI

Sport ad alta quota

Tra le regioni del Nord-Ovest dell'Italia, la **Valle d'Aosta** e il **Piemonte** condividono° il paesaggio alpino, una storia comune e molte tradizioni. A queste due regioni possiamo aggiungere i territori della **Svizzera italiana** che comprende° **il Canton Ticino**, la valle **Mesolcina** del Cantone dei Grigioni e le valli **Bregaglia** e di **Poschiavo**. Queste regioni anche se appartengono alla Svizzera sono considerate «italiane» perché ancora oggi la popolazione parla la lingua italiana, oltre ad altre lingue nazionali.

Geograficamente sono tutte regioni montuose ed è qui che le Alpi toccano il cielo con le cime° più alte: il **Gran Paradiso**, il **Monte Bianco**, il **Cervino** e le vette° del **Monte Rosa** superano i 4000 metri di altezza. Ed è sui versanti° di questi massicci sempre coperti di neve che il turismo invernale si è sviluppato, soprattutto a partire dagli anni '50 del XX secolo, diventando uno dei punti di forza° dell'economia di queste regioni.

Le possibilità di divertirsi, sperimentare e godere della neve sono molteplici e si evolvono rapidamente: ai materiali più tecnologici e sicuri si uniscono tecniche nuove o riscoperte che permettono un contatto sempre più diretto tra l'uomo e la natura imbiancata° in località come **Sestriere**, **Bardonecchia**, **Cervinia** e **Courmayeur**.

Per gli amanti dello **sci alpino** e dello **sci di fondo°** classici, queste regioni offrono chilometri di piste° sempre ben innevate° e impianti moderni. Chi pratica l'alpinismo può scalare le maggiori vette alpine con itinerari impegnativi° su roccia e ghiacciai°.

Nuove attività, anche di sport estremo, si sono aggiunte allo sci e allo **snowboard**. Il **telemark**, per esempio, offre maggiore libertà di movimento sugli sci mentre il **freeride** e il **backcountry** uniscono scalate° ad alta quota a

Monte Bianco

discese fuoripista°. Per gli appassionati di mountain bike, sulle Alpi è possibile praticare lo **snow-bike** che utilizza la bici con gomme chiodate° su percorsi° cross country. Stanno «prendendo il volo»° anche discipline come il **kiteski**, lo **snowkiting** e l'**eliski** che permettono di volare sui massicci innevati prima di intraprendere° temerarie° discese.

Per chi invece non ama gli effetti dell'adrenalina è possibile camminare in montagna con le «**ciaspole**» o **racchette da neve**, fare lo **sleddog**, o **pattinare sul ghiaccio** insieme alla famiglia. Insomma, Valle d'Aosta, Piemonte e Svizzera italiana possono soddisfare le passioni degli amanti degli sport invernali di tutte le età.

In più...

Il **Monte Bianco**, con i suoi 4.810,90 metri d'altezza, è la montagna più alta delle Alpi, d'Italia e d'Europa. Si trova tra la Valle d'Aosta, in Italia, e la regione della Savoia, in Francia. I fianchi° della montagna sono coperti da numerosi ghiacciai°, i più grandi dei quali sono sul versante francese. Le prime persone a conquistarne la vetta furono **Jacques Balmat** e **Michel Gabriel Paccard** l'8 agosto 1786.

condividono *share* **comprende** *includes* **cime** *summits* **vette** *peaks* **versanti** *mountainsides*
punti di forza *points of strength* **imbiancata** *whitened* **sci di fondo** *cross-country ski*
piste *slopes* **innevate** *snow-covered* **impegnativi** *challenging* **ghiacciai** *glaciers*
scalate *climbing* **fuoripista** *backcountry skiing* **gomme chiodate** *snow tires* **percorsi** *trails*
prendendo il volo *taking off* **intraprendere** *to start* **temerarie** *daredevil* **fianchi** *sides*
ghiacciai *glaciers*

Lugano **Lugano** è la città più grande e turisticamente più sviluppata del **Canton Ticino** ed il terzo polo finanziario° della Svizzera dopo Ginevra e Zurigo. Si trova sulla riva° nord del **Lago di Lugano** ed è circondata da montagne. È una città eclettica che unisce la vita aristocratica del **Casinò** e quella raffinata degli amanti dell'arte ad una realtà cittadina all'insegna della° natura e della vita all'aria aperta. Numerosi sono i parchi cittadini rigogliosi° di piante e fiori esotici e gli itinerari per escursioni sul lago e nei dintorni° della città.

Ferrero La **Ferrero S.p.A.** è una multinazionale italiana nel settore dei dolciumi°, con sede a Pino Torinese, in provincia di Torino, fondata nel 1946 da **Pietro Ferrero**. L'azienda nasce con l'idea di realizzare prodotti dolciari° usando materie fresche e locali, come le nocciole° piemontesi. Dalla lavorazione° delle nocciole con altri ingredienti, Pietro crea una crema spalmabile° che ha immediatamente grande successo. Negli anni la crema cambierà fino a diventare nel 1964 la famosa **Nutella**. Alla Nutella si aggiungeranno dolci di gran successo come i cioccolatini **Ferrero Rocher** e **Mon Cheri** e gli ovetti° **Kinder Sorpresa** e molti altri ancora!

polo finanziario *financial center* **riva** *shore* **all'insegna della** *characterized by* **rigogliosi** *blooming* **dintorni** *outskirts* **dolciumi** *sweets* **prodotti dolciari** *confectionery products* **nocciole** *hazelnuts* **lavorazione** *processing* **spalmabile** *spreadable* **ovetti** *chocolate eggs*

Vero o falso? Indica se ogni frase è **vera** o **falsa**. Correggi le frasi false. Some answers will vary.

1. La regione del Canton Ticino fa parte del territorio italiano. Falso. Fa parte del territorio svizzero.

2. Il Monte Bianco è la montagna più alta d'Italia e d'Europa. Vero.

3. Il backcountry ed il freeride si praticano su piste regolari. Falso. Si praticano fuoripista.

4. Sulle Alpi è possibile praticare mountain bike solo in estate. Falso. Si può praticare snow-bike in inverno.

5. Con le «ciaspole» è possibile sciare. Falso. È possibile fare escursioni a piedi.

6. Lugano è una città della Svizzera italiana. Vero.

7. Lugano è una città importante per l'attività finanziaria. Vero.

8. La Nutella è fatta con ingredienti locali del Piemonte. Vero.

Quanto hai imparato? Rispondi alle domande.
Some answers will vary.

1. Qual è la caratteristica principale delle regioni della Svizzera italiana? Si parla la lingua italiana.

2. Com'è il paesaggio naturale del Piemonte e della Valle d'Aosta? Ci sono soprattutto montagne.

3. Di che cosa hanno bisogno gli sportivi che vogliono praticare lo snow-bike? Hanno bisogno di una bicicletta con le gomme chiodate.

4. Quali sport possono praticare le persone più tranquille o i bambini? passeggiate sulla neve con le racchette da neve, pattinaggio

5. Quali attività all'aperto si possono praticare a Lugano? passeggiate nei parchi, escursioni in montagna, gite sul lago

6. Quali sono alcune caratteristiche della Nutella? È una crema spalmabile; è fatta con le nocciole.

Progetto

Registi per un giorno

A Torino c'è il Museo Nazionale del Cinema, uno dei musei più ricchi di collezioni e unico nella sua architettura verticale. Dopo aver visitato il sito del museo e ammirato Torino e il suo panorama dall'alto, immaginate di «essere dei registi» che devono preparare un documentario su Torino.

- Decidete il tema del documentario: storico, artistico o turistico.
- Scegliete un titolo per il documentario.
- Ricercate le informazioni necessarie per il vostro documentario.
- Preparate una presentazione da mostrare alla classe.

GALLERIA DI PERSONE ILLUSTRI

SCRITTORE, SEMIOLOGO
Umberto Eco (1932–2016)

Umberto Eco, nato ad Alessandria nel 1932, è stato un critico, saggista, scrittore e semiologo di fama internazionale. Inizia la sua carriera come editore di programmi culturali per la Rai, per poi passare all'insegnamento presso (*at*) varie università italiane finché nel 1975 viene nominato professore di Semiotica all'Università di Bologna. Insegna in prestigiose università, quali Northwestern, Yale e la Columbia University. Scrive numerosi saggi di semiotica, linguistica e filosofia e negli anni Ottanta esordisce nella narrativa con il romanzo *Il nome del rosa*. Il romanzo diventa un successo internazionale, viene tradotto in quarantasette lingue e vende più di cinquanta milioni di copie in trent'anni. Negli anni Ottanta e Novanta continua la sua intensa e prolifica attività narrativa e saggistica. Muore nel 2016 a Milano a seguito di un tumore che lo aveva colpito due anni prima.

BALLERINO
Roberto Bolle (1975–)

Roberto Bolle è un ballerino italiano di fama internazionale. Nato a Casale Monferrato, Bolle è il primo ballerino al mondo ad essere etoile (*star*) di due teatri contemporaneamente, il Teatro alla Scala di Milano e l'American Ballet Theatre di New York. Entra alla scuola di ballo dell'Accademia Teatro alla Scala all'età di dodici anni e nel 2004 ne diventa primo ballerino. Roberto Bolle si è da allora esibito in tutti i maggiori teatri del mondo e con le compagnie più note tra le quali l'American Ballet Theatre, il Balletto dell'Opéra di Parigi, il Royal Ballet a Londra. Dal 2008 Roberto si è esibito in location d'eccezione come il Colosseo, le Terme di Caracalla e Piazza San Marco, con il suo gala «Roberto Bolle and Friends».

NEUROLOGA, SCIENZIATA
Rita Levi-Montalcini
(1909–2012)

Rita Levi-Montalcini è stata una neurologa, accademica e premio Nobel per la medicina nel 1986. Ad oggi è stata l'unica donna italiana ad aver ricevuto il premio Nobel scientifico. La scienziata torinese si laurea in medicina nel 1936 e mentre si sta specializzando in Psichiatria e Neurologia è costretta ad emigrare per via delle leggi razziali perché è di origine ebrea. Dopo la guerra si stabilisce negli Stati Uniti e lavora presso la Washington University di Saint Louis dove scopre il Nerve Growth Factor (NGF), una proteina coinvolta (*involved*) nello sviluppo del sistema nervoso; questa ricerca le consentirà di aggiudicarsi il Nobel. Torna a vivere in Italia negli anni Ottanta dove fonda e dirige istituti di ricerca come il centro di ricerca sull'NGF e l'EBRI (European Brain Research Institute). Rita Levi-Montalcini muore a Roma nel 2012.

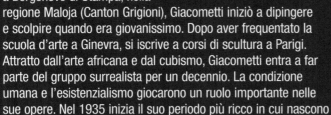

SCULTORE, PITTORE
Alberto Giacometti
(1901–1966)

Alberto Giacometti è stato uno scultore e pittore svizzero, tra i più importanti del XX secolo. Nato a Borgonovo di Stampa, nella regione Maloja (Canton Grigioni), Giacometti iniziò a dipingere e scolpire quando era giovanissimo. Dopo aver frequentato la scuola d'arte a Ginevra, si iscrive a corsi di scultura a Parigi. Attratto dall'arte africana e dal cubismo, Giacometti entra a far parte del gruppo surrealista per un decennio. La condizione umana e l'esistenzialismo giocarono un ruolo importante nelle sue opere. Nel 1935 inizia il suo periodo più ricco in cui nascono

le sue famose sculture filiformi, estremamente alte e sottili. L'amicizia con Picasso e Sartre lo riavvicina (*leads him back*) alla pittura, che però costituisce una piccola parte del suo lavoro. La scultura bronzea, *L'Homme qui marche I*, fece il record per il prezzo d'acquisto di 100 milioni di dollari. Il record venne successivamente battuto da un'altra sua scultura, *L'Homme au doigt*, che venne venduta per 141 milioni di dollari.

Comprensione

Completare Completa le seguenti frasi.

1. Roberto Bolle è primo ballerino di ___due___ teatri contemporaneamente.

2. Roberto Bolle si è esibito in tutti i ___maggiori teatri___ del mondo.

3. Umberto Eco è stato un ___critico, saggista, scrittore e semiologo___ di fama internazionale.

4. *Il nome della rosa* è stato tradotto in ___quarantasette lingue___.

5. Umberto Eco è autore di numerosi ___saggi___ di semiotica, linguistica e filosofia.

6. Rita Levi-Montalcini ha vissuto in Italia e ___negli Stati Uniti___.

7. Rita Levi-Montalcini è stata l'unica ___donna italiana___ a vincere il premio Nobel Scientifico.

8. Il Nerve Growth Factor è una ___proteina___ coinvolta nello sviluppo del sistema nervoso.

9. Alberto Giacometti è stato uno ___scultore___ e pittore svizzero.

10. *L'Homme qui marche I* di Giacometti è una ___scultura bronzea___ venduta per 100 milioni di dollari.

Scrittura

Scrivi sull'argomento Scegli uno dei seguenti argomenti e scrivi un paragrafo seguendo le indicazioni.

- **Scrittori famosi** L'Italia è la patria di numerosi autori di successo. Chi è il tuo scrittore favorito? Che libro ti ha colpito di più e perché? Scrivi un paragrafo sul tuo autore e libro preferito.

- **Donne straordinarie** Rita Levi-Montalcini è un grande esempio di donna che ha conquistato e rivoluzionato un settore solitamente dominato dagli uomini. Quali altre donne hanno ottenuto simili successi in professioni solitamente maschili? Stila un elenco e spiega brevemente il loro percorso (*path*) e traguardi (*goals*).

- ***L'Homme qui marche I*** Osserva l'immagine della celebre scultura di Giacometti. Descrivi l'opera d'arte e spiega cosa ne pensi.

 Practice more at **vhlcentral.com**.

INSTRUCTIONAL RESOURCES `10.1`
Audioscripts, Answer Keys, Lab MP3s, Grammar Presentation Slides
SAM/WebSAM: WB, LM

RIMANDO

The **si passivante** is presented in **Strutture 10.2, pp. 396–397**.

ATTENZIONE!

When forming the passive voice with a compound tense, remember to make both the past participle of **essere** and the past participle of the other verb agree with the subject.

La ragazza è stata invitata dal Principe Azzurro.
The girl was invited by Prince Charming.

ATTENZIONE!

The simple tenses of the verbs **venire** and **andare** are sometimes used instead of **essere** in passive sentences. When **andare** is used this way, it often expresses obligation.

L'inglese è/viene studiato da molti studenti italiani.
English is studied by many Italian students.

Le regole devono essere/vanno spiegate prima di cominciare il gioco.
The rules must be explained before starting the game.

ATTENZIONE!

Some common expressions using **andare** in the passive voice are:

va considerato — *it must be considered*

va detto — *it must be said*
va ripetuto — *it must be repeated*

Point out that the passive form of simple tenses consists of two words, while the passive voice of compound tenses consists of three words.

Passive voice

- A verb is in the active voice when the subject carries out the action of the verb. Transitive verbs can also be used in the passive voice. In the passive voice, the subject of the verb is acted upon. The agent (the person or thing carrying out the action) may not be mentioned. Passive voice de-emphasizes the agent and spotlights what would usually be the direct object in the active voice. The passive voice occurs more often in writing than in speech.

Active voice	**Passive voice**
SUBJECT + VERB + DIRECT OBJECT	SUBJECT + VERB + AGENT
Il topo **mangia** il formaggio.	Il formaggio **è mangiato** dal topo.
The mouse eats the cheese.	*The cheese is eaten by the mouse.*

- Form the passive voice using the appropriate tense of **essere** + [*past participle*]; the past participle of the verb must agree in number and gender with the subject of the verb. The agent, when mentioned, is introduced by the preposition **da**.

Le regole **saranno scritte** dal proprietario.
The rules will be written by the owner.

L'assegno è **stato cambiato** (da uno studente).
The check was cashed (by a student).

- Verbs can be conjugated in the passive voice in any tense or mood. The tense or mood is reflected in the form of the verb **essere**.

Tense	Examples
presente	Il latte **è bevuto** dai bambini. *The milk is drunk by the children.*
passato prossimo	La villa **è stata distrutta** dal terremoto. *The villa was destroyed by the earthquake.*
imperfetto	Cinquanta euro **erano dati** alla chiesa ogni domenica. *Fifty euros were given to the church every Sunday.*
futuro semplice	Tutte le città **saranno inquinate** dalle macchine. *All cities will be polluted by cars.*
futuro anteriore	Quando finirà lo sciopero, molti operai **saranno stati** già **licenziati**. *After the strike is over, many workers will have already been laid off.*
condizionale	Lo stesso stipendio minimo **sarebbe guadagnato** da tutti. *The same minimum wage would be earned by everyone.*
condizionale passato	Senza i problemi alla borsa, la recessione **sarebbe stata evitata**. *Without the problems in the stock market, the recession would have been avoided.*
congiuntivo presente	È necessario che il prestito **sia fatto** oggi. *It is necessary for the loan to be made today.*
congiuntivo passato	Siamo sorpresi che la risposta **sia stata ricevuta** così presto. *We are surprised that the answer was received so soon.*
congiuntivo imperfetto	Sarebbe meraviglioso se tu **fossi scelto**. *It would be great if you were chosen.*
congiuntivo trapassato	Sarebbe stato meglio se la telefonata **fosse stata fatta** dalla segretaria. *It would have been better if the call had been made by the secretary.*

Pratica e comunicazione

1

In cerca di lavoro A un anno dalla laurea, Sara non riesce a trovare lavoro e manda un'e-mail al suo amico Giovanni. Completa il brano con i verbi giusti alla forma passiva.

aiutare	assumere	fare	lodare (*praise*)
assistere	esaminare	fissare	tenere

Ciao Giovanni,

oggi sono molto triste perché dopo il colloquio della settimana scorsa, non
(1) __sono stata assunta__.
(2) __Sono stata lodata__ dal direttore per il mio ottimo curriculum, ma la domanda
(3) __era stata fatta__ da molti candidati e c'era molta concorrenza (*competition*). Mi
hanno detto però che (4) __sarò tenuta__ in considerazione per il prossimo posto libero.
Così sono andata in un'agenzia di collocamento. Le persone (5) __sono aiutate__ da
un consulente e (6) __sono assistite__ nella ricerca del lavoro ideale. Il mio curriculum
(7) __sarà esaminato__ da un esperto la prossima settimana e spero che un colloquio
(8) __sia fissato__ presto.

Ciao,

Sara

2

Al lavoro Riscrivi le frasi dalla forma attiva a quella passiva.

1. Il proprietario assumerebbe nuovi operai. Nuovi operai sarebbero assunti dal proprietario.
2. Credo che il dirigente abbia licenziato la segretaria. Credo che la segretaria sia stata licenziata dal dirigente.
3. È necessario che Giovanni chieda un mutuo. È necessario che un mutuo sia chiesto da Giovanni.
4. I lavoratori guadagnavano un buono stipendio. Un buono stipendio era guadagnato dai lavoratori.
5. Gli impiegati faranno lo straordinario. Lo straordinario sarà fatto dagli impiegati.
6. Il collega non aveva ottenuto le ferie. Le ferie non erano state ottenute dal collega.

3

Il giornale universitario In coppia, scegliete uno dei seguenti titoli e scrivete un articolo per il giornale universitario dove spiegate quando e dove è accaduto l'evento, chi ha partecipato e come è andata a finire. Utilizzate la forma passiva e le parole suggerite.

Siamo soli nello spazio?
scoprire, extraterrestri, navicella spaziale, mandare, astronauta, comunicare

Premiato il miglior film dell'anno
premiare, trattare, dedicare, interpretare, svolgersi, ispirare

Vivere senza tecnologia
Internet, cellulare, stress, ritmo, uscire, cambiare

S Practice more at **vhlcentral.com**.

INSTRUCTIONAL RESOURCES 10.2
Audioscripts, Answer Keys, Lab MP3s, Grammar Presentation Slides
SAM/WebSAM: WB, LM

Si passivante and *si impersonale*

—Non **si può fare** tutto.

Si passivante

RIMANDO

To review the passive voice, see **Strutture 10.1, p. 394.**

Remind students that the object of an active sentence becomes the subject of a passive sentence.
L'uomo d'affari affitta la macchina. (Active)
La macchina è affittata dall'uomo d'affari. (Passive)

To contrast the passive voice and the **si passivante**, provide (or have students come up with) the passive voice equivalents of the examples.

- The **si passivante** (passive **si**) is equivalent to the passive voice. It is used primarily when the agent is not expressed and it is used more frequently than the passive voice.

Active voice	Passive voice	*Si passivante*
Ricevono i regali.	I regali sono ricevuti.	Si ricevono i regali.
They receive the gifts.	*The gifts are received.*	*The gifts are received.*

- The **si passivante** is formed with the pronoun **si** and the third person singular or plural of a verb that takes a direct object (a transitive verb). The choice between singular and plural is determined by the subject of the sentence, which generally follows the verb.

Si beve l'acqua.   **Si mangiano** i piselli.
People drink water.   *People eat peas.*

- The **si passivante** is always conjugated with **essere** in compound tenses. The past participle agrees in number and gender with the subject of the verb.

La scorsa estate **si sono mangiati** molti gelati.
Last summer, a lot of ice cream was eaten.

Mi stupisco che **si siano chiusi** i negozi così presto.
I'm surprised the stores closed so early.

- When there are direct or indirect object pronouns used with the **si passivante**, they precede the pronoun **si**. Use the third person singular form of the verb with direct object pronouns. In sentences with **ne**, however, change the order and the spelling of the pronouns to **se ne**.

Si comprano francobolli all'ufficio postale. **Li si compra** anche alla tabaccheria.
You can buy stamps at the post office. You can also buy them at the drug store.

Si comprano molte cose, e **se ne buttano via** tantissime.
Much is bought and so much is thrown away.

- In compound tenses, the past participle agrees with the direct object pronoun.

Si è chiamato il dottore?
Has the doctor been called?

Sì, **lo si è chiamato** un'ora fa.
Yes, he was called an hour ago.

Si è servita già la cena?
Has dinner already been served?

Sì, **la si è servita** alle 8.00.
Yes, it was served at 8:00.

ATTENZIONE!

The **si passivante** is often used on signs to indicate something for sale, for rent, etc.

Si vendono appartamenti e monolocali vicino al mare.
Apartments and studios near the beach are for sale.

Affittasi camere doppie e singole in un appartamento per 5 persone.
Single and double rooms for rent in a five-person apartment.

Si impersonale

- An impersonal form is used when the subject of a sentence is non-specific or unimportant for the speaker. In English, words like *people, they, one, we,* and *you* can convey this meaning. In Italian, the impersonal form is most commonly expressed by using the **si impersonale**.

Dopo il lavoro, **si va** al bar.
After work, people go to the bar.

Si **mangia bene** in quel ristorante.
You eat well at that restaurant.

- The **si impersonale** is formed by using the pronoun **si** followed by the third person singular of any intransitive verb or of any transitive verb when the subject is not expressed.

Quando **si sta** male, **si va** dal dottore.
When you are sick, you go to the doctor's.

S'impara bene se **si studia** molto.
You learn a lot if you study a lot.

It is commonly used to request or to give information, instructions, and permission.

Non **si parla** con la bocca piena!
Don't talk with your mouth full!

Come **si fa** a creare un sito?
How do you make a website?

- When the **si impersonale** is used with a verb that expresses a state of being, such as **essere** or **diventare**, adjectives and nouns following the verb are always in the masculine plural form, even though the verb is singular.

Dalle mie parti, **si è molto generosi**.
Where I'm from, people are really generous.

Quando **si diventa vecchi**, tutto è più chiaro.
When you get old, everything is clearer.

Quando **si è studenti**, si dorme poco.
When you're a student, you don't sleep a lot.

Si lavora moltissimo quando **si diventa professori**.
You work a lot when you become a professor.

- When the **si impersonale** is used in compound tenses, a singular form of **essere** is always required as an auxiliary. For verbs normally conjugated with **avere**, use the masculine singular form of the past participle. For verbs conjugated with **essere**, use a plural past participle.

Si è viaggiato molto.
(La gente ha viaggiato molto.)
People have traveled a lot.

Quando **si è arrivati**, nessuno era lì.
(Quando la gente è arrivata, nessuno era lì.)
When people arrived, no one was there.

- Indirect object pronouns precede **si**. When **ne** is used, **si** becomes **se** and the order is always **se ne**.

Si discute di sport in ufficio?
Do people talk about sports in the office?

No, non **se ne parla** affatto!
No, they don't talk about them at all!

Si può telefonare ai clienti dopo le sei?
Can one call clients after six?

No, non **gli si può telefonare** così tardi!
No, one cannot call them so late!

- When using a reflexive or reciprocal verb with the **si impersonale**, avoid repeating **si** by replacing it with **ci**.

Come **ci si saluta** tra amici?
How does one say hello among friends?

Ci si saluta con due baci.
One says hello with two kisses.

ATTENZIONE!

The pronoun **si** precedes the conjugated forms of verbs such as **dovere**, **potere**, and **volere**.

Si deve andare a scuola alle 7.30.
One has to go to school at 7:30.

ATTENZIONE!

As an alternative to using the **si impersonale**, you may use **uno** or **la gente**.

La gente passa troppo tempo a guardare Facebook.
= **Si passa troppo tempo a guardare Facebook.**
People spend too much time on Facebook.

ATTENZIONE!

In spoken Italian, the **si impersonale** is sometimes used to mean **noi**.

Dove si va domani?
Where are we going out tomorrow?

Cosa si mangia oggi?
What are we eating today?

To make sure students use **essere** in compound tenses, give them some examples of the **passato prossimo** with **noi**, **la gente** or **tutti** as the subject. Example:
—**Tutti hanno mangiato bene.**
—**Si è mangiato bene.**

Give students additional examples of **si impersonale** with reflexive verbs. Example:
Se non ci si alza presto, non si mangia a casa mia.
Ci si è lavati, ci si è vestiti e dopo si è usciti.

Pratica

1

Cosa si fa...? Simona e Diana stanno organizzando una piccola gita a Torino. Cambia i verbi tra parentesi usando la forma del **si** impersonale.

SIMONA Ciao Diana, allora cosa si fa questo fine settimana?

DIANA (1) __Si va__ (andiamo) a Torino!

SIMONA Sì, che bella idea! Hai già deciso cosa (2) __si fa__ (facciamo)?

DIANA (3) __Ci si sveglia__ (ci svegliamo) presto, (4) __si parte__ (partiamo) alle sette così (5) __si arriva__ (arriviamo) presto.

SIMONA Bene, poi si visita il Museo Egizio e la Mole Antonelliana.

DIANA Va bene, poi per pranzo (6) __si mangia__ (mangiamo) al ristorante consigliato da Cristian.

SIMONA E nel pomeriggio?

DIANA Nel pomeriggio (7) __ci si riposa__ (ci riposiamo) in un caffè e poi (8) __si torna__ (torniamo) a casa.

SIMONA Non vedo l'ora di partire!

2

In ufficio Trasforma le frasi passive utilizzando il **si passivante**.

Modello **Le lettere sono spedite.**
Si spediscono le lettere.

1. Il candidato è stato assunto. Si è assunto il candidato.
2. Le e-mail saranno lette. Si leggeranno le e-mail.
3. Le ferie sono prese ad agosto. Si prendono le ferie ad agosto.
4. La promozione è stata ottenuta. Si è ottenuta la promozione.
5. Le imprese sono finanziate. Si finanziano le imprese.
6. I soldi saranno investiti. Si investiranno i soldi.

3 Have students restate the paragraph, applying it to their own lives.

3

Dopo il lavoro Completa il brano con i verbi forniti mettendoli nella forma del **si passivante** o del **si impersonale**.

andare	giocare	invitare	raccontare
bere	guardare	mangiare	rilassarsi
fare	incontrarsi	organizzare	

Ad Alessandria, dopo una lunga giornata di lavoro, (1) __ci si rilassa__ un po' prima di tornare a casa. (2) __Si va__ in palestra o (3) __si gioca__ a tennis o a calcio. Altre volte (4) __ci si incontra__ con gli amici, (5) __si beve__ un aperitivo, (6) __si mangiano__ gli stuzzichini e (7) __si fanno__ due chiacchiere. (8) __Si raccontano__ le ultime novità. Spesso (9) __si organizzano__ gite per il fine settimana. Nel fine settimana (10) __si va__ a cena fuori e (11) __si guarda__ un film o (12) __si invitano__ gli amici a casa.

4 Have students add more questions of their own.

4

Il tempo libero In coppia, a turno, fatevi le seguenti domande. Rispondete utilizzando il **si passivante** o il **si impersonale**.

- Come si passa la giornata nella tua città?
- Dove si incontrano gli amici?
- Cosa si fa per passare una serata tranquilla?
- Dove si mangiano i migliori gelati?

- Cosa si fa nel tempo libero?
- Cosa si fa la sera?
- Dove si ascolta buona musica?
- Dove si beve il miglior caffè?

Practice more at **vhlcentral.com**.

Comunicazione

5

Conversazione In coppia, inventate cinque domande da fare a un(a) amico/a. Utilizzate il **si** impersonale con **essere** o **diventare** più gli aggettivi.

> **Modello** —Come va il tuo nuovo lavoro? Lavori tanto? Si diventa nervosi quando si lavora molto!
>
> —Sì, sono stanco e quando si è stanchi si diventa nervosi!

5 Have students use the six questions as the basis for creating a short conversation that they can act out for classmates.

6

Inventa

A. In coppia, descrivete la scena e cosa fanno le persone nella foto, con almeno sei frasi. Utilizzate il **si** passivante e il **si** impersonale.

B. Confrontate le vostre frasi con il resto della classe.

7

Il ponte In coppia, inventate e poi mettete in scena una conversazione dove decidete cosa fare durante il prossimo ponte (*long weekend*) utilizzando il si impersonale. Potete usare le espressioni della lista.

7 Have groups of students share their directives; have students ask relevant questions while their classmate reads his/her conversation.

andare a sciare	scrivere e-mail importanti
incontrare i genitori	studiare per l'esame
lavorare ad un progetto	uscire con gli amici

> **Modello** —Ciao Paola, che si fa questo fine settimana?
>
> —Ciao Sara, si va…

8

Festa a sorpresa In coppia, scrivete cosa si deve fare per organizzare una perfetta festa a sorpresa.

> **Modello** Per prima cosa, si deve stabilire la data, poi si deve fare la lista degli invitati...

INSTRUCTIONAL RESOURCES | **10.3**
Audioscripts, Answer Keys, Lab MP3s, Grammar Presentation Slides
SAM/WebSAM: WB, LM

ATTENZIONE!

In addition to any changes in the verb tenses, depending on the context, you might have to make other changes in subject and object pronouns, reflexive pronouns, and possessive adjectives and pronouns.

Ha detto: «Non sono stato io!»
Ha detto che non era stato lui.

Disse: «È mio.»
Disse che era suo.

Ha detto: «Mi sono dimenticata.»
Ha detto che si era dimenticata.

Mi hai detto: «Voglio andare con te.»
Mi hai detto che volevi andare/ venire con me.

Disse: «Ti avevo visto.»
Disse che l'aveva visto.

ATTENZIONE!

When the verb introducing the indirect discourse is in the past, you might also need to make the following changes.

adesso	→	in quel momento
oggi	→	(in) quel giorno
ora	→	allora
domani	→	il giorno dopo/ seguente
fra poco	→	poco dopo
prossimo	→	seguente
ieri	→	il giorno prima
l'altro ieri	→	due giorni prima
poco fa	→	poco prima
scorso	→	prima/precedente
qui	→	lì
qua	→	là
questo	→	quello

Antonella ha detto: «Mia sorella partirà domani.»
Antonella said, "My sister will leave tomorrow."

Antonella ha detto che sua sorella sarebbe partita il giorno dopo.
Antonella said that her sister would leave the next day.

Indirect discourse

- Direct discourse reports exactly what someone says or has said. In writing, quotation marks enclose the person's words. Indirect discourse relates a person's words without repeating them verbatim; they are not set off in writing by quotation marks.

Direct discourse	Indirect discourse
Massimiliano dice: «Vado al bancomat.»	Massimiliano dice che va al bancomat.
Massimiliano says, "I am going to the ATM."	*Massimiliano says that he is going to the ATM.*

- Indirect discourse is often introduced by verbs such as **chiedere** (*to ask*), **dire** (*to say/tell*), **domandare** (*to ask*), **ripetere** (*to repeat*), **rispondere** (*to respond*), or **sostenere** (*to maintain*).

Mi **chiedono** quando andrò in pensione. *They are asking me when I will retire.*

Gli **rispondo** che non ne ho idea! *I keep telling them that I have no idea!*

- The change from direct to indirect discourse often requires a number of changes in a sentence. These changes may include a change of verb tense and/or mood, changes of possessive pronouns and adjectives, changes in personal pronouns, and changes in demonstrative adjectives and expressions of time and place.

- When the verb introducing indirect discourse is in the present or future tense, no change in the verb tense is needed.

Discorso diretto	Discorso indiretto
Barbara **domanda:** «Quando **arriverà** il nuovo motorino?»	Barbara **domanda** quando **arriverà** il nuovo motorino.
Barbara asks, "When does my new scooter get here?"	*Barbara asks when her new scooter will get here.*
Federico **risponderà:** «Non mi **alzerò** fino a mezzogiorno!»	Federico **risponderà** che non si **alzerà** fino a mezzogiorno.
Federico will answer, "I won't get up until noon!"	*Federico will answer that he won't get up until noon.*

- When introduced by a verb in the past tense, verbs in the **imperfetto** or **trapassato** do not change when changing from direct to indirect discourse. This rule applies both to verbs in the indicative and in the subjunctive.

Discorso diretto (imperfetto)	Discorso indiretto (imperfetto)
Ugo ha detto: «Silvia **voleva** dare le dimissioni.»	Ugo ha detto che Silvia **voleva** dare le dimissioni.
Ugo said, "Silvia wanted to quit."	*Ugo said that Silvia wanted to quit.*
Disse: «**Pensavo** che il contabile **avesse** la ricevuta.»	Disse che **pensava** che il contabile **avesse** la ricevuta.
He said, "I thought the accountant had the receipt."	*He said that he thought that the accountant had the receipt.*

Discorso diretto (trapassato)	Discorso indiretto (trapassato)
Abbiamo detto: «L'**aveva preparata**.»	Abbiamo detto che l'**aveva preparata**.
We said, "She had prepared it."	*We said that she had prepared it.*
Rispose: «Volevo sapere dove **fosse andata**.»	Rispose che voleva sapere dove **fosse andata**.
He replied, "I wanted to know where she had gone."	*He replied that he wanted to know where she had gone.*

- When the verb introducing indirect discourse is in a past tense, verb tenses other than the **imperfetto** or **trapassato** must also shift to the past tense. This is true whether the verb is in the indicative or subjunctive.

Discorso diretto (presente)	Discorso indiretto (imperfetto)
Giorgina ha risposto: «Non **voglio** pagare la tassa.» *Giorgina answered, "I don't want to pay the tax."*	Giorgina ha risposto che non **voleva** pagare la tassa. *Giorgina answered that she didn't want to pay the tax.*

Discorso diretto (futuro/condizionale)	Discorso indiretto (condizionale passato)
Pandora ha urlato: «Non **aprirò** mai questa scatola!» *Pandora yelled, "I will never open this box!"*	Pandora ha urlato che non **avrebbe** mai **aperto** quella scatola. *Pandora yelled that she would never open that box.*

Discorso diretto (passato prossimo/remoto)	Discorso indiretto (trapassato)
Pierluigi ha ammesso: «**Ho perso** la mia chiave.» *Pierluigi admitted, "I lost my key."*	Pierluigi ha ammesso che **aveva perso** la sua chiave. *Pierluigi admitted that he had lost his key.*
Maria Elena ha risposto: «Credo che questi bambini l'**abbiano trovata**.» *Maria Elena replied, "I think these children found it."*	Maria Elena ha risposto che credeva che quei bambini l'**avessero trovata**. *Maria Elena replied that she thought those children had found it.*

- There are two ways to indicate the change from an imperative in direct discourse to its equivalent in indirect discourse. You may use **di** + [infinitive] or the imperfect subjunctive.

Discorso diretto (imperativo)	Discorso indiretto (infinito/congiuntivo imperfetto)
Stefano gli **ha detto**: «**Fallo** subito!» *Stefano said to him, "Do it right away!"*	Stefano gli **ha detto di farlo** subito. Stefano gli **ha detto che lo facesse** subito. *Stefano told him to do it right away.*

- Hypothetical situations expressing reality, possibility, and impossibility undergo changes as shown in the shift from direct to indirect discourse. In indirect discourse, all three of the hypothetical situations are expressed with the same basic tenses: the past perfect subjunctive (**congiuntivo trapassato**) after **se**, and the past conditional (**condizionale passato**) in the result clause.

Discorso diretto	Discorso indiretto
Gianni disse: «Se **avremo** soldi, **compreremo** una bella casa.» *Gianni said, "If we have the money, we will buy a nice house."*	Gianni disse che se **avessero avuto** soldi, **avrebbero comprato** una bella casa. *Gianni said that if they had the money, they would buy a nice house.*
Marina rispose: «Se **avessi** soldi, **comprerei** una macchina!» *Marina replied, "If I had the money, I would buy a car!"*	Marina rispose che se **avesse avuto** soldi, **avrebbe comprato** una macchina. *Marina replied that if she had the money, she would buy a car.*
Paolo aggiunse: «Se **avessi avuto** soldi, **avrei comprato** una Ferrari.» *Paolo added, "If I had had the money, I would have bought a Ferrari."*	Paolo aggiunse che se **avesse avuto** soldi, **avrebbe comprato** una Ferrari. *Paolo added that if he had had the money, he would have bought a Ferrari.*

ATTENZIONE!

When the speaker is talking to or about him/herself, it is common to use **di** + [*infinitive*]. To indicate a past action, use **di** + [*past infinitive*].

Ugo dice: «Io non guadagno abbastanza.»
Ugo says, "I don't earn enough."

Ugo dice di non guadagnare abbastanza.
Ugo says he doesn't earn enough.

Pia ha detto: «Non ho ricevuto la lettera.»
Pia said, "I didn't receive the letter."

Pia ha detto di non aver ricevuto la lettera.
Pia said that she hadn't received the letter.

RIMANDO

To review hypothetical statements, see **Strutture 9.3, pp. 360–361**.

Pratica

1 Have students create original conversations and transform them into indirect discourse.

1

Al lavoro Riscrivi le conversazioni ascoltate al lavoro utilizzando il discorso indiretto. Some answers will vary.

> **Modello** Teresa: «Voglio un aumento di stipendio.»
> Il direttore: «Va bene, avrai l'aumento!»
>
> Teresa dice che vuole un aumento di stipendio.
> Il direttore risponde che va bene, avrà l'aumento.

1. Mario: «Voglio cambiare il mio orario di lavoro.» Mario dice che vuole cambiare il suo orario
   di lavoro.
   La segretaria: «Devi riempire il modulo.» La segretaria risponde che deve riempire il modulo.
2. Carlo: «La prossima settimana andrò in ferie.» Carlo dice che la settimana prossima andrà in ferie.
   Il collega: «Io ci sono andato il mese scorso.» Il collega risponde che lui ci è andato il mese precedente.
3. Lucia: «Ho mandato il fax.» Lucia dice che ha mandato il fax.
   Il capo: «Puoi fare la pausa.» Il capo risponde che può fare la pausa.
4. Matteo: «Dovrei uscire un momento.» Matteo dice che dovrebbe uscire un momento.
   La direttrice: «Va bene.» La direttrice risponde che va bene.

2 Have students add additional opinions in indirect discourse.

2

L'articolo Alcuni esperti esprimono la loro opinione sulla crisi economica. Tu sei un giornalista e scrivi un articolo su quello che hanno detto usando il discorso indiretto.

- Un economista: «Nel mese di luglio la crisi economica raggiungerà livelli altissimi. Gli effetti degli interventi dello stato non si fanno sentire.» Un economista ha detto che nel mese di luglio la crisi
  avrebbe raggiunto/avrà raggiunto livelli altissimi e che gli effetti degli interventi dello stato non si facevano sentire.
- Un politico: «La ripresa economica dovrebbe avvenire presto. Il periodo peggiore è già passato.» Un politico ha detto che la ripresa economica sarebbe dovuta avvenire presto e che il periodo peggiore era già passato.
- Un sindacalista: «Il tasso di disoccupazione è salito negli ultimi mesi. Tutto è iniziato a causa della crisi finanziaria.» Un sindacalista ha detto che il tasso di disoccupazione era salito negli ultimi
  mesi e che tutto era iniziato a causa della crisi finanziaria.

3 Give additional hypothetical statements that employees might have said during a meeting and have volunteers report what was said using a reporting verb in the **passato prossimo**.

3

Riunione Durante una riunione di lavoro alcuni impiegati fanno delle dichiarazioni (*statements*). Riscrivile in un promemoria usando il discorso indiretto.

1. I dipendenti avevano detto: «Vogliamo un orario di lavoro flessibile.»
   I dipendenti avevano detto che volevano un orario di lavoro flessibile.
2. La segretaria aveva detto: «Abbiamo bisogno di più impiegati.» La segretaria aveva
   detto che avevano bisogno di più impiegati.
3. Il direttore ha spiegato: «Pensavo che fossero stati assunti.» Il direttore ha spiegato
   che pensava che fossero stati assunti.
4. Un'impiegata ha proposto: «Se usassimo materiali più economici i costi di produzione diminuirebbero.» Un'impiegata ha proposto che se avessero usato materiali più economici i costi
   di produzione sarebbero diminuiti.
5. La dirigente aveva dichiarato: «La produzione è salita nell'ultimo mese.»
   La dirigente aveva dichiarato che la produzione era salita nell'ultimo mese.

4 Answers: **Il direttore ha detto a Martina di contattare i vecchi clienti, di controllare la posta elettronica ogni mattina e di mandare i nuovi cataloghi ai rappresentanti./ Il direttore ha detto a Martina che contattasse i vecchi clienti, che controllasse la posta elettronica ogni mattina e che mandasse i nuovi cataloghi ai rappresentanti./ Il direttore ha detto ai dipendenti di fare un'ora di straordinario, di ispezionare il materiale arrivato e di completare i progetti iniziati./Il direttore ha detto ai dipendenti che facessero un'ora di straordinario, che ispezionassero il materiale arrivato e che completassero i progetti iniziati.**

4

Disposizioni In coppia leggete la lista degli ordini lasciata dal direttore per i suoi dipendenti. Riscrivetela utilizzando le due forme di discorso indiretto.

> **Modello** Per il contabile: Paga gli stipendi.
>
> Il direttore ha detto al contabile di pagare gli stipendi./Il direttore ha detto al contabile che pagasse gli stipendi.

- **Per Martina:**

  Contatta i vecchi clienti.

  Controlla la posta elettronica ogni mattina.

  Manda i nuovi cataloghi ai rappresentanti.

- **Per i dipendenti:**

  Fate un'ora di straordinario al giorno.

  Ispezionate il materiale arrivato.

  Completate i progetti iniziati.

 Practice more at **vhlcentral.com**.

Comunicazione

SUGGESTION Revisit some
of the literature from earlier
lessons and assign stories
or chunks of stories for
students to rewrite in indirect
discourse. Selections with a
lot of dialogue (such as the
Dario Fo play in Lezione 6)
are particularly apt for
this activity.

5

Telefonata In coppia, raccontatevi a turno una conversazione telefonica che avete avuto di recente. Fatevi delle domande per saperne di più.

> Modello —Ieri sera ho parlato con mia madre e mi ha detto che lei e mio padre sarebbero venuti a trovarmi questo fine settimana.
>
> —Ti ha detto quanto tempo rimarranno?
>
> —Non proprio, ma ha detto che sarebbero rimasti fino a domenica pomeriggio.

6

Fumetti In gruppo, immaginate cosa stanno dicendo i personaggi nei fumetti e inseritelo nella nuvoletta. Poi riscrivetelo usando il discorso indiretto.

7

Recensione In gruppo, a turno raccontate brevemente la trama dell'ultimo film o telefilm che avete visto. Gli altri studenti ascoltano e riassumono in quattro o cinque frasi usando il discorso indiretto.

8

Tra avvocati Due avvocati si incontrano per curare gli interessi dei loro clienti e per negoziare le richieste della controparte. In coppia, scegliete una delle due situazioni e inventate una conversazione tra gli avvocati, utilizzando il discorso indiretto, per riportare cosa i clienti gli hanno detto.

> Modello —Il mio cliente ha detto che voleva tenere il cane.
>
> —Mi dispiace, ma il mio cliente ha detto che il suo cliente poteva tenere il gatto ma non il cane.

- Due avvocati che rappresentano moglie e marito che vogliono divorziare.

- Due avvocati che rappresentano l'azienda da una parte, e un dipendente che è stato licenziato dall'altra.

INSTRUCTIONAL RESOURCES **10.4**
Audioscripts, Answer Keys, Lab MP3s, Grammar Presentation Slides
SAM/WebSAM: WB, LM

ATTENZIONE!

To avoid ambiguity, use **da** instead of **a** to show who is performing the action.

Fate scrivere una poesia a Beatrice.
Have a poem written for/by Beatrice.

Fate scrivere una poesia da Beatrice.
Have Beatrice write a poem.

ATTENZIONE!

You may also use a disjunctive pronoun instead of an indirect object pronoun for clarification or emphasis.

Glielo faccio vedere.
I'm showing it to him/her.

Lo faccio vedere a lui, non a lei.
I'll show it to him, not to her.

ATTENZIONE!

Pronouns follow and attach to **fare** in three situations: the **tu**, **noi**, and **voi** forms of the imperative, when **fare** is an infinitive, and in the gerund.

Fallo venire subito!
Have him come right away!

Voglio farli capire.
I want to make them understand.

Facendoli ragionare, il professore li aiuta a ricordare.
By making them reason, the teacher helps them remember.

Give students an active sentence such as "**Preparo un panino**" and the name of another student, and ask them to tell who is now doing the action.
—**Preparo un panino / Barbara**
—**Faccio preparare un panino a/da Barbara.**

Fare, lasciare, and verbs of perception followed by the infinitive

—*Li **farei dormire** a casa tua.*

Fare followed by the infinitive

- **Fare** + [*infinitive*] indicates that the subject is causing something to be done or causing someone else to do something.

L'insegnante **fa parlare** Paolo.
The teacher makes Paolo talk.

Marco **fa lavare** la macchina a suo fratello.
Marco has his brother wash his car.

- When there is one object after **fare** + [*infinitive*], it is always a direct object. When there are two objects, the person or thing acted upon is the direct object and the person participating in the action is an indirect object.

	DIRECT OBJECT
Il padrone farà licenziare	**l'impiegato.**

The boss will have the employee fired.

	DIRECT OBJECT	INDIRECT OBJECT
Il padre fa aprire	**un conto**	**a sua figlia.**

The father is having his daughter open an account.

- Object pronouns do not attach to the infinitive. They normally precede the conjugated form of **fare**. Note that the past participle of **fare** agrees with preceding direct object pronouns.

Ho fatto presentare le sue qualifiche a Gina.
I had Gina present her qualifications.

Le ho fatte presentare a Gina.
I had Gina present them.

Hai fatto suonare la tromba a Salvatore?
Did you have Salvatore play the trumpet?

Gliel'hai fatta suonare?
Did you have him play it?

- **Farsi** + [*infinitive*] expresses the idea of having something done to or for oneself by another person. Use **da** + a person to indicate who is performing the action.

La nonna **si fa lavare** i capelli **dalla** nipote.
The grandmother has her hair washed by her granddaughter.

Mi farò cuocere una bella pastasciutta **da** Patrizia.
I will have Patrizia cook a nice pasta dish for me.

- If the infinitive after **fare** is a reflexive verb, the reflexive pronoun is dropped.

Non **fare alzare** papà.
Don't make Daddy get up.

Ho fatto pentire Maria.
I made Maria feel bad.

Lasciare followed by the infinitive

- **Lasciare** + [*infinitive*] means *to allow*, *to let* or *to permit* someone to do something.

> **Lascio piangere** il mio fratellino.
> *I let my little brother cry.*

- As with the **fare** construction, when there is one object after **lasciare** + [*infinitive*], it is always a direct object. If there are two objects, the person or thing acted upon is the direct object and the person doing the action is an indirect object.

> Abbiamo lasciato cantare **i nostri ospiti.**
> *We let our guests sing.*

> **La** lasciate mangiare.
> *You are letting her eat.*

> **Li** abbiamo lasciati cantare.
> *We let them sing.*

> **Le** lasciate mangiare **le patatine fritte.**
> *You are letting her eat French fries.*

- **Lasciarsi** expresses the idea of allowing something to be done by or for oneself. The person or thing who performs the action is introduced by **da**.

> Il mio collega **si lascia convincere** a comprare il caffè a tutti gli amici.
> *My coworker lets himself get talked into buying coffee for his friends.*

> **Mi sono lasciata** trasportare dalla musica.
> *I let myself drift away with the music.*

> Per il colloquio, **mi lascerò vestire da** mia moglie!
> *For the interview, I'll let my wife choose my clothes!*

- **Lasciare** may also be followed by **che**. When the two clauses have a different subject, a verb in the appropriate form of the subjunctive is used in the dependent clause.

> La professoressa **ha lasciato che** gli studenti **mangiassero** nell'aula.
> *The professor let the students eat in the classroom.*

Verbs of perception followed by the infinitive

- Verbs of perception such as **sentire** (*to hear*) and **vedere** (*to see*) may be followed by an infinitive. Additional verbs of perception are: **guardare** (*to watch*), **ascoltare** (*to listen to*), **udire** (*to hear*), and **osservare** (*to observe*).

> **Ho sentito gridare** il contabile.
> *I heard the accountant screaming.*

> **Ascoltiamo cantare** il nostro amico.
> *We are listening to our friend sing.*

> **L'ho sentito gridare.**
> *I heard him screaming.*

> **L'ascoltiamo cantare.**
> *We are listening to him sing.*

- The direct object follows the infinitive and the direct object pronoun precedes the conjugated verb of perception when there is only one object.

> Vedo arrivare **l'aereo.**
> *I see the plane coming.*

> **Lo** vedo arrivare.
> *I see it coming.*

- If the infinitive has its own object, place it after the infinitive and place the other noun after the verb of perception.

> Abbiamo visto il leone **mangiare** la gazzella.
> *We saw the lion eat the gazelle.*

> **ATTENZIONE!**

Two expressions, **lasciare perdere** and **lasciare stare**, are idiomatic. The first means *to let something go* or *to forget about something*, the second means *to let something be*.

Non troveremo mai quella lettera—lasciamo perdere!
We will never find that letter— let's forget about it.

Hai già riletto la tua risposta tre volte—lascia stare!
You've already read your answer three times—leave it!

Explain to students that **lasciarsi andare** has the idea of letting oneself go (as in not taking care of oneself). Example: **Quando suo marito è morto, si è lasciata andare.**

> **ATTENZIONE!**

Pronouns follow and attach to **lasciare** in three situations: the **tu**, **noi**, and **voi** forms of the imperative, when **lasciare** is an infinitive, and in the gerund.

Lascialo giocare in pace.
Let him play in peace.

Puoi lasciargli fare un dolce.
You can let them make dessert.

Lasciandole stare alzate fino a tardi, ci troveremo nei guai.
We'll be sorry if we let them stay up.

Point out that verbs of perception may also be followed by a relative clause introduced by **che** or **mentre**. Example: **Sento il cane che abbaia. Abbiamo osservato la ragazza mentre partiva.**

Pratica

1

Istruzioni Utilizza gli elementi forniti per fare delle frasi con **fare** + infinito.

> **Modello** La ditta firma il contratto. / il consulente
>
> Il consulente fa firmare il contratto alla ditta.

1. Gli operai lavorano. / il direttore Il direttore fa lavorare gli operai.
2. La segretaria ha mandato le e-mail. / il capo Il capo ha fatto mandare le e-mail dalla segretaria.
3. La stagista farà il colloquio di lavoro. / il consulente Il consulente farà fare il colloquio di lavoro alla stagista.
4. Il contabile ha depositato gli assegni. / il collega Il collega ha fatto depositare gli assegni al contabile.
5. L'assistente contatta i clienti. / il dirigente Il dirigente fa contattare i clienti all'assistente.

2

Primo giorno di lavoro Utilizza gli elementi forniti per fare delle frasi con **fare** + infinito o **farsi** + infinito, poi riscrivi le frasi utilizzando i pronomi diretti e indiretti.

> **Modello** La segretaria fa il caffè. (Il capo)
>
> Il capo fa fare il caffè alla segretaria./Il capo glielo fa fare.

1. L'assistente porta il contratto al direttore. (Il direttore) Il direttore si fa portare il contratto dall'assistente. Il direttore se lo fa portare.
2. La nuova impiegata firma il contratto. (Il direttore) Il direttore fa firmare il contratto alla nuova impiegata. Il direttore glielo fa firmare.
3. I dipendenti conoscono la nuova impiegata. (Il direttore) Il direttore fa conoscere la nuova impiegata ai dipendenti. Il direttore gliela fa conoscere.
4. La nuova impiegata vede il nuovo progetto. (I dipendenti) I dipendenti fanno vedere il nuovo progetto alla nuova impiegata. I dipendenti glielo fanno vedere.
5. L'assistente spiega i progetti alla nuova impiegata. (La nuova impiegata) La nuova impiegata si fa spiegare i progetti dall'assistente. La nuova impiegata se li fa spiegare.

3

Genitori e figli In coppia, usate gli elementi forniti per parlare di cosa vi lasciavano o non vi lasciavano fare i vostri genitori quando eravate adolescenti.

> **Modello** uscire la sera
>
> I miei genitori non mi lasciavano uscire la sera durante la settimana, ma mi lasciavano uscire solo il venerdì o il sabato sera.

- andare in vacanza da solo/a
- andare in discoteca con gli amici
- tornare a casa tardi senza avvertire
- guidare la loro macchina
- avere un indirizzo e-mail privato
- usare Internet senza limiti
- ?

4

Have students use the questions to role-play the detective/witness interview. Encourage students to add questions of their own. Have them write a report based on their interviews.

Una rapina C'è stata una rapina (*robbery*) in una banca e tu come testimone devi rispondere alle domande dell'investigatore. Some answers will vary.

> **Modello** Hanno fatto uscire i clienti?
>
> No, non li hanno fatti uscire.

1. Avete visto arrivare i ladri? No, non li abbiamo visti arrivare.
2. Avete sentito sparare un colpo di pistola? Sì, lo abbiamo sentito sparare.
3. I ladri hanno fatto aprire la cassaforte (*safe*) al cassiere? Non so se gliel'hanno fatta aprire.
4. Hanno fatto entrare tutti i clienti nell'ufficio del direttore? Sì, li hanno fatti entrare tutti.
5. Hanno fatto scattare (*go off*) l'allarme? No, non l'hanno fatto scattare.
6. Hanno fatto parlare gli ostaggi con i loro parenti? Sì, li hanno fatti parlare con i loro parenti.
7. Si sono fatti consegnare tutti i soldi dall'impiegato? No, non se li sono fatti consegnare tutti.
8. Avete visto cadere a terra la segretaria? Sì, l'abbiamo vista cadere.

Practice more at
vhlcentral.com.

Comunicazione

5

Questionario In coppia, rispondete alle seguenti domande.

1. Cosa ti fa ridere?
2. Che cosa ti fa perdere la pazienza?
3. Fai controllare la tua auto periodicamente?
4. Ti fai tagliare i capelli dal parrucchiere (*barber/hairdresser*)?
5. Lasci usare il tuo computer ai tuoi amici?
6. Lasci leggere il tuo diario personale ai tuoi amici?
7. Ti lasci convincere facilmente dagli altri?
8. Fai usare il tuo iPad ai tuoi amici?

5 Have students add questions of their own.

5 Have students summarize ways in which they are similar and share their conclusions in groups.

6

Il lavoro ideale In coppia, descrivete il vostro lavoro ideale, utilizzando **fare**, **lasciare** e i verbi di percezione più infinito.

> **Modello** Il mio lavoro ideale è quello che mi lascia iniziare alle 10 di mattina e non mi fa lavorare il venerdì.

7

Uno sguardo al futuro Fate una lista di sei cose che tu e la tua famiglia vi farete fare da altri tra vent'anni, quando sarete molto ricchi. Condividete la lista con i vostri compagni che vi faranno domande a riguardo.

> **Modello** Mi farò portare la colazione a letto tutte le mattine.
> Mio fratello si farà accompagnare dall'autista.

7 Have students in the group determine whose list is most imaginative, most practical, most outrageous, etc.

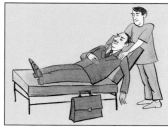

8

Qualcosa di strano Racconta qualcosa di strano che ti è successo di recente, puoi usare la tua immaginazione, utilizzando i verbi di percezione e **lasciare** + **infinito**.

> **Modello** Ieri pomeriggio ho sentito gridare la mia vicina di casa, ho visto correre un uomo con un cappello nel cortile e poi ho udito ridere il marito della vicina...

Sintesi

1

Parliamo In gruppo, leggete i quattro estratti e rispondete alle domande.

I giovani e il mondo del lavoro.

Francesco, 24 anni, Padova

È sempre più difficile per noi giovani trovare lavoro. Per me è importante scegliere un buon corso di laurea e soprattutto fare esperienza all'estero. Lavorare in un altro paese è un'occasione per crescere professionalmente e avere poi la possibilità di trovare un lavoro interessante e ben pagato.

Paola, 25 anni, Napoli

Mi sono laureata l'anno scorso e ancora non ho trovato lavoro, e nella mia stessa situazione si trovano la metà dei laureati. Purtroppo dobbiamo accettare lavori precari, spesso mal pagati e non adeguati agli studi fatti. Voglio essere indipendente ma non ci riesco e non capisco perché dovrei trasferirmi in un'altra città o in un altro paese.

Giacomo, 20 anni, Genova

Secondo me, i giovani laureati possono trovare lavoro; devono solo darsi da fare e cercare di fare esperienza anche durante gli anni dell'università invece di aspettare dopo la laurea. Ogni estate, io accetto qualsiasi lavoro che riesco a trovare per fare esperienza e cercherò il mio lavoro ideale dopo che mi sarò laureato.

Sara, 26 anni, Perugia

Purtroppo siamo in un circolo vizioso: le aziende vogliono giovani con esperienza, e così nessuno è disposto ad assumerli senza esperienza. Ma dove dovremmo maturare noi giovani questa esperienza? Secondo me, l'università e il mondo del lavoro dovrebbero lavorare insieme per dare questa occasione a noi giovani.

1. Qual è l'opinione degli intervistati riguardo alle difficoltà che hanno i giovani italiani a trovare lavoro?
2. Quali soluzioni suggeriscono per risolvere questo problema?
3. Secondo te, quali fattori influenzano la loro opinione?
4. Con quale degli intervistati ti identifichi di più? Perché?
5. Secondo te, questi sono problemi solo italiani o ci sono anche nel tuo paese?

2

Scriviamo Scegli uno dei seguenti argomenti e scrivi un tema di circa una pagina.

- Fai un resoconto (*summary*) delle opinioni dei quattro intervistati.
- Quale delle quattro opinioni è più vicina alla tua? Spiega perché.

Strategie per la comunicazione

Quando ti prepari a riportare quello che altre persone hanno detto, sia a voce che per iscritto, ricordati di non limitarti ad usare solo il verbo **dire**, ma utilizza altri sinonimi come: **raccontare**, **spiegare**, **chiarire**, **ricordare**, **far notare**, **affermare** ed **esprimere**.

Preparazione  Vocabulary Tools

Vocabolario della lettura

l'abbigliamento *clothing*
il capo (di abbigliamento) *article (of clothing)*
la griffe *designer label*
il look *dressing style*
la marca *brand*
la richiesta *demand*
il settore *sector*
la sfilata *(fashion) parade*
lo stile *style*
lo/la stilista *fashion designer*

Vocabolario utile

l'abito *(men's) suit*
la cravatta *tie*
i gioielli *jewelry*
la (mini)gonna *(mini)skirt*
gli orecchini *earrings*
i pantaloni (lunghi/corti) *(long/short) pants*
i sandali *sandals*
il tailleur (invar.) *(women's) suit*
il tatuaggio *tattoo*
il trucco *makeup*

1
Parole nuove Associa i sinonimi nelle due colonne.

_f_ 1. l'abbigliamento   a. la griffe
_e_ 2. i sandali   b. i creatori di moda
_a_ 3. la marca   c. la caratteristica, l'orientamento
_h_ 4. il look   d. il campo
_g_ 5. la richiesta   e. le scarpe aperte
_d_ 6. il settore   f. i vestiti
_c_ 7. lo stile   g. la domanda
_b_ 8. gli stilisti   h. lo stile nel vestirsi

2
Stile e look In coppia, rispondete alle domande.

1. Quali stilisti italiani conosci? Quali sono i prodotti che preferisci?
2. Ti piace seguire le mode nel vestirti?
3. Come descriveresti il tuo look? È simile a quello degli altri studenti?
4. Come descriveresti il look della tua celebrità preferita?

3
Sondaggio Cosa indosseresti in queste occasioni? Intervista altri studenti.

Situazione	Abbigliamento	Accessori	Scarpe
in ufficio			
a un matrimonio			
a un colloquio di lavoro			
a una festa			
all'università			
sulla spiaggia			
sulla neve			

Nota CULTURALE

Il più famoso museo italiano dedicato alla storia della moda è la **Galleria del costume**, che si trova a Palazzo Pitti a Firenze. È una grande collezione che include più di 6.000 manufatti°, fra abiti antichi e moderni, accessori, costumi teatrali e cinematografici a partire dal '700. Molti degli esemplari, creati da stilisti italiani e stranieri, sono rari o addirittura° unici. Il museo spesso organizza anche mostre temporanee speciali.

manufatti *handicrafts* **addirittura** *even*

LA MODA ITALIANA

Versace, collezione
autunno-inverno,
Milano Moda, 2009

Da molti anni, la scritta *Made in Italy* su un capo di abbigliamento è un sinonimo di qualità e prestigio, e l'industria della moda è diventata uno dei settori più importanti dell'economia italiana. Naturalmente il *Made in Italy* si riferisce anche a numerosi altri prodotti esportati dei settori industriali più disparati: la meccanica automobilistica e motociclistica, l'arredamento°, l'enogastronomia, che sono ormai diffusi e apprezzati in tutto il mondo. La moda però ha un ruolo privilegiato non solo nell'economia ma anche nell'immaginazione e nella società italiana: «moda», infatti, vuol dire anche «costume», che ha il doppio significato di abbigliamento e di caratteristiche socio-culturali.

Oltre a incrementare l'esportazione dei prodotti artigianali e industriali così contribuendo alla crescita economica del paese, il successo degli stilisti di moda ha anche cambiato l'immagine che gli stranieri hanno degli italiani. Il successo dell'industria della moda italiana nasce dalla piccola e media imprenditoria°: la tradizione tessile°, unita alla qualità dei materiali locali e alla creatività dei talenti individuali, ha ispirato un prodotto completamente *Made in Italy*.

La moda italiana nasce a Roma durante il boom economico degli anni '50. La seconda guerra mondiale è finita e il mercato italiano è in espansione. Con la loro boutique vicino a via Veneto, le sorelle Fontana sono le prime stiliste a conquistare una fama internazionale. Giovanni Battista Giorgini organizza la prima sfilata di alta moda italiana a Firenze. È l'inizio della crescita commerciale del settore: Giorgini riesce infatti a catturare l'interesse dei grandi magazzini statunitensi. Le sfilate fiorentine continuano ancora oggi, ospitate nel famoso Palazzo Pitti. Anche la grande produzione cinematografica di Cinecittà, la Hollywood romana, aumenta la richiesta di capi firmati per i registi, gli attori e

home furnishings (line 10)

small/medium business (line 26)
textile (line 27)

Eleganza al lavoro

In ufficio gli italiani si vestono sobriamente con abito e cravatta e le italiane in tailleur serio con colori classici. E le scarpe? Preferibilmente chiuse, anche d'estate, con tacchi bassi per le donne. Un look molto rigoroso, variato solo da accessori personalizzati ma non troppo vistosi°.

vistosi *loud*

le attrici del momento, visibili in tutto il mondo sia sul grande schermo che in televisione. I modelli indossati negli anni '60 da Ava Gardner, Jackie Kennedy Onassis, Audrey Hepburn, Grace di Monaco e Marilyn Monroe sono diventati dei classici.

Negli anni '60 e '70 si affermano Giorgio Armani e Valentino. Molti stilisti modificano i loro disegni per seguire anche i gusti dei più giovani. Per attrarre il maggior numero di clienti nasce così la moda pronta firmata dalle griffe più prestigiose ma che si può comprare a prezzi accessibili nei negozi più diffusi e non soltanto nelle carissime boutique degli stilisti di via Condotti, di fronte a piazza di Spagna a Roma.

Milano è diventata la capitale dello stile e della moda italiana dagli anni '80 in poi°. Nella zona del centro chiamata il «quadrilatero della moda», delimitato da via Montenapoleone, via Manzoni, via della Spiga e corso Venezia, si concentrano i negozi dei più famosi creatori di moda. Alla fine di settembre e all'inizio di ottobre, durante la «settimana della moda» si può assistere° alle sfilate milanesi. Davanti alle telecamere e agli occhi di tutto il mondo sfilano le modelle più conosciute, vestite da Prada, Gucci, Dolce e Gabbana, Versace e moltissimi altri stilisti ormai leggendari per le loro favolose collezioni. È il trionfo della moda *Made in Italy*. ■

from the 80s on (line 70)

attend (line 77)

1 Ask pairs to create three more true/false statements and then give them to a different group to check.

Analisi

Comprensione

A. Indica se le affermazioni sono **vere** o **false**.

Vero	Falso	
☐	☑	1. Il *Made in Italy* si riferisce solo alle creazioni di alta moda.
☑	☐	2. Il successo della moda italiana è anche dovuto alla forza della piccola e media imprenditoria.
☐	☑	3. Armani e Valentino sono i primi stilisti a diventare famosi anche all'estero.
☐	☑	4. Milano era la capitale della moda durante la produzione cinematografica di Cinecittà.
☑	☐	5. La prima sfilata di moda italiana è stata organizzata a Firenze.
☑	☐	6. Le attrici Ava Gardner, Audrey Hepburn, Grace di Monaco e Marilyn Monroe hanno tutte indossato vestiti di stilisti italiani.
☐	☑	7. Gli italiani si vestono in maniera stravagante per andare in ufficio.
☑	☐	8. Le sfilate più importanti di Milano avvengono ogni anno tra settembre e ottobre.

B. Correggete le affermazioni false.

2

Un look italiano? Guardate queste foto e descrivete il look e la personalità di ogni persona.

3 Ask students to form two teams and debate the issue after jotting down the main points of their respective arguments.

TEACHING OPTION
Ask students to organize a fashion show, taking turns being the designers, the models, and the announcers describing the outfits.

TEACHING OPTION
Ask students to create a fashion magazine. Divide the class in small groups and ask each one to write one section of the magazine (news, editorials, fashion show reports, gossip about what celebrities are wearing) using pictures from the web, actual fashion magazines, drawings, etc.

Dibattito In piccoli gruppi, scegliete un'opinione e difendetela.

Il mondo della moda è superficiale e corrotto.

Il mondo della moda è positivo per l'economia e l'immagine dell'Italia.

4

Scrittura Scegli uno di questi argomenti e scrivi un testo di una pagina.

- Qual è l'impatto dell'industria della moda sull'economia?

- Cosa pensi delle aziende che sfruttano la manodopera (*take advantage of workers*)? Pensi che sia importante non comprare prodotti a prezzi molto più bassi della norma? Perché?

- Secondo te, quale settore economico è in maggiore crescita? Perché? Quali saranno i prodotti più diffusi nel futuro?

Practice more at vhlcentral.com.

Preparazione

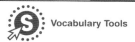 **Vocabulary Tools**

A proposito dell'autore

Italo Calvino (1923–1985) è uno scrittore molto amato da grandi e bambini. Infatti, molte delle sue favole allegoriche possono essere lette e apprezzate da un pubblico adulto o infantile. Nato a Cuba da genitori italiani, Calvino cresce in Liguria durante gli anni del fascismo e trova nell'allegoria un modo sicuro per esprimere le sue idee. È uno dei narratori italiani più importanti degli anni '50 e '60. Calvino ha scritto saggi, articoli, romanzi e racconti, e ha raccolto fiabe antiche della tradizione popolare italiana. Calvino è anche uno scrittore sperimentale molto attento ai meccanismi narrativi.

Vocabolario della lettura

coricarsi *to lie down*
la dolcezza *sweetness*
la fabbrica/l'officina *factory*
il guanciale *pillow*
rincasare *to go back home*
il rumore *noise*
la smorfia *smirk*
spogliarsi *to undress*
stirarsi *to stretch*
la vestaglia *robe*

Vocabolario utile

la confidenza *intimacy*
il fraintendimento *misunderstanding*
l'odore *smell*
la sveglia *alarm clock*
il turno di lavoro *work shift*

Nottambulo is someone who prefers to work at night, a night owl; **mattiniero** is an early bird. You could poll students and see how many of them prefer waking up early and why.

1
Definizioni Trovate la definizione adatta ad ogni parola.

_f_ 1. la sveglia
_b_ 2. la vestaglia
_a_ 3. spogliarsi
_d_ 4. il guanciale
_e_ 5. coricarsi
_c_ 6. la confidenza

a. togliersi i vestiti
b. indumento che si usa in casa
c. l'intimità che si ha con una persona
d. dove mettiamo la testa sul letto
e. mettersi in posizione orizzontale
f. strumento infernale che suona la mattina

2
Preparazione Fate a un(a) compagno/a le seguenti domande.
1. Com'è il tuo orario a scuola? Hai anche un lavoro?
2. Conosci coppie che fanno turni di lavoro diversi? Quando riescono a vedersi?
3. Quando studi e lavori, dove trovi il tempo per divertirti?
4. Che tipo di orario di lavoro vorresti avere a vent'anni? E a trenta? A quaranta?
5. È importante avere lo stesso orario del tuo partner e lo stesso lavoro?

3
Mattinieri o nottambuli? In coppia, rispondete alle seguenti domande.
1. A che ora preferisci svegliarti? Sei nottambulo/a o mattiniero/a?
2. Hai mai abitato con delle persone che hanno ritmi diversi dai tuoi?
3. Sei nervoso se ti svegli fuori dai tuoi orari e bioritmi naturali? È importante per te mantenere una routine?
4. Se tu e tua moglie o tuo marito aveste turni di lavoro diversi, cosa fareste per vedervi?
5. Quanto è importante avere gli stessi interessi e gli stessi orari del partner?

Nota CULTURALE

La raccolta° di racconti **Gli amori difficili** da cui è tratto° il racconto «L'avventura di due sposi» è composta da venti racconti di amori sospesi°, di coppie che non si incontrano la maggior parte delle volte, ma che si amano distrattamente, intensamente, disperatamente, dolcemente. «L'avventura di due sposi» racconta di una vita urbana, spersonalizzata°, con ritmi di lavoro costanti e difficili, in cui l'amore si trova nei piccoli spazi di pochi momenti.

raccolta *collection* è **tratto** *is taken* **sospesi** *suspended* **spersonalizzata** *depersonalized*

Gli amori difficili was written in 1971. The stories contained in it eloquently and accurately depict urban life in the years after the economic boom of the '60s.

 Practice more at **vhlcentral.com**.

L'avventura di due sposi

ITALO CALVINO

L'operaio Arturo Massolari faceva il turno della notte, quello che finisce alle sei. Per rincasare aveva un lungo tragitto°, che compiva° in bicicletta nella bella stagione, in tram nei mesi piovosi e invernali. Arrivava a casa tra le sei e tre quarti e le sette, cioè alle volte un po' prima alle volte un po' dopo che suonasse la sveglia della moglie, Elide.

Spesso i due rumori: il suono della sveglia e il passo di lui che entrava si sovrapponevano° nella mente di Elide, raggiungendola° in fondo al sonno, il sonno compatto della mattina presto che lei cercava di spremere° ancora per qualche secondo col viso affondato° nel guanciale. Poi si tirava su dal letto di strappo° e già infilava° le braccia alla cieca° nella vestaglia, coi capelli sugli occhi. Gli appariva così, in cucina, dove Arturo stava tirando fuori° i recipienti° vuoti dalla borsa che si portava con sé sul lavoro: il portavivande°, il termos, e li posava sull'acquaio°. Aveva già acceso il fornello e aveva messo su° il caffè. Appena lui la guardava, a Elide veniva da° passarsi una mano sui capelli, da spalancare° a forza gli occhi, come se ogni volta si vergognasse° un po' di questa prima immagine che il marito aveva di lei entrando in casa, sempre così in disordine, con la faccia mezz'addormentata°. Quando due hanno dormito insieme è un'altra cosa, ci si ritrova al mattino a riaffiorare° entrambi° dallo stesso sonno, si è pari°.

Alle volte° invece era lui che entrava in camera a destarla°, con la tazzina del caffè, un minuto prima che la sveglia suonasse; allora tutto era piú naturale, la smorfia per uscire dal sonno prendeva una specie° di dolcezza pigra°, le braccia che s'alzavano per stirarsi, nude, finivano per cingere° il collo di lui. S'abbracciavano. Arturo aveva indosso il giaccone impermeabile°; a sentirselo° vicino lei capiva il tempo che faceva: se pioveva o faceva nebbia o c'era neve, a seconda di° com'era umido e freddo. Ma gli diceva lo stesso: — Che tempo fa? — e lui attaccava° il suo solito brontolamento° mezzo ironico, passando in rassegna° gli inconvenienti° che gli erano occorsi°, cominciando dalla fine: il percorso° in bici, il tempo trovato uscendo di fabbrica, diverso da quello di quando c'era entrato la sera prima, e le grane° sul lavoro, le voci che correvano nel reparto°, e così via.

A quell'ora, la casa era sempre poco scaldata°, ma Elide s'era tutta spogliata, un po' rabbrividendo°, e si lavava, nello stanzino da bagno. Dietro veniva lui, più con calma, si spogliava e si lavava anche

---

...si davano un bacio, apriva la porta e già la si sentiva correre giù per le scale.

---

lui, lentamente, si toglieva di dosso° la polvere° e l'unto° dell'officina. Così stando tutti e due intorno allo stesso lavabo°, mezzo nudi, un po' intirizziti°, ogni tanto dandosi delle spinte°, togliendosi di mano il sapone, il dentifricio, e continuando a dire le cose che avevano da dirsi, veniva il momento della confidenza, e alle volte, magari° aiutandosi a vicenda° a strofinarsi° la schiena°, s'insinuava° una carezza, e si trovavano abbracciati.

Ma tutt'a un tratto° Elide: — Dio! Che ora è già! — e correva a infilarsi° il reggicalze°, la gonna, tutto in fretta, in piedi, e con la spazzola° già andava su e giù per i capelli, e sporgeva il viso allo specchio del comò°, con le mollette° strette tra le labbra. Arturo le veniva dietro°, aveva acceso una sigaretta, e la guardava stando in piedi, fumando, e ogni volta pareva un po' impacciato°, di dover stare lì senza poter fare nulla. Elide era pronta, infilava il cappotto nel corridoio, si davano un bacio, apriva la porta e già la si sentiva correre giù per le scale.

Margin glossary (left column):
- way/he used to cover
- overlapped
- reaching her
- squeeze
- buried
- abruptly
- slipped/blindly
- was taking out/containers
- lunch box
- kitchen sink
- put on (the stove)
- felt like
- open wide
- she were ashamed
- half asleep
- emerging/both
- both are equal
- Sometimes
- to wake her up
- sort
- slow
- hug
- rain jacket/feeling it
- according to
- began

Margin glossary (right column):
- grumbling
- going over/nuisances
- he had encountered
- journey
- troubles
- division
- heated
- shivering
- would take off
- dust/grease
- sink
- numb with cold
- pushes
- perhaps/reciprocally
- wash, scrub/back/would slip in
- all of a sudden
- put on
- garter belt
- brush
- dresser/hair pins
- would follow her
- clumsy

Arturo restava solo. Seguiva il rumore dei tacchi di Elide giù per i gradini°, e quando non la sentiva più continuava a seguirla col pensiero, quel trotterellare° veloce per il cortile°, il portone°, il marciapiede, fino alla fermata del tram. Il tram lo sentiva bene, invece: stridere°, fermarsi, e lo sbattere° della

steps
steps
courtyard/street door
screeching/slamming

———

...strisciava un piede verso il posto di suo marito, per cercare il calore di lui...

———

pedana° a ogni persona che saliva. «Ecco, l'ha preso», pensava, e vedeva sua moglie aggrappata° in mezzo alla folla d'operai e operaie sull'«undici»°, che la portava in fabbrica come tutti i giorni. Spegneva la cicca°, chiudeva gli sportelli° alla finestra, faceva buio, entrava in letto.

Il letto era come l'aveva lasciato Elide alzandosi, ma dalla parte sua, di Arturo, era quasi intatto°, come fosse stato rifatto allora. Lui si coricava dalla propria parte, per bene°, ma dopo allungava° una gamba in là, dov'era rimasto il calore di sua moglie, poi ci allungava anche l'altra gamba, e così a poco a poco si spostava° tutto dalla parte di Elide, in quella nicchia° di tepore° che conservava ancora la forma del corpo di lei, e affondava il viso nel suo guanciale, nel suo profumo, e s'addormentava.

Quando Elide tornava, alla sera, Arturo già da un po' girava° per le stanze: aveva acceso la stufa°, messo qualcosa a cuocere. Certi lavori li faceva lui, in quelle ore prima di cena, come rifare il letto, spazzare° un po', anche mettere a bagno° la roba da lavare. Elide poi trovava tutto malfatto°, ma lui a dir la verità non ci metteva nessun impegno° in più: quello che lui faceva era solo una specie di rituale per aspettare lei, quasi un venirle incontro° pur restando tra le pareti° di casa, mentre fuori s'accendevano le luci

wooden step
hanging
tram number eleven
cigarette butt/shutters
undisturbed
dutifully/would stretch
would move
niche/warmth
was walking around
stove
sweep/soak
badly done
did not put any effort into it
meeting her/walls

e lei passava per le botteghe° in mezzo a quell'animazione fuori tempo dei quartieri dove ci sono tante donne che fanno la spesa alla sera.

Alla fine sentiva il passo per la scala, tutto diverso da quello della mattina, adesso appesantito°, perché Elide saliva stanca dalla giornata di lavoro e carica° della spesa.

Arturo usciva sul pianerottolo°, le prendeva di mano la sporta°, entravano parlando. Lei si buttava° su una sedia in cucina, senza togliersi il cappotto, intanto che lui levava° la roba° dalla sporta. Poi: —Su, diamoci un addrizzo° lei diceva,— e s'alzava, si toglieva il cappotto, si metteva in veste da casa°. Cominciavano a preparare da mangiare: cena per tutt'e due, poi la merenda che si portava lui in fabbrica per l'intervallo° dell'una di notte, la colazione che doveva portarsi in fabbrica lei l'indomani°, e quella da lasciare pronta per quando lui l'indomani si sarebbe svegliato.

Lei un po' sfaccendava° un po' si sedeva sulla seggiola di paglia° e diceva a lui cosa doveva fare. Lui invece era l'ora in cui era riposato°, si dava attorno°, anzi voleva far tutto lui, ma sempre un po' distratto, con la testa già ad altro. In quei momenti lì, alle volte arrivavano sul punto di urtarsi°, di dirsi qualche parola brutta, perché lei lo avrebbe voluto più attento a quello che faceva, che ci mettesse più impegno, oppure che fosse più attaccato° a lei, le stesse più vicino, le desse più consolazione°. Invece lui, dopo il primo entusiasmo perché lei era tornata, stava già con la testa fuori di casa, fissato° nel pensiero di far presto perché doveva andare.

Apparecchiata° tavola, messa tutta la roba pronta a portata di mano per non doversi più alzare, allora c'era il momento dello struggimento° che li pigliava° tutti e due d'avere così poco tempo per stare insieme, e quasi non riuscivano° a portarsi il cucchiaio alla bocca, dalla voglia che avevano di star lì a tenersi per mano°.

shops
weighed down
loaded
landing
grocery bag
would throw herself
would take out/stuff
let's get a move on
apron
break
the day after
got busy
straw chair
was rested/would run around
hurt one another
attached
comfort
(trans)fixed
Set
anguish/would seize them
didn't manage
hold hands

was after

soft/warm

would hoist/crossbar 180

from top to bottom

shaking/head

175 Ma non era ancora passato tutto il caffè e già lui era dietro° la bicicletta a vedere se ogni cosa era in ordine. S'abbracciavano. Arturo sembrava che solo allora capisse com'era morbida° e tiepida° la sua sposa. Ma si caricava° sulla spalla la canna° della bici e scendeva attento le scale.

Elide lavava i piatti, riguardava la casa da cima a fondo°, le cose che aveva fatto il marito, scuotendo° il capo°.

Ora lui correva le strade buie, tra i radi° fanali°, forse era già dopo il gasometro°. Elide andava a letto, spegneva° la luce. Dalla propria parte, coricata°, strisciava° un piede verso il posto di suo marito, per cercare il calore di lui, ma ogni volta s'accorgeva° che dove dormiva lei era più caldo, segno che anche Arturo aveva dormito lì, e ne provava° una grande tenerezza°. ∎

185 *scarce*

head lights/gas station

turned off

lying down/would slither

190 *realized*

felt/tenderness

Analisi

1

Comprensione Metti in ordine i seguenti pezzi del racconto.

___4___ a. La mattina tutti e due si lavano in bagno.

___7___ b. I due cenano insieme.

___1___ c. L'operaio Arturo Massolari fa il turno di notte.

___8___ d. Quando Arturo va al lavoro in bicicletta, Elide lo segue con il pensiero.

___3___ e. Elide domanda che tempo fa.

___5___ f. Arturo ascolta i rumori in strada e immagina la moglie che va al lavoro.

___2___ g. Quando Arturo arriva a casa Elide dorme e Arturo le prepara il caffè.

___6___ h. Quando Elide torna, Arturo ha fatto qualche faccenda (*chore*) e si scambiano delle parole.

2

Interpretazione Scegli le risposte che ti sembrano giuste e poi confrontale con quelle di un(a) compagno/a.

1. Elide sente arrivare il marito perché _____.
   a. suona la sveglia   b. nel sonno sente i suoi passi in cucina
   c. non ha potuto dormire

2. Elide si vergogna un po' perché _____.
   a. non ha preparato lei il caffè   b. è ancora in vestaglia
   c. sembra che abbia sempre sonno mentre lui è sveglio

3. Dal giaccone di Arturo, Elide capisce _____.
   a. se Arturo ha fatto una doccia   b. se deve fare il bucato
   c. che tempo fa senza chiederlo

4. In bagno i due _____.
   a. condividono sapone, dentifricio, parole e carezze
   b. aspettano il proprio turno senza parlare   c. si rubano il sapone e litigano

5. Arturo cerca il lato di Elide nel letto perché _____.
   a. è un modo per sentirsi vicino a lei   b. è più comodo del suo lato
   c. lui non ha il comodino

6. Seduti a cena Arturo ed Elide _____.
   a. chiacchierano e si divertono   b. sono allegri perché hanno un po' di
   tempo insieme   c. sono tristi perché sanno che hanno poco tempo

3

I protagonisti In coppia, rispondete alle seguenti domande.

1. Perché Elide è imbarazzata la mattina?

2. Come sono i momenti di intimità tra Arturo ed Elide?

3. Quali gesti di affetto si scambiano? Fate almeno quattro esempi.

4. Perché sono nervosi prima di cena?

5. Che aggettivi usereste per descrivere Arturo ed Elide?

6. Quanti anni pensate che abbiano Arturo ed Elide?

7. Secondo voi, si vogliono bene? Da cosa lo deducete?

4

La routine di Arturo ed Elide Discuti con un(a) compagno/a i seguenti punti.

1. In che modo la routine dei due sposi è simile? Pensate a cosa fa Elide quando Arturo non c'è e viceversa.

2. Come sarebbe la loro routine se avessero dei bambini?

3. Perché viene usato l'imperfetto per raccontare questa storia?

4. Quanto interferisce la vita esterna con la loro vita di coppia?

5. La vita esterna dei due sposi non viene rappresentata in forma diretta attraverso la narrazione ma si racconta indirettamente. Come? Potete ricostruire il mondo esterno attraverso la routine di Arturo ed Elide?

6. C'è qualcosa di positivo nella routine della coppia? Cosa?

The imperfect underscores how the events told are routine: they are always the same, day in, day out. Ask how the story would be different if it were told in the **passato remoto** (or **prossimo**).

5

Relazioni personali e lavoro In piccoli gruppi, rispondete alle domande.

1. Immaginate che Arturo ed Elide siano già in pensione. Come sarebbe la loro vita? Pensate che gli mancherebbe il lavoro? Perché?

2. Che tipo di sacrifici fareste per le vostre famiglie? Fareste un lavoro che non vi piace o che vi porta lontano dalla famiglia?

3. Pensate ai vostri nonni e ai vostri genitori. Quanto interferiva il lavoro nella vita familiare? Quanto interferiva nel lavoro la vita familiare?

4. Fareste dei sacrifici personali per un lavoro molto importante? Perché?

6

La vita insieme In piccoli gruppi, scrivete e recitate una scenetta in cui due coppie di vicini di casa o di colleghi di lavoro si trovano a cena e parlano dei loro orari di lavoro (che devono essere completamente diversi). In caso siate in numero dispari, un marito o una moglie può essere sempre da solo/a perché l'altro è sempre in viaggio per lavoro. Considerate le seguenti idee.

6 Students may imagine any kind of scenario. This exercise can also be done as a take-home composition to be graded separately from an in-class "performance." Having students memorize short dialogues helps.

- turni di notte contro turni di giorno

- cosa spinge a scegliere un determinato lavoro: perché scegliere un lavoro con un orario difficile, quali sono i vantaggi

- lavoro in fabbrica, ufficio, scuola contro lavoro da casa

- pranzi a casa contro panino veloce al lavoro

7

Tema Scegli una di queste situazioni e scrivi un tema di almeno tre paragrafi.

- Ti hanno offerto un lavoro fantastico ma è dall'altra parte del paese. La tua relazione ne soffrirà sicuramente, ma per fortuna esistono gli aerei. Scrivi un e-mail al(la) tuo/a migliore amico/a per chiedere consigli. Esponi tutti i problemi del caso: distanza, situazione economica, vacanze, ecc.

- Ti hanno offerto un lavoro notturno. La paga è buona, ma riuscirai a mantenere intatta la tua relazione? Scrivi la lettera che daresti al(la) tuo/a partner per spiegare perché dovresti accettare il lavoro e quali saranno i sacrifici da fare.

Practice more at **vhlcentral.com**.

Pratica

Punti chiave per un buon saggio

Non esiste una formula infallibile per scrivere un buon saggio: ciò che imparerai con la pratica e leggendo buoni esempi ti aiuterà. Fai comunque attenzione ai seguenti elementi:

Concisione Evita la ridondanza sia del linguaggio che delle idee. Non ripetere quello che hai già detto. Evita le parole che non sono necessarie e semplifica il più possibile ogni frase.

Tono Usa un tono adeguato a seconda del pubblico e delle tue intenzioni. Non usare un tono eccessivamente informale né troppo elevato.

Linguaggio Usa parole definite e concrete. Concentrati sulle parole principali di ogni frase e chiediti quali associazioni di idee saranno suggerite al lettore dalle tue parole.

Fluidità Le tue argomentazioni devono scorrere chiaramente dall'inizio alla fine. Se ci sono frasi o paragrafi che potrebbero confondere (*to confuse*) il lettore, cambiali. Va bene presentare una varietà di idee e sorprendere il lettore ma bisogna fare attenzione a non confonderlo.

1

Preparazione Leggete il seguente paragrafo e confrontatelo con la biografia a **pagina 413**. Come sono diversi? Perché questa versione non è un esempio da seguire?

Calvino (1923–1985) era uno scrittore molto amato. È amato da grandi e bambini. Molte delle sue favole allegoriche possono essere lette e apprezzate da grandi e da bambini. Tutti lo apprezzano. Calvino è nato a Cuba. Cresce in Liguria durante gli anni del fascismo e trova un modo sicuro per raccontare le sue idee. È amico di Cesare Pavese ed Elio Vittorini. È un narratore importante degli anni '50 e '60. Ha scritto romanzi, saggi, racconti e articoli. Ha raccolto fiabe antiche della tradizione fiabistica popolare italiana. È anche uno scrittore sperimentale. È molto attento ai meccanismi narrativi.

2

Saggio Scegli uno di questi argomenti e scrivi un saggio.

- Il saggio deve far riferimento ad almeno due dei quattro brani studiati in questa lezione o nelle precedenti lezioni e contenuti in **Cortometraggio**, **Immagina**, **Cultura** e **Letteratura**.

- Il saggio deve essere lungo almeno tre pagine.

- Una volta concluso il saggio, rivedilo e controlla che sia conciso, fluido e che il tono e il linguaggio siano adeguati.

> Nella società in cui viviamo, l'apparenza e il successo sembrano contare più di chi siamo. Secondo te, quali fattori determinano l'essenza di una persona? Qual è il giusto equilibrio tra apparenza, posizione sociale e il vero «io»?

> Il lavoro serve per sostenere la famiglia, ma spesso porta via tempo agli affetti. Esiste una via di mezzo?

> Dai brani studiati in questa lezione, quali riflessioni sono possibili sul rapporto uomo/donna e lavoro?

Il lavoro e le finanze

 Vocabulary Tools

La ricerca di lavoro

l'agenzia di collocamento job agency
la carriera career
il colloquio di lavoro job interview
il curriculum (vitae) résumé
l'esperienza (professionale) (professional) experience
la formazione education; training
l'intervistatore/intervistatrice interviewer
il mestiere occupation; trade
il posto/la posizione job
le qualifiche qualifications
lo/la stagista intern

fare domanda (per un lavoro) to apply (for a job)
impiegare to employ

La gente al lavoro

il capo boss
il/la consulente consultant
il/la contabile accountant
il direttore/la direttrice manager
il/la dirigente executive
l'impiegato/a employee
il/la proprietario/a owner
il/la segretario/a secretary

Al lavoro

il/la collega colleague
la ditta/l'azienda company
le ferie holidays
il lavoro a orario normale/ridotto full-/part-time job
l'orario di lavoro work hours
la promozione promotion
lo sciopero strike
il sindacato labor union
lo stipendio (minimo) (minimum) wage
l'ufficio office

andare in pensione to retire
dare le dimissioni to quit
dirigere to manage
fare lo straordinario to work overtime
guadagnare to earn

licenziare to fire

Le finanze

la bancarotta bankruptcy
il bancomat ATM
la borsa stock exchange
la carta di credito credit card
la cifra figure, number
il conto (corrente) (checking) account
la crisi economica economic crisis
il debito debt
il mercato immobiliare real estate market
il prestito loan
la recessione recession
la ricevuta; lo scontrino receipt
il risparmio savings
lo sportello window; counter
la tassa tax
il tasso (d'interesse) (interest) rate

approfittare to take advantage of
aprire/chiudere un conto to open/close an account
avere dei debiti to be in debt
cambiare un assegno to cash a check
depositare/versare to deposit
fare un mutuo to take out a mortgage
fare un prelievo/deposito to make a withdrawal/deposit
investire to invest
risparmiare to save

a breve/lungo termine short-/long-term
finanziario/a financial
prospero/a successful

Cortometraggio

l'annuncio (di lavoro) (job) ad
la casalinga housewife
la direzione management
il fioraio florist
l'impegno commitment
gli occhiali da sole sunglasses
la piscina swimming pool
lo sguardo gaze

la società firm; society
il/la socio/a (business) partner

affidare to entrust
assumere to hire
rinunciare to give up

disoccupato/a unemployed

Cultura

l'abbigliamento clothing
l'abito (men's) suit
il capo (di abbigliamento) article (of clothing)
la cravatta tie
i gioielli jewelry
la (mini)gonna (mini)skirt
la griffe designer label
il look dressing style
la marca brand
gli orecchini earrings
i pantaloni (lunghi/corti) (long/short) pants
la richiesta demand
i sandali sandals
il settore sector
la sfilata (fashion) parade
lo stile style
lo/la stilista fashion designer
il tailleur (invar.) (women's) suit
il tatuaggio tattoo
il trucco makeup

Letteratura

la confidenza intimacy
la dolcezza sweetness
la fabbrica/l'officina factory
il fraintendimento misunderstanding
il guanciale pillow
l'odore smell
il rumore noise
la smorfia smirk
la sveglia alarm clock
il turno di lavoro work shift
la vestaglia robe

coricarsi to lie down
rincasare to go back home
spogliarsi to undress
stirarsi to stretch

APPENDICE

Punti per la revisione dei saggi

Per correggere il tuo lavoro, devi essere obiettivo e devi avere un buon occhio critico.

Prova a leggere il tuo saggio come se lo avesse scritto un'altra persona: ti convince? Ci sono elementi che ti lasciano perplesso o ti disturbano? Questa lista ti aiuterà a rivedere tutti gli aspetti del tuo saggio, dalle caratteristiche generali ai dettagli.

Primo passo: una visione generale

Tema

Il saggio risponde alla domanda o al tema assegnato?

Tesi

Hai comunicato chiaramente la tua tesi?

La tesi non è la stessa cosa del tema: è un argomento specifico che determina la struttura del saggio.

L'idea della tesi deve apparire nel primo paragrafo, deve essere presente in tutto il saggio e deve riassumersi, ma non semplicemente ripetersi, nella conclusione.

Logica e struttura

Leggi il saggio dall'inizio alla fine e concentrati sull'organizzazione delle idee.

Ogni idea si relaziona con la successiva? Elimina qualsiasi mancanza di continuità.

Ci sono parti irrilevanti o che devono essere spostate?

Hai sostenuto la tua tesi con un numero di argomenti sufficienti o mancano degli esempi?

Pubblico

Il saggio deve essere adeguato (*appropriate*) al tipo di lettore.

Se il lettore non è informato sul tema, assicurati di presentare un contenuto sufficientemente ricco perché possa seguire il tuo ragionamento. Spiega i termini che potrebbero confonderlo.

Adatta il tono e il vocabolario al tipo di pubblico. Pensa sempre al tuo lettore come a qualcuno intelligente e scettico che non accetterà le tue idee se non lo convincono. Il tono non deve essere eccessivamente colloquiale, affettato o frivolo.

Intenzione

Se vuoi informare o spiegare un tema, devi essere preciso e meticoloso. Un saggio argomentativo si deve distinguere per l'obbiettività: evita le opinioni personali e soggettive. Puoi cercare di persuadere il lettore con opinioni personali e giudizi di valore solo se sono sostenuti da argomenti logici.

Secondo passo: il paragrafo

Concentrati su ogni paragrafo con queste domande in mente:

Paragrafo

C'è una frase principale in ogni paragrafo? L'idea centrale non solo deve dare coerenza e unità al paragrafo, ma deve anche indirizzarlo verso la tesi principale del saggio.

Com'è la transizione da un paragrafo all'altro? Se è chiara, conferirà fluidità al saggio; se è brusca, può creare confusione e irritare il lettore.

Come inizia e come finisce il saggio? L'introduzione deve essere interessante e deve indicare chiaramente la tesi del saggio. La conclusione non deve limitarsi a ripetere quello che è stato detto: come qualsiasi altro paragrafo, deve presentare un'idea originale.

Leggi il paragrafo, se è possibile a voce alta, e presta attenzione al ritmo del linguaggio. Se tutte le frasi sono uguali, la lettura diventa monotona e noiosa. Cerca di variare la lunghezza delle frasi e il ritmo.

Terzo passo: la frase

Come ultimo passo, leggi minuziosamente tutte le frasi.

Frasi

Cerca le parole appropriate per ogni tipo di situazione. Considera i possibili sinonimi. Usa sempre un linguaggio diretto, preciso e completo.

Evita la ridondanza. Elimina ogni frase o parola che potrebbe creare distrazione o che potrebbe ripetere quello che hai già detto.

Controlla la grammatica. Assicurati che ci sia concordanza tra il soggetto e il verbo, tra i sostantivi e gli aggettivi e tra i pronomi e i loro antecedenti. Assicurati di usare le preposizioni giuste.

Controlla l'ortografia. Fai particolarmente attenzione agli accenti.

Valutazione e progresso

Revisione

Se è possibile, scambia il tuo saggio con un(a) compagno/a e ascolta i suggerimenti per migliorare il tuo lavoro. Considera quello che cambieresti, ma anche quello che ti piace.

Correzioni

Quando l'insegnante ti riconsegna (*gives back*) il saggio, leggi i commenti e le correzioni. Prepara una pagina dal titolo: **Note per migliorare i lavori di scrittura** e fai una lista dei tuoi errori più comuni. Conservala insieme al saggio in una cartella dei lavori e consultala regolarmente. In questo modo potrai valutare i tuoi progressi ed evitare di cadere sempre negli stessi errori.

Verb conjugation tables

Below you will find the infinitive of the verbs introduced as active vocabulary in **Immagina**, as well as other model verbs. Each verb is followed by a model verb conjugated on the same pattern. The number in parentheses indicates where in the verb tables, pages **A5–A16**, you can find the conjugated forms of the model verb. The phrase "**p.p. with essere**" after a verb means that it is conjugated with **essere** in the **passato prossimo** and all other compound tenses (see page **A6**). The reference "**1-3-3 verb**" in this table indicates that the verb is regular in all forms except the past participle, and the following forms of the **passato remoto**: first person singular, third person singular, and third person plural. The irregular forms for these types of verbs are listed on pages **A15–A16**. For reflexive verbs, the list usually points to a non-reflexive model and includes a reminder that compound tenses are formed with **essere**. A full conjugation of the simple forms of a reflexive verb is presented in Verb table 5 on page **A5**.

abbaiare like cambiare (13)
abbracciarsi like adorare (1)
 except **p.p.** with **essere**
abitare like adorare (1)
abituarsi like adorare (1)
 except **p.p.** with **essere**
abolire like capire (4)
abusare like adorare (1)
accogliere like togliere (49)
accomodarsi like adorare (1)
 except **p.p.** with **essere**
accorgersi like credere (2) *except*
 1-3-3 verb and **p.p.** with **essere**
adagiarsi like mangiare (27)
 except **p.p.** with **essere**
adattarsi like adorare (1)
 except **p.p.** with **essere**
addormentarsi like adorare
 (1) *except* **p.p.** with **essere**
adeguarsi like adorare (1)
 except **p.p.** with **essere**
adorare (1)
affidare like adorare (1)
aggiornare like adorare (1)
aggrapparsi like adorare (1)
 except **p.p.** with **essere**
aiutarsi like adorare (1) *except*
 p.p. with **essere**
allegare like litigare (26)
allenarsi like adorare (1)
 except **p.p.** with **essere**
allontanarsi like adorare
 (1) *except* **p.p.** with **essere**
alzare like adorare (1)
alzarsi (5)
amare like adorare (1)
amarsi like adorare (1) *except*
 p.p. with **essere**
andare (8)
andarsene like andare (8)
annoiarsi like cambiare (13)
 except **p.p.** with **essere**
apparire (9)
appartenere like tenere (48)
applaudire like dormire (3)
approfittare like adorare (1)
approfondire like capire (4)
approvare like adorare (1)
aprire (10)
arrabbiarsi like cambiare (13)
 except **p.p.** with **essere**

arrendersi like prendere (35)
 except **p.p.** with **essere**
arricchirsi like capire (4)
arrivare like adorare (1)
 except **p.p.** with **essere**
asciugarsi like litigare (26)
 except **p.p.** with essere
ascoltare like adorare (1)
aspettare like adorare (1)
aspettarsi like adorare (1)
 except **p.p.** with **essere**
assistere like credere (2) *except*
 past participle is **assistito**
assomigliare like cambiare (13)
assumere like credere (2)
 except **1-3-3** verb
assumersi like credere (2)
 except **p.p.** with **essere**
attraversare like adorare (1)
aumentare like adorare (1)
avere (6)
avvenire like venire (55)
avvicinarsi like adorare (1)
 except **p.p.** with **essere**
baciarsi like adorare (1)
 except **p.p.** with **essere**
bastare like adorare (1)
battere like credere (2)
bere (11)
bruciare like cominciare (16)
bussare like adorare (1)
buttare like adorare (1)
cadere (12)
cambiare (13)
campeggiare like mangiare (27)
cancellare like adorare (1)
cantare like adorare (1)
capire (4)
capitare like adorare (1)
censurare like adorare (1)
cercare (14)
cessare like adorare (1)
chattare like adorare (1)
chiacchierare like adorare (1)
chiamare like adorare (1)
chiamarsi like adorare (1)
 except **p.p.** with **essere**
chiedere (15)
clonare like adorare (1)
cogliere like togliere (49)
colonizzare like adorare (1)
coltivare like adorare (1)

combattere like credere (2)
cominciare (16)
comporre like porre (33)
condividere like credere (2)
 except **1-3-3** verb
condurre like produrre (36)
conformarsi like adorare (1)
 except **p.p.** with **essere**
conoscere like credere (2) *except*
 1-3-3 verb and **p.p.** with **essere**
conoscersi like adorare (1)
 except **p.p.** with **essere**
conquistare like adorare (1)
consigliare like cambiare (13)
contare like adorare (1)
continuare like adorare (1)
copiare like cambiare (13)
coprire di like aprire (10)
coricarsi like adorare (1)
 except **p.p.** with **essere**
correggere like credere (2)
 except **1-3-3** verb
correre like credere (2)
 except **1-3-3** verb
credere (2)
crescere like credere (2)
 except **1-3-3** verb
cuocere (17)
dare (18)
decidere like credere (2)
 except **1-3-3** verb
dedicarsi like adorare (1)
 except **p.p.** with **essere**
depositare like adorare (1)
desiderare like adorare (1)
difendere like prendere (35)
digitare like adorare (1)
dimenticarsi like dimenticare
 (19) *except* **p.p.** with **essere**
diminuire like capire (4)
dimostrare like adorare (1)
dipendere like prendere (35)
dipingere like dormire (3)
 except **1-3-3** verb
dire (20)
dirigere like credere (2) *except*
 1-3-3 verb
discutere like credere (2)
 except **1-3-3** verb
disfarsi like fare (23)
 except **p.p.** with **essere**
dispiacere like tacere (47)

dissentire like dormire (3)
disturbare like adorare (1)
divenire like venire (55)
diventare like adorare (1)
divertirsi like dormire (3)
 except **p.p.** with **essere**
dividere like credere (2) *except*
 1-3-3 verb
divorziare like cambiare (13)
dolere (21)
dormire (3)
dovere (22)
dubitare like credere (2)
educare like cercare (14)
eleggere like credere (2)
 except **1-3-3** verb
entrare like adorare (1)
ereditare like adorare (1)
esaurirsi like capire (4)
 except **p.p.** with **essere**
esigere like credere (2) *except*
 1-3-3 verb
espellere like credere (2)
 except **1-3-3** verb
essere (7)
fare (23)
farsi like fare (23) *except* **p.p.**
 with **essere**
ferirsi like capire (4) *except* **p.p.**
 with **essere**
fermare like adorare (1)
fermarsi like adorare (1)
 except **p.p.** with **essere**
festeggiare like mangiare (27)
fidanzarsi like adorare (1)
 except **p.p.** with **essere**
fidarsi like adorare (1)
 except **p.p.** with **essere**
filmare like adorare (1)
fingere like credere (2) *except*
 1-3-3 verb
finire like capire (4)
fregare like litigare (26)
fregarsene like litigare (26)
 except **p.p.** with **essere**
fucilare like adorare (1)
fuggire like dormire (3)
giocare (24)
girare like adorare (1)
giudicare like dimenticare (19)
giurare like adorare (1)
governare like adorare (1)

guadagnare like sognare (44)
guarire like capire (4)
guidare like adorare (1)
immaginare like adorare (1)
imparare like adorare (1)
impazzire like capire (4)
impedire like capire (4)
impiegare like litigare (26)
imporre like porre (33)
importare like adorare (1)
impoverirsi like capire (4)
  except **p.p.** with **essere**
imprigionare like adorare (1)
improvvisare like adorare (1)
incollare like adorare (1)
incontrarsi like adorare (1)
  except **p.p.** with **essere**
incoraggiare like mangiare (27)
indossare like adorare (1)
influenzare like adorare (1)
informarsi like adorare (1)
  except **p.p.** with **essere**
ingrassare like adorare (1)
innamorarsi like adorare (1)
  except **p.p.** with **essere**
insegnare like sognare (44)
insistere like crędere (2)
  except past participle is **insistito**
interessare like adorare (1)
intervistare like adorare (1)
invądere like crędere (2)
  except **1-3-3** verb
invecchiare like cambiare (13)
investire like dormire (3)
inviare (25)
invitare like adorare (1)
lamentare like adorare (1)
lamentarsi like adorare (1)
  except **p.p.** with **essere**
lasciare like cominciare (16)
lavarsi like adorare (1) *except*
  p.p. with **essere**
lęggere like crędere (2) *except*
  1-3-3 verb
legiferare like adorare (1)
liberare like adorare (1)
licenziare like adorare (1)
litigare (26)
lottare like adorare (1)
maledire like dire (20)
mancare like cercare (14)
mandare like adorare (1)
mangiare (27)
manifestare like adorare (1)
masterizzare like adorare (1)
mentire like dormire (3)
meritare like adorare (1)
męttere (28)
męttersi like męttere (28)
  except **p.p.** with **essere**
mobilitare like adorare (1)
mollare like adorare (1)
morire (29)
muǫvere (30)
muǫversi like muǫvere (30)
  except **p.p.** with **essere**
nąscere like crędere (2)
  except **1-3-3** verb

nascǫndere like crędere (2)
  except **1-3-3** verb
navigare like litigare (26)
nuǫcere (31)
obbligare like litigare (26)
occǫrrere like crędere (2)
  except **1-3-3** verb
occuparsi like adorare (1)
  except **p.p.** with **essere**
odiare like adorare (1)
offrire like dormire (3)
  except **1-3-3** verb
opprimere like dormire (3)
  except **1-3-3** verb
ottenere like tenere (48)
parare like adorare (1)
parcheggiare like mangiare (27)
pareggiare like mangiare (27)
parere (32)
parlare like adorare (1)
parlarsi like adorare (1)
  except **p.p.** with **essere**
partecipare like adorare (1)
partire like dormire (3)
passare like adorare (1)
passeggiare like mangiare (27)
penare like adorare (1)
pensare like adorare (1)
pentirsi like dormire (3) *except*
  p.p. with **essere**
pęrdere like crędere (2) *except*
  1-3-3 verb
pęrdersi like crędere (2) *except*
  1-3-3 verb and **p.p.** with **essere**
permęttere like męttere (28)
persuadere like crędere (2)
  except **1-3-3** verb
pescare like cercare (14)
piacere like tącere (47)
piąngere like crędere (2)
  except **1-3-3** verb
pianificare like adorare (1)
porre (33)
possedere like sedere (43)
potere (34)
predire like dire (20)
preferire like capire (4)
pregare like litigare (26)
pręndere (35)
preoccuparsi like adorare (1)
  except **p.p.** with **essere**
preparare like adorare (1)
prevedere like vedere (54)
produrre (36)
promęttere like męttere (28)
promuǫvere like muǫvere (30)
provare like adorare (1)
provarsi like adorare (1)
  except **p.p.** with **essere**
punire like capire (4)
raccǫgliere like tǫgliere (49)
realizzare like adorare (1)
reclamare like adorare (1)
registrare like adorare (1)
ręndersi like pręndere (35)
  except **p.p.** with **essere**
restare like adorare (1)
riciclare like adorare (1)

ricordarsi like adorare (1)
  except **p.p.** with **essere**
rįdere like crędere (2) *except*
  1-3-3 verb
riempire (37)
riflęttere like crędere (2) *except*
  1-3-3 verb
rimandare like adorare (1)
rimanere (38)
rimproverare like adorare (1)
rincasare like adorare (1)
ringraziare like cambiare (13)
rinunciare like cominciare (16)
riposarsi like adorare (1)
  except **p.p.** with **essere**
risǫlvere (39)
risparmiare like cambiare (13)
rispettare like adorare (1)
rispǫndere (40)
risultare like adorare (1)
ritenere like tenere (48)
ritornare like adorare (1)
riuscire like uscire (52)
rivǫlgersi like crędere (2)
  except **1-3-3** verb and **p.p.**
  with **essere**
rǫmpere like crędere (2)
  except **1-3-3** verb
rovesciare like cominciare (16)
rubare like adorare (1)
salire (41)
saltare like adorare (1)
salvare like adorare (1)
sapere (42)
sbagliare like cambiare (13)
sbrigarsi like litigare (26)
  except **p.p.** with **essere**
scalare like adorare (1)
scaricare like dimenticare (19)
scęgliere like tǫgliere (49)
scęndere like pręndere (35)
sciare like cominciare (16)
scolpire like capire (4)
scommęttere like męttere (28)
scomparire like apparire (9)
sconfįggere like crędere (2)
  except **1-3-3** verb
scrivere like crędere (2)
  except **1-3-3** verb
scriversi like crędere (2) *except*
  1-3-3 verb and **p.p.** with **essere**
sedere (43)
segnare like sognare (44)
sembrare like adorare (1)
sentirsi like dormire (3)
servire like dormire (3)
sfarsi like fare (23)
sgranchirsi like capire (4) *except*
  p.p. with **essere**
smęttere like męttere (28)
sminuire like capire (4)
soffrire like aprire (10)
sognare (44)
sopravvįvere like vįvere (57)
sormontare like adorare (1)
sorrįdere like crędere (2)
  except **1-3-3** verb
sparire like capire (4)
spęgnere (45)

sperare like adorare (1)
spettinare like adorare (1)
spiare like adorare (1)
spiegare like litigare (26)
spįngere like crędere (2)
  except **1-3-3** verb
spogliarsi like adorare (1)
  except **p.p.** with **essere**
sposarsi like adorare (1)
  except **p.p.** with **essere**
squillare like adorare (1)
stabilirsi like capire (4)
  except **p.p.** with **essere**
stare (46)
stirarsi like adorare (1)
  except **p.p.** with **essere**
strįngere like crędere (2)
  except **1-3-3** verb
studiare like adorare (1)
stufarsi like adorare (1)
  except **p.p.** with **essere**
stupire like capire (4)
suggerire like capire (4)
suonare like adorare (1)
superare like adorare (1)
svegliare like cambiare (13)
svegliarsi like cambiare (13)
  except **p.p.** with **essere**
svǫlgersi like crędere (2) *except*
  1-3-3 verb and **p.p.** with **essere**
tącere (47)
telefonarsi like adorare (1)
  except **p.p.** with **essere**
temere like crędere (2)
tenere (48)
tifare like adorare (1)
tirare like adorare (1)
tǫgliere (49)
tornare like adorare (1)
tracciare like cominciare (16)
tradurre like produrre (36)
trarre (50)
trasferirsi like capire (4)
  except **p.p.** with **essere**
trasmęttere like męttere (28)
trattarsi like adorare (1)
trovarsi like adorare (1)
  except **p.p.** with **essere**
truccarsi like cercare (14)
  except **p.p.** with **essere**
tutelare like adorare (1)
udire (51)
uscire (52)
valere (53)
vantarsi like adorare (1)
  except **p.p.** with **essere**
vedere (54)
vedersi like vedere (54)
  except **p.p.** with **essere**
venire (55)
vergognarsi like sognare (44)
  except **p.p.** with **essere**
versare like adorare (1)
vestirsi like dormire (3) *except*
  p.p. with **essere**
vįncere (56)
vįvere (57)
viziare like cambiare (13)
volere (58)
votare like adorare (1)

Regular verbs: simple tenses

1. adorare (*to adore*)
Participio passato: adorato
Gerundio presente: adorando
Infinito passato: avere adorato

	INDICATIVO				CONDIZIONALE	CONGIUNTIVO		IMPERATIVO
	Presente	Imperfetto	Passato remoto	Futuro	Presente	Presente	Imperfetto	
	adoro	adoravo	adorai	adorerò	adorerei	adori	adorassi	
	adori	adoravi	adorasti	adorerai	adoreresti	adori	adorassi	adora (non adorare)
	adora	adorava	adorò	adorerà	adorerebbe	adori	adorasse	adori
	adoriamo	adoravamo	adorammo	adoreremo	adoreremmo	adoriamo	adorassimo	adoriamo
	adorate	adoravate	adoraste	adorerete	adorereste	adoriate	adoraste	adorate
	adorano	adoravano	adorarono	adoreranno	adorerebbero	adorino	adorassero	adorino

2. credere (*to believe*)
Participio passato: creduto
Gerundio presente: credendo
Infinito passato: avere creduto

	INDICATIVO				CONDIZIONALE	CONGIUNTIVO		IMPERATIVO
	Presente	Imperfetto	Passato remoto	Futuro	Presente	Presente	Imperfetto	
	credo	credevo	credei, credetti	crederò	crederei	creda	credessi	
	credi	credevi	credesti	crederai	crederesti	creda	credessi	credi (non credere)
	crede	credeva	credé, credette	crederà	crederebbe	creda	credesse	creda
	crediamo	credevamo	credemmo	crederemo	crederemmo	crediamo	credessimo	crediamo
	credete	credevate	credeste	crederete	credereste	crediate	credeste	credete
	credono	credevano	crederono, credettero	crederanno	crederebbero	credano	credessero	credano

3. dormire (*to sleep*)
Participio passato: dormito
Gerundio presente: dormendo
Infinito passato: avere dormito

	INDICATIVO				CONDIZIONALE	CONGIUNTIVO		IMPERATIVO
	Presente	Imperfetto	Passato remoto	Futuro	Presente	Presente	Imperfetto	
	dormo	dormivo	dormii	dormirò	dormirei	dorma	dormissi	
	dormi	dormivi	dormisti	dormirai	dormiresti	dorma	dormissi	dormi (non dormire)
	dorme	dormiva	dormì	dormirà	dormirebbe	dorma	dormisse	dorma
	dormiamo	dormivamo	dormimmo	dormiremo	dormiremmo	dormiamo	dormissimo	dormiamo
	dormite	dormivate	dormiste	dormirete	dormireste	dormiate	dormiste	dormite
	dormono	dormivano	dormirono	dormiranno	dormirebbero	dormano	dormissero	dormano

4. capire (*to understand*)
Participio passato: capito
Gerundio presente: capendo
Infinito passato: avere capito

	INDICATIVO				CONDIZIONALE	CONGIUNTIVO		IMPERATIVO
	Presente	Imperfetto	Passato remoto	Futuro	Presente	Presente	Imperfetto	
	capisco	capivo	capii	capirò	capirei	capisca	capissi	
	capisci	capivi	capisti	capirai	capiresti	capisca	capissi	capisci (non capire)
	capisce	capiva	capì	capirà	capirebbe	capisca	capisse	capisca
	capiamo	capivamo	capimmo	capiremo	capiremmo	capiamo	capissimo	capiamo
	capite	capivate	capiste	capirete	capireste	capiate	capiste	capite
	capiscono	capivano	capirono	capiranno	capirebbero	capiscano	capissero	capiscano

Reflexive verbs

5. alzarsi (*to get up*)
Participio passato: alzato/a
Gerundio presente: alzandosi
Infinito passato: essersi alzato/a

	INDICATIVO				CONDIZIONALE	CONGIUNTIVO		IMPERATIVO
	Presente	Imperfetto	Passato remoto	Futuro	Presente	Presente	Imperfetto	
	mi alzo	mi alzavo	mi alzai	mi alzerò	mi alzerei	mi alzi	mi alzassi	
	ti alzi	ti alzavi	ti alzasti	ti alzerai	ti alzeresti	ti alzi	ti alzassi	alzati (non alzarti/ non ti alzare)
	si alza	si alzava	si alzò	si alzerà	si alzerebbe	si alzi	si alzasse	si alzi
	ci alziamo	ci alzavamo	ci alzammo	ci alzeremo	ci alzeremmo	ci alziamo	ci alzassimo	alziamoci
	vi alzate	vi alzavate	vi alzaste	vi alzerete	vi alzereste	vi alziate	vi alzaste	alzatevi
	si alzano	si alzavano	si alzarono	si alzeranno	si alzerebbero	si alzino	si alzassero	si alzino

Auxiliary verbs

6 avere (to have)

Infinito / Participio passato / Gerundio presente / Infinito passato		INDICATIVO				CONDIZIONALE	CONGIUNTIVO		IMPERATIVO
		Presente	Imperfetto	Passato remoto	Futuro	Presente	Presente	Imperfetto	
avere (to have)		ho	avevo	ebbi	avrò	avrei	abbia	avessi	
avuto		hai	avevi	avesti	avrai	avresti	abbia	avessi	abbi (non avere)
avendo		ha	aveva	ebbe	avrà	avrebbe	abbia	avesse	abbia
avere avuto		abbiamo	avevamo	avemmo	avremo	avremmo	abbiamo	avessimo	abbiamo
		avete	avevate	aveste	avrete	avreste	abbiate	aveste	abbiate
		hanno	avevano	ebbero	avranno	avrebbero	abbiano	avessero	abbiano

7 essere (to be)

Infinito / Participio passato / Gerundio presente / Infinito passato		Presente	Imperfetto	Passato remoto	Futuro	Presente	Presente	Imperfetto	IMPERATIVO
essere (to be)		sono	ero	fui	sarò	sarei	sia	fossi	
stato/a		sei	eri	fosti	sarai	saresti	sia	fossi	sii (non essere)
essendo		è	era	fu	sarà	sarebbe	sia	fosse	sia
essere stato/a		siamo	eravamo	fummo	saremo	saremmo	siamo	fossimo	siamo
		siete	eravate	foste	sarete	sareste	siate	foste	siate
		sono	erano	furono	saranno	sarebbero	siano	fossero	siano

Compound tenses

Ausiliare	INDICATIVO								CONDIZIONALE		CONGIUNTIVO			
	Passato prossimo		Trapassato prossimo		Trapassato remoto		Futuro anteriore		Passato		Passato		Trapassato	
avere	ho	adorato	avevo	adorato	ebbi	adorato	avrò	adorato	avrei	adorato	abbia	adorato	avessi	adorato
	hai	perduto	avevi	perduto	avesti	perduto	avrai	perduto	avresti	perduto	abbia	perduto	avessi	perduto
	ha	dormito	aveva	dormito	ebbe	dormito	avrà	dormito	avrebbe	dormito	abbia	dormito	avesse	dormito
	abbiamo	capito	avevamo	capito	avemmo	capito	avremo	capito	avremmo	capito	abbiamo	capito	avessimo	capito
	avete		avevate		aveste		avrete		avreste		abbiate		aveste	
	hanno		avevano		ebbero		avranno		avrebbero		abbiano		avessero	
essere	sono andato/a		ero andato/a		fui andato/a		sarò andato/a		sarei andato/a		sia andato/a		fossi andato/a	
	sei andato/a		eri andato/a		fosti andato/a		sarai andato/a		saresti andato/a		sia andato/a		fossi andato/a	
	è andato/a		era andato/a		fu andato/a		sarà andato/a		sarebbe andato/a		sia andato/a		fosse andato/a	
	siamo andati/e		eravamo andati/e		fummo andati/e		saremo andati/e		saremmo andati/e		siamo andati/e		fossimo andati/e	
	siete andati/e		eravate andati/e		foste andati/e		sarete andati/e		sareste andati/e		siate andati/e		foste andati/e	
	sono andati/e		erano andati/e		furono andati/e		saranno andati/e		sarebbero andati/e		siano andati/e		fossero andati/e	

Irregular verbs

8 — andare (*to go*); andato/a; andando; essere andato/a

	INDICATIVO Presente	Imperfetto	Passato remoto	Futuro	CONDIZIONALE Presente	CONGIUNTIVO Presente	Imperfetto	IMPERATIVO
	vado	andavo	andai	andrò	andrei	vada	andassi	
	vai	andavi	andasti	andrai	andresti	vada	andassi	vai, va' (non andare)
	va	andava	andò	andrà	andrebbe	vada	andasse	vada
	andiamo	andavamo	andammo	andremo	andremmo	andiamo	andassimo	andiamo
	andate	andavate	andaste	andrete	andreste	andiate	andaste	andate
	vanno	andavano	andarono	andranno	andrebbero	vadano	andassero	vadano

9 — apparire (*to appear*); apparso/a; apparendo; essere apparso/a

	INDICATIVO Presente	Imperfetto	Passato remoto	Futuro	CONDIZIONALE Presente	CONGIUNTIVO Presente	Imperfetto	IMPERATIVO
	appaio	apparivo	apparii, apparvi	apparirò	apparirei	appaia	apparissi	
	appari	apparivi	apparisti	apparirai	appariresti	appaia	apparissi	appari (non apparire)
	appare	appariva	apparì, apparve	apparirà	apparirebbe	appaia	apparisse	appaia
	appariamo	apparivamo	apparimmo	appariremo	appariremmo	appariamo	apparissimo	appariamo
	apparite	apparivate	appariste	apparirete	apparireste	appariate	appariste	apparite
	appaiono	apparivano	apparirono, apparvero	appariranno	apparirebbero	appaiano	apparissero	appaiano

10 — aprire (*to open*); aperto; aprendo; avere aperto

	INDICATIVO Presente	Imperfetto	Passato remoto	Futuro	CONDIZIONALE Presente	CONGIUNTIVO Presente	Imperfetto	IMPERATIVO
	apro	aprivo	aprii, apersi	aprirò	aprirei	apra	aprissi	
	apri	aprivi	apristi	aprirai	apriresti	apra	aprissi	apri (non aprire)
	apre	apriva	aprì, aperse	aprirà	aprirebbe	apra	aprisse	apra
	apriamo	aprivamo	aprimmo	apriremo	apriremmo	apriamo	aprissimo	apriamo
	aprite	aprivate	apriste	aprirete	aprireste	apriate	apriste	aprite
	aprono	aprivano	aprirono, apersero	apriranno	aprirebbero	aprano	aprissero	aprano

11 — bere (*to drink*); bevuto; bevendo; avere bevuto

	INDICATIVO Presente	Imperfetto	Passato remoto	Futuro	CONDIZIONALE Presente	CONGIUNTIVO Presente	Imperfetto	IMPERATIVO
	bevo	bevevo	bevvi	berrò	berrei	beva	bevessi	
	bevi	bevevi	bevesti	berrai	berresti	beva	bevessi	bevi (non bere)
	beve	beveva	bevve	berrà	berrebbe	beva	bevesse	beva
	beviamo	bevevamo	bevemmo	berremo	berremmo	beviamo	bevessimo	beviamo
	bevete	bevevate	beveste	berrete	berreste	beviate	beveste	bevete
	bevono	bevevano	bevvero	berranno	berrebbero	bevano	bevessero	bevano

12 — cadere (*to fall*); caduto/a; cadendo; essere caduto

	INDICATIVO Presente	Imperfetto	Passato remoto	Futuro	CONDIZIONALE Presente	CONGIUNTIVO Presente	Imperfetto	IMPERATIVO
	cado	cadevo	caddi	cadrò	cadrei	cada	cadessi	
	cadi	cadevi	cadesti	cadrai	cadresti	cada	cadessi	cadi (non cadere)
	cade	cadeva	cadde	cadrà	cadrebbe	cada	cadesse	cada
	cadiamo	cadevamo	cademmo	cadremo	cadremmo	cadiamo	cadessimo	cadiamo
	cadete	cadevate	cadeste	cadrete	cadreste	cadiate	cadeste	cadete
	cadono	cadevano	caddero	cadranno	cadrebbero	cadano	cadessero	cadano

13 — cambiare (*to change*); cambiato; cambiando; avere cambiato

	INDICATIVO Presente	Imperfetto	Passato remoto	Futuro	CONDIZIONALE Presente	CONGIUNTIVO Presente	Imperfetto	IMPERATIVO
	cambio	cambiavo	cambiai	cambierò	cambierei	cambi	cambiassi	
	cambi	cambiavi	cambiasti	cambierai	cambieresti	cambi	cambiassi	cambia (non cambiare)
	cambia	cambiava	cambiò	cambierà	cambierebbe	cambi	cambiasse	cambi
	cambiamo	cambiavamo	cambiammo	cambieremo	cambieremmo	cambiamo	cambiassimo	cambiamo
	cambiate	cambiavate	cambiaste	cambierete	cambiereste	cambiate	cambiaste	cambiate
	cambiano	cambiavano	cambiarono	cambieranno	cambierebbero	cambino	cambiassero	cambino

14 cercare (to look for) — cercato / cercando / avere cercato

INDICATIVO Presente	Imperfetto	Passato remoto	Futuro	CONDIZIONALE Presente	CONGIUNTIVO Presente	CONGIUNTIVO Imperfetto	IMPERATIVO
cerco	cercavo	cercai	cercherò	cercherei	cerchi	cercassi	
cerchi	cercavi	cercasti	cercherai	cercheresti	cerchi	cercassi	cerca (non cercare)
cerca	cercava	cercò	cercherà	cercherebbe	cerchi	cercasse	cerchi
cerchiamo	cercavamo	cercammo	cercheremo	cercheremmo	cerchiamo	cercassimo	cerchiamo
cercate	cercavate	cercaste	cercherete	cerchereste	cerchiate	cercaste	cercate
cercano	cercavano	cercarono	cercheranno	cercherebbero	cerchino	cercassero	cerchino

15 chiedere (to ask for) — chiesto / chiedendo / avere chiesto

INDICATIVO Presente	Imperfetto	Passato remoto	Futuro	CONDIZIONALE Presente	CONGIUNTIVO Presente	CONGIUNTIVO Imperfetto	IMPERATIVO
chiedo	chiedevo	chiesi	chiederò	chiederei	chieda	chiedessi	
chiedi	chiedevi	chiedesti	chiederai	chiederesti	chieda	chiedessi	chiedi (non chiedere)
chiede	chiedeva	chiese	chiederà	chiederebbe	chieda	chiedesse	chieda
chiediamo	chiedevamo	chiedemmo	chiederemo	chiederemmo	chiediamo	chiedessimo	chiediamo
chiedete	chiedevate	chiedeste	chiederete	chiedereste	chiediate	chiedeste	chiedete
chiedono	chiedevano	chiesero	chiederanno	chiederebbero	chiedano	chiedessero	chiedano

16 cominciare (to begin) — cominciato / cominciando / avere cominciato

INDICATIVO Presente	Imperfetto	Passato remoto	Futuro	CONDIZIONALE Presente	CONGIUNTIVO Presente	CONGIUNTIVO Imperfetto	IMPERATIVO
comincio	cominciavo	cominciai	comincerò	comincerei	cominci	cominciassi	
cominci	cominciavi	cominciasti	comincerai	cominceresti	cominci	cominciassi	comincia (non cominciare)
comincia	cominciava	cominciò	comincerà	comincerebbe	cominci	cominciasse	cominci
cominciamo	cominciavamo	cominciammo	cominceremo	cominceremmo	cominciamo	cominciassimo	cominciamo
cominciate	cominciavate	cominciaste	comincerete	comincereste	cominciate	cominciaste	cominciate
cominciano	cominciavano	cominciarono	cominceranno	comincerebbero	comincino	cominciassero	comincino

17 cuocere (to cook) — cotto / cuocendo / avere cotto

INDICATIVO Presente	Imperfetto	Passato remoto	Futuro	CONDIZIONALE Presente	CONGIUNTIVO Presente	CONGIUNTIVO Imperfetto	IMPERATIVO
cuocio	cuocevo	cossi	cuocerò	cuocerei	cuocia	cuocessi	
cuoci	cuocevi	cuocesti	cuocerai	cuoceresti	cuocia	cuocessi	cuoci (non cuocere)
cuoce	cuoceva	cosse	cuocerà	cuocerebbe	cuocia	cuocesse	cuocia
cuociamo	cuocevamo	cuocemmo	cuoceremo	cuoceremmo	cuociamo	cuocessimo	cuociamo
cuocete	cuocevate	cuoceste	cuocerete	cuocereste	cuociate	cuoceste	cuocete
cuociono	cuocevano	cossero	cuoceranno	cuocerebbero	cuociano	cuocessero	cuociano

18 dare (to give) — dato / dando / avere dato

INDICATIVO Presente	Imperfetto	Passato remoto	Futuro	CONDIZIONALE Presente	CONGIUNTIVO Presente	CONGIUNTIVO Imperfetto	IMPERATIVO
do	davo	diedi, detti	darò	darei	dia	dessi	
dai	davi	desti	darai	daresti	dia	dessi	dai, da', dà (non dare)
dà	dava	diede, dette	darà	darebbe	dia	desse	dia
diamo	davamo	demmo	daremo	daremmo	diamo	dessimo	diamo
date	davate	deste	darete	dareste	diate	deste	date
danno	davano	diedero, dettero	daranno	darebbero	diano	dessero	diano

19 dimenticare (to forget) — dimenticato / dimenticando / avere dimenticato

INDICATIVO Presente	Imperfetto	Passato remoto	Futuro	CONDIZIONALE Presente	CONGIUNTIVO Presente	CONGIUNTIVO Imperfetto	IMPERATIVO
dimentico	dimenticavo	dimenticai	dimenticherò	dimenticherei	dimentichi	dimenticassi	
dimentichi	dimenticavi	dimenticasti	dimenticherai	dimenticheresti	dimentichi	dimenticassi	dimentica (non dimenticare)
dimentica	dimenticava	dimenticò	dimenticherà	dimenticherebbe	dimentichi	dimenticasse	dimentichi
dimentichiamo	dimenticavamo	dimenticammo	dimenticheremo	dimenticheremmo	dimentichiamo	dimenticassimo	dimentichiamo
dimenticate	dimenticavate	dimenticaste	dimenticherete	dimentichereste	dimentichiate	dimenticaste	dimenticate
dimenticano	dimenticavano	dimenticarono	dimenticheranno	dimenticherebbero	dimentichino	dimenticassero	dimentichino

20 dire (to say) — detto / dicendo / avere detto

INDICATIVO Presente	Imperfetto	Passato remoto	Futuro	CONDIZIONALE Presente	CONGIUNTIVO Presente	CONGIUNTIVO Imperfetto	IMPERATIVO
dico	dicevo	dissi	dirò	direi	dica	dicessi	
dici	dicevi	dicesti	dirai	diresti	dica	dicessi	di', di (non dire)
dice	diceva	disse	dirà	direbbe	dica	dicesse	dica
diciamo	dicevamo	dicemmo	diremo	diremmo	diciamo	dicessimo	diciamo
dite	dicevate	diceste	direte	direste	diciate	diceste	dite
dicono	dicevano	dissero	diranno	direbbero	dicano	dicessero	dicano

21 dolere (to hurt)
Participio passato: doluto/a — Gerundio presente: dolendo — Infinito passato: essere doluto/a

	INDICATIVO				CONDIZIONALE	CONGIUNTIVO		IMPERATIVO
	Presente	Imperfetto	Passato remoto	Futuro	Presente	Presente	Imperfetto	
	dolgo	dolevo	dolsi	dorrò	dorrei	dolga, dogla	dolessi	
	duoli	dolevi	dolesti	dorrai	dorresti	dolga, dogla	dolessi	duoli (non dolere)
	duole	doleva	dolse	dorrà	dorrebbe	dolga, dogla	dolesse	dolga
	doliamo, dogliamo	dolevamo	dolemmo	dorremo	dorremmo	doliamo, dogliamo	dolessimo	doliamo
	dolete	dolevate	doleste	dorrete	dorreste	doliate, dogliate	doleste	dolete
	dolgono	dolevano	dolsero	dorranno	dorrebbero	dolgano	dolessero	dolgano

22 dovere (to have to; to owe)
Participio passato: dovuto — Gerundio presente: dovendo — Infinito passato: avere dovuto

	INDICATIVO				CONDIZIONALE	CONGIUNTIVO		IMPERATIVO
	Presente	Imperfetto	Passato remoto	Futuro	Presente	Presente	Imperfetto	
	devo, debbo	dovevo	dovei, dovetti	dovrò	dovrei	deva, debba	dovessi	*This verb is not used in the imperative.*
	devi	dovevi	dovesti	dovrai	dovresti	deva, debba	dovessi	
	deve	doveva	dové, dovette	dovrà	dovrebbe	deva, debba	dovesse	
	dobbiamo	dovevamo	dovemmo	dovremo	dovremmo	dobbiamo	dovessimo	
	dovete	dovevate	doveste	dovrete	dovreste	dobbiate	doveste	
	devono, debbono	dovevano	doverono, dovettero	dovranno	dovrebbero	devano, debbano	dovessero	

23 fare (to do; to make)
Participio passato: fatto — Gerundio presente: facendo — Infinito passato: avere fatto

	INDICATIVO				CONDIZIONALE	CONGIUNTIVO		IMPERATIVO
	Presente	Imperfetto	Passato remoto	Futuro	Presente	Presente	Imperfetto	
	faccio	facevo	feci	farò	farei	faccia	facessi	
	fai	facevi	facesti	farai	faresti	faccia	facessi	fai, fa' (non fare)
	fa	faceva	fece	farà	farebbe	faccia	facesse	faccia
	facciamo	facevamo	facemmo	faremo	faremmo	facciamo	facessimo	facciamo
	fate	facevate	faceste	farete	fareste	facciate	faceste	fate
	fanno	facevano	fecero	faranno	farebbero	facciano	facessero	facciano

24 giocare (to play)
Participio passato: giocato — Gerundio presente: giocando — Infinito passato: avere giocato

	INDICATIVO				CONDIZIONALE	CONGIUNTIVO		IMPERATIVO
	Presente	Imperfetto	Passato remoto	Futuro	Presente	Presente	Imperfetto	
	gioco, giuoco	giocavo	giocai	giocherò	giocherei	giochi, giuochi	giocassi	
	giochi, giuochi	giocavi	giocasti	giocherai	giocheresti	giochi, giuochi	giocassi	gioca, giuoca (non giocare)
	gioca, giuoca	giocava	giocò	giocherà	giocherebbe	giochi, giuochi	giocasse	giochi, giuochi
	giochiamo	giocavamo	giocammo	giocheremo	giocheremmo	giochiamo	giocassimo	giochiamo
	giocate	giocavate	giocaste	giocherete	giochereste	giochiate	giocaste	giocate
	giocano, giuocano	giocavano	giocarono	giocheranno	giocherebbero	giochino, giuochino	giocassero	giochino, giuochino

25 inviare (to send)
Participio passato: inviato — Gerundio presente: inviando — Infinito passato: avere inviato

	INDICATIVO				CONDIZIONALE	CONGIUNTIVO		IMPERATIVO
	Presente	Imperfetto	Passato remoto	Futuro	Presente	Presente	Imperfetto	
	invio	inviavo	inviai	invierò	invierei	invii	inviassi	
	invii	inviavi	inviasti	invierai	invieresti	invii	inviassi	invia (non inviare)
	invia	inviava	inviò	invierà	invierebbe	invii	inviasse	invii
	inviamo	inviavamo	inviammo	invieremo	invieremmo	inviamo	inviassimo	inviamo
	inviate	inviavate	inviaste	invierete	inviereste	inviate	inviaste	inviate
	inviano	inviavano	inviarono	invieranno	invierebbero	inviino	inviassero	inviino

26 litigare (to quarrel)
Participio passato: litigato — Gerundio presente: litigando — Infinito passato: avere litigato

	INDICATIVO				CONDIZIONALE	CONGIUNTIVO		IMPERATIVO
	Presente	Imperfetto	Passato remoto	Futuro	Presente	Presente	Imperfetto	
	litigo	litigavo	litigai	litigherò	litigherei	litighi	litigassi	
	litighi	litigavi	litigasti	litigherai	litigheresti	litighi	litigassi	litiga (non litigare)
	litiga	litigava	litigò	litigherà	litigherebbe	litighi	litigasse	litighi
	litighiamo	litigavamo	litigammo	litigheremo	litigheremmo	litighiamo	litigassimo	litighiamo
	litigate	litigavate	litigaste	litigherete	litighereste	litighiate	litigaste	litigate
	litigano	litigavano	litigarono	litigheranno	litigherebbero	litighino	litigassero	litighino

27 mangiare (to eat)
Participio passato: mangiato — Gerundio presente: mangiando — Infinito passato: avere mangiato

	INDICATIVO				CONDIZIONALE	CONGIUNTIVO		IMPERATIVO
	Presente	Imperfetto	Passato remoto	Futuro	Presente	Presente	Imperfetto	
	mangio	mangiavo	mangiai	mangerò	mangerei	mangi	mangiassi	
	mangi	mangiavi	mangiasti	mangerai	mangeresti	mangi	mangiassi	mangia (non mangiare)
	mangia	mangiava	mangiò	mangerà	mangerebbe	mangi	mangiasse	mangi
	mangiamo	mangiavamo	mangiammo	mangeremo	mangeremmo	mangiamo	mangiassimo	mangiamo
	mangiate	mangiavate	mangiaste	mangerete	mangereste	mangiate	mangiaste	mangiate
	mangiano	mangiavano	mangiarono	mangeranno	mangerebbero	mangino	mangiassero	mangino

28 — mettere

Infinito: mettere *(to put)*
Participio passato: messo
Gerundio presente: mettendo
Infinito passato: avere **messo**

INDICATIVO				CONDIZIONALE	CONGIUNTIVO		IMPERATIVO
Presente	**Imperfetto**	**Passato remoto**	**Futuro**	**Presente**	**Presente**	**Imperfetto**	
metto	mettevo	**misi**	metterò	metterei	metta	mettessi	
metti	mettevi	mettesti	metterai	metteresti	metta	mettessi	metti (non mettere)
mette	metteva	**mise**	metterà	metterebbe	metta	mettesse	metta
mettiamo	mettevamo	mettemmo	metteremo	metteremmo	mettiamo	mettessimo	mettiamo
mettete	mettevate	metteste	metterete	mettereste	mettiate	metteste	mettete
mẹttono	mettẹvano	**mịsero**	metteranno	metterẹbbero	mẹttano	mettẹssero	mẹttano

29 — morire

Infinito: morire *(to die)*
Participio passato: morto/a
Gerundio presente: morendo
Infinito passato: essere **morto/a**

INDICATIVO				CONDIZIONALE	CONGIUNTIVO		IMPERATIVO
Presente	**Imperfetto**	**Passato remoto**	**Futuro**	**Presente**	**Presente**	**Imperfetto**	
muọio	morivo	morii	morirò, **morrò**	morirei, **morrei**	**muọia**	morissi	
muori	morivi	moristi	morirai, **morrai**	moriresti, **morresti**	**muọia**	morissi	**muori** (non morire)
muore	moriva	morì	morirà, **morrà**	morirebbe, **morrebbe**	**muọia**	morisse	**muọia**
moriamo	morivamo	morimmo	moriremo, **morremo**	moriremmo, **morremmo**	moriamo	morissimo	moriamo
morite	morivate	moriste	morirete, **morrete**	morireste, **morreste**	moriate	moriste	morite
muọiono	morịvano	morirono	moriranno, **morranno**	morirẹbbero, **morrẹbbero**	**muọiano**	morịssero	**muọiano**

30 — muovere

Infinito: muovere *(to move)*
Participio passato: mosso/a
Gerundio presente: muovendo, **movendo**
Infinito passato: avere **mosso**

INDICATIVO				CONDIZIONALE	CONGIUNTIVO		IMPERATIVO
Presente	**Imperfetto**	**Passato remoto**	**Futuro**	**Presente**	**Presente**	**Imperfetto**	
muovo	muovevo, **movevo**	**mossi**	muoverò, **moverò**	muoverei, **moverei**	muova	muovessi, **movessi**	
muovi	muovevi, **movevi**	muovesti, **movesti**	muoverai, **moverai**	muoveresti, **moveresti**	muova	muovessi, **movessi**	muovi (non muovere)
muove	muoveva, **moveva**	**mosse**	muoverà, **moverà**	muoverebbe, **moverebbe**	muova	muovesse, **movesse**	muova
muoviamo, **moviamo**	muovevamo, **movevamo**	muovemmo, **movemmo**	muoveremo, **moveremo**	muoveremmo, **moveremmo**	muoviamo, **moviamo**	muovessimo, **movessimo**	muoviamo, **moviamo**
muovete, **movete**	muovevate, **movevate**	muoveste, **moveste**	muoverete, **moverete**	muovereste, **movereste**	muoviate, **moviate**	muoveste, **moveste**	muovete, **movete**
muọvono	muovẹvano, **movẹvano**	**mọssero**	muoveranno, **moveranno**	muoverẹbbero, **moverẹbbero**	muọvano	muovẹssero, **movẹssero**	muọvano

31 — nuocere

Infinito: nuocere *(to harm)*
Participio passato: nuociuto, nociuto
Gerundio presente: nuocendo, **nocendo**
Infinito passato: avere **nuociuto**, **nociuto**

INDICATIVO				CONDIZIONALE	CONGIUNTIVO		IMPERATIVO
Presente	**Imperfetto**	**Passato remoto**	**Futuro**	**Presente**	**Presente**	**Imperfetto**	
nuọccio, **nọccio**	nuocevo, **nocevo**	**nocqui**	nuocerò, **nocerò**	nuocerei, **nocerei**	**nuọccia**	nuocessi, **nocessi**	
nuoci	nuocevi, **nocevi**	nuocesti, **nocesti**	nuocerai, **nocerai**	nuoceresti, **noceresti**	**nuọccia**	nuocessi, **nocessi**	nuoci (non nuọcere)
nuoce	nuoceva, **noceva**	**nocque**	nuocerà, **nocerà**	nuocerebbe, **nocerebbe**	**nuọccia**	nuocesse, **nocesse**	nuoca
nuociamo, **nociamo**	nuocevamo, **nocevamo**	nuocemmo, **nocemmo**	nuoceremo, **noceremo**	nuoceremmo, **noceremmo**	nuociamo, **nociamo**	nuocessimo, **nocessimo**	nuociamo, **nociamo**
nuocete, **nocete**	nuocevate, **nocevate**	nuoceste, **noceste**	nuocerete, **nocerete**	nuocereste, **nocereste**	nuociate, **nociate**	nuoceste, **noceste**	nuocete, **nocete**
nuọcciono, **nọcciono**	nuocẹvano, **nocẹvano**	**nọcquero**	nuoceranno, **noceranno**	nuocerẹbbero, **nocerẹbbero**	**nuọcciano**	nuocẹssero, **nocẹssero**	**nuọcciano**

32 — parere

Infinito: parere *(to seem)*
Participio passato: parso/a
Gerundio presente: parendo
Infinito passato: essere **parso/a**

INDICATIVO				CONDIZIONALE	CONGIUNTIVO		IMPERATIVO
Presente	**Imperfetto**	**Passato remoto**	**Futuro**	**Presente**	**Presente**	**Imperfetto**	
paio	parevo	**parvi**	**parrò**	**parrei**	**paia**	paressi	
pari	parevi	paresti	**parrai**	**parresti**	**paia**	paressi	*This verb is not used in the imperative.*
pare	pareva	**parve**	**parrà**	**parrebbe**	**paia**	paresse	
paiamo	parevamo	paremmo	**parremo**	**parremmo**	**paiamo**	paressimo	
parete	parevate	pareste	**parrete**	**parreste**	**paiate**	pareste	
paiono	parẹvano	**pạrvero**	**parranno**	**parrẹbbero**	**paiano**	parẹssero	

Infinito — Participio passato / Gerundio presente / Infinito passato	INDICATIVO Presente	INDICATIVO Imperfetto	INDICATIVO Passato remoto	INDICATIVO Futuro	CONDIZIONALE Presente	CONGIUNTIVO Presente	CONGIUNTIVO Imperfetto	IMPERATIVO
33 porre *(to put)* / **posto** / ponendo / avere **posto**	**pongo** / **poni** / **pone** / **poniamo** / **ponete** / **pongono**	**ponevo** / **ponevi** / **poneva** / **ponevamo** / **ponevate** / **ponevano**	**posi** / **ponesti** / **pose** / **ponemmo** / **poneste** / **posero**	**porrò** / **porrai** / **porrà** / **porremo** / **porrete** / **porranno**	**porrei** / **porresti** / **porrebbe** / **porremmo** / **porreste** / **porrebbero**	**ponga** / **ponga** / **ponga** / **poniamo** / **poniate** / **pongano**	**ponessi** / **ponessi** / **ponesse** / **ponessimo** / **poneste** / **ponessero**	— / **poni** (non porre) / **ponga** / **poniamo** / **ponete** / **pongano**
34 potere *(to be able to)* / potuto / potendo / avere potuto	**posso** / **puoi** / **può** / **possiamo** / **potete** / **possono**	potevo / potevi / poteva / potevamo / potevate / potevano	potei, potetti / potesti / poté, potette / potemmo / poteste / poterono, potettero	**potrò** / **potrai** / **potrà** / **potremo** / **potrete** / **potranno**	**potrei** / **potresti** / **potrebbe** / **potremmo** / **potreste** / **potrebbero**	**possa** / **possa** / **possa** / **possiamo** / **possiate** / **possano**	potessi / potessi / potesse / potessimo / poteste / potessero	*This verb is not used in the imperative.*
35 prendere *(to take)* / **preso** / prendendo / avere **preso**	prendo / prendi / prende / prendiamo / prendete / prendono	prendevo / prendevi / prendeva / prendevamo / prendevate / prendevano	**presi** / prendesti / **prese** / prendemmo / prendeste / **presero**	prenderò / prenderai / prenderà / prenderemo / prenderete / prenderanno	prenderei / prenderesti / prenderebbe / prenderemmo / prendereste / prenderebbero	prenda / prenda / prenda / prendiamo / prendiate / prendano	prendessi / prendessi / prendesse / prendessimo / prendeste / prendessero	— / prendi (non prendere) / prenda / prendiamo / prendete / prendano
36 produrre *(to produce)* / **prodotto** / **producendo** / avere **prodotto**	**produco** / **produci** / **produce** / **produciamo** / **producete** / **producono**	**producevo** / **producevi** / **produceva** / **producevamo** / **producevate** / **producevano**	**produssi** / **producesti** / **produsse** / **producemmo** / **produceste** / **produssero**	**produrrò** / **produrrai** / **produrrà** / **produrremo** / **produrrete** / **produrranno**	**produrrei** / **produrresti** / **produrrebbe** / **produrremmo** / **produrreste** / **produrrebbero**	**produca** / **produca** / **produca** / **produciamo** / **produciate** / **producano**	**producessi** / **producessi** / **producesse** / **producessimo** / **produceste** / **producessero**	— / **produci** (non produrre) / **produca** / **produciamo** / **producete** / **producano**
37 riempire *(to fill)* / riempito / **riempiendo** / avere riempito	**riempio** / riempi / **riempie** / riempiamo / riempite / **riempiono**	riempivo / riempivi / riempiva / riempivamo / riempivate / riempivano	riempii / riempisti / riempì / riempimmo / riempiste / riempirono	riempirò / riempirai / riempirà / riempiremo / riempirete / riempiranno	riempirei / riempiresti / riempirebbe / riempiremmo / riempireste / riempirebbero	**riempia** / **riempia** / **riempia** / riempiamo / riempiate / **riempiano**	riempissi / riempissi / riempisse / riempissimo / riempiste / riempissero	— / riempi (non riempiere) / **riempia** / riempiamo / riempite / **riempiano**
38 rimanere *(to stay)* / **rimasto/a** / rimanendo / essere **rimasto/a**	**rimango** / rimani / rimane / rimaniamo / rimanete / **rimangono**	rimanevo / rimanevi / rimaneva / rimanevamo / rimanevate / rimanevano	**rimasi** / rimanesti / **rimase** / rimanemmo / rimaneste / **rimasero**	**rimarrò** / **rimarrai** / **rimarrà** / **rimarremo** / **rimarrete** / **rimarranno**	**rimarrei** / **rimarresti** / **rimarrebbe** / **rimarremmo** / **rimarreste** / **rimarrebbero**	**rimanga** / **rimanga** / **rimanga** / *rimaniamo* / *rimaniate* / **rimangano**	rimanessi / rimanessi / rimanesse / rimanessimo / rimaneste / rimanessero	— / rimani (non rimanere) / **rimanga** / rimaniamo / rimanete / **rimangano**

39 risolvere (to resolve)

Participio passato: **risolto** — Gerundio presente: risolvendo — Infinito passato: avere **risolto**

	INDICATIVO Presente	Imperfetto	Passato remoto	Futuro	CONDIZIONALE Presente	CONGIUNTIVO Presente	Imperfetto	IMPERATIVO
	risolvo	risolvevo	**risolvei, risolvetti, risolsi**	risolverò	risolverei	risolva	risolvessi	
	risolvi	risolvevi	risolvesti	risolverai	risolveresti	risolva	risolvessi	risolvi (non risolvere)
	risolve	risolveva	**risolvé, risolvette, risolse**	risolverà	risolverebbe	risolva	risolvesse	risolva
	risolviamo	risolvevamo	risolvemmo	risolveremo	risolveremmo	risolviamo	risolvessimo	risolviamo
	risolvete	risolvevate	risolveste	risolverete	risolvereste	risolviate	risolveste	risolvete
	risolvono	risolvevano	**risolverono, risolvettero, risolsero**	risolveranno	risolverebbero	risolvano	risolvessero	risolvano

40 rispondere (to answer)

Participio passato: **risposto** — Gerundio presente: rispondendo — Infinito passato: avere **risposto**

	INDICATIVO Presente	Imperfetto	Passato remoto	Futuro	CONDIZIONALE Presente	CONGIUNTIVO Presente	Imperfetto	IMPERATIVO
	rispondo	rispondevo	**risposi**	risponderò	risponderei	risponda	rispondessi	
	rispondi	rispondevi	rispondesti	risponderai	risponderesti	risponda	rispondessi	rispondi (non rispondere)
	risponde	rispondeva	**rispose**	risponderà	risponderebbe	risponda	rispondesse	risponda
	rispondiamo	rispondevamo	rispondemmo	risponderemo	risponderemmo	rispondiamo	rispondessimo	rispondiamo
	rispondete	rispondevate	rispondeste	risponderete	rispondereste	rispondiate	rispondeste	rispondete
	rispondono	rispondevano	**risposero**	risponderanno	risponderebbero	rispondano	rispondessero	rispondano

41 salire (to go up)

Participio passato: salito — Gerundio presente: salendo — Infinito passato: avere salito/essere salito (intransitive)

	INDICATIVO Presente	Imperfetto	Passato remoto	Futuro	CONDIZIONALE Presente	CONGIUNTIVO Presente	Imperfetto	IMPERATIVO
	salgo	salivo	salii	salirò	salirei	**salga**	salissi	
	sali	salivi	salisti	salirai	saliresti	**salga**	salissi	sali (non salire)
	sale	saliva	salì	salirà	salirebbe	**salga**	salisse	**salga**
	saliamo	salivamo	salimmo	saliremo	saliremmo	saliamo	salissimo	saliamo
	salite	salivate	saliste	salirete	salireste	saliate	saliste	salite
	salgono	salivano	salirono	saliranno	salirebbero	**salgano**	salissero	**salgano**

42 sapere (to know)

Participio passato: saputo — Gerundio presente: sapendo — Infinito passato: avere saputo

	INDICATIVO Presente	Imperfetto	Passato remoto	Futuro	CONDIZIONALE Presente	CONGIUNTIVO Presente	Imperfetto	IMPERATIVO
	so	sapevo	**seppi**	**saprò**	**saprei**	**sappia**	sapessi	
	sai	sapevi	sapesti	**saprai**	**sapresti**	**sappia**	sapessi	**sappi** (non sapere)
	sa	sapeva	**seppe**	**saprà**	**saprebbe**	**sappia**	sapesse	**sappia**
	sappiamo	sapevamo	sapemmo	**sapremo**	**sapremmo**	**sappiamo**	sapessimo	**sappiamo**
	sapete	sapevate	sapeste	**saprete**	**sapreste**	**sappiate**	sapeste	**sappiate**
	sanno	sapevano	**seppero**	**sapranno**	**saprebbero**	**sappiano**	sapessero	**sappiano**

43 sedere (to sit)

Participio passato: seduto — Gerundio presente: sedendo — Infinito passato: essere seduto

	INDICATIVO Presente	Imperfetto	Passato remoto	Futuro	CONDIZIONALE Presente	CONGIUNTIVO Presente	Imperfetto	IMPERATIVO
	siedo, seggo	sedevo	sedei, sedetti	sederò, **siederò**	sederei, **siederei**	**sieda, segga**	sedessi	
	siedi	sedevi	sedesti	sederai, **siederai**	sederesti, **siederesti**	**sieda, segga**	sedessi	**siedi** (non sedere)
	siede	sedeva	sedé, sedette	sederà, **siederà**	sederebbe, **siederebbe**	**sieda, segga**	sedesse	**sieda, segga**
	sediamo	sedevamo	sedemmo	sederemo, **siederemo**	sederemmo, **siederemmo**	sediamo	sedessimo	sediamo
	sedete	sedevate	sedeste	sederete, **siederete**	sedereste, **siedereste**	sediate	sedeste	sedete
	siedono, seggono	sedevano	sederono, sedettero	sederanno, **siederanno**	sederebbero, **siederebbero**	**siedano, seggano**	sedessero	**siedano, seggano**

44 sognare (to dream)

Participio passato: sognato — Gerundio presente: sognando — Infinito passato: avere sognato

	INDICATIVO Presente	Imperfetto	Passato remoto	Futuro	CONDIZIONALE Presente	CONGIUNTIVO Presente	Imperfetto	IMPERATIVO
	sogno	sognavo	sognai	sognerò	sognerei	sogni	sognassi	
	sogni	sognavi	sognasti	sognerai	sogneresti	sogni	sognassi	sogna (non sognare)
	sogna	sognava	sognò	sognerà	sognerebbe	sogni	sognasse	sogni
	sogniamo, sognamo	sognavamo	sognammo	sogneremo	sogneremmo	**sogniamo, sognamo**	sognassimo	sogniamo
	sognate	sognavate	sognaste	sognerete	sognereste	**sogniate, sognate**	sognaste	sognate
	sognano	sognavano	sognarono	sogneranno	sognerebbero	sognino	sognassero	sognino

Infinito / Participio passato / Gerundio presente / Infinito passato	INDICATIVO Presente	Imperfetto	Passato remoto	Futuro	CONDIZIONALE Presente	CONGIUNTIVO Presente	Imperfetto	IMPERATIVO
45 spegnere (to turn off) / **spento** / spegnendo / avere **spento**	**spengo** / spegni / spegne / spegniamo / spegnete / **spengono**	spegnevo / spegnevi / spegneva / spegnevamo / spegnevate / spegnevano	**spensi** / spegnesti / **spense** / spegnemmo / spegneste / **spensero**	spegnerò / spegnerai / spegnerà / spegneremo / spegnerete / spegneranno	spegnerei / spegneresti / spegnerebbe / spegneremmo / spegnereste / spegnerebbero	**spenga** / **spenga** / **spenga** / spegniamo / spegniate / **spengano**	spegnessi / spegnessi / spegnesse / spegnessimo / spegneste / spegnessero	spegni (non spegnere) / **spenga** / spegniamo / spegnete / **spengano**
46 stare (to stay; to be) / **stato/a** / stando / essere stato/a	sto / **stai** / sta / stiamo / state / **stanno**	stavo / stavi / stava / stavamo / stavate / stavano	**stetti** / **stesti** / **stette** / **stemmo** / **steste** / **stettero**	**starò** / **starai** / **starà** / **staremo** / **starete** / **staranno**	**starei** / **staresti** / **starebbe** / **staremmo** / **stareste** / **starebbero**	**stia** / **stia** / **stia** / stiamo / stiate / **stiano**	**stessi** / **stessi** / **stesse** / **stessimo** / **steste** / **stessero**	**stai, sta'** (non stare) / **stia** / stiamo / state / **stiano**
47 tacere (to be silent) / **taciuto** / tacendo / avere **taciuto**	**taccio** / taci / tace / **tacciamo** / tacete / **tacciono**	tacevo / tacevi / taceva / tacevamo / tacevate / tacevano	**tacqui** / tacesti / **tacque** / tacemmo / taceste / **tacquero**	tacerò / tacerai / tacerà / taceremo / tacerete / taceranno	tacerei / taceresti / tacerebbe / taceremmo / tacereste / tacerebbero	**taccia** / **taccia** / **taccia** / **tacciamo** / **tacciate** / **tacciano**	tacessi / tacessi / tacesse / tacessimo / taceste / tacessero	taci (non tacere) / **taccia** / **tacciamo** / tacete / **tacciano**
48 tenere (to hold) / **tenuto** / tenendo / avere **tenuto**	**tengo** / **tieni** / **tiene** / teniamo / tenete / **tengono**	tenevo / tenevi / teneva / tenevamo / tenevate / tenevano	**tenni** / tenesti / **tenne** / tenemmo / teneste / **tennero**	**terrò** / **terrai** / **terrà** / **terremo** / **terrete** / **terranno**	**terrei** / **terresti** / **terrebbe** / **terremmo** / **terreste** / **terrebbero**	**tenga** / **tenga** / **tenga** / teniamo / teniate / **tengano**	tenessi / tenessi / tenesse / tenessimo / teneste / tenessero	**tieni** (non tenere) / **tenga** / teniamo / tenete / **tengano**
49 togliere (to remove) / **tolto** / togliendo / avere **tolto**	**tolgo** / **togli** / toglie / **togliamo** / togliete / **tolgono**	toglievo / toglievi / toglieva / toglievamo / toglievate / toglievano	**tolsi** / togliesti / **tolse** / togliemmo / toglieste / **tolsero**	toglierò / toglierai / toglierà / toglieremo / toglierete / toglieranno	toglierei / toglieresti / toglierebbe / toglieremmo / togliereste / toglierebbero	**tolga** / **tolga** / **tolga** / **togliamo** / **togliate** / **tolgano**	togliessi / togliessi / togliesse / togliessimo / toglieste / togliessero	**togli** (non togliere) / **tolga** / **togliamo** / togliete / **tolgano**
50 trarre (to draw) / **tratto** / traendo / avere **tratto**	**traggo** / trai / trae / traiamo / traete / **traggono**	traevo / traevi / traeva / traevamo / traevate / traevano	**trassi** / traesti / **trasse** / traemmo / traeste / **trassero**	**trarrò** / **trarrai** / **trarrà** / **trarremo** / **trarrete** / **trarranno**	**trarrei** / **trarresti** / **trarrebbe** / **trarremmo** / **trarreste** / **trarrebbero**	**tragga** / **tragga** / **tragga** / traiamo / traiate / **traggano**	traessi / traessi / traesse / traessimo / traeste / traessero	trai (non trarre) / **tragga** / traiamo / traete / **traggano**
51 udire (to hear) / **udito** / udendo / avere udito	**odo** / **odi** / **ode** / udiamo / udite / **odono**	udivo / udivi / udiva / udivamo / udivate / udivano	udii / udisti / udì / udimmo / udiste / udirono	udirò, **udrò** / udirai, **udrai** / udirà, **udrà** / udiremo, **udremo** / udirete, **udrete** / udiranno, **udranno**	udirei, **udrei** / udiresti, **udresti** / udirebbe, **udrebbe** / udiremmo, **udremmo** / udireste, **udreste** / udirebbero, **udrebbero**	**oda** / **oda** / **oda** / udiamo / udiate / **odano**	udissi / udissi / udisse / udissimo / udiste / udissero	**odi** (non udire) / **oda** / udiamo / udite / **odano**

Infinito / Participio passato / Gerundio presente / Infinito passato	INDICATIVO				CONDIZIONALE	CONGIUNTIVO		IMPERATIVO
	Presente	Imperfetto	Passato remoto	Futuro	Presente	Presente	Imperfetto	
52 uscire (to go out) / uscito/a / uscendo / essere uscito/a	esco / esci / esce / usciamo / uscite / escono	uscivo / uscivi / usciva / uscivamo / uscivate / uscivano	uscii / uscisti / uscì / uscimmo / usciste / uscirono	uscirò / uscirai / uscirà / usciremo / uscirete / usciranno	uscirei / usciresti / uscirebbe / usciremmo / uscireste / uscirebbero	esca / esca / esca / usciamo / usciate / escano	uscissi / uscissi / uscisse / uscissimo / usciste / uscissero	esci (non uscire) / esca / usciamo / uscite / escano
53 valere (to be worth) / valso / valendo / avere valso	valgo / vali / vale / valiamo / valete / valgono	valevo / valevi / valeva / valevamo / valevate / valevano	valsi / valesti / valse / valemmo / valeste / valsero	varrò / varrai / varrà / varremo / varrete / varranno	varrei / varresti / varrebbe / varremmo / varreste / varrebbero	valga / valga / valga / valiamo / valiate / valgano	valessi / valessi / valesse / valessimo / valeste / valessero	vali (non valere) / valga / valiamo / valete / valgano
54 vedere (to see) / visto/veduto / vedendo / avere visto/veduto	vedo / vedi / vede / vediamo / vedete / vedono	vedevo / vedevi / vedeva / vedevamo / vedevate / vedevano	vidi / vedesti / vide / vedemmo / vedeste / videro	vedrò / vedrai / vedrà / vedremo / vedrete / vedranno	vedrei / vedresti / vedrebbe / vedremmo / vedreste / vedrebbero	veda / veda / veda / vediamo / vediate / vedano	vedessi / vedessi / vedesse / vedessimo / vedeste / vedessero	vedi (non vedere) / veda / vediamo / vedete / vedano
55 venire (to come) / venuto/a / venendo / essere venuto/a	vengo / vieni / viene / veniamo / venite / vengono	venivo / venivi / veniva / venivamo / venivate / venivano	venni / venisti / venne / venimmo / veniste / vennero	verrò / verrai / verrà / verremo / verrete / verranno	verrei / verresti / verrebbe / verremmo / verreste / verrebbero	venga / venga / venga / veniamo / veniate / vengano	venissi / venissi / venisse / venissimo / veniste / venissero	vieni (non venire) / venga / veniamo / venite / vengano
56 vincere (to win) / vinto / vincendo / avere vinto	vinco / vinci / vince / vinciamo / vincete / vincono	vincevo / vincevi / vinceva / vincevamo / vincevate / vincevano	vinsi / vincesti / vinse / vincemmo / vinceste / vinsero	vincerò / vincerai / vincerà / vinceremo / vincerete / vinceranno	vincerei / vinceresti / vincerebbe / vinceremmo / vincereste / vincerebbero	vinca / vinca / vinca / vinciamo / vinciate / vincano	vincessi / vincessi / vincesse / vincessimo / vinceste / vincessero	vinci (non vincere) / vinca / vinciamo / vincete / vincano
57 vivere (to live) / vissuto / vivendo / avere vissuto	vivo / vivi / vive / viviamo / vivete / vivono	vivevo / vivevi / viveva / vivevamo / vivevate / vivevano	vissi / vivesti / visse / vivemmo / viveste / vissero	vivrò / vivrai / vivrà / vivremo / vivrete / vivranno	vivrei / vivresti / vivrebbe / vivremmo / vivreste / vivrebbero	viva / viva / viva / viviamo / viviate / vivano	vivessi / vivessi / vivesse / vivessimo / viveste / vivessero	vivi (non vivere) / viva / viviamo / vivete / vivano
58 volere (to want) / voluto / volendo / avere voluto	voglio / vuoi / vuole / vogliamo / volete / vogliono	volevo / volevi / voleva / volevamo / volevate / volevano	volli / volesti / volle / volemmo / voleste / vollero	vorrò / vorrai / vorrà / vorremo / vorrete / vorranno	vorrei / vorresti / vorrebbe / vorremmo / vorreste / vorrebbero	voglia / voglia / voglia / vogliamo / vogliate / vogliano	volessi / volessi / volesse / volessimo / voleste / volessero	vogli (non volere) / voglia / vogliamo / vogliate / vogliano

Verbs that are irregular in the *participio passato* and *passato remoto*

These **–ere** and **–ire** verbs are irregular in the **participio passato** and in three forms of the **passato remoto**. All other forms of these verbs follow regular conjugation patterns. The full conjugation of some high-frequency verbs from this list —**chiedere** (15), **mettere** (28), **prendere** (35), **rispondere** (40), and **vincere** (56)— is presented in the preceding pages for your reference. On the list of active verbs on p. **A3**, these verbs are referenced as **1-3-3** verbs.

Infinito		Participio passato	Passato remoto (1st p. sing, 3rd p. sing, 3rd p. pl.)
accorgersi	*to realize*	accorto	accorsi, accorse, accorsero
affliggere	*to torment*	afflitto	afflissi, afflisse, afflissero
assumere	*to assume*	assunto	assunsi, assunse, assunsero
attendere	*to wait for*	attento	attesi, attese, attesero
chiedere	*to ask*	chiesto	chiesi, chiese, chiesero
chiudere	*to close*	chiuso	chiusi, chiuse, chiusero
concludere	*to conclude*	concluso	conclusi, concluse, conclusero
condividere	*to share*	condiviso	condivisi, condivise, condivisero
conoscere	*to meet, to know/ be familiar with*	conosciuto	conobbi, conobbe, conobbero
coprire	*to cover*	coperto	coprii/copersi, coprì/coperse, coprirono/copersero
correggere	*to correct*	corretto	corressi, corresse, corressero
correre	*to run*	corso	corsi, corse, corsero
crescere	*to grow*	cresciuto	crebbi, crebbe, crebbero
decidere	*to decide*	deciso	decisi, decise, decisero
difendere	*to defend*	difeso	difesi, defese, difesero
dipendere	*to depend on*	dipeso	dipesi, dipese, dipesero
dipingere	*to paint*	dipinto	dipinsi, dipinse, dipinsero
dirigere	*to manage*	diretto	diressi, diresse, diressero
discutere	*to discuss*	discusso	discussi, discusse, discussero
distruggere	*to destroy*	distrutto	distrussi, distrusse, distrussero
eleggere	*to elect*	eletto	elessi, elesse, elessero
emergere	*to emerge*	emerso	emersi, emerse, emersero
esigere	*to require*	esatto	esigei/esigetti, esigé/esigette, esigerono/esigettero
espandere	*to expand*	espanso	espansi, espanse, espansero
espellere	*to expel*	espulso	espulsi, espulse, espulsero
esplodere	*to explode*	esploso	esplosi, esplose, esplosero
esprimere	*to express*	espresso	espressi, espresse, espressero
evadere	*to evade*	evaso	evasi, evase, evasero
fingere	*to pretend*	finto	finsi, finse, finsero
friggere	*to fry*	fritto	frissi, frisse, frissero
giungere	*to arrive*	giunto	giunsi, giunse, giunsero
invadere	*to invade*	invaso	invasi, invase, invasero
leggere	*to read*	letto	lessi, lesse, lessero
mettere	*to put*	messo	misi, mise, misero
nascere	*to be born*	nato	nacqui, nacque, nacquero
nascondere	*to hide*	nascosto	nascosi, nascose, nascosero

Infinito		Participio passato	Passato remoto (1st p. sing, 3rd p. sing, 3rd p. pl.)
occorrere	*to be necessary*	occorso	occorsi, occorse, occorsero
offendere	*to offend*	offeso	offesi, offese, offesero
offrire	*to offer*	offerto	offrii/offersi, offri/offerse, offrirono/offersero
opprimere	*to oppress*	oppresso	oppressi, oppresse, oppressero
perdere	*to lose*	perso	persi, perse, persero
persuadere	*to convince*	persuaso	persuasi, persuase, persuasero
piacere	*to please, to like*	piaciuto	piacqui, piacque, piacquero
piangere	*to cry*	pianto	piansi, pianse, piansero
piovere	*to rain*	piovuto	piovve, piovvero
porgere	*to give*	porto	porsi, porse, porsero
prendere	*to take*	preso	presi, prese, presero
radere	*to shave*	raso	rasi, rase, rasero
redimere	*to redeem*	redento	redensi, redense, redensero
rendere	*to render*	reso	resi, rese, resero
ridere	*to laugh*	riso	risi, rise, risero
riflettere (*intrans.*)	*to reflect on, to ponder*	riflettuto	riflettei, rifletté, rifletterono
riflettere (*trans.*)/ riflettersi	*to reflect*	riflesso	riflessi, riflesse, riflessero
risolvere	*to resolve*	risolto	risolsi/risolvei, risolse/risolvé, risolsero/risolverono
rispondere	*to answer*	risposto	risposi, rispose, risposero
rompere	*to break*	rotto	ruppi, ruppe, ruppero
scendere	*to come down*	sceso	scesi, scese, scesero
sconfiggere	*to defeat*	sconfitto	sconfissi, sconfisse, sconfissero
scoprire	*to discover*	scoperto	scoprii/scopersi, scopri/scoperse, scoprirono/ scopersero
scrivere	*to write*	scritto	scrissi, scrisse, scrissero
scuotere	*to shake*	scosso	scossi, scosse, scossero
smettere	*to stop*	smesso	smisi, smise, smisero
soffrire	*to suffer*	sofferto	soffrii/soffersi, soffri/sofferse, soffrirono/soffersero
sorridere	*to smile*	sorriso	sorrisi, sorrise, sorrisero
sospendere	*to hang*	sospeso	sospesi, sospese, sospesero
spendere	*to spend*	speso	spesi, spese, spesero
spingere	*to push*	spinto	spinsi, spinse, spinsero
stringere	*to press*	stretto	strinsi, strinse, strinsero
succedere	*to happen*	successo	successi, successe, successero
svolgere	*to carry out, conduct*	svolto	svolsi, svolse, svolsero
trascorrere	*to spend*	trascorso	trascorsi, trascorse, trascorsero
uccidere	*to kill*	ucciso	uccisi, uccise, uccisero
vincere	*to win*	vinto	vinsi, vinse, vinsero
volgere	*to turn*	volto	volsi, volse, volsero

Vocabulary

This glossary contains the words and expressions listed on the **Vocabolario** page found at the end of each lesson in **Immagina**, as well as other useful vocabulary. A numeral following an entry indicates the lesson where the word or expression was introduced.

Abbreviations used in this glossary

adj.	adjective	*invar.*	invariable
adv.	adverb	*m.*	masculine
conj.	conjunction	*p.p.*	past participle
f.	feminine	*pl.*	plural
fam.	familiar	*prep.*	preposition
form.	formal	*pron.*	pronoun
indef.	indefinite	*v.*	verb

Italiano-Inglese

A

a *prep.* at; in; to
  a buon mercato *adj.* cheap **8**
  a condizione che *conj.* provided that **7**
  a meno che *conj.* unless **7**
  a patto che *conj.* provided that **7**
  a piedi *adv.* on foot
  a righe *adj.* striped
  a squarciagola *adv.* at the top of one's voice **3**
  a suo agio *adv.* at ease
  a tempo parziale *adj., adv.* part-time
  a tempo pieno *adj., adv.* full-time
  a tinta unita *adj.* solid-color
  a volte *adv.* sometimes
  al mare *adv.* at/to the beach
  al solito suo *adv.* as usual
  al vapore *adj.* steamed
  all'inizio *adv.* at first
  alla griglia *adj.* grilled
  alla moda *adj.* fashionable **3**
abbaiare *v.* to bark **1**
abbastanza *adv.* enough
  Abbastanza bene. Pretty well.
abbiente *adj.* affluent **5**
abbigliamento *m.* clothing **10**
abbonamento *m.* season ticket; subscription
abbracciare *v.* to hug
abbracciarsi *v.* to hug each other **2**
abbronzarsi *v.* to tan
abitare *v.* to inhabit, to live **8**
abitazioni *f., pl.* housing **5**
abito *m.* dress; suit (men's) **10**
  abito *m.* **da sera** evening dress **3**
abituarsi *v.* to get used to **7, 8**
abolire *v.* to abolish **8**

abusare *v.* to abuse **4**
abuso *m.* **di potere** abuse of power **4**
accadere *v.* to happen
accanto (a) *prep.* next to
accendere *v.* to turn on
accenno *m.* hint
accogliere *v.* to greet **1**
accomodarsi *v.* to make oneself comfortable **5**
accordo *m.* agreement **4**
accorgersi *v.* to realize **2**
  accorgersi di *v.* to notice **8**
acido/a: pioggia *f.* **acida** acid rain
acqua *f.* water
acquario *m.* aquarium
acquedotto *m.* aqueduct **2**
acquerello *m.* watercolor **8**
acquisito/a: parenti *m., pl.* **acquisiti** in-laws
acquisto *m.* purchase
acritico/a *adj.* acritical
adagiarsi *v.* to lie down
adattamento *m.* adaptation **9**
adattarsi *v.* to adapt **6**
adatto/a *adj.* suitable **8**
addormentarsi *v.* to fall asleep **2**
adeguarsi *v.* to adjust **6**
adesso *adv.* now
adorare *v.* to adore **1**
adottare *v.* to adopt
adottivo/a *adj.* adopted; adoptive **5**
aereo *m.* airplane
aeroporto *m.* airport
affare *m.* deal **4**
affascinante *adj.* charming **1**
affatto *adv.* completely
  non... affatto *adv.* not at all
affettuoso/a *adj.* affectionate **1**
affiatato/a *adj.* close-knit **5**
affidare *v.* to entrust **10**
affinché *conj.* so that **7**
affinità di coppia *f.* compatibility **9**
affittare *v.* to rent (owner)

affitto *m.* rent, lease
affollato/a *adj.* crowded **2**
affresco *m.* fresco **8**
affumicato/a *adj.* smoked
africano/a *adj.* African
agenda *f.* planner
agente *m., f.* agent
agenzia *f.* agency
  agenzia *f.* **di collocamento** job agency **10**
  agenzia *f.* **di somministrazione lavoro** temp agency
  agenzia *f.* **immobiliare** real estate agency
aggiornare *v.* to update **7**
aggiornato: essere aggiornato/a *v.* to be up-to-date **9**
aggiustare *v.* fix
aggrapparsi *v.* to hold on to, hang on to **6**
aglio *m.* garlic
agnostico/a *adj.* agnostic **6**
agosto *m.* August
agricoltore/agricoltrice *m., f.* farmer
agricoltura *f.* agriculture
  agricoltura *f.* **biologica** organic farming
agrodolce *adj.* sweet-and-sour
aiutare *v.* help
aiutarsi *v.* to help each other **2**
alba *f.* dawn, sunrise
albergo *m.* hotel
  albergo *m.* **a cinque stelle** five-star hotel
albero *m.* tree
alcuni/e *indef. adj.* some; a few **9**; *indef. pron.* some; a few **9**
alimentari *m., pl.* foodstuffs
allacciare *v.* to buckle (seatbelt)
allagamento *m.* flooding **7**
alleati *m., pl.* allies, allied troops **2**
allegare *v.* to attach **7**
allegramente *adv.* cheerfully

allegro/a *adj.* cheerful
allenarsi *v.* to train 3
allenatore/allenatrice *m., f.* coach 3
allontanarsi (da) *v.* to distance oneself 8
allora *adv., conj.* so, then
allusivo/a *adj.* suggestive
alluvione *f.* flood, inundation 7
alpinismo *m.* mountain climbing 3
alto/a *adj.* tall 9
altri/e *indef. pron.* others
altro *indef. pron.* something (anything else)
altro/a/i/e *indef. adj.* other
  l'altro ieri *adv.* the day before yesterday
  l'un l'altro each other
altroché *adv.* absolutely
alunno/a *m., f.* pupil, student
alzare *v.* to raise; lift 2
alzarsi *v.* to get up, to stand up 2
amabile *adj.* lovable 5
amante *m., f.* lover
amare *v.* to love 1
amaro/a *adj.* bitter
amarsi *v.* to love each other 2
ambientalismo *m.* environmentalism
ambiente *m.* environment
ambulanza *f.* ambulance
americano/a *adj.* American
amicizia *f.* friendship 1
amico/a *m., f.* friend
analfabeta *adj.* illiterate 4
ananas *(invar.) m.* pineapple
anche *conj.* also, as well, too
ancora *adv.* again, still, yet
  non... ancora *adv.* not yet
andare *v.* to go 1
  andare a cavallo *v.* to go horseback riding
  andare al cinema *v.* to go to the movies
  andare dal dottore *v.* to go to the doctor
  (non) andare di moda *v.* to (not) be in fashion
  andare in bicicletta *v.* to ride a bike
  andare in palestra *v.* to go to the gym 3
  andare in pensione *v.* to retire 10
  andarsene *v.* to leave (go away from it) 2, 6
angolo *m.* corner 2
  dietro l'angolo *adv.* around the corner
angoscia *f.* anguish 7
anima *f.* soul 5
  anima *f.* **gemella** soul mate 1
animalaccio *m.* monster 2

animale *m.* animal
  animale *m.* **domestico** pet
anno *m.* year
  avere ... anni *v.* to be ... years old
annoiarsi *v.* to get bored 2
annullare *v.* to cancel
annuncio *m.* ad
  annuncio *m.* **di lavoro** job ad 10
ansioso/a *adj.* anxious 1
antenato *m.* ancestor 5
anticipo: essere in anticipo *v.* to be early 2
anticonformista *adj.* nonconformist 6
antipasto *m.* appetizer, starter
antipatico/a *adj.* unpleasant
ape *f.* bee
apparecchiare la tavola *v.* to set the table
apparenza *f.* appearance 4
appartamento *m.* apartment 2
  appartamento *m.* **arredato** furnished apartment
appartenere (a) *v.* to belong (to) 6
appena *adv., conj.* hardly, just
applaudire *v.* to clap 3
applauso *m.* applause
apprendista *m., f.* apprentice 8
approfittare *v.* to take advantage of 10
approfondire *v.* to study in-depth 1
approvare una legge *v.* to pass a law 4
appuntamento *m.* date 1
  prendere un appuntamento *v.* to make an appointment
appunti *m., pl.* notes
aprile *m.* April
aprire *v.* to open 3
  aprire un conto *v.* to open an account 10
arabo/a *adj.* Arab
arancia *f.* orange
arancione *adj.* orange
arbitro *m.* referee 3
architetto *m., f.* architect
arma *f.* weapon 4
armadio *m.* closet
armate *f., pl.* armies 2
aroma *m.* aroma, flavoring
arrabbiarsi *v.* to get mad/angry 1, 2
arrabbiato/a *adj.* angry
arrampicata *f.* climbing
arrendersi *v.* to surrender 8
arricchirsi *v.* to become rich 6
arricciare *v.* to curl
arrivare *v.* to arrive 3
Arrivederci. Good-bye.
arrivi *m., pl.* arrivals
arrosto/a *adj.* roasted
arte *f.* art
  belle arti *f. pl.* fine arts 8
  opera *f.* **d'arte** work of art

artigiano/a *m., f.* artisan 8
artistico/a *adj.* artistic
ascensore *m.* elevator
asciugacapelli *(invar.) m.* hair dryer
asciugamano *m.* towel
asciugarsi *v.* to dry up 2
asciugatrice *f.* clothes dryer
ascoltare *v.* to listen 6
  ascoltare musica *v.* to listen to music
ascoltatore/ascoltatrice *m., f.* (radio) listener 9
aspettare *v.* to wait 8
  aspettare un figlio *v.* to be expecting (a baby) 5
aspettarsi *v.* to expect 8
aspirapolvere *m.* to vacuum
  passare l'aspirapolvere *v.* to vacuum
aspirina *f.* aspirin
assaggiare *v.* to taste 4
assassinio *m.* assassination 8
assegno *m.* check 4
  cambiare un assegno *v.* to cash a check 10
  pagare con assegno *v.* to pay by check
assicurazione *f.* **sulla vita** life insurance
assistente *m., f.* **amministrativo/a** administrative assistant
assistere a *v.* to attend 8
assolo *m.* solo
assomigliare a *v.* to resemble 5
assumere *v.* to hire 10
  assumersi una responsabilità *v.* to assume responsibility 5
assunzione *f.* hiring
astronauta *m., f.* astronaut 7
astronomo/a *m., f.* astronomer 7
ateo/a *adj.* atheistic 6; *m., f.* atheist
atletica *f.* track and field
atletico/a *adj.* athletic
attacco *m.* attack 2
attendere *v.* to wait (for)
attento/a *adj.* attentive
  essere attento/a *v.* to be careful 8
attenzione: fare attenzione *v.* to pay attention
atterrare *v.* to land
attesa *f.* waiting, wait 7
  restare in attesa *v.* to be on hold
attimo *m.* second, moment
attivista *m., f.* activist 4
attivo/a *adj.* active
atto *m.* act
attore/attrice *m., f.* actor/actress 9
attraente *adj.* attractive
attraversare *v.* to cross 2
attualità *f.* current affairs 9
audace *adj.* audacious, bold

aula *f.* classroom, lecture hall
aumentare *v.* to increase **6**
aumento *m.* raise
autobus *m.* bus
  salire sull'autobus *v.* to get on the bus **2**
  scendere dall'autobus *v.* to get off the bus **2**
automobile *f.* car
automobilismo *m.* car racing **3**
automobilista *m.,f.* driver
autonomia *f.* autonomy **6**
autonomo/a *adj.* self-governing **4**
autore/autrice *m., f.* author
autoritario/a *adj.* bossy **5**
autoritratto *m.* self-portrait **8**
autostrada *f.* highway
autosufficiente *adj.* self-sufficient **5**
autunno *m.* fall
avanspettacolo *m.* variety show, burlesque
avanti Cristo *adj.* BC **8**
avaro/a *adj.* greedy
avere *v.* to have **1**
  avercela con qualcuno *v.* to be angry at someone
  avere bisogno di *v.* to need **8**
  avere dei debiti *v.* to be in debt **10**
  avere fame *v.* to be hungry **1**
  avere fiducia (in) *v.* to trust **1**
  avere fretta (di) *v.* to be in a hurry **8**
  avere mal di pancia (schiena, testa) *v.* to have a stomachache (backache, headache)
  avere paura (di) *v.* to be afraid (of) **1**
  avere ragione *v.* to be right **8**
  avere sete *v.* to be thirsty **1**
  avere sonno *v.* to be sleepy **1**
  avere torto *v.* to be wrong **8**
  avere un incidente *v.* to have/be in an accident
  avere vergogna (di) *v.* to be ashamed (of) **1**
  avere voglia di *v.* to feel like **8**
  avere... anni *v.* to be... years old **1**
avvenire *v.* to happen **6**
avvicinarsi *v.* to go/come near **5**
avvocato *m., f.* lawyer **4**
azienda *f.* company **10**
azzurro/a *adj.* blue, sky blue

B

bacca *f.* berry
bacheca *f.* bulletin board
baciare *v.* to kiss
baciarsi *v.* to kiss each other **2**
baffi *m., pl.* moustache **9**
bagaglio *m.* **a mano** carry-on baggage

bagno *m.* bath, bathroom
  vasca *f.* **da bagno** bathtub
baita *f.* cabin (mountain shelter)
balconata *f.* dress circle
balcone *m.* balcony
ballare *v.* to dance
ballerino/a *m., f.* ballet dancer
balletto *m.* ballet; *m.* short dance performance
bambino/a *m., f.* baby, child
bambola *f.* doll **5**
banana *f.* banana
banca *f.* bank
  banca *f.* **dati** database **7**
bancario/a *adj.* bank
  conto *m.* **bancario** bank account
bancarotta *f.* bankruptcy **10**
banchiere/a *m., f.* banker
banco *m.* desk; *m.* check-in counter **5**
bancomat *m.* ATM **10**
banconota *f.* bill
bandiera *f.* flag **4**
bar *m.* café **1**
barba *f.* beard
  schiuma *f.* **da barba** shaving cream
barca *f.* boat
barista *m., f.* bartender
barocco/a *adj.* Baroque
basket *m.* basketball
basso/a *adj.* short **9**
bassotto *m.* basset hound **1**
bastare *v.* to be sufficient **3**
battaglia *f.* battle **8**
battere le mani *v.* to clap
batteria *f.* drums
batterista *m., f.* drummer
baule *m.* trunk
beige (*invar.*) *adj.* beige
bellezza *f.* beauty
  salone *m.* **di belleza** beauty salon
bellino/a *adj.* cute, pretty
bello/a *adj.* beautiful, handsome
  belle arti *f. pl.* fine arts **8**
benché *conj.* although **7**
bene *adv.* well **9**
  Abbastanza bene. Pretty well.
Benvenuto! Welcome!
benzinaio/a *m., f.* gas station attendant **7**
bere *v.* to drink **1**
bernoccolo *m.* bump
biancheria *f.* **intima** underwear
bianco/a *adj.* white
bibita *f.* drink
biblioteca *f.* library
bicchiere *m.* glass
bicicletta *f.* bicycle
bidello/a *m., f.* caretaker, custodian
biglietteria *f.* ticket office/window
biglietto *m.* ticket **3**
  biglietto *m.* **intero** full price ticket
  biglietto *m.* **ridotto** reduced ticket

biliardino *m.* foosball **3**
biliardo *m.* billiards **3**
bilocale *m.* two-room apartment
binario *m.* train track **1**
biochimico/a *m., f.* biochemist **7**
biografia *m.* biography **8**
biologia *f.* biology
biologo/a *m., f.* biologist **7**
biondo/a *adj.* blond(e)
birra *f.* beer
birreria *f.* pub
biscotto *m.* cookie **1**
bisnonno/a *m., f.* great-grandfather/ grandmother **1, 5**
bisogno: avere bisogno di *v.* to need **8**
bizantino/a *adj.* Byzantine
blu (*invar.*) *adj.* blue
bocca *f.* mouth
  In bocca al lupo. (*lit.* In the mouth of the wolf.) Good luck.
boccaglio *m.* snorkel **4**
bocciare *v.* to fail (an exam)
bollente *adj.* boiling hot **7**
bollette *f., pl.* bills
  pagare le bollette *v.* to pay the bills
bontà *f.* goodness **3**
borsa *f.* handbag; stock exchange **10**
  borsetta *f.* small purse
botolo *m.* mutt **1**
bottega *f.* shop **8**
bottiglia *f.* bottle
braccio (*pl.* braccia *f.*) *m.* arm
bravo/a *adj.* good; skilled
breve: a breve termine *adj.* short-term **10**
brevetto *m.* patent **7**
briciola *f.* crumb
brillante *adj.* bright
bruciare *v.* to burn **9**
bruciore *m.* **di stomaco** heartburn
bruno/a *adj.* dark-haired
brutto/a *adj.* ugly
bucato: fare il bucato *v.* to do the laundry **5**
bue (*pl.* i buoi) *m.* ox (oxen) **7**
buffo/a *adj.* funny **3**
bugia *f.* lie
bullo/a *m., f.* bully **3**
buono/a *adj.* good **9**
  buon affare *m.* good deal
  buon senso *m.* common sense **6**
  Buonanotte. Good night.
  Buonasera. Good evening.
  Buongiorno. Good morning, Hello.
burattinaio *m.* puppeteer **4**
burattino *m.* puppet **3**
burro *m.* butter
bussare *v.* to knock **5**
busta *f.* envelope

buttare: buttare di sotto *v.* to throw down/below **6**
buttare via *v.* to throw away **1**

C

C.V. *m.* résumé
c'è *there is*
  C'è il/la signor(a)…? Is Mr./ Mrs… there?
  C'è il sole. It's sunny.
  C'è il temporale. It's stormy.
  C'è vento. It's windy.
  Che c'è di nuovo? What's new?
  Che cosa c'è? What's wrong?
cabina *f.* cabin
  cabina *f.* **di controllo** cockpit **5**
  cabina *f.* **telefonica** phone booth
cadere *v.* to fall **3**
caffè *m.* coffee
caffettiera *f.* coffee maker
cafone/a *m., f.* slob; *adj.* rude, boorish
calcetto *m.* foosball **9**; five-player soccer **2**
calciatore *m.* soccer player **3**
calcio *m.* soccer **3**
  calcio *m.* **di rigore** penalty kick **3**
caldo/a *adj.* hot
  avere caldo *v.* to feel hot
  ondata *f.* **di caldo** heat wave
calli *f., pl* Venetian streets **7**
calza *f.* sock; stocking
cambiare *v.* to change; to exchange **3**
  cambiare un assegno *v.* to cash a check **10**
camera *f.* room
  camera *f.* **d'aria** inner tube **4**
  camera *f.* **da letto** bedroom
  camera *f.* **singola/doppia** single/double room
  servizio *m.* **in camera** room service
cameriere/a *m., f.* waiter/waitress
camicetta *f.* blouse
camicia *f.* dress shirt
camion *m.* truck
  camion *m.* **della nettezza urbana** garbage truck
camionista *m., f.* truck driver
camminare *v.* to walk
campagna *f.* campaign; countryside **2**
  campagna *f.* **elettorale** electoral campaign **3**
  campagna *f.* **pubblicitaria** advertising campaign
campeggiare *v.* to camp **3**
campeggio *m.* camping
campo *m.* cellular reception; field **9**
campo *m.* field **2**
  campi *m., pl.* Venetian squares/fields **7**
  campo *m.* **di/da gioco** playing field **3**
canadese *adj.* Canadian

canale *m.* channel, canal
  canale *m.* **televisivo** television channel
  canali *m., pl.* canals **7**
canarino *m.* canary
cancellare *v.* to erase **7**
candidato/a *m., f.* candidate
cane *m.* dog
  cane *m.* **da caccia** hunting dog **1**
canile *m.* dog shelter **1**
canottaggio *m.* rowing **3**
canottiera *f.* tank top
cantante *m., f.* singer
cantare *v.* to sing **1**
cantina *f.* wine cellar
cantucci *m., pl.* Tuscan almond biscotti **1**
canzone *f.* song
caos *m.* chaos **6**
capacità *f.* skill
capelli *m., pl.* hair
  capelli *m., pl.* **a spazzola** crew cut
  capelli *m., pl.* **raccolti** pulled back hair
  capelli *m., pl.* **sciolti** loose hair
  tagliarsi i capelli *v.* to cut one's hair
capire *v.* to understand **1**
capitare *v.* to happen **8, 9**
capitone *m.* large eel **6**
capo *m.* leader **4**, boss **10**; item, article
  capo *m.* **di abbigliamento** article of clothing **10**
capodanno *m.* New Year's Day
capolavoro *m.* masterpiece **9**
capolinea *m.* terminus
cappello *m.* hat
cappotto *m.* coat **3**
Cappuccetto Rosso *m.* Little Red Riding Hood **2**
capra *f.* goat
carabinieri *m., pl.* military police **5**
caraffa *f.* carafe
carattere *m.* personality **5**
carcere *m.* jail
carciofo *m.* artichoke
carica *f.* post **4**
  carica batteria *m.* battery charger
caricare *v.* to charge; to load
carie *f.* cavity
carino/a *adj.* cute
carne *f.* meat
  carne *f.* **di maiale** pork
  carne *f.* **di manzo** beef
carnevale *m.* carnival; Mardi Gras **9**
caro/a *adj.* expensive
carota *f.* carrot
carriera *f.* career **10**
carrozza *f.* car (train) **4**; carriage
carta *f.* card, paper
  carta *f.* **d'imbarco** boarding pass
  carta *f.* **di credito** credit card **10**
  carta *f.* **di debito** debit card

  carta geografica map **6**
  carta topografica city map **9**
  foglio *m.* **di carta** sheet of paper
  pagare con carta di credito/ debito *v.* to pay with a credit/ debit card
carte *f., pl.* playing cards
cartella *f.* folder
cartina *f.* map
cartoleria *f.* stationery store
cartolina *f.* post card
cartoni *m. pl.* **animati** *m.* cartoons **9**
caruccio *adj.* sweet, very dear
casa *f.* home, house
casale *m.* farmhouse **2**
casalinga *f.* housewife **10**
cascata *f.* waterfall
caserma *f.* barracks **8**
casino: Che casino! What a mess!
caso: nel caso che *conj.* in the case that **7**
cassa *f.* **automatica** ATM
cassata *f.* Sicilian dessert **1**
cassetta *f.* **delle lettere** mailbox
cassettiera *f.* dresser
cassetto *m.* drawer
castano/a *adj.* brown (hair)
catastrofe *f.* catastrophe
cattedrale *f.* cathedral **6**
cattivo/a *adj.* bad **9**; naughty
cattolico/a *adj.* Catholic **6**
cavallo *m.* horse
cavo *m.* cable
CD/compact disc *m.* CD
CD-ROM *m.* CD-ROM
celibe *adj., m.* single **1**
cellula staminale *f.* stem cell **7**
cellulare *m.* cell phone
cena *f.* supper
censura *f.* censorship **9**
censurare *v.* to censor **8**
centesimo *adj.* one-hundredth
cento *m.* one hundred
centomila *m.* one hundred thousand
centonovantotto *m.* one hundred ninety eight
centouno *m.* one hundred one
centoventicinque *m.* one hundred twenty five
centrale *f.* **nucleare** nuclear power plant
centravanti *m.* center forward **3**
centro *m.* center
  centro *m.* **commerciale** shopping mall **3**
  in centro *adj., adv.* downtown
cercare *v.* to look for **1, 5**
  cercare di *v.* to try **8**
certo/a *adj.* certain
cespuglio *m.* bush
cessare (di) *v.* to stop **8**
cestino *m.* wastebasket
chattare *v.* to chat online **9**

che *interr. pron.* what; *rel. pron.* that, which, who, whom
  che cosa *interr. pron.* what
chi *interr. pron.* who; whom; *rel. pron.* those who, the one(s) who
chiacchierare *v.* to chat **2**
chiacchiere *f., pl.* chit-chat
chiacchierone *m.* chatterbox
chiamare *v.* to call **2**
chiamarsi *v.* to be named; to call each other **2**
chiaro/a *adj.* clear; light
chiave *f.* key
chiavetta USB *f.* flash drive **7**
chic *adj.* chic
chiedere *v.* to ask (for) **3**
  chiedere un prestito *v.* to ask for a loan
chiesa *f.* church **6**
chilo *m.* kilo
chimico/a *m., f.* chemist **7**
chiocciola *f.* @ symbol **7**
chiosco *m.* kiosk, newstand
  chiosco *m.* **per le informazioni** information booth
chirurgo/a *m., f.* surgeon
chitarra *f.* guitar
chitarrista *m., f.* guitarist
chiudere *v.* to close
  chiudere un conto *v.* to close an account **10**
chiunque *indef. pron.* anyone, whoever **9**
chiuso: naso *m.* **chiuso** stuffy nose
ci: ci sono there are
  Ci sono 18 gradi. It is 18 degrees out.
  Ci vediamo! See you soon!
Ciao. Good-bye./Hi.
ciascuno/a *indef. adj.* each **9**; *indef. pron.* each **9**
cibo *m.* food
ciclismo *m.* cycling
ciclone *m.* cyclone
cielo *m.* sky
cifra *f.* figure, number **10**
ciglia *(invar.) f.* eyelash
Cin, cin! Cheers!
cineasta *m., f.* filmmaker **9**
cinema *m.* cinema
cinese *adj.* Chinese
cinquanta *m.* fifty
cinquantuno *m.* fifty-one
cinque *m.* five
cinquecentesimo *adj.* five-hundredth
cinquecento *m.* five hundred
cinquecentocinquantamila *m.* five hundred fifty thousand
cinquemila *m.* five thousand
cintura *f.* belt
  cintura *f.* **di sicurezza** seatbelt

ciò che *rel. pron.* that which, that, what **9**
cioccolateria *f.* cafè specializing in chocolate
cioè *conj.* that is **2**
cipolla *f.* onion
cipresso *m.* cypress
circolazione *f.* traffic **2**
città *f.* city
cittadinanza *f.* citizenship **4**
cittadino/a *m., f.* citizen **2**
ciuffo *m.* tuft of hair
civile *adj.* civil
  guerra *f.* **civile** civil war **4**
  stato *m.* **civile** marital status
civiltà *f.* civilization **8**
clandestino *m.* illegal (immigrant) **4**
claque *f.* professional clappers
clarinetto *m.* clarinet
classe *f.* class
  classe *f.* **economica** economy class
  classe *f.* **turistica** tourist class
  conflitto *m.* **di classe** class conflict **6**
  prima classe *adj.* first class
classico/a *adj.* classic; classical **8**
classifica *f.* chart **3**
cliente *m., f.* client, customer
clima *m.* climate
clonare *v.* to clone **7**
club *m.* **sportivo** sports club **3**
coda *f.* queue
  fare la coda *v.* to wait in line **3**
codardo/a *adj.* coward **5**
codice *m.* code **7**
  codice *m.* **deontologico** code of conduct/ethics **7**
codino *m.* ponytail
coercitivo/a *adj.* coercive
cofano *m.* hood
cogliere *v.* to pick **1**
  cogliere *v.* **in fallo** to catch out **8**
cognato/a *m.* brother-/sister-in-law
cognome *m.* last name
coincidenza *f.* coincidence **3**
coinquilino/a *m., f.* housemate; roommate **2**
colazione *f.* breakfast
  fare colazione *v.* to have breakfast **1**
collaboratrice *f.* **domestica** maid
collana *f.* necklace
collega *m., f.* colleague **10**
collegamento *m.* connection
collezione *f.* collection
colline *f., pl.* hills
collo *m.* neck
colloquio *m.* **di lavoro** job interview **10**
colonizzare *v.* to colonize **8**
colonna *f.* **sonora** soundtrack **9**
colore *m.* color
colpa *f.* fault **1**

colpevole *adj.* guilty **4**
colpire *v.* to hit
colpo *m.* **di fulmine** love at first sight **1**; lightning strike **9**
coltello *m.* knife
coltivare *v.* to grow **7**
combattere *v.* to fight **4**
come *adv.* how
cominciare (a) *v.* to begin (to); to start (to) **1**
commedia *f.* comedy
commessa *f.* saleswoman **1**
commettere *v.* commit
commissione *f.* commission **8**
commovente *adj.* moving, touching
comodino *m.* night table
compagno/a *m., f.* partner **1**
  compagno/a *m.f.* **di classe** classmate
comparsa *f.* appearance **6**
compassione *f.* compassion **2**
competenza *f.* ability; competence
competitivo/a *adj.* competitive **3**
compiti *m., pl.* homework
compleanno *m.* birthday
completo/a: al completo *adj.* no vacancies
comporre *v.* to compose; to dial
compositore/compositrice *m., f.* composer
composizione *f.* composition **8**
  composizione *f.* **demografica** demographic makeup **2**
comprare *v.* to buy
comprensione *f.* understanding **6**
comprensivo/a *adj.* understanding **1**
compressa *f.* tablet
compromesso *m.* compromise
computer *m.* computer **7**
  computer *m.* **portatile** laptop computer **7**
  computer *m.* **da tavolo** desktop computer **7**
comune *m.* town hall
comunicato *m.* **stampa** press release **9**
comunque *conj., adv.* however
con *prep.* with
concerto *m.* concert
concorrente *m.* contestant
condividere *v.* to share **1**
condizione *f.* condition
condurre *v.* to run
  condurre un'inchiesta *v.* to carry out an investigation
confidenza *f.* intimacy **10**
confine *m.* (national) boundary **4**
conflitto *m.* **di classe** class conflict **6**
conformarsi *v.* to conform **6**
conformismo *m.* conformism
conformista *adj.* conformist **6**
congedo *m.* leave

congelatore *m.* freezer
coniglio *m.* rabbit
coniuge *m., f.* spouse 9
connazionale *adj.* compatriot 8
conoscere *v.* to meet; know, be familiar with 3
  conoscere di vista *v.* to know by sight
  conoscere la strada *v.* to know the way
  conoscere... a fondo *v.* to know something inside and out
  Piacere di conoscerLa/ti. (*form./fam.*) Pleased to meet you.
conoscersi *v.* to know each other 2
conquistare *v.* to conquer 8
conservare *v.* to preserve
conservatore/conservatrice *adj.* conservative 4
consigliare (di) *v.* to advise 8
consiglio *m.* council 4
consulente *m., f.* consultant 10
conta *f.* counting rhyme 2
contabile *m., f.* accountant 10
contadino/a *m., f.* farmer 2
contanti *m., pl.* cash
  pagare in contanti *v.* to pay in cash
contare *v.* to be important 9
contare su *v.* to rely on, count on 1
contemporaneo/a *adj.* contemporary; modern
contento/a *adj.* content; happy
continuare *v.* to continue 8
conto *m.* account 10
  aprire/chiudere un conto *v.* to open/close an account 10
  conto *m.* **bancario** bank account
  conto *m.* **corrente** checking account 10
contorno *m.* side dish
contrariato/a *adj.* annoyed 1
contratto *m.* contract; lease
contravvenire a *v.* infringe
contributi *m., pl.* contributions; taxes
contro *prep.* against 8
controllare *v.* to check
  controllare la linea *v.* to watch one's weight
controllo *m.* control; check-up
  controllo *m.* **passaporti** passport control
controllore *m.* ticket collector
controverso/a *adj.* controversial 7
convalidare *v.* to validate (ticket)
conversazione *f.* conversation
convinto/a *adj.* earnest
coperto/a *adj.* overcast
copiare *v.* to copy 7
copione *m.* script 9
coppia *f.* couple 1
coprire (di) *v.* to cover (with) 8
coraggioso/a *adj.* courageous
coricarsi *v.* to lie down 10

cornetta *f.* receiver
coro *m.* chorus
corpo *m.* body
correggere *v.* to correct 3
correre *v.* to run 3
corridoio *m.* hallway
corriera *f.* long-distance bus 6
cortese *adj.* courteous
cortesia *f.* courtesy
corto/a *adj.* short (hair)
cortometraggio *m.* short film
cosa *f.* thing; *interr. pron.* what
  (Che) cos'è? What is it?
  Cosa vuol dire...? What does... mean?
  La solita cosa. The usual.
coscienza *f.* conscience 3
  coscienza *f.* **ambientale** environmental awareness
Così, così. So-so.
così... come *adv.* as
costa *f.* coast
costare *v.* to cost; to be worth
  Quanto costa(no)...? How much is/are... ?
costituzione *f.* constitution 6
costoso/a *adj.* expensive
costringere *v.* to coerce
costruire *v.* to build
costume *m.* **da bagno** bathing suit
cotone *m.* cotton
cravatta *f.* tie 10
credenza *f.* cupboard
credere *v.* to believe 6
credito *m.* credit
  carta *f.* **di credito** credit card 10
  pagare con carta di credito *v.* to pay with a credit card
crema *f.* lotion
Crepi. Thanks. (*lit.* May the wolf die.) (*answer to* **In bocca al lupo**.)
crescere *v.* to grow 3
crescita *f.* growth 4
cretino/a *m., f.* jerk
criminale *m., f.* criminal 4
criminalità *f.* crime 4
crimine *m.* crime 4
crisi *f.* **economica** economic crisis 10
critico *m.* critic 9
  critico *m.* **cinematografico** film critic 9
crociera *f.* cruise
cronaca *f.* news 9
  cronaca *f.* **sportiva** sports news 9
  cronaca *f.* **locale** local news 9
cronista *m., f.* reporter 9
crostata *f.* pie 8
crudele *adj.* cruel
crudeltà *f.* cruelty 4
cucchiaino *m.* teaspoon
cucchiaio *m.* spoon
cucina *f.* kitchen

cucinare *v.* to cook
cuffie *f., pl.* headphones
cugino/a *m., f.* cousin 5
cui *rel. pron.* which, whom
culmine *m.* height (fig.) 9
cuocere *v.* to cook 3
cuoco/a *m., f.* chef, cook
cuore *m.* heart
  stare a cuore *v.* to matter 2
curare *v.* to heal
curatore/curatrice *m., f.* curator 1
curioso/a *adj.* curious
curriculum (vitae) *m.* résumé 10

D

d.C. (dopo Cristo) *adj.* AD (Anno Domini) 2, 8
d'avanguardia *adj.* avant-garde 8
da *prep.* at; by; from, since
da non perdere must-see
  Da quanto tempo... For how long...
  Dàje! Come on! 2
danza *f.* **classica** classical dance
dare *v.* to give
  dare fastidio *v.* to annoy 1
  dare indicazioni *v.* to give directions 2
  dare le dimissioni *v.* to resign, to quit 10
  dare noia a *v.* to bother 8
  dare retta *v.* to pay attention 5
  dare un esame *v.* to take a test 1
  dare un passaggio *v.* to give a ride 2
  dare un'occhiata *v.* to take a look 3
darsi *v.* to give to each other
  può darsi it's possible
davanti (a) *prep.* in front of
davvero *adv.* really
debito *m.* debt 10
  avere dei debiti *v.* to be in debt 10
  pagare con carta di debito *v.* to pay with a debit card
debole *adj.* weak
debutto *m.* debut
decennio *m.* decade 8
decidere *v.* to decide 3
decidersi (a) *v.* to make up one's mind (to) 8
decimo *adj.* tenth
decisione: prendere una decisione *v.* to make a decision
decollare *v.* to take off
decreto *m.* decree
dedicarsi (a) *v.* to dedicate oneself to 4
degrado *m.* deterioration
delitto *m.* crime 6
deluso/a *adj.* disappointed 1
democratico/a *adj.* democratic 8

democrazia *f.* democracy **4**
denaro *m.* money
dente *m.* tooth
  lavarsi i denti *v.* to brush
  one's teeth
dentiera *f.* denture **5**
dentifricio *m.* tooth paste
dentista *m., f.* dentist
dentro *prep.* inside
deporre *v.* to testify **4**
depositare *v.* to deposit **10**
deposito: fare un deposito *v.*
  to make a deposit **10**
depressione *f.* depression
depresso/a *adj.* depressed **1**
depurare *v.* purify
deputato/a *m., f.* congressman/
  congresswoman **4**
deserto *m.* desert
desiderare *v.* to desire **6**
desiderio *m.* wish **1**
desolato/a *adj.* sorry
  essere desolato/a *v.* to be sorry **5**
destra *f.* right, right hand
di (d') *prep.* from; of
  di fronte a *prep.* across from
  di media statura *adj.* of average
  height
dialetto *m.* dialect **6**
dialogo *m.* dialogue **6**
dicembre *m.* December
diciannove *m.* nineteen
diciassette *m.* seventeen
diciottesimo *adj.* eighteenth
diciotto *m.* eighteen
dieci *m.* ten
dieta *f.* diet
  essere a dieta *v.* to be on a diet
dietro *prep.* behind **8**
difendere *v.* to defend **4**
difesa *f.* defense **2, 3**
differita: in differita *adv.*
  pre-recorded **9**
difficile *adj.* difficult
diffidente *adj.* mistrustful **2**
digitale *adj.* digital
  macchina *f.* **fotografica digitale**
  digital camera
digitare *v.* to type; dial
dignità *f.* dignity
dilemma *m.* dilemma, quandary
diluvio *m.* torrential downpour
dimenticabile *adj.* forgettable **1**
dimenticare *v.* to forget
dimenticarsi (di) *v.* to forget (to) **2**
diminuire *v.* to decrease **6**
dimissioni: dare le dimissioni *v.*
  to quit **10**
dimostrare *v.* to prove **7**
dinamico/a *adj.* dynamic
Dio *m.* God **6**
dipendere (da) *v.* to depend (on) **8**

dipingere *v.* to paint **3, 8**
  dipinto *n.* painting
diploma *m.* degree; diploma
dire *v.* to say **1**
dire la verità *v.* to tell the truth
diretta: in diretta *adv., adj.* live **9**
direttore *m., f.* manager **10**
direzione *f.* management **10**
dirigente *m., f.* executive **10**
dirigere *v.* to lead **8**; to manage **10**
diritto *m.* right; law
  diritti *m., pl.* **umani** human rights **4**
  diritto *m.* **d'autore** copyright **8**
disagio *v.* discomfort **8**
disboscamento *m.* deforestation
discarica *f.* dump
disco *m.* **rigido** hard drive
discreto/a *adj.* discreet
discutere *v.* to discuss **3**
disfarsi *v.* to get rid of **6**
disinvolto/a *adj.* confident
disoccupato/a *adj.* unemployed **10**
disonesto/a *adj.* dishonest **1**
dispensa *f.* pantry
dispiacere *v.* to mind, to be sorry **2**
disponibile *adj.* helpful
  stanza *f.* **disponibile** vacancy
dispositivo *m.* device **7**
dissentire *v.* to disagree; dissent **6**
distinguere *v.* to distinguish **6**
distributore automatico *m.*
  beverage dispenser **7**
disturbare *v.* to bother **1**
dito (*pl.* dita f.) *m.* finger
  dito *m.* **del piede** (*pl.*
  dita *f.*) toe
ditta *f.* company **10**
dittatura *f.* dictatorship **4**
divano *m.* couch
divenire *v.* to become **3**
diventare *v.* to become
  diventare indipendente *v.* to
  become independent **5**
divergenza *f.* difference
diversità *f.* diversity **6**
divertente *adj.* fun
divertirsi *v.* to have fun **2**
dividere *v.* to share **7**
divieto *m.* ban
divorziare (da) *v.* to divorce **1**
divorziato/a *adj.* divorced **1**
dizionario *m.* dictionary
DNA *m.* DNA **7**
doccia *f.* shower
docente *m., f.* lecturer; teacher
documentario *m.* documentary **9**
documento *m.* document; ID
dodici *m.* twelve
dogana *f.* customs
dolce *adj.* sweet; *m.* dessert
dolcezza *f.* sweetness **10**
dolore *m.* pain

domanda *f.* question
  fare domanda *v.* to apply **10**
  fare una domanda *v.* to ask
  a question
domandare *v.* to ask
domani *adv.* tomorrow
domenica *f.* Sunday
domestico/a *adj.* domestic
dominio *m.* domination **6**
donna *f.* woman
  donna *f.* **d'affari** businesswoman
dono *m.* gift
dopo *adv.* afterwards; *prep.* after **8**
  d.C. (dopo Cristo) *adj.* AD
  (Anno Domini) **2, 8**
dopodomani *adv.* the day
  after tomorrow
doppiaggio *m.* dubbing **9**
dormire *v.* to sleep **1**
dotato/a *adj.* gifted; talented
dottore(ssa) *m., f.* doctor
dove *prep.* where
dovere *v.* to have to; must **1**; *v.* to owe
dramma *m.* drama; play
  dramma *m.* **psicologico**
  psychological drama
drammatico/a *adj.* dramatic
drammaturgo/a *m., f.* playwright **8**
dubitare *v.* to doubt **7**
due *m.* two
duecento *m.* two hundred
duecentoquarantacinque *m.* two
  hundred forty five
duemila *m.* two thousand
durante *prep.* during **8**
durare *v.* to last
duro/a *adj.* hard; tough

E

e *conj.* and
ebreo/a *adj.* Jewish, Jew **6**
ecco *adv.* here
ecografia *f.* ultrasound **3**
ecologia *f.* ecology
economia *f.* economics
edicola *f.* newsstand **2**
edificio *m.* building **2**
editore/editrice *m., f.* publisher **9**
editoria *f.* publishing industry
educare *v.* to raise **5**
effetto *m.* effect
  effetti *m., pl.* **speciali** special
  effects **9**
  effetto *m.* **serra** greenhouse effect
egoista *adj.* selfish **5**
Ehilà! Hey there!
eleggere *v.* to elect **4**
elettricista *m., f.* electrician **9**
elettrodomestico *m.* appliance

elettrònica *f.* electronics **7**
elevato/a *adj.* high
elezione *f.* election
  pèrdere le elezioni *v.* to lose the election **4**
  vìncere le elezioni *v.* to win the election **4**
e-mail *f.* e-mail message
emicrania *f.* migraine
  emigrazione f. *emigration* **4**
emozionato/a *adj.* excited **1**
empatìa *f.* empathy **6**
energìa *f.* energy
  energìa f. eòlica wind power
  energìa f. nucleare nuclear energy
  energìa f. rinnovàbile renewable energy
  energìa f. solare solar energy
  energìa f. tèrmica thermal energy
  energìa pulita *f.* clean energy **7**
enèrgico/a *adj.* energetic
enoteca *f.* store specializing in wine
entrare *v.* to go in **3**
entusiasmo *m.* enthusiasm **1**
entusiasta *adj.* enthusiastic **1**
èpico/a: racconto *m.* **èpico** epic
equitazione *f.* horseback riding **3**
erba *f.* grass
ereditare *v.* to inherit **5**
errore *m.* error
eruzione *f.* eruption
  eruzione f. cutànea rash
esame *m.* test
  dare un esame *v.* to take a test **1**
esaurirsi *v.* to run out **7**
escursionismo *m.* hiking **3**
esèrcito *m.* army **4**
esercizio: fare esercizio *v.* to exercise
esibizione *f.* performance
esigente *adj.* demanding
esigenza *f.* requirement **2**
esigere *v.* to require **6**
espèllere *v.* to expel **8**
esperienza *f.* experience **10**
  esperienza f. professionale professional experience **10**
esperimento *m.* experiment **7**
esplorare *v.* explore
esposizione *f.* exhibit
espressione *f.* expression
èssere *v.* to be **3**
  èssere aggiornato/a *v.* to be up-to-date **9**
  èssere al verde *v.* to be broke
  èssere allèrgico (a) *v.* to be allergic (to)
  èssere attento/a *v.* to be careful **8**
  èssere ben/mal pagato/a *v.* to be well/poorly paid
  èssere desolato/a *v.* to be sorry **5**
  èssere in antìcipo *v.* to be early **2**

èssere in buona salute *v.* to be in good health
èssere in lìnea to be online
èssere in panne *v.* to break down
èssere in tour *v.* to be on tour
èssere in/fuori forma *v.* to be in/out of shape
èssere incinta *v.* to be pregnant **5**
èssere negato/a per *v.* to be no good at...
èssere pronto/a a *v.* to be ready to **8**
èssere sorpreso/a *v.* to be surprised **6**
estate *f.* summer
èstero *m.* foreign countries **6**
  all'èstero *adv.* abroad
estètico/a *adj.* aesthetic **8**
estràneo/a *m., f.* stranger **5**
età *f.* age; era **8**
  età adulta *f.* adulthood **5**
ètico/a *adj.* ethical **7**
etto *m.* one hundred grams
evitare (di) *v.* to avoid

F

fa *adv.* ago
fàbbrica *f.* factory **10**
faccende *f., pl.* chores
  fare i mestieri/le faccende *v.* to do household chores
faccia *f.* face
fàcile *adj.* easy
facoltà *f.* department; faculty
fagiolino *m.* green bean
falegname *m.* carpenter
fallire *v.* fail
fame: avere fame *v.* to be hungry **1**
famiglia *f.* family
fango *m.* mud
fantascientìfico/a *adj.* science fiction **7**
fantasma *m.* ghost **5**
fantoccio *m.* puppet **4**
fare *v.* to do, make **1**
  Fa caldo. It's hot.
  Fa freddo. It's cold.
  Fammi vedere. Let me see.
  fàrcela *v.* to make it **6**
  fare attenzione a *v.* to pay attention **8**
  fare bel/brutto tempo *v.* to be nice/nasty weather **1**
  fare colazione *v.* to have breakfast **1**
  fare commissioni *v.* to run errands **2**
  fare/comporre un nùmero *v.* to dial a number **9**
  fare domanda (per un lavoro) *v.* to apply (for a job) **10**
  fare due passi *v.* to take a short walk

fare finta *v.* to pretend
fare i compiti *v.* to do one's homework **1**
fare il bagno/la doccia *v.* to take a bath/shower
fare il bucato *v.* to do the laundry **5**
fare il buffone *v.* to act the fool
fare il letto *v.* to make the bed
fare il pendolare *v.* to commute
fare il ponte *v.* to take a long weekend
fare la coda *v.* to wait in line **3**
fare la fila *v.* to wait in line
fare la pòlvere *v.* to dust
fare la valigia *v.* to pack a suitcase
fare lo straordinario *v.* to work overtime **10**
fare meglio a *v.* to be better off **8**
fare progetti *v.* to make plans
fare spese *v.* to go shopping **1**
fare un abbonamento *v.* to subscribe **9**
fare un giretto *v.* to go for a stroll **2**
fare un mùtuo *v.* to take out a mortgage **10**
fare un picnic *v.* to have a picnic
fare un prelievo/depòsito *v.* to make a withdrawal/deposit **10**
fare un viaggio *v.* to take a trip
fare una domanda *v.* to ask a question
fare una foto *v.* to take a picture
fare una gita *v.* to take a short trip
fare una manifestazione *v.* to demonstrate **6**
fare una passeggiata *v.* to take a walk
fare vedere a *v.* to show **8**
farsi male *v.* to hurt oneself
fatto/a in casa *adj.* homemade
farmacista *m., f.* pharmacist
faro *m.* headlight; *m.* lighthouse **4**
farsi la barba *v.* to shave **2**
fascista *adj.* fascist **8**
fastidio: dare fastidio *v.* to annoy **1**
fatato/a *adj.* enchanted **3**
fattorìa *f.* farm
fàvola *f.* fairy tale **3**
fax *m.* fax
febbraio *m.* February
febbre *f.* fever
  avere la febbre *v.* to have a fever
fede *f.* faith **6**
fedele *adj.* faithful **1**; *m., f.* believer **6**
felice *adj.* happy
felpa *f.* sweatshirt
fèmmina *f.* female
femminista *adj.* feminist
fenòmeno *m.* phenomenon **3**
ferie *f., pl.* holidays **10**
ferirsi *v.* to injure oneself **3**
ferita *f.* injury; wound

fermare *v.* to stop **2**
fermarsi *v.* to stop **2**
fermata *f.* stop **2**
  fermata *f.* **a richiesta** stop
    on request
  fermata *f.* **dell'autobus/della**
  metro/del treno *f.* bus/subway/train
ferragosto *m.* August 15
  (holiday); August vacation **9**
ferro (da stiro) *m.* iron
ferroviere *m.* railway employee **6**
festa *f.* holiday; party
  Festa del santo patrono *f.* Feast
    of the Patron Saint
  Festa *f.* **del lavoro** Labor Day
  Festa *f.* **della Repubblica**
    Republic Day
festeggiamenti *m., pl.* festivities **9**
festeggiare *v.* to celebrate **3**
festival *m.* festival
fetta *f.* slice
fiaba *f.* fairy tale **3**
fidanzarsi (con) *v.* to get
  engaged (to) **1**
fidanzato/a *adj.* engaged **1**;
  m., f. boyfriend/girlfriend **5**;
  m., f. fiancé(e) **1**
fidarsi (di) *v.* to trust (in) **8**
fiducia *f.* trust **4**
  avere fiducia (in) *v.* to trust **1**
fieno *m.* hay
figliastra *f.* stepdaughter
figliastro *m.* stepson
figlio/a *m., f.* son/daughter **5**
  figlio/a unico/a *m., f.* only child **5**
figlioccio/a *m., f.* godson/
  goddaughter **5**
fila *f.* line
  fare la fila *v.* to wait in line
  stare in fila *v.* to stand in line
film *m.* film, movie
  film *m.* **di fantascienza/**
  dell'orrore horror/sci-fi film
filmare *v.* to film **9**
filmino *m.* short film
finanziario/a *adj.* financial **10**
fine *f.* end
  saldi *m., pl.* **di fine stagione**
    end-of-season sales **3**
finestra *f.* window
fingere *v.* to pretend
finire *v.* to finish **4**
fino a *prep.* until
fioraio *m.* florist **10**
fiore *m.* flower
fiorista *m.* florist; flower shop
firmare *v.* to sign
firmato/a *adj.* designer **3**
fisarmonica *f.* accordion
fisico/a *m., f.* physicist **7**
  fisico/a *m., f.* **nucleare** nuclear
    physicist **7**
fiume *m.* river

flauto *m.* flute
focacceria *f.* store specializing
  in focaccia
foglia *f.* leaf
folclore *m.* folklore **9**
folla *f.* crowd **2**
fondamenta *f., pl.* foundations **6**
fondo *m.* bottom
fontana *f.* fountain
football *m.* **americano** football
forchetta *f.* fork
foresta *f.* forest
formaggio *m.* cheese
formazione *f.* education; training **10**
forno *m.* oven
forte *adj.* strong
Forza! Come on!
foschia *f.* mist
foto(grafia) *f.* photo(graph)
fotocopiare *v.* to photocopy
fotografo *m.* photographer
fra/tra *prep.* among; between; in **8**
  fra di loro each other, among/
    between them
  fra poco *adv.* in a little while
fragola *f.* strawberry
fraintendimento *m.*
  misunderstanding **10**
francese *adj.* French
francobollo *m.* stamp
frangia *f.* bangs
fratellastro *m.* half brother;
  stepbrother
fratellino *m.* little/younger brother
fratello *m.* brother
frattura *f.* fracture
freccette *f., pl.* darts
freddo/a *adj.* cold
  avere freddo *v.* to feel cold
fregarsene *v.* to not care (about) **2, 6**
frenare *v.* to brake
freni *m., pl.* brakes
frequentare *v.* to attend
frequentemente *adv.* frequently
fresco/a *adj.* cool
fretta *f.* haste
  avere fretta (di) *v.* to be in a hurry **8**
frettoloso/a *adj.* in a hurry **2**
friggere *v.* to fry
frigo *m.* fridge
fritto/a *adj.* fried
frizione *f.* clutch
frizzante: acqua *f.* **frizzante**
  sparkling water
fronte *f.* front
frutta *f.* fruit
  frutti *m., pl.* **di mare** seafood
fucilare *v.* to execute **8**
fuggire *v.* to flee **3**
fulmine lightning
  colpo *m.* **di fulmine** love at
    first sight **1**; lightning strike **9**

fumetto *m.* comic strip **9**
fungo *m.* mushroom
funzionare *v.* function; work
funzionario/a *m., f.* civil servant
fuori *prep.* outside
  fuori posto *adj.* out of place **8**
furbo/a *adj.* sly, shrewd **5**
furto *m.* theft **7**
  furto *m.* **d'identità** identity theft **7**
futurista *adj.* Futurist
futuro *m.* future

G

gabbia *f.* cage **1**
gabbiano *m.* seagull
gabinetto *m.* toilet
galleria *f.* gallery
gamba *f.* leg
  in gamba *adj.* smart
gamberetto *m.* shrimp
gara *f.* race **3**
garage *(invar.)* *m.* garage
gatto/a *m., f.* cat
gelateria *f.* ice cream shop
geloso/a *adj.* jealous **1**
gemello/a *adj.* twin **5**
  anima *f.* **gemella** soul mate **1**
gene *m.* gene **7**
genere *m.* genre; kind **8**
  in genere *adv.* generally
genero *m.* son-in-law **5**
generoso/a *adj.* generous
genetica *f.* genetics **3**
gengiva *f.* gum **5**
geniale *adj.* great **1**
genio/a *m., f.* genius
genitore *m.* parent **5**
  genitore *m.* **single** single parent **5**
gennaio *m.* January
genocidio *m.* genocide
gentile *adj.* kind
geologo/a *m., f.* geologist **7**
gesso *m.* chalk
gestore *m., f.* manager
gettare *v.* to throw
già *adv.* already
giacca *f.* jacket
giallo *m.* thriller **8**; *adj.* mystery **9**
giallo/a *adj.* yellow
giapponese *adj.* Japanese
giardiniere/a *m., f.* gardener
giardino *m.* garden
  giardini *m., pl.* **pubblici** public
    gardens **2**
ginnastica *f.* gymnastics
ginocchio (*pl.* ginocchia *f.*) *m.* knee
giocare *v.* to play **8**
  giocare a nascondino *v.* to play
    hide-and-seek **5**
  giocare in casa/trasferta *v.* to
    play a home/away game **3**

giocatore/giocatrice *m., f.* player **2, 3**
gioco *m.* game
campo *m.* **di/da gioco** playing field **3**
gioco *m.* **a premi** quiz show
gioco *m.* **di società** board game **3**
gioielleria *f.* jewelry store
gioielli *m., pl.* jewelry **10**
giornale *m.* newspaper **9**
giornale *m.* **radio** radio news **9**
giornale *m.* **scandalistico** tabloid
giornalista *m., f.* journalist **9**
giorno *m.* day
giorno *m.* **festivo** public holiday
giovane *adj.* young; *m., f.* young man/woman
giovedì *m.* Thursday
gioventù: ostello *m.* **della gioventù** youth hostel
giovinezza *f.* youth **5**
girare *v.* to film **9**
girare (a destra/sinistra) *v.* to turn (right/left) **2**
giro *m.* tour; turn
in giro *adv.* around; out and about
prendere in giro *v.* to tease
gita *f.* short trip
giudicare *v.* to judge **4**
giudice *m., f.* judge **4**
giugno *m.* June
giurare (su) *v.* to swear (on) **8**
giuria *f.* jury **4**
giurisprudenza *f.* law
giustizia *f.* justice **4**
giusto/a *adj.* fair, right **4**
globalizzazione *f.* globalization **6**
gola *f.* throat
golf *m.* sweater **9**
goloso/a *adj.* food-loving **4**
gomito *m.* elbow
gomma *f.* eraser
gonna *f.* skirt **10**
gotico/a *adj.* Gothic
governare *v.* to govern **4**
governo *m.* government **4**
gradinata *f.* tier
gradino *m.* step
grado *m.* degree
graffetta *f.* paper clip; staple
graffettatrice *f.* stapler
granata *f.* grenade
grande *adj.* big **9**
grande magazzino *m.* department store
grandine *f.* hail
grasso/a *adj.* fat
gratis *(invar.) adj.* free
gratitudine *f.* gratitude **7**
grattacielo *m.* skyscraper **2**
grave *adj.* serious

Grazie. Thank you.
Grazie mille. Thanks a lot.
greco/a *adj.* Greek
grembo *m.* womb
griffe *f.* designer label **10**
grigio/a *adj.* grey
griglia *f.* grill
gruppo *m.* group
gruppo *m.* **(musicale)** band **3**
gruppo *m.* **rock** rock band
guadagnare *v.* to earn **10**
guanciale *m.* pillow **10**
guanto *m.* glove
guardare *v.* to look at
guardarsi *v.* to look at oneself/each other
guardia *f.* **costiera** coast guard **4**
guarire *v.* to cure; heal **7**
guerra *f.* war
guerra *f.* **civile** civil war **4**
guerra *f.* **mondiale** world war **4**
guidare *v.* to drive **2**
gusti *m., pl.* tastes, preferences **9**
gusto *m.* flavor
gustoso/a *adj.* tasty

I

idea *f.* idea
idealista *adj.* idealistic **1**
idraulico *m.* plumber
ieri *adv.* yesterday
ieri sera last night
illegale *adj.* illegal **4**
imbianchino *m.* painter
imbonitore *m.* huckster
imbucare una lettera *v.* to mail a letter
immaginare *v.* to imagine **7**
immaturo/a *adj.* immature **1**
immigrante *m., f.* immigrant **2**
immigrazione *f.* immigration **4**
immobiliare: agente *m., f.* **immobiliare** real estate agent
immondizia *f.* trash
immorale *adj.* unethical **7**
impanare *v.* to bread
imparare *v.* to learn **8**
imparentato/a *adj.* related **5**
imparziale *adj.* impartial; unbiased **9**
impatto *m.* impact
impatto ambientale *m.* environmental impact **7**
impazzire *v.* to go mad **3**
impedire *v.* to prevent; incapacitate
impegno *m.* commitment **10**
imperatore/imperatrice *m., f.* emperor/empress **8**
impermeabile *m.* raincoat **3**
impianto *m.* **stereo** stereo system
impiegare *v.* to employ **10**

impiegato/a *m., f.* employee **10**
impiegato/a *m., f.* **postale** postal worker
impiego *m.* job **4**
imporre *v.* to impose **4**
importante *adj.* important
importare *v.* to be important; matter **2**
impossibile *adj.* impossible **7**
impoverirsi *v.* to become poor **6**
impressione *f.* impression
imprigionare *v.* to imprison **4**
improbabile *adj.* unlikely **7**
improvvisare *v.* to improvise **3**
in *prep.* at; in; to
In bocca al lupo. *(lit.* In the mouth of the wolf.) Good luck.
in gamba *adj.* sharp
in modo che *conj.* so that
inaffidabile *adj.* unreliable **4**
inaspettato/a *adj.* unexpected **1**
incartare *v.* to wrap
incassare *v.* to cash **4**
incertezza *f.* uncertainty **6**
inchiesta: condurre un'inchiesta *v.* to carry out an investigation
incidente *m.* accident
incinta: essere incinta *v.* to be pregnant **5, 8**
incollare *v.* to paste **7**
incomprensione *f.* lack of understanding **6**
incontrare *v.* to meet
incontrarsi *v.* to get together **2**
incoraggiare *v.* to encourage **8**
incosciente *adj.* irresponsible **6**
incoscienza *f.* recklessness **6**
incredibile *adj.* incredible
incrocio *m.* intersection **2**
indaffarato/a *adj.* busy **2**
indicazioni: dare indicazioni *v.* to give directions **2**
indimenticabile *adj.* unforgettable **1**
indipendente *adj.* independent
diventare indipendente *v.* to become independent **5**
indirizzo *m.* address
indirizzo *m.* **e-mail** e-mail address **7**
indossare *v.* to wear **1**
indovinare *v.* to guess
ineguale *adj.* unequal **4**
infanzia *f.* childhood **5**
infedele *adj.* unfaithful **1**
inferiore *adj.* lower, shorter; inferior **9**
infermiere/a *m., f.* nurse
infezione *f.* infection
infimo/a *adj.* lowest **9**
infilarsi *v.* to slip on (clothing) **9**
influente *adj.* influential **9**
influenza *f.* flu
influenzare *v.* to influence **4**
informarsi *v.* to keep oneself informed **9**

informatica *f.* computer science **7**
informativa *f.* report **8**
infradito *f., pl.* flip-flops **3**
infrastruttura *f.* infrastructure **2**
ingegnere *m.* engineer **2**
ingegneria *f.* engineering **7**
ingenuità *f.* naïveté **5**
ingenuo/a *adj.* naïve
ingiusto/a *adj.* unfair **4**
inglese *adj.* English
ingolfare (motore) *v.* to flood
ingordigia *f.* gluttony **4**
ingorgo *m.* **stradale** traffic jam **2**
ingrassare *v.* to gain weight **8**
inizio *m.* beginning
innamorarsi (di) *v.* to fall in love (with) **1**
innanzitutto *adv.* first of all
inno *m.* anthem **4**
innocente *adj.* innocent **4**
innovativo/a *adj.* innovative
inopportuno/a *adj.* inappropriate
inquietante *adj.* disturbing
inquilino/a *m., f.* tenant
inquinamento *m.* pollution **7**
insalata *f.* salad
insegnante *m., f.* professor; teacher
insegnare *v.* to teach **8**
insensibile *adj.* insensitive
insetto *m.* insect
insicuro/a *adj.* insecure **1**
insieme *adv.* together
insipido/a *adj.* bland
insistere *v.* to insist **6**
insonnia *f.* insomnia
insopportabile *adj.* unbearable **5**
integrazione *f.* integration **4, 6**
intelligente *adj.* intelligent
intelligenza *f.* intelligence
intelligenza *f.* **artificiale** artificial intelligence (A.I.) **7**
interessante *adj.* interesting
interessare *v.* to interest **2**
interessarsi (a/di) *v.* to be interested in **8**
interesse: tasso *m.* **di interesse** interest rate
Internet caffè *m.* internet cafè
interpellare *v.* to consult
interpretare *v.* to perform
interrogatorio *m.* interrogation **8**
intervallo *m.* intermission
intervento *m.* intervention; operation **7**
intervista *f.* interview **9**
intervistatore/intervistatrice *m., f.* interviewer **10**
intorno *prep., adv.* around
intrattenitore *m.* entertainer
invadere *v.* to invade **8**
invecchiare *v.* to age **5**
invece *adv.* instead; on the other hand
inventare *v.* invent

inverno *m.* winter
investigazione *f.* investigation **8**
investimento *m.* investment
investire *v.* to invest **10**
inviare *v.* to send **1**
inviato/a *m., f.* **speciale** correspondent **9**
invitare (a) *v.* to invite (to) **8**
invito *m.* invitation **8**
irlandese *adj.* Irish
irresponsabile *adj.* irresponsible
isola *f.* island
istantaneo/a: messaggio *m.* **istantaneo** instant message
istruzione *f.* education
italiano/a *adj.* Italian

J

jeans *m., pl.* jeans

L

là *adv.* there
labbro (*pl.* labbra *f.*) *m.* lip
laboratorio *m.* lab
laggiù *adv.* down there **6**
ladro/a *m., f.* thief **4**
lagnone/a *m., f.* whiner
lago *m.* lake
lamentare *v.* to regret, to lament **6**
lamentarsi (di) *v.* to complain (about) **2**
lamentoso/a *adj.* whiny
lampada *f.* lamp
lampo *m.* flash of lightning
lana *m.* wool
largo/a *adj.* big; loose
lasciare *v.* to allow, to let; to leave **1**
Lasciami in pace. Leave me alone.
lasciare un messaggio *v.* to leave a message
lasciarsi *v.* to break up
lassie *m.* collie **1**
lassù *adv.* up there **6**
latte *m.* milk
lattuga *f.* lettuce
laurearsi *v.* to graduate from college/university
lavagna *f.* blackboard
lavanderia *f.* dry cleaner **9**
lavanderia *f.* dry cleaner; laundromat
lavare *v.* to wash
lavare i piatti *v.* to wash the dishes
lavarsi *v.* to wash oneself **2**
lavarsi i denti *v.* to brush one's teeth
lavastoviglie *f.* dishwasher
lavatrice *f.* washing machine **5**
lavavetri *m.* window cleaner
lavorare *v.* to work
lavoro *m.* job; work
annuncio *m.* **di lavoro** job ad **10**

colloquio *m.* **di lavoro** job interview **10**
lavoro *m.* **a orario normale/ ridotto** full-/part-time job **10**
leale *adj.* loyal **3**
legale *adj.* legal **4**
legge *f.* law
approvare/passare una legge *v.* to pass a law **4**
leggere *v.* to read **3**
leggero/a *adj.* light; slight
legiferare *v.* legislate **4**
legno *m.* wood **5**
legumi *m., pl.* legumes
lenti a specchio *f., pl.* mirrored lenses **3**
lento/a *adj.* slow
lettera *f.* letter
lettera *f.* **di presentazione** cover letter
letteratura *f.* literature
lettere *f., pl.* arts (humanities)
letto *m.* bed
lettore *m.* reader
lettore CD/DVD/MP3 *m.* CD/DVD/MP3 player **7**
lettura *f.* reading
lezione *f.* class; lesson
liberale *adj.* liberal **4**
liberare *v.* to liberate **8**
libertà *f.* freedom **4**
libertà *f.* **di culto** freedom of worship **6**
libertà *f.* **di stampa** freedom of the press **9**
libreria *f.* bookstore
libro *m.* book
libro *m.* **elettronico** *m.* e-Book **7**
licenziare *v.* to fire **10**
liceo *m.* high school
limite *m.* **di velocità** speed limit
linea *f.* line
lingua *f.* language
lingua *f.* **dei segni** sign language
lingua *f.* **madre** native language **6**
lingue *f., pl.* languages (subject)
liscio/a *adj.* straight (hair)
litigare *v.* to quarrel, fight **5**
livello: passaggio *m.* **a livello** level crossing
livido *m.* bruise
locale *m.* **notturno** nightclub
località *f.* resort
località *f.* **balneare** ocean resort
località *f.* **di villeggiatura** resort
lontano/a *adj.* distant **5**; *adv.* far
look *m.* dressing style **10**
lottare *v.* to fight, struggle
luglio *m.* July
luna *f.* moon
luna park *m.* amusement park **3**
lunedì *m.* Monday
lungo *prep.* along **8**

lungo/a *adj.* long
  a lungo termine *adj.* long-term **10**
luogo *m.* place
  luoghi comuni *m., pl.* commonplaces
lupo *m.* wolf **1**
lusso *m.* luxury **4**

M

ma *conj.* but
macchiare *v.* to stain
macchiato/a *adj.* stained
macchina *f.* car
  macchina *f.* **ibrida** hybrid car
  salire in macchina *v.* to get in the car **2**
  scendere dalla macchina get out of the car **2**
  macchina *f.* **fotografica (digitale)** (digital) camera
macelleria *f.* butcher shop
madre *f.* mother
madrina *f.* godmother **5**
maggio *m.* May
maggiore *adj.* bigger; older **9**
magia *f.* magic **3**
maglia *f.* jersey **2, 3**
maglietta *f.* t-shirt
maglione *m.* sweater
magro/a *adj.* thin
mai *adv.* ever
malato/a *adj.* ill
malattia *f.* ailment; disease
male *adv.* badly **9**; *m.* pain
  mal *m.* **di gola** sore throat
  mal *m.* **di mare** sea-sickness
  mal *m.* **di testa** headache
  Non c'è male. Not bad.
  Sto male. I am not well.
maledire *v.* to curse
maledizione *f.* curse
maleducato/a *adj.* bad-mannered **5**
malgrado *conj.* although **7**
maltempo *m.* bad weather **6**
maltrattamento *m.* abuse; mistreatment **6**
mamma *f.* mom
mammone *m.* mama's boy **5**
mancare *v.* to be missing **2**
mandare *v.* to send
  mandare in onda *v.* to broadcast
mandria *f.* herd **7**
mangiare *v.* to eat **6**
manica *f.* sleeve
  maglietta *f.* **a maniche corte/ lunghe** short-/long-sleeved t-shirt
manifestare *v.* to demonstrate **6**
manipolazione *f.* manipulation
mano (*pl.* **le mani)** *f.* hand
mansarda *f.* attic
mantenersi *v.* to provide for oneself

mappa *f.* map
marca *f.* brand **10**
marciapiede *m.* sidewalk **2**
mare *m.* sea
marea *f.* tide **7**
marito *m.* husband **5**
  primo/secondo marito *m.* first/ second husband
marmellata *f.* jam
marmo *m.* marble **8**
marrone *adj.* brown (eyes)
martedì *m.* Tuesday
martello *m.* hammer **8**
marziano/a *m., f.* Martian **7**
marzo *m.* March
maschera *f.* mask **4**
maschio *m.* male
massima *f.* maxim
massimo/a *adj.* greatest **9**
masterizzare *v.* to burn **7**
matematica *f.* mathematics
matematico/a *m., f.* mathematician **7**
materia *f.* subject
materiale *m.* **edile** building material **2**
materno/a *adj.* maternal **5**
matita *f.* pencil
matrigna *f.* stepmother
matrimonio *m.* wedding **1**
mattina *f.* morning
maturità *f.* maturity **5**
maturo/a *adj.* mature **1**
meccanico/a *m., f.* mechanic
mecenate *m.* patron **8**
media *m., pl.* media
mediante *prep.* by means of **8**
medicina *f.* drug; medicine
medico *m.* **di famiglia** family doctor
medio/a: di media statura *adj.* of average height
Medioevo *m.* Middle Ages **6**
meglio *adv.* better **9**
mela *f.* apple
melanzana *f.* eggplant
melone *m.* melon
mendicante *m., f.* beggar **2**
meno *adv.* less; *adv.* minus
mensa *f.* cafeteria
mensile *f.* monthly magazine **9**
mensilità *f.* monthly paycheck; salary
mentire *v.* to lie **1**
mentre *conj.* while
menu *m.* menu
mercato *m.* market
  mercato *m.* **immobiliare** real estate market **10**
mercoledì *m.* Wednesday
merenda *f.* afternoon snack
merendina *f.* snack **3**
meridionale *adj.* southern **6**
meritare *v.* to deserve **1**

mese *m.* month
messaggio *m.* message
  messaggio *m.* **istantaneo** IM, instant message
messicano/a *adj.* Mexican
mestiere *m.* occupation; trade **10**
  mestieri *m., pl.* chores
metro *m.* tape measure **8**
metro(politana) *f.* subway **2**
metropoli *f.* big city **2**
mettere *v.* to put **2**
  mettere in scena *v.* to put on a play
  mettere sotto *v.* to run over **7**
  mettersi *v.* to put on (clothing, shoes) **1**
mezzanotte *f.* midnight
mezzo *m.* means
  mezzo *m.* **di trasporto** means of transportation
  mezzo *m.* **pubblico** public transportation **2**
mezzogiorno *m.* noon
mezz'ora *f. m.* half hour
microfono *m.* microphone
microonda: (forno a)
  microonde *m.* microwave oven
miglio *m.* mile
migliorare *v.* to improve
migliore *adj.* better **9**
mille *m.* one thousand
millecento *m.* one thousand one hundred
millesimo *adj.* one-thousandth
minaccia *f.* threat **4**
minestrone *m.* thick soup
minigonna *f.* miniskirt **10**
minimo/a *adj.* least, lowest **9**
minore *adj.* smaller; younger **9**
miracolo *m.* miracle **5**
miseria *f.* misery, poverty
mobili *m., pl.* furniture
mobilità *f.* transfer
mobilitare *v.* to mobilize **6**
moda *f.* fashion
  passato/a di moda *adj.* out-of-style **3**
moderato/a *adj.* moderate **4**
modesto/a *adj.* modest
modo *m.* way
modulo *m.* form
  riempire un modulo *v.* to fill out a form
moglie *f.* wife **5**
mollare *v.* to let go **6**
molto *adv.* a lot **9**
molto/a/i/e *indef. adj., pron.* a lot of; many; much
monarchico/a *adj.* monarchic **8**
moneta *f.* change; coin
monolocale *m.* studio apartment
montagna *f.* mountain
montano/a: località *f.* **montana** mountain resort

morale *adj.* ethical **7**; *f.* moral **3**
morbillo *m.* measles
morire *v.* to die **3**
morso *m.* bite
morte *f.* death **5**
moschea *f.* mosque **6**
mosso/a *adj.* wavy
mostra *f.* exhibition **3, 8**
mostrare *v.* to show
motore *m.* engine; motor
motorino *m.* scooter
mucca *f.* cow
multa *f.* traffic ticket **9**; fine
multilingue *adj.* multilingual **6**
multilinguismo *m.* multilinguism **4**
municipio *m.* city hall **2**
muovere *v.* to move **2**
muoversi *v.* to get going **2**
mura *f., pl.* **di cinta** city walls **2**
muratore *m.* bricklayer
muschio *m.* moss
muscoloso/a *adj.* muscular
musica *f.* music
musicista *m., f.* musician
muso *m.* muzzle **1**
musulmano/a *adj.* Muslim **6**
muta *f.* wet suit **4**
mutuo *m.* mortgage

N

nanotecnologia *f.* nanotechnology **7**
narratore *m.* narrator **8**
nascere *v.* to be born **3**
nascita *f.* birth **5**
nascondere *v.* to hide
nascosto/a *adj.* hidden **4**
naso *m.* nose
  naso *m.* **chiuso** stuffy nose
nastro *m.* ribbon
  nastro *m.* **adesivo** adhesive tape
  nastro *m.* **trasportatore** luggage
  carousel; moving walkway **5**
Natale *m.* Christmas
natura *f.* nature
  natura *f.* **morta** still life **8**
naturale *adj.* natural
  acqua *f.* **naturale** still water
naufrago *m.* castaway **4**
nausea *f.* nausea
nave *f.* ship
navigare *v.* to navigate
  navigare in rete *v.* to surf the Web
  navigare su Internet/sulla rete
  v. to browse /surf the Internet/Web **7**
navigatore satellitare *m.* GPS
nazionalismo *m.* nationalism **6**
né: non... né... né *conj.*
  neither... nor
neanche: non... neanche *adv.*
  not even
necessario/a *adj.* necessary

necessità: di prima
  necessità *adj.* absolutely necessary **5**
negozio *m.* store
  negozio *m.* **d'alimentari**
  grocery store
nemico *m.* enemy **2**
nemmeno *conj.* not even
neoclassico/a *adj.* Neoclassical
neoplatonismo *m.* Neoplatonism **8**
neppure *conj.* not even
nero/a *adj.* noir, black
nervoso/a *adj.* nervous
nessuno/a *indef. adj.* no, not any **9**;
  indef. pron. no one, not anyone **9**
netturbino/a *m., pl.* garbage collector
neve *f.* snow
nevicare *v.* to snow
niente *indef. pron.* nothing **9**
  Niente di nuovo. Nothing new.
ninnananna *f.* lullaby **3**
nipote *m., f.* nephew/niece;
  grandson/granddaughter **5**
no *adv.* no
noia *f.* boredom
  Che noia! How boring!
  dare noia a *v.* to bother **8**
noioso/a *adj.* boring
noleggiare *v.* to rent (car)
noleggio *m.* lease
non *adv.* not
  non... più *adv.* no more, no longer
nonno/a *m., f.* grandfather/
  grandmother **5**
nono *adj.* ninth
nonostante *conj.* although **7**
norma *f.* law; norm
nostalgia *f.* nostalgia **1**
notevole *adj.* remarkable, important **7**
notizia *f.* news story **9**
notiziario *m.* radio/TV news, news
  program **2, 9**
notorietà *f.* fame
notte *f.* night
novanta *m.* ninety
nove *m.* nine
novecento *m.* nine hundred
novella *f.* short novel **8**
novembre *m.* November
nubile *adj., f.* single **1**
nucleo familiare *m.* family unit **5**
nulla *indef. pron.* nothing **9**
numero *m.* number
  numero *m.* **di telefono**
  phone number
nuora *f.* daughter-in-law **5**
nuotare *v.* to swim
nuoto *m.* swimming
nuovo/a *adj.* new
  di nuovo *adv.* again
nuvola *f.* cloud
nuvoloso/a *adj.* cloudy

O

o *conj.* or
obbediente *adj.* obedient **4**
obbligare (a) *v.* to oblige, compel **8**
occhiali *m., pl.* glasses
  occhiali da sole *m., pl.*
  sunglasses **10**
occhiata: dare un'occhiata *v.* to
  take a look **3**
occhio *m.* eye
occorrere *v.* to be necessary **6**
occuparsi di *v.* to take care of **8**
occupazione *f.* occupation
  prima occupazione *f.* first job
oceano *m.* ocean
odiare *v.* to hate **1**
odiarsi *v.* to hate each other
odio *m.* hatred
odore *m.* smell **10**
officina *f.* factory **10**
offrire *v.* to offer **3**
oggettivo/a *adj.* objective **8**
oggi *m., adj., adv.* today
ogni *indef. adj.* every, all **9**
Ognissanti *m.* All Saints' Day
ognuno/a *indef. pron.* everyone **9**
olio *m.* oil
olio d'oliva *m.* olive oil
oltre *prep.* beyond **8**
ombrello *m.* umbrella
omicida *adj.* homicidal **8**
onesto/a *adj.* honest **1**
onirico/a *adj.* dream-like **9**
opera *f.* work (of art); opera **8**
operaio/a *m., f.* factory worker
opinione *f.* opinion
  opinione *f.* **pubblica** public
  opinion **6**
opportuno/a *adj.* appropriate
oppresso/a *adj.* oppressed **4**
opprimere *v.* to oppress **8**
oppure *conj.* or
ora *f.* hour
orario *m.* schedule **1**
  orario *m.* **di lavoro** work hours **10**
orchestra *f.* orchestra
  orchestra *f.* **da camera** chamber
  orchestra **8**
  orchestra *f.* **sinfonica**
  symphony **8**
ordigno *m.* bomb **5**
ordinare *v.* to order
orecchini *m., pl.* earrings **10**
orecchio (*pl.* orecchie *f.*) *m.* ear
orgoglio *m.* pride **3**
orgoglioso/a *adj.* proud **1**
orientarsi *v.* to get one's bearings
orizzonte *m.* horizon
ormai *adv.* by now, already
orologio *m.* clock; watch
oroscopo *m.* horoscope **9**

orrore: film m. **dell'orrore** m. horror film
ospedale m. hospital
ospizio m. nursing home 6
osteria f. small restaurant
ottanta m. eighty
ottantaduesimo adj. eighty-second
ottantuno m. eighty-one
ottavo adj. eighth
ottenere v. to obtain 6
ottico m. optician 3
ottimista adj. optimistic 1
ottimo/a adj. very good 9
otto m. eight
otto milioni m. eight million
ottobre m. October
ottocento m. eight hundred
ovunque adv. all over; wherever

P

pacco m. package
pace f. peace 4
pacifico/a adj. peaceful 4
pacifista adj. pacifist 4
padre m. father
padrino m. godfather 5
padrone m. owner, boss 4
padrone/a di casa m., f. landlord/ landlady
paesaggio m. landscape 8
paesano/a m., f. village/ (fellow) countryman/woman 2
paese m. village 2
pagare v. to pay
pagare con assegno v. to pay by check
pagare in contanti v. to pay in cash
pagare le bollette v. to pay the bills
paio m. pair
palazzo m. building, palace 2
palestra f. gymnasium
andare in palestra v. to go to the gym 3
palla f. ball 2
pallacanestro f. basketball
pallavolo f. volleyball
pallone m. soccer; (soccer) ball 2, 3
palpebra f. eyelid 5
panchina f. bench
pane m. bread
panetteria f. bakery
panettone m. Christmas cake 6
paninoteca f. sandwich shop
pannello m. **solare** solar panel
pannolino m. diaper 2
panorama m. landscape; panorama
pantaloncini m., pl. shorts
pantaloni m., pl. pants
pantaloni corti m., pl. short pants 10
pantaloni lunghi m., pl. long pants 10

pantofole f., pl. slippers
papa m. pope 6
papà m. dad
parabrezza m. windshield
parapendio m. paragliding
parare v. to save; block 2, 3
parcheggiare v. to park 2
pareggiare v. to tie 3
pareggiare una partita v. to tie a game 3
pareggio m. tie 3
parente m., f. relative 5
parentela f. relatives; family relationship 5
parenti m., pl. relatives
parere v. to appear; seem 2
parete f. wall
parlamento m. parliament 6
parlare (di) v. to talk (about) 8
parlarsi v. to speak to each other 2
parrucchiere/a m., f. hairdresser
parte f. part
Da questa parte. This way.
partecipare (a) v. to participate (in) 8
partenze f., pl. departures
particolare m. detail 8
partigiano m. resistance fighter 2; partisan 8
partire v. to leave 3
partire in vacanza v. to go on vacation
partita f. game
vincere/perdere/pareggiare una partita v. to win/lose/tie a game 3
partito m. **politico** political party 4
parziale adj. partial; biased 9
pascolo m. pasture, grazing land 7
Pasqua f. Easter
pasquetta f. Easter Monday 9
passaggio m. passage
dare un passaggio v. to give a ride 2
passare v. to pass 2, 3; to spend (time)
passare una legge v. to pass a law 4
passato/a di moda adj. out of style 3
passeggero/a m. passenger 2
passeggiare v. to take a walk 2
passeggiata f. walk
passerella f. footbridge 7
passo m. pass; step
a due passi da not far from
pasta(sciutta) f. pasta
laboratorio m. **di pasta fresca** store specializing in homemade pasta
pasticceria f. pastry shop
pasto m. meal
patata f. potato
patente f. driver's license
paterno/a adj. paternal 5
patria f. homeland 2
patrigno m. stepfather

patrimonio m. **culturale** cultural heritage 9
pattinaggio m. skating 3
pattinaggio m. **sul ghiaccio** ice-skating 3
patto m. pact
paura f. fear 4
avere paura (di) v. to be afraid (of) 1
pavimento m. floor
paziente adj. patient; m., f. patient
pazzo/a adj. crazy
peccato m. pity
pecora f. sheep
pedone m., f. pedestrian 2
peggio adv. worse
peggiore adj. worse 9; adv. worse 9
pelle f. skin; leather
pelliccia f. fur 5
penare v. to suffer 6
penna f. pen
pennello m. paintbrush 8
pensare v. to think 8
pensare a v. to think about 8
pensare di v. to plan to 8
pensionato/a m., f. retiree
pensione f. boarding house; pension
pensione: andare in pensione v. to retire 10
pentirsi v. to regret 5
pepe m. pepper (spice)
peperone (rosso, verde) m. (red, green) pepper
per prep. for, in order to, through
per favore adv. please
pera f. pear
perché conj. why; so that 7
perciò conj. so
perdere v. to lose 3
perdere le elezioni v. to lose the election 4
perdere una partita v. to lose a game 3
perdersi v. to get lost 2
perdita f. loss 2
pericolo m. danger 4
pericoloso/a adj. dangerous 2
periferia f. suburb 2
permettere v. to allow 6
persona f. person
personaggio m. character 8
personaggio m. **principale** main character
persuadere (a) v. to persuade (to) 8
pesante adj. heavy; rich
pesca f. peach
pescare v. to fish 4
pesce m. fish
pescheria f. fish/seafood shop
peso m. weight
pessimista adj. pessimistic 1
pessimo/a adj. very bad 9
pettegolezzi m. gossip 1
pettinare v. to brush

pettinarsi *v.* to brush/comb one's hair
pettine *m.* comb
petto *m.* chest
pezzo *m.* piece **3**
piacere *m.* pleasure; *v.* to be pleasing, like **6**
pianeta *m.* planet
  salvare il pianeta *v.* to save the planet
piangere *v.* to cry **3**
pianificare *v.* to plan **6**
pianista *m., f.* pianist
piano *m.* **di cottura** stovetop
piano *m.* **urbanistico** city plan **2**
pianta *f.* plant
piattaforma *f.* platform **1**
piatto *m.* course; plate
  primo/secondo piatto *m.* first/second course
piccante *adj.* spicy
piccolo/a *adj.* small **9**
piede *m.* foot
pieno/a *adj.* full
pietanza *f.* dish **4**
pietra *f.* rock
pigmento *m.* pigment **8**
pigro/a *adj.* lazy
PIL *m.* GDP
pillola *f.* pill
pinne *f., pl.* flippers **4**
pioggia *f.* rain
piovere *v.* to rain
piovoso/a *adj.* rainy
piscina *f.* swimming pool **10**
pittore/pittrice *m., f.* painter **8**
pittura *f.* paint; painting **8**
  pittura *f.* **a olio** oil painting **8**
  pittura *f.* **a pastello** pastel painting **8**
più *adj., adv.* more; most
  non... più *adv.* no more, no longer
pizzeria *f.* pizza shop
pizzico *m.* pinch
platea *f.* stall
pneumatico *m.* **sgonfio** flat tire
poco *adv.* little **9**
poco/a (po'): po' (di) *adj.* little (not much) (of)
podere *m.* farmhouse
poema *m.* poem
poesia *f.* poetry **8**
poeta/poetessa *m., f.* poet
poi *adv.* later; then
polemica *f.* controversy **6**
politico/a *m., f.* politician **4**
politica *f.* politics **4**
polizia *f.* police
poliziotto/a *m., f.* police officer **2**
pollici *m./pl* inches (*lit.* thumbs) **7**
polpo *m.* octopus
poltrona *f.* armchair; seat

polvere *f.* dust
pomeriggio *m.* afternoon
pomodoro *m.* tomato
pompiere *m.* fireman **7**
ponte *m.* bridge
popolazione *f.* population **6**
popolo *m.* people
poppa *f.* stern **4**
porre *v.* to put **1**
porta *f.* door
portare *v.* to bring; to wear
  portare fuori la spazzatura *v.* to take out the trash
  portare un vestito *v.* to wear a suit
portatile *adj.* portable
  computer *m.* **portatile** laptop computer **7**
portiera *f.* car door
portiere/a *m.* goalkeeper **2, 3**
portiere/a *m., f.* caretaker; doorman
posizione *m., f.* job **10**
possedere *v.* to own **4**; to possess
possessivo/a *adj.* possessive **5**
possibile *adj.* possible **7**
posta *f.* mail
poster *m.* poster
postino/a *m., f.* mail carrier
posto *m., f.* job **10**
potente *adj.* powerful **4**
potenza *f.* power **4**
potere *v.* to be able, can **1**; *m.* power
povero/a *adj.* poor
povertà *f.* poverty **2, 6**
pranzo *m.* lunch
  sala *f.* **da pranzo** dining room
prato *m.* meadow
precisione *f.* precision **8**
predire *v.* to predict **7**
preferibile *adj.* preferable
preferire *v.* to prefer **6**
preferito/a *adj.* favorite
prefisso *m.* area code **9**
pregare *v.* to pray **6**
preghiera *f.* prayer
pregiudizio *m.* prejudice **6**
preistorico *adj.* prehistoric **8**
prelievo: fare un prelievo *v.* to make a withdrawal **10**
premiato/a *adj.* award-winning **8, 9**
premio *m.* prize
prenatale *adj.* prenatal **3**
prendere *v.* to take **1**
  prendere in affitto *v.* to rent (tenant)
  prendere l'iniziativa *v.* to take initiative **5**
  prendere qualcosa da bere/ mangiare *v.* to get something to drink/eat **3**
  prendere un congedo *v.* to take leave time
prenotare *v.* to make a reservation

prenotazione *f.* reservation
preoccuparsi (di) *v.* to worry (about) **2**
preoccupato/a *adj.* worried **1**
preoccupazione *f.* worry **7**
preparare *v.* to prepare **8**
prepararsi *v.* to get oneself ready
presentare *v.* to introduce; to present
presentazione *f.* introduction
preservare *v.* to preserve
presso *prep.* near, with **8**
prestare *v.* to lend
presidente *m., f.* president **4**
prestito *m.* loan **10**
presto *adv.* quickly; soon
  A presto. See you soon.
prete *m.* priest **6**
prevedere *v.* to predict **7**
prigionia *f.* imprisonment
prigioniero/a *m., f.* prisoner **2**
prima *adv.* beforehand; *adv.* first, before; *f.* opening night, premiere **3**; *prep.* before
  prima che *conj.* before **7**
primavera *f.* spring
primo/a *adj.* first
primogenito/a *m., f.* first-born
principale *adj.* main; *m., f.* boss; director
prioritario/a: posta *f.* **prioritaria** priority mail
probabile *adj.* likely **7**
probabilità *f.* probability **9**
problema *m.* problem
professione *f.* profession
professore(ssa) *m., f.* professor
profumeria *f.* cosmetics/perfume shop
programma *m.* plan; program
proibito/a *adj.* forbidden
proiezione *f.* screening
promesso *p.p., adj.* promised **4**
promettere (di) *v.* to promise (to) **8**
promozione *f.* promotion **10**
promuovere *v.* to promote **4**
pronto/a *adj.* ready
  essere pronto/a a *v.* to be ready to **8**
  pronto soccorso *m.* first aid; emergency room
  Pronto. Hello. (on the phone)
proporre *v.* to propose
proprietario/a *m., f.* owner **10**
prosa *f.* prose **8**
prosciutto *m.* ham
proseguire *v.* to continue
prospero/a *adj.* successful **10**
prossimo/a *adj.* next
protagonismo *m.* desire to be in the limelight

protestante *adj.* Protestant **6**
protettore *m.* protector
provarci (con) *v.* to flirt (with) **2**
provare *v.* to feel **1**
  provare a *v.* to try to **8**
provarsi *v.* to try on **3**
proverbio *m.* proverb **6**
provincia *f.* province **6**
provino *m.* screen test
prua *f.* bow **4**
prudente *adj.* careful **1**
pseudonimo *m.* screen/pen name
psicologo/a *m., f.* psychologist
pubblicare *v.* to publish
pubblicità *f.* commercial;
  advertisement **9**
pubblico *m.* audience, public
pugilato *m.* boxing **3**
pulire *v.* to clean
pulito/a *adj.* clean
  energia *f.* **pulita** clean energy **7**
pullman *m.* bus; coach
punire *v.* to punish **5**
puntata *f.* episode **9**
punto *m.* point
  punto *m.* **di riferimento**
    reference point **4**
  punto *m.* **di vista** point of view **8**
puntuale *adj.* on-time
puntura: fare una puntura *v.*
  to give a shot
purché *conj.* so that **7**
pure *adv.* also; even
puzza *f.* stench

Q

qua *adv.* here
quaderno *m.* notebook
quadro *m.* painting; picture **8**
qualche *indef. adj.* some, a few **9**
  qualche volta *adv.* sometimes
qualcosa *indef. pron.* something **9**
qualcuno/a *indef. pron.* someone **9**
quale *adj., pron., adv.* what, which
qualifiche *f., pl.* qualifications **10**
qualsiasi *indef. adj.* any, whatever,
  whichever **9**
qualunque *indef. adj.* any, whatever,
  whichever **9**
quando *conj., adv.* when
quanti *rel. pron.* everyone, all who,
  all that **9**
quanti/e *adj.* how many
  Quanti gradi ci sono? What is
    the temperature?
quanto *adj., pron., adv.* how much;
  rel. pron. that which, that, what **9**
  Da quanto tempo... For how
    long...
quaranta *m.* forty
quartiere *m.* neighborhood **1, 2;**
  m. quarter

quarto *adj.* fourth; quarter hour
quattordici *m.* fourteen
quattro *m.* four
quattrocchi *m., f.* four eyes **3**
quattrocento *m.* four hundred
quel(lo) che *rel. pron.* that which,
  that, what **9**
quello/a *adj.* that
questo/a *adj.* this
questura *f.* police headquarters
qui *adv.* here
  qui vicino *adv.* nearby
quindici *m.* fifteen
quinto *adj.* fifth
quotidiano/a *adj.* daily **2**

R

rabbino *m.* rabbi **6**
raccogliere *v.* to pick **3**
raccomandare *v.* to recommend;
  to urge
raccomandata *f.* registered mail
raccomandazione *f.*
  recommendation
racconto *m.* short story
radersi *v.* to shave
radice *f.* root **5**
radio *f.* radio
  stazione *f.* **radio** radio station **9**
raffinato/a *adj.* refined **3**
raffreddore *m.* cold
  avere il raffreddore *v.* to have
    a cold
rafting *m.* rafting
ragazza *f.* girl; girlfriend
ragazzaccio *m.* bad boy
ragazzo *m.* boy; boyfriend
ragione *f.* reason
  avere ragione *v.* to be right **8**
ramo *m.* branch
rana *f.* frog
rapina *f.* robbery **4**
rapinare *v.* to rob **4**
rapporto *m.* relationship **9**
rappresentazione *f.* **dal vivo**
  live performance
raramente *adv.* rarely
rasoio *m.* razor
rassegna *f.* festival **9**
rata *f.* installment; payment
razza *f.* race **1**
razzismo *m.* racism **6**
re/regina *m., f.* king/queen **8**
realismo *m.* realism **6**
realista *adj.* realistic **8**
reality *m.* reality show
realizzare *v.* to fulfill; achieve **6**
recensione *f.* review **9**
recessione *f.* recession **10**
recitare *v.* to act; to recite
  recitare un ruolo *v.* to play a role

reclamare *v.* to complain, protest;
  claim **6**
redattore/redattrice *m., f.* editor **9**
referenze *f., pl.* references
regalare *v.* to give (as a gift)
regime *m.* regime **8**
regista *m., f.* director **9**
registrare *v.* to record **9**
registratore *m.* recorder (tape,
  CD, etc.)
regno *m.* kingdom **6, 8**
regolamento *m.* regulations **3**
relitto *m.* relic
remare *v.* to row
remissivo/a *adj.* submissive **5**
rendersi *v.* to become
  rendersi conto di *v.* to realize **8**
reperto *m.* find (archeol.) **2**
resistente *adj.* sturdy **1**
Resistenza *f.* Resistance **8**
responsabile *adj.* responsible
restare *v.* to have left **2;** to remain,
  to stay
restituire *v.* to give back
retaggio *m.* heritage **1**
rete *f.* goal; net **3**
  rete *f.* **senza fili** wireless network **7**
retta: dare retta *v.* to pay attention **5**
riattaccare: riattaccare il
  telefono *v.* to hang up the phone
ribalta *f.* proscenium, downstage
ribelle *adj.* rebellious **5**
riccio/a *adj.* curly
ricco/a *adj.* rich
ricerca *f.* research **7**
ricercatore/ricercatrice *m., f.*
  researcher **7**
ricetta *f.* prescription; recipe
ricevere *v.* to receive; to get
ricevimento *m.* reception **8**
ricevuta *f.* receipt **10**
richiesta *f.* demand **10**
riciclare *v.* to recycle **7**
riciclo *m.* recycling
riconoscere *v.* to acknowledge,
  to recognize
ricordare *v.* to remember
ricordarsi (di) *v.* to remember (to) **2**
ricordo *m.* memory **1**
ridere *v.* to laugh **3**
riempire (di) *v.* to fill (with) **8**
rifiuto *m.* garbage
  vietato buttare rifiuti no littering
riflettere (su) *v.* to reflect (on) **8**
rifugio *m.* shelter
riga *f.* part, stripe
rigore: calcio *m.* **di rigore**
  penalty kick **3**
rima *f.* rhyme **8**
rimandare *v.* to postpone **5**
rimanere *v.* to stay **1**
rimborso *m.* refund

rimproverare *v.* to scold **5**
rinascimentale *adj.* Renaissance
Rinascimento *m.* Renaissance **6**
rincasare *v.* to go back home **10**
rincorrere *v.* to chase
rinforzo *m.* reinforcement **5**
ringraziare (di) *v.* to thank (for) **8**
rinunciare (a) *v.* to give up **10**
riordinare *v.* to tidy up
riparare *v.* to repair
ripetere *v.* to repeat
riposarsi *v.* to rest **2**
riscaldamento *m.* **globale** global warming **7**
riso *m.* rice
risolvere *v.* to solve **6**
Risorgimento *m.* Resurgence (Italian unification) **6**
risparmiare *v.* to save **10**
risparmio *m.* saving **10**
  conto *m.* **di risparmio** savings account
rispettare *v.* to respect
rispondere *v.* to answer **3**
  rispondere al telefono *v.* to answer the phone
ristorante *m.* restaurant
risultare *v.* to result **3**
ritardo *m.* delay **2**
ritenere *v.* to maintain **6**
ritirare dei soldi *v.* to withdraw money
ritirata *f.* retreat **2**
ritornare *v.* to go back, to return **3**
ritratto *f.* portrait
ritrovato *m.* discovery, finding **7**
riunione *f.* meeting
riuscire (a) *v.* to succeed in, manage to **1**
rivedere *v.* to recognize
rivista *f.* magazine **9**
rivolgersi *v.* to address **8**
robotica *f.* robotics **7**
romanico/a *adj.* Romanesque
romantico/a *adj.* romantic
romanzo *m.* novel **8**
rompere *v.* to break **3**
  rompere con *v.* to break up with **1**
rompersi *v.* to break
rondine *f.* swallow
rosa *adj.* romance **9**; *(invar.)* pink; *f.* rose
rosolare *v.* to brown
rossetto *m.* lipstick
rosso/a *adj.* red
rotonda *f.* rotary
rovesciare *v.* to overturn **4**; to overthrow **8**
rovine *f., pl.* ruins **2**
rozzo/a *adj.* crude
rubare *v.* to steal **5**
rubrica *f.* address book

rubrica (di cultura e società) *f.* (lifestyle) section **9**
rumore *m.* noise **10**
rumoroso/a *adj.* noisy **2**
ruolo *m.* role **5**
ruscello *m.* stream
russo/a *adj.* Russian

S

sabato *m.* Saturday
sacco *m.* sack
  sacco (di) *adj.* ton (of)
saggista *m., f.* essayist **8**
sala *f.* hall, room
  sala *f.* **d'emergenza** emergency room
salario *m.* salary
  salario *m.* **elevato/basso** high/low salary
salato/a *adj.* salty
saldi *m., pl.* sales **3**
  saldi *m., pl.* **di fine stagione** end-of-season sales **3**
sale *m.* salt
salire *v.* to go up **1**
  salire in macchina *v.* to get in the car **2**
  salire le scale *v.* to climb stairs **2**
  salire sul treno *v.* to get on the train **2**
  salire sull'autobus *v.* to get on the bus **2**
saltare *v.* to jump **3**
  saltare la lezione *v.* to skip class **2**
salto *m.* **generazionale** generation gap **5**
salumeria *f.* delicatessen
salutare *v.* to greet
salutarsi *v.* to greet each other
salute *f.* health
saluto *m.* greeting
salvare *v.* to save **4**
Salve. *(form.)* Hello.
salvo *prep.* except (for) **8**
  salvo che *conj.* unless **7**
salvo/a *adj.* safe **4**
sandali *m., pl.* sandals **10**
sangue *m.* blood **5**
sano/a *adj.* healthy
santo/a *m., f.* saint **6**
  santo/a *m., f.* **patrono/a** patron saint **9**
sapere *v.* to know **1**
sapone *m.* soap
sapore *m.* flavor **4**
saporito/a *adj.* tasty
sartoria *f.* tailor's shop **8**
sasso *m.* stone
sassofono *m.* saxophone
satirico/a *adj.* satirical **8**
sbadigliare *v.* to yawn

sbadiglio *m.* yawn **7**
sbagliare *v.* to make a mistake **1**
sbagliato/a *adj.* wrong **7**
sbarazzarsi di *v.* to get rid of
sbrigarsi *v.* to hurry **2**
scacchi *m., pl.* chess **3**
scaffale *m.* bookshelf
scala *f.* ladder; staircase **8**
  scale *f., pl.* stairs
  salire/scendere le scale *v.* to climb/go down stairs
scalare *v.* to climb **3**
scambio *m.* exchange **4**
  scambio *m.* **di idee** exchange of opinions **8**
scandalo *m.* scandal **4**
scappamento *m.* exhaust
scaricare *v.* to download **7**
scarpe *f., pl.* **da ginnastica/tennis** sneakers **3**
scatola *f.* box **1**
scavo *m.* excavation **2**
scegliere *v.* to choose **1**
scelta *f.* choice **1**
scemo/a *adj.* dim-witted
scena *f.* stage, scene
  mettere in scena *v.* to put on a play
scendere *v.* to go down
  scendere dal treno get off the train **2**
  scendere dalla macchina *v.* to get out of the car **2**
  scendere dall'autobus *v.* to get off the bus **2**
  scendere in campo *v.* to start the game **3**
sceneggiatura *f.* screenplay **9**
scenetta *f.* skit
schema *m.* diagram; scheme
schermo *m.* screen **9**
scherzare *v.* to joke
scherzo *m.* joke
scherzoso/a *adj.* playful
schiavitù *f.* slavery **8**
schiena *f.* back
schifoso/a *adj.* disgusting
schizzo *m.* sketch **8**
sci *m.* skiing **3**; *m. (inv.)* ski
  sci *m.* **di fondo** cross-country skiing **3**
sciare *v.* to ski **1**
sciarpa *f.* scarf
scienze *f., pl.* science
scienziato/a *m., f.* scientist
Sciò! Shoo!
sciopero *m.* strike **10**
scivolare *v.* to slide
scodella *f.* bowl
scogliera *f.* cliff
scoiattolo *m.* squirrel
scolpire *v.* to sculpt **8**; *engrave*

scommettere (su) *v.* to bet (on) **6, 8**
scomparire *v.* to disappear **7**
scomparsa *f.* disappearance **6**
sconfiggere *v.* to defeat **8**
sconfitta *f.* defeat **4**
scontrino *m.* receipt **10**
scopa *f.* broom
scoperta *f.* discovery **7**
scopo *m.* aim; goal **7**
scoraggiamento *m.*
  discouragement **7**
scoria *f.* waste
scorso/a *adj.* last
scortese *adj.* discourteous
scottatura *f.* burn
scrittore/scrittrice *m., f.* writer
scrivere *v.* to write **3**
scriversi *v.* to write each other **2**
scultore/scultrice *m., f.* sculptor **8**
scultura *f.* sculpture **8**
scuola *f.* school
scuro/a *adj.* dark
scusare *v.* to excuse
  Scusi/a. *(form./fam.)* Excuse me.
sdegnarsi *v.* to become indignant **9**
sdegno *m.* contempt
se *conj.* if
sé *disj. pron., m., f., sing., pl.* herself;
  himself; itself; themselves; yourself
sebbene *conj.* although **7**
secchione/a *m., f.* student who
  studies too hard **3**
secco/a *adj.* dry
secolo *m.* century **2**
secondo *prep.* according to **8**
secondo/a *adj.* second
sedersi *v.* sit down
sedia *f.* chair
sedicesimo *adj.* sixteenth
sedici *m.* sixteen
seducente *adj.* attractive
segnale *m.* signal **7**
  segnale *m.* **analogico** analog
    signal **7**
  segnale *m.* **digitale** digital signal **7**
  segnale *m.* **stradale** road sign **2**
segnare (un gol) *v.* to score
  (a goal) **2, 3**
segretario/a *m., f.* secretary **10**
seguire *v.* to follow; to take (a class)
sei *m.* six
seicento *m.* six hundred
selciato *m.* cobblestones
selvaggi *m. pl.* savages
semaforo *m.* traffic light **2**
sembrare *v.* to seem **2**
seminterrato *m.* basement;
  garden-level apartment
sempre *adv.* always
sensibile *adj.* sensitive **1**
senso *m.* sense
  buon senso *m.* common sense **6**

senso *m.* **unico** one way
sentiero *m.* path
sentire *v.* to feel; to hear
sentirsi *v.* to feel **1**
senza *prep.* without **8**
  senza che *conj.* without **7**
separato/a *adj.* separated
sera *f.* evening
serio/a *adj.* serious
serpente *m.* snake
servire *v.* to serve
  servire a *v.* to be good for **8**
servizio *m.* service
  stazione *f.* **di servizio**
    service station
sessanta *m.* sixty
sesto *adj.* sixth
seta *m.* silk
sete: avere sete *v.* to be thirsty **1**
settanta *m.* seventy
sette *m.* seven
settecento *m.* seven hundred
settembre *m.* September
settentrionale *adj.* northern **6**
settimana *f.* week
  settimana *f.* **bianca** ski vacation
settimanale *m.* weekly magazine **9**
settimo *adj.* seventh
settore *m.* sector **10**
severo/a *adj.* strict **5**
sfarsi *v.* to fall apart
sfida *f.* challenge **7**
sfilata *f.* (fashion) parade **10**
sfogliatella *f.* Neapolitan pastry **1**
sfollati *m., pl.* evacuees **2**
sforzo *m.* effort **9**
sgranchirsi *v.* to stretch out **7**
sguardo *m.* gaze **10**
shampoo *(invar.) m.* shampoo
si *pron.* one; *ref. pron. m., f., sing.,*
  pl. herself, himself, itself, onself,
  themselves
siccità *f.* drought
sicurezza *f.* security, safety **4**
sicuro *adj.* certain
significare *v.* to mean
signor... *m.* Mr....
signora... *f.* Mrs....
la Sua/vostra signora *(form.)* your
  wife **8**
simpatico/a *adj.* likeable, nice
sinagoga *f.* synagogue **6**
sincero/a *adj.* sincere
sindacato *m.* labor union **10**
sindaco *m.* mayor **2**
sinistra *f.* left
sintomo *m.* symptom
sipario *m.* curtain
sistema *m.* system
sistemare *v.* to put together
sito *m.* **Internet** Web site
smaltire *v.* to drain

smettere *v.* to stop **3**
sminuire *v.* to play down **3**
smog *m.* smog
smorfia *f.* smirk **10**
SMS *m.* text message **7**
soccorso: pronto soccorso *m.*
  emergency room
società *f.* firm; society **10**
socievole *adj.* sociable; friendly **5**
socio/a *m., f.* (business) partner **10**
sofferenza *f.* suffering
soffriggere *v.* to fry lightly
soffrire (di) *v.* to suffer (from) **7, 8**
soggettivo/a *adj.* subjective **8**
soggiorno *m.* living room
sognare *v.* to dream **1**
soldato *m.* soldier **2**
soldi *m., pl.* money
sole *m.* sun
soleggiato/a *adj.* sunny
solito/a *adj.* usual
  di solito *adv.* usually
solo *adj.* alone; lonely
soltanto *adv.* only
soluzione *f.* solution
sommerso/a *adj.* submerged **7**
sondaggio *m.* opinion poll **9**
sopra *prep., adv.* above; over
sopracciglio (pl. sopracciglia f.)
  m. eyebrow
soprannome *m.* nickname **5**
sopravvivenza *f.* survival **2**
sopravvivere *v.* to survive **5**
sordo/a *adj.* deaf **5**
sorella *f.* sister
  sorellastra *f.* half sister, stepsister
  sorellina *f.* little/younger sister
sorgere *v.* to rise (sun)
sormontare *v.* to overcome **5**
sorpreso/a: essere
  sorpreso/a *v.* to be surprised **6**
sorridere *v.* to smile **5**
sottaceto *adj.* pickled
sott'olio *adj.* in oil
sotto *prep.* under **8**; *adv.* underneath
sottosviluppo *m.*
  underdevelopment **6**
sottotitolo *m.* subtitle **9**
sovrappopolazione *f.*
  overpopulation **6**
spagnolo/a *adj.* Spanish
spalla *f.* shoulder
sparare *v.* to shoot **4**
sparecchiare la tavola *v.* to clear
  the table
sparire *v.* to dissapear **3**
spazzare *v.* to sweep
spazzatura *f.* garbage
  portare fuori la spazzatura *v.*
    to take out the trash
spazzino/a *m., f.* street sweeper
spazzola *f.* brush

spazzolino *m.* **(da denti)** tooth brush
specchio *m.* mirror
specialista *m., f.* specialist
specializzazione *f.* specialization
spedire *v.* to send
spegnere *v.* to turn off
spendere *v.* to spend (money)
sperare *v.* to hope **6**
sperimentale *adj.* experimental **9**
spesa: fare la spesa *v.* to buy
  groceries
spesso *adv.* often
spettacolo *m.* show, performance **3**
spettatore/spettatrice
  m., f. spectator
spettinare *v.* to muss hair **5**
spia *f.* spy **2, 8**
spiaggia *f.* beach
spiare *v.* to spy **4**
spiccioli *m., pl.* small change **3**
spiegare *v.* to explain **1**
spigola *f.* bass fish **4**
spingere *v.* to push **6**
spinotto *m.* plug **3**
spiritoso/a *adj.* clever; funny
spogliarsi *v.* to undress **10**
spolverare *v.* to dust
sporcare *v.* to soil
sporco/a *adj.* dirty
sport *m.* sport
  sport *m., pl.* **estremi** extreme sports
sportello *m.* window; counter **10**
sportivo/a *adj.* active
  club *m.* **sportivo** sports club **3**
  cronaca *f.* **sportiva** sports news **9**
sposare *v.* to marry
sposarsi (con) *v.* to get married (to) **1**
sposato/a *adj.* married **1**
sposo/a *m., f.* groom/bride **5**
sprecare *v.* to waste
spumone *m.* a type of gelato **1**
spuntare (i capelli) *v.* to trim
  (one's hair)
spuntino *m.* snack
squadra *f.* team **3**
  squadra *f.* **di calcio** soccer team **2**
squillare *v.* to ring (telephone) **9**
squisito/a *adj.* exquisite
stabilirsi *v.* to settle **6**
stadio *m.* stadium **2**
stage *m.* internship
stagione *f.* season
stagista *m., f.* intern **10**
stampa: comunicato *m.* **stampa**
  press release **9**
stampante *f.* printer
stampare *v.* to print
stanco/a *adj.* tired
stanza *f.* room
stare *v.* to stay **1**
  stare a cuore *v.* to matter **2**
  stare bene/male *v.* to be well/ill **1**

stare in fila *v.* to stand in line **5**
stare per *v.* to be about to **1**
stare zitto *v.* to be/stay quiet **2**
starnutire *v.* to sneeze
statista *m.* statesman **6**
statua *f.* statue
stazione *f.* station
  stazione *f.* **di polizia** police
    station **2**
  stazione *f.* **radio** radio station **9**
stella *f.* star
stereotipo *m.* stereotype **6**
stile *m.* style **10**
stilista *m., f.* fashion designer **10**
stipendio *m.* wage **10**
  stipendio *m.* **minimo** minimum
    wage **10**
stirare *v.* to iron
stirarsi *v.* to stretch **10**
stivale *m.* boot
stoffa *f.* fabric **8**
stomaco *m.* stomach
storia *f.* history
storico/a *adj.* historic **8**
strada *f.* street **2**
  conoscere la strada *v.* to know
    the way
strafare *v.* to overdo things
straniero/a *adj.* foreign
strano/a *adj.* strange **5**
stretto/a *adj.* tight; tight-fitting
stringere la mano a *v.* to shake
  hands with **8**
strisce *f., pl.* **pedonali** crosswalk **2**
strofa *f.* stanza **8**
strumento *m.* instrument
  strumento *m.* **musicale**
    musical instrument
studente(ssa) *m., f.* student
studi *m., pl.* studies
studiare *v.* to study **1**
studio *m.* office; study
studioso/a *adj.* studious
stufarsi *v.* to be fed up **2**
stufo/a *adj.* fed up **1**
stupire *v.* to surprise **7**
su *prep.* in; on
  su Internet online
subacqueo *m.* scuba diver **4**
subaffittare *v.* to sublet
subito *adv.* immediately; right away
succedere *v.* to happen
successo *m.* success
succo *m.* juice
  succo *m.* **d'arancia** orange juice
suggerire *v.* to suggest **6**
suocero/a *m., f.* father-/mother-
  in-law **5**
suonare *v.* to play (instrument) **3**
suora *f.* nun **3**
superare *v.* to overcome **6**; *v.* to
  pass (an *exam*)

superato/a *adj.* old-fashioned
superiore *adj.* higher; superior **9**
supermercato *m.* supermarket
supplemento *m.* excess fare
supplente *m.* substitute teacher
supremo/a *adj.* supreme **9**
sussurro *m.* whisper; murmur
sveglia *f.* alarm clock **10**
svegliare *v.* to wake someone **2**
svegliarsi *v.* to wake up **2**
sviluppare *v.* to develop
sviluppo *m.* advance; development **6, 7**
svizzero/a *adj.* Swiss
svolgersi *v.* to take place **8**

T

tacca *f.* cellular reception bar **9**
tacchi *m., pl.* heels **3**
  tacchi *m., pl.* **alti** high heels **1**
  tacchi *m., pl.* **bassi** low heels **1**
taccuino *m.* notebook
taglia *f.* clothing size
tagliare *v.* to cut
  tagliare i capelli *v.* to cut one's hair
taglia *f.* size **1**
taglio *m.* cut **8**
tailleur *m.* (women's) suit **10**
tamburo *m.* drum
tana *f.* burrow
tanto *adj.* so much, so many
  di tanto in tanto *adv.* off and on
  tanto… quanto *adv.* as
tappeto *m.* carpet
tardi *adv.* late
  A più tardi. See you later.
tariffa *f.* fare
tassa *f.* tax **10**
tassì *m.* taxi
tassista *m.* taxi driver **6**
tasso *m.* rate
  tasso *m.* **d'interesse** interest rate **10**
  tasso *m.* **di natalità** birthrate **6**
tastiera *f.* keyboard
tata *f.* nanny
tatuaggio *m.* tattoo **10**
tavola *f.* table
  sparecchiare la tavola *v.* to clear
    the table
  tavola *f.* **calda** cafeteria; snack bar
tavolo *m.* table
  computer *m.* **da tavolo** desktop
    computer **7**
taxi *m.* taxi
tazza *f.* cup; mug
tè *m.* tea
teatrale *adj.* theatrical
teatro *m.* theater
tecnico *m., f.* technician
tecnologia *f.* technology
tedesco/a *adj.* German **8**
tela *f.* canvas

telecomando *m.* remote control
telecomunicazioni *f., pl.* telecommunications **7**
telefonare *v.* to telephone
telefonarsi *v.* to phone each other **2**
telefonico/a: segreteria *f.* **telefonica** answering machine
telefonino *m.* cell phone **9**
telefono *m.* telephone
telegiornale *m.* TV news **9**
telenovela *f.* soap opera
telespettatore/telespettatrice *m., f.* television viewer **9**
televisione *f.* television **9**
televisione *f.* **via cavo** cable TV **9**
televisione *f.* **satellitare** satellite TV **9**
tema *m.* essay; theme
temere *v.* to fear, be afraid **6**
tempaccio *m.* bad weather
tempo *m.* weather
temporale *m.* storm **9**
tenace *adj.* tenacious
tenda *f.* curtain
tenere *v.* to hold **1**
tenere a *v.* to care about **8**
tenero/a *adj.* sweet; tender
tennis *m.* tennis
tenore di vita *m.* standard of living **6**
teorema *m.* theorem
tergicristallo *m.* windshield wiper
terme *f., pl.* (thermal) baths **2**
termine: breve/lungo **termine** *adj.* short-/long-term **10**
termometro *m.* thermometer
terra: surriscaldamento *m.* **della terra** global warming
terremoto *m.* earthquake
terrorismo *m.* terrorism **4**
terrorista *m., f.* terrorist **4**
terzo *adj.* third
tesina *f.* essay; term paper
testa *f.* head
testardo/a *adj.* stubborn **5**
testimone *m., f.* witness **4**
testo *m.* textbook
tiepido *adj.* lukewarm **4**
tifare (per) *v.* to be a fan of, root for **3**
tifoso/a *m., f.* fan **2; 3**
timbrare *v.* to stamp
timido/a *adj.* shy **1**
tinta *f.* color; dye
tintoria *f.* dry cleaner
tipo *m.* guy
tiramisù *m.* "pick-me-up" coffee dessert **1**
tirare *v.* to kick **2**
tirare avanti *v.* to forge ahead **6**
tirocinio *m.* professional training
tivù *f.* TV
toccare *v.* to touch

togliere *v.* to remove **1**
tonno *m.* tuna
tonto/a *adj.* dumb
topo *m.* mouse
topografia *f.* topography **2**
tormenta *f.* bilizzard
tornado *m.* tornado
tornare *v.* to go back, to return **3**
torneo *m.* tournament **3**
toro *m.* bull
tosse *f.* cough
tossico/a: rifiuti *m., pl.* **tossici** toxic waste
tossire *v.* to cough
tostapane *m.* toaster
tostare *v.* to toast
tovaglia *f.* tablecloth **4**
tovagliolo *m.* napkin
tra *prep.* among, between, in
tracciare *v.* to trace **6**
tradizione *f.* tradition **6**
tradurre *v.* to translate **1, 8**
traffico *m.* traffic **2**
tragedia *f.* tragedy
traghetto *m.* ferry **7**
tragico/a *adj.* tragic **8**
tram *m.* cable car **2**
trama *f.* plot **8**
tramontare *v.* set (sun)
tramonto *m.* sunset
tranne *prep.* except **8**
tranquillo/a *adj.* calm **1**
trarre *v.* to draw, bring **9**
trasferirsi *v.* to move (change residence) **2, 5**
traslocare *v.* to move
trasmettere *v.* to broadcast **9**
trasmissione *f.* broadcast **7**
trasporto *m.* transportation
trasporto *m.* **pubblico** public transportation
trattarsi di *v.* to be about, deal with **8**
trattato *m.* treaty **4**
trattoria *f.* small restaurant, family run
trauma *m.* trauma
tre *m.* three
treccia *f.* braid
treccine *f., pl.* dreadlocks
trecento *m.* three hundred
tredicesima *f.* year-end bonus
tredici *m.* thirteen
trendy *adj.* trendy
treno *m.* train
salire sul treno *v.* to get on the train **2**
scendere dal treno *v.* get off the train **2**
trenta *m.* thirty
trentacinque *m.* thirty-five
trentadue *m.* thirty-due

trentanove *m.* thirty-nine
trentaquattro *m.* thirty-four
trentasei *m.* thirty-six
trentasette *m.* thirty-seven
trentatré *m.* thirty-three
trentatreesimo *adj.* thirty-third
trentotto *m.* thirty-eight
trentuno *m.* thirty-one
tribuna *f.* stand
tribunale *m.* courthouse **2**
triste *adj.* sad
troppo *adj., adv., indef. pron.* too much
trovare *v.* to find
trovare lavoro *v.* to find a job
trovarsi *v.* to be located **2**
truccarsi *v.* to put on make up **1**
trucco *m.* makeup **10**
truppa *f.* troop **7**
tuono *m.* thunder
turista *m., f.* tourist
turno *m.* **di lavoro** work shift **10**
tutelare *v.* to protect, defend **6**
tutto *indef. adj.* every, all **9**; *indef. pron.* everything **9**
tutti quanti *rel. pron.* everyone, all who, all that **9**
tutti quelli che *rel. pron.* everyone, all who, all that **9**
tutti/e *indef. pron.* everyone; everything **9**
tutto ciò che *rel. pron.* everything that, all that **9**
tutto esaurito *adj.* sold out **3**
tutto quanto *rel. pron.* everything that, all that **9**
tutto quel(lo) che *rel. pron.* everything that, all that **9**
TV *f.* TV
guardare la TV *v.* to watch TV

uccello *m.* bird
ufficio *m.* office **10**
ufficio *m.* **informazioni turistiche** tourist information office
ufficio *m.* **postale** post office
uguaglianza *f.* equality **4**
uguale *adj.* equal **4**
ultimo/a *adj.* last
Umanesimo *m.* Humanism **8**
umano/a: risorse *f., pl.* **umane** human resources
umidità *f.* humidity
umido/a *adj.* humid
in umido *adj.* stewed
umile *adj.* humble **1**
umorismo *m.* humor **6**
umoristico/a *adj.* humorous **8**
undicesimo *adj.* eleventh

ụndici *m.* eleven
unito/a *adj.* united
università *f.* university
uomo (*pl.* uọmini) *m.* man
  uomo *m.* **d'affari** businessman
uovo (*pl.* uova *f.*) *m.* egg
urbanịstica *f.* city planning 2
usanza *f.* custom 9
usare *v.* to use
uscire *v.* to come out 1; to be
  released 9
  uscire (da) *v.* to leave 8
  uscire con *v.* to go out with 1
uscita *f.* exit
ụtile *adj.* useful 1
uva *f.* grapes

V

vacanza *f.* vacation
vaccino *m.* vaccine 7
vagare *v.* to roam, to wander 9
valere *v.* to be worth 6
  valere la pena *v.* to be worth it 3
valigetta *f.* briefcase
valigia: fare la valigia *v.* to pack
  a suitcase
valle *f.* valley
valletta *f.* TV host assistant
valuta *f.* currency 4
vanitoso/a *adj.* vain 5
vantaggio *m.* advantage 4
vantarsi *v.* to boast, brag 2
vaporetto *m.* motor boat (used for
  public transportation in Venice) 7
varicella *f.* chicken-pox
vaso *m.* vase
vassọio *m.* tray 1
vecchiạia *f.* old age 5
vecchio/a *adj.* old
vedere *v.* to see 3
vedersi *v.* to see each other 2
  vedersi con *v.* to date
vẹdovo/a *adj.* widowed; widower/
  widow 1
velato/a *adj.* veiled
veloce *adj.* fast
velocemente *adv.* quickly
vẹndere *v.* to sell
vendicativo/a *adj.* vengeful 1
venditore/venditrice *m., f.* vendor 2
  venditore/venditrice *m., f.*
    ambulante street vendor 2
venerdì *m.* Friday
venire *v.* to come 1
  venire da *v.* to come from 8
ventẹsimo *adj.* twentieth
venti *m.* twenty
venticinque *m.* twenty-five
ventidue *m.* twenty-two
ventinove *m.* twenty-nine
ventiquattro *m.* twenty-four

ventisei *m.* twenty-six
ventisette *m.* twenty-seven
ventitré *m.* twenty-three
vento *m.* wind
ventoso/a *adj.* windy
ventotto *m.* twenty-eight
ventre *m.* abdomen
ventuno *m.* twenty-one
veramente *adv.* truly
verbale *m.* police report 8
verde *adj.* green
verdura *f.* vegetable
vergogna *f.* shame 2
  avere vergogna (di) *v.* to be
    ashamed (of) 1
vergognarsi *v.* to be ashamed 1, 2
versare *v.* to deposit 10
verso *m.* line (of poetry) 8;
  prep. toward
vestaglia *f.* robe 10
vestirsi *v.* to get dressed 2
vestito *m.* suit; dress
  vestiti *m., pl.* clothing
  vestito *m.* **da donna** suit 3
  vestito *m.* **da sposa** wedding
    dress
  vestito *m.* **da uomo** suit 3;
    suit/dress 3
veterinario/a *m., f.* veterinarian
vetrina *f.* shop window 1
vetro *m.* car window
vetturino *m.* coachman
vịa *f.* street 2; *adv.* away
  buttare vịa *v.* to throw away 1
viaggiare *v.* to travel
viaggiatore *m.* traveler
viaggio *m.* trip
  agente *m.,f.* **di viaggio** travel
    agent
vicino/a *adj.* near; *m., f.* neighbor;
  adv. near, close
  vicino a *prep.* close (to)
vịcolo *m.* alley
videocạmera *f.* camcorder
videogioco *m.* videogame 3
videoteca *f.* video store
vịgile *v.* alert 8
  vịgile *m., f.* **del fuoco** firefighter 2
  vịgile/vigilessa *m., f.* **urbano/a**
    traffic officer
vigilia *f.* eve 6
vignetta *f.* cartoon 9
villa *f.* single-family home; villa
vịncere *v.* to win
  vịncere le elezioni *v.* to win the
    election 4
  vịncere una partita *v.* to win a
    game 3
vino *m.* wine
viola *(invar.) adj.* purple
violenza *f.* violence 4
violinista *m., f.* violinist

violino *m.* violin
visitare *v.* to visit
viso *m.* face
vista *f.* sight
  conọscere di vista *v.* to know
    by sight
vita *f.* life; waist
vịttima *f.* victim 4
vitto: vitto e alloggio room and
  board (lit. food and apartment) 5
vittoria *f.* victory 4
vittorioso/a *adj.* victorious 4
vivace *adj.* lively 2, 5
vịvere *v.* to live 5
  vịvere di *v.* to live on 8
viziare *v.* to spoil 5
voce *f.* voice 4
voglia *f.* desire
  avere voglia di *v.* to feel like 8
volante *m.* steering wheel
volere *v.* to want 1
  volerci *v.* to take, require 8
  volere bene a *v.* to feel affection
    for 1
volo *m.* flight
volontà *f.* willingness, will, wish 4, 6
volpe *f.* fox 1
volpino *m.* Pomeranian 1
volta *f.* time; turn
volto *m.* face 9
vọngola *f.* clam
votare *v.* to vote 4
voto *m.* grade
vulạnico/a: eruzione *f.* **vulcạnica**
  volcanic eruption

W

windsurf *m.* windsurfing

Y

yogurt *m.* yogurt

Z

zainetto *m.* small backpack 5
zaino *m.* backpack
zampa *f.* paw 1
zeppe *f., pl.* wedge shoes 3
zịo/a *m., f.* uncle/aunt 5
zoọlogo/a *m., f.* zoologist 7
zuppa *f.* soup

English-Italian

A

@ symbol chiocciola *f.* 7
abdomen ventre *m.*
ability competenza *f.*
abolish abolire *v.* 8
above sopra *prep., adv.*
abroad all'estero *adv.*
absolutely altroché *conj.*
abuse abusare *v.* 4;
  maltrattamento *m.* 6
  abuse of power abuso *m.* di
    potere 4
accident incidente *m.*
  to have/be in an accident avere
    un incidente *v.*
according to secondo *prep.* 8
accordion fisarmonica *f.*
account conto *m.* 10
  checking account conto *m.*
    corrente 10
  to open/close an account
    aprire/chiudere *v.* un conto 10
accountant contabile *m., f.* 10
achieve realizzare *v.* 6
acid rain pioggia *f.* acida
acknowledge riconoscere *v.*
acritical acritico/a *adj.*
across from di fronte a *prep.*
act atto *m.;* recitare *v.*
active attivo/a *adj.;* sportivo/a *adj.*
activist attivista *m., f.* 4
actor/actress attore/attrice *m., f.* 9
ad annuncio *m.* 10
  job ad annuncio *m.* di lavoro 10
AD (Anno Domini) d.C. (dopo
    Cristo) *adj.* **2, 8**
adapt adattarsi *v.* 6
adaptation adattamento *m.* 9
address rivolgersi *v.* 8; indirizzo *m.*
  address book rubrica *f.*
adhesive tape nastro *m.* adesivo
adjust adeguarsi *v.* 6
administrative assistant assistente
    m., f. amministrativo/a
adopt adottare *v.*
adopted adottivo/a *adj.* 5
adoptive adottivo/a *adj.* 5
adore adorare *v.* 1
adulthood età *f.* adulta 5
advance sviluppo *m.* **6, 7**
advantage vantaggio *m.* 4
advertisement pubblicità *f.* 9
advertising campaign campagna
    f. pubblicitaria
advise consigliare (di) *v.* 8
aesthetic estetico/a *adj.* 8
affectionate affettuoso/a *adj.* 1
affluent abbiente *adj.* 5
afraid: be afraid (of) avere paura

(di) *v.* 1
African africano/a *adj.*
after dopo *prep.* 8
afternoon pomeriggio *m.*
  afternoon snack merenda *f.*
afterwards dopo *adv.*
again ancora; di nuovo *adv.*
against contro *prep.* 8
age età *f.* 8; invecchiare *v.* 5
agency agenzia *f.*
agent agente *m., f.*
agnostic agnostico/a *adj., m., f.* 6
ago fa *adv.*
agreement accordo *m.* 4
agriculture agricoltura *f.*
ailment malattia *f.*
aim scopo *m.* 7
airplane aereo *m.*
airport aeroporto *m.*
alarm clock sveglia *f.* 10
alert vigile *adj.* 8
all ogni; tutto *indef. adj., indef. pron.* 9
  all over ovunque *adv.*
  All Saints' Day Ognissanti *m.*
  all that tutto ciò che, tutto quanto,
    tutto quel che, tutto quello che *rel.*
    pron. 9
  all that/who quanti, tutti quanti,
    tutti quelli che, tutti/e *rel. pron.* 9
allergic: to be allergic (to) essere
    allergico (a) *v.*
alley vicolo *m.*
allies (allied troops) alleati *m., pl.* 2
allow lasciare *v.;* permettere *v.* 6
allusive allusivo/a *adj.*
alone; lonely solo *adj.*
along lungo *prep.* 8
already già *adv.*
  by now, already ormai *adv.*
also anche; pure *conj.*
although benché, malgrado,
    nonostante, sebbene *conj.* 7
always sempre *adv.*
ambulance ambulanza *f.*
American americano/a *adj.*
among fra, tra *prep.*
amusement park luna park *m.* 3
analog signal segnale *m.*
    analogico 7
ancestor antenato *m.* 5
and e *conj.*
angry arrabbiato/a *adj.*
  to be angry at someone avercela
    con qualcuno *v.*
anguish angoscia *f.* 7
animal animale *m.*
annoy dare fastidio *v.* 1
annoyed contrariato/a *adj.* 1
answer rispondere *v.* 3
  to answer the phone rispondere
    al telefono *v.*
answering machine segreteria *f.*
    telefonica

anthem inno *m.* 4
anxious ansioso/a *adj.* 1
any qualsiasi, qualunque *indef. adj.* 9
anyone chiunque *indef. pron.* 9
apartment appartamento *m.* 2
  studio apartment monolocale *m.*
appear parere *v.* 2
appearance apparenza *f.* 4;
  comparsa *f.* 6
appetizer antipasto *m.*
applause applauso *m.*
apple mela *f.*
appliance elettrodomestico *m.*
apply fare domanda *v.*
  apply for a job fare domanda per
    un lavoro *v.* 10
appointment: to make an
    appointment prendere un
    appuntamento *v.*
apprentice apprendista *m., f.* 8
appropriate opportuno/a *adj.*
April aprile *m.*
aquarium acquario *m.*
aqueduct acquedotto *m.* 2
Arab arabo/a *adj.*
architect architetto *m., f.*
area code prefisso *m.* 9
arm braccio (*pl.* braccia *f.*) *m.*
armchair poltrona *f.*
armies armate *f., pl.* 2
army esercito *m.* 4
aroma aroma *m.*
around intorno *prep., adv.*
  around (out and about) in giro
arrivals arrivi *m., pl.*
arrive arrivare *v.* 3
art arte *f.*
  fine arts belle arti *f., pl.* 8
artichoke carciofo *m.*
article: article of clothing capo *m.*
    di abbigliamento 10
artificial intelligence (A.I.)
    intelligenza *f.* artificiale 7
artisan artigiano/a *m., f.* 8
artistic artistico/a *adj.*
arts (humanities) lettere *f., pl.*
as così… come *adv.;* tanto…
    quanto *adv.*
  as well anche *conj.*
ask chiedere *v.* 3; domandare *v.*
  to ask a question fare una
    domanda *v.*
  to ask, consult interpellare *v.*
aspirin aspirina *f.*
assassination assassinio *m.* 8
assume responsibility assumersi
    una responsabilità *v.* 5
astronaut astronauta *m., f.* 7
astronomer astronomo/a *m., f.* 7
at a; da; in *prep.*
  @ symbol chiocciola *f.* 7
atheistic ateo/a *adj.* 6
athletic atletico/a *adj.*

ATM bancomat *m.* **10;** cassa *f.* automatica
attach allegare *v.* **7**
attack l'attacco *m.* **2**
attend assistere a *v.* **8;** frequentare *v.*
attention: to pay attention dare retta, fare attenzione a *v.* **5**
attentive attento/a *adj.*
attic mansarda *f.*
attractive attraente *adj.* **1**
audacious audace *adj.*
audience pubblico *m.*
August agosto *m.*
aunt zia *f.* **5**
author autore/autrice *m., f.*
autonomy autonomia *f.* **6**
avant-garde d'avanguardia *adj.* **8**
average: of average height di media statura *adj.*
avoid evitare (di) *v.*
award-winning premiato/a *adj.* **8, 9**
awareness: environmental awareness coscienza *f.* ambientale

B

baby bambino/a *m., f.*
back schiena *f.*
backpack zaino *m.*
  small backpack zainetto *m.* **5**
bad cattivo/a *adj.* **9**
  bad boy ragazzaccio *m.*
  bad weather maltempo *m.* **6;** tempaccio *m.*
  bad-mannered maleducato/a *adj.* **5**
  very bad pessimo/a *adj.* **9**
badly male *adv.* **9**
bakery panetteria *f.*
balcony balcone *m.*
ball palla *f.*; pallone *m.* **2, 3**
ballet balletto *m.*
ballet dancer ballerino/a *m., f.*
ban divieto *m.*
banana banana *f.*
band gruppo *m.* (musicale) **3**
  rock band gruppo *m.* rock
bangs frangia *f.*
bank banca *f.*; bancario/a *adj.*
  bank account conto *m.* bancario
banker banchiere/a *m., f.*
bankruptcy bancarotta *f.* **10**
bark abbaiare *v.* **1**
Baroque barocco/a *adj.*
barracks caserma *f.* **8**
bartender barista *m., f.*
basement seminterrato *m.*
basketball basket, pallacanestro *m.*
bass (fish) spigola *f.* **4**
basset hound bassotto *m.* **1**
bath bagno *m.*
bathing suit costume *m.* da bagno
bathroom bagno *m.*

bathtub vasca *f.* da bagno
battery charger carica batteria *m.*
battle battaglia *f.* **8**
BC(E) a.C. (avanti Cristo) *adj.* **8**
be essere *v.* **3**
  to be... years old avere... anni *v.* **1**
  to be a fan of, root for tifare (per) *v.* **3**
  to be able, can potere *v.* **1**
  to be about to stare per *v.* **1**
  to be about, deal with trattarsi di *v.* **8**
  to be afraid (of) avere paura (di) *v.* **1**
  to be afraid temere *v.* **6**
  to be ashamed vergognarsi *v.* **1, 2**
  to be ashamed (of) avere vergogna (di) *v.* **1**
  to be better off fare meglio a *v.* **8**
  to be born nascere *v.* **3**
  to be careful essere attento/a *v.* **8**
  to be early essere in anticipo *v.* **2**
  to be expecting (a baby) aspettare un figlio *v.* **5**
  to be fed up stufarsi *v.* **2**
  to be good for servire a *v.* **8**
  to be hungry avere fame *v.* **1**
  to be important contare *v.* **9**
  to be important, to matter importare *v.* **2**
  to be in a hurry avere fretta (di) *v.* **8**
  to be in debt avere dei debiti *v.* **10**
  to be informed, up-to-date essere aggiornato/a *v.* **9**
  to be interested in interessarsi (a/di) *v.* **8**
  to be located trovarsi *v.* **2**
  to be missing mancare *v.* **2**
  to be named chiamarsi *v.* **2**
  to be necessary occorrere *v.* **6**
  to be pregnant essere incinta *v.* **5**
  to be ready essere pronto/a a *v.* **8**
  to be released uscire *v.* **9**
  to be right avere ragione (di) *v.* **8**
  to be sorry dispiacere *v.* **2;** essere desolato/a *v.* **5**
  to be sufficient bastare *v.* **3**
  to be surprised essere sorpreso/a *v.* **6**
  to be thirsty avere sete *v.* **1**
  to be well/ill stare bene/male *v.* **1**
  to be worth valere *v.* **6**
  to be worth it valere la pena *v.* **3**
  to be wrong avere torto *v.* **8**
beach spiaggia *f.*
  at/to the beach al mare *adv.*
beard barba *f.*
bearings: to get one's bearings orientarsi *v.*
beautiful bello/a *adj.*
beauty bellezza *f.*
  beauty salon salone *m.* di belleza
become divenire *v.* **3;** diventare;

rendersi *v.*
  to become independent diventare indipendente *v.* **5**
  to become indignant sdegnarsi *v.* **9**
  to become poor impoverirsi *v.* **6**
  to become rich arricchirsi *v.* **6**
bed letto *m.*
bedroom camera *f.* da letto
bee ape *f.*
beef carne *f.* di manzo
beer birra *f.*
before prima *prep., adv.;* prima che *conj.* **7**
beforehand prima *adv.*
beggar mendicante *m., f.* **2**
begin (to) cominciare (a) *v.* **1**
beginning inizio *m.*
behind dietro *prep., adv.* **8**
beige beige *(invar.) adj.*
believe credere *v.* **6**
believer fedele *m., f.* **6**
belong (to) appartenere (a) *v.* **6**
belt cintura *f.*
bench panchina *f.*
berry bacca *f.*
bet (on) scommettere (su) *v.* **6, 8**
better meglio *adv.* **9;** migliore *adj.* **9**
between fra/tra *prep.*
beverage dispenser distributore automatico *m.* **7**
beyond oltre *prep., adv.* **8**
biased parziale *adj.* **9**
bicycle bicicletta *f.*
big grande *adj.* **9;** largo/a *adj.*
  big city metropoli *f.* **2**
  bigger maggiore *adj.* **9**
bill banconota *f.;* conto *m.*
billiards biliardo *m.* **3**
bills bollette *f., pl.*
  to pay the bills pagare le bollette *v.*
biochemist biochimico/a *m., f.* **7**
biography biografia *m.* **8**
biologist biologo/a *m., f.* **7**
biology biologia *f.*
bird uccello *m.*
birth nascita *f.* **5**
birthday compleanno *m.*
birthrate tasso *m.* di natalità **6**
bite morso *m.*
bitter amaro/a *adj.*
black nero/a *adj.*
blackboard lavagna *f.*
bland insipido/a *adj.*
blizzard tormenta *f.*
blonde biondo/a *adj.*
blood sangue *m.* **5**
blouse camicetta *f.*
blue azzurro/a; blu *(invar.) adj.*
board game gioco *m.* di società **3**
boarding house pensione *f.*
boarding pass carta *f.* d'imbarco *f.*
boast vantarsi *v.* **2**

boat barca *f.*
body corpo *m.*
boiling hot bollente *adj.* 7
bomb ordigno *m.* **5**, bomba *f.*
book libro *m.*
bookshelf scaffale *m.*
bookstore libreria *f.*
boot stivale *m.*
boredom noia *f.*
boring noioso/a *adj.*
  How boring! Che noia!
boss padrone *m.* **4**; capo *m.* **10**;
  principale *m., f.*
bossy autoritario/a *adj.* 5
bother disturbare *v.* **1**; dare noia a *v.* 8
bottle bottiglia *f.*
bottom fondo *m.*
boundary confine *m.* 4
bow prua *f.* 4
bowl scodella *f.*
box scatola *f.* 1
boxing pugilato *m.* 3
boy ragazzo *m.*
boyfriend fidanzato *m.* **5**; ragazzo *m.*
brag vantarsi *v.* 2
braid treccia *f.*
brake frenare *v.*
brakes freni *m., pl.*
branch ramo *m.*
brand marca *f.* 10
bread impanare *v.;* pane *m.*
break rompere *v.* **3**; rompersi *v.*
  to break up with rompere con *v.* 1
break down essere in panne *v.*
breakfast colazione *f.*
  to have breakfast fare
    colazione *v.* 1
break up lasciarsi *v.*
bricklayer muratore *m.*
bride sposa *f.* 5
bridge ponte *m.*
briefcase valigetta *f.*
bright brilliante *adj.*
bring portare *v.*, trarre *v.* 9
broadcast mandare in onda;
  trasmettere *v.* **9**; trasmissione *f.* 7
broke: to be broke essere al verde *v.*
broom scopa *f.*
brother fratello *m.*
  brother-in-law cognato *m.*
  little/younger brother fratellino *m.*
brown rosolare *v.*
  brown (*eyes*) marrone *adj.*
  brown (*hair*) castano/a *adj.*
browse the Internet/Web navigare
  su Internet/sulla rete *v.* 7
bruise livido *m.*
brush pettinare *v.;* spazzola *f.*
  to brush one's hair pettinarsi *v.*
  to brush one's teeth lavarsi
    i denti *v.*
buckle (*seatbelt*) allacciare *v.*

build costruire *v.*
building edificio *m.* **2**; palazzo *m.* **2**;
  immobiliare *adj.*
  building material materiale
    m. edile 2
bull toro *m.*
bulletin board bacheca *f.*
bully bullo *m., f.* 3
bump bernoccolo *m.*
burn bruciare *v.* 9
burn bruciare; masterizzare *v.* **7**;
  scottatura *f.*
burrow tana *f.*
bus autobus *m.;* pullman *m.*
  get off a bus scendere
    dall'autobus *v.* 2
  long-distance bus corriera *f.* 6
  to get on a bus salire
    sull'autobus *v.* 2
bush cespuglio *m.*
businessman uomo *m.* d'affari
businesswoman donna *f.* d'affari
busy indaffarato/a *adj.* 2
but ma *conj.*
butcher macelleria *f.;* macellaio *m.*
butter burro *m.*
buy comprare *v.*
by da *prep.*
  by now; already ormai *adv.*
Byzantine bizantino/a *adj.*

C

cabin (*mountain shelter*) baita *f.*
cable cavo *m.*
  cable car tram *m.* 2
  cable TV televisione *f.* via cavo 9
café bar *m.* 1
  café specializing in
  chocolate cioccolateria *f.*
cafeteria mensa; tavola *f.* calda *f.*
cage gabbia *f.* 1
cake: Christmas
  cake panettone *m.* 6
call chiamare *v.* 2
calm tranquillo/a *adj.* 1
camcorder videocamera *f.*
camera: digital camera
  macchina *f.* fotografica digitale
camp campeggiare *v.* 3
campaign campagna *f.*
  electoral campaign campagna *f.*
    elettorale 3
camping campeggio *m.*
Canadian canadese *adj.*
canals canali *m., pl.* 7
canary canarino *m.*
cancel annullare *v.*
candidate candidato/a *m., f.*
canvass tela *f.*
car automobile *f.;* macchina *f.*
  car racing automobilismo *m.* 3
  get out of a car scendere dalla

  macchina *v.* 2
  to get in a car salire in macchina *v.* 2
  car door portiera *f.*
carafe caraffa *f.*
card carta *f.*
  playing cards carte *f., pl.* (da gioco)
care (about) tenere a *v.* 8
  to not care (about) fregarsene
    (di) *v.* **2, 6**
career carriera *f.* 10
careful prudente *adj.* 1
caretaker bidello/a; portiere/a *m., f.*
carnival carnevale *m.* 9
carpenter falegname *m.*
carpet tappeto *m.*
carriage carrozza *f.*
carrot carota *f.*
carry: carry out an investigation
  condurre un'inchiesta *v.*
carry-on baggage bagaglio *m.*
  a mano
cartoon vignetta *f.* 9
  cartoons cartoni *m. pl.* animati 9
cash contanti *m., pl.*
  to cash incassare *v.* 4
  to cash a check cambiare un
    assegno *v.* 10
  to pay in cash pagare in contanti *v.*
castaway naufrago *m.* 4
cat gatto/a *m., f.*
catastrophe catastrofe *f.*
catch out cogliere *v.* in fallo 8
cathedral cattedrale *f.* 6
Catholic cattolico/a *adj.* 6
cavity carie *f.*
CD CD/compact disc *m.*
CD-ROM CD-ROM *m.*
celebrate festeggiare *v.* 3
celebrations festeggiamenti *m., pl.*
cell phone cellulare *m.,*
  telefonino *m.* 9
cellular reception bar tacca *f.* 9
cellular reception, field campo *m.* 9
censorship censura *f.* 9
censor censurare *v.* 8
center centro *m.*
  center forward centravanti *m.* 3
century secolo *m.* 2
certain certo/a, sicuro/a *adj.*
chair sedia *f.*
chalk gesso *m.*
challenge sfida *f.* 7
chamber orchestra orchestra *f.*
  da camera 8
change cambiare *v.;* moneta *f.*
  small change spiccioli *m., pl.* 3
channel canale *m.*
chaos caos *m.* 6
character personaggio *m.* 8
  main character personaggio
    m. principale
charge caricare *v.*

charming affascinante *adj.* **1**
chart classifica *f.* **3**
chase rincorrere *v.*
chat chiacchierare *v.* **2**
chat online chattare *v.* **9**
chatterbox chiacchierone *m.*
cheap a buon mercato *adj.* **8**
check assegno *m.* **4;** controllare *v.*
  to cash a check cambiare un
    assegno *v.* **10**
  to pay by check pagare con
    assegno *v.*
check-in counter banco *m.* **5**
cheerful allegro/a *adj.*
cheerfully allegramente *adv.*
Cheers! Cin, cin!
cheese formaggio *m.*
chef cuoco/a *m., f.*
chemist chimico/a *m., f.* **7**
chess scacchi *m., pl.* **3**
chest petto *m.*
chic chic *adj.*
chicken-pox varicella *f.*
child bambino/a *m., f.*
  only child figlio/a unico/a *m., f.* **5**
childhood infanzia *f.* **5**
Chinese cinese *adj.*
chit-chat chiacchiere *f., pl.*
choice scelta *f.* **1**
choose scegliere *v.* **1**
chores faccende *f., pl.,*
  mestieri *m., pl.*
  to do household chores fare i
    mestieri/le faccende *v.*
chorus coro *m.*
Christmas Natale *m.*
  Christmas bread panettone *m.* **6**
church chiesa *f.* **6**
cinema cinema *m.*
citizen cittadino/a *m., f.* **2**
citizenship cittadinanza *f.* **4**
city città *f.*
  big city metropoli *f.* **2**
  city hall municipio *m.* **2**
  city map carta topografica *f.* **9**
  city plan piano *m.* urbanistico **2**
  city planning urbanistica *f.* **2**
  city walls mura *f., pl.* di cinta **2**
civil civile *adj.*
  civil servant funzionario/a *m., f.*
  civil war guerra *f.* civile **4**
civilization civiltà *f.* **8**
claim reclamare *v.* **6**
clam vongola *f.*
clap applaudire *v.* **3;** battere le mani *v.*
clapper: professional clappers
  claque *f.*
clarinet clarinetto *m.*
class classe; lezione *f.*
  class conflict conflitto *m.* di classe **6**
classic; classical classico/a *adj.* **8**
classmate compagno/a *m., f.* di classe

classroom aula *f.*
clean pulire *v.;* pulito/a *adj.*
  clean energy energia *f.* pulita **7**
clear chiaro/a *adj.*
  to clear the table sparecchiare la
    tavola *v.*
clever spiritoso/a *adj.*
client cliente *m., f.*
cliff scogliera *f.*
climate clima *m.*
climb scalare *v.* **3**
  to climb stairs salire le scale *v.*
climbing arrampicata *f.*
clock orologio *m.*
clone clonare *v.* **7**
close chiudere *v.*
  to close an account chiudere
    un conto *v.* **10**
close (to) vicino (a) *prep.*
close-knit affiatato/a *adj.* **5**
closet armadio *m.*
clothes dryer asciugatrice *f.*
clothing abbigliamento *m.* **10;**
  vestiti *m., pl.*
  clothing size taglia *f.*
cloud nuvola *f.*
cloudy nuvoloso/a *adj.*
clutch frizione *f.*
coach allenatore/allenatrice *m., f.* **3**
  coach (*bus*) pullman *m.*
coachman vetturino *m.*
coast costa *f.*
  coast guard guardia *f.* costiera **4**
coat cappotto *m.* **3**
cobblestones selciato *m.*
cockpit cabina *f.* di controllo **5**
code codice *m.* **7**
  code of conduct/ethics codice
    m. deontologico **7**
coerce costringere *v.*
coercive coercitivo/a *adj.*
coffee caffè *m.*
  coffee maker caffettiera *f.*
coin moneta *f.*
coincidence coincidenza *f.* **3**
cold freddo/a *adj.;* raffreddore *m.*
  It's cold. Fa freddo.
  to feel cold avere freddo *v.*
  to have a cold avere il
    raffreddore *v.*
colleague collega *m., f.* **10**
collection collezione *f.*
collie lassie *m.* **1**
colonize colonizzare *v.* **8**
color colore *m.;* tinta *f.*
comb pettine *m.*
  to comb one's hair pettinarsi *v.*
come venire *v.* **1**
  Come on! Forza!; Dàje! **2**
  to come from venire da *v.* **8**
  to come near avvicinarsi *v.* **5**
  to come out uscire *v.* **1**

comedy commedia *f.*
comic strip fumetto *m.* **9**
commercial pubblicità *f.* **9**
commission commissione *f.* **8**
commit commettere *v.*
commitment impegno *m.* **10**
common sense buon senso *m.* **6**
commonplaces luoghi *m., pl.*
  comuni
commute fare il pendolare *v.*
company azienda, ditta *f.* **10**
compassion compassione *f.* **2**
compatibility affinità di coppia *f.* **9**
compatriot compatriot *adj.* **8**
compel obbligare (a) *v.* **8**
competence competenza *f.*
competitive competitivo/a *adj.* **3**
complain lamentarsi (di) *v.* **2;**
  reclamare *v.* **6**
completely affatto;
  completamente *adv.*
compose comporre *v.*
composer compositore/
  compositrice *m., f.*
composition composizione *f.* **8**
compromise compromesso *m.*
computer computer *m.* **7**
  computer science informatica *f.* **7**
  desktop computer computer *m.*
    da tavolo **7**
  laptop computer computer *m.*
    portatile **7**
concert concerto *m.*
condition condizione *f.*
confident disinvolto/a *adj.*
conform conformarsi *v.* **6**
conformism conformismo *m.*
conformist conformista *adj.* **6**
congressman/congresswoman
  deputato/a *m., f.* **4**
connection collegamento *m.*
conquer conquistare *v.* **8**
conscience coscienza *f.* **3**
conservative conservatore/
  conservatrice *adj.* **4**
constitution costituzione *f.* **6**
consult interpellare *v.*
consultant consulente *m., f.* **10**
contemporary contemporaneo/a *adj.*
contempt sdegno *m.*
content contento/a *adj.*
contestant concorrente *m., f.*
continue continuare *v.* **8;**
  proseguire *v.*
contract contratto *m.*
contravene contravvenire a *v.*
contributions contributi *m., pl.*
control controllo *m.*
controversial controverso/a *adj.* **7**
controversy polemica *f.* **6**
conversation conversazione *f.*
cook cucinare *v.;* cuocere *v.* **3**
cook cuoco/a *m., f.*

cookie biscotto *m.* 1
cool fresco/a *adj.*
copy copiare *v.* 7
copyright diritto *m.* d'autore 8
corner angolo *m.* 2
  around the corner dietro
    l'angolo *adv.*
correct correggere *v.* 3
correspondent inviato/a *m., f.*
  speciale 9
cosmetics shop profumeria *f.*
cost costare *v.*
cotton cotone *m.*
couch divano *m.*
cough tosse *f.;* **tossire** v.
council consiglio *m.* 4
count on contare su *v.* 1
counting rhyme conta *f.* 2
countryman/countrywoman
  paesano/a *m., f.* 2
countryside campagna *f.* 2
couple coppia *f.* 1
courageous coraggioso/a *adj.*
course piatto *m.*
  first/second course primo/
    secondo piatto *m.*
courteous cortese *adj.*
courtesy cortesia *f.*
courthouse tribunale *m.* 2
cousin cugino/a *m., f.* 5
cover (with) coprire (di) *v.* 8
cow mucca *f.*
coward codardo/a *adj.* 5
craftsman artigiano/a *m., f.*
crazy pazzo/a *adj.*
credit credito *m.*
  credit card carta *f.* di credito 10
  to pay with a credit card pagare
    con carta di credito *v.*
crew cut capelli *m., pl.* a spazzola
crime criminalità *f.* 4; crimine 4;
  delitto *m.* 6
criminal criminale *m., f.* 4
crisis: economic crisis crisi *f.*
  economica 10
critic critico *m.* 9
cross attraversare *v.* 2
cross-country skiing sci *m.* di
  fondo *m.* 3
crosswalk strisce *f., pl.* pedonali 2
crowd folla *f.* 2
crowded affollato/a *adj.* 2
crude rozzo/a *adj.*
cruel crudele *adj.*
cruelty crudeltà *f.* 4
cruise crociera *f.*
crumb briciola *f.*
cry piangere *v.* 3
cultural heritage patrimonio
  culturale *m.* 9
cup tazza *f.*
cupboard credenza *f.*

curator curatore/curatrice *m., f.* 1
cure guarire *v.* 7
curious curioso/a *adj.*
curl arricciare *v.*
curly riccio/a *adj.*
currency valuta *f.* 4
current affairs attualità *f.* 9
curse maledire *v.;* maledizione *f.*
curtain sipario *m.;* tenda *f.*
custom usanza *f.* 9
customer cliente *m., f.*
customs dogana *f.*
cut tagliare *v.* taglio *m.* 8
  to cut one's hair tagliare i capelli *v.*
cute bellino/a, *m., f.* carino/a *adj.*
cycling ciclismo *m.*
cyclone ciclone *m.*
cypress cipresso *m.*

D

dad papà *m.*
daily quotidiano/a *adj.* 2
dance ballare *v.*
  classical dance danza *f.* classica
  short dance performance
    balletto *m.*
danger pericolo *m.* 4
dangerous pericoloso/a *adj.* 2
dark scuro/a *adj.*
  dark-haired bruno/a *adj.*
darts freccette *f., pl.*
database banca *f.* dati 7
date appuntamento *m.* 1
  be up-to-date essere
    aggiornato/a *v.* 9
date vedersi con *v.*
  daughter figlia *f.* 5
  daughter-in-law nuora *f.* 5
dawn alba *f.*
day giorno *m.*
deaf sordo/a *adj.* 5
deal affare *m.* 4
  good deal buon affare *m.*
dear: sweet, very dear
  caruccio *adj.*
death morte *f.* 5
debit card carta *f.* di debito
  to pay with a debit card pagare
    con carta di debito *v.*
debt debito *m.* 10
  to be in debt avere dei debiti *v.* 10
debut debutto *m.*
decade decennio *m.* 8
December dicembre *m.*
decide decidere *v.* 3
decision: to make a
  decision prendere una decisione *v.*
decrease diminuire *v.* 6
decree decreto *m.*
dedicate oneself (to) dedicarsi
  (a) *v.* 4

defeat sconfiggere *v.* 8; sconfitta *f.* 4
defend difendere *v.* 4; tutelare *v.* 6
defense difesa *f.* 2, 3
deforestation disboscamento *m.*
degree diploma; grado *m.*
  It is 18 degrees out. Ci sono
    18 gradi.
delay ritardo *m.* 2
delicatessen (negozio di)
  gastronomia *f.*
demand richiesta *f.* 10
demanding esigente *adj.*
democracy democrazia *f.* 4
democratic democratico/a *adj.* 8
demographic makeup
  composizione *f.* demografica 2
demonstrate fare una manifestazione,
  manifestare *v.* 6
dentist dentista *m., f.*
denture dentiera *f.* 5
department facoltà *f.*
  department store grande
    magazzino *m.*
departures partenze *f., pl.*
depend (on) dipendere (da) *v.* 8
deposit depositare, versare *v.* 10
depressed depresso/a *adj.* 1
depression depressione *f.*
desert deserto *m.*
deserve meritare *v.* 1
designer firmato/a *adj.* 3
  designer label griffe *f.* 10
desire desiderare *v.* 6; voglia *f.*
  desire to be in the limelight
    protagonismo *m.*
desk banco *m.*
desktop computer computer *m.*
  da tavolo 7
dessert dolce *m.*
detail particolare *m.* 8
deterioration degrado *m.*
develop sviluppare *v.*
development sviluppo *m.* 6, 7
device dispositivo *m.* 7
diagram schema *m.*
dial comporre *v.;* digitare *v.*
dial a number fare/comporre un
  numero *v.* 9
dialect dialetto *m.* 6
dialogue dialogo *m.* 6
diaper pannolino *m.* 2
dictatorship dittatura *f.* 4
dictionary dizionario *m.*
die morire *v.* 3
diet dieta *f.*
  to be on a diet essere a dieta *v.*
difference divergenza; differenza *f.*
difficult difficile *adj.*
digital digitale *adj.*
  digital camera macchina *f.*
    fotografica digitale
  digital signal segnale *m.* digitale 7

dignity dignità *f.*
dilemma dilemma *m.*
dim-witted scemo/a *adj.*
dining room sala *f.* da pranzo
diploma diploma *m.*
directions: to give directions
dare indicazioni *v.* 2
director regista *m., f.* 9;
principale *m., f.*
dirty sporco/a *adj.*
disagree dissentire *v.* (da, su) 6
disappear sparire *v.* 3;
scomparire *v.* 7
disappearance scomparsa *f.* 6
disappointed deluso/a *adj.* 1
discomfort disagio *m.* 8
discouragement
scoraggiamento *m.* 7
discourteous scortese *adj.*
discovery ritrovato *m.* 7; scoperta *f.* 7
discreet discreto/a *adj.*
discuss discutere *v.* 3
disease malattia *f.*
disgusting schifoso/a *adj.*
dish pietanza *f.* 4
dishonest disonesto/a *adj.* 1
dishwasher lavastoviglie *f.*
dissent dissentire *v.* 6
distance oneself allontanarsi (da) *v.* 8
distant lontano/a *adj.* 5
distinguish distinguere *v.* 6
disturbing inquietante *adj.*
diversity diversità *f.* 6
divorce divorziare (da) *v.* 1
divorced divorziato/a *adj.* 1
DNA DNA *m.* 7
do fare *v.* 1
to do one's homework fare
i compiti *v.* 1
to do the laundry fare il
bucato *v.* 5
doctor dottore(ssa) *m., f.*
family doctor medico *m.* di famiglia
to go to the doctor andare
dal dottore *v.*
document documento *m.*
documentary documentario *m.* 9
dog cane *m.*
dog shelter canile *m.* 1
doll bambola *f.* 5
domestic domestico/a *adj.*
domination dominio *m.* 6
door porta *f.*
doorman portiere/a *m., f.*
doubt dubitare *v.* 7
down there laggiù *adv.* 6
download scaricare *v.* 7
downstage ribalta *f.*
drain smaltire *v.*
drama dramma *m.*
dramatic drammatico/a *adj.*
draw (*bring*) trarre *v.* 9

drawer cassetto *m.*
dreadlocks treccine *f., pl.*
dream sognare *v.* 1
dream-like onirico/a *adj.* 9
dress abito *m.;* vestito *m.* 3
dress circle balconata *f.*
dress shirt camicia *f.*
evening dress abito *m.* da sera 3
woman's dress vestito *m.*
da donna 3
dresser cassettiera *f.*
dressing style look *m.* 10
drink bere *v.* 1; bibita *f.*
to get something drink/
eat prendere qualcosa da bere/
mangiare *v.* 3
drive guidare *v.* 2
driver automobilista *m., f.* 2
driver's license patente *f.*
drought siccità *f.*
drug medicina *f.*
drum tamburo *m.*
drums batteria *f.*
drummer batterista *m., f.*
dry secco/a *adj.*
dry cleaner lavanderia, tintoria *f.* 9
dry up asciugarsi *v.* 2
dryer (*clothes*) asciugatrice *f.*
dubbing doppiaggio *m.* 9
dumb tonto/a *adj.*
dump discarica *f.*
during durante *prep.* 8
dust fare la polvere, spolverare *v.;*
polvere *f.*
dye tinta *f.*
dynamic dinamico/a *adj.*

E

each ciascuno/a *indef. adj., pron.* 9
each other l'un l'altro, fra di loro
ear orecchio (*pl.* orecchie *f.*) *m.*
earn guadagnare *v.* 10
earnest convinto/a *adj.*
earrings orecchini *m., pl.* 10
earthquake terremoto *m.*
ease: at ease a proprio agio *adv.*
Easter Pasqua *f.*
Easter Monday pasquetta *f.* 9
easy facile *adj.*
eat mangiare *v.* 6
to get something to drink/
eat prendere qualcosa da bere/
mangiare *v.* 3
e-Book libro *m.* elettronico 7
ecology ecologia *f.*
economics economia *f.*
economy class classe *f.* economica
editor redattore/redattrice *m., f.* 9
education formazione *f.* 10;
istruzione *f.*
eel: large eel capitone *m.* 6

effect effetto *m.*
effort sforzo *m.* 9
egg uovo (*pl.* uova *f.*) *m.*
eggplant melanzana *f.*
eight otto *m.*
eight hundred ottocento *m.*
eight million otto milioni *m.*
eighteen diciotto *m.*
eighteenth diciottesimo *adj.*
eighth ottavo *adj.*
eighty ottanta *m.*
eighty-one ottantuno *m.*
eighty-second ottantaduesimo *adj.*
elbow gomito *m.*
elect eleggere *v.* 4
election elezione *f.*
to lose the election perdere le
elezioni *v.* 4
electrician elettricista *m., f.* 9
electronics elettronica *f.* 7
elevator ascensore *m.*
eleven undici *m.*
eleventh undicesimo *adj.*
e-mail address indirizzo *m.* e-mail 7
e-mail message e-mail *f.*
emergency room sala *f.*
d'emergenza; pronto soccorso *m.*
emigration emigrazione *f.* 4
empathy empatia *f.* 6
emperor/empress imperatore/
imperatrice *m., f.* 8
employ impiegare *v.* 10
employee impiegato/a *m., f.* 10
enchanted fatato/a *adj.* 3
encourage incoraggiare *v.* 8
end fine *f.*
enemy nemico *m.* 2
energetic energico/a *adj.*
energy energia *f.*
clean energy energia *f.* pulita 7
engaged fidanzato/a *adj.* 1
engine motore *m.*
engineer ingegnere *m.* 2
engineering ingegneria *f.* 7
English inglese *adj.*
engrave scolpire *v.*
enough abbastanza *adv.*
entertainer intrattenitore *m.*
enthusiasm entusiasmo *m.* 1
enthusiastic entusiasta *adj.* 1
entrust affidare *v.* 10
envelope busta *f.*
environment ambiente *m.*
environmental impact impatto *m.*
ambientale 7
environmentalism ambientalismo *m.*
epic racconto *m.* epico
episode puntata *f.* 9
equal uguale *adj.* 4
equality uguaglianza *f.* 4
era età *f.*
erase cancellare *v.* 7

eraser gomma *f.*
error errore *m.*
eruption eruzione *f.*
essay tema *m.;* tesina *f.*
essayist saggista *m., f.* **8**
ethical etico/a; morale *adj.* **7**
evacuees sfollati *m., pl.* **2**
eve vigilia *f.* **6**
even pure, persino *adv.*
  not even non… neanche *adv.*
  not even non… nemmeno, non… neppure *conj.*
evening sera *f.*
  Good evening. Buonasera.
ever mai *adv.*
every ogni; tutto *indef. adj.* **9**
everyone ognuno/a; tutti *indef. pron.* **9** quanti, tutti quanti, tutti quelli che, tutti/e *rel. pron.* **9**
everything tutto, tutti/e *indef. pron.* **9**
  everything that tutto ciò che, tutto quanto, tutto quel che, tutto quello che *rel. pron.* **9**
excavation scavo *m.* **2**
except tranne *prep.* **8**
  except (for) salvo *prep.* **8**
exchange cambiare *v.* **3**; scambio *m.* **4**
  exchange of opinions scambio *v.* di idee **8**
excited emozionato/a *adj.* **1**
excuse scusare *v.*
  Excuse me. Scusi/a. (*form./fam.*)
execute fucilare *v.* **8**
executive dirigente *m., f.* **10**
exercise fare esercizio *v.*
exhaust scappamento *m.*
exhibit esposizione *f.*
exhibition mostra *f.* **3, 8**
exit uscita *f.*
expect aspettarsi *v.* **8**
expel espellere *v.* **8**
expensive caro/a, costoso/a *adj.*
experience esperienza *f.* **10**
  professional experience esperienza *f.* professionale **10**
experiment esperimento *m.* **7**
experimental sperimentale *adj.* **9**
explain spiegare *v.* **1**
explore esplorare *v.*
expression espressione *f.*
exquisite squisito/a *adj.*
extreme sports sport *m., pl.* estremi
eye occhio *m.*
eyebrow sopracciglio (*pl.* sopracciglia *f.*) *m.*
eyelash ciglio *(pl.* ciglia *f.) m.*
eyelid palpebra *f.* **5**

F

fabric stoffa *f.* **8**
face faccia *f.;* viso *m.;* volto *m.* **9**

face viso *m.*
factory fabbrica; officina *f.* **10**
  factory worker operaio/a *m., f.*
faculty facoltà *f.*
fail fallire *v.*
  to fail (exam) bocciare *v.*
fair giusto/a *adj.* **4**
fairy tale favola, fiaba *f.* **3**
faith fede *f.* **6**
faithful fedele *adj.* **1**
fall autunno *m.;* cadere *v.* **3**
  to fall apart sfarsi *v.*
  to fall asleep addormentarsi *v.* **2**
  to fall in love (with) innamorarsi (di) *v.* **1**
fame notorietà *f.*
family famiglia *f.*
  family relationship parentela *f.* **5**
  family unit nucleo *m.* familiare **5**
fan tifoso/a *m., f.* **2; 3**
fare tariffa *f.*
  excess fare supplemento *m.*
farm fattoria *f.*
farmer agricoltore/agricoltrice *m., f.;* contadino/a *m., f.* **2**
farmhouse casale *m.* **2**; podere *m.*
fascist fascista *adj.* **8**
fashion moda *f.*
  to (not) be in fashion (non) andare di moda *v.*
  fashion designer stilista *m.* **10**
fashionable alla moda *adj.* **3**
fast veloce *adj.*
fat grasso/a *adj.*
father padre *m.*
father-in-law suocero *m.* **5**
fault colpa *f.* **1**
favorite preferito/a *adj.*
fax fax *m.*
fear paura *f.* **4**; temere *v.* **6**
Feast of the Patron Saint Festa del santo patrono *f.*
February febbraio *m.*
fed up stufo/a *adj.* **1**
feel sentire *v.;* provare *v.* **1**; sentirsi *v.* **1**
  to feel affection for volere bene a *v.* **1**
  to feel like avere voglia di *v.* **8**
female femmina *f.*
feminist femminista *adj.*
ferry traghetto *m.* **7**
festival festival *m.;* rassegna *f.* **9**
festivities festeggiamenti *m., pl.* **9**
fever febbre *f.*
  to have a fever avere la febbre *v.*
few: a few qualche, alcuni/e *indef. adj.* **9** alcuni/e *indef. pron.* **9**
fiancé(e) fidanzato/a *m., f.* **1**
field campo *m.* **2**
  playing field campo *m.* di/da gioco **3**
fifteen quindici *m.*
fifth quinto *adj.*

fifty cinquanta *m.*
fifty-one cinquantuno *m.*
fight combattere *v.* **4**; litigare *v.* **5**; lottare *v.* **6**
figure cifra *f.* **10**
fill (with) riempire (di) *v.* **8**
  to fill out a form riempire un modulo *v.*
film film *m.;* filmare, girare *v.* **9**
  film critic critico *m.* cinematografico **9**
  horror/sci-fi film film *m.* di fantascienza/dell'orrore
filmmaker cineasta *m., f.* **9**
financial finanziario/a *adj.* **10**
find trovare *v.*
  find (archeol.) reperto *m.* **2**
finding ritrovato *m.* **7**
fine multa *f.*
  fine arts belle arti *f., pl.* **8**
finger dito (*pl.* dita *f.*) *m.*
finish finire *v.* **4**
fire licenziare *v.* **10**
firefighter vigile *m., f.* del fuoco **2**
fireman pompiere *m.* **7**
firm società *f.* **10**
first prima *adv.;* primo/a *adj.*
  at first all'inizio *adv.*
  first aid pronto/primo soccorso *m.*
  first-born primogenito/a *m., f.*
  first class prima classe *adj.*
  first of all innanzitutto *adv.*
fish pescare *v.* **4**; pesce *m.*
  fish shop pescheria *f.*
five cinque *m.*
five hundred cinquecento *m.*
five hundred fifty thousand cinquecentocinquantamila *m.*
five thousand cinquemila *m.*
five-hundredth cinquecentesimo *adj.*
five-player soccer calcetto *m.* **2**
fix aggiustare *v.*
flag bandiera *f.* **4**
flash drive chiavetta USB *f.* **7**
flash of lightning lampo *m.*
flavor sapore *m.* **4**; gusto *m.*
flavoring aroma *m.*
flee fuggire *v.* **3**
flight volo *m.*
flip-flops infradito *f., pl.* **3**
flippers pinne *f., pl.* **4**
flirt (with) provarci (con) *v.* **2**
flood alluvione *f.* **7**; ingolfare (motore) *v.*
flooding allagamento *m.* **7**
floor pavimento *m.*
florist fioraio, fiorista *m.* **10**
flower fiore *m.*
  flower shop fiorista *m.*
flu influenza *f.*
flute flauto *m.*
folder cartella *f.*

folklore folclore *m.* **9**
follow seguire *v.*
food cibo *m.*
food-loving goloso/a *adj.* **4**
foodstuffs alimentari *m., pl.*
fool: to act the fool fare il buffone *v.*
foosball biliardino *m.* **3**
foosball calcetto *m.* **9**
foot piede *m.*
  on foot a piedi *adv.*
football football *m.* americano
footbridge passerella *f.* **7**
for per *prep.*
  For how long… Da quanto tempo…
forbidden proibito/a *adj.*
foreign straniero/a *adj.*
  foreign countries estero *m.* **6**
forest foresta *f.*
forge ahead tirare avanti *v.* **6**
forget dimenticare *v.;* dimenticarsi
  (di) *v.* **2**
forgettable dimenticabile *adj.* **1**
fork forchetta *f.*
form modulo *m.*
forty quaranta *m.*
foundations fondamenta *f., pl.* **6**
fountain fontana *f.*
four quattro *m.*
four eyes quattrocchi *m., f.* **3**
four hundred quattrocento *m.*
fourteen quattordici *m.*
fourth quarto *adj.*
fox volpe *f.* **1**
fraction parte, frazione *f.*
fracture frattura *f.*
free gratis *(invar.) adj., adv.*
freedom libertà *f.* **4**
  freedom of the press libertà *f.*
  di stampa **9**
  freedom of worship libertà *f.*
  di culto *f.* **6**
freezer congelatore *m.*
French francese *adj.*
frequently frequentemente *adv.*
fresco affresco *m.* **8**
Friday venerdì *m.*
fridge frigo *m.*
fried fritto/a *adj.*
friend amico/a *m., f.*
friendly socievole *adj.* **5**
friendship amicizia *f.* **1**
frog rana *f.*
from da, di (d') *prep*
front fronte *f.*
  in front of davanti (a) *prep.*
fruit frutta *f.*
fry friggere *v.*
  to fry lightly soffriggere *v.*
fulfill realizzare *v.* **6**
full pieno/a *adj.*
  full price ticket biglietto *m.* intero
  full-time a tempo pieno *adj., adv.*

fun divertente *adj.*
function funzionare *v.*
funny buffo/a *adj.* **3;** spiritoso/a *adj.*
fur pelliccia *f.* **5**
furnished apartment
  appartamento *m.* arredato
furniture mobili *m., pl.*
future futuro *m.*
Futurist futurista *adj.*

G

gain weight ingrassare *v.* **8**
gallery galleria *f.*
game gioco *m.;* partita *f.*
  to win/lose/tie a game vincere/
  perdere/pareggiare una partita *v.* **3**
garage garage *(invar.) m.*
garbage rifiuto *m.;* spazzatura *f.*
  garbage collector
  netturbino/a *m., pl.*
  garbage truck camion *m.* della
  nettezza urbana
garden giardino *m.*
  garden-level apartment
  seminterrato *m.*
  public gardens giardini *m., pl.*
  pubblici **2**
gardener giardiniere/a *m., f.*
garlic aglio *m.*
gas station attendant
  benzinaio/a *m., f.* **7**
gaze sguardo *m.* **10**
GDP PIL *m.*
gene gene *m.* **7**
generally in genere *adv.*
generation gap salto *m.*
  generazionale **5**
generous generoso/a *adj.*
genetics genetica *f.* **3**
genius genio/a *m., f.*
genocide genocidio *m.*
genre genere *m.* **8**
geologist geologo/a *m., f.* **7**
German tedesco/a *adj.* **8**
get ricevere *v.*
  to get angry arrabbiarsi *v.* **1**
  to get bored annoiarsi *v.* **2**
  to get dressed vestirsi *v.* **2**
  to get embarrassed vergognarsi
  v. **1**
  to get engaged (to) fidanzarsi
  (con) *v.* **1**
  to get going muoversi *v.* **2**
  to get in a car salire in macchina *v.* **2**
  to get lost perdersi *v.* **2**
  to get mad/angry arrabbiarsi *v.* **2**
  to get married (to) sposarsi
  (con) *v.* **1**
  to get off the bus scendere
  dall'autobus *v.* **2**
  to get off the train scendere dal
  treno *v.* **2**

to get on the bus salire
  sull'autobus *v.* **2**
to get on the train salire sul
  treno *v.* **2**
to get out of the car scendere
  dalla macchina *v.* **2**
to get rid of disfarsi di *v.* **6**
to get something to drink/
  eat prendere qualcosa da bere/
  mangiare *v.* **3**
to get together incontrarsi *v.* **2**
to get up alzarsi *v.* **2**
to get used to abituarsi *v.* **7, 8**
ghost fantasma *m.* **5**
gift dono *m.*
gifted dotato/a *adj.*
girl ragazza *f.*
girlfriend ragazza *f.;* fidanzata *m., f.* **5**
give dare *v.*
  to give (*as a gift*) regalare *v.*
  to give a ride dare un passaggio *v.* **2**
  to give back restituire *v.*
  to give directions dare
  indicazioni *v.* **2**
  to give to each other darsi *v.*
  to give up rinunciare (a) *v.* **10**
glass bicchiere *m.*
glasses occhiali *m., pl.*
global warming riscaldamento *m.*
  globale *m.* **7;** surriscaldamento *m.*
  della Terra
globalization globalizzazione *f.* **6**
glove guanto *m.*
gluttony ingordigia *f.* **4**
go andare *v.* **1**
  to go back home rincasare *v.* **10**
  to go back/return (ri)tornare *v.* **3**
  to go down scendere *v.*
  to go down the stairs scendere
  le scale *v.*
  to go for a stroll fare un giretto *v.* **2**
  to go in entrare *v.* **3**
  to go mad impazzire *v.* **3**
  to go near avvicinarsi *v.* **5**
  to go out with uscire con *v.* **1**
  to go shopping fare spese *v.* **1**
  to go to the gym andare in
  palestra *v.* **3**
  to go up salire *v.* **1**
goal rete *f.* **3;** scopo *m.* **7**
goalkeeper portiere/a *m.* **2, 3**
goat capra *f.*
God Dio *m.* **6**
godfather padrino *m.* **5**
godmother madrina *f.* **5**
godson/goddaughter figlioccio/a
  m., f. **5**
good bravo/a *adj.;* buono/a *adj.* **9**
  good deal buon affare *m.*
  Good evening. Buonasera.
  Good luck. In bocca al lupo.
  (*lit.* In the mouth of the wolf.)
  Good morning. Buongiorno.

Good night. Buonanotte.
to be no good at... essere negato/a per *v.*
very good ottimo/a *adj.* **9**
Good-bye. Arrivederci., Ciao.
goodness bontà *f.* **3**
gossip pettegolezzi *m.* **1**
Gothic gotico/a *adj.*
govern governare *v.* **4**
government governo *m.* **4**
GPS navigatore satellitare *m.*
grade voto *m.*
graduate: to graduate from college/university laurearsi *v.*
grandfather/grandmother nonno/a *m., f.* **5**
grandson/granddaughter nipote *m., f.* **5**
grapes uva *f.*
grass erba *f.*
gratitude gratitudine *f.* **7**
grazing land pascolo *m.* **7**
great geniale *adj.* **1**
greatest massimo/a *adj.* **9**
great-grandfather/grandmother bisnonno/a *m., f.* **1, 5**
greedy avaro/a *adj.*
Greek greco/a *adj.*
green verde *adj.*
green bean fagiolino *m.*
greenhouse effect effetto *m.* serra
greet accogliere *v.* **1**; salutare *v.*
to greet each other salutarsi *v.*
greeting saluto *m.*
grenade granata *f.*
grey grigio/a *adj.*
grill griglia *f.*
grilled alla griglia *adj.*
groceries: to buy groceries fare la spesa *v.*
grocery store negozio *m.* d'alimentari
groom sposo *m.* **5**
group gruppo *m.*
grow coltivare *v.* **7**; crescere *v.* **3**
growth crescita *f.* **4**
guess indovinare *v.*
guilty colpevole *adj.* **4**
guitar chitarra *f.*
guitarist chitarrista *m., f.*
gum gengiva *f.* **5**
guy tipo *m.*
gym: to go to the gym andare in palestra *v.* **3**
gymnasium palestra *f.*
gymnastics ginnastica *f.*

H

hail grandine *f.*
hair capelli *m., pl.*
to cut one's hair tagliare i capelli *v.*
hair dryer asciugacapelli (*invar.*) *m.*

hairdresser parrucchiere/a *m., f.*
half brother fratellastro *m.*
half hour mezz'ora *m.*
half sister sorellastra *f.*
hall sala *f.*
hallway corridoio *m.*
ham prosciutto *m.*
hammer martello *m.* **8**
hand mano (*pl.* le mani) *f.*
on the other hand invece *adv.*
handbag borsa *f.*
handsome bello/a *adj.*
hang: to hang up the phone riattaccare il telefono *v.*
happen accadere, succedere *v.;* avvenire *v.* **6**
happen capitare *v.* **8, 9**
happy contento/a; felice *adj.*
hard duro/a *adj.*
hard drive disco rigido *m.*
hardly appena *adv., conj.*
haste fretta *f.*
hat cappello *m.*
hate odiare *v.* **1**
to hate each other odiarsi *v.*
hatred odio *m.*
have avere *v.* **1**
to have a stomachache (backache, headache) avere mal di pancia (schiena, testa) *v.*
to have breakfast fare colazione *v.* **1**
to have fun divertirsi *v.* **2**
to have left restare *v.* **2**
to have to; must dovere *v.* **1**
hay fieno *m.*
head testa *f.*
headache mal *m.* di testa
headlight faro *m.*
headphones cuffie *f., pl.*
heal curare *v.;* guarire *v.* **7**
health salute *f.*
to be in good health essere in buona salute *v.*
healthy sano/a *adj.*
hear sentire *v.*
heart cuore *m.*
heartburn bruciore *m.* di stomaco
heat wave ondata *f.* di caldo
heavy pesante *adj.*
heels tacchi *m., pl.* **3**
high heels tacchi alti *m., pl.* **1**
low heels tacchi bassi *m., pl.* **1**
height (fig.) culmine *m.* **9**
of average height di media statura *adj.;*
Hello. Buongiorno.; Salve. (*form.*)
Hello. (on the phone) Pronto.
help aiutare *v.*
to help each other aiutarsi *v.* **2**
helpful disponibile *adj.*
herd mandria *f.* **7**

here ecco *adv.;* qua, qui *adv.*
heritage retaggio *m.* **1**
Hey there! Ehilà!
Hi. Ciao.
hidden nascosto/a *adj.* **4**
hide nascondere *v.*
high elevato/a *adj.*
high school liceo *m.*
higher superiore *adj.* **9**
highway autostrada *f.*
hiking escursionismo *m.* **3**
hills colline *pl*
hint accenno *m.*
hire assumere *v.* **10**
hiring assunzione *f.*
historic storico *adj.* **8**
history storia *f.*
hit colpire *v.*
hold tenere *v.* **1**
to hold on to, hang on to aggrapparsi *v.* **6**
to be on hold restare in attesa *v.*
holiday festa *f.*
public holiday giorno *m.* festivo
holidays ferie *f., pl.* **10**
home casa *f.*
homeland patria *f.* **2**
homemade fatto/a in casa *adj.*
homework compiti *m., pl.*
homicidal omicida *adj.* **8**
honest onesto/a *adj.* **1**
hood cofano *m.*
hope sperare *v.* **6**
horizon orizzonte *m.*
horoscope oroscopo *m.* **9**
horror film film *m.* dell'orrore *m.*
horse cavallo *m.*
horseback riding equitazione *f.* **3**
to go horseback riding andare a cavallo *v.*
hospital ospedale *m.*
hot caldo/a *adj.*
It's hot. Fa caldo.
to feel hot avere caldo *v.*
hotel albergo *m.*
five-star hotel albergo *m.* a cinque stelle
hour ora *f.*
house casa *f.*
househusband casalingo *m.*
housemate coinquilino/a *m., f.* **2**
housewife casalinga *f.* **10**
housing abitazioni *f., pl.* **5**
how come *adv.*
For how long... Da quanto tempo...
how many quanti/e *adj., pron.*
how much quanto *adj., pron., adv.*
How much is/are... ? Quanto costa(no)...?
however comunque *conj., adv.*
huckster imbonitore *m.*
hug abbracciare *v.;* abbracciarsi *v.* **2**

human resources risorse *f., pl.* umane
human rights diritti *m., pl.* umani **4**
Humanism Umanesimo *m.* **8**
humanities lettere *f., pl.*
humble umile *adj.* **1**
humid umido/a *adj.*
humidity umidità *f.*
humor umorismo *m.* **6**
humorous umoristico/a *adj.* **8**
hungry: to be hungry avere fame *v.* **1**
hunting dog cane *m.* da caccia **1**
hurry sbrigarsi *v.* **2**
  in a hurry frettoloso/a *adj.* **2**
  to be in a hurry avere fretta (di) *v.* **8**
hurt: to hurt oneself farsi male *v.*
husband marito *m.* **5**
  first/second husband primo/secondo marito *m.*
hybrid car macchina *f.* ibrida

I

ice cream shop gelateria *f.*
ice-skating pattinaggio *m.* sul ghiaccio **3**
ID documento *m.*
idea idea *f.*
idealistic idealista *adj.* **1**
identity theft furto *m.* d'identità **7**
if se *conj.*
ill malato/a *adj.*
illegal illegale *adj.* **4**
  illegal immigrant clandestino *m.* **4**
illiterate analfabeta *adj.* **4**
IM messaggio *m.* istantaneo *m.*
imagine immaginare *v.* **7**
immature immaturo/a *adj.* **1**
immediately subito *adv.*
immigrant immigrante *m., f.* **2**
  illegal immigrant clandestino *m.* **4**
immigration immigrazione *f.* **4**
impact impatto *m.*
impartial imparziale *adj.* **9**
important importante *adj.;* notevole *adj.* **7**
impose imporre *v.* **4**
impossible impossibile *adj.* **7**
impression impressione *f.*
imprison imprigionare *v.* **4**
imprisonment prigionia *f.*
improve migliorare *v.*
improvise improvvisare *v.* **3**
in a; fra/tra; in; su *prep.*
  in a hurry frettoloso/a *adj.* **2;** di/in fretta *adv.*
  in order to per *prep.*
  in the case that nel caso che *conj.* **7**
inappropriate inopportuno/a *adj.*
incapacitate impedire *v.*
inches pollici *m./pl* **7**
increase aumentare *v.* **6**

incredible incredibile *adj.*
independent indipendente *adj.*
  to become independent diventare indipendente *v.* **5**
indignant: to become indignant sdegnarsi *v.* **9**
infection infezione *f.*
inferior inferiore *adj.* **9**
influence influenzare *v.* **4**
influential influente *adj.* **9**
information booth chiosco *m.* per le informazioni
informed: to keep oneself informed informarsi *v.* **9**
infrastructure infrastruttura *f.* **2**
infringe contravvenire a *v.*
inhabit abitare *v.* **8**
inherit ereditare *v.* **5**
injure oneself ferirsi *v.* **3**
injury ferita *f.*
in-laws parenti *m., pl.* acquisiti
inner tube camera *f.* d'aria **4**
innocent innocente *adj.* **4**
innovative innovativo/a *adj.*
insect insetto *m.*
insecure insicuro/a *adj.* **1**
insensitive insensibile *adj.*
inside dentro *prep., adv.*
insist insistere *v.* **6**
insomnia insonnia *f.*
installment rata *f.*
instant message messaggio *m.* istantaneo
instead invece *adv.*
instrument strumento *m.*
  musical instrument strumento *m.* musicale
insurance: life insurance assicurazione *f.* sulla vita
integration integrazione *f.* **4, 6**
intelligence intelligenza *f.*
intelligent intelligente *adj.*
interest interessare *v.* **2**
  interest rate tasso *m.* di interesse
interested: to be interested in interessarsi (a/di) *v.* **8**
interesting interessante *adj.*
intermission intervallo *m.*
intern stagista *m., f.* **10**
Internet cafè Internet caffè *m.*
internship stage *m.*
interrogation interrogatorio *m.* **8**
intersection incrocio *m.* **2**
intervention intervento *m.*
interview intervista *f.* **9**
  job interview colloquio *m.* di lavoro **10**
interviewer intervistatore/intervistatrice *m., f.* **10**
intimacy confidenza *f.* **10**
introduce presentare *v.*
introduction presentazione *f.*
inundation alluvione *f.* **7**

invade invadere *v.* **8**
invent inventare *v.*
invest investire *v.* **10**
investigation investigazione *f.* **8**
investment investimento *m.*
invitation l'invito *m.* **8**
invite (to) invitare (a) *v.* **8**
Irish irlandese *adj.*
iron ferro *m.* (da stiro); stirare *v.*
irresponsible incosciente *adj.* **6;** irresponsabile *adj.*
island isola *f.*
Italian italiano/a *adj.*

J

jacket giacca *f.*
jail carcere *m.*
jam marmellata *f.*
January gennaio *m.*
Japanese giapponese *adj.*
jealous geloso/a *adj.* **1**
jeans jeans *m., pl.*
jerk cretino/a *m., f.*
jersey maglia *f.* **2, 3**
jewelry gioielli *m., pl.* **10**
  jewelry store gioielleria *f.*
Jewish ebreo/a *adj.* **6**
job lavoro *m.;* impiego *m.* **4,** posto *m.,* posizione *f.* **10**
  first job prima occupazione *f.*
  full-/part-time job lavoro *m.* a orario normale/ridotto **10**
  job ad annuncio *m.* di lavoro **10**
  job agency agenzia *f.* di collocamento **10**
  job interview colloquio *m.* di lavoro **10**
  to find a job trovare lavoro *v.*
joke scherzare *v.;* **scherzo** *m.*
journalist giornalista *m., f.* **9**
judge giudicare *v.* **4;** giudice *m., f.* **4**
juice succo *m.*
July luglio *m.*
jump saltare *v.* **3**
June giugno *m.*
jury giuria *f.* **4**
just appena *adv., conj.*
justice giustizia *f.* **4**

K

keep: keep oneself informed informarsi *v.* **9**
key chiave *f.*
keyboard tastiera *f.*
kick tirare *v.* **2**
kilo chilo *m.*
kind genere *m.;* gentile *adj.*
king re *m.* **8**
kingdom regno *m.* **6, 8**
kiosk chiosco *m.*
kiss baciare *v.*

kiss each other baciarsi *v.* **2**
kitchen cucina *f.*
knee ginocchio (*pl.* ginocchia *f.*) *m.*
knife coltello *m.*
knock bussare *v.* **5**
know sapere *v.* **1** (*be familiar with*)
conoscere *v.* **3**
  to know by sight conoscere
  di vista *v.*
  to know each other conoscersi *v.* **2**
  to know something inside and
  out conoscere… a fondo *v.*
  to know the way conoscere la
  strada *v.*

L

lab laboratorio *m.*
Labor Day Festa *f.* del lavoro
labor union sindacato *m.* **10**
lack of understanding
incomprensione *f.* **6**
ladder scala *f.*
lake lago *m.*
lament lamentare *v.* **6**
lamp lampada *f.*
land atterrare *v.*
landlord/landlady padrone/a *m., f.*
di casa
landscape paesaggio *m.* **8**;
panorama *m.*
language lingua *f.*
  languages (*subject*) lingue *f., pl.*
  native language lingua *f.* madre **6**
  sign language lingua *f.* dei segni
  laptop computer computer *m.*
  portatile **7**
last durare *v.;* scorso/a, ultimo/a *adj.*
  last name cognome *m.*
  last night ieri sera
late tardi *adv.*
later poi *adv.*
laugh ridere *v.* **3**
laundromat lavanderia *f.*
laundry: to do the laundry fare il
bucato *v.* **5**
law giurisprudenza; legge *f.;* norma *f.*
  to pass a law approvare/passare
  una legge *v.* **4**
lawyer avvocato *m., f.* **4**
lazy pigro/a *adj.*
leader capo *m.* **4**
lead dirigere *v.* **8**
leaf foglia *f.*
learn imparare *v.* **8**
lease affitto, noleggio *m.*
least minimo/a *adj.* **9**
leather pelle *f.*
leave congedo *m.;* lasciare *v.* **1**;
partire *v.* **3**; uscire (da) *v.* **8**
  Leave me alone. Lasciami in pace.

to leave (*go away from it*)
andarsene *v.* **2, 6**
to leave a message lasciare un
messaggio *v.*
to take leave time prendere un
congedo *v.*
lecture hall aula *f.*
lecturer docente *m., f.*
left sinistra *f.*
leg gamba *f.*
legal legale *adj.* **4**
legislate legiferare *v.* **4**
legumes legumi *m., pl.*
lend prestare *v.*
less meno *adj., adv.*
lesson lezione *f.*
let lasciare *v.*
  Let me see. Fammi vedere.
  to let go mollare *v.* **6**
letter lettera *f.*
  cover letter lettera *f.* di presentazione
lettuce lattuga *f.*
level livello *m.*
liberal liberale *adj.* **4**
liberate liberare *v.* **8**
library biblioteca *f.*
lie bugia *f.*
lie mentire *v.* **1**
  to lie down adagiarsi *v.;* sdraiarsi
  v. **2**; coricarsi *v.* **10**
life vita *f.*
lift alzare *v.* **2**
light chiaro/a; leggero/a *adj.*
lighthouse faro *m.* **4**
lightning fulmine *m.*
lightning strike colpo *m.* di
fulmine **9**
like piacere *v.* **6**
likeable simpatico/a *adj.*
likely probabile *adj.* **7**
line fila; linea *f.*
  line (*poetry*) verso *m.* **8**
  to wait in line fare la coda, fare
  la fila *v.*
lip labbro (*pl.* labbra *f.*) *m.*
lipstick rossetto *m.*
listen ascoltare *v.* **6**
  to listen to music ascoltare
  musica *v.*
listener: radio listener ascoltatore/
ascoltatrice *m., f.* **9**
literature letteratura *f.*
littering: no littering vietato
buttare rifiuti
little poco *adj., adv., indef. pron.* **9**
  in a little while fra poco *adv.*
  little sister sorellina *f.*
  little (*not much*) (of) po' (di) *adj.*
Little Red Riding Hood
Cappuccetto Rosso *m.* **2**
live abitare *v.* **8**; vivere *v.* **5**;
in diretta *adj., adv.* **9**

live performance
rappresentazione *f.* dal vivo
to live on vivere di *v.* **8**
lively vivace *adj.* **2, 5**
living room soggiorno *m.*
load caricare *v.*
loan prestito *m.* **10**
  to ask for a loan chiedere un
  prestito *v.*
located: to be located trovarsi *v.* **2**
long lungo/a *adj.*
  no more, no longer non… più *adv.*
long-term a lungo termine *adj.* **10**
look at guardare *v.*
  to look at oneself/each other
  guardarsi *v.*
look for cercare *v.* **1, 5**
loose largo/a *adj.*
  loose hair capelli *m., pl.* sciolti
lose perdere *v.* **3**
  to lose a game perdere una
  partita *v.* **3**
  to lose the election perdere le
  elezioni *v.* **4**
loss perdita *f.* **2**
lot: a lot molto *adv.* **9**
a lot of molto/a/i/e *indef. adj., pron.*
lotion crema *f.*
lovable amabile *adj.* **5**
love volere bene a *v.* **1**
  love at first sight colpo *m.* di
  fulmine **1**
  to love each other amarsi *v.* **2**
lover amante *m., f.*
lower inferiore *adj.* **9**
lowest infimo/a; minimo/a *adj.* **9**
loyal leale *adj.* **3**
luck: Good luck. Buona fortuna.;
In bocca al lupo. (*lit.* In the mouth
of the wolf.)
luggage carousel nastro *m.*
trasportatore **5**
lukewarm tiepido *adj.*
lullaby ninnananna *f.* **3**
lunch pranzo *m.*
luxury lusso *m.* **4**

M

magazine rivista *f.* **9**
  monthly magazine mensile *m.* **9**
  weekly magazine settimanale *m.* **9**
magic magia *f.* **3**
maid collaboratrice *f.* domestica
mail posta *f.*
  mail carrier postino/a *m., f.*
  to mail a letter imbucare una
  lettera *v.*
mailbox cassetta *f.* delle lettere
main principale *adj.*
maintain ritenere *v.* **6**
make fare *v.* **1**

to make a mistake sbagliare *v.* **1**
to make a withdrawal/deposit fare un prelievo/deposito *v.* **10**
to make it farcela *v.* **6**
to make oneself comfortable accomodarsi *v.* **5**
to make the bed fare il letto *v.*
to make up one's mind (to) decidersi (a) *v.* **8**
makeup trucco *m.* **10**
male maschio *m.*
mama's boy mammone *m.* **5**
man uomo (*pl.* uomini) *m.*
manage dirigere *v.* **10**
  manage (to) riuscire (a) *v.* **1**
management direzione *f.* **10**
manager direttore/direttrice **10**; gestore *m.*
manipulation manipolazione *f.*
many molto/a/i/e *indef. adj., pron.*
  how many quanti/e *adj., pron.*
  so many tanti/e *adj.*
map carta *f.* geografica **6**; cartina, mappa *f.*
  city map carta topografica *f.* **9**
marble marmo *m.* **8**
March marzo *m.*
Mardi Gras carnevale *m.* **9**
marital status stato *m.* civile
market mercato *m.*
married sposato/a *adj.* **1**
marry sposare *v.*
Martian marziano/a *m., f.* **7**
mask maschera *f.* **4**
masterpiece capolavoro *m.* **9**
maternal materno/a *adj.* **5**
mathematician matematico/a *m., f.* **7**
mathematics matematica *f.*
matter stare a cuore *v.* **2**
mature maturo/a *adj.* **1**
maturity maturità *f.* **5**
maxim massima *f.*
May maggio *m.*
mayor sindaco *m.* **2**
meadow prato *m.*
meal pasto *m.*
mean significare *v.*
means mezzo *m.*
  by means of mediante *prep.* **8**
  means of transportation mezzo *m.* di trasporto
measles morbillo *m.*
meat carne *f.*
mechanic meccanico/a *m., f.*
media media *m., pl.*
medicine medicina *f.*
meet conoscere *v.* **3**; incontrare *v.;* conoscersi *v.*
meeting riunione *f.*
melon melone *m.*
memory ricordo *m.* **1**
mention accenno *m.*
menu menù *m.*

mess: What a mess! Che casino!
message messaggio *m.*
Mexican messicano/a *adj.*
microphone microfono *m.*
microwave oven (forno a) microonde *m.*
Middle Ages Medioevo *m.* **6**
midnight mezzanotte *f.*
migraine emicrania *f.*
mile miglio *m.*
military police carabinieri *m., pl.* **5**
milk latte *m.*
mind dispiacere *v.* **2**
miniskirt minigonna *f.* **10**
minus meno *adv.*
minute minuto *m.*
miracle miracolo *m.* **5**
mirror specchio *m.*
mirrored lenses lenti *f., pl.* a specchio **3**
missing: to be missing mancare *v.* **2**
mist foschia *f.*
mistreatment maltrattamento *m.* **6**
mistrustful diffidente *adj.* **2**
misunderstanding fraintendimento *m.* **10**
mobilize mobilitare *v.* **6**
moderate moderato/a *adj.* **4**
modern contemporaneo/a *adj.*
modest modesto/a *adj.*
mom mamma *f.*
moment attimo *m.*
monarchic monarchico/a *adj.* **8**
Monday lunedì *m.*
money denaro *m.;* soldi *m., pl.*
monster animalaccio *m.* **2**
month mese *m.*
moon luna *f.*
moral morale *f.* **3**
more più *adj., adv.*
  no more, no longer non… più *adv.*
morning mattina *f.*
  Good morning. Buongiorno.
mortgage mutuo *m.*
mosque moschea *f.* **6**
moss muschio *m.*
most più *adj., adv.*
mother madre *f.*
mother-in-law suocera *f.* **5**
motor motore *m.*
motor boat (*used for public transportation in Venice*) vaporetto *m.* **7**
mountain montagna *f.*
  mountain climbing alpinismo *m.* **3**
mouse topo *m.*
moustache baffi *m., pl.* **9**
mouth bocca *f.*
move muovere *v.* **2**
  to move (*change residence*) trasferirsi *v.* **2, 5**; traslocare *v.*

movie film *m.*
  to go to the movies andare al cinema *v.*
moving commovente *adj.*
moving walkway nastro *m.* trasportatore **5**
Mr.... signor… *m.*
Mrs.... signora… *f.*
much molto/a/i/e *indef. adj., pron.*
  how much quanto *adj., pron., adv.*
  How much is/are… ? Quanto costa(no)…?
  so much tanto *adj., adv.*
  too much troppo *adj., adv.*
mud fango *m.*
mug tazza *f.*
multilingual multilingue *adj.* **6**
multilinguism multilinguismo *m.* **4**
murmur sussurro *m.*
muscular muscoloso/a *adj.*
mushroom fungo *m.*
music musica *f.*
musician musicista *m., f.*
Muslim musulmano/a *adj.* **6**
muss hair spettinare *v.* **5**
must-see da non perdere *adj.* **3**
mutt botolo *m.* **1**
muzzle muso *m.* **1**
mystery giallo/a *adj.* **9**

N

naïve ingenuo/a *adj.*
naïveté ingenuità *f.* **5**
name: last name cognome *m.*
named: to be named chiamarsi *v.* **2**
nanny tata *f.*
nanotechnology nanotecnologia *f.* **7**
napkin tovagliolo *m.*
narrator narratore *m.* **8**
nationalism nazionalismo *m.* **6**
natural naturale *adj.*
nature natura *f.*
naughty cattivo/a *adj.*
nausea nausea *f.*
navigate navigare *v.*
Neapolitan pastry sfogliatella *f.* **1**
near presso *prep.* **8**; vicino/a *adj.*
nearby qui vicino *adv.*
necessary necessario/a *adj.*
  absolutely necessary di prima necessità *adj.* **5**
  to be necessary occorrere *v.* **6**
neck collo *m.*
necklace collana *f.*
need avere bisogno di *v.* **8**
neighborhood quartiere *m.* **1, 2**
neither: neither... nor non… né… né *conj.*
Neoclassical neoclassico/a *adj.*
Neoplatonism neoplatonismo *m.* **8**
nephew nipote *m.* **5**

nervous nervoso/a *adj.*
net rete *f.* **3**
new nuovo/a *adj.*
  New Year's Day capodanno *m.*
news cronaca *f.* **9**
  (radio/TV) news (program)
    notiziario *m.* **2, 9**
  local news cronaca *f.* locale **9**
  news story notizia *f.* **9**
newspaper giornale *m.* **9**
newsstand edicola *f.* **2**; chiosco *m.*
  dei giornali
next prossimo/a *adj.*
  next to accanto (a) *prep.*
nice simpatico/a *adj.*
  Have a nice day Buona giornata!
nickname soprannome *m.* **5**
niece nipote *f.* **5**
night notte *f.*
  Good night. Buonanotte.
  night table comodino *m.*
nightclub locale *m.* notturno
nine nove *m.*
nine hundred novecento *m.*
nineteen diciannove *m.*
ninety novanta *m.*
ninth nono *adj.*
no nessuno/a *indef. adj.* **9**; no *adv.*
no one nessuno/a *indef. pron.* **9**
noir nero *adj.*
noise rumore *m.* **10**
noisy rumoroso/a *adj.* **2**
nonconformist anticonformista *adj.* **6**
noon mezzogiorno *m.*
norm norma *f.*
northern settentrionale *adj.* **6**
nose naso *m.*
  stuffy nose naso *m.* chiuso
nostalgia nostalgia *f.* **1**
not non *adv.*
  not any nessuno/a *indef. adj.* **9**
  not anyone nessuno/a *indef. pron.* **9**
  not at all non... affatto *adv.*
  Not bad. Non c'è male.
  not far from a due passi da
  not yet non... ancora *adv.*
notebook quaderno *m.*; taccuino *m.*
notes appunti *m., pl.*
nothing niente, nulla *indef. pron.* **9**
  Nothing new. Niente di nuovo.
notice accorgersi di *v.* **8**
novel romanzo *m.* **8**
  short novel novella *f.* **8**
November novembre *m.*
now adesso *adv.*
nuclear nucleare *adj.*
  nuclear energy energia *f.* nucleare
  nuclear power plant centrale *f.*
    nucleare
number cifra *f.* **10**; numero *m.*
nun suora *f.* **3**

nurse infermiere/a *m., f.*
nursing home ospizio *m.* **6**

O

obedient obbediente *adj.* **4**
objective oggettivo *adj.* **8**
oblige obbligare (a) *v.* **8**
obtain ottenere *v.* **6**
occupation mestiere *m.* **10**;
  occupazione *f.*
ocean oceano *m.*
October ottobre *m.*
octopus polpo *m.*
of di (d') *prep.*
off: off and on di tanto in tanto *adv.*
offer offrire *v.* **3**
office studio *m.;* ufficio *m.* **10**
often spesso *adv.*
oil olio *m.*
  in oil sott'olio *adj.*
old vecchio/a *adj.*
  old age vecchiaia *f.* **5**
  to be ... years old avere ... anni *v.*
older maggiore *adj.* **9**
old-fashioned superato/a *adj.*
olive: olive oil olio *m.* d'oliva
on su *prep.*
one hundred cento *m.*
  one hundred grams etto *m.*
one hundred ninety eight
  centonovantotto *m.*
one hundred one centouno *m.*
one hundred thousand
  centomila *m.*
one hundred twenty five
  centoventicinque *m.*
one thousand mille *m.*
one thousand one hundred
  millecento *m.*
one way senso *m.* unico
one-hundredth centesimo *adj.*
one-thousandth millesimo *adj.*
onion cipolla *f.*
online su Internet *adj., adv.*
  to be online essere in linea *v.*
only soltanto *adv.*
on-time puntuale *adj., adv.*
open aprire *v.* **3**
  to open an account aprire un
    conto *v.* **10**
opening night prima *f.* **3**
opera opera *f.*
operation intervento *m.* **7**
opinion opinione *f.*
  opinion poll sondaggio *m.* **9**
  public opinion opinione *f.*
    pubblica **6**
oppress opprimere *v.* **8**
oppressed oppresso/a *adj.* **4**
optician ottico *m.* **3**
optimistic ottimista *adj.* **1**

or o; oppure *conj.*
orange arancia *f.;* arancione *adj.*
  orange juice succo *m.* d'arancia
orchestra orchestra *f.*
order ordinare *v.*
organic farming agricoltura *f.*
  biologica
other altro/a/i/e *indef. adj.*
  others altri/e *indef. pron.*
out of place fuori posto *adj.* **8**
out-of-style passato/a di moda *adj.* **3**
outside fuori *prep., adv.*
oven forno *m.*
over sopra *prep., adv.*
overcast coperto/a *adj.*
overcome sormontare *v.* **5**;
  superare *v.* **6**
overdo strafare *v.*
overpopulation sovrappopolazione
  f. **6**
overthrow rovesciare *v.* **8**
overturn rovesciare *v.* **4**
owe dovere *v.*
own possedere *v.* **4**
owner padrone *m.* **4**; proprietario/a
  m., f. **10**
ox (oxen) bue (*pl.* buoi) *m.* **7**

P

pacifist pacifista *m., f., adj.* **4**
pack: to pack a suitcase fare la
  valigia *v.*
package pacco *m.*
pact patto *m.*
paid: to be well/poorly paid
  essere ben/mal pagato/a *v.*
pain dolore; male *m.*
paint dipingere *v.* **3**; pittura *f.* **8**
paintbrush pennello *m.* **8**
painter imbianchino *m.;* pittore/
  pittrice *m., f.* **8**
painting dipinto *m.* **8**;
  quadro *m.* **8**; pittura *f.* **8**
  oil painting pittura *f.* a olio **8**
  pastel painting pittura *f.* a
    pastello **8**
pair paio *m.*
palace palazzo *m.* **2**
panorama panorama *m.*
pantry dispensa *f.*
pants pantaloni *m., pl.*
  long pants pantaloni *m., pl.*
    lunghi **10**
  short pants pantaloni *m., pl.*
    corti **10**
paper clip graffetta *f.*
parade: fashion parade sfilata *f.* **10**
paragliding parapendio *m.*
parent genitore *m.* **5**
  single parent genitore *m.* single **5**
park parcheggiare *v.* **2**

parliament parlamento *m.* **6**
part parte; riga *f.*
partial parziale *adj.* **9**
participate (in) partecipare (a) *v.* **8**
partisan partigiano/a *m., f.* **8**
partner compagno/a *m., f.* **1**
  business partner socio a *m., f.* **10**
part-time a tempo parziale *adj., adv.*
party festa *f.*
pass passare *v.* **2, 3**; passo *m.*
  to pass (*exam*) superare *v.*
  to pass a law approvare/passare
    una legge *v.* **4**
passage passaggio *m.*
passenger passeggero/a *m.* **2**
passport control controllo *m.*
  passaporti
pasta pasta(sciutta) *f.*
paste incollare *v.* **7**
pastry shop pasticceria *f.*
pasture pascolo *m.* **7**
patent brevetto *m.* **7**
paternal paterno/a *adj.* **5**
path sentiero *m.*
patient paziente *adj.*; paziente *m., f.*
patron mecenate *m.* **8**
  patron saint santo/a *m., f.*
    patrono/a **9**
paw zampa *f.* **1**
pay pagare *v.*
  to pay attention dare retta *v.* **5**;
    fare attenzione a *v.* **8**
  to pay by check pagare con
    assegno *v.*
  to pay in cash pagare in contanti *v.*
  to pay the bills pagare le bollette *v.*
  to pay with a credit/debit card
    pagare con carta di credito/
    debito *v.*
paycheck: monthly paycheck
  mensilità *f.*
payment rata *f.*
peace pace *f.* **4**
peaceful pacifico/a *adj.* **4**
peach pesca *f.*
peak (*fig.*) culmine *m.*
pear pera *f.*
pedestrian pedone *m.* **2**
pen penna *f.*
penalty kick calcio *m.* di rigore **3**
pencil matita *f.*
pension pensione *f.*
people popolo *m.*
pepper: (red, green) pepper
  peperone (rosso, verde) *m.*
  (*spice*) pepe *m.*
perform interpretare *v.*
performance esibizione *f.*;
  spettacolo *m.* **3**
perfume shop profumeria *f.*
person persona *f.*
personality carattere *m.* **5**

persuade (to) persuadere (a) *v.* **8**
pessimistic pessimista *adj.* **1**
pet animale *m.* domestico
pharmacist farmacista *m., f.*
phenomenon fenomeno *m.* **3**
phone booth cabina *f.* telefonica
phone number numero *m.*
  di telefono
photo(graph) foto(grafia) *f.*
photocopy fotocopiare *v.*
photographer fotografo *m.*
physicist fisico/a *m., f.* **7**
  nuclear physicist fisico/a
    m., f. nucleare **7**
pianist pianista *m., f.*
pick cogliere *v.* **1**; raccogliere *v.* **3**
pickled sottaceto *adj.*
picnic: to have a picnic fare un
  picnic *v.*
picture quadro *m.*
pie crostata *f.* **8**
piece pezzo *m.* **3**
pigment pigmento *m.* **8**
pill pillola *f.*
pillow guanciale *m.* **10**
pinch pizzico *m.*
pineapple ananas *(invar.) m.*
pink rosa *(invar.) adj.*
pity peccato *m.*
pizza shop pizzeria *f.*
place luogo *m.*
plan pensare di *v.* **8**; pianificare *v.* **6**;
  programma *m.*
  to make plans fare progetti *v.*
planet pianeta *m.*
planner agenda *f.*
plant pianta *f.*
plate piatto *m.*
platform piattaforma *f.* **1**
play giocare *v.* **8**; dramma *m.*
  to play (*instrument*) suonare *v.* **3**
  to play a home/away game
    giocare in casa/trasferta *v.* **3**
  to play a role recitare un ruolo *v.*
  to play down sminuire *v.* **3**
  to play hide-and-seek giocare a
    nascondino *m.* **3**
  to put on a play mettere in scena *v.*
player giocatore/giocatrice *m., f.* **2, 3**
  CD/DVD/MP3 player lettore *m.*
    CD/DVD/MP3 **7**
playful scherzoso/a *adj.*
playing field campo *m.* di/da gioco **3**
playwright drammaturgo/a *m., f.* **8**
please per favore *adv.*
pleasure piacere *m.*
  Pleased to meet you. Piacere di
    conoscerLa/ti. (*form./fam.*)
plot trama *f.* **8**
plug spinotto *m.* **3**
plumber idraulico *m.*
poem poema *m.*

poet poeta/poetessa *m., f.*
poetry poesia *f.* **8**
point punto *m.*
  point of view punto *m.* di vista **8**
  reference point punto *m.* di
    riferimento **4**
police polizia *f.*
  military police carabinieri *m., pl.* **5**
  police headquarters questura *f.*
  police officer poliziotto/a *m., f.* **2**
  police report verbale *m.* **8**
  police station stazione *f.* di
    polizia **2**
political party partito *m.* politico **4**
politician politico/a *m., f.* **4**
politics politica *f.* **4**
pollution inquinamento *m.* **7**
Pomeranian volpino *m.* **1**
ponytail codino *m.*
pool piscina *f.* **10**
poor povero/a *adj.*
  to become poor impoverirsi *v.* **6**
pope papa *m.* **6**
population popolazione *f.* **6**
pork carne *f.* di maiale
portable portatile *adj.*
portrait ritratto *f.*
position posto *m.*, posizione *f.*
possess possedere *v.* **4**
possessive possessivo/a *adj.* **5**
possible possibile *adj.* **7**
  it's possible può darsi
post carica *f.* **4**
post card cartolina *f.*
post office ufficio *m.* postale
postal worker impiegato/a *m., f.*
  postale
poster poster *m.*
postpone rimandare *v.* **5**
potato patata *f.*
poverty povertà *f.* **2, 6**
power potenza *f.* **4**; potere *m.*
powerful potente *adj.* **4**
pray pregare *v.* **6**
prayer preghiera *f.*
precision precisione *f.* **8**
predict predire, prevedere *v.* **7**
prefer preferire *v.* **6**
preferable preferibile *adj.*
preferences gusti *m., pl.* **9**
pregnant incinta *adj.* **5, 8**
  to be pregnant essere incinta *v.*
prehistoric preistorico *adj.* **8**
prejudice pregiudizio *m.* **6**
premiere prima *f.* **3**
prenatal prenatale *adj.* **3**
prepare preparare *v.* **8**
pre-recorded in differita *adj., adv.* **9**
prescription ricetta *f.*
present presentare *v.*
preserve conservare; preservare *v.*
president presidente *m., f.* **4**

press release comunicato *m.* stampa **9**
pretend fare finta *v.*
pretend fingere *v.*
pretty bellino/a *adj.*
  Pretty well. Abbastanza bene.
prevent impedire *v.*
pride orgoglio *m.* **3**
priest prete *m.* **6**
print stampare *v.*
printer stampante *f.*
priority mail posta *f.* prioritaria
prisoner prigioniero/a *m., f.* **2**
prize premio *m.*
probability probabilità *f.* **9**
problem problema *m.*
profession professione *f.*
professor insegnante;
  professore(ssa) *m., f.*
program programma *m.*
prohibition divieto *m.*
promise (to) promettere (di) *v.* **8**
promised promesso *p.p., adj.* **4**
promote promuovere *v.* **4**
promotion promozione *f.* **10**
propose proporre *v.*
proscenium ribalta *f.*
prose prosa *f.* **8**
protect tutelare *v.* **6**
protector protettore *m.*
protest reclamare *v.* **6**
Protestant protestante *adj.* **6**
proud orgoglioso/a *adj.* **1**
prove dimostrare *v.* **7**
proverb proverbio *m.* **6**
provide: to provide for oneself
  mantenersi *v.*
provided that a condizione che,
  a patto che *conj.* **7**
province provincia *f.* **6**
psychological drama dramma *m.*
  psicologico
psychologist psicologo/a *m., f.*
pub birreria *f.*
public pubblico *m.*
  public transportation mezzo *m.*
  pubblico **2**; trasporto *m.* pubblico
publish pubblicare *v.*
publisher editore/editrice *m., f.* **9**
publishing industry editoria *f.*
pulled back hair capelli *m., pl.*
  raccolti
punish punire *v.* **5**
pupil alunno/a *m., f.*
puppet burattino *m.* **3**, fantoccio *m.* **4**
puppeteer burattinaio *m.* **4**
purchase acquisto *m.*
purify depurare *v.*
purple viola (*invar.*) *adj.*
purse: small purse borsetta *f.*
push spingere *v.* **6**

put mettere *v.* **2**; porre *v.* **1**
  to put on (clothing, shoes)
  mettersi *v.* **1**
  to put on a play mettere in scena *v.*
  to put on make up truccarsi *v.* **1**
  to put together sistemare *v.*

Q

qualifications qualifiche *f., pl.* **10**
quandary dilemma *m.*
quarrel litigare *v.* **5**
quarter quartiere *m.*
  quarter hour quarto
queen regina *f.* **8**
question domanda *f.*
  to ask a question fare una
  domanda *v.*
queue coda *f.*
quickly presto, velocemente *adv.*
  to be/stay quiet stare zitto *v.* **2**
quit dare le dimissioni *v.* **10**
quiz show gioco *m.* a premi

R

rabbi rabbino *m.* **6**
rabbit coniglio *m.*
race razza *f.* **1**; gara *f.* **3**
racism razzismo *m.* **6**
radio radio *f.*
  radio news giornale *m.* radio **9**
  radio station stazione *f.* radio **9**
rafting rafting *m.*
railway employee ferroviere *m.* **6**
rain pioggia *f.*; piovere *v.*
raincoat impermeabile *m.* **3**
rainy piovoso/a *adj.*
raise alzare *v.* **2**; aumento *m.*;
  educare *v.* **5**
rarely raramente *adv.*
rash eruzione *f.* cutanea
rate tasso *m.*
  interest rate tasso *m.*
  d'interesse *m.* **10**
razor rasoio *m.*
read leggere *v.* **3**
reader lettore *m.*
reading lettura *f.*
ready pronto/a *adj.*
  to be ready essere pronto/a a *v.* **8**
  to get oneself ready prepararsi *v.*
real estate immobiliare *adj.*
  real estate agency agenzia *f.*
  immobiliare
  real estate agent agente *m., f.*
  immobiliare
  real estate market mercato *m.*
  immobiliare **10**
realism realismo *m.* **6**
realistic realista *adj.* **8**

reality show reality *m.*
realize accorgersi *v.* **2**; rendersi
  conto (di) *v.* **8**
really davvero *adv.*
reason ragione *f.*
rebellious ribelle *adj.* **5**
receipt ricevuta *f.* **10**; scontrino *m.* **10**
receive ricevere *v.*
receiver cornetta *f.*
reception ricevimento *m.* **8**
recession recessione *f.* **10**
recipe ricetta
recite recitare *v.*
recklessness incoscienza *f.* **6**
recognize rivedere *v.*; riconoscere *v.*
recommend raccomandare *v.*
recommendation
  raccomandazione *f.*
record registrare *v.* **9**
recorder (tape, CD, etc.)
  registratore *m.*
recycle riciclare *v.* **7**
recycling riciclo *m.*
red rosso/a *adj.*
reduce: reduced ticket biglietto
  m. ridotto
referee arbitro *m.* **3**
reference point punto di
  riferimento *m.* **4**
references referenze *f., pl.*
refined raffinato/a *adj.* **3**
reflect (on) riflettere (su) *v.* **8**
refund rimborso *m.*
regime regime *m.* **8**
registered mail raccomandata *f.*
regret lamentare *v.* **6**; pentirsi *v.* **5**
regulations regolamento *m.* **3**
reinforcement rinforzo *m.* **5**
related imparentato/a *adj.* **5**
relationship rapporto *m.* **9**
relative parente *m., f.* **5**
  relatives parentela *f.* **5**; parenti *m., pl.*
relic relitto *m.*
rely on contare su *v.* **1**
remain restare
remarkable notevole *adj.* **7**
remember ricordare *v.*; ricordarsi
  (di) *v.* **2**
remote control telecomando *m.*
remove togliere *v.* **1**
Renaissance rinascimentale *adj.*;
  Rinascimento *m.* **6**
renewable energy energia *f.*
  rinnovabile
rent affitto *m.*
  to rent (car) noleggiare *v.*
  to rent (owner) affittare *v.*
  to rent (tenant) prendere in affitto *v.*
repair riparare *v.*
repeat ripetere *v.*
report informativa *f.* **8**

reporter cronista *m., f.* **9**
require esigere *v.* **6**; volerci *v.* **8**
requirement esigenza *f.* **2**
research ricerca *f.* **7**
researcher ricercatore/ricercatrice *m., f.* **7**
resemble assomigliare a *v.* **5**
reservation prenotazione *f.*
  make a reservation prenotare *v.*
resign dare le dimissioni *v.*
Resistance Resistenza *f.* **8**
resistance fighter partigiano *m.* **2**
resort località *f.* di villeggiatura
  mountain resort località *f.* montana
  ocean resort località *f.* balneare
respect rispettare *v.*
responsible responsabile *adj.*
rest riposarsi *v.* **2**
restaurant ristorante *m.*
  small restaurant osteria *f.*
  small restaurant, family run trattoria *f.*
result risultare *v.* **3**
résumé C.V. *m.*; curriculum *m.* (vitae) **10**
Resurgence Risorgimento *m.* **6**
retire andare in pensione *v.* **10**
retiree pensionato/a *m., f.*
retreat ritirata *f.* **2**
return tornare *v.*
review recensione *f.* **9**
rhyme rima *f.* **8**
ribbon nastro *m.*
rice riso *m.*
rich pesante; ricco/a *adj.*
  to become rich arricchirsi *v.* **6**
rid: to get rid of sbarazzarsi di *v.*
ride: to give someone a ride dare un passaggio *v.*
  to ride a bike andare in bicicletta *v.*
right destra *f.*; giusto/a *adj.* **4**
  right away subito *adv.*
  to be right avere ragione (di) *v.* **8**
ring (telephone) squillare *v.* **9**
rise (sun) sorgere *v.*
river fiume *m.*
road sign segnale *m.* stradale **2**
roam vagare *v.* **9**
roasted arrosto/a *adj.*
rob rapinare *v.* **4**
robbery rapina *f.* **4**
robe vestaglia *f.* **10**
robotics robotica *f.* **7**
rock pietra *f.*
role ruolo *m.* **5**
romance rosa *adj.* **9**
Romanesque romanico/a *adj.*
romantic romantico/a *adj.*
room camera, stanza, sala *f.*
  single/double room camera *f.* singola/doppia

room and board vitto e alloggio (lit. *food and apartment*) **5**
room service servizio *m.* in camera
roommate coinquilino/a *m., f.* **2**
root radice *f.* **5**
rotary rotonda *f.*
row remare *v.*
rowing canottaggio *m.* **3**
ruins rovine *f., pl.* **2**
rumor sussurro *m.*
run condurre *v.*; correre *v.* **3**
  to run errands fare commissioni *v.* **2**
  to run out esaurirsi *v.* **7**
  to run over mettere sotto *v.* **7**
Russian russo/a *adj.*

S

sack sacco *m.*
sad triste *adj.*
safe salvo/a *adj.* **4**
safety sicurezza *f.* **4**
saint santo/a *m., f.* **6**
salad insalata *f.*
salary salario *m.*; mensilità *f.*
  high/low salary salario *m.* elevato/basso
sales saldi *m., pl.* **3**
  end-of-season sales saldi *m., pl.* di fine stagione **3**
saleswoman commessa *f.* **1**
salt sale *m.*
salty salato/a *adj.*
sandals sandali *m., pl.* **10**
sandwich shop paninoteca *f.*
satellite TV televisione *f.* satellitare **9**
satirical satirico/a *adj.* **8**
Saturday sabato *m.*
savages selvaggi *pl*
save parare *v.* **2, 3**; risparmiare *v.* **10**; salvare *v.* **4**
  to save the planet salvare il pianeta *v.*
saving risparmio *m.* **10**
  savings account conto *m.* di risparmio
saxophone sassofono *m.*
say dire *v.* **1**
scandal scandalo *m.* **4**
scarf sciarpa *f.*
scene scena *f.*
schedule orario *m.* **1**
scheme schema *m.*
school scuola *f.*
science scienze *f., pl.*
  computer science informatica *f.* **7**
  science fiction fantascientifico/a *adj.* **7**
scientist scienziato/a *m., f.*

scold rimproverare *v.* **5**
scooter motorino *m.*
score (a goal) segnare (un gol) *v.* **2, 3**
screen schermo *m.* **9**
  screen name pseudonimo *m.*
  screen test provino *m.*
screening proiezione *f.*
screenplay sceneggiatura *f.* **9**
script copione *m.* **9**
scuba diver subacqueo *m.* **4**
sculpt scolpire *v.* **8**
sculptor scultore/scultrice *m., f.* **8**
sculpture scultura *f.* **8**
sea mare *m.*
seafood frutti *m., pl.* di mare
  seafood shop pescheria *f.*
seagull gabbiano *m.*
sea-sickness mal *m.* di mare
season stagione *f.*
  season ticket abbonamento *m.*
seat poltrona *f.*
seatbelt cintura *f.* di sicurezza
second secondo/a *adj.*
secretary segretario/a *m., f.* **10**
section: lifestyle section rubrica *f.* di cultura e società **9**
sector settore *m.* **10**
security sicurezza *f.* **4**
see vedere *v.* **3**
  See you later. A più tardi.
  See you soon. Ci vediamo./ A presto.
  to see each other vedersi *v.* **2**
seem sembrare, parere *v.* **2**
selfish egoista *adj.* **5**
self-governing autonomo/a *adj.* **4**
self-portrait autoritratto *m.* **8**
self-sufficient autosufficiente *adj.* **5**
sell vendere *v.*
send inviare *v.* **1**; mandare, spedire *v.*
sense senso *m.*
sensitive sensibile *adj.* **1**
separated separato/a *adj.*
September settembre *m.*
serious grave, serio/a *adj.*
serve servire *v.*
service servizio *m.*
  service station stazione *f.* di servizio
set (sun) tramontare *v.*
  to set the table apparecchiare la tavola *v.*
settle stabilirsi *v.* **6**
seven sette *m.*
seven hundred settecento *m.*
seventeen diciassette *m.*
seventh settimo *adj.*
seventy settanta *m.*
shake hands with stringere la mano a *v.* **8**
shame vergogna *f.* **2**

shape: to be in/out of shape essere in/fuori forma *v.*

share condividere *v.* 1; dividere *v.* 7

sharp in gamba *adj.*

shave farsi la barba *v.* 2; radersi *v.*

shaving cream schiuma *f.* da barba

sheep pecora *f.*

sheet: sheet of paper foglio *m.* di carta

shelter rifugio *m.*

ship nave *f.*

Shoo! Sciò!

shop bottega *f.* 8; fare spese *v.*

  shop window vetrina *f.* 1

shopping center/mall centro commerciale *m.* 3

short basso/a *adj.* 9

  short (hair) corto/a *adj.*

  short film cortometraggio; filmino *m.*

  short story racconto *m.*

  short-term a breve termine *adj.* 10

  short trip gita *f.*

shorter inferiore *adj.* 9

shorts pantaloncini *m., pl.*

shot: to give a shot fare una puntura *v.*

shoulder spalla *f.*

show fare vedere a *v.* 8; mostrare *v.;* spettacolo *m.* 3

shower doccia *f.*

shrewd furbo/a *adj.* 5

shrimp gamberetto *m.*

shy timido *adj.* 1

side dish contorno *m.*

sidewalk marciapiede *m.* 2

sight vista *f.*

  to know by sight conoscere di vista *v.*

sign firmare *v.*

signal segnale *m.* 7

silk seta *m.*

since da *prep*

sincere sincero/a *adj.*

sing cantare *v.* 1

singer cantante *m., f.*

single celibe *adj., m.* 1; nubile *adj., f.* 1

single-family home villa *f.*

sister sorella *f.*

  little/younger sister sorellina *f.*

sister-in-law cognata *f.*

sit down sedersi *v.*

six sei *m.*

six hundred seicento *m.*

sixteen sedici *m.*

sixteenth sedicesimo *adj.*

sixth sesto *adj.*

sixty sessanta *m.*

size taglia *f.* 1

skating pattinaggio *m.* 3

sketch schizzo *m.* 8

ski sciare *v.* 1; sci *(invar.) m.*

skiing sci *m.* 3

skill capacità *f.*

skilled bravo/a *adj.*

skin pelle *f.*

skip: to skip class saltare la lezione *v.*

skirt gonna *f.* 10

skit scenetta *f.*

sky cielo *m.*

  sky blue azzurro/a *adj.*

skyscraper grattacielo *m.* 2

slavery schiavitù *f.* 8

sleep dormire *v.* 1

sleepy: to be sleepy avere sonno *v.* 1

sleeve manica *f.*

slice fetta *f.*

slide scivolare *v.*

slight leggero/a *adj.*

slip on (clothing) infilarsi *v.* 9

slippers pantofole *f., pl.*

slob cafone/a *m., f.*

slow lento/a *adj.*

sly furbo/a *adj.* 5

small piccolo/a *adj.* 9

  small change spiccioli *m., pl.* 3

  smaller minore *adj.* 9

smart in gamba *adj.*

smell odore *m.* 10

smile sorridere *v.* 5

smirk smorfia *f.* 10

smog smog *m.*

smoked affumicato/a *adj.*

snack spuntino *m.;* merendina *f.* 3

  snack bar tavola *f.* calda

snake serpente *m.*

sneakers scarpe *f., pl.* da ginnastica/ tennis 3

sneeze starnutire *v.*

snorkel boccaglio *m.* 4

snow neve *f.;* nevicare *v.*

so allora *adv., adj.;* perciò *conj.*

  so much, so many tanto *adj.*

  so that in modo che *conj.*

  so that affinché, benché, purché *conj.* 7

soap sapone *m.*

soap opera telenovela *f.*

soccer calcio *m.* 3;

  soccer ball pallone *m.* 3

  soccer player calciatore *m.* 3

  soccer team squadra *f.* di calcio 2

sociable socievole *adj.* 5

society società *f.* 10

sock calza *f.*

soil sporcare *v.*

solar: solar energy energia *f.* solare

  solar panel pannello *m.* solare

sold out tutto esaurito *adj.* 3

soldier soldato *m.* 2

solid-color tinta unita *adj.*

solo assolo *m.*

solution soluzione *f.*

solve risolvere *v.* 6

some qualche, alcuni/e *indef. adj.* 9; alcuni/e *indef. pron.* 9

someone qualcuno/a *indef. pron.* 9

something qualcosa *indef. pron.* 9; **(anything else)** altro *indef. pron.*

sometimes a volte, qualche volta *adv.*

son figlio *m.* 5

song canzone *f.*

son-in-law genero *m.* 5

soon presto *adv.*

sorry desolato/a *adj.*

  to be sorry dispiacere *v.* 2; essere desolato/a *v.* 5

So-so. Così, così.

soul anima *f.* 5

  soul mate anima *f.* gemella 1

soundtrack colonna sonora *f.* 9

soup zuppa *f.*

  thick soup minestrone *m.*

southern meridionale *adj.* 6

Spanish spagnolo/a *adj.*

shoot sparare *v.* 4

sparkling water acqua *f.* frizzante

speak: to speak to each other parlarsi *v.* 2

special effects effetti *m., pl.* speciali 9

specialist specialista *m., f.*

specialization specializzazione *f.*

spectator spettatore/spettatrice *m., f.*

speed limit limite *m.* di velocità

spend (*money*) spendere *v.;* **(*time*)** passare *v.*

spicy piccante *adj.*

spoil viziare *v.* 5

spoon cucchiaio *m.*

sport sport *m.*

  sports club club *m.* sportivo 3

  sports news cronaca *f.* sportiva 9

spouse coniuge *m., f.* 9

spring primavera *f.*

spy spia *f.* 2, 8; spiare *v.* 4

squirrel scoiattolo *m.*

stadium stadio *m.* 2

stage scena *f.*

stain macchiare *v.*

stained macchiato/a *adj.*

staircase scala *f.*

stairs scale *f., pl.*

  to climb/go down stairs salire/scendere le scale *v.*

stall platea *f.*

stamp francobollo *m.;* timbrare *v.*

stand tribuna *f.*

  stand in line stare in fila *v.* 5

standard of living tenore di vita *m.* 6

stanza strofa *f.* 8

staple graffetta *f.*

stapler graffettatrice *f.*

star stella *f.*
start (to) cominciare (a) *v.* **1**
  to start the game scendere in
  campo *v.* **3**
starter antipasto *m.*
statesman statista *m.* **6**
station stazione *f.*
  radio station stazione *f.* radio **9**
stationery store cartoleria *f.*
statue statua *f.*
stay rimanere, stare *v.* **1**; restare *v.*
steal rubare *v.* **5**
steamed al vapore *adj.*
steering wheel volante *m.*
stem cell cellula *f.* staminale **7**
stench puzza *f.*
step gradino; passo *m.*
stepbrother fratellastro *m.*
stepdaughter figliastra *f.*
stepfather patrigno *m.*
stepmother matrigna *f.*
stepsister sorellastra *f.*
stepson figliastro *m.*
stereo system impianto *m.* stereo
stereotype stereotipo *m.* **6**
stern poppa *f.* **4**
stewed in umido *adj.*
still ancora *adv.*
  still life natura *f.* morta **8**
  still water acqua *f.* naturale
stock exchange borsa *f.* **10**
stomach stomaco *m.*
stone sasso *m.*
stop cessare (di) *v.* **8**; fermare; fermarsi
  v. **2**; smettere *v.* **3**; fermata *f.* **2**
  bus/subway/train stop fermata
  f. dell'autobus/della metro/del
  treno *f.* **2**
  stop on request fermata *f.* a richiesta
store negozio *m.*
  store specializing in focaccia
  focacceria *f.*
  store specializing in homemade
  pasta laboratorio *m.* di pasta fresca
  store specializing in wine
  enoteca *f.*
storm temporale *m.* **9**
  It's stormy. C'è il temporale.
stovetop piano *m.* di cottura
straight (*hair*) liscio/a *adj.*
strange strano/a *adj.* **5**
stranger estraneo/a *m., f.* **5**
strawberry fragola *f.*
stream ruscello *m.*
street strada, via *f.* **2**
  Venetian streets calli *f., pl* **7**
stretch stirarsi *v.* **10**
  stretch out sgranchirsi *v.* **7**
strict severo/a *adj.* **5**
strike sciopero *m.*
stripe riga *f.*
striped a righe *adj.*

strong forte *adj.*
struggle lottare *v.* **4**
stubborn testardo/a *adj.* **5**
student studente(ssa), alunno/a *m., f.*
  student who studies too hard
  secchione/a *m., f.* **3**
studies studi *m., pl.*
studio apartment monolocale *m.*
studious studioso/a *adj.*
study studiare *v.* **1**; studio *m.*
  to study in-depth approfondire *v.* **1**
stuffy nose naso *m.* chiuso
sturdy resistente *adj.* **1**
style stile *m.* **10**
subject materia *f.*
subjective soggettivo/a *adj.* **8**
sublet subaffittare *v.*
submerged sommerso/a *adj.* **7**
submissive remissivo/a *adj.* **5**
subscribe fare un abbonamento *v.* **9**
subscription abbonamento *m.*
substitute teacher supplente *m.*
subtitle sottotitolo *m.* **9**
suburbs periferia *f.* **2**
subway metro(politana) *f.* **2**
succeed in riuscire a *v.* **1**
success successo *m.*
successful prospero/a *adj.* **10**
suffer penare *v.* **6**; soffrire *v.* **7**
  to suffer (from) soffrire (di) *v.* **8**
suffering sofferenza *f.*
sufficient: to be sufficient
  bastare *v.* **3**
suggest suggerire *v.* **6**
suggestive allusivo/a *adj.*
suit abito *m.* **10**; vestito *m.* (da uomo) **3**
  women's suit tailleur *m.* **10**
suitable adatto/a *adj.* **8**
suitcase: to pack a suitcase fare
  la valigia *v.*
summer estate *f.*
sun sole *m.*
  It's sunny. C'è il sole.
Sunday domenica *f.*
sunglasses occhiali *m., pl.* da sole **10**
sunny soleggiato/a *adj.*
sunrise alba *f.*
sunset tramonto *m.*
superior superiore *adj.* **9**
supermarket supermercato *m.*
supper cena *f.*
supreme supremo/a *adj.* **9**
surf: to surf the Internet/Web
  navigare su Internet/sulla rete *v.* **7**;
  navigare in rete *v.*
surgeon chirurgo *m.*
surprise stupire *v.* **7**
  to be surprised essere
  sorpreso/a *v.* **6**
surrender arrendersi *v.* **8**
survival sopravvivenza *f.* **2**
survive sopravvivere *v.* **5**

swallow rondine *f.*
swear (on) giurare (su) *v.* **8**
sweater golf *m.* **9**; maglione *m.*
sweatshirt felpa *f.*
sweep spazzare *v.*
  street sweeper spazzino/a *m., f.*
sweet caruccio; dolce; tenero/a *adj.*
  sweet-and-sour agrodolce *adj.*
sweetness dolcezza *f.* **10**
swim nuotare *v.*
swimming nuoto *m.*
  swimming pool piscina *f.* **10**
Swiss svizzero/a *adj.*
symphony orchestra *f.* sinfonica **8**
symptom sintomo *m.*
synagogue sinagoga *f.* **6**
system sistema *m.*

T

table tavola *f.;* tavolo *m.*
  to clear the table sparecchiare la
  tavola *v.*
tablecloth tovaglia *f.* **4**
tablet compressa *f.*
tabloid giornale *m.* scandalistico
tailor's shop sartoria *f.* **8**
take prendere *v.* **1**; volerci *v.* **8**
  to take (*a class*) seguire *v.*
  to take a bath/shower fare il
  bagno/la doccia *v.*
  to take a long weekend fare il
  ponte *v.*
  to take a look dare un'occhiata *v.* **3**
  to take a picture fare una foto *v.*
  to take a short trip fare una gita *v.*
  to take a short walk fare due
  passi *v.*
  to take a test dare un esame *v.* **1**
  to take a trip fare un viaggio *v.*
  to take a walk passeggiare *v.* **2**;
  fare una passeggiata *v.*
  to take advantage of
  approfittare *v.* **10**
  to take care of occuparsi di *v.* **8**
  to take initiative prendere
  l'iniziativa *v.* **5**
  to take off decollare *v.*
  to take out a mortgage fare un
  mutuo *v.* **10**
  to take out the trash portare
  fuori la spazzatura *v.*
  to take place svolgersi *v.* **8**
talented dotato/a *adj.*
talk (about) parlare (di) *v.* **8**
tall alto/a *adj.* **9**
tan abbronzarsi *v.*
tank top canottiera *f.*
tape measure metro *m.* **8**
taste assaggiare *v.* **4**
  tastes gusti *m., f.* **9**
tasty gustoso/a, saporito/a *adj.*

tattoo tatuaggio *m.* **10**
tax tassa *f.* **10**
taxes contributi *m., pl.*
taxi tassì; taxi *m.*
  taxi driver tassista *m.* **6**
tea tè *m.*
teach insegnare *v.* **8**
teacher docente; insegnante *m., f.*
team squadra *f.* **3**
tease prendere in giro *v.*
teaspoon cucchiaino *m.*
technician tecnico *m., f.*
technology tecnologia *f.*
telecommunications
  telecomunicazioni *f., pl.* **7**
telephone telefonare *v.;* telefono *m.*
  to (tele)phone each other
    telefonarsi *v.* **2**
television televisione *f.* **9**
  television channel canale
    m. televisivo
  television viewer telespettatore/
    telespettatrice *m., f.* **9**
  TV host assistant valletta *f.*
  TV news telegiornale *m.* **9**
tell the truth dire la verità *v.*
temp agency agenzia *f.* di
  somministrazione lavoro
ten dieci *m.*
tenacious tenace *adj.*
tenant inquilino/a *m., f.*
tender tenero/a *adj.*
tennis tennis *m.*
tenth decimo *adj.*
term paper tesina *f.*
terminus capolinea *m.*
terrorism terrorismo *m.* **4**
terrorist terrorista *m., f.* **4**
test esame *m.*
testify deporre *v.* **4**
text message SMS *m.* **7**
textbook libro *m.* di testo
thank (for) ringraziare (di) *v.* **8**
  Thank you. Grazie.
  Thanks a lot. Grazie mille.
  Thanks. Crepi. (*answer to* In bocca
    al lupo.) (lit. *May the wolf die.*)
that che; ciò che, quanto, quel che,
  quello che *rel. pron.* **9**; quello/a *adj.*
  that which ciò che, quanto, quel
    che, quello che *rel. pron.* **9**
that is cioè *conj.* **2**
theater teatro *m.*
theatrical teatrale *adj.*
theft furto *m.* **7**
theme tema *m.*
then allora; poi *adv.*
theorem teorema *m.*
there là *adv.*
  Is Mr./Mrs. ... there? C'è il/la
    signor(a)…?

  there are ci sono
  there is c'è
thermal baths terme *f., pl.* **2**
thermal energy energia *f.* termica
thermometer termometro *m.*
thief ladro/a *m., f.* **4**
thin magro/a *adj.*
think pensare *v.* **8**
  to think about pensare a *v.* **8**
third terzo *adj.*
thirsty: to be thirsty avere sete *v.* **1**
thirteen tredici *m.*
thirty trenta *m.*
thirty-eight trentotto *m.*
thirty-five trentacinque *m.*
thirty-four trentaquattro *m.*
thirty-nine trentanove *m.*
thirty-one trentuno *m.*
thirty-seven trentasette *m.*
thirty-six trentasei *m.*
thirty-third trentatreesimo *adj.*
thirty-three trentatré *m.*
thirty-two trentadue *m.*
this questo/a *adj.*
threat minaccia *f.* **4**
three tre *m.*
three hundred trecento *m.*
thriller giallo *m.* **8**
throat gola *f.*
  sore throat mal *m.* di gola
through per *prep.*
throw gettare *v.*
  to throw away buttare via *v.* **1**
  to throw down/below buttare di
    sotto *v.* **6**
thunder tuono *m.*
Thursday giovedì *m.*
ticket biglietto *m.* **3**
  ticket collector controllore *m.*
  ticket office/window biglietteria *f.*
  traffic ticket multa *f.* **9**
tide marea *f.* **7**
tidy: to tidy up riordinare *v.*
tie cravatta *f.* **10**; pareggiare *v.* **3**;
  pareggio *m.* **3**
  to tie a game pareggiare una
    partita *v.* **3**
tight: tight-fitting stretto/a *adj.*
time volta *f.*
  times età *f.*
tire: flat tire pneumatico *m.* sgonfio
tired stanco/a *adj.*
to a; in *prep.*
toast tostare *v.*
toaster tostapane *m.*
today oggi *m., adv.*
toe dito *m.* del piede (*pl.* dita *f.*) *m.*
together insieme *adv.*
  to get together incontrarsi *v.* **2**
toilet gabinetto *m.*
tomato pomodoro *m.*

tomorrow domani *m., adv.*
  the day after tomorrow
    dopodomani *m., adv.*
ton (of) sacco (di) *adj.*
too anche *conj.*
  too much troppo *adj., adv.*
tooth dente *m.*
  to brush one's teeth lavarsi i
    denti *v.*
  tooth brush spazzolino *m.* (da denti)
  tooth paste dentifricio *m.*
topography topografia *f.* **2**
tornado tornado *m.*
torrential downpour diluvio *m.*
touch toccare *v.*
touching commovente *adj.*
tough duro/a *adj.*
tour giro *m.*
  to be on tour essere in tour *v.*
tourist turista *m., f.*
  tourist class classe *f.* turistica
  tourist information office
    ufficio *m.* informazioni turistiche
tournament torneo *m.* **3**
toward verso *prep.*
towel asciugamano *m.*
town città *f.,* paese *m.*
  in town in centro *adv.*
  town hall comune *m.*
toxic waste rifiuti *m., pl.* tossici
trace tracciare *v.* **6**
track and field atletica *m.*
trade mestiere *m.* **10**
tradition tradizione *f.* **6**
traffic circolazione *f.,* traffico *m.* **2**
  traffic jam ingorgo *m.* stradale **2**
  traffic light semaforo *m.* **2**
  traffic officer vigile/vigilessa *m.,*
    f. urbano/a
  traffic ticket multa *f.* **9**
tragedy tragedia *f.*
tragic tragico/a *adj.* **8**
train allenarsi *v.* **3**; treno *m.*
  get off the train scendere dal
    treno *v.* **2**
  to get on the train salire sul
    treno *v.* **2**
  train car carrozza *f.* **4**
  train track binario *m.* **1**
training formazione *f.* **10**
  professional training tirocinio *m.*
transfer mobilità *f.*
translate tradurre *v.* **1, 8**
transportation trasporto *m.*
trash immondizia *f.*
  to take out the trash portare
    fuori la spazzatura *v.*
trauma trauma *m.*
travel viaggiare *v.*
  travel agent agente *m., f.* di viaggio
traveler viaggiatore *m.*

tray vassoio *m.* **1**
treaty trattato *m.* **4**
tree albero *m.*
trendy trendy *adj.*
trim (one's hair) spuntare (i capelli) *v.*
trip viaggio *m.*
troop truppa *f.* **7**
truck camion *m.*
  truck driver camionista *m., f.*
truly veramente *adv.*
trunk baule *m.*
trust avere fiducia (in), fidarsi (di) *v.* **1**; fiducia *f.* **4**
try to cercare di *v.* **8**; provare a *v.* **8**
  to try on provare, provarsi *v.* **3**
t-shirt maglietta *f.*
  short-/long-sleeved t-shirt maglietta *f.* a maniche corte/lunghe
Tuesday martedì *m.*
tuft of hair ciuffo *m.*
tuna tonno *m.*
turn volta *f.*; svolta *f.*; girare *v.*
  to turn off spegnere *v.*
  to turn on accendere *v.*
  to turn (right/left) girare (a destra/sinistra) *v.* **2**
Tuscan almond biscotti cantucci *m., pl.* **1**
TV tivù, TV *f.*
twelve dodici *m.*
twentieth ventesimo *adj.*
twenty venti *m.*
twenty-eight ventotto *m.*
twenty-five venticinque *m.*
twenty-four ventiquattro *m.*
twenty-nine ventinove *m.*
twenty-one ventuno *m.*
twenty-seven ventisette *m.*
twenty-six ventisei *m.*
twenty-three ventitré *m.*
twenty-two ventidue *m.*
twin gemello/a *adj.* **5**
two due *m.*
two hundred duecento *m.*
two hundred forty five duecentoquarantacinque *m.*
two thousand duemila *m.*
two-room apartment bilocale *m.*
type digitare *v.* **7**

U

ugly brutto/a *adj.*
ultrasound ecografia *f.* **3**
umbrella ombrello *m.*
unbearable insopportabile *adj.* **5**
unbiased imparziale *adj.* **9**
uncertainty incertezza *f.* **6**
uncle zio *m.* **5**; **under** sotto *adv., prep.* **8**

underdevelopment sottosviluppo *m.* **6**
understand capire *v.* **1**
understanding comprensione *f.* **6**; comprensivo/a *adj.* **1**
underwear biancheria *f.* intima
undress spogliarsi *v.* **10**
unemployed disoccupato/a *adj.* **10**
  to be unemployed essere disoccupato/a *v.*
unequal ineguale *adj.* **4**
unethical immorale *adj.* **7**
unexpected inaspettato/a *adj.* **1**
unfair ingiusto/a *adj.* **4**
unfaithful infedele *adj.* **1**
unforgettable indimenticabile *adj.* **1**
united unito/a *adj.*
university università *f.*
unless a meno che, salvo che *conj.* **7**
unlikely improbabile *adj.* **7**
unpleasant antipatico/a *adj.*
unreliable inaffidabile *adj.* **4**
until fino a *prep.*
up there lassù *adv.* **6**
update aggiornare *v.* **7**
urge raccomandare *v.*
use usare *v.*
useful utile *adj.* **1**
usual solito/a *adj.*
  as usual al solito suo *adv.*
  The usual. La solita cosa.
usually di solito *adv.*

V

vacancy stanza *f.* disponibile
vacation vacanza *f.*
  ski vacation settimana *f.* bianca
  to go on vacation partire in vacanza *v.*
vaccine vaccino *m.* **7**
vacuum aspirapolvere *m.*; passare l'aspirapolvere *v.*
vain vanitoso/a *adj.* **5**
validate (*ticket*) convalidare *v.*
valley valle *f.*
variety show avanspettacolo *m.* varietà *f.*
vase vaso *m.*
vegetable verdura *f.*
veiled velato/a *adj.*
vendor venditore/venditrice *m., f.* **2**
  street vendor venditore/venditrice *m., f.* ambulante **2**
Venetian veneziano *m., f.*
  Venetian squares/fields campi *m., pl.* **7**
  Venetian streets calli *f., pl.* **7**
vengeful vendicativo/a *adj.* **1**
veterinarian veterinario/a *m., f.*
victim vittima *f.* **4**
victorious vittorioso/a *adj.* **4**

victory vittoria *f.* **4**
video store videoteca *f.*
videogame videogioco *m.* **3**
viewer telespettatore *m.* **9**
villa villa *f.*
village paese *m.* **2**
villager/(fellow) countryman/ woman paesano/a *m., f.* **2**
violence violenza *f.* **4**
violin violino *m.*
violinist violinista *m., f.*
visit visitare *v.*
voice voce *f.* **4**
  at the top of one's voice a squarciagola *adv.* **3**
volcanic eruption eruzione *f.* vulcanica
volleyball pallavolo *f.*
vote votare *v.* **4**

W

wage stipendio *m.* **10**
  minimum wage stipendio *m.* minimo **10**
waist vita *f.*
wait attesa *f.* **7**; aspettare *v.* **8**
  to wait (for) attendere *v.*
  to wait in line fare la coda *v.* **3**; fare la fila *v.* **1**
waiter/waitress cameriere/a *m., f.*
waiting attesa *f.*
wake (*someone*) svegliare *v.* **2**
  to wake up svegliarsi *v.* **2**
walk camminare *v.*; passeggiata *f.*
wall parete *f.*
wander vagare *v.* **9**
want volere *v.* **1**
war guerra *f.*
  civil war guerra *f.* civile **4**
  world war guerra *f.* mondiale **4**
wash lavare *v.*
  to wash the dishes lavare i piatti *v.*
  to wash oneself lavarsi *v.* **2**
washing machine lavatrice *f.* **5**
waste scoria *f.*; sprecare *v.*
wastebasket cestino *m.*
watch orologio *m.*
  to watch one's weight controllare la linea *v.*
  to watch TV guardare la TV *v.*
water acqua *f.*
watercolor acquerello *m.* **8**
waterfall cascata *f.*
wavy mosso/a *adj.*
way modo *m.*
  This way. Da questa parte.
  to know the way conoscere la strada *v.*
weak debole *adj.*
weapon arma *f.* **4**

wear indossare *v.* **1**; portare *v.*
  to wear a suit portare un vestito *v.*
weather tempo *m.*
  to be nice/nasty (*weather*)
    fare bel/brutto tempo *v.* **1**
Web site sito *m.* Internet
wedding matrimonio *m.* **1**
  wedding dress vestito *m.* da
    sposa
wedge shoes zeppe *f., pl.* **3**
Wednesday mercoledì *m.*
week settimana *f.*
weight peso *m.*
Welcome! Benvenuto!
well bene *adv.* **9**
  I am not well. Sto male.
  Pretty well. Abbastanza bene.
wet suit muta *f.* **4**
what che, che cosa, cosa *interr. pron.;*
  quale *adj., pron., adv.;* ciò che, quanto,
  quel che, quello che *rel. pron.* **9**
  What does . . . mean? Cosa
    vuol dire…?
  What is it? (Che) cos'è?
  What is the temperature?
    Quanti gradi ci sono?
  What's new? Che c'è di nuovo?
  What's wrong? Che cosa c'è?
whatever/whichever qualsiasi,
  qualunque *indef. adj.* **9**
wheel: steering wheel volante *m.*
when quando *conj., adv.*
where dove *adv., conj.*
wherever ovunque *adv.*
which che; cui *rel. pron.;* quale *adj.,*
  pron., adv.
while mentre *conj.*
whiner lagnone/a *m., f.*
whiny lamentoso/a *adj.*
whisper sussurro *m.*
white bianco/a *adj.*
who che *rel. pron.;* chi *interr. pron.*
  those who, the one(s) who
    chi *rel. pron.*

whoever chiunque *indef. pron.* **9**
whom che; cui *rel. pron.;* chi *rel. pron.*
why perché *conj.*
widowed vedovo/a *adj.* **1**
widower/widow vedovo/a *m., f.* **1**
wife moglie *f.* **5**
  your wife la Sua/vostra
    signora *(form.)* **8**
willingness volontà *f.* **4, 6**
win vincere *v.*
  to win a game vincere una
    partita *v.* **3**
  to win the election vincere le
    elezioni *v.* **4**
wind vento *m.*
  It's windy. C'è vento.
  wind power energia *f.* eolica
window finestra *f.*
  window (*bank*) sportello *m.* **10**
  window cleaner lavavetri *m.*
windshield parabrezza *m.*
  windshield wiper tergicristallo *m.*
windsurfing windsurf *m.*
windy ventoso/a *adj.*
wine vino *m.*
  wine cellar cantina *f.*
winter inverno *m.*
wireless network rete *f.* senza fili **7**
wish desiderio *m.* **1**
with con *prep.;* presso *prep.* **8**
withdraw: to withdraw money
  ritirare dei soldi *v.*
without senza *prep.* **8**; senza che *conj.* **7**
witness testimone *m., f.* **4**
wolf lupo *m.* **1**
woman donna *f.*
womb grembo *m.*
wood legno *m.* **5**
wool lana *m.*
work lavoro *m.;* funzionare; lavorare *v.*
  to work overtime fare lo
  straordinario *v.* **10**
  work (of art) opera *f.* (d'arte) **8**

work hours orario *m.* di lavoro **10**
  work shift turno *m.* di lavoro **10**
worker operaio/a *m., f.*
worried preoccupato/a *adj.* **1**
worry (about) preoccuparsi
  (di) *v.* **2**; preoccupazione *f.* **7**
worse peggiore *adj.* **9**; peggio *adv.* **9**
worth: to be worth valere *v.* **6**;
  costare *v.*
  to be worth it valere la pena *v.* **3**
wound ferita *f.*
wrap incartare *v.*
write scrivere *v.* **3**
  to write each other scriversi *v.* **2**
writer scrittore/scrittrice *m., f.*
wrong sbagliato/a *adj.* **7**
  to be wrong avere torto *v.* **8**

Y

yawn sbadigliare *v.;* sbadiglio *m.* **7**
year anno *m.*
  to be … years old avere… anni *v.*
year-end bonus tredicesima *f.*
yellow giallo/a *adj.*
yesterday ieri *m., adv.*
  the day before yesterday
    l'altro ieri *m., adv.*
yet ancora *adv.*
yogurt yogurt *m.*
young giovane *adj.*
  younger sister sorellina *f.*
younger minore *adj.* **9**
youth giovinezza *f.* **5**
  youth hostel ostello *m.*
    della gioventù

Z

zoologist zoologo/a *m., f.* **7**

Index

Credits

Literature Credits

page 36 Courtesy of Susanna Tamaro.
page 76 Courtesy of Claudio Gianini.
page 116 Copyright © Giangiacomo Feltrinelli Editore, 1988, First published as Il bar sotto il mare in January 1988 by Giangiacomo Feltrinelli Editore, Milan, Italy.
page 158 Courtesy of Dacia Maraini.
page 200 © Elsa Morante Estate. All rights reserved handled by Agenzia Letteraria Internazionale, Milan, Italy. Published in Italy by Giulio Einaudi Editore, Milano.
page 240 © 2020 Ugo Guanda Editore S.r.l. – Gruppo editoriale Mauri Spagnol; "Disegno di Dario Fo © Archivio Storico Rame Fo – C.T.F.R. srl."
page 328 Courtesy of Einaudi Editore.
page 372 © 1962, 1966, 1972, 1984, 1998, 2012 and 2015 Giulio Einaudi editore s.p.a., Torino.
page 414 Courtesy of The Wylie Agency.

Short Film Credits

page 8   By permission of Andrea Rovetta.
page 48 Courtesy of Isabella Salvetti.
page 88 By permission of Nuvola Films.
page 128 By permission of Elimi Dei Mulini.
page 172 By permission of Gianluca Arcopinto.
page 212 Courtesy of Premium Films.
page 254 Courtesy of Mattia Riccio.
page 298 Courtesy of ContentLine/Feelsales.
page 342 By permission of Associazione Culturale Premio Solinas.
page 386 By permission of Nuvola Films.

Every effort has been made to trace the copyright holders of the works published herein. If proper copyright acknowledgment has not been made, please contact the publisher and we will correct the information in future printings.

Photography and Art Credits

All images © by Vista Higher Learning unless otherwise noted.

Cover: (sculpture) *Teseo Screpolato* (2011), Igor Mitoraj. Bronze, 295 x 188 x 180 cm. Susanne Kremer Photography LLC/©2018 Artists Rights Society (ARS), New York/ADAGP, Paris; (sky) Primeimages/E+/Getty Images.

Front Matter (IAE): IAE-16: Rido/123RF.

Lesson 1: 2: Oneinchpunch/Shutterstock; **3:** (b) Hybrid Images/Cultura/Corbis; **4:** (tl, b) Martín Bernetti; (tm) Vanessa Bertozzi; (tr) Dmitri Mikitenko/Fotolia; **12–13:** Ed Rooney/Alamy; **13:** (left col: t, right col) María Eugenia Corbo; (left col:b) Mary Evans Picture Library/Alamy; **14:** (l) Gabriele Putzu/EPA-EFE/REX/Shutterstock; (tr) Andreas Rentz/Getty Images; (br) Swan Gallet/WWD/REX/Shutterstock; **15:** (t) *Lorenzo Da Ponte* (ca. 1830), Samuel Morse. Detail. New York Yacht Club/The Picture Art Collection/Alamy; (m) Jorge Villegas/AGE Fotostock; (b) *Christopher Columbus* (1519), Sebastiano del Piombo. Oil on canvas, 42 x 34 3/4 in. Metropolitan Museum of Art, New York/Everett Historical/Shutterstock; **19:** Blend Images/Alamy; **25:** (tl) Nancy Camley; (tr) Ana Cabezas Martín; (bl) John DeCarli; (br) Katie Wade; **26:** Roy Morsch/AGE Fotostock; **29:** (all) Anne Loubet; **31:** (all) María Eugenia Corbo; **32:** Hybrid Images/ Cultura/Corbis; (background) Zagreb/Fotolia; **33:** (t, b) Annie Pickert Fuller; (background) Zagreb/Fotolia; **34:** (l, m) Nicolás Corbo; (r) Gaby Corbo; **35:** Luciano Movio/Marka/Alamy; **36:** Martin-dm/E+/Getty Images.

Lesson 2: 42: Richard I'Anson/Lonely Planet Images/Getty Images; **43:** (b) Fabiomax/Fotolia; **44:** (tl, r, bl) Katie Wade; (m) Anne Loubet; **52–53:** Andrés Vanegas; **52:** (b) Ana Cabezas Martín; **53:** (left col: t) Nancy Camley; (left col: b) Terry Wilson/iStockphoto; (right col) Ana Cabezas Martín; **54:** (t) Marka/Alamy; (b) Slim Aarons/Premium Archive/Getty Images; **55:** (t) Keystone-France/Gamma-Keystone/Getty Images; (bl) Maria Laura Antonelli/REX/Shutterstock; (br) Fototeca Gilardi/AGE Fotostock; **58:** (tl, tr, bm) Martín Bernetti; (tm) Nikada/iStockphoto; (bl) Ali Burafi; (br) Ana Cabezas Martín; **61:** (all) Martín Bernetti; **62:** (tl, tm, bl) Vanessa Bertozzi; (tr, br) Martín Bernetti; (bm) Image Source/AGE Fotostock; **63:** (l) Paolo Cipriani/iStockphoto; (r)

Vanessa Bertozzi; **67:** Anne Loubet; **69:** (t) John DeCarli; (bl) Rossy Llano; (bm) Pascal Pernix; (br) Anne Loubet; **70:** (tl) Katie Wade; (tr) Peter M. Wilson/Alamy; (bl) Goodshoot/Alamy; (br) Vanessa Bertozzi; **71:** (l) Andrew Paradise; (r) Bruno Mosconi/AP/REX/Shutterstock; **72:** (foreground) Clara/Fotolia; Fabiomax/ Fotolia; **73:** VHL; **75:** Courtesy of Claudio Gianini; **76:** Jacques LOIC/Photononstop/Getty Images.

Lesson 3: 82: Dennisdvw/iStockphoto; **83:** (b) Mipan/Fotolia; **84:** (t) VCG/Corbis; (m) Martín Bernetti; (b) Charlie Borland/Photolibrary; **92–93:** Werner Hilpert/Fotolia; **92:** (b) Jessica Beets; **93:** (left col: t) Ray Levesque; (left col: b) Vaclav Janousek/Fotolia; (right col) Andrew Paradise; **94:** (tl) *Mona Lisa (La Gioconda)* (c. 1503–19), Leonardo da Vinci. Oil on panel, 0.77 x 0.53 m. Musée du Louvre, Paris, France/Exotica im/ AGE Fotostock; (tr) *Portrait of Michelangelo Buonarroti* (early 17th cen.), Domenico Passignano. Oil on canvas. Galleria Enrico Lumina, Bergamo, Italy/Heritage Images/Hulton Fine Art Collection/Getty Images; (bl) *Self-portrait (red chalk on paper)* (c. 1512) Leonardo da Vinci. Biblioteca Reale, Turin, Italy/B.A.E. Inc/ Alamy; (br) *The Creation of Adam* (1511-12), detail from the *Sistine Chapel Ceiling* (1508-12), Michelangelo Buonaroti. Fresco. Vatican Museums and Galleries, Vatican City, Italy/John Dambik/Alamy; **95:** (t) Massimo Sestini/Mondadori Portfolio/Getty Images; (m) *Portrait of Dante Alighieri* (16th cen.), Anonymous. Portraitgalerie, Schloss Ambras, Innsbruck, Austria/Leemage/Corbis Historical/Getty Images; (b) Courtesy of Edizioni Polistampa; **105:** Ana Cabezas Martín; **108:** Ana Cabezas Martín; **109:** (l) Jessica Beets; (ml) John DeCarli; (mr) Hulton-Deutsch Collection/Corbis Historical/Getty Images; (r) Alessandra Benedetti/Corbis Historical/Getty Images; **110:** (tl, br) Corel/Corbis; (tr) Imag'in Pyrenees/Fotolia; (bl) Martín Bernetti; **112:** Mipan/Fotolia; **113:** Rick Friedman/Corbis Sport/Getty Images; **115:** Sophie Bassouls/Corbis Entertainment/Getty Images; **116:** Lawrence Manning/Corbis.

Lesson 4: 122: Eugenio Marongiu/Shutterstock; **123:** (b) Klaus Hackenberg/Corbis/Getty Images; **124:** (tl) Teresa Garrido; (tm) Katie Wade; (bl) Image Source/Corbis; (br) Ana Cabezas Martín; **125:** Katie Wade; **132–133:** Atlantide Phototravel/Corbis Documentary/Getty Images; **132:** (b) Nancy Camley; **133:** (left col: t) Vision images/Fotolia; (left col: b) Skowron/Shutterstock; (right col) Albo/Shutterstock; **134:** (l) *Antonio Stradivari (Stradivarius) in His Atelier* (1886), Antonio Rinaldi. Detail. Museo Civico Ala Ponzone, Cremona, Italy/Leemage/Corbis Historical/Getty Images; (r) Karwai Tang/WireImage/Getty Images; (m) Dominique Charriau/WireImage/Getty Images; **135:** (t) *The Calling of St. Matthew* (1599-1600), Caravaggio. Oil on canvas, 322x340 cm. Chiesa di San Luigi dei Francesi, Cappella Contarelli, Rome, Italy/Leemage/ Universal Images Group/Getty Images; (b) Fototeca Gilardi/Marka/AGE Fotostock; **139:** (l) Vanessa Bertozzi; (r) Nancy Camley; **148:** Ana Cabezas Martin; **149:** (tl) Martín Bernetti; (tr) Vanessa Bertozzi; (bl) Rafael Ríos; (br) Mark Adams/123RF; **151:** (l) Darrin Henry/123RF; (m) Martín Bernetti; (r) Viacheslav Nikolaenko/Shutterstock; **154:** Klaus Hackenberg/Corbis/Getty Images; **157:** Ulf Anderson/Getty Images.

Lesson 5: 166: WestEnd61/Media Bakery; **167:** (b) Michael Blann/Photodisc/Getty Images; **168:** (l) Corbis; (m) Anne Loubet; (r) SW Productions/Getty Images; **169:** Anne Loubet; **176–177:** Ollirg/Shutterstock; **176:** Christian Suhrbier/Imagebroker/Alamy; **177:** (left col: t) John Miller/Robert Harding/Getty Images; (left col: b) Uroszunic/Deposit Photos; (right col) Tobias Machhaus/Shutterstock; **178:** (bl) Ernesto Ruscio/ Getty Images; (tl) A7A Collection/Photo 12/Alamy; (tr) Sueddeutsche Zeitung Photo/Alamy; (br) ITAR-TASS News Agency/Alamy; **179:** (t) Keystone /Hulton Archive/Getty Images; (b) Laski Diffusion/Hulton Archive/Getty Images; **183:** Dragan Trifunovic/Gizmo/E+/Getty Images; **186:** Bloodua/Deposit Photos; **187:** Tomo Jesenicnik/Shutterstock; **194:** (l) Martín Bernetti; (r) Monkeybusiness/Deposit Photos; **196:** Michael Blann/Photodisc/Getty Images; **197:** Rachel Distler; **199:** Pictorial Parade/Staff/Getty Images; **200:** Siri Stafford/DigitalVision/Getty Images; **203:** Pixtal/AGE Fotostock.

Lesson 6: 206: JohnnyGreig/E+/Getty Images; **208:** (t) Nancy Camley; (bl) Randall Fung/Corbis; (br) Masterfile; **209:** Katie Wade; **210:** (l) Ray Levesque; (r) EzeePics Studio/Shutterstock; **216–217:** Vanessa Bertozzi; **216:** Vanessa Bertozzi; **217:** (left col: t) Sailorr/Fotolia; (left col: b) Davide Chiarito/iStockphoto/Getty Images; (right col) Zbynek/Shutterstock; **218:** (t) Corner/Fotogramma/Ropi/ZUMA Press/Newscom; (bl) Courtesy of Mondadori Editore; (bm) Victor Watts/Alamy; (br) Daniel Simon/Gamma-Rapho/Getty Images; **219:** (tl) JT Vintage/Glasshouse Images/Alamy; (tr) Everett Collection; (bl) Italy Photo Press/ZUMA Press/ Newscom; (br) Indigo Film/Photo 12/Alamy; **223:** (all) Nancy Camley; **233:** Martín Bernetti; **236:** Fototeca Storica Nazionale/Getty Images; **237:** Bob Thomas/Popperfoto/Getty Images; **239:** Colin McPherson/Corbis Entertainment/Getty Images; **245:** María Eugenia Corbo.

Lesson 7: 248: Shots Studio/Shutterstock; **249:** (b) Mary Clarke/Alamy; **250:** (tl) Suravid/Shutterstock; (m) Ifeelstock/Deposit Photos; (tr) Vanessa Bertozzi; (b) Comstock/Fotosearch; **258–259:** Olena Z/Shutterstock; **258:** (b) Janet Dracksdorf; **259:** (left col: t) Mikhail Nekrasov/Shutterstock; (left col: b) Adriano Bacchella/ AGF RM/AGE Fotostock; (right col) Sebastiano Bettio/Fotolia; **260:** (l) *Portrait of Marco Polo* (1867), Enrico Podio. Museo di Palazzo Doria-Tursi, Genoa, Italy/Fine Art Images /Heritage Image/AGE Fotostock; (r) Bartolomeo/Deposit Photos; **261:** (t) Mondadori Portfolio Editorial/Getty Images; (m) Illustration: Mikel Casal for Newton Compton Editori srl/©2014 Newton Compton Editori srl; (bl) Basso Cannarsa/Agence Opale/Alamy; (br) CJM Photography/Alamy; **266:** (l) Martín Bernetti; (r) Aaron Amat/Fotolia; (tablet image) Ana Cabezas Martín; **267:** Enrico Fianchini/Getty Images; **275:** Sean Justice/Corbis/VCG/Getty Images;

278: Blinkstock/Alamy; 279: Jessica Beets; 280: Mary Clarke/Alamy; 283: De Agostini Editore/Biblioteca Ambrosiana/AGE Fotostock; 284: Larry Moore/Illustration Source; 287: Michelangelus/Shutterstock.

Lesson 8: 292: Don Mammoser/Shutterstock; **293:** (b) *David* (1910), Luigi Arrighetti. Detail. Replica of *David* (1501-1504) by Michelangelo Buonarroti. Piazza della Signoria, Florence, Italy/INSADCO Photography/Alamy; **294:** (t) Janet Dracksdorf; (ml) Laurent Hamels/Studio Grand Ouest/Fotolia; (mr) Ana Cabezas Martín; (bl) Fotofoster1/Deposit Photos; (br) Corbis; **295:** Bryan Busovicki/Shutterstock; **302–303:** DEA/R.Carnovalini/Getty Images; **302:** John DeCarli; **303:** (left col: t) Perov Stanislav/Shutterstock; (left col: b) Neil Harrison/Mountainpix/Shutterstock; (right col) Rossandhelen/Deposit Photos; **304:** (t) Bruno Bebert/AP/Shutterstock; (bl) Karwai Tang/Wire Image/Getty Images; (br) WWD/Shutterstock; **305:** (tr) *Portrait of Giuseppe Verdi* (1886), Giovanni Boldini. Detail. Casa di Riposo per Musicisti di Milano/Fondazione Giuseppe Verdi, Milan, Italy/Fine Art Images/Heritage Image Partnership Ltd/Alamy; (tl) Jean Marc Zaorski/Gamma-Rapho/Getty Images; (br) Alberto Berti/Marka/AGE Fotostock; (bl) Universal/Courtesy Everett Collection; **309:** (t) Rafael Rios; (ml, mr, br) Martín Bernetti; (bl) VHL; **321:** (l) Elnur/Deposit Photos; (ml) Thomas Northcut/Digital Vision/Getty Images; (mr) Anne Loubet; (r)Martín Bernetti; **322:** *Sfera con sfera* (1989-1990), Arnaldo Pomodoro. Bronze, 400 cm. Alex Garaev/Shutterstock/©2018 Fondazione Arnaldo Pomodoro; **323:** *The Prophet Ezekiel* (1510), detail from the *Sistine Chapel Ceiling* (1508-12), Michelangelo Buonarroti. Fresco. Vatican Museums and Galleries, Vatican City, Italy/Fratelli Alinari IDEA S.p.A./Alinari Archives/Corbis Historical/Getty Images; **324:** *David* (1910), Luigi Arrighetti. Detail. Replica of *David* (1501-1504) by Michelangelo Buonarroti. Piazza della Signoria, Florence, Italy/INSADCO Photography/Alamy; **327:** Mimmo Frassineti/AGF/Shutterstock; **329:** Filippo Monteforte/AFP/Getty Images; **330:** Deborah Pendell/Arcangel Images.

Lesson 9: 336: Pixdeluxe/E+/Getty Images; **337:** (b) Carlo Bavagnoli/Time & Life Pictures/Getty Images; **338:** (tl) Rafael Rios; (tr) Vanessa Bertozzi; (m) Corbis; (bl) Sergey Nivens/Shutterstock; (br) Janet Dracksdorf; **346–347:** Leonardo Viti/Shutterstock; **346:** (b) CuboImages s.r.l/Alamy; **347:** (left col: t) Venturelli/Getty Images; (left col: b) Rainer Binder/Ullstein bild/Getty Images; (right col) AP/REX/Shutterstock; **348:** (l) *Portrait of Nicolò Paganini,* Andrea Cefaly (1827-1907). Oil on canvas, 65 x 51 cm. Conservatorio di Musica San Pietro a Majella, Napoli, Italy. De Agostini Editore/A. Dagl/AGE Fotostock; (br) Giorgio Lotti Mondadori Portfolio/Newscom; (tr) Courtesy of Mondadori Editore; **349:** (t) Courtesy of Renzo Piano Building Workshop s.r.l. Stefano Goldberg; (m) AlanStix64/Deposit Photos; (b) Fototeca Gilardi/Marka/AGE Fotostock; **355:** (all) Katie Wade; **359:** (all) Rafael Rios; **361:** Martín Bernetti; **365:** (l) Frederic Cirou/Media Bakery; (m) Franckreporter/E+/Getty Images; (r) Skynesher/iStockphoto; **368:** Carlo Bavagnoli/Time & Life Pictures/Getty Images; **369:** Marka/Alamy; **371:** Basso Cannarsa/Agence Opale/Alamy; **372:** Stanislav Mikhalev/Getty Images; (inset) Matt Carr/Getty Images; **375:** Sylvain Sonnet/Getty Images.

Lesson 10: 380: Hero Images/Getty Images; **381:** (b) Giovanni Giannoni/Penske Media/REX/Shutterstock; **382:** (tl) Image Source/Alamy; (tm) PhotoAlto/Alamy; (tr) Katie Wade; (ml) Martín Bernetti; (mr) Vanessa Bertozzi; (bl) Nancy Camley; **390–391:** C./Shutterstock; **390:** (b) Macumazahn/Shutterstock; **391:** (left col: t) John DeCarli; (left col: b) Mrohana/iStock Editorial/Getty Images; (right col) María Eugenia Corbo; **392:** (l) AGF s.r.l./REX/Shutterstock; (m) Graziano Arici/AGE Fotostock; (r) Courtesy of Bompiani/Giunti Editore 2018; **393:** (t) Vittoriano Rastelli/Corbis Historical/Getty Images; (m) Paul Almasy/Corbis Historical/Getty Images; (b) *L'homme qui marche I* (1960), Alberto Giacometti. Bronze, 180.5 x 27 x 97 cm. Boris Roessler/dpa/AGE Fotostock/©2018 Alberto Giacometti Estate/VAGA at Artists Rights Society (ARS), NY; **398:** María Eugenia Corbo; **399:** NakoPhotography/Deposit Photos; **408:** (tl) Rui Vale de Sousa/Fotolia; (tr) Corbis/Veer; (bl) Fotolia; (br) Blend Images/Fotolia; **410:** Giovanni Giannoni/Penske Media/REX/Shutterstock; **411:** Katie Wade; **412:** (l) Ustyujanin/Shutterstock; (m) Paul Hakimata Photography/Shutterstock; (r) Konstantynov/Shutterstock; **413:** Jean-Paul Guilloteau/Kipa/Sygma/Getty Images; **414:** Leslie Richard Jacobs/Corbis; **417:** Rob Goldman/Corbis; **419:** Eric Audras/Media Bakery.

Back Cover: Demaerre/iStockphoto.

About the Authors

Anne Cummings is a Professor Emeritus of French and Italian at El Camino College in California. She has over thirty years of teaching experience at universities, community colleges, and in the private sector in both the US and abroad. Anne is widely published in the field of foreign language education. She has degrees from the University of Southern California and the University of California at Los Angeles, and a diploma from the **Centro di Lingua e Cultura Italiana "Giacomo Leopardi."** Anne resides in Southern California.

Gloria Pastorino is Professor of Italian and French at Fairleigh Dickinson University, where she also teaches World Literature, Drama, and Film. She holds MAs from the University of New Mexico and the **Istituto Universitario di Lingue Moderne** in Milan as well as a PhD in Comparative Literature from Harvard University. Gloria specializes in theater and has written articles on Italian and French theater, migration, Italian cinema, masculinity, and zombies. She is a renowned literary translator who has translated, among others, plays by Luigi Pirandello and Dario Fo. Her other accomplishments include earning numerous honors for distinction in teaching. Gloria is originally from Milan and lives in New York City.